D0848636

JOHN JAY

John Jay, by "B.B.E.", one of the earliest portraits of Jay, by an artist now known only by his initials.

JOHN JAY
Founding Father

Walter Stahr

Hambledon and London

New York and London

Hambledon and London
175 Fifth Avenue
New York 10010

102 Gloucester Avenue
London NW1 8HX

First Published 2005

ISBN 1 85285 444 8

A description of this book is available from the Library of Congress and from the British Library.

Typeset by Carnegie Publishing Ltd, Lancaster, and printed in the United States of America by R. R. Donnelley & Sons Company.

Distributed in the United States and Canada exclusively by Palgrave Macmillan, a division of St. Martin's Press.

Contents

Illustrations

Text Illustrations

Illustration Acknowledgements

The author and publishers are grateful to the following institutions for permission to reproduce illustrations: The Maryland Historical Society, Baltimore, Maryland, pl. 1; New York State Department of Parks and Recreation, pls. 2, 3, pp. 222, 369; Jay Heritage Center, Rye, New York, pl. 4; University Archives and Columbiana Collection, Columbia University, pl. 5; The New-York Historical Society, pls. 6, 7 and 9 and p. 23; Fraunces Tavern® Museum, pl. 8; Kirby Collection of Historical Paintings, Lafayette College, Easton, Pennsylvania, pl. 10; National Portrait Gallery, Smithsonian Institution, pls. 11, 12; Winterthur Museum, Gift of Henry Francis DuPont, pl. 13; Images © Board of Trustees, National Gallery of Art, Washington, pls. 14 (gift of the Avalon Foundation), 17 (gift of Mrs. Robert Homans) and 18 (lent by Peter A. Jay); Franklin Delano Roosevelt Library, pl. 15; Colonial Williamsburg Foundation, pl. 16; Library of Congress, p. ii; Historical Society of Pennsylvania, p. 95; Rare Book and Manuscript Library, Columbia University, p. 235; Emmet Collection, Miriam and Ira D. Wallach Division of Art, Print and Photographs, The New York Public Library, Astor, Lenox and Tilden Foundations, pp. 268, 343 (top); Museum of the City of New York, p. 343 (bottom).

Acknowledgements

IT IS A PLEASURE to thank some of those who have helped me to research, write and publish this book. I did most of the research at the Library of Congress and in the Rare Book and Manuscript Room of the Butler Library of Columbia University; at both institutions the staff members were most helpful. John Kaminski and his colleagues on the Documentary History of the Ratification of the Constitution, and Kenneth Bowling and colleagues at the Documentary History of the First Federal Congress, were generous both with their time and their materials. Chris Mackay at the Bank of New York and Gwynned Cannan at Trinity Church cheerfully helped me with their records. Various people have read the manuscript. I would like especially to thank Kevin Butterfield, Carolyn Campbell, Landa Freeman, John Kaminski, Jack Lange, John McGinnis, Louisa North, David Strubbe and Janet Wedge for their helpful comments. The responsibility for the errors which remain is of course mine alone. My employer, Emerging Markets Partnership, allowed me to maintain my position as an international lawyer while I worked on this book. I was fortunate to find at Hambledon and London such pleasant and professional editors as Martin Sheppard and Tony Morris. Last but most important, I must thank my family: my parents for their inspiration and my wife and children for their patience.

Introduction

O N A FINE SPRING DAY in April 1789, on the balcony of Federal Hall in New York City, George Washington was sworn in as the first President of the United States. Many of those now known as the Founding Fathers were with Washington on that day, including John Adams, Henry Knox, Robert Livingston, James Madison and Roger Sherman. John Jay was there in his role as the nation's Secretary for Foreign Affairs. The crowd on Wall and Broad Streets below was "so dense that it seemed one might literally walk on the heads of the people." When Washington stepped out onto the balcony, he was greeted with "universal shouts of joy and welcome." He came forward to the edge of the balcony, "laid his hand upon his heart, bowed several times, and then retired to an arm chair near the table." The crowd "seemed to understand that the scene had overcome him, and were at once hushed into profound silence." Washington then came forward again, placed his hand upon the large Bible, and repeated after Chancellor Livingston the oath prescribed by the Constitution. "I solemnly swear that I will faithfully execute the office of the President of the United States, and will, to the best of my ability, preserve, protect, and defend the Constitution of the United States." Washington added "so help me God" and bent down to kiss the Bible. As he did so, Livingston turned to the crowd and shouted out: "Long live George Washington, President of the United States!" The crowd responded with equal emotion, with long and repeated cheers. "All the bells in the city rang out a peal of joy," and ships in the harbor added their cannon to the din. After a minute or so, Washington and the others turned and went back inside Federal Hall.[1]

John Jay knew all the men on the balcony that day: he was their friend, their colleague, and in some cases their mentor. Jay and Livingston had attended school together at nearby King's College and had worked as law partners in New York before the Revolution. Jay, Washington, Adams and Sherman had met in the fall of 1774, when they had all gathered in Philadelphia for the First Continental Congress. Jay and Livingston had drafted the first constitution for New York State and then served in the first state government. Jay and Washington had worked side by side in 1779, when one was President of the Continental Congress and the other head of the Continental Army. Jay, Adams and Franklin had negotiated the treaty that ended the Revolutionary War and secured America's boundaries. During the past few years, Jay as Secretary for Foreign Affairs and Knox as Secretary of War had shared offices in New York City. Jay, Madison and Alexander Hamilton had collaborated on *The Federalist*, the most thorough explanation and defense of the Constitution. Indeed, the very balcony on which they were standing was in some sense Jay's work, since he had been one of those who advanced funds to turn New York's City Hall into the nation's Federal Hall.

Many hoped and expected at this time that Jay would continue to handle the nation's foreign affairs. Instead, Washington appointed him later that year the first Chief Justice of the United States Supreme Court, and in this role he helped organize the federal court system and decided some of its key early cases. In 1794, when faced with imminent war with Britain, Washington again turned to Jay, sending him to Britain, where he negotiated and signed Jay's Treaty. Elected Governor of New York in 1795, while he was on his way back from England, Jay resigned his position as Chief Justice to guide and shape the rapidly growing and changing state. In 1801, he retired to his farm in Bedford, New York, where he lived as a respected elder statesman until his death in 1829.

Jay's personal life, while less dramatic than that of some of his friends, was equally interesting. He was a leader of various social and religious causes, most notably the effort to encourage the gradual end of slavery and to improve the lives of free blacks. His wife, Sarah Livingston Jay, was an educated, accomplished and adventurous woman. Among other things, she was America's first diplomatic spouse, accompanying her husband on his wartime voyage to Spain, and almost paying with her life when their ship was dismasted in the North

Atlantic. Her letters show that Sarah was almost as expert in politics as she was in fashion. She has recently been recognized as one of the "Founding Mothers" and fully deserves the compliment.[2]

John Jay's contemporaries recognized his remarkable skills and contributions. George Washington knew Jay had the "talents, knowledge, and integrity which are so necessary" to serve as the nation's first Chief Justice. John Adams believed that, in the process of developing and adopting the federal Constitution, Jay was "of more importance than the rest, indeed of almost as much weight as the rest." John Marshall admired his predecessor's "sound judgment" and "unyielding firmness and inflexible integrity." A French diplomat, while Jay was Secretary for Foreign Affairs, complained that "it is as difficult to obtain anything [from Congress] without the cooperation of that minister, as to bring about the rejection of a measure proposed by him."[3]

Today, however, Jay is largely forgotten and sometimes misrepresented. David McCullough, in his biography of Adams, states that Jay was in Spain for a year before Adams arrived there en route to France. In fact Jay did not arrive in Spain until Adams was on his way out of the country. Joseph Ellis, in his book on the "Founding Brothers," excludes Jay from his list of the "eight most prominent political leaders in the early republic," naming instead Aaron Burr, who would be forgotten today if he had not killed Alexander Hamilton. Histories of the American Revolution generally mention Jay a few times; they devote many pages to Hamilton, Jefferson and Madison.[4]

One reason for this neglect may be that John Jay was the most conservative of the leading founders. He was a reluctant revolutionary, and many of his friends and relatives became Loyalists. In Jay's view, Britain forced America into the war, giving the Americans no choice but to fight to defend their traditional *British* liberties. Jay was also a reluctant democrat: he believed that elections were the best way to select leaders, but he also believed that the people would often choose poor leaders, and he deplored the popular democracy which emerged during the early nineteenth century. Unlike many of the other Founders, Jay was an openly religious man. He quoted from and paraphrased the Bible in his political papers; he served as a leader of his parish church and of the national church; and he was a president of the American Bible Society.

Another reason Jay has been neglected is that his personal papers are less available than those of the other Founders. In part, this was Jay's intent: he was cautious in his correspondence and directed that many personal papers be destroyed. In part, this is because, alone among the major Founders, Jay is not the subject of an ongoing effort to find and publish all his papers. It may be that the neglect has something to do with Jay's quiet personal life. He was a dutiful son, a faithful husband, a loving father. He did not die in a duel, like Hamilton, or sleep with a slave, like Jefferson. He was a good man, but not always an easy subject for the biographer.

Whatever the reason, it has been a long time, almost seventy years, since Jay has been the subject of a biography. There have been articles and theses on aspects of his life, such as his work as Secretary for Foreign Affairs, but no attempt to integrate these into a full life. There are also many interesting primary sources that were not available or were not used in prior biographies. The purpose of this book is to use all this material to tell the story of Jay's life to a new generation of Americans.

CHAPTER I

New York

NEW YORK CITY, at the time that John Jay was born there in 1745, was
a tiny town at the edge of an empire. Its population was only about eleven
thousand, its area only a few acres on the southern tip of Manhattan. The
colony of New York, of which the city was the capital, was a vast area on the
map, but very lightly settled, with a white population of only about fifty
thousand. (There was also a black population of about ten thousand slaves and
an Indian population of unknown size.) Most white residents of the colony
were small-scale farmers, growing mainly for themselves and their families.
The trade of the colony, carried on by merchants such as Jay's father and
grandfather, was largely the export of timber, wheat, corn and meat to the
West Indies, and the import of finished goods from Britain. New York was one
of about twenty British colonies in North America, ranging from Nova Scotia
in the north to the sugar islands in the south. The colonies had no formal legal
relations with one another; they were each separate, looking mainly not to one
another but back across the ocean to Great Britain.[1]

In 1745, the British empire was once again at war with the French empire,
as it would be off and on for the next seventy years. New York City, because
it was so easily accessible by water, was very much at risk. Only a month
before Jay's birth, the French and Indians raided Saratoga, about two hundred
miles up the Hudson River. The residents of New York City had therefore
erected, on the northern edge of town, a new fourteen-foot wooden palisade.
The southern tip of the island was defended by the massive if somewhat ancient
Fort George. The harbor was filled with privateers, ships owned and outfitted
by private merchants, but officially authorized to capture French merchant or

warships. Although the Jays were not military men, war was a constant element of their lives.[2]

Indeed, it had been a war, a religious civil war, which drove the Jay family out of France. Jay's great-grandfather Pierre was one of the thousands of French Protestants, known as Huguenots, who fled to and settled in Britain in the late seventeenth century. Jay did not have any British ancestors, but he never forgot that it was Britain that "afforded my ancestors an asylum from persecution." Jay's grandfather Auguste was one of the far smaller group of Huguenots that fled to America instead of Britain or Holland. Auguste stopped first in South Carolina, where he found the climate "intolerable," then in Philadelphia, which he found "in an infant state," and finally settled in New York, with which he was "much pleased."[3]

Augustus Jay, as he soon called himself, worked first as a supercargo, or shipboard junior merchant, for Frederick Philipse, the richest man in New York at this time. Philipse had started life as a carpenter, then began trading on his own account and purchasing land, so that by 1693 he owned over two hundred square miles in what is today Westchester County, New York. Philipse was, at the time that Augustus Jay worked for him, making immense sums trading with pirates in Madagascar, sending them supplies such as rum, wine, beer, tobacco and clothing, and bringing back furniture, spices and slaves. It is almost certain that Augustus Jay was, to some extent, involved in the slave trade which his descendant came to deplore and decry.[4]

In 1697, Augustus Jay married Anna Maria Bayard at the Dutch Church in New York City. Anna was the "exceedingly lovely" daughter of Balthazar Bayard, a merchant and a brewer. She was related to many of the most prominent Dutch families in the colonies: the Stuyvesants, the Van Cortlandts, and others. "By his marriage," John Jay later wrote, "Augustus became encircled with friends who from their situations were able, and from the attachment to consanguinity ... were disposed, to promote his interest as a merchant, and his social happiness as a man."[5] Although they married in the Dutch Church, it appears that Augustus and his wife Anna worshipped in several churches. Two of their children were baptized in the French Church, three in the Dutch Church. Augustus himself served as a member of the vestry of the Anglican church, Trinity Church, from 1727 through 1746. In this respect, Augustus followed the pattern of many Huguenots, who drifted away from the French language and the French church.[6]

John Jay's maternal grandfather, Jacobus Van Cortlandt, was born in New Amsterdam, as it then was, in 1658. He married Eva Philipse, the adopted daughter of Frederick Philipse, and like his father and father-in-law, worked as a merchant and a political leader. Van Cortlandt served in the New York Assembly off and on from 1691 through 1715; he served twice as Mayor of New York City; and he held various judicial and military positions. It would appear that he did not speak English very well, for at one point the English Governor complained that Van Cortlandt and two other candidates for office "scarce speak English." But of course the Dutch accounted, at this time, for more than half the population of New York City, so perhaps it would have been more appropriate for them to complain that the English could not speak Dutch. Jacobus and his wife Eva had five children, two of whom, their son Frederick and their daughter Mary, married children of Augustus and Anna Jay. Jacobus and Eva lived in a substantial town house on Broadway just north of Trinity Church. Jacobus died in 1739, so his grandson John never knew him, but his wife Eva lived on until the boy was in his early teens.[7]

Jay's father Peter was born in New York City in 1704. He learned the trade of a merchant at his father's side and on an extended overseas voyage, during which he spent several months with his cousins David and John Peloquin in Bristol, England, and also visited cousins in Paris and La Rochelle, France. In later life, Peter Jay was a severe man, but his letters from this period show a lighter side, such as when his cousin David asked him to report on how he was "greeted by those charming and beautiful American girls of whom you told me so often." Peter was soon a prosperous New York merchant in his own right, trading in cloth and clothing from England and Holland, flax seed from Ireland, and timber, furs and wheat from the colonies. Peter married Mary Van Cortlandt in 1728, in the Dutch Church, but they baptized their children at Trinity Church and, starting in 1732, Peter served on the vestry there, like his father.[8]

Peter and Mary Jay raised a large family; by the time of John's birth in December 1745, there were six other children, ranging in age from Eve at seventeen to Anna at eight. Four of these children were in some way troubled. Eve was prone to fits of hysterics, and Augustus was slow or lazy or both. Peter sent Augustus away to study with the Reverend Samuel Johnson in Connecticut, but Johnson found it hard to work with Augustus and his "bird-witted humor," and after two years Augustus returned home. Two other children, Peter and Anna, were blinded by smallpox in 1739. Reverend Johnson wrote to their father to comfort and congratulate him "upon that truly Christian temper with which" he faced "this heavy visitation."[9]

Mary Jay is an elusive figure. Several hundred letters to or from her husband Peter survive, but there is not one surviving letter from Mary, and indeed perhaps she could not write. According to her grandson William, she "had a cultivated mind and fine imagination; mild and affectionate in her temper and manners, she took delight in the duties was well as the pleasures of domestic life; while a cheerful resignation to the will of Providence, during many years of sickness and suffering, bore witness to the strength of her religious faith." Peter's letters certainly confirm that his wife was often ill; in one he wrote that her "rheumatic disorder continues as usual, but I thank God she seems now relieved of the hectic fever she was taken with last fall."[10]

In November 1745, Peter reported to his Peloquin cousins that, because of the dangers of the war, and the "helpless condition of part of my family," he had suspended trade and moved to the country, "where I've a delightful place twenty odd miles out of town, which affords a pretty good living." Jay's "place" was a farm near the Long Island Sound in Rye, Westchester County. Mary Jay must have returned from there into the city to give birth to her baby John, perhaps to have access to a better doctor or favorite midwife. John was probably born at 66 Pearl Street, in the substantial Dutch house in which his family had been living for several years. He was baptized at Trinity Church a few days after his birth.[11]

The village of Rye, New York, was at this time like many other American villages: a small central core, with an inn and pair of churches, surrounded by scattered farms and farm houses. Peter Jay owned a farm of about four hundred acres, with a large white farm house, about two miles from the center of town. On one side of the house, the Boston post road was close enough that the family could "call out" to friends they saw on the road. On the other side of house, the Jay land stretched down to the water more than half a mile away, and the view extended across the sound to Long Island. According to a descendant, it "was a lovely place for the boy John to grow up in. The house was surrounded by woods full of birds, and the seashore beckoned just below." [12]

Although Peter Jay owned a farm, he does not seem to have been much of a farmer. His letters almost never mention the weather or his crops. In one letter, however, he complained that "the sickness among my negroes during these three last months, and which still continues, having from three to five always down at a time, gives me more trouble and fatigue than I can well undergo." Peter named a few slaves, described their medical problems, then noted that because of "this distressed condition of my family, I cannot be spared from home to visit my friends in town." Peter's attitude towards his slaves is revealing: they were both part of his family and troublesome. [13]

At about the same time that he moved his family to Rye, Peter Jay ceased to trade actively. He was still busy, however, seeking payment for earlier trades. Because he usually did not purchase British goods, but rather acted as agent for British merchants, the debts were owed not to Jay himself but to the various British merchants. Peter Jay used all the means at his disposal, including lawsuits and debtors' prison, to enforce these debts. He reported to his cousins in Bristol that he had obtained a judgment against one debtor and hoped "a close confinement would have the desired effect." He informed another correspondent that he was willing to arrest a well-known Jewish merchant, but not in Rhode Island, where "actions for debt are endless." The sums involved were substantial. In 1746, Peter Jay was chasing over £4,000 owed to British merchants; two years later he had worked the amount down to about £500. John Jay, later in life, would make himself unpopular by insisting that Americans had to pay their debts to British creditors, and surely some of his views on these issues were formed by watching his father at work. [14]

In the spring of 1749, John's older brother James left home to study medicine in Edinburgh, Scotland. Peter wrote often to his distant son, and these letters show how he parented all his children, including John. Peter wanted James to be diligent and economical. "I know that [the] usual fees at the college must be paid, but then you must be very sparing in your other expenses, which cannot amount to too much, if you apply close to your studies." James should not compare his allowance with that of richer students. "Others whose affluence affords them a greater expense are no examples for us." But Peter wanted James to room with a respectable family, even if this cost somewhat more than a boarding house, and not to study so hard as to risk his health.[15]

Illness and death were frequent themes in Peter's letters. In one, Peter wrote that his father Augustus had died after a long illness, and instructed James to wear "suitable mourning" for his grandfather. In his next letter, Peter reported that his daughter Eve had "just recovered from a severe case of pleurisy, and is still unwell after an attack of hysterics." A few months later, Peter wrote that "it pleased God to take to himself your little sister Mary after six days of illness of a sore throat." Religion was another frequent theme. The Jays were now Anglicans, but Anglicans with Calvinist severity. Peter urged James to attend church regularly and to pray daily. Mary Jay's mother Anna Van Cortlandt was so pious that, according to family tradition, "she died on her knees while in prayer." From both sides of the family, therefore, John Jay inherited strong, simple religious faith.[16]

Although Rye was isolated, Peter Jay followed the news of the wider world, and especially the almost constant wars between Britain and France. In 1746, Peter reported to his English cousins that forces were being gathered in New York to join "an expedition against Canada, which I hope will be attended with good success." In 1748, he noted that the peace treaty, because it returned Cape Breton to the French, was not popular in America. In 1754, he related how "Major Washington with between three and four hundred Virginian troops under his command" was attacked "within English limits by a body of about eight hundred French and Indians." In 1756, he hoped that Britain would attack and capture Quebec, since after that "the remainder of the country [French Canada] would soon fall of course into our hands." In 1760, he opined that the Indian war in South Carolina was "a bad affair," and expressed the hope that General Amherst would soon "chastise and bring to reason the savages there." In 1761, he wrote that a fleet of a hundred ships and seven thousand men had left New York harbor, bound for Martinique, where the fighting might cost "many lives" if the island was well defended. In 1762, Peter exulted in the British capture of Havana, which would humble "the haughty Spaniard" and also weaken France. Peter Jay was a strong, even passionate, supporter of Britain in her wars against France and Spain, an attitude his son almost certainly shared.[17]

Jay and Livingston Genealogy

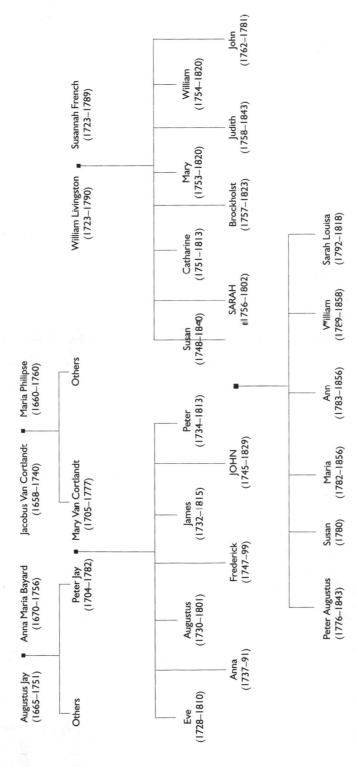

This genealogy omits those who died young.

Like most children at this time, John began his studies at home, with his parents. When he was only six, his father wrote that he was "of a very grave disposition and takes to learning exceeding well. He has lately gone through the five [Latin] declensions etc. with much ease and is now in the verbs." A year later, his father reported to his cousins that "my Johnny also gives me a very pleasing prospect. He seems to be endowed with a very good capacity, is very reserved and quite of his brother James's disposition for books. He has made a beginning at the Latin and gives reason to expect that he will succeed very well." [18]

When John was not quite eight years old, Peter sent him away to school in New Rochelle, about eight miles south and west of Rye, also on the edge of the Long Island Sound. Most residents of New Rochelle were descendants of the French Huguenot refugees who had settled there in the 1680s and 1690s. By the 1750s, English was the main language of the town and the Anglican church was its main church, but there was still a French tone to the town and to its religion. This tone was reinforced, for young John, by his schoolmaster Pierre or Peter Stoupe. Stoupe was born in 1690 in Geneva, and he had served in his youth as pastor of the Huguenot church in Charleston, South Carolina, before he converted to Anglicanism and moved to New Rochelle. [19]

William Jay, in his biography of his father, gave a rather unkind account of Stoupe and his school:

> Ignorant of the world, regardless of money, and remarkable for absence of mind, [Stoupe] devoted every moment of his leisure to his studies, and particularly to the mathematics; and he left the undisputed government of himself and his household to his wife, who was as penurious as he was careless. The parsonage and everything about it was suffered to decay, and the boys were treated with little food and much scolding. Little as he was, John contrived to prevent the snow from drifting upon his bed, by closing the broken panes of glass with pieces of wood.

Like most boys, however, John found small pleasures even in adverse circumstances. "His health was robust; and in after-life he used to mention the pleasure he at this time enjoyed in roaming through the woods and gathering nuts, which he carried home in his stockings, which he stripped off for this purpose." [20]

A somewhat different picture of Stoupe emerges from the files of the Anglican Church. In 1750, for example, Stoupe reported to the church authorities in London that many of his parishioners would "prefer the hearing a sermon to all idle and vain amusements." Although there were only about sixty regular communicants at this time, Stoupe was pleased that they are "still the same people, very devout, constant and steady members of the Church." In 1756, Stoupe reported that the church in New Rochelle continued to do well, that the number of communicants had increased to eighty, and that he had baptized within the past twelve months thirty-four white and six black children.[21]

Given the short distance between Rye and New Rochelle, John probably went home frequently during the three years that he attended Stoupe's school. In 1756, perhaps having reached the limit of what Stoupe could offer, John returned home and continued his studies for the next few years under George Murray, a private tutor.[22]

In 1760, at the age of fourteen, Jay entered King's College in New York City. The choice of King's was probably an easy one for Peter Jay. It was an Anglican institution, under the control of his friend Samuel Johnson, and it was in New York City, where he still had many friends and family members. The other colleges in America at this time, such as Harvard, were both more distant from Rye and under the control of other religious denominations. The other option was education in Britain, but this would be far more expensive, and Peter Jay was not a man to undertake expenses lightly.

King's College, at the time Jay entered it in 1760, was utterly unlike the grand institution it later became, under the name of Columbia University. The college was only six years old and was still viewed with suspicion by many, who considered it an improper extension of Anglican influence in New York. The college did have an impressive new building, standing near what is today the intersection of Broadway and Murray Street. But the college did not have many students to fill this building: only six boys started with Jay during the summer of 1760 and the total student body was about twenty at this time. The boys were young, generally entering at the age of fourteen, and the faculty consisted of only three, Samuel Johnson and two younger men.[23]

Johnson was an Anglican minister, a tall, heavy man, and an avid reader not only of theology but also of philosophy, literature and history. He was an active correspondent, writing to Bishop Berkeley about philosophy and to Benjamin Franklin about educational issues. Jay got to know him well, for Johnson handled the first-year students himself. In theory, boys entering the college already had a fair command of Greek and Latin, but Johnson found that most of the boys were "very raw," so that much of the first year was spent "reviewing" the languages the boys ideally should have learned before they arrived. For the Greek course, Johnson used the New Testament as his text; for the Latin course a reader on moral philosophy, with sections on virtues such as prudence and fortitude. Thus, at the same time that Johnson was teaching or reviewing languages, he was also teaching religion and philosophy. For Johnson, almost every aspect of the college curriculum was aimed at turning out devout and virtuous young men.[24]

The curriculum in the first year also covered rhetoric, oratory and logic. Rhetoric included not only learning to write and speak persuasively, but also learning to read and listen critically. Oratory was the vital art of public speaking. Jay's "articulation was indistinct, and his mode of pronouncing the letter L exposed him to ridicule." So he "purchased a book written by Sheridan, probably his *Lectures on Elocution*, and, shutting himself up daily in his room, studied it till his object was accomplished." In logic, Johnson emphasized the "new logic," which considered the deductive reasoning necessary for history and science as well as the syllogisms of Aristotle. During the second year, students continued to study Latin, Greek, English and related subjects with Johnson. Jay was so serious that, "when about to write an English exercise, he placed a piece of paper and pencil by his bedside [so] that if, while meditating on his subject in the night, a valuable idea occurred to him, he might make some note of it, even in the dark." Students also started during their second year to study "higher classics" with Leonard Cutting and mathematics and science with Robert Harpur. The mathematics problems would have been familiar from the family's commercial background. "A, B and C, trading to Guinea, with £480, £680, and £840 in three years time did gain £1010, how much is each man's share of the gain?" Of particular use, given that Jay would be involved in negotiating so many boundaries, there was instruction in surveying and mapmaking.[25]

In the first part of their third year, students studied "natural philosophy" with Harpur. Their text covered mechanics, hydrostatics, pneumatics, optics, and astronomy. Johnson was particularly proud of the college's scientific "apparatus," so it seems likely that Harpur supplemented the lectures with experiments. Johnson was keen for his students to learn some physical science, but he did not want them to become so scientific that they questioned their Anglican faith. Voltaire, Montesquieu and Rousseau formed no part of the curriculum at King's College. Jay probably read these authors, especially Montesquieu, at some point, but they never touched his firm religious faith. In later life, he was not particularly interested in science, with the exception of agriculture.[26]

John Jay's third year at King's College was overshadowed by the arrival of Myles Cooper and departure of Samuel Johnson. Cooper was a young classics scholar from Oxford, an Anglican minister, not as learned a man as Johnson, but a plausible successor. Cooper arrived in New York City in October 1762, and Johnson hoped to use the remainder of the academic year to train Cooper to be President. The board of governors, however, had other ideas: they demanded that Johnson resign so that Cooper could start immediately. Johnson resisted, and his supporters among the governors were able to restrain his opponents, but in February 1763 Johnson's second wife died of smallpox, and within a few weeks Johnson retired to Connecticut.[27]

President Cooper changed the curriculum of King's College, increasing the emphasis on the classical authors and reducing the study of natural sciences. Thus, instead of spending the spring of 1763 doing physics experiments with Harpur, young John probably found himself reading Homer with Cooper. Moreover, Cooper was keen to tighten discipline at the college, and apparently required John to take his meals at the college, like all the other students. In his fourth and final year John would have read the classical historians Herodotus and Thucydides. It also appears that, at about this time, he read Grotius on international law, the key text on the subject.[28]

Although the academic side of King's College was serious, students found time for other activities. They were living in New York City, which was the second largest city in America after Philadelphia, now with a population of about 18,000. The city was filled at this time with British troops fighting the war with France, and with sailors manning warships and privateers. Soldiers

and sailors need entertainment, and there were more than two hundred taverns
and perhaps as many brothels. Indeed, one visitor a few years later observed
that the area around King's College was a particular haunt of "ladies of
pleasure," many of whom were "fine well-dressed women."[29]

Young John did not partake of these pleasures. His father, whose standards
were strict, described his son as "a youth remarkably sedate." It appears that
he attended services at Trinity Church regularly; in one letter his father
complained to the church authorities that John and his brother Frederick were
denied access to what he viewed as the Jay family pew. John also visited often
with his uncle, John Chambers, a prominent New York lawyer and another
member of Trinity Church vestry. And John enjoyed the company of his
college friends, one of whom noted that he never had "such real pleasure as I
do in the conversation of the few select ones who visit Jay's room, which might
very justly be called a receptacle of agreeable fellows."[30]

John Jay's closest college friend was Robert R. Livingston Jr., a year
younger than John, but in many respects the senior member of the pair. He was
named after his great-grandfather, who had arrived in New York in 1674
"without family, friends or patrons," and by his death was called Lord of
Livingston Manor. Robert's father was a leader of New York society, owner of
a substantial estate at Clermont, and a justice of the Supreme Court. Young
Robert himself was tall and slim, with the confidence of one who stands to
inherit substantial wealth.[31]

A few years later, Jay wrote Livingston a letter contrasting their characters
at this time:

> When our friendship first commenced ... and for some time after I took it into my
> head that our dispositions were in many respects similar. Afterwards I conceived a
> different opinion. It appeared to me that you had more vivacity. Bashfulness and pride
> rendered me more hard, both equally ambitious but pursuing it in different roads.
> You flexible I pertinacious but equally sensible of indignities, you less prone to
> sudden resentment – both possessed of warm passions, but you of more self-posses-
> sion, you formed for a citizen of the world I for a college or a village, you fond of
> large acquaintance, I careless of all but a few. You could forbid your countenance to
> tell tales, mine was a babbler. You understood men and women early, I knew them
> not. You had talents and inclination for intrigue, I had neither. Your mind (and body)
> received pleasures from variety of objects, mine from few. You was naturally easy of

access and advances, I in neither. Unbounded confidence kept us together – may it
ever exist!

He no doubt meant in this letter to compliment his friend, but he also portrayed
himself as being somewhat more serious and principled than his high-born,
high-living friend. His admission that he did not understand women was
seconded by another friend, who noted at this time that "every one who has
the happiness of his acquaintance must know him to be more ignorant [of
women] than in any other art whatsoever."[32]

Jay met many of his lifelong friends and colleagues through King's College.
Egbert Benson would go on to be a leader of the Revolution in New York, a
member of the Continental Congress, and a prominent judge in the federal
court system. Peter Van Schaack would serve in New York revolutionary
committees and later in life as Jay's personal lawyer. Gouverneur Morris would
serve in the New York legislature, in the Continental Congress, and most
notably in the Philadelphia constitutional convention, where he penned the
immortal preamble to the Constitution.

It would be wrong to assume, however, that all the boys at the college were
future lawyers and leaders. In Jay's class, for example, six boys entered in the
fall of 1760, but only Jay and Harison were graduated in the spring of 1764.
None of the four who departed before graduation went on to any notable
achievements. And it would be very wrong to assume, from the presence of a
few future leaders of the Revolution, that King's College raised revolutionaries.
On the contrary, well over half of the alumni of the college became Loyalists,
far more than for any other American college. The King's alumni who were
revolutionary leaders, including John Jay, Alexander Hamilton, Gouverneur
Morris and Robert Livingston, were not leaders of street riots, but opponents of
popular violence. It is hard to say whether students learned respect for authority
at King's College, or whether the college only admitted students who respected
authority, but in any case the men who emerged from the early college were
conservative, even authoritarian.[33]

Jay himself had one conflict with the college authorities, late in his fourth
year, a fight which almost prevented him from graduating. William Jay
recounts that some of the students, while in the dining hall, "began to break the
table." The noise attracted President Cooper, who interrogated the students

one by one. None of them admitted to breaking the table, nor to knowing who had broken the table. When Cooper reached Jay, however, and asked who was at fault, he responded: "I do not choose to tell you, sir." Cooper was outraged, but Jay maintained that the rules of the college "did not require him to inform against his companions, and that therefore his refusal to do so was not an act of disobedience." Cooper disagreed and suspended him for a time.[34]

If the suspension had been allowed to turn into expulsion, Jay's career might have been quite different. A few years later, a student wrote that expulsion would "be an almost insuperable obstacle to my being received into any employment." But Jay was allowed to return after a suspension of a few weeks, and graduated with honor a few weeks later. Cooper no doubt reflected that the college would look foolish holding a graduation ceremony for a single student, Jay's classmate Harison. Cooper probably also considered Jay's overall good record, both academic and disciplinary.[35]

John Jay, in addition to his other activities, served as his father's agent in New York City. In one letter, for example, Peter asked his son to call upon a cousin and "desire him to pay you my share of the money" for a certain piece of land. In another letter, Peter asked John to buy him one hundred limes, the usual flavoring for rum at this time. In yet another letter, Peter asked John to "require" from a Jewish merchant his "final answer" as to whether he wished to remain in the house leased to him by Peter Jay. If the merchant left the house, John was to "immediately put an advertisement over the door" and in the newspapers. A few days later an advertisement appeared informing readers that the house and store house were available and that those interested should "enquire of John Jay," in care of his uncle.[36]

In May 1762, Peter wrote to his cousins that John "prosecutes his studies to satisfaction" at college. "He is endowed with very good natural parts and is bent upon a learned profession, I believe it will be the law." Neither Peter nor John explained the choice, but it is not hard to guess at the reasons. The law was a prestigious profession, and lawyers dominated the political life of the small colony. Young John could use his academic skills to learn the law, and could use his personal connections to build up a law practice. In August 1763, Peter wrote to John that, since he intended to read law, "I hope you'll closely attend to it with a firm resolution that no difficulties in prosecuting that study shall discourage you from applying very close to it, and if possible taking a delight in it." [37]

There were, at this time, no law schools: the only way to become a lawyer was to serve as a clerk to a senior lawyer. Because the lawyers of New York, in an effort to restrict access and raise fees, had agreed that none of them would accept clerks from 1756 through 1769, Peter Jay was forced to look to London or Bristol for a potential placement for his son. He was particularly hopeful about Bristol, where his cousins the Peloquins lived, and "where I conceive it will be far less expensive in regard to his board etc., than in London, and where the end will be answered as well." The responses he received, however, were not at all encouraging. David Peloquin wrote back that he did not know many lawyers, but his impression was that they were "so thick set in this city that most people wonder in what manner many of them get their bread." Peter Jay started to think about London, either "the Temple or one of the Inns of Court"; he confessed to his other son James that "my thoughts are indeed too much perplexed about what to do for him." [38]

But in January 1764 the lawyers in New York changed their policy, allowing for a clerkship in New York itself. Peter and John Jay promptly decided that John would clerk with Benjamin Kissam, a leading lawyer, probably known to Peter in his earlier life as a city merchant. Peter wrote to John, outlining in some detail what he thought would be fair terms. The Jays would pay Kissam £200, but the contract should specify that the money would be returned to Peter Jay if either Kissam or Jay died before the clerkship started. The term of the clerkship would be five years, but during the last two years John would be "at liberty" to have time off to read law on his own. [39]

John Jay was graduated from King's College on May 22, 1764. That morning, he joined the fifty boys from the college's new grammar school, his classmate Richard Harison, President Cooper and the other faculty members in an impressive academic procession. They marched out the east gate of the college yard, along what is now Park Place, across Broadway, across the southern corner of the triangular common, across the Boston road, and down to St. George's Chapel. The chapel was a new building, in the latest style, with elegant windows and a hexagonal steeple. It was crowded that morning, for the audience included the commander of the British troops in North

America, His Excellency General Thomas Gage, "accompanied by several of the Members of his Majesty's Council, the Judges of the Supreme Court, the President and Governors of the college, and many of the Clergy and Gentlemen of the City and Country." Jay's parents were *not* present, however; his father apparently decided to stay in Rye with his invalid wife and other children.[40]

President Cooper opened the ceremony with a prayer, related the events of the academic year, and then gave an "instructive exhortation to the young gentlemen who were to be graduated." After a speech by Harison, Jay gave a "spirited and sensible English dissertation on the happiness and advantages from a state of peace," no doubt touching on the recent end of the French and Indian War. The two young men then "entertained" the audience with a debate on "the subject of national poverty, opposed to national riches." After speeches by two graduates from earlier years, who by virtue of the passage of time were receiving their masters' degrees, Cooper closed the ceremony with another prayer. The academics then processed back to the college hall, where they "dined together in honor of the day." The bill from the previous year's meal suggests that it was a grand feast. On that occasion, fifty-nine diners managed to drink fifty-six bottles of Madeira, eleven bottles of claret and fourteen bottles of cider. The food was probably equally extensive.[41]

John Jay was eighteen years old, about to embark upon his career as a law clerk and then a lawyer. He was a smart, serious, studious young man. His college degree already made him part of an educated elite: at this time probably only one man out of a hundred in the colonies graduated from college. Unlike his brother, and some of his contemporaries, he had completed his education in America, giving him a less international perspective. Although he excelled in his studies, he was not a narrow academic, as shown by his commercial work for his father in New York City. He was sociable with his college friends, but not yet particularly comfortable with young ladies. He was somewhat stubborn, as he had shown in the table incident. All these qualities would come into play in his later life as a lawyer, diplomat, politician and statesman.

CHAPTER 2

The Law

In JUNE 1764, John Jay started work as a law clerk for Benjamin Kissam. The life of a law clerk in the eighteenth century was not easy. Every document had to be written out by hand, and the "hand" was usually that of one of the clerks. Research was difficult because there were relatively few books to work from, and these books were written in almost impenetrable legal language. The senior lawyers were often busy or away, so that they had limited time to guide their clerks. Peter Van Schaack (who started his clerkship a few years later) complained about "how many hours have I hunted, how many books turned up, for what three minutes of explanation from any tolerable lawyer would have made evident to me." Lindley Murray (the other clerk in Kissam's office) observed that the law "contains many barren and uninviting tracts, and extensive fields of laborious employment. It abounds with discordant views, with intricate and perplexing discussions, and requires deep and patient investigation." [1]

Although the hours were long and the work tedious, Jay immediately developed a strong relationship with Kissam. In October 1764, Peter Jay reported to a friend that his son was "very happily placed, with a gentleman who is extremely fond of him and who spares no pains in instructing of him." Murray remembered years later that his colleague was "remarkable for strong reasoning powers, comprehensive views, indefatigable application, and uncommon firmness of mind." He also had the advantage of having access to a good library, left to him by his late uncle John Chambers. [2]

Outside the office, Jay continued to see friends, especially Robert Livingston. His letters to Livingston from this period read somewhat like love letters. In April 1765, for example, he wrote:

> Convinced that friendship was one of the greatest blessings as well as advantages this life can boast, I have long since thought seriously of engaging in a connection of this kind with one, whom I might have reason to think qualified for such an intimacy, by being not only of a similar profession and circumstance with myself, but one whose disposition would concur with his fidelity and good sense, in rendering that tie firm and indissoluble, which once entered into, ought ever to be preserved inviolable.

He had hesitated, however, since he was not sure whether Livingston "had entered into a connection of this kind already, and I thought it imprudent to make the proposal, without having a very good reason to think it would meet with a favorable reception." He was pleased beyond words that Livingston had "himself removed all these difficulties, when he himself opened wide those doors of friendship, into which I had long desired to enter." They had now "entered into a connection of the most delicate nature, a connection replete with happiness and productive of very extensive advantages." Livingston apparently found these warm words too much, and suggested that they write on other themes, which Jay was quite willing to do, since he was sure that his friend was "as capable of maintaining a correspondence upon other subjects, as the person whom you honor with the name of friend." These letters suggest that, for Jay at least, the relationship was at this time very serious. Sadly, the friendship did not prove "inviolable" or "indissoluble": it cooled in the 1780s and they were political enemies during the 1790s.[3]

While Kissam was away during the summer of 1766, he asked for "some account of the business of the office." Jay responded:

> If by wanting to know how matters go on in the office, you intend I shall tell you how often your clerks go into it, give me leave to remind you of the old law maxim, that a man's own evidence is not to be admitted in his own cause ... If I should tell you that I am all day in the office, and as attentive to your interests as I could be to my own, I suspect you would think it such an impeachment of my modesty as would not operate very powerfully in favor of my veracity. And if, on the other hand, I should tell you that I make hay while the sun shines ... I should be much mistaken, if you did not think the confession looked too honest to be true.

At the end of the letter, he noted that some people would consider his style "too free, considering the relation we stand in to each other." Kissam wrote back, however, that he was pleased with his clerk's "humor and freedom," that he did not want the "adventitious circumstance" of his age and seniority to limit their friendship.[4]

In May 1767, John received his master's degree from King's College. No further course work, indeed no further work, was required for this honor, only to have behaved "soberly and decently" in the three years after one's initial graduation. Jay delivered a speech to the "very numerous and splendid audience" about "the usefulness of the passions," and then he and his classmate debated whether "a man ought to engage in war without being persuaded of the justness of his cause." The newspaper reported that the "masterly sentiments that were exhibited on both sides of the question entertained the audience with particular pleasure."[5]

Public speaking was an important art for a lawyer or leader in the 1700s, and Jay refined his speaking skills by joining a debating society. The group met every Thursday evening for debates on political and moral issues. In January 1768, for example, there was a debate on whether "in an absolute monarchy it is better that the crown should be elective than hereditary." Jay argued that elections would lead to better rulers, and that people would not "risk by rebellion their lives and property to get rid of a good King." Later in the year, the debate was about the Roman leader Virginius, who had killed his daughter Virginia to save her from becoming the mistress of the tyrant Appius. Jay argued that Appius had "usurped" power by extending his rule beyond its allotted period and "putting to death all who opposed him." To "destroy this extensive and unconstitutional power it was necessary to raise a general opposition," and the otherwise unthinkable action of Virginius was thus justifiable.[6]

Jay signed on for a clerkship with Kissam of five years, the minimum permitted under the rules at the time. Midway through this period, however, the rules changed, allowing college graduates to qualify as lawyers after a legal clerkship of only three years. The two men discussed the situation and agreed to "split the difference" at four years. With only about thirty active lawyers in New York City, and only a couple of candidates for admission to their ranks each year, bar examinations were rarely needed: the lawyers relied on personal knowledge to determine who should be admitted to their ranks. In October

1768, Governor Henry Moore, "being well assured of the ability and learning of John Jay, Gentleman," appointed him an attorney at law and authorized him to appear before all the provincial courts. A few days later, Jay appeared with his friend Livingston in the Supreme Court to be sworn in as members of the bar.[7]

The four years during which John Jay was a law clerk roughly coincided with a period of tension between Britain and its American colonies, especially New York. The initial controversy was over the American Revenue Act, or Sugar Act, of 1764. Parliament hoped that this law would increase customs revenue in several ways: by improving the enforcement of the customs laws; by imposing new duties on several articles; and above all by reducing to an enforceable level the duty on French molasses. Americans were accustomed to importing molasses from the French West Indies without paying the statutory duty of six pence per gallon; instead they paid bribes of about one or two pence per gallon to the customs officers. The Act lowered the duty to three pence per gallon, but the intent was to *enforce* the duty, something rather shocking to the Americans. The new Act also provided that customs cases would be tried in admiralty courts, by judges appointed by the King, rather than in common law courts, by juries selected from local citizens. The New York Assembly, in a petition to Parliament, argued that even "conquered vassals, upon the principle even of natural justice, may claim a freedom from assessments unbounded and unassented to." They claimed, as British citizens, this same freedom from taxes imposed by anybody other than their own elected representatives. Without this right, they feared they would see their "liberty, property, and all the benefits of life, tumble into insecurity and ruin."[8]

New Yorkers at this time saw threats to their liberty not only from Parliament but also from local officials. Only a week after the petition just quoted, a civil trial started in New York City, the result of a bloody waterfront argument in which Waddell Cunningham stabbed and nearly killed Thomas Forsey. Cunningham apparently expected the jury to decide against him, because he took the unusual step of hiring notaries to take down the testimony. Since his mentor Kissam "filled in" for one of these notaries for part of the trial,

Jay may well have been present. As expected, the jury returned a verdict for Forsey, at which point one of Cunningham's notaries asked the court to allow an appeal from the jury's decision to the Governor. The Chief Justice rejected this unusual request, saying that under English law there was no appeal from a jury's decision on the facts.[9]

The acting Governor, the aged and irascible Cadwallader Colden, now entered the fray. Colden was the most learned man in the colony, an expert in history, medicine, botany and philosophy. He may not have been particularly interested in the dispute between Cunningham and Forsey, but he *was* interested in increasing the Governor's control over the local legal system. He directed the judges to appear before him to explain their conduct in the Cunningham case, and he started working with the Attorney General to devise some way in which he could hear and decide the appeal.[10]

William Livingston, a leading lawyer and politician, took to the papers to ensure that this was not merely a dispute between the Governor and the lawyers. In a series of articles from February through August 1765, Livingston argued that, if the losing side could appeal from a jury verdict, citizens would effectively lose the right to have their cases decided by a "jury of their peers." This right, he argued, was sacred, "matured by ages, founded as it were upon a rock." Americans should "oppose arbitrary rule in every shape by every lawful method in our power. Never let us sit supine and indolent while our precious privileges are abridged." Even most of Colden's "friends" thought that he should not attempt to review the jury's verdict. John Watts, father of one of Jay's friends and a member of Colden's council, reported that Colden "was always disliked enough," but now the people "would prefer Beelzebub himself." [11]

It was against this background of threats and tensions that New Yorkers learned, in May 1765, of the passage of the Stamp Act. This Act required the use of special stamps for various papers in the American colonies, including all legal papers. As in the case of the Revenue Act, the colonists argued that Parliament could not impose an internal tax upon them. Peter Jay, writing to his Peloquin cousins in England, described the Stamp Act as a "hard measure" which was "considered here by the most judicious" as likely to lay "the foundation for much trouble." A few weeks later, he wrote them again to say that he feared "the proceedings of the colonies" in response to the Act would "doubtless be highly resented by those in power, at home." Although he was born in and had lived almost all his life in New York, England was still "home" for Peter Jay, and most other Americans.[12]

Among the unusual "proceedings" in America was the Stamp Act Congress, which convened in New York City in early October 1765. This was the first gathering of delegates from various colonies since the far less controversial Albany Congress of 1754. The final resolutions of the Stamp Act Congress, sent to Parliament but not publicized for a while in America, respectfully but firmly argued that taxes could not be imposed without the consent of the colonies. As the delegates dispersed at the end of October, broadsides appeared on New York streets warning the "first man that either distributes or makes use of stamped paper" to "take care of his house, person, and effects." On the last day of October, the day before the effective date of the Stamp Act, a newspaper announced in black the "death of liberty" and a mob roamed the streets breaking windows. On the next day, a mob of about two thousand gathered at Fort George, taunting the troops guarding the stamps there. The troops held their fire, but the mob proceeded to Bowling Green, where they made an immense bonfire, and then to Vauxhall, where they gutted the house of a British officer, and for good measure drank all his wine.[13]

John Jay and his parents Peter and Mary were in New York City at the time of this riot. Peter reported to his cousin that they "witnessed a most surprising ferment on account of the stamp papers, and as violent attempts were intended to get them out of the Fort, I thought it most prudent for us to withdraw immediately to our more peaceable habitation in the country." Britain and its colonies "may both have reason to curse the first promoters of [the Stamp Act] who by this impolitic act have united the several colonies into the strongest ties of mutual interest and friendship." It seems that the son, like the father, disapproved of both the Stamp Act and the riots.[14]

Jay wrote a long letter to Livingston on the last day of October 1765 but surprisingly did not mention the Stamp Act. At the end, he noted that "the office will prevent my adding any thing in the morning." It thus appears that Kissam's office was open for business in early November. The lawyers, however, had no access to stamped papers, so they could not prepare pleadings,

A section of the Montresor map of New York City, 1775. Although it had about 25,000 inhabitants at the time, New York City was still quite compact, occupying only the southern tip of the island of Manhattan.

contracts or other documents that would be valid. They also had no place to file papers, since the courts were closed, due to the same lack of stamps. After a while, the lawyers ceased work, not so much in protest, as has sometimes been suggested, but rather in frustration.[15]

Jay and Livingston used the suspension of legal work to take a tour, a "New England frolic." Jay then spent some time in Rye, riding his horse and reading his law books, and urging his friend Livingston to make better use of his leisure. "Recollect for a moment what time has elapsed since we have been free from the drudgery of business, that such an opportunity will probably not again offer, and therefore that it was by no means to be neglected." In late April 1766, Kissam wrote to Jay from the city, reporting that his sleep had been disturbed the night before by an early and erroneous report of the repeal of the Stamp Act. He urged his clerk, as soon as they received a real report of repeal, to return immediately to the city, for at that time "we shall doubtless have a luxuriant harvest of the law." The welcome news of repeal arrived in late May, and Jay resumed the "drudgery of business" in the New York office.[16]

At about this same time, in early 1766, there were riots and rebellions on various Hudson Valley estates. During the summer of 1766, Kissam undertook the unpopular task of defending one of the leaders of these tenant rebellions, William Prendergast. Kissam wrote to his clerk from Albany, where forty-seven of the rioters were on trial: "What their fate will be, God only knows; it is terrible to think that so many lives should be at stake upon the principles of a constructive murder." In the trial, Kissam argued that Prendergast could not be convicted of treason because he was acting upon a private grievance against the landlords, not raising arms against the King.[17]

The political tensions of the 1760s shaped young Jay. He observed how America's resistance to the Stamp Act had led to its repeal by Parliament, how American protests of the Revenue Act had led to amendments which reduced the duties, and how the firm stance of New York's lawyers had led to a revision of the royal instructions, clarifying that the Governor could not review a jury verdict. This analysis may have confused chronology with causation, for there were many factors other than American resistance which caused these changes in British policy. But Jay did not consider these complexities. He was so certain that properly expressed resistance would change British policy that he would later become one of the last American leaders to be converted from "resistance" to "revolution."[18]

Jay also learned in the 1760s various lessons about democracy. He saw what were deemed the proper procedures for protesting an Act of Parliament, in the form of the Stamp Act Congress and the Assembly's respectful petition. But he also saw at first hand more "popular" forms of protest, such as the Stamp Act riots, and as much as he deplored violence, he must have noticed its power. It was not the polite petitions of the Stamp Act Congress, but rather the mob threatening his life, which forced Governor Colden to abandon any hope of distributing the stamps. Jay would, throughout his life, have an uneasy relationship with popular democracy.[19]

In November 1768, as soon as they were qualified as lawyers, John Jay and Robert Livingston agreed to work together as partners. Partnerships of this type were rare in New York at this time; most lawyers worked alone. The two young men probably believed that, by combining their connections, they were more likely to obtain enough work. They also knew that, although they were the only two lawyers admitted in 1768, there were a number of others who would be admitted over the next few years. Many of them would not survive as lawyers, because there simply was not enough legal work in New York City to keep sixty or seventy lawyers busy. Indeed Jay and Livingston were themselves not particularly busy. In the April 1769 term of the New York Supreme Court, they had only four cases on the calendar.[20]

Jay spent much of that year working as clerk to the commission appointed to resolve the boundary dispute between New York and New Jersey. The boundary had been in dispute for decades and the territory at issue was immense. New York claimed much of what is today northern New Jersey, and New Jersey countered with claims to some of what is today Orange County and Rockland County, New York. The appointment as clerk was probably obtained through Kissam, one of the lawyers representing New York before the commission. The main task of the clerk was to take notes and prepare the official record, which ran to over seven hundred pages of questions, answers and arguments.[21]

The seven commissioners who attended the initial sessions in New York

City were an impressive group. They included Peyton Randolph, the speaker of the Virginia legislature, and Jared Ingersoll, a senior lawyer from Connecticut. The lawyers who argued the case before them were almost as impressive, with New York being represented by Kissam, John Morin Scott and James Duane. The commission considered an amazing variety of evidence: ancient Dutch land grants, learned texts on surveying and determining latitude, and the testimony of several dozen witnesses from the disputed territory. New Jersey, for example, presented John Demarest, who testified that he had been born and still lived near Hackensack, that he and his neighbors all paid taxes to New Jersey, and that the lands thereabout had been part of New Jersey "for as long as he could remember." New York presented similar witnesses, arguing especially that the area around Tappan had long been part of New York. The questions and answers were neat and tidy, suggesting that the testimony was "cleaned up" by the clerk after it was taken down.

The commission met for the last week of July, recessed for several weeks, then met again for a month, until late September. At that time, the commission received the report of the surveyors, who fixed the boundary essentially along the line argued for by New Jersey. After deliberating for five days, the commission decided to accept this proposed line, and refused to accept the immediate appeals of the two colonies, setting its next session for early December in Hartford, Connecticut. When he arrived in Hartford in December, Jay found that there were not enough commissioners to form a quorum. Lawyers for both colonies sought permission to appeal to London, but the commission, or more precisely the few commissioners present, decided that they would not allow appeals yet, but rather hold another session in New York City in July 1770. On the appointed day in July, only one commissioner was present. Jay was probably not surprised: by this time many people in both New York and New Jersey favored accepting the proposed line. But he had to be concerned that, without a commission, he would not be paid his fee, and at about this time he sent out two bills, one to each of the two colonies.

In February 1772, the New York Assembly passed a law accepting the commission's line. Governor William Tryon of New York met with Governor William Franklin of New Jersey and persuaded him to accept the commission's line. The New Jersey Assembly promptly passed legislation accepting the commission's line. The only barrier to the settlement now was to get the formal, certified copy of the commission's record to London. But even though two Governors and two Assemblies had agreed upon the line, Jay refused to release the record. There is no written explanation of his concerns, but they probably related in part to his unpaid bills, in part to the question of his authority. He was appointed by the commission and answerable to it, and he had no instruction or authorization from the commission to release the record. In the end, it took a special law, passed by the New York legislature in February 1773, to pry the record loose from his grasp.

Some have suggested that Jay learned from this experience the value of arbitration commissions in resolving boundary disputes. More likely, he learned the weakness of such commissions in resolving colonial disputes, particularly given the lack of clear procedures. The commission had no authority to impose its decision upon New York and New Jersey; all it had done was suggest a solution which, in the end, both colonies agreed to accept. Other border disputes were not resolved during the colonial period and contributed to confusion and violence. The border disputes between New York and New England, for example, contributed to riots in the disputed territory. When he argued, years later, that a national government was necessary to resolve state border disputes, Jay was arguing from personal experience.[22]

The boundary commission was not the only work Kissam directed to his former clerk. After injuring his leg, Kissam asked him to handle his cases in northern New York. "You have now a call to go forth into my vineyard; and this you must do too upon an evangelical principle, that the master may receive the fruits of it." Kissam could not tell him much about these cases. "One is about a horse race, in which I suppose there is some cheat; another is about an eloped wife; another of them also appertains unto horseflesh. These are short hints; they may serve for briefs. If you admire conciseness, here you have it."[23]

In November 1770, a group of about fifteen to twenty lawyers gathered for the first of many meetings of "the Moot." This group included both senior lawyers, such as William Livingston, William Smith, and John Morin Scott, and more junior men, such as John Jay, Egbert Benson and Peter Van Schaack. Jay was generally present, and often a speaker, at the meetings. Many of the difficult legal issues discussed at the Moot involved relations between the

separate colonies. For example, they debated the effect of a New Jersey bank-
ruptcy upon creditors residing in New York. The consensus view was that an
order issued by a Jersey court would release debts contracted there, but could
not release or affect debts contracted in New York.[24]

These intercolonial issues were not of merely academic interest. At about this
same time, Jay was representing a plaintiff who had obtained a judgment in
New York on the basis of a judgment in Massachusetts. In a letter to his co-
counsel, he reported that many "of our best lawyers doubt whether an action in
one province on a judgment obtained in another can be supported." He noted
that the English courts generally would not accept judgments rendered by the
Irish courts. He thus could not have been too surprised when the New York
Supreme Court, at the time the highest court in the colony, ruled against him,
in essence requiring him to fight the case a second time. This problem was not
solved until the federal Constitution went into effect in 1789 and required each
state to give "full faith and credit" to the final decisions of other state courts.[25]

At some point in 1770, Jay and Livingston, perhaps feeling they were each
on their way to legal success, decided to dissolve their partnership. Jay started
at this point to secure substantial numbers of new cases. In the November 1770
session of the Supreme Court he opened eighteen cases, and another eighteen
in the June 1771 session. Perhaps as a result of overwork, his health suffered.
He wrote to a medical friend overseas that he had consulted with three different
doctors for a swelling in his neck and a persistent fever. The friend urged him
to exercise more, and the family tradition is that Jay cured himself by renting
a house six miles from his office, riding his horse each way each day. As to
work, he wrote that "I am as well circumstanced as I have a right to expect;
my old friends contribute much to my happiness, and upon the whole I have
reason to be satisfied with my share of the attention of Providence."[26]

Among his cases at this time was that of Reverend Joshua Bloomer. The
Governor had appointed Bloomer over the objection of the vestry, which
refused to pay his salary, and Bloomer sued the vestry, seeking an order
requiring them to pay. The case is mainly of interest because it occasioned a
dispute between Jay and his co-counsel John Tabor Kempe, the colony's
Attorney General at the time. Jay complained to Kempe that he "had not been
consulted in any one stage of the suit." Kempe's conduct suggested to the legal

world that Jay was "insignificant" and Jay demanded an "explanation" from Kempe. Kempe wrote back the same day, saying this was the "first instance I ever met with of such an address." Kempe accepted that it was "incumbent on every gentleman to explain his conduct when it is misunderstood, and such explanation is desired in proper terms, the want of which on your part is the only reason for my not doing it in the present instance." Jay, a few days later, did not "deny that I was warm, or if you please, that I am warm still." But "warmth excited by attacks on reputation, or inspired by a sense of indelicate treatment," was perfectly proper. He concluded that a "rupture" with Kempe would "be very disagreeable to me," but he would "rather reject the friendship of the world than purchase it by patience under indignities offered by any man in it." Somehow the two men resolved their differences short of a duel, but they were never friends.[27]

At about this same time, Jay found himself as opposing counsel to Kempe in an interesting assault case. According to the complaint, the defendants, after hiring the plaintiff as a schoolteacher for their children in White Plains, failed to pay him his agreed salary, then arranged for him to be arrested and beaten while in prison. The teacher had brought his case to Kempe, who declined to bring criminal charges, but agreed to represent the teacher as a private lawyer in a civil action. Jay, representing the defendants, arranged to have the case transferred to the defendants' local court. He turned the case into a trial of the plaintiff, arguing that he deceived the defendants into hiring him and was caught in the very act of stealing a bag of corn. The jury, perhaps sympathetic to their neighbors, acquitted them.[28]

Jay's legal practice was not built, however, on embattled ministers and schoolteachers. The majority of his cases were simple actions to recover commercial debts. And there were many, many such cases: in 1773 he had more than a hundred cases pending in the Supreme Court and another hundred pending in the Westchester court. Over the six years starting in 1770, he handled more than three hundred cases in the Mayor's Court in New York City, another local court in which smaller debt cases were handled.[29]

Many of the judges at this time were not trained as lawyers, and Jay complained that they were "taken from among the farmers," so that one could not guide them "through the mazes and intricacies of the law." In late 1772, the

Governor and Council considered a proposal by Jay and Livingston that
lawyers be appointed to ride circuit as advisers to the common pleas judges.
The lawyers whom they had in mind were themselves: Jay hoped to serve in
Orange, Richmond, and Westchester counties, and Livingston to serve in
Dutchess and three other northern counties. After a heated debate over two
sessions, however, the Governor and his Council did not approve the proposal.
Even after this defeat, Jay did not entirely give up hope. In early 1774, he wrote
to a friend in Britain that, if the government were "to establish this office and
provide for its support, it would evince an attention to the interests of the
colony" that would tend to "place the ministry in somewhat a more favorable
point of view than they now appear."[30]

By the time he wrote this letter, Jay was earning about £1000 a year from
his law practice, more than almost any other lawyer in the colony. From
today's perspective, Jay's interest in a quasi-judicial position, which would pay
far less, is somewhat curious. But in colonial days government service and
private practice were not mutually exclusive; indeed government service
helped advance a lawyer's private career. Moreover, service as a judicial
adviser would be a first step towards a position as a judge, a position that was
well paid, prestigious, and less demanding than private practice.[31]

Jay somehow found time not only to handle all his legal work, but also to have
an active social life. He was a leading member of the "Social Club," a group
which met in the wintertime at Fraunces Tavern and in the summer at Kip's
Bay. He was also the manager of a dancing assembly, a role which led him to
the edge of another possible duel, when he denied an applicant admission to the
assembly. Jay recognized that the applicant might view his rejection as a
personal insult, and offered that "if any reasonable person will say I have
injured you or that you have a right to satisfaction, I will either ask your
pardon or fight you." In a second letter, he urged that they submit the matter
to several of their contemporaries for a "fair determination of our difference."
Duels were not uncommon at the time, but Jay in this case, and indeed
throughout his life, avoided them.[32]

Dancing assemblies of course involved young women as well as young men,
and it was probably at a dance that John Jay met Sarah Livingston in late 1772

or early 1773. Sarah or Sally was one of the eight living children of William Livingston and his wife Susannah French Livingston, ranging in age from Susan and Catharine, in their early twenties, down to John, only ten at this time. William Livingston, a grandson of the immigrant Robert Livingston, was a leader in New York law and politics from the early 1750s through his retirement to northern New Jersey in early 1772. Although there were several other Livingstons active in New York politics during this period, and they were occasionally derided as the "Livingston faction," most scholars today believe that such labels are too simple to capture the complexities of New York's colonial politics. William Livingston, for example, was a staunch Presbyterian, and an early and ardent foe of the Anglican King's College. Yet one of William's brothers served as one of the college's first governors, and many of the Livingstons, including John's friend Robert, attended the college. During the brief period in which he served in the Assembly, William sometimes voted with, and sometimes against, his Livingston cousins.[33]

As for Sarah herself, she was only sixteen years old at this time: intelligent, articulate, beautiful, flirtatious. One of John's friends, the witty and elegant Gouverneur Morris, wrote at this time to Catharine Livingston that "never was a little creature so admired" as her sister Sally at New York. "As to her heart, when in the midst of her admirers, it singeth with joy … The rosy fingers of pleasure paint her cheeks with double crimson. Her eyes sparkle with delight. And so it will continue if the whim does not take her to get in love." Her suitors were, in Morris's view, poor creatures. "One bending forwards rolling up his eyes and sighing most piteously. Another at a distance sitting side long upon his chair with melancholic and despondent phiz [face] prolonged unto the seventh button hole of his waistcoat." A few weeks later, a distant cousin of Sally's described her in similar terms, as "that opening rose, who if so angelic now, what must she be when all expanded."[34]

It is possible that John was, at this time, flirting with women other than Sally Livingston. Thomas Jones, a Loyalist historian writing after the Revolution, asserted that, because he was "disappointed in two several attempts to marry in the DeLancey family," Jay retaliated by taking "a wife in [the family] of the Livingstons, a family ever opposed to the politics of the DeLanceys, turned republican, espoused the Livingston interest, and ever after opposed all legal government." Jones is simplistic in suggesting that Jay's entire political future was determined by his decision to marry a Livingston rather than a DeLancey. But he does highlight the differences between the Anglican and authoritarian Jay and the Presbyterian and iconoclastic Livingston. There were religious and political differences between the two men, differences which they somehow managed to bridge, and indeed to obliterate over time.[35]

John Jay married Sarah Livingston in the parlor of Liberty Hall, William Livingston's home in Elizabeth Town, on April 28, 1774. The couple then left to visit various relatives, stopping in Rye, where Sarah met John's immediate family for the first time. Sarah was worried about meeting her husband's two blind siblings, but they had "such an appearance of cheerfulness and good humor in all they say that instead of depressing they raised my spirits." She found John's mother "extremely ill" and "amazingly affected at seeing me," but "after a little chat she appeared much better." The couple traveled north, stopping among other places at an inn in Poughkeepsie, where Sarah complained that "it is not [in] my power to write well in this room where there is such a collection of country-men talking politics."[36]

Her husband was twenty-eight years old in the spring of 1774. Physically, he was a tall man, perhaps nearly six feet, with a prominent nose and sharp eyes. Professionally, he was one of New York City's leading lawyers, handling difficult commercial and political cases. His friends and relatives included many of the leaders of New York, and now, through his new wife, he was part of the Livingston family. But Jay was not, in the spring of 1774, a political man. His early letters only rarely mention the political issues which roiled New York. But politics were about to overturn his comfortable life. Indeed, his legal career basically ended in 1774, although his law office would remain open until 1776, and he would always retain the cautious approach he learned as a lawyer. The very same newspaper which reported that "John Jay, eminent barrister of this City," married "Miss Sally Livingston, third daughter of William Livingston," also reported speeches in Parliament denouncing the "real and actual rebellion" in Massachusetts, which would soon spread to New York City.[37]

CHAPTER 3

Resistance Leader

NEW YORK enjoyed a period of political peace from late 1770 through early 1773. In October of that year, however, New York learned of a new Act of Parliament, imposing a modest tax on tea imported into the colonies. Many New Yorkers saw this as yet another example of improper "taxation without representation." A poster signed by the "Sons of Liberty" appeared, pledging that the group would "treat as enemies" anyone who imported, purchased or used tea which had paid the duty. At a mass meeting outside the City Hall, the crowd shouted that it would not allow East India tea to be landed in New York. Several months passed, however, before the first ships bearing tea arrived in New York harbor. When they did, following the earlier example of Boston, some New Yorkers boarded a ship and dumped the tea into the harbor. "It was not without some risk of his life" that the captain escaped to another ship in the harbor.[1]

This New York City tea party was held in late April 1774, just a few days before the Elizabeth Town wedding of John Jay and Sarah Livingston. The newly-weds spent most of May in rural New York, visiting relatives and attending to John's law practice. He probably read in a newspaper at some point during May how Parliament, in retaliation for the Boston Tea Party, had closed Boston harbor and suspended civil government in Massachusetts. But he was not aware, until he returned to the city from the northern counties in late May, that he had been named to "the committee appointed by the city to take into consideration the measures of Parliament relative to Boston."[2]

The fifty-one members of this committee ranged from radicals such as Alexander McDougall and Isaac Sears to conservatives such as John DeLancey and Peter Van Schaack. When the full committee met for the first time, it appointed a subcommittee of four, including John Jay and James Duane, to prepare a response by eight that evening to a letter from Boston. How to respond was far from obvious. The radicals wanted to support Boston by agreeing that New York would immediately cease to import British goods. But New York's merchants were unwilling to agree to such a boycott, at least not until the rest of the colonies agreed to a similar measure. It is thus perhaps not surprising that the subcommittee called for a general continental congress. The New York letter, drafted by Duane based on Jay's notes, called for a meeting of delegates from all colonies to consider the "deplorable circumstances" of Boston and how best to protect "our common rights."[3]

After attending this initial meeting, and assisting in drafting this letter, Jay attended only four of the many meetings of the committee from late May through late August. In some cases he missed meetings because he was out of town. In late June, for example, he wrote to Sarah from Albany, saying his trip up the Hudson by sloop had been "as agreeable as absence from you and the filth of twenty dirty lousy Scotch passengers would admit." In other cases, however, he was in New York, but either busy with his work or with his wife. He did not disregard politics completely. In July, for example, he helped draft instructions which would give the delegates to the proposed congress broad discretion, saying that it would be "premature" for any one colony to take a fixed position before the "joint councils." When these draft instructions were denounced by John Morin Scott as "pusillanimous," Jay angrily demanded an explanation from Scott. A few days later, at a rather confused meeting, the committee of fifty-one nominated Jay and four others to represent New York City at the Continental Congress. In late July, the voters of the city confirmed this slate through an election.[4]

Jay was in some ways an unlikely choice to represent New York at this inter-colonial meeting. He was by far the youngest of the delegates representing New York. One of these delegates, Philip Livingston, an uncle of Sarah Livingston Jay, was almost sixty at the time, and had served for many years in the Assembly and briefly served as its Speaker. Another delegate, James Duane, had among other things served as the colony's Attorney General. Nor was Jay an experienced merchant, like John Alsop and Isaac

Low, the two other New York delegates. It may be that the key factor in the choice of Jay was his very *lack* of political experience. He was neither a member of the DeLancey nor the Livingston faction, neither a radical no a conservative. Or perhaps he was already displaying the politician's ability to speak like a radical when with radicals and like a conservative with conservatives.[5]

His acceptance of the appointment was also somewhat curious, since it was a critical step on the path that would lead to his becoming a Revolutionary rather than a Loyalist. But of course that is not how Americans viewed the imminent congress. They thought of this new congress as a parallel to the Stamp Act Congress, a one-time gathering designed to bring Britain to its senses. Although there were diverse opinions about how best to handle the crisis, there was as yet no clear division between Loyalists and Revolutionaries. On the contrary, there was remarkable consensus throughout America that a congress was necessary to draft petitions and to devise a trade boycott, and that these together would persuade Parliament to repeal the sanctions against Massachusetts. Jay looked forward to the chance to do his part in resolving the differences between the "mother country" and the "daughter colonies."[6]

Although some of the New York delegates were saluted by cannon and escorted out of the town by crowds, Jay himself left simply and quietly one morning in late August, "without the inhabitants being apprised of his departure." He rode to Elizabeth Town, where he joined his father-in-law, William Livingston, also a delegate, and they traveled together to Philadelphia. Philadelphia was at this time somewhat more populous than New York, a neat and compact city of about twenty-five thousand people. The streets were straight, parallel, lined by tall trees, and illuminated at night by lamps. The houses were handsome and close set, with over six thousand dwellings in an area of less than a square mile. A few days after arriving, Jay joined some of the other delegates on a trip to see the famous falls at Schuykill.[7]

The main work of these first few days in Philadelphia, however, was getting to know the other delegates. There were only a few delegates with any kind of an "inter-colonial" reputation at this time. Samuel Adams was the leader of the Massachusetts delegation, known as having radical views and backroom skills.

George Washington was generally respected for his military exploits during the French and Indian wars. John Dickinson of Pennsylvania, who would join the Congress within a few weeks, was famous for the letters he had published under the pen name of the "Pennsylvania Farmer." But most of the delegates, even those who had years of experience in their colonial legislatures, were not known outside their own colonies. Indeed, for many this was their first trip outside their own colony or region.[8]

On September 5, 1774, a cool morning after a hard rain, about fifty delegates gathered at City Tavern. On this first day, they resolved some relatively easy questions: where to meet (they chose Carpenters' Hall over the State House), and who should serve as their secretary (they chose Charles Thomson rather than Jay's new friend Silas Deane).[9] On the next day, Congress tackled a far harder issue: whether each colony should have one vote, or whether votes should be weighted in some way according to the population of the colonies. Patrick Henry of Virginia, the most populous colony, was all in favor of voting by population. Henry argued that "the distinctions between Virginians, Pennsylvanians, New Yorkers and New Englanders are no more. I am not a Virginian, but an American." Samuel Ward of Rhode Island, the smallest colony, insisted that every colony should have an equal vote. Richard Henry Lee of Virginia noted that they did not have "the materials" to ascertain the population of each colony. Henry responded that in his view "government is at an end" and "all America thrown into one mass." Jay politely disagreed: in his view they were not there "to frame an American constitution." The "measure of arbitrary power is not full, and I think it must run over, before we undertake to frame a new constitution." He softened his remarks by adding: "To the virtue, spirit, and abilities of Virginia we owe much. I should always therefore from inclination as well as justice, be for giving Virginia its full weight." In the end, the delegates agreed to give each colony one vote.[10]

This debate is sometimes cited as an early example of the conflict between radicals and conservatives in the Continental Congress. But such simple terms do not capture the complexity of the Congress. To be sure, there *were* radical delegates and conservative delegates. But there were also large colony delegates from Virginia and small colony delegates from Rhode Island; there were northern delegates and southern delegates; there were commercial delegates and agricultural delegates. The various divisions among the delegates made the debates interesting and unpredictable. Perhaps more important than all these divisions was the strong desire of most delegates to find compromises and consensus. Jay shared this desire; he did not agree with Henry, but he did praise Virginia and even suggested he would be willing to agree to give it a more than equal vote.[11]

The delegates' search for common ground is shown by how they resolved, later that same day, the question of whether to start their sessions with a prayer. John Jay and John Rutledge of South Carolina expressed concern that "we were so divided in religious sentiments, some Episcopalians, some Quakers, some Anabaptists, some Presbyterians, and some Congregationalists," that it would be uncomfortable for some to "join in the same act of worship." Samuel Adams, not known as particularly devout, rose and said he "was no bigot, and could hear a prayer from a gentleman of piety and virtue." Adams suggested that they hear the next morning from a local Anglican priest. Jay and Rutledge, both devout Anglicans, could not object, and the prayers the next day were generally agreed to be fitting and moving.[12]

One reason the delegates were moved to pray was that they had received alarming news by an express rider from the north. According to this rider, there had been a skirmish between British and Americans near Boston, and even now British "troops and fleets [were] cannonading the town of Boston." He also reported that armed men from all over New England were converging on Boston to support the people there. The Congress and Philadelphia were thrown into "utmost confusion" and "bells muffled rung" all afternoon. The delegates believed that war had started and their faces showed "the most unfeigned marks of sorrow." The reports of fighting were soon proved false, but this "war scare" showed that many Americans were ready not only for resolutions and boycotts, but even military action.[13]

A committee of twenty-four members, including Jay, was appointed to prepare a statement of America's rights, its grievances, and the means of redress. At the debates of this committee on the next day, Jay agreed with John Adams of Massachusetts and others that it was necessary to "recur to the law of nature," as well as the British constitution, to define and defend American rights. On the other side, Joseph Galloway and James Duane argued that

American rights derived only from the British constitution and the colonial charters. Again, a simple division of the delegates into conservatives and radicals does not capture the complexity of the debate. Although Jay was generally conservative, as were Galloway and Duane, on this issue Jay sided with the radicals like Adams. The "ingenious" debates of this committee continued at such length that a subcommittee was formed to move matters forward; after its report debates continued in the "great committee." [14]

A few days later, another rider arrived from the north: Paul Revere brought with him a copy of the Suffolk Resolves. The preamble to this document called upon the people of Massachusetts to resist "the unparalleled usurpation of unconstitutional power" by which "our capital is robbed of the means of life, whereby the streets of Boston are thronged with military executioners, whereby our coasts are lined and harbors crowded with ships of war." The resolutions themselves, however, "cheerfully" affirmed that King George was "our rightful sovereign" and asked the Philadelphia Congress to adopt measures which would renew "that harmony and union between Great Britain and the colonies, so earnestly wished for by all good men." [15] After only a day of debate, the Congress "unanimously" ratified the resolves. Congress urged the people of Massachusetts to continue "in the same firm and temperate conduct," trusting that the "united efforts of North America in their behalf" would persuade Britain "quickly to introduce better men and wiser measures." Congress published both the Suffolk Resolves and its approval of them, the first public statement by the Congress. [16]

At first, it is not easy to see why the conservatives accepted these radical resolutions. Of course, we cannot be sure of each delegate's views, since voting was by states, and the votes of individual delegates were not recorded. Moreover, in the context of the emerging consensus in Philadelphia, the resolves were not really that radical. They did not advocate armed action; indeed they effectively prohibited armed action other than "merely upon the defensive." The delegates viewed the resolves as a useful way of signaling to Britain that they would stand firmly behind the people of Massachusetts, as long as the resistance in Massachusetts was not provocative. [17]

Consensus among the delegates developed not merely during formal discussions, but also, and perhaps especially, during informal conversations in taverns and at tables. One evening, some of the gentlemen of Philadelphia gave a grand dinner at the State House for the delegates, and about five hundred people dined at once. More often, the delegates were entertained at the houses of wealthy Philadelphians. John Adams described one dinner as a "mighty feast" with "the very best of claret, madeira, and burgundy," as well as "melons, fine beyond description, and pears and peaches as excellent." Thomas Cushing reported to his wife that, after Congress ceased work at around three or four in the afternoon, we "then dine with the nobles of Philadelphia, with seldom less than ten, twelve or fifteen in company." [18]

There are no similar comments from Jay because only one of his letters from this period survives. In this letter, to John Vardill in England, Jay reported that the "indignation of all ranks of people is very much roused by the Boston and Canada bills. God knows how the contest will end. I sincerely wish it may terminate in a lasting union with Great Britain." He was "obliged to be very reserved on this subject by the injunction of secrecy laid on all members of the Congress" but hoped in another letter to "be able to be more explicit." [19]

In late September, Congress began debating when and how the American colonies should cease to export goods to and import goods from Britain. Although it has been suggested that Jay opposed a trade boycott, the limited evidence proves precisely the opposite. [20] According to notes taken by John Adams, Jay argued that "negotiation, suspension of commerce, and war are the only three things. War is by general consent to be waived at present. I am for negotiation and suspension of commerce." [21] There was, indeed, almost complete consensus within the Congress in favor of both non-importation and non-exportation. The critical questions were timing and scope. The Virginian delegates wanted to be allowed to continue exports until late 1775, to allow time for the Virginia tobacco crop in the ground to be exported to Britain. Many delegates objected that a delay in the boycott would delay Britain's reaction. As Samuel Chase of Maryland put it, "non-exportation at a future day cannot avail us." In the end, the other colonies had to yield to Virginia, and the date set for the end of exports was September 1775. [22]

The resolutions were turned into an "association," a detailed set of rules regarding trade, to be enforced by committees of inspection, elected "in every county, city and town" by those entitled to vote in regular legislative elections.

This administrative provision in the association was perhaps the most important action of the first Congress. Thousands of people participated in the election of these local committees, and the committees themselves involved thousands of others in leading the resistance at the local level. During the fall and winter of 1774 and early 1775, as the crisis continued and deepened, these local committees gradually supplanted the royal governments as the effective government of the colonies.[23]

Although in Jay's view war was "by general consent" to be avoided, there were delegates who favored more warlike measures. In early October, Richard Henry Lee moved that the Congress recommend that the colonies arm and equip their militias. Patrick Henry supported the motion, arguing that "arms are a resource to which we shall be forced." Various delegates opposed them: John Rutledge called the proposal "in degree, a declaration of war," and Benjamin Harrison said that arming the militia would "tend only to irritate, whereas our business is to reconcile." The motion was rejected. A few days later, Paul Revere again arrived, this time with the news that General Gage had begun to fortify the narrow neck of land which connected Boston with the mainland. Samuel Adams suggested that Congress should demand that Gage cease his works or face "consequences of the most serious nature," including "the horrors of a civil war." Most of the delegates were not ready for such warlike language, however, so they responded in a far less strident tone.[24]

As Congress was debating the trade boycott and rejecting military measures, it was also drafting petitions and statements, and it was here that Jay made his major contribution. Congress appointed Jay, Livingston, and Lee as a committee to prepare two documents: an address to the British people and a memorial to the American people. According to Thomas Jefferson, both Lee and Jay prepared drafts of the British address, but when read to Congress, his friend Lee's draft met with a "dead silence" followed by a few "faint compliments." Livingston then rose "and observed that a friend of his had been sketching what he had thought might be proper for such an address" and read Jay's draft out to the Congress. "There was but one sentiment of admiration" and the draft was "adopted with scarce an alteration." It is a nice story, but probably not true. Jefferson's information was second-hand and his account written thirty years later. None of the delegates who were present in Philadelphia, in their contemporary notes or letters, mentioned rejection of a Lee draft and acceptance of a Jay draft. Jay's own recollection, years later, was that the committee had agreed that Lee would prepare the memorial to the Americans and he would prepare the address to the British, "both of which were done accordingly." [25]

The final address (the draft unfortunately does not survive) provides interesting insights into the thinking of Jay and the Congress at this time. Jay started by reminding his British readers of American support in the French and Indian wars. "Did we not, in the last war, add all the strength of this vast continent to the force which repelled our common enemy? Did we not leave our native shores, and meet disease and death, to promote the success of British arms in foreign climates?" Rather than thank the Americans, Britain immediately after the war attempted to "drain this country of all its money" through the unfair and unconstitutional Revenue Act. Jay reserved special scorn for the provisions of the Act which deprived Americans of the right to be "tried by an honest uninfluenced jury" and subjected them instead "to the sad necessity of being judged by a single man, a creature of the Crown." [26]

Jay essentially admitted that the Boston radicals should not have destroyed the tea, but he argued that the proper response was a civil lawsuit against those responsible. Instead, the East India Company had persuaded Parliament to punish the whole town of Boston. "Without incurring or being charged with a forfeiture of their rights, without being heard, without being tried, without law, and without justice, by an Act of Parliament, their charter is destroyed, their liberties violated, their constitution and form of government changed." He was equally critical of the Quebec Act, which in his view would make the Canadians "fit instruments" to be used by Britain "to reduce the ancient free Protestant Colonies to the same state of slavery with themselves." And he was "astonished" that Britain would establish in Canada the Catholic religion, "a religion that has deluged your island in blood, and dispersed impiety, bigotry, persecution, murder and rebellion through every part of the world." [27]

The people of Britain may have heard that the Americans were "seditious, impatient of government and desirous of independence." They should rest "assured that these are not facts, but calumnies." If Britons would permit

Americans to "be as free as yourselves" then "we shall ever esteem a union
with you to be our greatest glory and our greatest happiness." But if "neither
the voice of justice, the dictates of the law, the principles of the constitution, or
the suggestions of humanity can restrain your hands from shedding human
blood in such an impious cause," then Britons should know that "we will never
submit to be hewers of wood or drawers of water for any ministry or nation in
the world." The Americans prayed that Britain would elect a Parliament of
"wisdom, independence and public spirit," which could "restore that harmony,
friendship and fraternal affection between all the inhabitants of his Majesty's
kingdoms and territories, so ardently wished for by every true and honest
American." [28]

The Address to the People of Great Britain was an impressive first effort for
someone who, only a few months before, had been uninterested in politics. Not
surprisingly, in his address, Jay emphasized legal and procedural issues, such
as the right to a jury trial and a voice in legislation. He also echoed themes he
had heard over the years from his father: strong support of Britain in its wars
against France and strong hatred of Catholics.

When Congress completed its work, there was a dinner at City Tavern to
celebrate. Although not everyone in Congress had agreed on every issue, delegates from twelve diverse colonies (Georgia was not present) had achieved a
remarkable degree of unity. The actions and addresses of the Congress, considered as a whole, were both firm and temperate. Most of the delegates believed
that the political and commercial pressure from the colonies would force some
concessions from Britain, in the same way that such pressure had worked ten
years ago in the Stamp Act crisis. For himself, Jay could reflect that only a few
weeks ago he had been an unknown commercial lawyer. Now he had proved
himself, during this Congress, able to hold his own with the best debaters and
writers of the colonies.[29]

When he returned to New York in November of 1774, Jay found a city increasingly divided between Patriots and Loyalists. Many of the most vocal Loyalists
were Anglicans, including Myles Cooper, Jay's former teacher at King's College, Samuel Seabury, a young Anglican minister in Westchester, and Thomas
Chandler, who argued in an anonymous essay that the Bible "requir[es] us on

pain of damnation to be duly subject to the higher powers, and not to resist their lawful authority." One of those who responded in print was Jay's young friend Alexander Hamilton, a student at King's College at this time. Jay and Hamilton had probably met in 1773, when Hamilton was a student at Elizabeth Town Academy. Hamilton arrived in America from the Caribbean in late 1772 or early 1773 with neither family nor fortune, and only a few friends, but he had a brilliant mind, intense ambition, and limitless energy. Like Jay, he found the Livingston women attractive; a few years later he would challenge Kitty Livingston "to meet me in whatever path you dare" especially "the flowery walks and roseate bowers of Cupid." In late 1774 and early 1775, Hamilton published his first political pamphlets, lengthy anonymous responses to the anonymous essays of Seabury. Many people assumed these essays were the work of Jay.[30]

Jay himself, however, was not very active in politics in late 1774 or early 1775. In a letter to Robert Livingston, he confessed that he "ought to say something to you about politics," but would not because he was "sick of the subject." He was a member of New York's "committee of sixty," elected to enforce the Congress's trade restrictions, but not very active in its work. When the committee received a letter from Connecticut expressing concern about reported divisions of opinion in New York, it was Jay who drafted the reply, arguing that "the people in general are zealous in the cause." New Yorkers were, in his words, "as sensible of the blessings of liberty as any people on the continent."[31]

In reassuring the Connecticut committee, Jay was considerably understating the strength of Loyalism in New York. Indeed, many of his friends were or would become Loyalists. One of them, William Laight, wrote to another, John Vardill, regretting that Jay, who used to be sound and loyal, had now become a "Blue Skin" or Revolutionary.

> How to account for [the] change I know not, unless it is owing to his too sudden elevation to a popular character ... Popularity must be the object at which Jay is aiming, and to please the populace he must have thrown aside his old principles. Will you believe me when I tell you that a few nights ago he was chairman, and appeared to be highly proud of his station, at a meeting, where Lamb, Sears, Barclay the Barber, Roorback etc. etc. were the principal orators? A further evidence of his

defection is that the Blues trumpet his merits and patriotism at every corner of the streets.

Laight urged Vardill not to confront Jay, since it was the hope and "prayer of his friends that he should see his error." [32]

Some believed that Jay himself was among the Loyalists at this time. Benjamin Franklin, writing from London to Joseph Galloway in Pennsylvania, noted that it was "whispered by ministerial people that yourself and Mr. Jay of New York are friends to their measures, and give them private intelligence of the views of the popular or country party in America." These whispers show how imperfectly London understood America. Jay was indeed a friend of Britain in the way that many other Americans were at this time, in that he ardently hoped for some compromise and reconciliation. But he was no friend of the recent Acts of Parliament. And he was not providing "private intelligence" about the affairs of Congress, unless his innocuous letter to Vardill could be called intelligence. [33]

In late April 1775, Jay attended the first two days of a provincial convention, held at the Exchange Building in New York, to discuss instructions for and select delegates to the next Continental Congress. He was apparently not present, however, on the day when this convention selected twelve delegates, including himself, his friend Robert Livingston, Robert's cousin Philip Livingston, and Jay's distant cousin Philip Schuyler. The Convention gave these men "or any five of them" authority to decide at the Continental Congress on "such measures as shall be judged most effectual for the preservation and re-establishment of American rights and privileges, and the restoration of harmony between Great Britain and the colonies." [34]

On Sunday April 23, 1775, a rider from the north galloped south into New York City and finally reined in his horse on Broadway. There he announced, to all who would listen, that General Gage had sent British regulars out of Boston to seize American weapons in Lexington and Concord, that the regulars had fired on the American militiamen, that the Americans had returned fire, and that dozens of men were dead and injured. When pressed for proof, he showed dispatches signed by respected committee members in Massachusetts. War had started in Boston, and people naturally assumed that New York would be next. "Tales of all kinds [were] invented, believed, denied, discredited." A crowd went to the wharves, where they emptied two ships of flour and bread intended for the British army. Later in the day a crowd broke into City Hall and carried off more than five hundred muskets, along with bayonets and ammunition. A few days later, an armed mob forced the customs collector to hand over his keys to Isaac Sears, who then declared the port closed.[35]

The committee of sixty, formed to enforce the continental association, was not able to control of the situation. They urged an election of a new, larger committee, with one hundred members, to govern the city. Jay, Duane and Van Schaack drafted a new "association" for New York City. In it, the inhabitants solemnly agreed to "follow the advice" of the new committee for "the preservation of peace and good order, and the safety of individuals and private property." A thousand New Yorkers signed this document within a few days. On the first of May, the city elected the committee of one hundred, including Jay.[36]

This committee met almost daily in early May 1775, but Jay was busy getting his legal and personal affairs in order before leaving for Philadelphia, so he attended only twice. He was also missing on the morning when the New England and New York delegates were accompanied across the Hudson River by a cheering crowd of five hundred people, including two hundred armed militia men. Perhaps Jay left a day or two earlier to spend some time with his wife in Elizabeth Town; perhaps he left a day or two later to finish up his legal work in New York City; perhaps he simply did not want to be part of this political spectacle.[37]

John Jay joined the Continental Congress in Philadelphia in the middle of May 1775. Instead of meeting in Carpenters' Hall, this second Congress met in the Assembly Room of the Pennsylvania State House, the building now known as Independence Hall. The members of the second Congress were basically the same as those of the first, although there were a few significant additions. Benjamin Franklin, the most famous American of the day, nearly seventy years old and recently returned from a long stay in England, joined the Pennsylvania delegation in May. Perhaps because he was angry at the way he had been treated in his last months in England, perhaps to prove that he was American not English, Franklin soon joined the radical wing of the Congress. John

Adams wrote home to his wife Abigail that Franklin "does not hesitate at our boldest measures, but rather seems to think us too irresolute and backward." Thomas Jefferson, a quiet young planter from Virginia with varied intellectual interests, joined the Virginia delegation in Philadelphia in June. He was silent during debates, but in committees he soon showed himself to be "prompt, frank, explicit, and decisive." [38]

This new Congress faced many difficult questions. One was whether, given Britain's failure to answer the prior petitions, it made any sense to petition Britain again. Another question was whether Congress should take formal control of and responsibility for the Americans outside Boston, an "army" without proper officers, training, or provisions. A related question was whether Congress should attempt to defend New York and the Hudson River against the expected arrival there of an armada of British warships. A few days after they gathered, the delegates learned that a small group of men, under Ethan Allen and Benedict Arnold, had captured the forts at Ticonderoga and Crown Point in northern New York. When asked in whose name he had seized Ticonderoga, Allen replied "in the name of the Great Jehovah and the Continental Congress." But Congress had not instructed the attack, and now had to consider whether to attempt to retain the forts. [39]

Congress spent most of its first month debating these issues behind closed doors; only scattered notes survive. Richard Henry Lee of Virginia started the debate by moving for creation of an army, a motion supported by several others. Jay's friend Livingston asked whether it made sense to raise an army before they decided upon the goals of armed resistance. Dickinson admitted that a "vigorous preparation for war" was necessary, but argued that Congress should also attempt another "plan for a reconciliation," and if necessary concede that Britain alone had the right to regulate American trade. A week later, Jay was one of the moderates, supporting Dickinson's argument that Congress should send agents to Britain to negotiate a peace treaty. Among those who attacked this idea was Jay's friend Rutledge, who was "against any concession whatever," and treated Dickinson's argument "with utmost contempt." [40]

By the end of May Congress had resolved some of these issues. First, Congress instructed New York to raise a militia force and build forts on the Hudson with a view to blocking British ships. In a cover letter drafted by Jay, the New York delegates stressed that the resolution should not be read to authorize the seizure of British military provisions. Second, after initially declining to accept Ticonderoga and Crown Point, Congress decided to attempt to hold the forts. Congress sent a letter, also drafted by Jay, to "the people of Canada" to assure them that the Americans did not intend to use these forts to threaten Canada. "You may rely on our assurances, that these colonies will pursue no measures whatever, but such as friendship and a regard for our mutual safety and interest may suggest." Third, Congress agreed that it would prepare another petition to the King, and in early June appointed a committee including Dickinson, Franklin and Jay to draw up the petition.[41]

Although Jay was busy in Philadelphia, he kept in touch with events in and around New York. From his brother Frederick, Jay learned that "some people in disguise" had attempted to "lay hands upon" his former teacher, Myles Cooper, and the editor of a Loyalist newspaper, James Rivington. Cooper managed to escape through a back door of the college (aided, according to tradition, by Alexander Hamilton) and a few days later boarded a ship for England, never to return. From his father, Jay learned that "1700 inhabitants of [Westchester] County have signed the Association" and "that the companies of militia have weekly their military exercises." Jay urged his wife to be "cheerful and in spirits" notwithstanding their separation. And he asked her, in her letters, to be "as particular as may be consistent with prudence, for in times like these we should be cautious what we commit to paper."[42]

Jay himself was cautious as he put pen to paper on a draft petition to the King. The colonists were "bound to Your Majesty by the strongest ties of allegiance and affection" and they had "the utmost confidence in the paternal care of their prince." (Jay would have been less confident if he had known that the King had already declared that the "die is now cast" and the colonists "must either submit or triumph.") Jay claimed that the colonies did not intend "to question the right of the British Parliament to regulate the commercial concerns of Empire" and suggested that the King should "commission some good and great men" to meet with commissioners appointed by the colonial legislatures to attempt to "devise some means of accommodating those unhappy dissentions."[43]

Jay's draft was found among the papers of Dickinson, suggesting that

Dickinson had it in hand as he drafted the "Olive Branch Petition" ultimately adopted by Congress. Like Jay, Dickinson set the petition up for signature by the individual delegates, rather than signature by the Congress, sensing that this would seem more proper. Dickinson also followed Jay's deferential tone and lifted a few of Jay's phrases. But Dickinson omitted Jay's concession that Parliament could regulate commerce and his suggestion that commissioners should be appointed. In short, a comparison of these two documents suggests that Jay was more conciliatory than even the member of Congress known as the leader of the conciliators.[44]

Jay was on another important committee at this time, to consider a letter from the Massachusetts Provincial Congress requesting advice from the Continental Congress as to whether it should form a new government. Although some of the more radical delegates wanted to urge Massachusetts to form a new constitution, most realized that this would suggest a final break with Britain. The compromise devised was to argue that the actions of the Governor invalidated his commission, allowing the provincial congress to govern as a provisional legislature under the colony's charter. It was a clever argument, perhaps too clever, but it postponed a definite break with Britain.[45]

In June, Congress made its most important decision of the year, naming George Washington to head the Continental Army, and sending him to Boston to organize the troops there. Congress followed up by appointing generals and other officers to serve under Washington, including Jay's cousin Philip Schuyler. Congress developed and adopted a detailed set of military regulations to govern the conduct of the war. It issued the first "continental" bills to raise funds to pay for the troops. The determination of Congress to arm itself was reinforced when news arrived of the fighting at Bunker Hill in Boston, fighting which left more than four hundred Americans dead.[46]

Jefferson recalled, many years later, an argument at about this time between Jay and Richard Henry Lee. Jefferson had urged William Livingston to take on a drafting assignment because Livingston was reputed the author of the *Address to the People of Great Britain*, which Jefferson considered "the first composition in the English language." Livingston relayed this comment to Jay, who naturally assumed that it was Lee, the other member of the prior year's committee, who was denying Jay credit for the draft. A few days later, while Jefferson and Lee were talking in the legislative lobby, Jay approached them. "Taking [Lee] by a button of the coat, [Jay] said to him pretty sternly 'I understand, sir, that you informed this gentleman that the Address to the People of Great Britain, presented to the committee by me, was drawn by Governor Livingston.'" Jefferson attempted to calm Jay down, assuring him that "though indeed I had been so informed, it was not by Mr. Lee, whom I had never heard utter a word on the subject." Presumably this eased the tension so that Jay released Lee's coat.[47]

In early July 1775, Jay and the other New York delegates in Philadelphia received a proposed plan of accommodation devised by the New York Provincial Congress. This plan, like Jay's draft petition to the King, conceded to Parliament the right to regulate trade for the "general benefit of the whole" empire, but reserved to the colonial legislatures the right to impose taxes in the colonies. The plan, like Jay's address of the prior year, criticized the Quebec Act, arguing that "the indulgence and establishment of popery" in Canada would "weaken the security" of the American colonies. In a side letter to Jay, Gouverneur Morris said this provision was "the most arrant nonsense" which he "opposed until I was weary." If this plan had arrived a few weeks earlier, before the news of Bunker Hill, Jay would probably have pressed the whole Congress to adopt it. But now Congress's course was more or less set: it would focus its energies on military matters. So Jay and the other New Yorkers did not bother to introduce the plan. They thanked the Provincial Congress and, in a postscript drafted by Jay, urged them to avoid religious issues, "which have for ages had no tendency other than that of banishing peace and charity from the world."[48]

Congress recessed for a few weeks in August and September 1775: Jay spent this time with his wife and her family in New Jersey. When Congress resumed its work in September 1775, it focused for several weeks on trade. Britain had closed the ports in most but not all the colonies, allowing those of New York, the Carolinas and Georgia to remain open. The key question was whether Congress should also allow those ports to remain open, so that the colonies could earn some money to purchase arms and other supplies, or whether all the ports should be closed in the name of fairness. Jay urged that the proper course was for the "other colonies [to] avail themselves of the custom houses in the exempted colonies." Closing all the ports would be "like cutting the foot to the shoe, not making a shoe for the foot."[49]

To complicate matters, under the British trade laws, the colonies were by and large required to trade only with Britain and British colonies. America could not expect to obtain military supplies now from Britain, nor could it expect its own meager factories to provide it the necessary supplies. But trading with other nations, especially in military goods, could be viewed as at least a *de facto* declaration of independence. Although Jay opposed a declaration of independence at this time, he favored trade, and indeed offered what was for the time a very broad argument for free trade. "We have more to expect from the enterprise, activity and industry of private adventurers than from the luke-warmness of assemblies. We want French woolens, Dutch worsteds, duck for tents, German steel, etc ... Shall we shut the door against private enterprise?"[50]

Another issue involved that controversial commodity, tea. Many New York merchants had large quantities of Dutch tea on hand, smuggled into the colony in violation of British law, which now could not be exported or used without violation of American law. Waiting for Jay and his colleagues, upon their return to Philadelphia, was a letter from the New York Provincial Congress, urging that the New York merchants be allowed to sell their tea, to raise funds to purchase ammunition and other supplies. The New York delegates thus argued for an exemption for this tea.[51]

After much debate, Congress decided all these issues against "free trade." In late October and early November 1775, Congress adopted a general ban on exports from the colonies, other than trade with the explicit permission of Congress and certain limited trade with the non-British West Indies. In early December, Jay complained that "Congress have at length determined against the tea holders, a measure in my opinion neither just nor politic."[52]

At about this time, Jay received an interesting letter from William Laight, the friend who had regretted his "blue" tendencies. Laight, recently returned from England, reported that there were many there who "hesitate not to declare that the Americans are in a state of rebellion, and that the most coercive measures ought to be used in order to bring them to a sense of their duty." There were others in Britain who "speak in favor of America, in general terms, but at the same time declare, that while the colonies are protected by this Kingdom, they ought to contribute in a constitutional manner their proportion of the expenses of the Empire." Perhaps most worrisome for Jay, his friend claimed that "the commerce of this kingdom has as yet been very little affected by the non-importation agreement. This is accounted for by the demand for British manufactures from various parts of Europe." In other words, American efforts to pressure Britain through trade restrictions were not having much effect.[53]

In spite of this and other discouraging news, Jay did not give up hope for reconciliation. In December, he urged that the official New York assembly should make a formal statement regarding its desire to "see peace between Great Britain and the colonies re-established." He drafted a paper at this time to refute the "ungenerous and groundless charge" that the colonies were "aiming at independence or a total separation from Great Britain." In this paper, he quoted from the journal of the Continental Congress a dozen passages which "abundantly prove the malice and falsity of such a charge." And in January 1776, he devoted many hours to secret negotiations with an unofficial representative from Britain, part of the "last effort before the Declaration of Independence to reconcile the American colonies with Great Britain."[54]

This unofficial representative, Lord Drummond, had lived in New York City and mingled in its upper society from 1768 through 1774. After a year in England, he arrived in Philadelphia in late December 1775, and presented to a few selected delegates a six-point "Plan of Accommodation." Under Drummond's plan, the colonies would provide the King "a perpetual grant" of revenue derived from taxes the colonies designed and imposed upon themselves. In return, Parliament would relinquish "all future claims of taxation" over the colonies, a major concession. Drummond claimed that his proposed plan was approved by Britain's most senior ministers, including Lord North, Lord Dartmouth and Lord Chief Justice Mansfield.[55]

Drummond was careful in selecting the delegates with whom he spoke, and one of those he selected was Jay. Drummond explained in his notes that Jay represented "moderate men" who hoped he would "prove some check to violent measures." He had, "in the course of the former session rendered himself much considered in [Congress] by his readiness in debate as well as in composition," and he was now "much inclined to reconciliation." Jay's initial reaction to Drummond's proposal was that it was improper to take "any fresh steps on any business of this sort while a petition as yet unanswered lay before the King." Drummond responded that the ministers intended to answer the petition, and outlined the anticipated answer. At this, Jay "entered readily" into discussions with Drummond on the terms of his plan. He thought the article on a "perpetual grant might alarm," but "when he came to view the compensations on the other hand in their fullest extent his apprehensions subsided." He "saw the salutary effect that would be produced by a removal of the dread of taxation."[56]

Reconciliation, it seemed, was not out of reach. At their meetings in early January, Drummond, Duane and Jay discussed how to deal with the anticipated opposition of some of the more radical, southern delegates. They agreed that, if the proposed terms were accepted by "a *majority* of the American representatives," but rejected on the part of "any *particular* colonies," then the delegates to Congress would "*adjourn* for the purpose of taking the sense of their respective colonies." Jay believed that the people of the southern colonies, if faced with a choice between "the re-establishment of peace founded on such liberal terms on one hand" and "all the horrors of a civil war on the other," would choose peace rather than the war desired by "a set of people who were obnoxious to them." In other words, he intended to appeal to the people of the southern colonies over the heads of their own delegates. He urged Drummond to return to Britain to carry "overtures from the colonies on the subject of accommodation." Drummond responded that it would be better if Congress sent its own "deputation" to Britain.[57]

Even while Jay was pursuing reconciliation with Britain, he was also working to develop relations with France. In late November 1775, Congress named Franklin, Jay and three others to a committee to correspond "with our friends in Great Britain, Ireland and other parts of the world." Franklin was in every way the senior member of this committee, and the committee's first action was to write to several of Franklin's friends. In a letter to Charles William Frederic Dumas, a Frenchman who had lived for many years among the diplomats at The Hague, they asked whether France and other nations would support the Americans "if, as it seems likely to happen, we should be obliged to break off all connection with Britain, and declare ourselves an independent people." A few days later the committee sent a similar letter to Arthur Lee, then in London, asking him to inquire discreetly about "the disposition of the foreign powers towards us." On this same day, Franklin sent a letter to the son of the Spanish King, thanking him for a handsome edition of the Roman historian Sallust. Franklin regretted that there was, as yet, nothing written by an American to compare with Sallust, but the colonies were "a rising state which seems likely to act a part of some importance on the stage of human affairs, and furnish materials for a future Sallust." Franklin hoped that this American state would "form a close and firm alliance with Spain." [58]

In this same month, December 1775, Jay and the other committee members had several secret nighttime meetings with a Frenchman who had recently arrived in Philadelphia, Achard de Bonvouloir. De Bonvouloir told the committee members that he was merely a French officer, traveling on his own, but the committee members sensed that he was at least semi-official, and indeed he had official instructions. The committee members asked de Bonvouloir whether France would aid the Americans and what France would expect in return for such aid. De Bonvouloir was cautious in his response: France wished America well, it might provide assistance, but what the assistance would be he could not say. De Bonvouloir in turn had questions for the Americans, about the strength and disposition of their forces, both at land and at sea. De Bonvouloir was favorably impressed with the American army, which he estimated at more than fifty thousand armed men, and with the determination of the Americans to be free "whatever it cost." [59]

Jay was thus, in late 1775 and early 1776, working to reconcile with Britain *and* to establish relations with Britain's mortal enemy, France. He did not see these parallel efforts as inconsistent. While he hoped and prayed that Britain and the colonies would compromise and reconcile, with each passing week he recognized that this was less likely. It made sense, in this context, to begin building up the diplomatic contacts, as well as the armies, that would be necessary for war. He summed up his views in a brief letter to his brother James, who had now been in Britain for many years, and who John feared would side with Britain if there was a war. "Though we desire reconciliation, [we] are well prepared for contrary measures. This is an unnatural quarrel and God only knows why the British Empire should be torn to pieces by unjust attempts to subjugate us." Instead of a customary closing, John wrote only "adieu, dear brother."[60]

The fall and early winter of 1775 were a difficult period for John personally. Sarah was pregnant with their first child, but John could not be with her. His letters were full of tender concern. "Again let me beg your never ceasing attention to your health. Reflect on its *importance!*" By early December, John was looking forward to the holidays "as much as a school boy ever did." A few days before Christmas, however, he wrote with bitter disappointment that Congress "refused to give me leave of absence." "My horses were new shod, wheels greased, clothes put up and every thing ready to set off." Leave was denied, however, because there were only five New York delegates present, the minimum number required to represent New York under the current instructions. John assured Sarah that "nothing but actual imprisonment" would prevent him from coming soon, in time to be present for the birth of their child.[61]

John was worried not only about his pregnant wife but also about his aged and infirm parents. In December, he received a letter from his father, who clearly feared the coming conflagration. "I once expected to pass the remainder of my life in the enjoyment of happy days with my family, which to my inexpressible grief I have now no prospect of." In January, John received another reminder of mortality, a letter from his friend Robert reporting the death of his own father, Judge Livingston. Robert wrote that death had deprived him "at one stroke of the warmest friend, the tenderest parent, and the most instructive and agreeable companion." John wrote back that his feelings, on reading Robert's letter, "mock[ed] the force of philosophy."[62]

Finally, John Jay was concerned about his law practice, which was languishing in his absence. One of his law clerks, Robert Troup, wrote that "when I reflect upon the present business of the office, I am filled with the deepest sorrow. Formerly it was extensive, and attended with much profit. Now it is confined within very narrow bounds, and of course accompanied by little gain." Jay was not even, at this point, being paid for attending the Continental Congress. When the Provincial Congress finally decided to pay its delegates four dollars a day for attending the Continental Congress, John commented to Sarah that this "does by no means equal the loss I have sustained by the appointment, but the convention I suppose consider the honor as an equivalent for the residue." [63]

In early January 1776, word reached Philadelphia that the New York Provincial Congress had decided that any three New York delegates would suffice to represent the colony in the Continental Congress. Since there were four others in Philadelphia, Jay was at last free to leave, and he left immediately for Elizabeth Town. There, in late January, Sarah gave birth to their first child, Peter Augustus Jay. John was pleased to have a son but concerned about his wife's health. Soon his fears had a basis, for Sarah fell ill. John's father Peter was also ill, so ill that John's brother Frederick feared the old man had only another month or two. But Peter was pleased to learn that his grandson bore both his name and his father's name. Frederick reported that the "old people would give half their estate to see [Sarah] and the colt." [64]

Although Jay's focus in the first two months of 1776 was on his family, he found some time for politics. His young friend Alexander Hamilton wrote from New York City that there would probably be an assembly election in February. Hamilton feared that the resistance leaders, so busy with their "new institutions," would think the old official assembly of "little importance," allowing the Tories to "elect their own creatures." Jay agreed that the patriots should name their own candidates and was himself among those named and elected from New York City. This official assembly, however, never met; Governor Tryon postponed its meeting several times, until he could no longer do so from his British warship. Jay urged Livingston, still grieving for his father, to focus on politics. "The spring advances fast and as soon as the roads will permit you, go to camp, to Philadelphia, in short anywhere, so that you are but moving." [65]

In early January, news arrived of the disastrous defeat of the small American force which was attempting to capture Quebec City. The American commander, the dashing young Richard Montgomery, had been killed and his colleague, Benedict Arnold, severely wounded. At about the same time, news arrived that British warships had bombarded and destroyed Norfolk, Virginia. In early February, when two British warships arrived in New York harbor, New Yorkers feared that the whole fleet had arrived, and the streets were jammed with people fleeing the city. A few weeks later, Americans learned of the Prohibitory Act, which instructed the Royal Navy to treat all American ships as enemies, subject to capture and sale as prizes. With each passing month, reconciliation seemed less likely and war more imminent.[66]

Jay returned to Philadelphia in March 1776 after "a most disagreeable journey" on "intolerable bad roads." Today, the work of the Congress in this period is generally viewed as the prelude to the Declaration of Independence in July 1776. At the time, however, Jay did not view his work this way; he saw only the host of issues that had to be resolved day by day. For example, on the very day he arrived, he attended a meeting of the committee on foreign correspondence and helped draw up instructions for his friend Silas Deane, who was going to France to acquire war supplies and explore the possibility of an alliance. Among other things, Deane carried with him to France "a mode of invisible writing" devised by James Jay. A few days later, Congress debated how to deal with a letter from Lord Drummond, requesting passports for an unnamed peace delegation to Britain. During the course of the debate, which lasted for at least four hours, it emerged that several moderate delegates, including Duane and Rutledge, had discussed peace with Drummond in January. This information angered many other delegates, and prompted one to move that Congress condemn any peace negotiations by any "public bodies or private persons other than the Congress." The debate must have been uncomfortable for Jay, one of Drummond's main interlocutors.[67]

Now that Britain had declared war on American shipping, most delegates favored allowing American privateers to attack British shipping. Jay was one of those who argued for privateers, but he also argued for continued trade with Britain, to the extent that it provided arms to the American patriots. The final resolution followed his suggestion, exempting "any vessel bringing settlers, arms, ammunition, or warlike stores to and for the use of these colonies." Once the resolution passed, Jay wrote to a friend in New York, Alexander McDougall, saying that he hoped New York could send out dozens of privateers to prey on enemy shipping, as it had in the wars against France. "I feel so much for the honor our calumniated colony that it would give me pleasure to see them distinguished by vigorous exertion."[68]

A similar question of "honor" was involved in the issue of the "loyalty oaths" which General Charles Lee demanded from suspected New York Tories. Jay was angered by Lee's policy, not because he held modern notions about freedom to hold personal political views. Lee was merely a military officer, with no authority from the New York legislature. In Jay's view, to "impose a test is a sovereign act of legislation, and when the army become our legislators, the people that moment become slaves." Also, Lee was an outsider, and Jay resented his assertion of a right to control New Yorkers. Jay and Duane persuaded Congress to resolve that "no oath by way of test be imposed upon, exacted, or required of any of the inhabitants of these colonies, by any military officers."[69]

Recognizing by April 1776 that it was likely that "the sword must decide the controversy," Jay focused increasingly on military matters. He helped to secure a commission for his friend Alexander Hamilton as an artillery captain, a role in which he quickly distinguished himself. He found in Philadelphia a sample of a pike, a stake with a spear head that could be used until sufficient guns were available, and sent it to New York by coach, so that it could be replicated there. When he heard that people on Staten Island were providing supplies to the British warships, he suggested that the rebels should attempt to deny the British supplies and water. He asked for numbers regarding troop strengths in New York; he pressed a contractor to fulfill his commitment to make muskets; and he urged the creation of a plant to produce saltpeter.[70]

One of the less admirable aspects of the American army was the obsessive concern of the officers about their relative ranks. Congress was forever dealing with officers who thought themselves slighted by another's promotion, and Jay had to deal with his share of such issues. McDougall wrote him in March complaining that, by virtue of a rule basing rank on first continental appointment, he would rank beneath those "who have been appointed eight months after" he had started to serve in the provincial forces. Jay wrote back that the rule was necessary to ensure equality among continental officers and that no personal slight was intended. In response to a similar complaint from another officer, he "regretted that all human affairs are liable to errors and imperfections, and that real as well as imaginary evils are so widely spread throughout the world."[71]

On a more positive note, Jay was called upon by Congress to draft a letter thanking Washington for his services. Washington would not accept pay, but his countrymen could "without your permission bestow upon you the largest share of their affections and esteem." History would record that "under your direction an undisciplined band of husbandmen in the course of a few months became soldiers," and that Washington and his men had prevented the British army from working their intended "desolation against the country" around Boston. This letter suggests that the process of making Washington a secular saint was already in progress.[72]

Jay continued to have some slight hope, through the spring of 1776, that there would be a reconciliation with Britain. In March, when Congress was considering instructions to its commissioners to Canada, some suggested that they urge the Canadians to form a new government. Jay argued against this suggestion, saying that this would look as if the Americans were encouraging the Canadians to "independency," and "there was much argument on this" point, unfortunately now lost to history. In April, he noted that some people were hoping for the arrival of peace commissioners from Britain. "As to those gentlemen, I sometimes think their coming questionable, and should they arrive, I suspect their powers will be too limited to promise us much from negotiation." By this time, a month before Congress recommended this critical step, he believed that the Americans should "erect good and well-ordered governments in all the colonies, and thereby exclude that anarchy which already too much prevails."[73]

In early May, John Jay left Philadelphia to spend time with Sarah, who was ill in Elizabeth Town, and with his father, who was ill in Rye. Instead of returning to the Continental Congress in Philadelphia, he decided to attend the sessions of the Provincial Congress in New York City. In part this was a question of proximity: he wanted to be near to his family. But it was also a question of priority: he believed that the New York Provincial Congress needed him more than the Continental Congress.[74]

New York City in May 1776 was utterly unlike the city he had left only a year before. Most of the civilian population had fled. A couple of British warships guarded the mouth of the harbor and a British fleet was expected to arrive any day. The city was far from empty, however, for it was occupied by an American army of about fifteen thousand men. Soldiers tore down fences for firewood and building material; open spaces were filled with tents and trash; and officers occupied elegant town houses and country estates. There were frequent tensions between shopkeepers, keen to profit from the situation, and troops, who accused them of profiteering. Trade of another kind, with "bitch-foxy jades" or prostitutes, flourished.[75]

Jay started attending the sessions of the Provincial Congress in late May. More than one hundred men had been elected to this Congress, but on an average day only about thirty were present at City Hall. By virtue of his education and national experience, Jay quickly emerged as the leader of this small group. The Congress faced three main issues: how to deal with the many known or suspected Tories; whether and how to form a new government for New York; and what stand to take on independence.[76]

After discussing for several months how best to deal with "internal enemies," the Congress in early June adopted two lists, one of those who should be arrested immediately, and one of those who should be summoned for questioning. The committee charged with these tasks, however, did little, and soon the lists were published, eliminating any surprise. At this point, a New York City mob decided to take matters into its own hands. The mob "hunted out half a dozen Tories, tarred and feathered two of them, rode some on rails, beat them, abused them, and paraded them, in a most disorderly fashion, through the streets in the direction of the commons." Continental troops finally arrived at the commons and restored order, but on the next day there was a similar, smaller riot. Perhaps in response to the riots, the Provincial Congress assigned Jay to the committee on conspiracies.[77]

He started his work by taking testimony from two men who confirmed earlier rumors that the British were paying men to "stand ready" to fight the rebels. One of these witnesses testified that Gilbert Forbes, a well-known gunsmith, was in charge of paying the recruits, and that Forbes in turn was being paid by David Matthews, Mayor of New York. Jay immediately wrote to Washington, asking him to arrest Matthews, who "stands charged with dangerous designs and treasonable conspiracies." Washington instructed, and his officers ensured, that Matthews was arrested at one o'clock in the morning.[78]

On the next day, Jay questioned Mayor Matthews, who explained that, a few

weeks ago, while he had been aboard a British warship, Governor Tryon had
"put a bundle of paper money into his hands," and asked him to pay it to
Forbes for guns. Matthews, an appointee of the Governor, had taken the
money, but had then refused to pay it over to Forbes. Indeed, Matthews
claimed that he warned Forbes that if he was providing guns to the British "he
would be hanged if he was found out." But Forbes pestered him until
Matthews, "finding there was no way of getting rid of him," gave him the
money. When Forbes was questioned, he admitted that he had sold the guns,
but claimed they were only bad ones that would not shoot straight.[79]

   All told in this period of two weeks, Jay and his colleagues on the committee
interrogated more than twenty men. One of the men who came before the
committee, William Hickey, was handed over to the army, tried, convicted,
and hanged on questionable evidence. Many of the other men questioned,
including Matthews and Forbes, were banished from New York to jails in
Connecticut, without formal trial or sentence. Usually no man was more interested in fairness than Jay, but these were unusual and dangerous days, so he
may perhaps be forgiven for focusing on results rather than process.[80]

On May 15, 1776, a few days before Jay joined the New York Provincial
Congress, the Continental Congress published a resolution finding that it was
necessary for the colonies to form new governments "for the preservation of
internal peace, virtue and good order, as well as for the defense of their lives,
liberties, and properties." John Adams believed that this was "the most important resolution that was ever taken in America," for by forming their own
governments the colonies were effectively declaring their independence.
Duane, who opposed the resolution, and evidently believed that Jay would
have opposed it as well, wrote him that there was "no reason that our colony
should be too precipitate in changing the present mode of government."[81]

   When the Provincial Congress took up the recommendation, Jay's friend
Morris gave a long speech, urging the necessity of independence, and
suggesting that an election be held for a convention to "frame a government."
Morris was opposed by John Morin Scott, who argued that "this Congress has
the power to form a government." Jay and five others were named to a
committee to consider this issue. The committee's report, probably drafted by

Jay, started with the proposition that the right of "framing, creating or remodeling" a government rests "in the people." The present government, in his view, had many defects. But because "doubts have arisen whether this Congress are invested with sufficient authority" to "institute a new form of internal government," the people of New York should elect a new congress with explicit authority to write a new constitution. The Congress approved the report and published it on the last day of May.[82]

Several other colonies were at this same time instructing, or at least authorizing, their delegates in Philadelphia to vote for independence. But the New York Provincial Congress, in a message perhaps drafted by Jay, was cool. "We are of the opinion that the Continental Congress alone have that enlarged view of our political circumstances which will enable them to decide upon these measures which are necessary for the general welfare." When the delegates in Philadelphia requested instructions, the Provincial Congress responded that they should take no position one way or the other until the results of the imminent election were known. This was somewhat disingenuous, since the voters were not being asked to consider independence, but only whether to form a new state government. Jay moved that the question posed to the voters should be amended, so that they should be asked to consider "the great question of independency." This resolution passed, but then curiously the Provincial Congress determined not to publish it "until after the election of deputies with powers to establish a new form of government." It is hard to know exactly what New Yorkers thought they were voting on, when they voted in late June 1776, but they probably understood that it was both statehood and independence.[83]

Jay's friends in Philadelphia kept him posted on the independence issue and urged him to come to Philadelphia. In early June, Edward Rutledge reported that the Congress had met until seven that evening to consider Lee's motion "resolving ourselves free and independent states." "I wish you had been here," Rutledge wrote, for he and a few others had to oppose independence against "the power of all New England, Virginia and Georgia." Rutledge wrote Jay again in late June "for the express purpose" of requesting his presence in Philadelphia. Congress was about to consider a Declaration of Independence, Articles of Confederation, and a draft treaty with foreign powers. "Whether we shall be able effectually to oppose the first, and infuse wisdom into the others will depend in great measure upon the exertions of the honest and sensible part of the members." Rutledge apparently believed that Jay would, if he was present, vote against a declaration of independence, as Rutledge himself did on the first of July, before changing his vote the next day "for the sake of unanimity." [84]

Jay, however, remained in New York, since he viewed the formation of a new state government as more important than the wording of a declaration of independence. He was thus not in Philadelphia in early July, when delegates from other states, but not New York, voted in favor of the declaration. But he was in New York for what he considered a more important event: the arrival in late June of the first part of the expected British fleet. More than one hundred ships, bearing more than ten thousand British troops, sailed into the lower part of the harbor. As one observer put it, it seemed like "a wood of pine trees" was in the harbor, as if "all London was afloat." [85]

As the British fleet sailed in, Jay went to Elizabeth Town to check on his wife and child. When he returned to the city the next day, he was outraged to learn that the delegates, at the suggestion of Morris, had left for the safety of White Plains. "This stroke of Morrisania politics quite confounds me." He was also annoyed to learn that Philip Livingston had left New York, in its hour of danger, for Philadelphia. "The ways of some men, like Solomon's serpent on the rock, are past finding out." [86]

The new Provincial Congress met for the first time on July 9, 1776, in White Plains. The first question to consider was the Declaration of Independence, the text of which had just arrived from Philadelphia. It would have been easy to argue that the New York voters had still not explicitly instructed their delegates on the question of independence. It would have been easy to argue that, with a hundred British warships and thousands of British troops a few miles away, a quiet silence was prudent. The normally cautious Jay, however, now turned bold. He drafted a resolution, unanimously adopted by his colleagues, that declared that, "while we lament the cruel necessity which has rendered" the Declaration of Independence "unavoidable," they "approve the same, and will, at the risk of our lives and fortunes, join with the other colonies in supporting it." [87]

How did it happen that Jay, cautious conservative, came to commit his life and his fortune to American independence? Years later, Jay wrote that Britain gave the Americans no choice other than to declare and fight for independence. But of course each individual American *did* have a choice, and many of his own family and friends chose loyalty rather than rebellion. He himself was completely sincere, from 1774 through early 1776, when he declared his personal loyalty to Britain and the British King. But he was also utterly committed to preserving what he saw as traditional *British* rights, such as the right to elect one's own legislators, or to be tried by one's own peers. When faced with the difficult choice between the British King and British freedom, he chose freedom. More precisely, he chose to *fight* for freedom: for it was far from clear in the summer of 1776 that the American rebels, opposed not only by British troops but also German mercenaries and Loyalist enemies, could defend their independence and their freedom.[88]

CHAPTER 4

Revolutionary Leader

THE FIRST PRIORITY for John Jay and other New York leaders in the summer of 1776 was military defense. On July 12, two British warships sailed past Manhattan, firing into the city, terrorizing the citizens, and laughing at the Americans' attempts to fire back. Indeed, five Americans were killed when one of their cannons exploded. The British ships continued north and anchored in the Tappan Zee, only about ten miles from where Jay and the other delegates were meeting in White Plains. At first the New York convention reacted hardly at all: they saw "no great reason to apprehend any considerable incursions." General Washington, however, realized that the British objective might be not merely a few provisions in Westchester County but control of key points along the Hudson River. He admonished the convention that a "greater misfortune could hardly befall the service and army." Duly chastened, the convention on July 15 named Jay, Livingston, and a few others to a committee to "devise and carry into execution" measures for "obstructing the channel of Hudson's River, or annoying the navigation of the enemy's ships in the navigation up the said River."[1]

This committee gathered a few days later at Fort Montgomery, on the west bank of the Hudson River, about fifty miles north of New York City. It was a curious group to discuss military problems, for at least five of the eight men were lawyers. In addition to Jay and Livingston, those present included George Clinton, a young lawyer serving as a general in the New York militia, and Robert Yates, an Albany lawyer and political leader. The committee reported regretfully to General Washington that, "notwithstanding the importance and advantageous situation" of Fort Montgomery, it was "by no means in a proper state of defense." In particular, the fort lacked cannon and ammunition, without which it could neither block the Hudson nor defend itself.[2]

On the next day, the committee decided to send Jay to Connecticut to "procure there twenty of the heaviest cannon which can be had" as well as "a proper quantity of shot and trucks for the said cannon." He was authorized to "impress carriages, teams, sloops and horses" and if necessary to "call out detachments of the militia" to transport the cannon. Jay rode rapidly, reaching Salisbury, Connecticut, in one day. He was disappointed, however, to learn there that the foundry would not provide anything without orders from either General Washington or Governor Trumbull. So he rode on to Lebanon, Connecticut, where he persuaded the Governor to lend New York ten twelve-pound and ten six-pound cannons, along with shot and trucks. When he returned to Salisbury, the overseers of the furnace agreed to provide the cannon and the ammunition on hand, but they refused to make more ammunition or any wheels. Having arranged for horse teams to handle the cannon, Jay hurried ahead to Livingston Manor, where his friend's workers could make trucks and ammunition. He then returned to Poughkeepsie, where he spent the first two weeks of August, working among other things on a chain to block the Hudson at Fort Montgomery.[3]

To the extent he could, John kept in touch with his wife Sarah, who was with her family in northern New Jersey. He started one letter to her by saying that he was "in a hot little room" where "in spite of importunities to hear the pompous [local minister] preach, and in defiance of the god of sleep, whom the bugs and fleas banished from my pillow last night, I sit down to write a few lines to my good little wife." In another, he asked whether she was "provided with a secure retreat in case Elizabeth Town should cease to be a place of safety?" He urged her not to worry too much about the future. "A person must possess no great share of sagacity who in this whirl of human affairs would account that certain, which in the nature of things cannot be so." Then he caught himself and added that this "looks more like writing an essay than a letter."[4]

On August 27, 1776, ten thousand British and Hessian soldiers soundly defeated an American army, of roughly equal size, in the Battle of Brooklyn.

More than a thousand Americans were killed, wounded or captured in the chaos. If the British general, William Howe, had pressed his advantage, he might well have captured the entire American army, and perhaps forced an early end to the rebellion. At the end of the day, Washington and his Americans were surrounded in Brooklyn, with their backs to the East River, and only light trenches between them and the British. As one British officer later wrote, "it cannot be denied that the American army lay almost entirely at the will of the English." But instead of attacking, Howe settled in for a siege, and Washington was able, under cover of darkness and fog, to get his force across the river to Manhattan.[5]

On the day after this battle, while Washington debated whether to retreat or attempt to maintain his position, the New York Provincial Convention met at Harlem, not ten miles away, and debated a similar issue: whether to remain or move to some safer place. William Duer argued that "it would be very practicable for a small party of men to surprise this defenseless town, and to remove all its inhabitants." Jay and others apparently objected that the proposed move would send the wrong message to Patriots in the southern part of the state. The proposal was carried, however, over their objection, and the convention prepared to move to Fish Kill.[6]

Fish Kill was at this time a "pleasant little village" more than eighty miles north of New York and five miles east of the Hudson River. The last fifteen miles of the road took the traveler "among the rugged hills and shapeless rocks" until the "village and plain of Fish Kill suddenly open upon his view with the effect of enchantment." The village itself consisted of about fifty "neat white farm houses" and two small churches. The first members of the convention to arrive met for a few days in the Episcopal church, but found that it was "very foul with the dung of doves and fowls," so they moved across the road to the Dutch church, where Jay found them when he arrived in early September.[7]

During the next few weeks, the convention debated how best to strengthen the Highland forts, how to remain in contact with the southern part of the state, and how to deal with certain specific Tories. The convention directed, for example, that a militia officer "remove" the Reverend Samuel Seabury, the "notoriously disaffected" Anglican priest in Westchester, "to this place," and appointed Jay to interrogate Seabury. It soon became clear that the convention could not do its other work if it considered suspects one by one, so Jay and a few others were named to a committee to "devise ways and means for preventing the dangers which may arise from the disaffected in this state." This "conspiracies committee" was soon meeting daily at Connor's Tavern: summoning suspected Tories, questioning them, and sending many of them into exile.[8]

Jay evidently liked Fish Kill, or at least felt that it was safe, for he soon gathered his family there. He traveled to northern New Jersey in September and returned with his wife, but not his son, whom he left with the Livingstons there. "I suspect," he wrote to his mother-in-law, "that the little woman's imagination will ere long begin to dwell on the pleasure of conversing with her mama and sisters and playing with her little son and heir." He hoped that such thoughts might lead "the fair daughters of Liberty Hall" to visit them in Fish Kill. A few days later, Jay left again, this time for Rye, where he retrieved his father and mother, and moved them into a farm he had rented near Fish Kill. In early November, John wrote to his sister-in-law that Sarah had taken "so little thought for the morrow as to bring only one pair of shoes with her. They are almost worn out, and shoemakers are as scarce here as saints were in Sodom. Be so obliging as to get a couple of neat pair, at any price, made for her, and send them by the first good opportunity."[9]

There was in fact a Yankee shoemaker in Fish Kill, well known to Jay, but he did not have much time to make shoes, for he was working as a spy. Jay first met Enoch Crosby in October 1776, a few weeks after he was appointed to the conspiracies committee. Crosby explained to the committee how he had posed as a Tory, had joined a Loyalist company being formed in Westchester, had passed information about the company to a Patriot leader, and then had been captured with his "comrades" near White Plains. The committee, recognizing a natural spy when they met one, immediately enlisted Crosby and sent him across the Hudson to "make such inquiries and discoveries as he could."[10]

Crosby went across the river and repeated the feat. He ingratiated himself with a British officer, indeed shared a cave with him for a week, as they recruited Loyalists for a new company. On the night before the company was to march south, Crosby suggested that, to avoid capture, they should all sleep

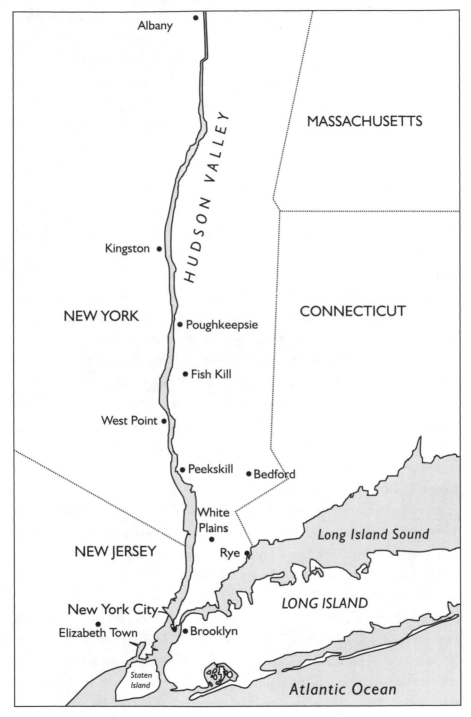

Map of New York City and the Hudson Valley.

separately. Crosby used the night to pass information to the committee, which sent a company to intercept the Loyalists. Crosby returned to Fish Kill and lived for a while in the home of a Dutch farmer, where he "went to work at making shoes." Jay arranged to meet with Crosby at the home of a nearby doctor. He "inquired for the Doctor, who was absent, inquired for medicine, but found none that he wanted. He came out of the house, and went to his horse near which [Crosby] stood, and as he passed he said in a low voice 'it won't do, there are too many around.'" A few days later, however, the committee got word to Crosby that they wanted him to check on a well-known Tory leader.

Crosby went north and found this leader, but could not get much out of him other than a list of Tories further south. In late February 1777, however, Crosby joined a *third* Loyalist company in formation and passed information about it to a nearby Patriot leader, Colonel Andrew Morehouse. Morehouse and his men captured the Loyalists, including Crosby. When Crosby protested that he was lame, Morehouse shouted that Crosby would go "dead or alive, and if in no other way you shall be carried on my horse with me." Morehouse carried Crosby off in this way, but released him later that night, and Crosby made his way to Fish Kill, where he reported to the committee.[11]

Crosby's account shows that Jay was far closer to the "front lines" of the Revolution than is generally assumed. Captured officers were treated, often with considerable respect, as prisoners of war; captured spies, like Nathan Hale or John André, were almost always executed. Certainly Crosby, if he had been caught by the British, would have been executed, and probably Jay himself was in some danger as a "spymaster." Many years later, Jay told a family friend, James Fenimore Cooper, the story of Crosby and his work. Cooper turned the story into his novel *The Spy*, a book which proved "instantly and phenomenally popular," and created an enduring image of the virtuous Americans fighting the treacherous British.[12]

Much of the committee's work involved people who were not really spies, but simply "men in the middle" of the conflict, such as Jay's friend Peter Van Schaack. Van Schaack had joined in the early stages of the resistance, serving on various committees in 1774 and 1775. In early 1775, because his eyesight was failing, he had left his law practice and moved to his family farm in Kinderhook. In May 1776, Van Schaack was among those asked by the

New York Provincial Congress to confirm that they would support the American cause. Van Schaack refused. He had been "disposed to go along with the Congress to a certain limited extent, hoping in that way to fix what they conceived to be the rights of their country upon the firmest foundation," but could not do so now that it appeared that the Americans intended "nothing short of a dissolution of the union between Britain and her Colonies."[13]

In December 1776, at a meeting Jay attended, the conspiracies committee noted that Peter Van Schaack, his brother Henry, and two others "have long maintained an equivocal neutrality in the present struggles and are in general supposed unfriendly to the American cause." The conspiracies committee directed that the Albany committee summon these four men and ask whether they "consider themselves as subjects of the State of New York, or of the King of Great Britain." If they called themselves New Yorkers, and were willing to take the prescribed oath of allegiance, they were to be released. If not, however, the Albany committee should "remove them" to Boston. Peter Van Schaack again refused, and was exiled to New England.[14]

Another case involving a friend, indeed a relative, was that of Beverly Robinson, married to the former Susanna Philipse, first cousin of Mary Jay. In February 1777, when summoned before the committee to answer questions about his loyalties, Robinson claimed that he was and wanted to remain neutral. Jay responded that "we have passed the Rubicon and it is now necessary every man take his part, cast off all allegiance to the King of Great Britain, and take an oath of allegiance to the states of America, or go over to the enemy, for we have declared ourselves independent." Robinson said that he could not take the American oath, but he would be "exceedingly glad to stay in the country," for he would have "no way to maintain my family" if he was "obliged to go over to the enemy." Jay politely gave Robinson a few days to consider the question, and assured him that "we should be exceedingly happy to have you with us."[15]

A few days later, Robinson wrote to say that he was "going down" to Westchester County, to confer there "with my friends on the unhappy and distracted state of my poor bleeding country." Jay now tried a different approach, writing to Susanna Philipse Robinson, warning her of the risks involved in moving their family to New York City. "Picture to your imagination a city besieged, yourself and children mixed with contending armies.

Should it be evacuated, where, with whom, and in what manner are you next to fly?" He conceded that Britain might be victorious, but asked his relative whether she could, even in this case, reconcile herself "to the mortifying reflection of being the mother of slaves? For who are slaves but those who in all cases without exception are bound to obey the uncontrollable mandates of a man, whether styled King or called peasant?" This eloquence had no effect: Beverly Robinson was already in New York City, working to raise a Loyalist regiment.[16]

Jay remained actively involved with the conspiracies committee from its formation in September 1776 through February 1777, when he started to devote most of his time to the new state constitution. The committee both gathered useful intelligence and performed critical counter-intelligence, identifying and neutralizing Tories.* While Jay and his colleagues were questioning suspected spies in late 1776, the American army was suffering defeat at almost every turn. In November, the British captured Fort Washington, and with it complete control of Manhattan. Jay did not view the loss as disastrous. Indeed, he wished "our army [was] well stationed in the Highlands, and all the lower country desolated; we might then bid defiance to all the further efforts of the enemy in that quarter." After capturing Fort Washington, the British crossed the Hudson and chased Washington's army across New Jersey. In early December, the Americans crossed the Delaware River into Pennsylvania, then destroyed all the boats on the New Jersey side. This stopped the British for a while, but there was every reason to expect that in the spring they would renew the attack.[17]

This was the background for Jay's most passionate paper of the war, the *Address of the Convention of the Representatives of the State of New York to Their Constituents*, printed in New York in December 1776. He admitted that the Americans had lost many battles, and hinted that they would lose more, but argued that they were sure to win the war, if they remained united and determined. "Even suppose that Philadelphia, which many believed to be of such great importance, suppose it was taken or abandoned, the conquest of America would still be at a great distance. Millions, determined to be free, still remain

---

* Indeed, the Central Intelligence Agency recently honored Jay by naming a conference room for "America's first counter-intelligence chief."

to be subdued, millions who disdain to part with their liberties, their consciences, and the happiness of their posterity in future ages, for infamous protections and dishonorable pardons." He mocked the idea that King George desired peace. "If there be one single idea of peace in his mind, why does he order your cities to be burned, your country to be desolated, your brethren to starve, and languish, and die in prison? If any thing were intended besides destruction, devastation, and bloodshed, why are the mercenaries of Germany transported near four thousand miles to plunder your houses, ravish your wives and daughters [and] strip your infant children?"[18]

Jay cited examples from the Bible and much of the address had a biblical tone. "If then, God hath given us freedom, are we responsible to Him for that, as well as other talents? If it be our birthright, let us not sell it for a mess of pottage, nor suffer it to be torn from us by the hand of violence! If the means of defense are in our power and we do not make use of them, what excuse shall we make to our children and our Creator?" New Yorkers should "be persuaded that divine Providence will not permit this western world to be involved in the horrors of slavery." Those who failed to heed "the calls of liberty, virtue and religion," those who were "forgetful of the magnanimity of their ancestors and the happiness of their children," should "be assured that they deserve to be slaves, and are entitled to nothing but anguish and tribulation." (Jay was using slavery here as a metaphor, but his choice of metaphor is itself revealing.) But those who did their duty at this dark hour could "cheerfully refer your cause to the great and righteous Judge," knowing that if successful they would enjoy "all the blessings of freedom" and if not "you will be happy with God and liberty in heaven."[19]

Jay's main work in late 1776 and early 1777 was on the first New York state constitution. The very concept of a written constitution was new at this time; Britons generally used the word "constitution" to refer to the unwritten basic principles of their government. But the Americans, in part because they had suffered from ambiguities in this implicit constitution, wanted to have explicit charters. American leaders considered these new constitutions critical, for they viewed the states as their basic, permanent governments, and the Continental Congress as only a temporary wartime device. Jefferson wrote in May 1776 that he longed to be home in Virginia, working on the state constitution, rather than in Philadelphia, working on a declaration of independence. Jay was equally alive to the importance of the task in New York state. Other forms of government, he wrote, were merely the result of "violence or accidental circumstances." But the "Americans are the first people whom Heaven has favored with an opportunity of deliberating upon, and choosing the forms of government under which they should live." In a lighter tone, he wrote to a friend that "we have a government, you know, to form, and God only knows what it will resemble. Our politicians, like some guests at a feast, are perplexed and undetermined to which dish to prefer."[20]

On the first of August, while Jay was in Connecticut seeking cannon, the New York convention named him to the committee to devise a "new form of government." Many of the fourteen members of this committee were lawyers who had known one another in New York City: Jay, Morris, Livingston, Hobart, Scott and Duane. A few of the members were lawyers from other parts of the state, including Abraham Yates of Albany. And a few men had no legal background at all, such as William Duer, who had served as a military aide in India before moving to New York and starting a business there.[21]

The more radical members of this committee wanted all or almost all men to vote, and favored a single, strong assembly. They had in mind something like the new Pennsylvania constitution, with a single assembly and a weak executive council. Jay disapproved of this approach, saying that Pennsylvania was "sick unto death" because "weak and bad constitutions incline to chronical disorders." Conservatives favored limiting those who could vote, splitting the legislature into a lower and upper house, and giving substantial power to the Governor. Jay generally agreed with his friend Rutledge, who wrote him that "when a state abounds in rascals (as is the case with too many at this day) you must suppress a little of that popular spirit, vest the executive powers of government in an individual that they may have vigor, and let them be as ample as is consistent with the great outlines of freedom."[22]

In spite of repeated reminders from the convention, the committee took several months to discuss and prepare the constitution. Many members of the committee had other duties and interests, so it was difficult to get together enough members to have a discussion. Jay himself was busy first with the

Hudson, then with spies. The convention itself did not meet often in January and February 1777. When the committee members did get together, they often disagreed. According to Abraham Yates, "a diversity of opinion soon took place in this committee, not whether the government should be of a republican form, partaking of monarchy, aristocracy and democracy, but what proportion of ingredients of each should make up the compound." Moreover, some conservatives favored delay, hoping that more settled times would produce a more considered document. Robert Livingston, commenting later about Pennsylvania, said that "nothing but well timed delays, indefatigable industry, and a minute attention to every favorable circumstance could have prevented our being in exactly their situation." [23]

In late February and early March 1777, Jay left the convention for a while to prepare the clean draft of the constitution, which was presented to the convention. Neither the committee's last draft nor his own draft survive, so it is not possible to be precise about the changes he made at this time. His role in producing the final draft led some early scholars to give Jay all credit for the constitution. More recent scholars have tended to emphasize that the committee worked as a whole and downplay Jay's role; one claimed that his main contribution was "clarity and economy of language." But this may understate his role, since he was involved not only in preparation of this last draft, but in all the committee work which had gone into the prior drafts, and in the convention debates which would refine the draft. [24]

The convention was, at this time, meeting in the court house in Kingston, New York, yet another small town in the Hudson Valley, about halfway between New York City and Albany. The frequent movement of the convention (from New York City to White Plains to Fish Kill to Kingston in the space of less than a year) was necessary because almost no part of the state was safe from British attack. This was underscored in late March of 1777, when the delegates learned that several hundred British troops had come ashore at Peekskill, just fifty miles south of Kingston. John wrote immediately to Sarah, who was at Fish Kill only about a dozen miles from the British, urging caution. Sarah had already written John a letter which shows both her calm and her caution. She reported that "not less than twelve hundred of the enemy landed at Peckskill," and that the Americans were removing their supplies from

Fish Kill. "I wish I knew," she said, "what is to be done with your white chest," presumably filled with sensitive political papers. Fortunately, the British did not attack Fish Kill. A few days later, Jay learned from a former law clerk, now serving with the provincial militia, that the leader of the British raid was none other than that "vile, infamous, rascally, hypocritical friend to America, Beverly Robinson." [25]

It was in this atmosphere of interruptions and danger that the delegates at Kingston debated the proposed New York state constitution. Perhaps reflecting the military situation, the constitution as it emerged from the committee gave the Governor more power than that of any other state leader at this time. Some states did not even have a "Governor" at this time, merely a "President" whose role was largely limited to presiding over sessions of the legislature. New York's Governor, in contrast, would be elected by the people, for a three-year term, and have considerable military and civil authority. [26]

The Governor's appointment power, under the committee draft, was curious: he could "name" persons to the legislature which would "if they think proper appoint them." If the legislature rejected four nominees in a row for a position, it could "proceed to appoint without waiting for [the Governor's] further nomination." According to Jay, the convention "disapproved" of this proposal, and "many other methods were devised by different members," none of which elicited much support. Jay, Morris and Livingston discussed the issue one evening and Jay drafted a provision creating a "Council of Appointment," composed of the Governor and four Senators. In his mind, the Governor would present names to the other members of the Council, whose only role would be to accept or reject these choices. That is not quite what his draft said, however. The draft provided for appointments by the Council, of which the Governor would be "president" with a "casting voice, but no other vote," and would "with the advice and consent of said council" make appointments. The Council of Appointment provision was a compromise, one which would not work very well in practice. [27]

Another, similar question was whether the Governor should have a veto on legislation. The convention at one point amended the draft to make the Governor part of the legislature, without the "power to originate or amend any law, but simply to give his assent or dissent thereto." Jay persuaded the convention to reverse the amendment, perhaps because the language was unclear on the effect of the Governor's "dissent." The convention then accepted a proposal, drafted by Livingston and supported by Jay, to create a Council of Revision. This Council (composed of the Governor, the Chancellor, and the members of the Supreme Court) would consider whether laws passed by the legislature were "inconsistent with the spirit of this constitution or with the public good." If the Council disapproved of a law, it could return it to the legislature for reconsideration, but the legislature could override the veto by a two-thirds vote in both houses. Like the Council of Appointment, the Council of Revision was a compromise, one which would soon cause difficulties.[28]

Much of the draft and the debate concerned the legislature and voting for legislators. The draft constitution provided for two houses: an Assembly of at least seventy members to be elected each year on a county-by-county basis, and a Senate of at least twenty-four members, elected from four large districts, with each Senator serving a four-year term. The Assembly was fairly closely based on the colonial assembly, although it was twice as large, and the committee carefully provided for a periodic census to ensure that each county had a fair representation. The Senate, on the other hand, was only loosely based on the Governor's Council, which of course was not an elected body, and had executive and judicial as well as legislative responsibilities. Jay helped the convention to refine these draft provisions. For example, after the convention adopted voting qualifications which would have disenfranchised the freemen of New York City and Albany, who had for many years voted for Assembly members, he proposed, and the convention accepted, an amendment to protect their franchise. After the convention adopted a provision continuing colonial election practices, including the practice of voice voting, he proposed, and the convention accepted, a section providing for election by paper ballot, to take effect once the war was over. He argued that election by ballot would "tend more to preserve the liberty and equal freedom of the people."[29]

The draft constitution did not say much about the judiciary: it generally assumed that the various colonial courts would continue in the new state system. The constitution did create one new office, that of Chancellor, to exercise the equity jurisdiction previously exercised by the Governor, and created one new court, to handle impeachments, reflecting the revolutionary concern with potential official misconduct. Jay proposed and the convention adopted an amendment to tighten the wording of the provision allowing judges to hold their offices during good behavior. He also proposed an exception to the prohibition on acts of attainder to allow such acts "during the present war."[30]

In many ways Jay showed himself, during this constitutional debate, to be a progressive thinker. He proposed, and the convention adopted, a provision protecting Indians against fraudulent contracts. He also supported a proposal by Gouverneur Morris, not adopted by the convention, to abolish slavery over time. In one important respect, however, Jay showed himself a reactionary. Perhaps reflecting the views of his father, Jay was the proponent of several anti-Catholic amendments.[31]

As it emerged from committee, the draft constitution provided that "the free toleration of religious profession and worship be forever allowed within this state to all mankind." This was too sweeping for Jay, who proposed that religious freedom would not extend to sects whose doctrines were "inconsistent with the safety of civil society" as determined by the legislature. When this proposal was not accepted, he advanced a more explicit proposal, that would deprive Catholics of the right to own land or participate in government, unless they swore that "no pope, priest, or foreign authority on earth" could "absolve the subjects of this state from the allegiance to the same" or "absolve men from sins described in and prohibited by the Holy Gospel." After this proposal was roundly rejected, he suggested that freedom of religion "not be construed to encourage licentiousness or be used in such a manner as to disturb or endanger the safety of the state." With some minor wording changes, this comparatively modest proposal was accepted, and indeed is still part of the New York constitution.[32]

Jay was not yet through with the Catholics, however. The committee's draft constitution provided that anyone who moved into the state could become a citizen by purchasing or renting land and then taking an oath of allegiance to the state. Jay now proposed a requirement that new citizens "abjure and renounce all allegiance and subjection to all and every foreign king, prince, potentate, and state in all matters, ecclesiastical as well as civil." Few could doubt that Catholics would find it hard to renounce their subjection to the Pope in ecclesiastical matters. The convention, however, accepted this restrictive proposal.[33]

In mid-April, as the Kingston convention was nearing the end of its work on the constitution, Jay learned that his mother had died at Fish Kill. He immediately left for Fish Kill, where he remained with his grieving father for the next three weeks. A few days after his departure, the convention finished its work and voted, with only one objection, to adopt and publish the new constitution. When Jay reviewed the final constitution in the newspapers, he noticed a few changes of which he disapproved. He discussed his objections first with two colleagues who were in Fish Kill at the time. One of them wrote back to Kingston that "Jay is exceedingly unhappy" with the provision "which puts the appointment of the clerks of courts in the power of the respective judges ... He alleges that [it is] putting in the power of the respective judges to provide for sons, brothers, dependents, etc." Jay also objected to the provision allowing each court to license its own attorneys.[34]

Livingston and Morris, on hearing of and reading these objections, immediately wrote to Jay, saying they had not "the most distant idea" that the provisions in question would "meet with your disapprobation." They reminded him that the constitution had now been formally adopted and published, so it was too late to consider minor technical amendments. "Judge then our amazement at reading a letter ... in which your sentiments against the power vested in the courts are blazoned in glowing colors, and consider how far your reputation may or may not contribute to make this constitution a living or dead law according to the scale in which you shall choose to place it."[35]

Jay responded in a long and heated letter to Livingston and Morris. On the substance of the provisions, he was very firm. The clause regarding clerks would allow judges to give these positions to their "children brothers relatives and favorites" and to "continue them in office against the public good." The clause about the licensing of attorneys was the "most whimsical crude indigested thing I have met with." It would force lawyers to seek separate qualifications from thirty or forty courts around the state, rather than qualifying before a single court, the Supreme Court. But after stating his objections at length, Jay assured his friends that he would support the new constitution. "Though the birth of the constitution is in my opinion premature,

I shall nevertheless do all in my power to nurse and keep it alive, being far from approving the Spartan law which encouraged parents to destroy such of their children as perhaps by some cross accident, might come into the world defective or misshapen." [36]

When Jay returned to Kingston in early May, he learned that the convention had elected him Chief Justice of New York, that he was part of a Council of Safety to administer the state until a Governor and legislature were elected, and that he was among those under discussion as a possible Governor. Although he conceded that the position of Governor would be "more respectable, as well as more lucrative" than that of Chief Justice, he reminded a friend that his "object in the course of the present great contest neither has been, nor will be, either rank or money." Since he was "persuaded that I can be more useful to the state in the office I now hold than in the one alluded to," he viewed it as his "duty to continue in it." Soon he started not only to *discourage* talk of his own election but to *encourage* the election of his cousin Philip Schuyler. "Unless the government be committed to proper hands, it will be weak and unstable at home, and contemptible abroad. For my own part, I know of no person at present whom I would prefer to General Schuyler." He was able to persuade the other members of the Council of Safety to endorse Schuyler for Governor and George Clinton for Lieutenant Governor. The Council recommended them because "their attachment to the cause is confessed and their abilities unquestionable." [37]

In late June, as the votes were being counted, Jay wrote to Schuyler that he expected soon to be able to address him as Governor of New York. A few days later, however, Schuyler wrote back that "General Clinton I am informed has a majority of votes for the chair. If so, he has played his cards better than was expected." And indeed Clinton had won. He received more than 1800 votes for Governor, while Schuyler received only about 1200. Clinton ran particularly well among the farmers of and soldiers from Dutchess, Orange and Ulster counties. Schuyler complained that Clinton's "family and connections do not entitle him to so distinguished a predominance." Schuyler and Jay were still working in an old style of politics, relying on family and connections; Clinton was developing a new style of politics, relying on rapport with the common people. [38]

In total, fewer than four thousand men voted in this first election in New York state history. The paltry number underlines an important fact: the state government at this time only reached a few people in a few counties. The British controlled New York City and the surrounding regions; the Americans were in control of Albany and the farming regions on either side of the Hudson. General John Burgoyne, with about five thousand British soldiers, was marching south along the line of Lake Champlain and the Hudson River. By late July Burgoyne was only about a hundred miles upriver from Albany. British soldiers and their Indian allies were also marching east from Oswego, along the line of the Mohawk River, about a hundred miles east of Albany. At any time the British could easily send troops north up the Hudson. In sum, it looked like three British armies might soon meet at Albany to celebrate their conquest of the upstart state of New York.[39]

In late July, the Council of Safety wrote to General Washington that it feared New York would prove an "easy conquest" for the British and asked for "a reinforcement from the southern states." On the next day, Gouverneur Morris returned to Kingston from a tour of the northern front. Morris presented an "appalling picture" to Jay and the other members of the Council. Morris estimated that Burgoyne had ten thousand men and reported that American militia men were "restive" and "unreliable." The Council immediately asked Morris and Jay to go to the headquarters of General Washington, to confer with him "about the state of the northern army," to seek reinforcements, and to "return with all convenient speed."[40]

Jay and Morris set out the next day from Kingston for Philadelphia, a horseback journey of at least two hundred miles each way. When they reached Washington's camp on the outskirts of the city, however, he flatly refused their request, saying that "if the matter were coolly and dispassionately considered, there would be found nothing so formidable in Mr. Burgoyne," nothing that could not be handled by additional militia raised in New York and New England. Jay and Morris decided to go over Washington's head, the one instance in Jay's life when he was disloyal to his Virginia friend. The two New Yorkers went in to Philadelphia, met with their friends there in the Congress, and persuaded Congress to send five hundred riflemen north to strengthen New York's defenses. After only a few days in the capital, Jay and Morris started back north, stopping for a day or two in northern New Jersey (where Sarah was staying with her family), and returning to Kingston by late August. Unfortunately, the journal of the New York convention does not detail their day-by-day itinerary, but it does note that the two men spent $139 on horses and taverns during their three-week journey.[41]

In early September 1777, Chief Justice Jay opened the first session of the new state Supreme Court at Kingston. As was the custom at the time, he started the court session with an elaborate charge to the grand jury, which was printed and circulated in the newspapers. He started with a brief history of the Revolution, "a revolution which, in the whole course of its rise and progress, is distinguished by so many marks of the Divine favor and interposition, that no doubt can remain of its being finally accomplished." History would find it "extraordinary" that thirteen colonies, "divided by variety of governments and manners, should immediately become one people ... unanimously determine to be free and, undaunted by the power of Britain, refer their cause to the Almighty and resolve to repel force by force." The "many remarkable and unexpected means and events by which our wants have been supplied and our enemies repelled or restrained," were "strong and striking proofs of the interposition of Heaven," which "like the emancipation of the Jews from Egyptian servitude" should fill American breasts with "a flame of gratitude and piety which may consume all remains of vice and irreligion." Many Americans interpreted the Revolution in religious terms, but Jay was unusual, among American leaders, in his use of religious images and eloquence.[42]

Jay praised the new constitution, saying that the "disposition of the legislative, executive, and judicial powers of government" promised "permanence to the constitution." And the convention (to some extent over his own objection) had secured religious freedom, so that "no opinions are dictated, no rules of faith prescribed, no preference given to one sect to the prejudice of others." His main point was that the constitution was at present only a piece of paper, waiting to be made real by the people:

> But let it be remembered, that whatever marks of wisdom, experience, and patriotism there may be in your constitution, yet like the beautiful symmetry, the just proportion, and elegant forms of our first parents before their Maker breathed into them the

breath of life, it is yet to be animated, and till then may indeed excite admiration, but will be of no use. From the people it must receive its spirit, and by them be quickened. Let virtue, honor, the love of liberty and of science be, and remain, the soul of this constitution, and it will become the source of great and extensive happiness to this and future generations.[43]

On the next day, Governor Clinton addressed both houses of the new state legislature. Clinton's brief speech (far shorter than Jay's grand jury charge) stressed recent military successes and mentioned several areas for immediate legislative action. Both the legislature and the court then got down to work. Jay and the court, over the next few days, held several preliminary hearings and one criminal trial. There were two murder cases, a case involving passing counterfeit continental bills, a major theft case, and a case of attempted rape. The defendant in the rape case, "Jack, a male Negro slave," was alleged to have assaulted and attempted to rape Catherine Helme, "a spinster." There were four witnesses for the government, including Helme, and six witnesses for the defendant, including his former owner, presumably as a character witness. Jack was convicted and sentenced to imprisonment.[44]

Jay and the other members of the new state government, however, were only in Kingston for about a month before they were forced to flee. In early September 1777, General John Burgoyne and his British and German troops crossed to the west side of the Hudson near Saratoga, only about a hundred miles north of Kingston. General Horatio Gates and the Americans dug themselves into solid positions south of the British. Robert Troup, serving as an aide to Gates, reported to Jay that if Burgoyne was "so rash" as to attack "it might end the war in the northern department." When Burgoyne did attack a few days later, the result was, if not an end to the northern war, at least a severe setback for the British, who lost more than five hundred men. Burgoyne now asked General Henry Clinton to bring troops north from New York City, believing that a threat from the south would draw off the American army facing him. Four thousand British troops in forty ships started up the Hudson River from New York City in early October. Many of them returned to New York City after they captured Fort Montgomery, but a smaller force, under General John Vaughan, continued north towards Kingston. When word reached there of the British advance, Jay and most of the other members of the state government left in haste. Jay wrote a brief note on October 8 to his friend Charles DeWitt, asking him to keep his baggage, and promising to return "to aid his country" as soon as he could find a safe place for his family. A week later, as Vaughan approached the town, he learned that, after a second battle at Saratoga, Burgoyne and all his troops had surrendered. In futile retaliation, Vaughan and his men burned Kingston to the ground, "not leaving a house."[45]

Saratoga is generally viewed today as the turning point in the war, because it was not long after news of Saratoga reached Paris that France decided to join the war on the American side. But that is not how Jay and his friends viewed Saratoga in late 1777 and early 1778. Jay probably agreed with his sister-in-law Susan, who wrote to denounce the generous surrender terms Gates offered to Burgoyne, allowing all the troops to leave America. "The [British] troops will go home and garrison the forts abroad, and let those garrisons come to America, so it will be only an exchange of men." Jay probably also agreed with his friend James Duane, who wrote to rejoice in "Burgoyne's total defeat" but also to caution that Washington's troops at Valley Forge were "ill clad and the weather is uncommonly severe." Duane was writing from York, Pennsylvania, to which Congress itself had fled when the British captured Philadelphia.[46]

John and Sarah Jay, when they left Kingston and Fish Kill, apparently went to Kent, Connecticut, about forty miles east. By December, however, they were back in Fish Kill, from which Jay wrote to his friend Schuyler that "the place where my family now reside is by no means desirable or convenient if secure, which is also doubtful." At Christmas James Duane, visiting the Livingston family at Livingston Manor, urged Jay to bring his family across the river. "Can you not then hasten your visit so as to pass the holidays at the Manor? In spite of our enemies you will find us cheerful and sociable." Duane did not mention, but Jay was probably aware, that the guests at the Manor included William Smith, formerly a leader of the New York bar, now a Tory sympathizer. Perhaps because Jay did not want to dine with Smith, perhaps for other reasons, the Jays remained at Fish Kill.[47]

During 1778, Jay presided over two sessions of the Supreme Court, one in April and one in August. He also presided over at least two special criminal courts to handle cases which could not wait until the next regularly scheduled circuit court. From Albany in April, he wrote to Morris that he was "engaged in the most disagreeable part of my duty: trying criminals. They multiply exceedingly. Robberies become frequent. The woods afford them shelter and the Tories food. Punishments must of course become certain and mercy dormant, a harsh system repugnant to my feelings, but nevertheless necessary."[48] In fact, however, in appropriate circumstances, he would show mercy. At the end of the Albany session, Jay and the other judges sentenced eleven men to death for various offenses, including murder and horse theft; they also recommended, in a report drafted by Jay, that Governor Clinton pardon three of these men. For example, Jay recommended that Clinton pardon one man because "his character was heretofore uniformly that of a domestic inoffensive young man" and "he appears to have had very little agency in the robbery." Clinton, who accepted all these recommendations, reported to Morris that Jay "fills the bench with great dignity and pronounces the sentences of the court with becoming grace. It is to be lamented that he has had already so many opportunities to display his abilities in that way but it is unavoidable."[49]

In addition to holding courts, Jay's other official duty was to review legislation as part of the Council of Revision. This position involved him in several severe disagreements with the legislature. The New York legislature started work in September 1777, but then fled Kingston as the British approached, leaving authority in the hands of a Council of Safety. The legislature did not meet again until January 1778, when it gathered in yet another town, Poughkeepsie, and affirmed and continued a grain embargo that had been imposed in the meantime by the Council of Safety. The Council of Revision, in a message drafted by Jay, objected that the Council of Safety had no constitutional basis. Now that a proper government was in place, under the new constitution, the legislature was the only body which could legislate, and it could not "dispense with or suspend the government established by the constitution." Jay also objected to the "court" established by the law, since it allowed the person who had seized the goods to act as both prosecutor and judge, and to proceed without notice to the owner of the goods. The legislators, some of whom had served on the Council of Safety, were not about to accept the argument that the Council was unconstitutional. They passed the bill into law over the veto. The weakness of the Council of Revision was now apparent to Jay and others. Here was a law which was clearly contrary to the constitution, for reasons Jay had explained carefully to the legislature. Yet the legislature could and did simply enact the law over the Council's objections.[50]

In late March, Jay and the Council objected to a law which disqualified from voting any man who had, after July 1776, declared his allegiance to the King; the constitution clearly allowed men to vote if they, at the time of the election, took an oath of allegiance to the state. The Council was particularly outraged by the "ex post facto" nature of the law. "To punish men for acts by laws made subsequent to the commission of such acts has, by all civilized nations, been deemed arbitrary and unjust." The Council rightly observed that the law "savor[ed] too much of resentment and revenge to be consistent with the dignity or good of a free people." On the same day, the Council objected to a special tax of five percent on profits of "traders and manufacturers." Jay declared that the constitution's guarantee of an "equal right to life, liberty and property" meant that "no member of this state can with justice be constrained to contribute more to the support thereof, than in like proportion with other citizens." In his view, it was "repugnant to the very idea of justice" to impose upon people merely because they were "traders" or "manufacturers" such "large penalties, not incurred on conviction of disobedience to any known law, and couched under the specious name of tax." In both cases, however, the legislature passed the law despite his objections.[51]

At the end of its session in April, the legislature added insult to injury by passing a bill which ratified all actions of the former Council of Safety. The Council of Revision sent a note to the legislature, asking it for a copy of all of the "orders and resolutions" which were ratified by this bill. Since the legislature was not in session, the Council did not have to react to this bill within the standard ten-day time frame. To prevent the bill from becoming law, however, the Council had to present its objections to the legislature on the first day of the new legislative session. When the legislature reconvened in June, only Governor Clinton and Chief Justice Jay were present in Poughkeepsie. Without a quorum, the Council could not act on the bill. Jay was more than a little annoyed with his friend Chancellor Livingston, whose absence allowed this outrageous bill to become law.[52]

The tax on traders and manufacturers proved unworkable or inadequate, so in November 1778 the legislature passed a second, similar tax bill. The legislature did not attempt to specify the tax, but rather authorized the assessors to impose and collect whatever tax they "shall in their judgment think proper." Jay and the Council again objected to the unfairness of the unequal taxation; they also insisted that the legislature could not "delegate the right of determining, at discretion, how much shall be levied." Jay's argument here is an early, indeed perhaps the first, American statement of the principle that a legislature cannot delegate unbounded discretion to an administrator or agency. In this case, his objections were effective, for the legislature did not pass the bill over the objections.[53]

In addition to his formal role as a member of the Council of Revision, Jay also served as an informal adviser to the legislature, and in at least one case his advice was heeded. In early 1778 he drafted a "hint" to the legislature on the "practice of impressing horses, teams and carriages by the military." He did not deny that the army needed horses and carriages, but in his view the only question was "whether the army shall at their mere will and pleasure furnish themselves, and that at the point of a bayonet." He urged the legislature to enact a law, to address the issue fairly, and a few weeks later it passed a law along the lines he suggested.[54]

Like many patriots, Jay had friends among the Loyalists, and like many, he remained to some extent in touch with these men on the other side. For example, he wrote James DeLancey, a prisoner at Hartford, that "notwithstanding the opposition of our sentiments and conduct relative to the present contest, the friendship which subsisted between us is not forgotten; nor will the good offices formerly done by yourself and family cease to excite my gratitude." Peter Van Schaack asked Jay to help persuade Governor Clinton to allow him and his ailing wife to visit New York City. Although Clinton often granted such requests, particularly to women, he denied this request, saying he had to prevent "all intercourse between the inhabitants and the enemy." A few months later, Jay wrote to Van Schaack that he wished they could "smoke a few pipes together," for then "you would perhaps be in better humor with many things in the world." But Van Schaack was understandably *not* in good humor, for a law passed at this time effectively banished him from the state. Van Schaack wrote to Jay at length, arguing that the legislature was not justified in punishing him for mere opinions. "I think that in a question depending on opinion only, and wherein every man has a right and is bound to determine according to his own opinion, he is accountable only for the fair and impartial exercise of his judgment, and as no human tribunal can examine this, so they ought not to punish him for the result."[55]

Jay was also in touch with Gouverneur Morris throughout 1778. In January, when Morris was at Valley Forge, he reported to Jay that he found just a "skeleton of an army," in a "naked, starving condition, out of health and out of spirits." Jay responded that he was glad to "hear that you were at head-quarters, especially on a business so important and perplexed." In April, Morris reported from York, Pennsylvania, where Congress was then meeting, that he believed a treaty had been signed with France. Jay's initial reaction to the French alliance was cool. "What the French treaty may be, I know not. If Britain would acknowledge our independence, and enter into a liberal alliance with us, I should prefer a connection with her to a league with any power on earth." He added that the "destruction of old England would hurt me; I wish it well: it afforded my ancestors asylum from persecution."[56]

Later in the year, Morris urged Jay to return to the Continental Congress, which had returned to Philadelphia after the British vacated the city. Congress was "at length fairly setting about our finances and our foreign affairs. For the latter particularly I much wish you were here." But Jay was reluctant to return to Philadelphia, far from his family and friends. In March, he wrote to his sister-in-law Susan, who was watching young Peter, that when he next saw his son he expected he would "have been taught to damn the King and say the [Presbyterian] Confession." Sarah must have been looking over John's shoulder, for he continued: "Sally says that if I write such things she wishes I would conclude my letter." Sarah then added her own amusing postscript, noting that she was perhaps guilty of "petty treason" for contradicting the "assertions of my lord and master."[57]

John Jay's public career began in 1769 with a border dispute, between New York and New Jersey. In late 1778, another state border dispute, this time involving New Hampshire, sent him from New York back into national poli-tics. New Yorkers argued that the proper border between New York and

New Hampshire was at the Connecticut River. Starting in about 1750, however, the Governor of New Hampshire issued grants for land west of the river, claiming that the western border of New Hampshire should be in line with the border between New York and Massachusetts. The Governor of New York raised the issue with the Privy Council, which ruled that the border was at the Connecticut River. New York then started issuing its own land grants for the same territory. Indeed, Jay himself applied without success for a portion of this land in 1771. Some of the settlers claiming under New Hampshire, however, refused to honor the Privy Council order or New York court orders. With the onset of the Revolution, the settlers declared themselves a new state, Vermont. They argued that they had as much right to secede from New York as New York had to secede from the British Empire.[58]

During 1778, Governor George Clinton grew increasingly anxious for assistance from the Congress in suppressing the "rebels" in Vermont. In April, Clinton requested an "explicit and unequivocal declaration of the sense of the Congress" on Vermont. In June, Ethan Allen, a Vermont leader, had himself appointed Attorney General of Vermont so that he could prosecute David Redding, a New York Loyalist. James Duane, in a letter to Jay, conceded that Redding was "very unworthy," but he was outraged to see Vermonters sitting in judgment on a New Yorker. Duane urged Jay to consider returning to Congress to raise the issue there. In July, Governor Clinton wrote again to Philadelphia complaining that "after many fruitless applications" Congress had still not acted. And in October Clinton asked, and the legislature agreed, that Jay should go as a delegate to Congress, mainly to obtain action on the Vermont issue.[59]

Jay's own attitude towards Vermont at this time is hard to discern. He reminded Morris from time to time to press the issue in Congress, but he also described a pamphlet by Ethan Allen on the issue as having "quaintness, impudence, and art," not quite a compliment, but not the condemnation that Clinton or Duane would have made. He recognized that, as time passed, "Vermont will gain strength," and that Congress would probably defer action on the issue "unless some collateral circumstance constrains them." In short, he seems to have accepted the New York position, but without much passion.[60]

Jay traveled from Poughkeepsie down to Philadelphia with mixed emotions.

He had accomplished much in the past two years, especially in the strong new state constitution. He believed that he and his conservative friends had achieved as much as they could on that front, that "another turn of the winch would have cracked the cord." He was also disgusted, however, with the way in which the New York legislature sometimes disregarded the state constitution or the national situation. The seeds of Jay's nationalism were already present in his disgust at this time with state politics. They would grow over the next year, as he observed from the President's chair the weakness and indecision of the national Congress.[61]

CHAPTER 5

President of the
Continental Congress

As JOHN JAY made his way south in late November and early December 1778, he was delayed by "several unavoidable accidents." He did not describe these accidents for his reader, but they are not hard to imagine. The British controlled the lower Hudson and New York City, so that, instead of taking the usual route down the river, a rebel like Jay had to travel by small roads to the west. As he crossed New Jersey, he saw the destruction caused by two years of intense fighting and foraging there. Philadelphia itself was still recovering at this time from a year of British occupation, during which dead horses were piled in the State House yard, churches robbed of their pews and plate, and many houses destroyed.[1]

When he reached Philadelphia, Jay saw an article in the prior day's newspaper, written and signed by his friend Silas Deane. Deane had spent much of 1777 and 1778 in France, where he had obtained some useful supplies but also quarreled with another American representative, Arthur Lee. When Deane returned to Philadelphia in the summer of 1778, he was eager to explain his side of the dispute to Congress. After sending a dozen letters to Congress, however, without getting the hearing he believed he deserved, Deane decided to go public. Deane alleged in his article that Lee's manners "gave universal disgust to the nation whose assistance we solicited." More seriously, Deane alleged that Lee had frequent contact with an apparent British spy.[2]

On the day after Jay's arrival, his first day back in Congress, President Henry Laurens moved that Congress appoint a special committee to consider

Deane's charges. Laurens was annoyed with Deane, who suggested in his article that Laurens had delayed consideration of his case, and annoyed with Congress, when it failed to vote on his motion. Two days later, Laurens startled the delegates by reading out to them a long, bitter resignation letter. Laurens argued that Deane's letter was not only an attack on Lee but an attack on "the honor and dignity of this House, the great representative of an infant empire." Laurens felt "my own honor, and much more forcibly the honor of the public, deeply wounded by Mr. Deane's address."[3]

After this "extraordinary event," Congress adjourned for the day and the delegates discussed informally who should be the next President. When they reconvened the next day, they elected Jay by a vote of eight states to four. According to James Duane, a "great majority of Congress immediately deter-mined that one of the New York delegates should succeed in the chair," and, since Philip Schuyler was not present, "Jay was prevailed on to take the chair." Gouverneur Morris gave more credit to Jay, saying that the "weight of his personal character contributed as much to his election as the respect for the state." Jay had the support not only of the friends of Deane, but also of some of the friends of Lee. Samuel Adams, a staunch supporter of Lee, wrote to his wife that he had "cheerfully" given his vote for Jay. It seems, from these and other brief comments, that the delegates selected Jay for several reasons: because they believed that the office should rotate among the states; because they thought the calm and judicious Jay would be a better President than the excitable and partisan Laurens; and because he managed to remain friendly with men, such as Samuel Adams, with whom he often disagreed.[4]

The Continental Congress, of which Jay served as President for the next several months, was not the legislative branch of a national government. There really was no national government at this time, only a confederation of states, something like the European Union today. The Congress had certain limited areas of authority: to raise and direct the army; to conduct foreign policy; to borrow or print money; and to resolve disputes among states. But Congress did not have the power to collect taxes; it could only request funds from the states. More generally, Congress did not have the power to write laws; it could only recommend legislation to the states. The Articles of Confederation (which had by this time been approved by many but not all of the states) provided that "each state retains its sovereignty, freedom and independence, and every power, jurisdiction, and right, which is not by this confederation expressly delegated to the United States, in Congress assembled."[5]

The Continental Congress also suffered from high turnover and frequent absences. Jay must have noticed the turnover when he returned in December 1778 and found that only nine of the fifty delegates with whom he served in early 1776 were still present.[6] Delegates left the Congress for many reasons, but perhaps the main reason was that it was hard work. Congress generally met six days a week for at least six hours a day. Before and after these sessions, members attended meetings of the numerous committees. Most members devoted at least another hour a day to writing letters, for they were expected to keep friends and colleagues informed. The distances made it impossible for most members to go home during short recesses. Members were stuck in Philadelphia week after week, month after month; when they grew tired of this, they often simply went home, either for a brief visit or for good.[7]

The role of the President of the Congress was limited and to some extent unclear. His principal duty was to preside over the sessions of the Congress. The President sat in a large, elevated chair facing the other members; he recognized them as they rose to speak, and they addressed him rather than one another. The President generally did not participate in debates, and Laurens once complained he was a mere "silent auditor and spectator." But prior to each important vote, the President would summarize the issue, somewhat like a judge summarizing for a jury. In January 1779, one delegate wrote that "as usual we looked to the President to give his opinion before balloting. Mr. Jay is more judicious than his predecessor in the chair and less prolix." Presumably the President could, through a careful summary, influence votes to an extent.[8]

Another major duty of the President was correspondence. During his ten months as President, Jay wrote over five hundred letters on behalf of Congress. In most cases, Jay had guidance from Congress on what to write. In some cases, the guidance was very specific, in the form of a draft letter reviewed and edited by the whole Congress. In other cases, the guidance was more general. For example, Congress would often ask President Jay to send copies of recent resolutions to the state governors. Jay had the services of a secretary, his brother-in-law Brockholst Livingston, to turn the views of Congress into drafts.[9] But he did not follow the guidance of Congress slavishly. In at least one case, a letter to Lafayette, Jay completely disregarded the official draft and sent his own letter. More often, he simply added a personal line or two. In addition to all his official correspondence, he had an extensive unofficial correspondence. He corresponded with Robert Livingston about the "little paltry party politics" of the New York legislature in Poughkeepsie; he urged Philip Schuyler not to resign his continental commission; he thanked Anthony Benezet, a leader of the Philadelphia Quakers, for some anti-slavery pamphlets; and he helped Alexander Hamilton and John Laurens with their scheme to offer slaves freedom in return for military service. "An essential part of the plan," Hamilton wrote to Jay, "is to give them their freedom with their muskets." Jay ensured that Congress passed a supportive resolution, but Congress could not legislate on this issue, and the South Carolina legislature rejected out of hand such a "very dangerous and impolitic step."[10]

The President was also expected to meet with and entertain foreign ministers, military leaders, and other members of Congress. Until Jay assumed the office, the Presidents paid for their entertainment expenses on their own. Laurens estimated that he spent more than fifty dollars a day hosting "delegates, strangers and sometimes ministers plenipotentiary." Jay must have mentioned to his colleagues that he could not afford this kind of expense, for the day after his election a committee was appointed to consider an allowance for the President. Congress resolved to hire a "convenient dwelling house" for the President and to provide "a table, carriage and servants" at public expense. Jay soon hired a steward, William Young, and rented a house, from Francis Gurney, so he could entertain in a style appropriate to his position.[11]

Although the presidency was a prestigious position, it was not a particularly powerful one. Presidents were elected by Congress and they could be removed by Congress. In practice, Congress did not remove its Presidents, but there was an expectation that they would resign after about a year in office. The President did not have a staff of any kind, other than his personal secretary and his steward. The President did not set the agenda of Congress, nor could he influence policy by naming favored members to committees. Perhaps most limiting, the President could not influence events through his political party, because there really *were* no political parties. There were, to be sure,

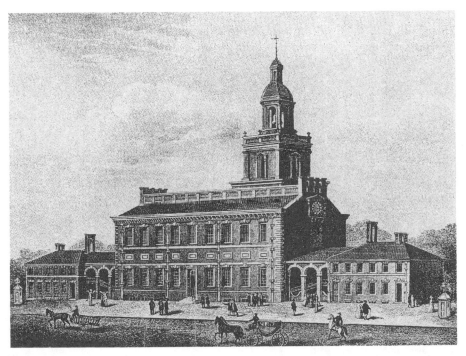

Pennsylvania State House. Jay knew the State House well: he served there in the Continental Congress off and on from early 1775 through late 1779. In a private letter to Washington, he commented that "there is as much intrigue in this State House as in the Vatican, but as little secrecy as in a boarding school."

predictable patterns on some issues, such as when the New England delegates voted to defend their fishing rights. But on many other issues, voting was far from predictable. Delegates who voted together on one issue would often vote against one another on another issue. Indeed, the delegates viewed the very words "party" or "faction" as insults.[12]

While Jay was its President, Congress devoted itself, in about equal measure, to personal disputes and foreign policy questions. The bickering made it far harder for Congress to deal with foreign policy, and policy issues, especially the demands of the French Minister, tended to lead to new personal disputes. Jay tried, with only limited success, to focus on policy rather than personalities.[13]

The United States and France were now allies, and France was represented in Philadelphia by a Minister Plenipotentiary, Conrad Alexandre Gérard. Gérard was a veteran French diplomat, nearly fifty, smooth, self-confident, self-centered. Jay immediately recognized that one of his main tasks as President was to confer with and defer to Gérard. On the day after he became President, Jay wrote to Gérard that it would be an honor to correspond with one so "high in the favor with the Protector of the Rights of Mankind" and "endeared to every American by his friendship for these United States." Jay's kind words and frequent visits helped keep Gérard's reports positive, but they also made other delegates question Jay's motives. When James Lovell of Massachusetts complained about the "lickspittles of the plenipotentiary," he probably had Jay in mind.[14]

Although Gérard was the most visible and active diplomat in Philadelphia, he was not the only one, for Spain was represented unofficially by Don Juan de Miralles. Miralles was born in Spain of French parents, but had lived most of his life in Cuba, where he had traded extensively with Europe and the American colonies. Although Spain did not yet recognize the United States, and was not yet at war, Spain was keenly interested in the war, so senior Spanish officials asked Miralles to go to Philadelphia as an observer. Miralles was ostensibly in the United States to pursue private trading opportunities, and indeed he did trade actively, but Americans generally understood that Miralles was also providing political, military and commercial information to Spain, and they treated him as if he were a diplomat. Miralles was convivial and pleasant, generous with brandy and cigars, and this of course helped his cause in Philadelphia.[15]

During December 1778, Gérard, Miralles and Jay discussed two issues of particular concern to Spain: the West, where Spanish interests in Louisiana collided with America's westward expansion; and Florida, recently ceded by Spain to Britain and now claimed by the United States. As to Louisiana, Jay said he expected that within a few years there would be more than twenty thousand American settlers there, and implied that Spain could not hold the territory against this human flood. Miralles countered that "before long those new settlers would shake off the yoke of the central government by creating a new republic" and suggested that, given this, perhaps the United States should renounce its claims in return for hard cash. As to Florida, Jay envisaged that it would soon become another state. Miralles said that because it "was a former possession," Spain could never "complacently see other nations possess it." If, however, the United States would work with Spain to recapture it, perhaps Spain would compensate the United States "for the expenses incurred."[16]

Thomas Paine, famed throughout America for his pamphlet *Common Sense*, which had made the case in early 1776 for independence, was living at this time in Philadelphia, and working part-time as secretary to the Foreign Affairs Committee of Congress. He was also publishing, under the rather obvious pseudonym "Common Sense," a series of letters in the *Pennsylvania Packet*, supporting Lee and attacking Deane. In one of these letters, Paine claimed that France had *given* rather than *sold* supplies to America before their alliance. Gérard was annoyed because France's official position was that it had not provided any governmental aid to the Americans before the alliance, although in fact such aid had been extensive. He was also annoyed because Paine's position, however minor, gave greater weight to the article. He wrote to President Jay to demand that Congress take action against Paine and his "indiscreet assertions."[17]

On the next morning, with the city covered by a new snow, Congress assembled to investigate and debate the issue. The printer John Dunlap was called into the hall and asked by President Jay whether he was the publisher of the *Pennsylvania Packet*. "Yes indeed," Dunlap replied. "Who," Jay asked, "was the author of the recent pieces signed 'Common Sense?'" "Thomas Paine,"

replied Dunlap. Jay dismissed Dunlap and summoned in Paine. Glaring down
at Paine, Jay raised a newspaper in his hand: "Here is the *Pennsylvania Packet*
of December 29. In it is a piece entitled 'Common Sense to the Public on Mr.
Deane's Affairs.' I am directed by Congress to ask whether you were the
author." Standing like a prisoner at the bar, Paine answered that he was the
author. Jay asked the same question about two more recent articles, received
the same answer, and then dismissed Paine as well. Congress spent much of the
next few days debating how to deal with Paine. Jay almost certainly agreed
with his friend Gouverneur Morris, who argued that Paine was a "mere adven-
turer from England, without fortune, without family or connections, ignorant
even of grammar." Congress *had* to dismiss Paine, "for without this in
contradicting him we shall not be believed."[18]

To avoid being dismissed, Paine attempted to resign. Paine said he had
learned "from the journals of this house" that he was "not to be heard." This
statement provoked further furious debate: how had Paine learned about a
secret session of Congress? President Jay asked Secretary Thomson whether
Paine had seen the draft journal. Thomson replied that nobody, other than
himself, had seen yesterday's notes, which he had taken home with him in the
evening and brought back in the morning. Someone moved that the President
should question the members "on their honor" to determine "whether they
have communicated the resolutions of yesterday to Mr. Thomas Paine." As this
motion was nearing a vote, Laurens reluctantly admitted that he had discussed
yesterday's proceedings with Paine. Now there was further debate and further
motions, including one by Jay himself that "the journals of this House contain
no determination denying Mr. Paine a hearing."[19]

Gérard, annoyed by the delay in Congress, wrote again to Jay, demanding
action. Jay replied that he had a "sincere desire as well as expectation of your
speedily receiving an explicit and satisfactory answer." A few days later, Jay
could finally write to Gérard "with real satisfaction" to send him the resolutions adopted by Congress to disavow and disapprove Paine's publications. But
Jay and the other critics of Paine failed in their attempt to disregard the resignation and have him dismissed. With the states divided evenly, and New Jersey
not present, a motion to dismiss failed.[20]

This episode shows how Jay was drawn into quarrels, even if he did not participate in debates. His insistence on an answer for Gérard, his tone in his questions to Paine, and his vote in favor of Paine's dismissal, all combined to anger those who supported Paine and Lee. The episode also shows that, much as Gérard claimed to deplore personal quarrels, he was a major cause of them. Congress did not have to debate Paine's letters; nor did Paine's letters really injure France. But Gérard thought they did and he insisted that Congress disavow Paine. And one quarrel often led to others. Even before Congress voted on whether to dismiss Deane, one of the most prominent former members of Congress, the Philadelphia merchant Robert Morris, published a long letter responding to an allegation by Paine about how Morris had handled public funds. Laurens then claimed that Morris had defamed him in one passage in this letter. This led to further debate, and indeed to a duel between Laurens and John Penn, whom Laurens viewed as having slighted him by failing to confirm certain statements against Morris.[21]

It was into this hothouse atmosphere that Gérard introduced the heated questions of peace terms and peace commissioners. Gérard informed Jay in early February that Spain would soon deliver an ultimatum to Britain: either accept Spain as the mediator of the dispute, and begin peace negotiations, or Spain would enter the war on the side of France. According to Gérard, Jay expressed "great pleasure at the prospect of peace negotiations," and suggested that Gérard should explain the situation to the whole Congress in a private session. At this session, Gérard formally asked Congress to take two steps: to appoint a "proper person to take part in the expected negotiations" and to determine its minimal peace terms.[22]

Although transatlantic communication was slow, Gérard probably at least sensed that peace negotiations were not imminent. In fact, France and Spain were at this very time negotiating the final points of their secret alliance against Britain, which they signed at the Spanish palace of Aranjuez in early April 1779. Gérard's real purpose was not to facilitate immediate peace discussions, but instead to lock Congress into narrow peace objectives, and thus to simplify France's task in any future peace negotiations. It is easy to understand why France wanted to limit America's ambitions; it is less easy to understand why Congress, particularly when defining peace objectives proved so difficult, did not simply postpone the issue.[23]

Congress referred the issue of peace terms to a committee of five, including Jay's friend Gouverneur Morris, and this committee reported back promptly. The committee suggested that the Americans should insist, in any peace treaty with Britain, on six key points: recognition of American independence; acceptance of boundaries reaching north to Canada, west to the Mississippi and south to Florida; evacuation of all British forces and forts in this American territory; a "right of fishing and curing fish on the banks and coasts of Newfoundland"; the right to navigate the Mississippi; and "free commerce" at New Orleans or some similar port. The first three propositions, although they to some extent exceeded what France or Spain would have wished, were readily agreed to by Congress. After some debate, Congress reluctantly decided that free navigation of the Mississippi and free trade at New Orleans were not *absolutely* necessary for peace. The fisheries question, however, proved far more difficult.[24]

From March through August, the delegates devoted day after day to "a long struggle about cod and haddock." The question was in a sense simple: should the United States insist that any peace treaty guarantee Americans the right to fish on the rich North Atlantic banks? The question was also sectional, since the fishermen were almost all from the New England. Their delegates argued that the fisheries were as vital to their states as tobacco to Virginia or rice to South Carolina. Southern delegates feared that the fighting over the next few years would be mainly in the south; Georgia was already occupied and South Carolina and Virginia threatened. Although a few southern delegates, notably Lee and Laurens, supported the New England position, most of them did not want to see the war unduly prolonged for the sake of a few fish. The middle state delegates, including Jay, found themselves literally in the middle on this issue. Because Congress was so closely divided, and the gain or loss of a single delegate could change a state's vote, those who lost one day would raise the issue again on another.[25]

The fishery question was debated not merely behind the closed doors of Congress, but in the newspapers as well. In June 1779, "Americanus" revealed in the *Pennsylvania Packet* that Congress had been debating peace terms since February, and that the major obstacle was the insistence of the New England delegates on fishing rights. If these delegates, by insisting on unreasonable conditions, delayed a peace negotiation, they would be "justly responsible for the consequences." Thomas Paine, writing again as "Common Sense," defended the fishing rights and attacked "Americanus" for breaching the confidences of Congress. "Without the fishing rights," Paine claimed, "independence would be a mere bubble." [26]

Jay visited Gérard one evening in July to discuss the fisheries issue. Gérard, who did not want the peace process complicated by the fisheries issue, argued that France would not continue the war simply "to obtain a small addition to the fortunes of some arms makers in New England." Jay, who wanted to see some compromise between the north and south on this issue, responded that a peace treaty which did not deal with the fisheries issue would not secure a lasting peace; it was "better to decide this great quarrel now than to see the flame of war rekindled after two or three years of peace." But Gérard was not persuaded; he thought Jay and his colleagues were merely exhausted by the "threats and the audacity of the English party." In Gérard's curious view, those who opposed France must favor England, so he called the New Englanders the "English party," although he knew they hated "the very name of England." [27]

Gérard may have delayed a compromise on the fisheries issue, but he could not prevent it. At the end of July, the middle states joined the northern states to resolve that if Great Britain some day interfered with Americans fishing in the North Atlantic, such "molestation" would be a "common cause" of the United States, and the "force of the union" would be "exerted to obtain redress." Then the middle states joined the southern states to resolve that the United States would *not* make fishing rights an absolute condition of a peace treaty. As in many compromises, the partisans on both sides were unhappy: New England had failed to make the fishing rights a precondition of peace, and the South was bound to join in defending the fishing rights, by force if necessary. Jay voted in favor of both resolutions: he was one of the compromisers. [28]

During this same period, from March through September 1779, Congress debated the second issue raised by Gérard: who should represent Congress abroad? A committee suggested in late March that Congress should vacate the appointments of *all* its current representatives, including Benjamin Franklin, Ralph Izard and Arthur Lee. The most bitter and prolonged debate concerned Lee. Gérard favored the recall from France of Lee, whom he privately termed "very troublesome if not dangerous." Lee's supporters viewed it as outrageous that he should be recalled merely because he had placed America's interests above those of France. They sought to downplay Gérard's concerns, and Samuel Adams told Congress that he had it on "highest authority" that Lee had the "full confidence of the court of France." When Gérard learned of this statement, he showed two delegates a letter from the French Foreign Minister, stating that he "feared" Lee "and those around him."[29]

Jay was drawn into the debate because of his close relation with Gérard and his role as President. In late April, he announced one morning that the pending question was "whether you will recall Mr. Lee." Laurens immediately disagreed, saying the question was instead the motion made by William Paca a few days earlier, that Congress should formally ask Gérard to state whether Lee "possesses the confidence of the courts of Versailles and Madrid." Paca now attempted to withdraw his motion, but Laurens insisted on a recorded vote. Jay opined that Paca, as author of the motion, could withdraw the motion without a vote. Laurens (who noted in his diary that he "was by no means surprised at the President's leanings") then "appealed to the rules, and said nothing less than violence could deprive him of his right" to a recorded vote. Duane deplored the tone of these remarks, and Laurens for once backed down, and allowed Paca to withdraw his motion.[30]

In early May, Jay was one of the twenty-two delegates who voted in favor of the recall of Arthur Lee. Laurens was among the fourteen delegates who voted to retain Lee. Because the states divided evenly on the motion, however, it did not pass. A few days later, the *Pennsylvania Packet* published an anonymous letter, presumably from a delegate, which showed how each delegate voted on this critical motion. The purpose of this unprecedented breach of secrecy was to discredit Lee and his supporters, by showing that they were in the minority. Lee's supporters responded quickly, disclosing in a letter to the *Packet* that Congress was considering the recall of even the illustrious Franklin. Obviously, the newspaper war raging outside made compromise inside the halls of Congress that much harder.[31]

Although the vote in early May ended for a while the debate on the recall of Lee, the question continued to color delegates' views of Jay. During a debate in June, a delegate characterized the motion to recall Lee as having been "lost."

Jay "hastily" and, in the opinion of Laurens "very rudely," stated that the motion was not "lost" because the "house equally divided." Laurens responded, probably equally rudely, that the consistent practice of Congress was to consider a question "lost" when the states divided equally. Jay "objected and appeared much chagrined." In August, a letter from Lee defending himself was read aloud to the Congress. William Whipple recorded that "envy, malice, and every vindictive passion" were on the faces of Lee's opponents, and in particular that Jay "changed color at every sentence." In September, in yet another of his *Common Sense* letters, Paine complained that Jay's attitude towards him earlier in the year had been "groundless and ungrateful." Paine argued that he was a true Patriot while Jay was merely lukewarm. "If America had had no better friends than [Jay] to bring about independence, I fully believe she never would have succeeded in it." [32]

During August, Congress learned that Spain had been at war with Britain since June. It was finally clear that there would be no peace negotiations in 1779 or perhaps 1780. Congress still viewed it as necessary, however, to name one or more peace commissioners, and to send someone to Spain, in search of funds and arms. Gérard hoped that Jay would be named the Peace Commissioner, since he had come to view Jay as pliable and pro-French. The New England delegates hoped that John Adams would be named the Peace Commissioner, since he could be counted on to defend the fisheries, whatever the instructions said. The Virginians hoped that Arthur Lee would be asked to go to Madrid, where he might redeem his damaged reputation. [33]

Adams was in Massachusetts and Lee was in France, so neither of them could agree or disagree with their selection. Jay was in Philadelphia, however, and it is worth pausing to consider why he was willing to accept an overseas assignment. Part of the answer is that he could not go on being President for ever, since there was an unwritten rule that a President should serve for only a year. Part of the answer is that he was tired of the politics of Congress and longed to be far from its intrigues and interference. Above all, however, he wanted to achieve American independence, and sensed that he could do more to help the cause in Paris or Madrid than he could in Philadelphia. Events would prove him right.

On a Saturday in late September, both Adams and Jay were nominated for the post of Peace Commissioner. Because "of the differences of opinions, the

voting was postponed" until an unusual Sunday session, when there were two
votes on who should be commissioner. On the first vote there were five states
for Adams, four for Jay, and three divided delegations; on the second vote six
states favored Adams, four Jay, and two states were divided. Since neither
candidate could command the required seven votes, Congress moved on to the
question of who should serve as commissioner in Spain. Adams, Jay and Lee
were all nominated, but apparently no votes were taken on this issue on
Sunday. That afternoon and evening, as the delegates dined and talked, a
compromise emerged: Adams would handle the peace negotiations and Jay
would go to Spain, with the prestigious title of "Minister Plenipotentiary." On
Monday, the delegates confirmed this compromise: Jay was elected Minister by
eight states, with three states divided; and Adams was elected to negotiate
peace by eleven states.[34]

Lee's partisans were bitter that their man had been excluded from any role.
James Lovell complained that Jay would "take the post of a man murdered on
purpose to make room." In general, however, members were pleased with their
choices, and pleased to have the contentious issue behind them. Gérard
reported that the choice of Jay "left nothing to be desired" because "to ample
intelligence and the best intentions, [Jay] joins a flexible and conciliatory character." Indeed, Gérard liked Jay so well that he made arrangements to travel
across the Atlantic with him, so that he could return to France while Jay went
to Spain. Miralles reported back to Spain that Congress showed its "respect for
our King by sending the leader of Congress to him, since as republicans they
have neither dukes nor other grandees as do the kingdoms of the first rank."[35]

From the perspective of the average American, the most pressing issue facing
Congress was neither peace terms nor peace commissioners, but the devasta-
ting depreciation of the continental dollar. In January 1778, it took four
continental dollars to purchase one dollar in hard currency. In January 1779, it
took eight continental dollars to purchase one hard dollar. By January 1780,
it took *thirty* continental dollars to obtain a hard dollar. The United States was
on the verge of hyperinflation.[36]

In one sense, Congress was the cause of the depreciation, because it was
Congress that was printing more and more continental dollars. Congress issued

$13 million of new currency in 1777, $63 million in 1778, and more than $124 million in 1779. In another sense, however, the depreciation was caused by circumstances beyond the control of Congress. Congress could not control the cost of the war; it had to pay for troops and their supplies. Congress had no power to impose taxes directly upon the American people. Congress could and did request that the states impose taxes and pass the revenues over to Congress. Most states attempted to comply with these requests, but the nominal amounts the states collected declined in value because of depreciation, and the states had to pay their own war expenses first before sending money to Congress.[37]

Not long after Jay arrived, Congress adopted a set of resolutions it hoped would slow or stop the depreciation of the continental currency. Congress resolved that the states should, in the course of 1779, raise $15 million through taxes. It also "called in" two series of continental currency which had been frequently counterfeited. People holding these series had a limited time within which to turn their notes in and receive either new currency or loan certificates. In sending these resolutions to the states, Jay stressed the "importance of the objects" of the resolutions and the need for "support and countenance" from "every virtuous citizen."[38]

The currency continued to lose value daily. General Washington wrote President Jay in April "that a wagon load of money will scarcely purchase a wagon load of provisions." Jay responded that the "state of our currency is really serious" but noted bitterly that "the conduct of some men really indicate[s] at least great indifference about it." Indeed, Congress was having difficulty focusing on its finances at this time. Days were lost to "trifling" debates about the fisheries and to personal quarrels. When Congress voted on whether to call upon the states for another $60 million in tax revenues, Jay was one of only a dozen delegates willing to ask the states to impose such substantial taxes. In late May, amidst street protests in Philadelphia, Congress finally decided to request $45 million, apportioned among the states by population. In sending this request to the states, Jay exhorted them to act. "While the great purposes for which the money was originally issued are remembered, there can be no doubt that every measure calculated to support its credit and preserve the public faith will be readily adopted."[39]

In spite of these resolutions, and some efforts by the states, the currency continued to depreciate throughout the summer of 1779. In early September, Jay reported to Governor Clinton that Congress had agreed to "stop the press at two hundred million" continental dollars, or "as far short of it, as the state of their other resources will permit." Since this limit was only about forty million more than was already in circulation, Congress would soon have to devise other means of financing the war. Although Presidents did not normally undertake drafting assignments, in this case Congress asked Jay to draft a letter from Congress to its constituents. Congress adopted and published, in both English and German, Jay's lengthy letter.[40]

Jay started by reminding Americans of why Congress had been forced to print continental dollars in the first place. To fight the war, Congress had to pay for an army. Congress could not raise money in the early days through loans: "of no nation in the world could you then borrow." Congress could not raise money at this stage through state taxes, since for this purpose "regular governments were essential" and "of these you were also destitute." America had "no other resource but the natural value and wealth of your fertile country," and this was the backing for the first continentals. Jay provided precise figures on the amount of continental currency issued, the amount raised through loans, and the amounts which had to date been contributed by the states to Congress. He warned that, once the two hundred million limit was reached, the states would bear the main responsibility for providing both troops and supplies in the next campaign.[41]

Most of his letter is a detailed discussion of the causes of the depreciation. He admitted that part of the depreciation was "natural," due to the excessive supply of continental dollars. He argued, however, that much of the depreciation was "artificial," due to doubts about whether America would become an independent nation and whether such a nation would pay its debts. Jay proceeded to dispel these doubts.[42] "The independence of America is now as fixed as fate," he declared, "and the petulant efforts of Britain to break it down are as vain and fruitless as the raging of the waves which beat against their cliffs." Among the factors which made this "certain" were that "that these states are daily increasing in power; that their armies have become veteran; that their governments, founded in freedom, are established; that their fertile country and their affectionate ally furnish them with ample supplies; [and] that the Spanish monarch, well prepared for war, with fleets and armies ready for combat, and a treasury overflowing with wealth, has entered the lists against Britain." Anyone who considered "these things, instead of doubting the issue of the war, will rejoice in the glorious, the sure and certain prospect of success."[43]

There was also no doubt, in Jay's view, that the independent United States would be able to pay its war debts. The population of the United States was already three million people, and this number was doubling roughly every twenty years. The people, and the land, would be productive: "Extensive wildernesses, now scarcely known or explored, remain yet to be cultivated, and vast lakes and rivers, whose waters have for ages rolled in silence and obscurity to the ocean, are yet to hear the din of industry, become subservient to commerce, and boast delightful villas, gilded spires, and spacious cities rising on their banks."[44]

Having established that the United States would have the *ability* to pay, Jay turned to the question of whether the United States would have the "political capacity" to pay. He noted that some "enemies" argued that "the confederation of the states remains yet to be perfected," that the "union may be dissolved," and that the states might in this scenario repudiate the bills and debts of the Continental Congress. These "enemies" had a point: Maryland had so far refused to sign the Articles of Confederation, and it was far from clear whether it could be enticed to sign without alienating other states. But Jay, in this case at least, ignored these legal details. "For every purpose essential to the defense of these states in the progress of the present war ... these states now are as fully, legally, and absolutely confederated as it is possible for them to be." The delegates and the states had pledged "their lives, their fortunes, and their sacred honor" to the cause of independence, and they could not and would not renege on their commitments. Moreover, as time progressed, a "sense of common permanent interest" and "ties of consanguinity" would "forever bind us together."[45]

Jay concluded by requesting, almost insisting, that the states and the people provide funds through "loans and taxes." Justice Holmes would later write that "taxes are what we pay for a civilized society." Jay now said that taxes were "the price of liberty, the peace and the safety of yourselves and posterity." Americans should never let it be said "that America had no sooner become independent than she became insolvent," or that "her infant glories and growing fame were obscured and tarnished by broken contracts and violated faith." [46] One leading scholar has said that "among the many state papers put forth by the Continental Congress," Jay's letter "ranks among the first." Certainly the letter was an eloquent argument as to why the United States would prevail in the war and become a great nation. But the letter, for all its eloquence, did nothing to stem the continued depreciation of the continental dollar. Within a little more than a year, the rate between the hard dollar and the continental dollar had reached one to one hundred. [47]

John Jay's most important relationship as President was not with other members of Congress, nor with foreign diplomats, but with George Washington. The two men had known one another since 1774, when they were both delegates to the first Continental Congress. Washington had impressed other delegates at that time with his size, his strength and his silence. He was above all a soldier, an impression he reinforced by wearing his uniform. He was "not a harum-scarum, ranting, swearing fellow, but sober, steady, and calm." There was a rumor at the time, which Washington did not deny, that he had "offered to raise and arm and lead one thousand men himself at his own expense." Jay and Washington were both present in the Congress in June 1775, when John Adams rose to urge that the army in Boston become a national army, headed by a general appointed by the Continental Congress. Adams explained that he had in mind a man "among us and very well known to all of us, a gentleman whose skill and experience as an officer, whose independent fortune, great talents and excellent universal character would command the approbation of all America." Washington left the hall as soon as Adams started this speech, but Jay stayed on for the discussion and debate, ending in a unanimous vote of the states in favor of Washington's appointment. In the three intervening years, Washington had been with his troops, and Jay mainly in New York, and they had seen one another only once, when Jay requested more troops for the northern front. [48]

Now, however, the two men would have to work together closely. The relationship was not a simple one. Washington was more than ten years older than Jay, and he was already famed and revered throughout America. Indeed Jay himself had drafted for Congress, in early 1776, a letter to Washington praising his work, saying that "the annals of America will record your title to a conspicuous place in the temple of fame." But in another sense Washington was merely a general, answerable to the Continental Congress, represented by its President. Jay's task now would be to preserve the proper *formal* subordination of the military to the civilian while at the same time showing the proper *informal* deference due to General Washington.[49]

He turned to this task immediately, writing to Washington that a "particularly agreeable" part of his new position would be to correspond with "those public characters whom I most esteem." Washington wrote back that his high opinion of Jay's "public character concurs with every personal consideration" in making his election as President "pleasing to me." Within a few days, they could speak face to face, when Washington came to Philadelphia to confer with Congress.[50]

The two men were together often over the next six weeks. As one officer noted, Philadelphia provided Washington "the most splendid entertainment imaginable: large assemblies, evening balls," and Jay was generally present at these events. Washington and Jay conferred privately about the issues facing Washington, the army and the nation: how to stop the depreciation of the currency; how to obtain adequate supplies for the army; and whether and how to attack the British in the spring. Washington was depressed by what he saw in Congress. "Party disputes and personal quarrels are the great business of the day," he wrote, while the "great and accumulated debt, ruined finances, depreciated money, and want of credit" were secondary issues, "postponed from day to day, from week to week as if our affairs wore the most promising prospect."[51]

Few military decisions were taken while Washington was in Philadelphia. As he noted sadly, the "depreciated condition of our money" and the "exhausted state of our resources" would likely require that the army "lie quiet in some favorable position" for several months in order to "save expenses." Congress and Washington did resolve that there would be no invasion of Canada. Jay justified the decision to Lafayette, who had hoped to lead the invading force, by noting the strength of the British defenses and the weakness of the American armies. "Prudence therefore dictates that the arms of America should be employed in expelling the enemy from her own shores, before the liberation of a neighboring province is undertaken."[52]

After Washington returned in early February to his headquarters in New Jersey, Washington and Jay wrote one another often, sometimes almost daily. Most of this correspondence was official: Washington sent the army's requests and reports through Jay, and Congress sent its instructions through Jay. Jay's letters from late February give a sense of the range and frequency of this correspondence. On one day, Jay relayed to Washington papers regarding alleged misconduct by several officers, with a request from Congress that the men be tried by court martial; a few days later, he forwarded a French report from the West Indies about British losses there; the next day, he reported that Congress had agreed to a request for a thousand dollars from General McDougall and would forward the sum to McDougall directly; two days later, he passed along resolutions defining the duties of the inspector general and urging defense of the western frontiers against Indian raids.[53]

Occasionally, the two men wrote one another more personal letters. Their most interesting exchange was started by a letter to Congress from General Horatio Gates, who commanded America's northern army, and who aspired to Washington's position. Gates complained that Washington was not keeping him adequately informed and argued in favor of an invasion of Canada, presumably led by Gates, as commander of the northern forces. Jay forwarded part of this letter to Washington, who responded with a long, emotional attack on the "artifices employed by some men to prejudice me in the public esteem." The President was "well acquainted" with the reasons against an expedition to Canada, and "they seem to have met the full approbation of Congress." Washington noted that, in the last seven months of 1778, he had written more than fifty letters to Gates and received more than forty from him. "I think," he noted sarcastically, "it will be acknowledged that the correspondence was frequent enough during that period." More recently, the pace of letters had slackened, but both armies were in winter quarters, which "afforded very little matter for epistolary intercourse." In closing, Washington said he was aware of the "delicacy" of Jay's situation, since the President was expected to share all official correspondence with Congress, and he asked Jay to treat the letter as "for your own private information." The letter did not make its way into the papers of the Continental Congress.[54]

Jay responded that he was "grateful" to know that Washington had "more than [the] usual degree of confidence" in him. He reassured Washington that Congress had taken no notice of the offending letter from Gates. Then, as he often did, he turned philosophical. "New modes of government not generally understood, nor in certain instances approved, want of moderation and information in the people, want of abilities and rectitude in some of their rulers ... men raised from low degrees to high stations, and rendered giddy by elevation ... laws dictated by the spirit of the times, not the spirit of justice and liberal policy," all of these factors and others "portend evils which much prudence, vigor and circumspection are necessary to prevent or control." In his view, there was "reason to expect a long storm, and difficult navigation" but after that he and Washington would some day find themselves "citizens of a better ordered state." "Things will come right, and these states will be great and flourishing." Even in the darkest days of the revolutionary war, Jay looked forward to the peace, prosperity and greatness of the United States.[55]

Even before he received this letter, Washington wrote with some concrete suggestions and questions. Why, Washington asked, was Congress "keeping the Continental frigates in port?" If the problem was lack of naval hands, would it not be better to "lend them to commanders of known bravery and capacity for a limited term," allowing these men as privateers to attack British shipping? And why was Congress allowing vessels from Bermuda to trade in the Delaware and Chesapeake bays? The British "will not and cannot let their people [in Bermuda] starve." Above all, what was Congress doing to "restore the credit of our currency?"[56]

Jay replied with a letter full of his frustrations with Congress. The Marine Committee, like many others, had "new members constantly coming in and old ones going out." Moreover "few of the members understand even the state of our naval affairs, or have time or inclination to attend to them." "Why," he asked rhetorically, was "not this system changed?" Because it is "convenient to the family compact," by which he meant the Lee family and their allies. As to the currency, he agreed that the situation was "serious," and he was "uncertain" whether or how "the progress of depreciation will be prevented." In short, "there is as much intrigue in this State House as in the Vatican, but as little secrecy as in a boarding school."[57]

The two men continued to correspond, both officially and personally, throughout the summer and early fall of 1779. As John and Sarah Jay were preparing to board their ship for Spain, letters arrived for each of them from the General. Washington hoped that the new Minister to Spain would have "a pleasant and an agreeable passage," the "most perfect and honorable accomplishment of your ministry," and "a safe return to the bosom of a grateful country." He wrote even more warmly to Sarah, wishing that "prosperous gales, unruffled sea, and every thing pleasing and desirable, may smooth the path she is about to walk in." As requested by Sarah, he enclosed a lock of his hair, which she cherished for the rest of her life.[58]

Among the many issues facing Congress, Jay did not forget Vermont, the issue which had brought him back to Congress. When he arrived in Philadelphia, he learned that most delegates were not inclined to intervene in the dispute between New York and Vermont. Many argued that Congress should focus its efforts on winning the war, not on interstate quarrels. Others argued that Congress should not act until all the states ratified the Articles of Confederation, since one article provided an explicit procedure for resolving interstate disputes. Some of the members now had a personal stake on the Vermont side of the dispute, because Ethan Allen had been in Philadelphia in November, bribing members with land grants issued by the "state government" of Vermont. Moreover, as Jay later explained, Congress was for "the greater part of the winter so heated by party divisions," that it would "have been improper and imprudent to have called upon them" to consider Vermont. In sum, as he reported to Governor Clinton, the "season for bringing on the affair of Vermont is not yet arrived."[59]

In May 1779, after Congress calmed down, the New York delegates proposed a resolution that no part of a state could "separate therefrom, and become independent thereof, without the express consent and approbation of such state." Another resolution would have requested the residents of the "pretended state of Vermont" to "return peaceably to their former jurisdictions." Jay wrote to Clinton to report that New York's resolutions had now been introduced, that he was "by no means without hopes of success," and that Clinton could "rely on our utmost exertions and care."[60]

When Congress took up the issue again, President Jay started the discussion by reading aloud some letters describing how Vermonters were seizing land and livestock from New Yorkers. Clinton's covering letter to Congress argued that events in Vermont were "fast approaching to a very serious crisis which nothing but the immediate interposition of Congress can possibly prevent." How much longer, Clinton asked bitterly, could the loyal inhabitants of Vermont be expected to wait for New York and the Congress to defend them? New Yorkers did not want to use force, but they could not remain "passive spectators of the violences committed upon our fellow citizens." [61]

According to Morris, his colleagues Jay and Duane presented New York's case "with a clearness and force irresistible unless by prejudice and blindness." But Jay's own notes show that there *were* a few delegates who resisted his "irresistible" arguments. John Fell of New Jersey argued that Congress should not interfere, at least not until "the other party can have an opportunity of defending themselves." Roger Sherman of Connecticut noted that the Articles of Confederation were not yet in force and that, even if they were, Congress would not have a right to "judge" the matter directly, but only to consider an appeal from a decision by commissioners. Elbridge Gerry of Massachusetts said that, although he was "always disposed to do justice to New York," a "present decision might be extrajudicial and give discontent." [62]

The only agreement Congress reached on this day was to discuss the issue again on the next Tuesday. During the debate that morning, an express letter arrived from Governor Clinton and was read out by President Jay. Ethan Allen and five hundred militia men had marched into several towns loyal to New York, arrested many of their leading citizens, and berated the townspeople for their failure to acknowledge the state of Vermont. Allen declared that he and his men would "establish their state by the sword, and fight all who shall attempt to oppose them." This finally forced Congress to act. Although Congress did not adopt the resolutions proposed by the New Yorkers, it did form a committee to travel to Vermont to seek a solution. Jay "with great pleasure" forwarded a copy of the resolutions to Clinton and urged upon the committee members the importance of their task, since the "contending parties" in Vermont were "now on the point of hostilities." [63]

The committee was a failure. Two members arrived in Bennington in mid-June and conferred there with Thomas Chittenden, the Governor of Vermont.

Chittenden said that New Yorkers would not be harassed if they would agree to serve in the Vermont militia. For the New Yorkers, this was an utterly unacceptable condition, since by serving in the Vermont militia they would recognize the existence and validity of Vermont. These two committee members left Vermont, and two other members of the committee arrived, but finding none of the others, departed for home. By mid-July, Congress had received two competing reports, each from two committee members. Jay had also received an even angrier letter from Clinton, suggesting that perhaps Allen was coordinating his attacks on the New Yorkers with British attacks on the frontier.[64]

After considering the issue for a while, Jay wrote to Clinton with a new approach: New York and New Hampshire should, "by acts of their respective legislatures authorize Congress to settle the line between them." In essence, he was suggesting a new version of the New York and New Jersey boundary commission for which he had served as secretary as a young lawyer. He hoped the New York legislature would take the issue up as soon as they convened and that "they will not be too nice and critical in their reservations and restrictions." In his view, the key goal was to establish an agreed boundary. If necessary, New York could concede the land itself to those claiming under the New Hampshire grants, since "we have vacant lands enough to do justice to individuals who may suffer by a decision against them."[65]

When Congress took up the Vermont issue again, in late September 1779, it adopted Jay's approach. In a set of unanimous resolutions, Congress called on New York, New Hampshire and Massachusetts to adopt laws "expressly authorizing Congress to hear and determine all differences between them relative to their respective boundaries." If the states would enact such laws, Congress would start hearings on Vermont before February 1780, and would decide the issue "according to equity." The Vermont government and its militia should "abstain in the meantime from exercising any power over any of the inhabitants" who were loyal to New York or the other states. The people of Vermont should avoid "violences and breaches of the public peace" and instead "cultivate harmony and concord among themselves."[66]

In a lengthy letter to Clinton, Jay explained, justified and defended these resolutions. He conceded that it might have been possible to use the outrages committed by Allen to obtain what "some among you would call very spirited and pointed resolutions." But such resolutions would have been "very imprudent ones" since they "would not have been unanimous." In his view, which he knew Clinton did not share, it was "better for New York to gain a permanent peace" rather than, by "an impolitic adherence to strict rights ... remain exposed to perpetual dissentions and encroachment." Given the overall weakness of the United States, "peace and established boundaries" were of "inestimable" importance.[67]

Jay's approach was thoughtful and balanced, but it failed. New York enacted the requested law in October 1779, but Massachusetts and New Hampshire refused to do so, and Congress could not proceed without their participation. A few years later, writing to his friend Egbert Benson about Vermont, Jay used unusual vulgarity: the issue was "*bitched* in its last as well as first stages."[68]

The first four months of John Jay's presidency required another painful separation from his family. Not knowing how long he would be in Congress, and knowing that housing would be scarce in Philadelphia, John left his wife and son with her family in northern New Jersey. Sarah wrote to John from there at the end of December, congratulating him upon his election to "the first office on the Continent," but complaining that she had learned about this through the newspaper, rather than by letter from him. If John had consulted her about the appointment ("as some men have their wives about public measures"), she would have advised him to limit his public service, for she was not such a "Roman matron" that she could give her husband over "so entirely to the public." Sarah's tone was light, but her point was important: she *was* in some sense a Roman matron, giving her husband over to the American cause, and she expected in return that he would confer with her about his career and even about public measures. Before she sent this, however, she received a letter from John, telling her that the "greatest gratification you derive from the honor of your late appointment is its being an additional recommendation to my esteem." "Do you really imagine," she asked her husband, "that my esteem for you can be heightened by any public testimony of your merit? No no my dear, my sentiments of esteem have long since been confirmed."[69]

John started to look for a house to rent in Philadelphia, a house large enough to accommodate his wife, his brother-in-law Brockholst, serving as his personal secretary, and his sister-in-law, the lively Catharine Livingston. But in mid-January he had to write to Sarah that he had "no home yet." He also did not know, at this stage, whether New York would extend his term in Congress beyond the first of March. If his term was not extended, he questioned whether it would be worthwhile for Sarah and Catharine to come "for the sake of only a week in Philadelphia." Sarah responded that she longed to see her husband, and that her sister also wanted "to know her fate," whether she would "spend the months of March and April agreeably at Philadelphia or waste them in obscurity and dullness."[70] Six weeks later, Jay still had no house. He explained to his sister-in-law that he had "hired Mr. Gurney's in January. He promised to move the tenth February. About that time Mrs. Gurney fell sick, and still continues so." He hoped that the "approach of spring" would entice the Gurneys out "to the country," so that he and his family could have the promised house. Finally, in late March, he could write to Sarah that he expected to have the house within a week, and that he would send Brockholst to collect her and her sister. "Believe me my love, my solicitude for the pleasure of seeing you is such that not a moment shall be lost."[71]

John, Sarah, Catharine and Brockholst lived for the next six months in the Gurney house, at the intersection of Front and Union streets, near the busy Philadelphia waterfront.[72] They often entertained other delegates at their new home, making use of the three thousand dollars a month provided to the President by the Congress. On other days, John and Sarah were entertained at homes or inns. For example, in early May, the Massachusetts delegation hosted a group including President Jay, former President Laurens, Minister Gérard, Don Juan de Miralles, and Dr. John Witherspoon, President of Princeton College and delegate from New Jersey.[73]

On the Fourth of July, John and Sarah, along with "many ladies and leading citizens of Philadelphia," attended a Catholic mass organized by the French Minister. The French chaplain "chanted the *Te Deum*, accompanied by the organ and an orchestra of many instruments." The celebrations continued on the next day, when Congress adjourned at noon to hear a eulogy on "the brave men who have fallen in the contest with Great Britain." Congress then hosted a dinner at City Tavern, at which there were thirteen toasts, each accompanied by a volley from a militia company. That night there were "brilliant fireworks," including a few rockets which, "after ascending to an amazing height in the air, burst and displayed thirteen stars."[74]

Sarah played her part in her husband's efforts to entertain the diplomats. Don Juan de Miralles reportedly won a small wager with Minister Gérard over the question of her complexion. Gérard insisted that it benefited from rouge, Miralles that it was natural; Sarah happily confirmed that it was indeed her own. William Livingston wrote to Sarah asking her to give his "compliments to Don Juan" de Miralles, and to "tell him that I long to hear the Spanish cannons roaring in the English channel." Livingston also wrote to his daughter Catharine, cautioning her against too close an association with the British prisoners then in Philadelphia. There were "a number of flirts in Philadelphia, equally famed for their want of modesty as want of patriotism," who would consort with the British officers. "I hope none of my connections will imitate them, either in the dress of their heads or the still more Tory feelings of their hearts."[75]

In late September, when Congress named him Minister to Spain, John and Sarah faced difficult questions. Should John go alone to Spain, to spare Sarah the dangers of wartime travel and difficulties of life abroad? Should Sarah travel with John, to provide him company and counsel? And what should they do about their son Peter, not yet three? In the end they decided that Sarah would go to Spain but Peter would remain in the care of the Livingston family. Sarah was unusual, unique, in deciding to join her husband on his revolutionary diplomatic mission. Other similarly situated wives, including Elizabeth Deane and Abigail Adams, remained at home.[76] The reasons why wives stayed in America are not hard to understand: crossing the Atlantic was dangerous at any time during the eighteenth century, and more dangerous in wartime, when any American ship could legitimately be captured or destroyed by the British. Later in the war, two of Sarah's brothers would suffer such fates: John died when the naval ship on which he was serving sank in a sudden storm off Bermuda in early 1781; Brockholst was captured by the British at sea and imprisoned in New York City in early 1782. Women faced additional difficulties, including the lack of privacy on board the ship, and the likelihood of pregnancy and childbirth in a foreign land. Sarah herself became pregnant just before or after she boarded the ship for Spain, and would give birth to three children during their years abroad, only two of whom would live.[77]

We do not, unfortunately, have Sarah's own explanation of why she decided to join her husband. But we do have letters from her family which give some sense of her reasons. Her father wrote to her that it was "with great pain that I am obliged to part with you across a wide ocean." Indeed, "considering the mortality of man and my time of life," he thought it "probable I may never see you again." Livingston, not usually religious in his letters, said that he prayed God would keep his daughter "in His holy protection." Sarah's mother wrote that the news of their immediate departure, without so much as a farewell visit to New Jersey, had shocked and distressed her beyond words. But she was now "reconciled" to Sarah's voyage, seeing that it was her "duty and happiness to accompany your best friend." Sarah's younger brother William wrote in a lighter vein, saying that her friends would approve her decision "to gratify a laudable curiosity and to travel in the pursuit of knowledge." The Livingston family had already been tracing the intended route, from Philadelphia to Madrid via Paris. "What think you," he asked his sister, "of the Pyrenean mountains? But your fortitude I suppose has before this leveled them with the plains. But what think you of your inveterate foe the *flea*? *France* abounds with them. *Spain* too is infested with that hostile animal. But this say you shall not terrify the mind of an American: very right." As her mother said, Sarah viewed it has both a "duty" and a "happiness" to travel with her husband. And as her brother said, she did so as "an American," to aid and advise her husband in his mission.[78]

The year of Jay's Presidency of the Congress has been called the "year of division." Certainly the Congress was divided in many ways at this time, both by personal quarrels and legitimate policy differences. Given the limited role and power of the President, however, there was little that Jay could have done to resolve divisions. Congress was cursed at this time with an unusually fractious group of members. Gérard, by insisting that Congress develop peace terms and appoint peace commissioners, exacerbated the problems. Jay performed capably the basic tasks of the President: presiding over the sessions, handling the correspondence, and meeting the dignitaries. Indeed, he sometimes went beyond the customary role of the President, such as when he drafted for the Congress the eloquent address on currency issues, or when he brokered a compromise on Vermont. Perhaps his greatest contribution may have been in preventing a quarrelsome Congress from descending into fistfights. In light of the circumstances, he was a good President, indeed one of the better Presidents of the Congress.[79]

Jay's year as President was important in another way: it helped prepare him for the next few years. He was far stronger, in his negotiations in Madrid and Paris, because he knew what would be acceptable to the Congress in Philadelphia. His frustrations as President also furthered his thinking about how to strengthen the national government, and in particular how to create a true President for the United States. A decade later, Jay would help to turn these thoughts into the new federal Constitution. His friendship with George Washington, formed during the difficult year of his Presidency, would lead to his appointment as Chief Justice. So even if Jay could not make much difference as President of the Congress, his year as President altered the course of his own life.

CHAPTER 6

Minister to Spain

As JAY PACKED TO LEAVE for Spain in October 1779, he must have lamented how little he knew about his destination. He knew, of course, that Spain was one of the world's major powers, with a population of about ten million at home and an empire that included almost all of South and Central America. Americans assumed that, with this vast empire, Spain itself was wealthy, but the expense of maintaining and defending the empire probably exceeded the value of the gold and silver it sent back to Spain. Only a few Americans or Britons visited Spain, so there was not much information available about it in print in English. As a result, the country seemed remote and romantic. Billy Livingston, in his departure letter to his sister Sally, said she would be traveling "to the land of the renowned Don Quixote," the "fairy land of fancy, [where] imagination frolics in all her wantonness." She must write to her family about "the ravishing wit and beauty of the ladies and the valorous gallantry of the men." [1]

Jay knew that Spain usually joined France in its wars against Britain, but not always or immediately. In the Seven Years' War, for example, Spain had allowed France to fight on its own for more than six years, until early 1762. Only at that time, and only after Britain declared war on Spain, did Spain declare war on Britain, after which Spanish and French armies invaded Britain's ally Portugal. In the summer of 1762, after a long and costly siege, British forces captured Havana from Spain, along with its gold and a dozen ships. A few weeks later, on the far side of the world, a small British force defeated the Spanish at Manila; the local Spanish commander was not even aware, before he was attacked, that Spain and Britain were at war. Spain recovered both Havana and Manila at the peace table in 1763, in return for French and Spanish concessions elsewhere. More recently, in 1770, when Spain and England quarreled over the Falkland Islands, France declined to support Spain, forcing the Spanish to yield.[2]

Jay knew nothing, however, of the complex negotiations, starting in 1776 and continuing through early 1779, by which France persuaded Spain to join its current war against Britain. Spain was reluctant for many reasons. First, she was deeply dependent upon shipments of gold and silver from her American colonies, and these would be vulnerable to seizure during a war. As one Spanish official put it to another in early 1778, "how depressed would our nation be if a rich convoy from New Spain were intercepted at sea?" Second, many Spaniards were loath to enter a war in support of the American rebels, fearing (rightly) that the example would some day be followed in their own colonies. Third, although Spain coveted some bits of British territory, most notably Gibraltar, none of them were essential. In the end, however, the French persuaded the Spanish that the American war presented an excellent opportunity to defeat their traditional enemy. In the secret convention of Aranjuez of April 1779, Spain agreed to join France in the war, and in particular in a joint invasion of Britain itself, for which plans were far advanced. France agreed not to end its war against Britain unless and until, as part of the peace, Spain recovered Gibraltar. Spain's other war aims included regaining Florida, expelling the British from Honduras, and recovering the island of Minorca.[3]

As to the progress of the war itself in Europe, Jay had read the reports in the Philadelphia newspapers: that a grand French and Spanish fleet had sailed from Cadiz and Brest; that 25,000 men had been landed in Ireland; and that "King George had by proclamation ordered the cattle to be driven from his seacoast, fearing a descent of the French, who have at least 60,000 men between Brest and Dunkirk." But these reports, as Jay no doubt suspected, were somewhat exaggerated. A French and Spanish fleet had indeed sailed from Cadiz, and threatened the English coast during the summer of 1779, causing considerable panic in England. But not one French or Spanish soldier was landed in England or Ireland; the French and Spanish fleet was decimated by illness and accident; and eventually retreated to its own ports to rest and regroup.[4]

Jay's instructions required him to seek recognition, alliance and financial support from Spain. He had very little to offer in return. For example, he was allowed to offer Spain, in return for its financial aid, either promises to repay a war loan or recognition of Spain's right to the Floridas. He knew from his discussions with Miralles and Gérard, however, that Spain would probably insist upon free navigation of the Mississippi as a price for an alliance. He was also supposed to obtain Spanish recognition of the United States, but he must have known how difficult it would be to persuade the Spanish monarch to recognize the American revolutionaries. Indeed, he knew that the most recent American emissary to Spain, Arthur Lee, had not even been allowed to remain on Spanish soil; he had been met near the border in early 1777 and escorted out of the country. Jay observed to Washington that the objectives of his mission, "however just, will not be easily attained, and therefore its success will be precarious, and probably partial." Even these modest expectations were to prove too high.[5]

John and Sarah Jay boarded the *Confederacy* at Chester, a port on the Delaware River just south of Philadelphia, in late October 1779. The thirty-two gun frigate, with a crew of about three hundred men, was under the nominal command of Captain Seth Harding. Harding's instructions from Congress, however, required him to "consult" with his two diplomatic passengers, Conrad Gérard and John Jay, and to "be governed by their orders with respect to any occurrences which may happen and the port to which you are to proceed." In a sense, therefore, Gérard and Jay were in joint command of the ship.[6]

There were about a dozen other passengers on the *Confederacy*, including Chevalier Roche, a knight of the order of St. Louis, and Captain Remuy of Marseille. The Americans included Sarah Livingston Jay, Brockholst Livingston, Peter Jay Munro and William Carmichael. Brockholst Livingston, twenty-two at this time, had spent the past year as Jay's private secretary in Philadelphia, and would now continue in this role abroad. Brockholst was a bright young man, but perhaps too old and too headstrong to serve as private secretary to his famous brother-in-law. Peter Jay Munro, twelve years old, was the son of John's sister Eve and the Reverend Harry Munro. Reverend Munro had left his family a few years before this time to join the British forces, been captured by the Americans and imprisoned, then escaped and made his way to

Britain. Eve Munro, effectively a widow, was pleased to entrust young Peter to his uncle John. William Carmichael, roughly the same age as Jay, was born in Maryland, but had lived in London for many years, where he was known for his drinking and womanizing. During the early part of the Revolution, Carmichael had been an unpaid assistant to Silas Deane in London and Benjamin Franklin in Paris; he was also probably a paid British informer. He returned to Maryland in 1778, served for a year in the Continental Congress, which then appointed him as Jay's secretary. Even putting aside the question of his loyalty, which apparently none doubted at this time, Carmichael was not a good choice as secretary, for he viewed himself as a diplomat in his own right.[7]

It took the *Confederacy* five "very tedious days" to sail the first forty miles south along the Delaware River and Bay. Brockholst complained that he was "closely and dully employed" in learning Spanish, while Sarah was making great strides in French, under the genial guidance of Gérard. Jay promised his friend Robert Livingston that they would have a "regular and constant correspondence" and sent him a cipher to use for this purpose. As the vessel rounded Cape May, it was "launched out to sea with a brisk gale," and the passengers were all quite seasick. Sarah and her brother soon recovered, but her "dear Mr. Jay suffered exceedingly" and was "surprisingly reduced."[8]

At four o'clock one November morning, Jay and the other passengers were awakened by the crack of timbers and the cries of wounded men. The passengers rushed up to the deck, where they saw that all the masts had toppled, and several crew members were injured. With no sails aloft, the ship was rolling in the heavy sea like an immense log. The captain set the crew to work to clear away the debris and get up a small sail. The crew finished these tasks by evening, but the next morning the ship was again out of control, not responding to her rudder. The shank of the rudder had split, a "greater misfortune," the captain told Jay, than the loss of the masts. The crew attempted to steer the ship using a bolt on the rudder, but this bolt "broke nearly in the middle and pulled out." Fortunately, there were two other eye bolts on the rudder, and the crew was able to attach chains to these bolts, and lines from these chains to the sides of the ship. These lines allowed the crew to control the rudder, but the lines frequently snapped, and the crashing rudder opened holes through which water poured. A few days after the initial accident, one of the injured crew members died, and all hands and passengers attended a short, somber service, at the end of which the body was committed to the sea.[9]

The situation was dangerous but Jay remained calm. Sarah told her parents that, although they loved her husband, they were "not acquainted with half his worth." "It is the property of a diamond," she wrote, "to appear most brilliant in the dark, and surely a good man never shines to greater advantage than in the gloomy hour of adversity." Sarah was comforted and a little awed by the "firmness" and "serenity of mind" which John displayed in these days.[10]

Jay's main task, during the days while the crew was rigging the rudder and the masts, was to consider with Gérard and Harding which way the ship should sail, once it was ready to do so. Gérard was anxious and impatient to proceed east for Europe. Jay, Harding and his officers all favored heading south for the French West Indies. Gérard argued that, even if they could not make Spain, they could at least make the Azores, where Jay and Gérard could get a ship to France, leaving Harding and the crew to fend for themselves. But even one of the Frenchmen admitted that, if they steered east this late in the year, they would "run a very great risk of perishing in the ocean." Jay learned all he could about the issues through careful questioning of the officers. At Harding's request, the officers explained in writing why they did not believe the ship could safely head east for Europe. Jay gave Gérard a copy of this opinion, but Gérard now refused to express a view, saying "it was not convenient for him to give any opinion or direction on the subject." Jay informed the captain that, since the diplomats could not agree on joint instructions, he should follow his own judgment. The *Confederacy* headed south.[11]

Gérard now, in Jay's words, "ceased to observe that cordiality and frankness which had before attended his conduct to me." Moreover, Carmichael sided with Gérard in the dispute, and this understandably angered the Jays. As Sarah put it later, "the friendly part [Carmichael] had assumed while we were at Philadelphia was thrown aside soon after the *Confederacy* was dismasted, and though the mask has at times been re-assumed, the cloven foot [of the devil] was not concealed as formerly." In an effort to lighten the mood, the Jays organized a birthday party for Madame Gérard. The day started with "a small band of music" and "the discharge of a number of cannon," followed by a "very genteel breakfast." The party then amused themselves with "chess, cards, and drafts," until dinner-time, after which "a number of pertinent toasts were drunk." This was also the day on which the ship crossed the tropic of Cancer, when the sailors followed their tradition of "shaving and ducking every person who had not crossed it before."[12]

The *Confederacy* arrived safely in Martinique in mid-December. It was, in Sarah's words, "the most verdant romantic country I ever beheld." William Bingham, who had worked with John in Congress, and was now the agent of Congress in Martinique, welcomed John and Sarah into his own home. Sarah shopped in the picturesque markets, toured a sugar mill, studied the beekeepers, and watched a wild native dance. John worked on his letters to Congress and others, and on organizing the repair of the *Confederacy* and their onward voyage on a French warship. He also saw something of Martinique, including slavery as it was practiced on sugar plantations, with men collared at the neck and chained at the ankle. His disgust did not prevent him from purchasing what he termed a "very fine negro boy of fifteen years old" called Benoit to serve as his own slave.[13]

Jay was troubled to learn that the officers and men of the *Confederacy* were almost without funds. "The idea of our officers being obliged to sneak, as they phrase it, from the company of French officers, for fear of running in debt with them for a bottle of wine or a bowl of punch ... was too humiliating to be tolerable." So he drew a bill on Franklin for one hundred guineas, as an advance on his own salary, and distributed the proceeds among the officers. He was also dismayed to learn that Congress had failed to pay Bingham for any of the supplies he had obtained. Bingham had attempted to draw bills upon Franklin to cover the costs of refitting two American warships, but these bills had been returned unpaid, with no explanation from Franklin. Bingham had been forced to use a personal note to raise funds. Jay could not do much to help Bingham, other than urging Congress to pay the "debts unavoidably contracted here" to refit American ships.[14]

The Jays left Martinique in late December on the French warship *Aurora*. Their voyage across the Atlantic was swift and pleasant; Sarah had "never known Mr. Jay [to] enjoy his health more perfectly than at present." Young Peter was "quite the favorite among the officers," to whom he was teaching

English, and from whom he was learning French. Two days before reaching the bay of Cadiz in southern Spain, the *Aurora* was "chased by an English frigate." As the sailors cleared for action, the excited Sarah went on deck, and "stayed there till the chase was over," catching cold in the night air.[15]

The *Aurora*'s intended destination was Toulon, France's main naval base in the Mediterranean. Jay planned to travel north from there to Paris, to confer with Franklin, before traveling south to Madrid. When the *Aurora* stopped in the Spanish port of Cadiz, however, he learned that a British fleet under Admiral Rodney had recently defeated the Spanish navy and controlled the nearby roads. The *Aurora* had been lucky to make it to Cadiz. Rather than test his luck further, Jay decided to stay there, and travel overland to Madrid. As he put it in a letter home, "Admiral Rodney had saved us the necessity of going that round about way to Madrid."[16]

Since he did not want to meet the same fate as his predecessor Lee, Jay did not depart immediately from Cadiz for Madrid, but rather sent Carmichael ahead with a letter. In this obsequious epistle, he said the United States hoped to "enter into such treaties of alliance, amity, and commerce, as would become the lasting foundations of perpetual peace to Spain and the United States, and the source of extensive advantages to both." He wanted to come to Madrid to present his credentials and begin negotiations, but would wait in Cadiz until he received some official response, since "on this as on every other occasion, it shall be my study to execute the trust reposed in me, in the manner most pleasing to his Majesty." Jay also asked Carmichael separately to investigate and report on various subjects, including the state of Spain's finances, armies and navies and the identity of the King's key advisers.[17]

John and Sarah Jay spent two months in Cadiz, the main seaport of Spain at this time, but they did not spend much time exploring. Sarah's first few days were particularly unpleasant, since she was "constantly confined" by a "severe cold" and by pregnancy, for she was expecting their second child sometime in the summer. John spent much of his time indoors as well, working on his correspondence. Brockholst reported that "the fleas here are so numerous, that I have frequently by walking once or twice across my chamber seen above six or seven at a time on my stockings." All of them commented that the sights of Spain made them appreciate America more. Sarah wrote to her sisters:

> Do you think, girls, that distance diminishes my affection for Americans, or my concern for their interest? Oh! no; it increases my attachment even to enthusiasm. Where is the country (Switzerland excepted) where justice is so impartially administered, industry encouraged, health and smiling plenty so bounteous to all as in our much favored country? And are not these blessings each of them resulting from, or matured by freedom, worth contending for? But whither, my pen, are you hurrying me? What have I to do with politics? Am I not myself a woman, and writing to ladies? Come then, ye fashions to my assistance! Alas! Sisters, it mortifies me exceedingly that the vessel which sails tomorrow is bound for Boston, and will therefore prevent me from sending you a specimen of them. The prevailing mode, however, is here the same as it was in America last winter, with only a trifling variation.

This passage captures Sarah perfectly: the ardent American, the eager politician, and the lady of fashion, all in one.[18]

In late February, Jay finally heard from Carmichael. It had taken him more than two weeks to travel from Cadiz to Madrid, due to the heavy rains. Carmichael explained that the formal letter should have been addressed to the Conde de Floridablanca, the King's principal Minister, rather than to Don José de Galvez, and that there was some jealousy between these two Ministers. In his next letter, however, Carmichael reported that he had met both Galvez and Floridablanca, and that the latter seemed "perfectly satisfied" with his explanation as to why the letter had been addressed to the former, and promised a response within a few days.[19]

In early March, Floridablanca's elaborate and somewhat evasive answer arrived in Cadiz. The King was pleased to learn of Jay's appointment, since he was already known in Spain for his "integrity, abilities, and station." He was welcome to come "to this court to explain your goals and those of the Congress, and to hear those of His Majesty." But until it was clearer whether there would be an agreement, it was "not fitting that your Excellency be granted a public character." In other words, since Spain did not recognize the United States, it would not officially receive Jay as a Minister, merely as a private citizen. Jay commented to Congress that it looked as if Spain would not acknowledge American independence simply "because we are independent, which would be candid and liberal," but rather would only do so in return for certain concessions. He was determined that he would not yield the Mississippi merely to obtain recognition. "There was a time when it might have been proper to have given that country for their making common cause with us, but that day is now past. Spain is at war with Britain." [20]

The Jays started for Madrid in great style: they crossed the bay at Cadiz in a "very handsome barge ... ornamented by a crimson damask canopy handsomely fringed, and the benches covered with cushions of the same." Sarah was enchanted by the "regularity of the oars, the music, the serenity of the weather, the mildness of the sea, and the beautiful prospect presented from the bay." When they reached the other side, they were greeted by Count Alejandro O'Reilly, an Irishman who had served Spain most of his life, and who hosted them that night for an elaborate dinner. On the next morning, however, there was a rude awakening. According to Sarah, the "two carriages in which we were to travel were the first *outré* figures that caught my attention: they have the impudence to call them coaches, [and] it is true they are made of wood and have four wheels, but there the resemblance ceases." The coachmen and mules were, in Sarah's view, equally outrageous: "in short drivers, mules, and carriages are admirably suited to each other, and not to be equaled elsewhere." At one point along the way, according to Brockholst, the coachman "either drunk or asleep" allowed the mules to trot down a hill, and the coach overturned. Sarah "had the good fortune not to receive the least hurt." John received a "bruise in the forehead" and Brockholst "a black eye, a bruised side, and a squeezed foot." [21]

The Jays brought with them "beds, hams, tea, sugar, chocolate, and other articles of provision," for they had been advised that they would not find adequate food along the way. But on their very first evening Sarah found that another article, a broom, was "absolutely essential." Her servants purchased one in the village, then swept their rooms with vigor, clearing it of "several loads of dirt, in which were contained not [less than] two or three thousand fleas, lice, bugs etc., if we may form any judgment by what still remained." The beds the Jays had brought with them were reasonably comfortable, but they could not sleep much, for the mules were in the adjoining room, and "serenaded" the Jays all night with the "tinkling" of their bells. At one inn, Jay was charged for fourteen beds, though his party including servants numbered only eight. When he complained, the innkeeper responded "that there were many beds in the rooms in which we had slept and that we might have used them all if we pleased. We remarked that it was impossible for eight people to use fourteen beds; they replied that was not their fault." There was nothing to do except pay the bill and keep it as a "curiosity." [22]

The journey must have been particularly difficult for Sarah, six months pregnant, but she did not complain. On the contrary, she wrote home that she "never saw anything more enchanting" than their initial view of Cordova, from a height a few miles outside the city, with the "vineyards and groves of olive trees ... here and there interspersed as if with matchless art." On the next day they toured the city, including the famous cathedral, with its "nine hundred and ninety-nine pillars of polished marble, elegantly wrought and of every kind that has been discovered." But since "Mr. Jay's maxim is to prefer business to pleasure," they hurried on the next day towards Madrid, which they reached in early April. [23]

Madrid was at this time a city of about 150,000 people, more than three times larger than Philadelphia. The rich of Madrid were far richer than the richest Americans, and the poor, who were of course much more numerous, far poorer. King Charles III was remaking Madrid, creating parks, boulevards and public buildings, as part of his campaign to make Spain a modern nation. Sarah reported to her father that "the trees alone with which he has adorned the roads and walks would be to you sufficient proof of his tastes." The Jays rented a "very convenient house" on Calle San Mateo, the former home of the legation of Saxony. It had "the advantage of a fountain in the yard, a circumstance," Sarah noted, "that but few of the inhabitants can boast as they are supplied with all the water they use from the public fountains." [24]

Carmichael handed Jay several letters upon his arrival, of which the most daunting was one from Floridablanca. "Before entering into a discussion" the Spanish King would need answers to a long list of questions about the population, politics, finances, and military forces of the United States. Jay worked for the next three weeks on his response, which ran to more than sixty thousand words. He described the United States carefully if positively, stressing that the people were united and determined to obtain their independence. On financial issues, he made the best of a bad situation, arguing that the "confederated states have no fixed revenues, nor are such revenues necessary, because all the private property in the country is at the public service." [25]

Jay was somewhat troubled that he did *not* have, among the letters waiting for him, anything from Benjamin Franklin, America's representative in Paris. Within two weeks, however, he received two friendly letters from Franklin, which confirmed among other things that Franklin had put French funds on deposit to pay Jay and Carmichael their salaries for the next few months. Jay wrote back immediately, thanking both Franklin and France, to which he now felt himself "attached" to a "degree that I could not have thought myself capable of ten years ago." He also asked Franklin to send along for Sarah one of the recent French prints of himself. "There is no man of your age in Europe so much a favorite with the ladies." [26]

Jay was prepared to be patient, but he soon learned that Congress had drawn bills of exchange on him for at least £100,000. Each bill was a promise by Congress that Jay would pay the bearer a certain sum on a certain date. Congress sold these bills at a discount in the United States, and the bills passed from merchant to merchant until they were presented to Jay. Congress did not really intend that Jay should reach into his own pocket to pay the bills; it hoped and expected that Spain would provide him the necessary funds. As the bills arrived, however, Jay did not know whether Spain would provide funds. He did not want to refuse the bills, which would weaken America's credit, but he also did not want to accept them, which would commit his personal credit for amounts far greater than his personal means. [27]

Jay was in Madrid when he received this initial letter, but King Charles and all his ministers were at Aranjuez, one of the four palaces around Madrid at which the King pursued his passion for hunting. Jay left his pregnant wife behind in Madrid and hurried the twenty miles to Aranjuez. When he arrived, he wrote to Floridablanca, explaining as best he could why Congress had adopted the "extraordinary" and "indelicate" measure of drawing bills without knowing whether funds would be available to satisfy them. "The eyes of America are now drawn towards [the Spanish King] by their opinion of his virtues and the situation of their affairs, and I flatter myself it will not be long before their hearts and affections will also be engaged by such marks of his

Majesty's friendship as his wisdom and liberality may prompt and their occasions render expedient." Of course, the "mark of friendship" which he had in mind was money.[28]

While he waited anxiously for a response, Jay had some time to explore Aranjuez, especially its gardens. One evening, while most people were "enjoying a bull feast," he took a "long solitary walk" among the gardens, finding himself alone except for a few gardeners. The *"beau monde,"* he reported, generally preferred "a grand public walk" where "every evening they pass and repass each other, where the courtier bows to his patron, the belle displays her charms, the *petit maître* his pretty person, [and] the grandee his equipage." Among this crowd, one could find a princess taking "her evening ride in a splendid carriage, drawn by six fine horses, richly caparisoned, and surrounded by guards well dressed and well mounted, and holding naked sabers in their hands." These "naked sabers," and the "fixed bayonets" of the soldiers, were grim reminders that this was "not America," that a "genius of a different character from that which presides at your hills and gardens, reigns over these." [29]

In May of 1780, four months after arriving in Spain, Jay finally met the Spanish Foreign Minister, the Conde de Floridablanca. Floridablanca was fifty-one years old at the time, a "little man," but one who immediately impressed the visitor as having "more than a common share of understanding." He had been born José Monino, the son of a merchant, and had started life as a lawyer, helping the government, especially in its legal battles with the Jesuits, which ended in the expulsion of the order from Spain. Not content to have the Jesuits out of Spain, King Charles sent Monino to Rome to argue that the order should be disbanded. When he succeeded, the King made him a count and his principal Minister. In this role, Floridablanca helped devise and implement many of the King's reforms: opening trade to other Spanish ports, revising the curriculum at the universities, and improving legal administration.[30]

Floridablanca explained to Jay and Carmichael that, although "last year he should have found no difficulty" in paying the £100,000, now he could not. He detailed for the Americans the "enormous expense of supporting thirty-five ships of the line" in the failed attempt to invade Great Britain. But perhaps Spain and the United States could enter into a contract, in which the United

States would provide Spain with "light frigates," delivered to Spain "loaded with tobacco or other produce." The King might be able, by the end of the year or early in the new year, to pay as much as £40,000 for such frigates. As to a treaty, Floridablanca said that there was only one obstacle: the Mississippi. He spoke "amply of the King's anxiety, resolution, and firmness on this point," but also hoped that "some middle way might be hit on which would pave the way to get over this difficulty." He promised to provide his views in writing in a few days.[31]

Jay returned to Madrid, where was concerned to hear that Thomas Hussey, an Irish priest, and Richard Cumberland, a minor British official, were about to arrive, bearing peace overtures from the British government. Learning of Jay's concern, Floridablanca summoned him back to Aranjuez, where he assured him that Hussey and Cumberland were on purely personal business. Jay suspected that this was not true, and that Floridablanca was in fact pleased at the presence of Hussey and Cumberland, hoping it might persuade Jay to be more reasonable. There was nothing he could do, however, other than to hope that Floridablanca would show his mission some favor, in an effort to persuade the British to be more reasonable as well.[32]

After several weeks, Jay received Floridablanca's promised written response, which unfortunately offered *less* than was discussed at the initial conference. If the United States could provide "handsome frigates and other smaller vessels of war," fully loaded and delivered, Spain could possibly pay the various bills in two years, with interest if necessary. Jay's reply was polite but firm. The merchants who held the bills would never wait two years to be paid; they would instead protest the bills, which would injure the "credit, operations, and feelings of the United States." As to the frigates, he explained patiently that building them would cost money, and the United States had no money to spare. He closed by hinting that Britain would be happy to learn that Spain would not, or could not, provide the modest sum necessary to satisfy the bills.[33]

In early July, news arrived in Madrid that the British had captured Charleston, South Carolina. Jay himself was not worried, as he knew that the British could capture all America's cities and not conquer America. The Spaniards, however, assumed that the loss of a major city was a major disaster. The effect in the negotiations was, in Jay's words, "as visible the next day as that of a hard night's frost on young leaves." Floridablanca, at their next meeting, made various unkind comments about America's failure to defend Charleston and organize its finances. He said he expected that the King would soon name a successor for Don Juan de Miralles, and that this new representative would, before departing for the United States, handle the negotiations with Jay.[34]

In early July 1780, Sarah gave birth in Madrid to a baby girl. The Jays were ecstatic: John wrote to his father-in-law that they would not follow the local custom of naming the child after a saint, but rather "name it after some sinner who will probably have more affection for it." Sarah wrote that her "whole heart overflowed with joy and gratitude for the birth of a lovely daughter." But, on the first day of August, the girl had "a fit," and the next day "the convulsions increased." Then "she was the whole day in one continued fit, nor could she close her little eye-lids until Friday morning the fourth of August at 4 o'clock, when wearied with pain, the little sufferer found rest in ..." Here Sarah had to break off her letter, and ask her mother to excuse her tears, for she too had "wept on similar occasions." John was equally grieved by the death of their daughter, but more reserved. Sarah described him as "resigned in affliction" and "possessing a cheerful disposition in every circumstance."[35]

John and Sarah remained at Madrid while the court went to San Ildefonso. Jay wrote often to Floridablanca, informing him of the arrival of various bills, and seeking guidance as to whether he should accept them. Floridablanca's rare replies simply deferred any action until the appointment of the new emissary. The creditors grew more and more insistent, and Jay finally went to San Ildefonso in late August. He sought out the French Ambassador, Montmorin, with whom he had often spoken about his difficulties, and who had served as a useful go-between with Spain. Montmorin now explained that the Spanish Minister had "been of late much occupied and perplexed with business" and advised Jay to "write the minister another letter *praying* an audience."[36]

At this Jay lost his temper, or at least pretended to lose it. He said firmly that he had come to Spain "to make propositions, not supplications." America was "independent in fact" and Congress would not "purchase from Spain the acknowledgment of an undeniable fact at the price she demanded for it." Indeed, he questioned whether the United States should have any treaties with

European nations, whether it would not be better to "remain free from the influence of their disputes and politics." Montmorin sat in stunned silence, then asked if Jay was at least content with the conduct of France. Jay replied that France should do more to act as a mediator between the United States and Spain. Montmorin said that he did not see how he could mediate unless there were particular issues in dispute. Jay replied that the task was not to resolve particular disputed points: it was somehow to *start* the negotiation.[37]

Floridablanca heard from Montmorin about this exchange, and a few days later Don Diego de Gardoqui, a member of a prominent merchant family, appeared at Jay's quarters, with an official note stating that he would carry on the discussions. He suggested that America should offer the Mississippi in return for the £100,000 of financial aid under discussion. Jay scorned the suggestion. "The Americans, almost to a man, believed that God Almighty had made that river a highway for the people of the upper country to go to the sea." Perhaps because of this and similar comments, perhaps because Spain was indeed impecunious, Gardoqui informed him a few days later that Spain could not provide further funds at this time.[38]

It was now clear that he needed help from France, so Jay wrote both to Vergennes, the French Foreign Minister, and to Franklin. He apologized for seeking further help from France, which was already assisting "with her fleets, her armies, her treasure, and her blood." But he argued that default on the bills would ruin America's credit, and that this "would be a matter of triumph to our common enemy and of pain to our friends." He sounded the same theme with Franklin. "Almost anything will be better than a protest, for exclusive of disgrace, which is intolerable, the consequences of it would cost Congress more than the expense of saving their credit."[39]

Jay's fourth meeting with Floridablanca, in September at San Ildefonso, started well, with the Minister thanking him for the help the Americans had recently provided at Havana. Since there seemed little point discussing money, Jay raised the topic of an alliance, and suggested that they should use as a model the treaty of alliance between France and the United States. Floridablanca reacted with surprising anger. Spain would "never consent" to use that treaty as the basis for anything, for it had been made "without the knowledge" of Spain, and had indeed caused "a rupture" between France and

Spain. Floridablanca was equally adamant on the Mississippi. The King of Spain would "never relinquish it"; it was "the principal object to be obtained by the war." Floridablanca reminded Jay that Congress had at one point been ready to give up navigation of the river as part of a treaty, and suggested that he get Congress to revert to this position, so that there would be some basis for agreement with Spain.[40]

In early November 1780, Jay summarized the past few months in a long report to Congress. Jay stressed that Congress should not draw further bills upon him, since he was unsure whether he could pay those which continued to arrive. Congress should disregard Spain's assurances of good will. Indeed, the United States would "always be deceived if we believe that any nation in the world has or will have a disinterested regard for us." This was especially true of "absolute monarchies, where the temporary views or passions of the prince, his ministers, his women, or his favorites, not the voice of the people, direct the helm of state." The United States should "endeavor to be as independent on the charity of our friends, as on the mercy of our enemies."[41]

Jay's personal situation in Spain was as difficult as the diplomatic deadlock. His salary was not adequate for his expenses, especially the expense of following the court from place to place. In Aranjuez, for example, where other diplomats stayed in rented homes, Jay lived in one room in a posada with one servant. Since the United States was not recognized, Jay could not be recognized, and he was not invited to dinners or other official events. With a few exceptions, Spaniards disliked Americans. "Many have even serious doubts of our being civilized," Jay wrote, and in particular "they could scarcely believe that the Roman Catholic religion was even tolerated."[42]

The Jays expected, as they left America, that their separation from friends and family there would cause difficulties. They probably expected that correspondence would be difficult, and it was: many letters did not make it across the Atlantic, and almost all letters were opened and read by the Spanish authorities. They did not expect, however, and were deeply hurt by, the actions of three Americans who joined them in Madrid: William Carmichael, Brockholst Livingston, and Lewis Littlepage.

Jay never really liked his official secretary Carmichael. In part this was a question of personal style: while Jay spent his evenings at home with his books and his wife, Carmichael spent his evenings in taverns and sometimes brothels. Jay may have envied his secretary's fluency in French and Spanish; he apparently never learned Spanish and his French was only fair. He was often annoyed by the way in which Carmichael seemed to conduct his own mission, meeting with Spanish and French officials without Jay present, or writing to Congress on his own. As time went on, dislike hardened into a fixed hatred. In late 1781, Jay wrote in cipher to his friend Morris that Carmichael was "the most faithless and dangerous [man] that I have ever met with, in all my life. This is strong language, but twenty-two months' constant experience assures me it is just."[43]

The relation with Brockholst Livingston was if anything more painful than that with Carmichael, for Brockholst was family. In a long letter to her father, never delivered, Sarah described how she and her husband had hoped that her brother would benefit from time in Europe; he could "perfect himself in two useful languages, gain a knowledge of mankind, form useful connections, and at the same time [progress] in the study of the law." But "instead of an affectionate and cheerful brother we too soon discovered a discontent and disgust which astonished us."[44]

One incident in particular outraged Sarah. Brockholst and a French friend were dining with the Jays, and the conversation turned to the topic of national drinking habits. Brockholst said it "was more rational to drink wine like the French with their dinner, than to oblige their guests to get drunk after, as was the custom in England and America." The guest said that this was no longer the custom in England, and Sarah "took the liberty of rescuing my countrymen from the same disgrace." The Frenchman asked about drinking among members of Congress, and Brockholst laughed that he had "seen them all drunk at a time." Sarah insisted that, although perhaps members drank to celebrate special days, "you would not infer from that, that it was a practice they were often guilty of." Brockholst persisted: the members of Congress were just "like other men, and he doubted not but that there were among them as great rascals as in other assemblies, and that indeed he knew some." At this, Sarah wheeled on her younger brother: he was no longer in America; he should not insult his country in front of foreigners; and he should in any event not contradict her in her own house. Brockholst was not at all ashamed: he and his guest excused themselves to go to Carmichael's house, where "we can say what we please." [45]

Lewis Littlepage arrived at the Jays' home on San Mateo Street in October 1780. Although the Jays had never met the youth, he was not unexpected, since Jay had agreed, at the request of a Virginia friend, to provide a home for the boy if he came to Spain. Relations were apparently good for the first few months, but in June 1781 Littlepage decided that life in Madrid was too dull, and that he would join the Spanish force being assembled in Cadiz. Jay was strongly opposed to this, but did not really expect that Floridablanca would allow the Protestant Littlepage to join the Catholic Spanish army. When Floridablanca granted the request, Jay had to decide whether to lend Littlepage money. As he later put it in a letter to Littlepage, "without money, you could not proceed, and without proceeding, you would suffer disgrace." He loaned Littlepage $150, placing a credit of this amount with Harrison, an American at Cadiz. [46]

Littlepage had hardly left Madrid, however, when he wrote to demand more money. His expenses "so greatly exceed my expectations, that I must absolutely request you to double my credit on Mr. Harrison." This was followed by a letter reporting that he had drawn bills on Jay. When the bills arrived, Jay refused them, which led to an angry outburst from Littlepage, who claimed that he had only left America because of Jay's assurances of support. Jay responded with a lawyer's brief, explaining in great detail that, although he had offered hospitality, he had not offered to be a banker. They exchanged similar letters throughout the winter of 1781 and 1782. In a typical exaggeration, Littlepage claimed that his only refuge from his poverty would be death in front of a British cannon. He finally returned to Madrid in April, and resumed living with the Jays, with whom he was at least temporarily reconciled. [47]

As best they could, John and Sarah kept in touch with family and friends back in America. Sarah's letters contain some interesting descriptions of Spain, but John's contain almost none. Instead, letters from both husband and wife were filled with questions and comments about America. Sarah asked for news about mutual friends in Philadelphia, and praised the efforts of women there to raise money for the American troops. "I am prouder than ever of my charming country-women. Excellent women!" John asked correspondents in New York for news about Vermont; he pressed friends in Philadelphia for political news; he pleaded with his family to keep him informed of their health and safety. In some of his letters, he managed to keep a light tone. After learning that his amorous friend Gouverneur Morris had lost his leg in an accident, he wrote that he heard that "Mrs. Plater, after having much use of your legs, has occasioned your losing one of them." But in other letters, he frankly admitted his gloom. "My eyes and affections are constantly turned towards America, and I think I shall return to it with as much real and cordial satisfaction as ever an exiled Israelite felt on returning to his land of promise." [48]

Jay's second year in Spain, 1781, was as difficult and fruitless as the first. During the early part of the year, Jay could pay the bills as they were presented, for Floridablanca provided him some funds as promised in December 1780. In mid-March, in keeping with the custom of the past few months, Jay sent Floridablanca a list of the bills which would come due in April, more than $89,000. There was no response until late March, when Jay received a short letter from Gardoqui. There was an "absolute impossibility" in making any funds available for the next few months, although Spain would provide Jay the balance of the sum promised in December in six months' time. Jay had no choice but to turn again to France, both through Montmorin in Madrid and Franklin in Paris. Montmorin met several times with Floridablanca, and extracted promises to pay the bills coming due in April. This saved Jay from immediate default, but more bills were coming due in May, so he sent a letter by courier to Franklin, pleading for funds. [49]

Franklin again rescued Jay; he promised funds to pay the bills coming due over the next few months. He cautioned, however, that there were many competing needs for funds, so that Jay should "not relax in your application for funds from Spain." Franklin also provided a copy of a letter in which he explained to Congress that, because of his age and illness, he wished to resign, and suggested that Jay should succeed him in Paris. Franklin urged Jay, if this "change would be agreeable to you," to write to his friends in Congress seeking the appointment. Though tempted, Jay advised Congress that it should not even dream of replacing Franklin. "The letters I have received from him," Jay wrote, "bear no marks of age and there is an acuteness and contentious

brevity in them which do not [indicate] an understanding injured by years."
Congress left Franklin in place, but it did name Jay, Adams, Jefferson and
Laurens to work with him in the peace negotiation.[50]

In May 1781, a letter from James Lovell, a Massachusetts delegate to
Congress, arrived in Spain, enclosing a resolution authorizing Jay, if absolutely
necessary, to allow Spain free navigation of the Mississippi south of the thirty-
first parallel. The letter was unofficial, however, and Jay feared that the lack of
an official letter meant that Congress had changed its mind. Moreover, he realized, as perhaps most members of Congress did not, that Spain could not
provide much aid, and that any attempt to share the Mississippi would "render
a future war with Spain unavoidable." When he met with Floridablanca on the
day after receiving Lovell's letter, Jay sensed from the Minister's comments
that he too had read the letter. Jay waited for an official letter, but when
nothing arrived, other than a dismal report about America's financial difficulties, he delayed no longer. He wrote to Floridablanca that Congress had
now "authorized me to agree to such terms relative to [the Mississippi] as to
remove the difficulties to which it has hitherto given occasion." At their
meeting a few days later, Floridablanca said that he would not have time to
consider the issue until the court removed to San Ildefonso. He also handed Jay
some letters, including official letters, all of which had been opened.[51]

Jay followed the court to San Ildefonso and again waited, this time for
Floridablanca to set a day for a conference. In early September, Jay wrote to
remind him that, since their meeting two months ago, "the affairs of the United
States at this court have made no progress." Jay noted that he had with him an
army major, who would return soon to Philadelphia, and that he hoped "to
make him the bearer of welcome tidings." Floridablanca met with Jay and the
major, but spent most of the time asking military questions, so that the conference was for Jay "as fruitless as the last." When another week passed, Jay
drafted a long letter to Floridablanca, complaining that he was at least entitled
to the courtesy of a "candid answer." Jay showed this letter in draft to
Montmorin, who persuaded him to tone it down, but probably also relayed the
original tone to Floridablanca. At a meeting a few days later, Floridablanca
apologized to Jay that "ill health" and the "multiplicity of business" had so
long delayed their discussion. He suggested that Jay should try his hand at a

"set of propositions" on the three main topics: financial aid, commercial relations, and territorial issues.[52]

With a speed which must have shocked the Spaniard, Jay drafted and presented within three days the outline of a full treaty. Jay did not attempt to describe the financial assistance Spain would provide to the United States, which would depend upon how much Spain *could* provide. Jay proposed that each nation should have access to the other's ports and colonies on a "most favored nation" basis. The United States was ready to "relinquish" to Spain the southern part of the Mississippi River, but only in return for *immediate* assistance from Spain in the war against Britain. Jay carefully provided that, if resolution of these issues should be delayed until "a general peace," the United States would not be "bound by any proposition or offers which he may now make."[53]

This proviso was the most important part of Jay's letter, indeed perhaps the most important action of his years in Spain. He knew that Spain meant, if possible, "to delay forming any political connections with us till a general peace, thereby avoiding advances of money which they are not very able to make, [and] a precedent which may one day be turned against them by their own colonies." He thus ensured that, if necessary, the United States could later disavow his offer. And this is indeed what Jay himself did when, as Secretary for Foreign Affairs, he was again negotiating with Spain.[54]

Like most people in Europe, Jay knew almost nothing about the progress of the war in the United States in the fall of 1781: how Washington marched his men all the way from New York to Virginia in a month; how the French navy prevented the British navy from entering the Chesapeake; how the Americans and French besieged the British at Yorktown. In late November, however, he received a hopeful letter from his friend Elbridge Gerry, who reported that "the superior force of our allies at sea [and] the strength of the allied army in Virginia" gave "every reason to expect" that "Cornwallis with his army will be captured." A few days later, in early December, Jay had a letter from Washington himself, written from Yorktown, sending the news that General Cornwallis and his force of almost eight thousand men had just surrendered there. Jay rejoiced at this "glorious, joyful, and important event," but also expected that there would be further fighting before a serious peace negotiation. He hoped that the news of the American victory would make

Floridablanca more inclined to negotiate. When he met with Floridablanca a few days later, however, the Minister explained that he would have to rely on his aide, Bernardo Del Campo, to talk with Jay. Del Campo, when he met with Jay in late December, told him that "it was very uncertain when our conferences could commence." Indeed, according to Del Campo, he did not yet have instructions from Floridablanca. Jay did not argue too hard; he knew well now that the Spaniards did not intend to deal with him.[55]

Jay spent the first few months of 1782 trying and in the end failing to avoid default on the bills drawn on him by Congress. The issue was partly diplomatic; if there was a default, the world would know that Spain was so uninterested in the United States that it would not provide it with a few thousand dollars. And the issue was partly personal; as Jay noted to Montmorin, because he had no diplomatic status in Spain, "the holders of the bills might commence actions against me on them." Debtors' prison was a remote but real possibility.[56]

A prominent Spanish banker, Francisco Cabarrus, was prepared to lend the money necessary to pay the bills coming due in March, but only if France or Spain guaranteed the loan, and only if the loan was repayable in a reasonable time. Jay described these terms to Montmorin, who relayed them to Floridablanca, and reported back that Floridablanca would "make every effort" but "cannot answer for his success." But Jay "should be perfectly easy in regard to personal consequences." Jay replied that he was not worried about personal issues, except insofar "as they may affect the political interests of the two countries."[57]

In early March, he wrote directly to Floridablanca, describing again the offer of Cabarrus. A week later, he met Floridablanca, who received him "with great cordiality" and said with a smile "that when I found myself very hard pressed, I should desire Cabarrus to wait upon him." As the due date approached, Jay sent Cabarrus to meet the minister. Floridablanca was indignant; he said that Jay must have misunderstood him; Cabarrus was not to approach him "until the last extremity." On the March due date of the bills, Jay wrote again to the Minister, saying that he had secured a day's grace from the creditors, and asking what help he could expect. Montmorin met the next morning with

Floridablanca, and reported that Spain would guarantee $50,000, provided Cabarrus would accept payment over a long period. Cabarrus, however, now insisted on repayment in four months, in four monthly installments. On the next day, word came back through Montmorin that Spain "could not possibly comply with Cabarrus's terms." [58]

At this, Jay gave up, and issued a statement explaining that when he accepted the bills "he had good reason to expect to be supplied with the funds necessary to pay them," that he had "been disappointed in the expectations he was encouraged to entertain," and that, although the amount involved was less than £25,000, he had no choice but to allow the creditors to protest nonpayment. Montmorin begged him not to include the amount, but Jay replied that he would let the world know how small the sums involved were. [59]

A few weeks later Jay was saved from further embarrassments by a letter from Franklin reporting that he had paid all the notes Jay had given to Cabarrus, and would now be in a position to pay all the other bills Congress had drawn upon Jay. Franklin was almost as bitter as Jay about the way in which Spain had treated them. "Since Spain does not think our friendship worth cultivating, I wish you would inform me of the whole sum we owe to her, that we may think of some means of paying it off speedily." Jay immediately informed the bankers that he was now in a position to pay them, and thus "our credit here was re-established." [60]

While Jay was struggling to find funds in Madrid, the government in London was debating, after the defeat at Yorktown, whether to make war or peace with the United States. In February, Jay heard from Franklin that Britain was "mad" for a separate peace with the United States, so that "they may more effectually take revenge on France and Spain." Franklin was "deaf" to these overtures, for the United States had promised France it would not make a separate peace, and could not renege on this promise. Jay agreed: "I should be ashamed of the country I now glory in, if she could for a moment forget her obligations to France ... our first and as yet faithful ally." In March, news reached Madrid that the British Parliament had decided to cease offensive operations in North America. Jay rejoiced at the news, and at the change this news brought in Spain, for it "made a deeper impression here in our favor than any event" since his arrival. [61]

In April, Jay learned from the Paris newspapers that there had been a complete change of ministry in Britain. He was still unsure, however, whether Britain was ready for a serious peace negotiation, and he urged Congress to "persevere vigorously in our military operations." But, in early May, he received two letters from Franklin, urging him to come to Paris. "Here you are greatly wanted, for messengers begin to come and go, and there is much talk of a treaty proposed, but I can neither make or agree to propositions of peace without the assistance of my colleagues." Congress had named five men to the peace commission, but it appeared that the other three would not be able to come to Paris, at least not for several months. Franklin observed that "Spain has taken four years to consider whether she should treat with us or not. Give her forty. And let us in the mean time mind our own business." Jay and his family (including little Maria, born in February) left Madrid in the middle of May 1782.[62]

Jay's mission to Spain is generally viewed as a complete failure. He worked hard, and he asked for funds politely, but in the end he obtained only a few thousand dollars. It is difficult to find any real errors in how Jay handled himself in Spain. Perhaps the real error was with Congress, which should have realized that he would not be able to secure recognition or assistance. Unfortunately, except for the brief and barren visit by Lee in early 1777, Congress had no representative in Spain until Jay arrived there in early 1780, and thus no real information about Spanish policies or finances. Without hard facts, Congress had to rely on soft words from Miralles, and on its own erroneous assumptions about Spain's immense wealth. Moreover, although Spain did not provide the financial help Jay requested, it *did* help the Americans through its own war against the British. Spain fought Britain in the Caribbean, the Mediterranean, and elsewhere, and thus helped prevent Britain from throwing all its force against the Americans. Jay's mission in Madrid at least educated him in the ways of European diplomacy, an education which would prove valuable in Paris.[63]

CHAPTER 7

Peace Commissioner

HE JAYS entered France, the most populous and powerful nation in Europe, south of Bayonne, on the Bay of Biscay. Other travelers at this time often remarked on the poverty of rural France; one reported that many children were "terribly ragged, if possible worse clad than if with no clothes at all." The Jays, however, were favorably impressed. John wrote to his friend Robert Livingston that "Spanish and French Biscay contain a number of romantic pretty scenes" and that he and his wife were "perfectly disposed to enjoy the beauties of the charming season." Sarah wrote to her mother that France was "one of the favorite spots of nature" with many "enchanting prospects and fertile fields." They paused for a few days at Bayonne and then at Bordeaux; in both places John noted the bustling ports and the possibilities of trade with America.[1]

They finally reached Paris in late June of 1782. Paris was at this time the largest city of continental Europe, with at least half a million and perhaps almost a million people. It was an immense city, a maze of narrow, crooked, dirty, foul streets. But there were also grand public spaces, such as the new Place Louis XV (now the Place de la Concorde), with statues, fountains and an imposing pair of classical buildings on its northern side. The wealthy of Paris lived in impressive stone houses, largely in the Faubourg Saint-Honoré and Faubourg Saint-Germain, and the poor lived everywhere else. Locals and visitors alike commented on the gap between rich and poor. "What a contrast between these immense and magnificent residences," wrote one novelist, "which reflect the greatness, luxury and corruption of their masters, and those humble forests inhabited by misery, and sometimes despair." Another described Paris as "dominated simultaneously by the most sumptuous opulence and the most deplorable misery."[2]

Jay did not pause to see the sights, however. After leaving his family at the Hôtel de la Chine, he went "immediately" to Passy, to meet with Franklin. Jay found him in "good health," at seventy-six, with a mind "more vigorous than that of any other man of his age I have known." He had known Franklin somewhat in Philadelphia, when they served together in the Continental Congress, but Franklin in France was a different and greater man. He was known and respected and indeed loved by the French; it was not uncommon for women to approach him on the street and kiss him. Franklin's house in rural Passy swarmed with friends and visitors: diplomats, philosophers, military officers, wealthy widows and total strangers. Adams complained that, between the press of visitors at Passy and Franklin's daily dinners in Paris, it was impossible to get the man to focus on work. But this was unfair to Franklin, because his social life was a key part of his diplomacy, and because he spent much of each day at his writing desk. Since arriving in France in late 1776, Franklin had secured French recognition of and assistance for the American cause, negotiated prisoner exchanges, handled America's finances in Europe, and generally supervised the entire American effort in Europe.[3]

Franklin loved to play chess, and indeed wrote an excellent essay on chess, in which he argued that the game was not merely "an idle amusement" but a way to learn "valuable qualities of the mind, useful in the course of human life." In one famous story about Franklin, he played a long chess game in the bathroom of his friend Madame Brillon, oblivious to the lady watching from her covered bathtub. In another such story, when Franklin's opponent checked his king, Franklin declined to defend it, saying the king was a mere tyrant, and that he would "fight out the rest of the battle *en républicain*." The diplomatic position which Franklin described for Jay (also an excellent chess player) on this afternoon was as complex as any that either had ever seen on the board.[4]

British troops were not on the attack in America at this time, but the war was far from over. British troops still occupied New York City, Charleston and various forts in the north and west, including Forts Niagara, Oswego and Oswegatchie. These troops could, at any time, resume their attacks, and Britain could at any time send more troops and ships across the Atlantic. Britain was still at war against France, Spain and the Netherlands. Not long before this time, a British fleet had defeated a French force in the West Indies, and Franklin feared this would encourage the British to continue the war. Spain had recently beaten the British at Minorca, and there were now rumors that Spain was planning an attack on Gibraltar.[5]

All five of the belligerents had representatives in Paris. Britain indeed had two representatives present, acting for two competing factions in the British government. Richard Oswald, a Scottish merchant, was in Paris at the behest of the Earl of Shelburne, Secretary for Colonial Affairs; and Thomas Grenville, a young aristocrat, was in Paris on behalf of Charles James Fox, Secretary for Foreign Affairs. As Jay reported to Livingston, now serving as the first American Secretary for Foreign Affairs, the "intentions of the British ministry with respect to us are by no means clear." It was "said that Mr. Fox and his friends incline to meet us on the terms of independence, but that Lord Shelburne and his adherents entertain the idea of making a compact with us, similar to that between Britain and Ireland." Franklin had spoken several times with each of the two British representatives, and he found Oswald quite congenial, but since neither of the Britons had formal authority to negotiate with the Americans, each side was merely testing the other's positions.[6]

Spain was represented in Paris by its Ambassador, the Conde d'Aranda, and the Netherlands by its Ambassador, who reportedly went "out but little" and had "little credit at home." The Foreign Minister of France was Charles Gravier, Comte de Vergennes, and his principal secretary was Joseph-Mathias Gérard de Rayneval. Both Vergennes and Rayneval had extensive diplomatic experience; and Rayneval was the younger brother of Conrad-Alexandre Gérard, with whom Jay had dealt in Philadelphia. The United States, for the time being, was represented only by Franklin and Jay. Congress had appointed five men as its Peace Commissioners: Thomas Jefferson had declined the honor and was still in Virginia; Henry Laurens had been captured on his way to Europe, spent more than a year in the Tower of London, and was now recuperating in the south of France; and John Adams was still working on a commercial treaty with and loan from the Netherlands. So, as Jay put it to Livingston, he and Franklin would have to handle "at least the skirmishing business" on their own.[7]

Perhaps the most difficult issue facing Franklin and Jay was how to work with France. The United States had promised, when it was seeking French aid, that it would not sign a peace treaty with Britain before France signed its peace treaty with Britain. Franklin and Jay were determined to live up to this commitment. As Jay put it to Franklin, "as long as France continues faithful to us I am clear that we ought to continue hand in hand to prosecute the war ... for I would rather see America ruined than dishonored." Congress had gone far beyond this, by instructing its commissioners to "make the most candid and confidential communications" to the French ministers and "to undertake nothing in the negotiations for peace or truce without their knowledge and concurrence." When Jay had received this instruction in Spain, he was outraged and protested vigorously. "As an American," he wrote to the President of the Congress, "I feel an interest in the dignity of my country, which renders it difficult for me to reconcile myself to the idea of the sovereign independent states of America, submitting in the persons of their ministers to be absolutely governed by the advice and opinions of the servants of another sovereign, especially in a case of such national importance." [8]

Franklin had not protested the instructions from Congress, but he had quietly begun to disregard them. Knowing full well France's hope that it would regain Canada in the peace negotiations, Franklin had already suggested to Britain that it cede Canada to the United States. Franklin had informed Vergennes that he would be having separate discussions with the British, though Vergennes insisted that "for our common security" the discussions should "go hand in hand." The key question for the Americans, however, was what Vergennes meant by his proviso about the discussions going "hand in hand." For example, since France had agreed that it would not make peace until Spain made peace, would France try to delay any treaty between Britain and America until after Spain had made its attempt to recapture Gibraltar? [9]

On the day after Jay's arrival, Franklin took him out to Versailles to meet Vergennes. Jay wrote not a word about the immense if somewhat run-down palace, at the time the largest building in the western world, nor about its King and Queen, the young Louis XVI and Marie Antoinette. Instead, he reported simply to Livingston that Foreign Minister Vergennes "gave me a very friendly reception" and "entered pretty fully with us into the state of the negotiation." Over the next few days, Jay met with some of the other diplomats in Paris, including the Spanish Ambassador Aranda, the British representative Grenville, and the Marquis de Lafayette, who was acting as a self-appointed liaison between the Americans and the French.[10]

Before Jay could do any real work in the peace negotiations, he fell ill, one of the thousands of victims of an influenza epidemic. He spent most of the month of July in his hotel room. The whole family was ill: Sarah with a cold and then with the flu, and their infant daughter Maria with whooping cough. Their physician told Sarah that "he had not seen any persons so severely attacked as Mr. Jay and myself." The weather outside was cold and rainy, more like winter than summer, and the mood inside was darkened by the news that Jay's father had died in New York. Peter Jay's death was "not unexpected," but still painful.[11] During this month, there were several developments, including a change of the British government, in which Shelburne emerged as Prime Minister, and the division of responsibility for the negotiation ended. Franklin (after consulting Jay) outlined for Oswald the terms he thought were necessary in a peace treaty, including independence, adequate boundaries, and the right to fish off Newfoundland. Franklin suggested various terms he thought were "advisable," including cession of all of Canada. Two days later, however, perhaps at Jay's suggestion, Franklin wrote Oswald to say that, until Britain acknowledged American independence, "propositions and discussions seem on consideration to be untimely." Franklin added that he could not "enter into particulars without Mr. Jay, who is now ill with the influenza."[12]

In late July and early August, as he regained his health, Jay had several important meetings, the first being with Benjamin Vaughan. Although Vaughan was only thirty-one at this time, he could claim a long friendship with Franklin, dating back to his boyhood, when the two met at the Vaughan home in London. Vaughan was a friend of and unofficial emissary from Shelburne, the new British Prime Minister. The Vaughan family was known to Jay, for Vaughan's brother John had recently appeared in Madrid, asking to be made an American citizen. John Jay and Benjamin Vaughan liked one another immediately. Vaughan described Jay as "a truly amiable and sensible man" with "frankness and decision that do him considerable honor." In the coming months, Vaughan served as an important "back channel" between the Americans and the British Prime Minister.[13]

Jay's second significant meeting was with the Spanish Ambassador Aranda. Aranda was an older man, more than seventy at this time, with a distinguished military and diplomatic record. Jay had heard that Aranda was "a little obstinate," but for his part he preferred "plain dealing obstinate men to those unstable ones who like the moon change once every fortnight." Aranda started by spreading on the table a large map of North America, a copy of the famous Mitchell map, first printed in London in 1755. Their initial task, Aranda said, was "to draw a line of demarcation between the territories that would be kept by Spain and those by the thirteen United States." They should not, in Aranda's view, quibble about "a hundred leagues more or less" in such an immense territory. He asked Jay to indicate the line he had in mind. Jay started at the source of the Mississippi in the north, and ran his finger down that great river almost to its mouth, to the thirty-first parallel. He then ran his finger east along the thirty-first parallel to the St. Mary's River, the generally accepted boundary between Spanish Florida and American Georgia. When Aranda protested, Jay referred to the terms of the original British charters. They were merely lines on the map, replied Aranda; Spain could just as easily draw lines running north from its territories "to the less known and frozen country of the north." When Jay asked what line Aranda had in mind, he said he would have to consider the issue for a few days. A few days later, Aranda's map arrived at Jay's rooms, with a red line running roughly due south from what is today Toledo, Ohio, to what is today Tallahassee, Florida. Aranda was suggesting that everything to the west, including what are today the states of Illinois, Indiana, Tennessee, Kentucky and Mississippi, would belong to Spain.[14]

Jay's third important meeting was with Richard Oswald, now the official British representative in Paris. Like Aranda, Oswald was an older man, well over seventy at this time. Before Shelburne asked him to go to Paris, Oswald had no prior government or diplomatic experience; he was a simply a successful merchant. Oswald had traded all his life with America, and indeed had lived there for five years in the 1730s and 1740s. In the 1760s, Oswald had tried and failed to make a fortune by buying land in Florida. In the 1770s, he had urged that Britain deal harshly with the "despicable rabble of rioters" and the

Map of the Central United States after the Revolution.

"confederacy of smugglers" in the American colonies. Now, however, in his discussions with Franklin and Jay, Oswald emphasized his desire for reconciliation.[15]

Oswald showed Jay a draft of his commission and a letter explaining why it was as yet only in draft form. Immediately noting that the draft commission did not describe the United States as independent, but rather referred to them as mere "colonies or plantations," Jay objected strenuously. In his view American independence "ought to be no part of a treaty" but "ought to have been expressly granted by Act of Parliament, and an order [given] for all troops to be withdrawn, previous to any proposal for treaty." Since Parliament was on its summer recess, the King "ought to do it now by proclamation." He went on at some length about how Britain's failure, at an early stage, to recognize American independence had caused most Americans "the loss of blood of some relation or other, devastation of their estates, and other misfortunes."[16]

During the course of this speech, Jay stressed that the key point was "to make such a peace as should be lasting." When Oswald asked him what he meant by this, he explained that he had in mind not a mere "parchment security," but rather a fair peace treaty, such that "it should not be in the *interest* of either party to violate it." He argued that France was entitled, as part of the peace, to more than just the independence of the United States; France had made conquests and Britain "could not expect to get back all we had lost." Jay, of all people, even argued that the United States owed "great obligations" to Spain for "advance of money."[17]

Oswald, who was used to the affable Franklin, was horrified by his first meeting with the adamant Jay. He now feared that the Americans would not be satisfied merely by a fair treaty between themselves and Britain, but would make demands on how Britain dealt with France and Spain. Oswald was concerned that Jay, "being a much younger man and bred to the law," would now lead the negotiation. Jay's "determined style of language" and strong "disapprobation of our conduct at home and abroad" suggested that "we have little to expect from him in the way of indulgence." Indeed, in Oswald's view, Jay was "as much alienated from any particular regard for England, as if he had never heard of it in his life."[18]

Franklin and Jay rode out to Versailles, a few days after this meeting with

Oswald, to discuss both the British and Spanish issues. Vergennes urged the Americans to start to negotiate with Oswald as soon as the original British commission arrived. Jay politely disagreed, saying that "it would be descending from the ground of independence to treat [negotiate] under the description of colonies." Vergennes responded that "names signified little," so little that France was prepared to negotiate with King George even though he styled himself King of Britain *and* France. Besides, Vergennes added, if the Americans exchanged formal commissions with the British, the British would accept an American commission styling the United States as an independent nation, and thereby implicitly recognize American independence. Franklin said that he thought the current commission "would do," but Jay insisted that he "did not like it" and that "it was best to proceed cautiously." As they turned to the question of the western border, Jay unrolled Aranda's map. Franklin and Jay both argued against Aranda's line, calling it "extravagant." Vergennes "was very cautious and reserved," but his secretary Rayneval said "he thought we claimed more than we had a right to." Having argued this same ground with Gérard in Philadelphia, Jay was not surprised to find his brother Rayneval now supporting the view that the West belonged to anyone *but* the Americans.[19]

On the way back to Passy, and then at Franklin's house there, Jay and Franklin discussed and debated the issues. Jay argued that France "did not want to see our independence acknowledged by Britain until they had made their uses of us," and in particular that France hoped to control the Americans until Spain had achieved its territorial goals. Jay "could not otherwise account" for the comments by Vergennes about Oswald's commission, which in Jay's view Vergennes "had too much understanding not to see the fallacy of." Franklin defended Vergennes and reminded Jay of their instructions, which required them to consult with and obey the French officials. At this Jay lost his temper, arguing that the instructions were the result of undue French influence in Philadelphia. If there was any conflict between the interests of America and the instructions, he would break the instructions "like this." And with that he threw his long clay pipe into the fireplace, where it shattered into a hundred pieces.[20]

The disagreement between Jay and Franklin is interesting, but not as important as their *agreement* on how to proceed. They agreed to drop Jay's more dramatic demands, such as a prior royal declaration of American independence, but they also agreed to insist on Jay's minimum condition: a new commission for Oswald, one that recognized that the United States was an independent nation. When Oswald tried the next day to persuade Franklin that Jay was being too rigid on the commission question, Franklin would not second guess his colleague. "Mr. Jay was a lawyer, and might think of things that did not occur to those who were not lawyers." Jay and Franklin soon learned that Adams agreed with their approach. "We ought not to treat at all," he wrote from the Netherlands, "until we see a minister authorized to treat with the *United States of America*, or their ministers." Only through "firmness, firmness, and patience for a few months," Adams wrote, could they achieve their goal of "sovereignty universally acknowledged by all the world." [21]

A few days after this, Oswald visited Jay, whom he found "in the best humor, and disposed to enter into a friendly discussion." To be sure, Jay was firm on "the great impropriety, and consequently the utter impossibility, of our ever treating with Great Britain on any other than an equal footing." But Jay abandoned his demands for a royal declaration and British withdrawal, and suggested that Oswald's commission itself could be revised to recognize American independence. Oswald "liked the idea" and asked Jay to draft the language, which he immediately did. On the next day, Oswald stopped by again to say that perhaps his instructions authorized him to make the declaration himself, without a new commission, though he would have to confer with London. Jay replied that, once Britain "cut this knot of independence," the other issues in the negotiation would fall into place quickly. Britain could then be "sure of recovering and preserving a solid and beneficial friendship with the Americans." Jay may have been too eager at this time, for he gave Oswald the impression that he would accept some kind of "recognition" of independence less than a new commission. [22]

Jay made similar comments at this time to Benjamin Vaughan, asking why Britain did not simply "cut the cord that ties us to France." He argued that, "while on the one hand little was to be got by bargaining with America, that much would be done by conceding this one point to her, and that the best way of England's making a good bargain with France was by making a good agreement with America." He cautioned, however, that if Britain promised independence, and then reneged on the promise, "there was an end to all confidence; and he would rather the war should go on to his grandson than that independence be given up." As Jay hoped and expected, Vaughan reported all these comments back to Shelburne, urging the requested recognition.[23]

In parallel with these discussions with Oswald and Vaughan, Jay continued his discussions with Rayneval and Aranda about the West. At a meeting in late August, Aranda pressed Jay to indicate some line, other than the Mississippi, that he would accept as the western boundary of the United States. Jay refused to do so, "saying that I had no authority to cede any lands" east of the Mississippi to Spain. Aranda expressed surprise, saying that Jay, as a former President of Congress, and as Minister Plenipotentiary to Spain, *surely* had authority to decide on a mere boundary. Jay responded that he doubted that any minister had authority to cede the territory of his sovereign. During the course of their debate, Aranda reminded Jay of the assistance that Spain had given the United States during the war. Jay replied "very coldly" that Spain had provided some financial assistance, but he did not see how Spain's activities in the Mississippi and Florida had helped the United States at all. Indeed, Jay "wished [Spain] had not taken Pensacola, because then the British troops were removed to New York, and their strength provided a considerable reinforcement for the English."[24]

In early September, Jay met with Rayneval, who lectured him at length about the history of the British and French claims to the western lands, arguing that the Americans could only "inherit" what the British had, and that the British themselves never had "good title" to the territory in question. As a "compromise," Rayneval proposed a complex line along various southern rivers, ending at the intersection of the Cumberland and Ohio Rivers. The "savages to the westward of this line should be free under the protection of Spain," and those to the east "under the protection of the United States." Rayneval was not very clear about the immense region *north* of his proposed line, at one point suggesting that it would be open to American settlement, at another stating that its "fate must be regulated by the court of London." Jay reiterated his basic position: the Mississippi was the only rightful western border.[25]

At this same time, Jay met "frequently" with Oswald to discuss the independence issue. Oswald showed Jay a few lines from his new instructions, which confirmed that Britain would grant "to America full, complete and unconditional independence in the most explicit manner, as an article of treaty." By this time, however, Jay was determined that he would only negotiate with Oswald once his commission recognized the United States as an independent nation. It was a question of national honor: it would be beneath the dignity of the United States to negotiate with someone who was only authorized to negotiate with colonies. Oswald "used every argument in [his] power" to get Jay over this point, but without success. At Oswald's request, Jay drafted a letter to Oswald, explaining that if Britain did not recognize American independence until it signed the treaty, it would imply "that we are not to be considered in that light until after the conclusion of the treaty," which "can not be reconciled" with America's "national honor." Jay showed this letter in draft form to Franklin, who was suffering at this time with severe kidney stones. Franklin questioned whether they should give it to Oswald, asking Jay what would happen if the British remained firm and the Americans were forced to negotiate on the British terms. Jay decided, however, to give the draft to Oswald anyway, along with a draft of Oswald's revised commission. Oswald, keen to avoid any misunderstanding, asked Jay whether he and Franklin would negotiate with him once he had a new commission in this form. Jay said they would, and "would not be long about it, and perhaps would not be over hard upon us [the British] in the conditions."[26]

In early September, Jay learned from Matthew Ridley, an American friend in Paris, that Rayneval had left two days earlier on a secret mission to London. Jay also learned that, on the day of his departure, Rayneval had spent two or three hours closeted with Aranda and Vergennes. Vergennes had recently told a British representative that there was no need for a new commission for Oswald, that "independence might be part of the treaty." Jay suspected the worst. Not only was he afraid that Rayneval would persuade the British not to issue the new commission he had so carefully worked out with Oswald; he feared that Rayneval would also work out with Shelburne a division of the western lands among Britain, France and Spain, and of the North Atlantic fishery between Britain and France.[27]

Jay's suspicions on the fishery issue were heightened by an intercepted French dispatch, sent to him at this time by one of the British representatives. This letter, written by the French secretary Marbois at Philadelphia in March 1782, argued that France should act soon to prevent the Americans from insisting on a right to the fishery as part of the peace treaty. According to Marbois, there were still "sensible people" in America with whom "one can speak of abandoning the fisheries and the western lands for the love of peace," but their numbers would decrease, and that of the "enthusiasts" who insisted on both fish and land would increase, "after the expulsion of the British from this continent."[28]

Jay raised his concerns with Franklin, but Franklin was not much troubled, and indeed expressed a "great degree of confidence" in the French. He also talked with Oswald, knowing that word would make its way back to Shelburne. But he was still worried, so he persuaded Vaughan to return to Britain to speak directly with Shelburne. During the two days before his departure, Vaughan and Jay discussed all the issues in the negotiation. Jay stressed that, "since every idea of conquest had become absurd, nothing remained for Britain to do, but to make friends of those whom they could not subdue." The first way to befriend the Americans was "treating with us on an equal footing." It would "not be wise" for Britain "to think of dividing the fishery with France and exclude us," for this would "perpetuate" American "resentments" and would induce America "to use every possible means of retaliation." It would also not be wise for Britain to conspire with France and Spain regarding the West for, whatever the treaty said, Americans would settle the West. If Britain in some way remained there, it would "sow the seeds of future war in the very treaty of peace."[29]

While waiting for word to arrive from England, either from Vaughan or Rayneval, Jay worked on a long letter to Vergennes, almost ten thousand words, explaining why Oswald's current commission was inadequate. More than half the letter was a rather long-winded diplomatic history of the formation of the Netherlands. According to Jay, this history proved that "the Dutch, ever after their declaration of independence in July 1581, uniformly treated with the neighboring nations on an *equal footing*, and also that they constantly and firmly refused to negotiate ... with Spain until she consented to treat with them in *like manner*." Jay delivered this letter in draft form to Franklin, who was still considering it when it was rendered moot.[30]

In late September, Jay went out to Versailles to meet with Vergennes, and found both Aranda and Lafayette in the waiting room. When Aranda asked Jay "when we should proceed to do business," he answered that he was ready as soon they exchanged commissions. Aranda said that "could not be expected in our case, for Spain had not yet acknowledged [American] independence." Lafayette and Aranda were arguing this point when Vergennes came into the room. Vergennes again urged Jay to disregard the question of commission, saying that Spanish recognition of American independence could be the first article of the treaty. Jay flatly refused: "he was the minister of an independent power and would treat as no other." Later, when they were alone, Vergennes offered Jay a general explanation of Rayneval's mission to England: he had gone "to judge whether a pacific disposition really prevailed in the British court" and had learned that Shelburne "was sincerely desirous of peace." Vergennes commented that, once Oswald received the promised new commission, the Americans could "go on to prepare [the] preliminaries." Vergennes then returned to the question of the western boundary, urging Jay to talk with Aranda, but Jay doubted that discussions would be productive, for "we should be content with no boundary short of the Mississippi."[31]

On the next day, Vaughan hurried back to Paris, along with the courier bearing Oswald's new commission, which formally authorized him to negotiate peace with commissioners appointed by the "thirteen United States of America." According to Vaughan, Shelburne had asked him whether the new commission was really necessary. When Vaughan answered "yes" it was "instantly granted." Jay was "very happy" that Oswald was now properly authorized to negotiate on an equal footing, and he urged Adams to come to Paris "soon, very soon."[32]

Adams would not arrive for a while, however, and Franklin's health was weak, so Jay carried on alone in the negotiation with the British. Oswald hoped, on the basis of earlier conversations with Franklin, that the United States would be satisfied with the right to fish in the North Atlantic, and not request the right to dry fish in Newfoundland and Nova Scotia. Jay, however, insisted that the Americans should have the right to dry their fish, "there being room enough for both of us, as well as the French." Oswald hoped that the United States might compensate the Loyalists, either by granting them some western land, or by giving them the profit from the sale of western land. Jay firmly declined, saying that all this land belonged to the United States. Oswald similarly hoped that the United States would compensate British merchants for their losses in the war. Again, Jay refused, claiming that this was a question of state law, although he "seemed not to approve of" a Maryland confiscation law.[33]

Although they disagreed on some issues, Jay and Oswald agreed on others. Oswald, who had a long personal interest in Florida, asked Jay whether the United States would object to Britain as a neighbor in West Florida. Jay "greatly approved of the proposal," and was "indeed anxious that Britain should regain control of that colony," since he thought Britain would make a more congenial neighbor than Spain. He suggested that Britain should "embark some of the troops from New York and Charleston and retake it." This was remarkable: he was urging Britain, with which America was still technically at war, to attack Spain, with which it was aligned if not allied.[34]

Like most lawyers, Jay preferred to prepare the first draft himself, and he now prepared the first draft of America's first peace treaty. Jay showed the draft to Franklin, who approved with one small reservation, regarding the northeast boundary. Franklin suggested that they show the draft to the French, but Jay "objected to communicating anything relative to [the draft] to the Comte de Vergennes. He merited no such confidence." Franklin reluctantly agreed.[35]

Jay handed the draft to Oswald in early October 1782. Although there were many later changes, much of Jay's first draft survived into the final document. In the preamble, Jay provided that the preliminary articles were "to be inserted in and to constitute" the treaty of peace between Britain and the United States, if and when Britain and France signed their own separate peace treaty. This language was critical, for it allowed the Americans both to negotiate with Britain and to honor their treaty with France. By using the word "constitute," Jay ensured that the preliminary articles would *become* the final treaty once Britain and France signed their final treaty. The preamble also explained Jay's view of the proper basis of peace:

> Whereas reciprocal advantages and mutual convenience are found by experience to form the only permanent foundation of peace and friendship between states, it is

agreed to frame the articles of the proposed treaty on such principles of liberal
equality and reciprocity, as that partial advantages (those seeds of discord) being
excluded, such a beneficial and satisfactory intercourse between the two countries
may be established, as to promise and secure to both, the blessings of perpetual peace
and harmony.

Jay's words were not only an explanation of this particular treaty, but a preview
of the long and vital friendship between Britain and the United States.[36]

In the first article, Jay proposed that the King acknowledge that the several
American states were "free, sovereign and independent." To prevent any future
disputes, the draft went on to define the boundaries of the United States. For the
northeast boundary, which would prove a difficult issue, Jay proposed a line
following the St. John's River to its source, then along the mountain ridges to
the source of the Connecticut River. For the northern boundary, Jay suggested
a line along the forty-fifth parallel west from the Connecticut River to the
St. Lawrence River, then west to Lake Nipissing, and then west to the source of
the Mississippi River. This line, if it had been accepted, would have resulted in
all of what is today southern Ontario, including Toronto, becoming part of the
United States. The western boundary, of course, was the Mississippi River,
from its source down to the thirty-first parallel. The southern boundary suggested
was generally along the thirty-first parallel, although Oswald strongly urged
that this line be reconsidered if Britain indeed recaptured West Florida.[37]

The second article of the draft promised a "firm and perpetual peace"
between Britain and the United States, and for this purpose required Britain
"forthwith" to withdraw all its armies from the United States. The third article
provided that fishermen from both nations should "continue to enjoy un-
molested the right to take fish of every kind on the banks of Newfoundland"
and the right to "dry and cure" their fish "at the accustomed places," whether
in Canada or the United States. The fourth article provided that the navigation
of the Mississippi "shall forever remain free and open" to both the United
States and Britain, a bold claim at a time when Spain owned New Orleans. Jay
also suggested that Britain should treat American ships and merchants like their
own "in any part of the world," and that America should provide reciprocal
rights to British ships and merchants. This would have opened for American
ships and merchants the whole of the British Empire, excepting only the

Hudson Bay and East India monopolies. It would equally have opened for British ships and merchants the whole of the United States, including the inland rivers of the Mississippi and its tributaries. It was an aggressive vision of the free trade future.[38]

Jay not only persuaded Oswald to send the draft back to London, but to support it strongly. Oswald asked that, if the enclosed draft was "found to be right in the main," he receive authority to sign it, with minor variations. Vaughan also argued for Jay's draft treaty in a lengthy letter to Shelburne. Since Americans would settle the western lands, regardless of what the treaty said, they were "not worth the cavil" for Britain. Similarly, Vaughan argued there was no point trying to exclude American fishermen from the fisheries: "we might as well think of making game laws for them." Vaughan was especially enthusiastic about Jay's trade proposal, predicting that Britain had much to gain by trading with a rapidly growing America. "Our own realms at home are bounded by nature, but not so America, who in forty years will probably have as many people as ourselves, and in eighty years more may have eighty millions." Vaughan's predictions proved remarkably correct, for the population of the United States did exceed that of Britain by about 1830.[39]

There was now a brief break in the discussions, while Oswald waited for London's reaction to the draft. Jay wrote to Morris with customary caution that "we may, and we may not, have peace this winter." He also urged the Congress to maintain strong armies until "every idea of hostility and surprise shall have completely vanished." Jay's caution was justified when, in late October, he learned from Oswald that the British government would *not* accept the draft. The government would be sending over another representative, Henry Strachey, to explain their objections. Jay pressed Oswald for details, but he declined to provide any, although he did say he feared that the French "had found means to put a spoke in our wheel." Oswald asked Jay whether they could somehow keep Strachey's arrival secret. Jay "told him it was not possible, and that it would be best to declare the truth about it, that he was coming with books and papers relative to our boundaries."[40]

At dinner that day, Rayneval pressed the two Americans for details of their discussions with the British. They responded that they "could not agree about all our boundaries," and mentioned as an example "the one between us and

Nova Scotia." When Rayneval asked what line they had in mind, they answered that "Canada should be reduced to its ancient bounds," that is its boundaries before 1763. Rayneval "contested our right to these back lands." He asked "what we expected as to the fisheries," and the Americans said "the same right we had formerly enjoyed." Here again, Rayneval thought the Americans were asking too much, suggesting they should "be content with the coastal fishery." This meeting confirmed for Jay, if he needed any confirmation, that the Americans should *not* confer in detail with the French, for the latter would take positions more extreme than the British.[41]

The third member of the American peace commission, John Adams, finally arrived in Paris in late October. Adams was nearly fifty years old at the time, short, stout, balding and blunt. Like Jay, he had spent the past few years in Europe on diplomatic assignments, in France and in the Netherlands, from which he had at last secured a commercial treaty and loan. But Adams was not a natural diplomat; as one friend put it "he cannot dance, drink, game, flatter, promise, dress, swear with the gentlemen ... or flirt with the ladies." (The friend added that the average diplomat was far less intelligent and honest than Adams.) While in Paris in 1778 and early 1780, Adams had chafed at the fame and the style of Franklin, whom he privately termed the "Old Conjuror." Indeed, when he returned to Paris in 1782, Adams refused at first to go out to Passy to call upon Franklin. "There was no necessity," he told Jay's friend Ridley, and "after the usage he had received from [Franklin] he could not bear to go near him." [42]

Adams approached Jay with caution too. They had served together in the Continental Congress, but they had (in the words of Adams) been members of "different sects" and had disagreed "with ardor." More recently, they had written one another from time to time, but their letters were generally cool and formal. Adams feared that he would now find himself "between two as subtle spirits, as any in this world, the one malicious, the other I think honest." So Adams approached Jay indirectly, speaking first with Ridley, who told him about Jay's firmness in dealing with the French and the Spanish, and hinted at differences between Jay and Franklin.[43]

On the Monday morning after his Saturday evening arrival, Adams called on Jay at his hotel. The two men spoke for more than three hours, and were surprised to find they agreed completely in their suspicions of France and their views as to the treaty with Britain. They went to a dinner to which they were both invited, then returned to Jay's room and spent the evening "in very interesting communications to each other." Adams later wrote that "nothing that has happened since the beginning of the controversy in 1761 has ever struck me more forcibly or affected me more intimately, than that entire coincidence of principles and opinions" which he and Jay now discovered.[44]

On the next day, Oswald brought the new British representative Strachey to Jay's rooms to introduce him. Henry Strachey was in "vigorous middle age," with many years of parliamentary and official experience. Strachey did not have Oswald's wide knowledge of America, but he had at least been there, and indeed he had met Franklin and Adams, when he served as the secretary of the unsuccessful peace talks in September 1776. Strachey was nominally in Paris merely to assist Oswald with "maps and boundaries," but it quickly became apparent that he was now the lead negotiator for the British side.[45]

Jay received Strachey politely, and soon Adams arrived. According to Jay's journal, the four men had some "loose conversation about the refugees, English debts, drying fish." There were at least two important comments, however. On the debts, Adams volunteered that he "had no notion of cheating anybody." Oswald and Strachey were pleased to hear this; indeed Strachey smiled with "every line of his face." At another point in the conversation, the British suggested that perhaps America's western boundary should be limited "by a longitudinal line east of the Mississippi." Jay fired back that, if the British insisted upon such a line, "it was needless to talk of peace, for we never would yield that point."[46]

On the next day, the three Americans gathered to discuss issues among themselves before meeting the British. Adams, the prior evening, had lectured Franklin about why the Americans should negotiate on their own, without referring every issue to France. Franklin now "turned to Mr. Jay and said, I am of your opinion and will go on with these gentlemen [the British] in the business without consulting this court [the French.]" From this point forward, the three Americans worked together closely and harmoniously.[47]

Soon thereafter, Franklin, Adams, Jay, Oswald and Strachey sat down in a conference room at Oswald's hotel, surrounded by "books, maps and papers relative to the boundaries." The five men negotiated "night and day" for the next week. They also dined together often; on one afternoon Jay hosted dinner for the five negotiators as well as Benjamin Vaughan and Matthew Ridley. Adams later recalled that they "lived together in perfect good humor" and that if they had merely been travelers thrown together at an inn "nothing could have been more agreeable." Adams also remembered, however, that the "sense of the immense responsibility that rested on every man on both sides made his heart tremble in his breast." The Americans preferred the genial Oswald to the argumentative Strachey. Adams described Strachey as "artful and insinuating," a man who "pushes and presses every point as far as it can possibly go." Strachey returned the favor, describing Jay and Adams as "the greatest quibblers I ever knew." [48]

On the question of the northern and western boundaries, the British now argued that the United States should be limited by the proclamation of 1763 (essentially along the Appalachian Mountains) or by the Quebec Act of 1774 (essentially along the Ohio River). Jay and the others rejected these sugges- tions, just as Jay had rejected them when advanced by Spain and France. The Americans offered two alternatives. One line would run along the forty-fifth parallel from the St. Lawrence all the way west to the Mississippi. If accepted, this would have made the settled regions of southern Ontario part of the United States, but given the unsettled forests of Minnesota to Canada. The second proposed line would run through the middle of the Great Lakes to the Lake of the Woods, then due west to the Mississippi. This line, which ultimately was agreed as part of the final treaty, let Canada retain southern Ontario, but gave the United States a more northerly northwest corner, at the Lake of the Woods. It was this northwest corner which later formed the basis of the forty-ninth parallel as the main border between the United States and Canada, and thus of the inclusion of what are now the northern tier of states. [49]

On the question of the southern boundary, the negotiators agreed at this point on a "separate article" reflecting the discussions between Jay and Oswald regarding West Florida. This provision, as drafted by Jay, stated that if Britain "shall recover, or be put in possession of, West Florida," the northern boundary of that province would run from the junction of the Yazoo and Mississippi Rivers "due east" to the Appalachiola River. In essence, the provision would have granted to Britain what are today southern Alabama and Mississippi, regardless of whether it obtained West Florida by conquest or negotiation. If Britain did not "recover" West Florida, however, the boundary would run along the thirty-first parallel, limiting Spain to a narrow strip of land along the Gulf.[50]

The most difficult boundary was the northeast boundary, between Maine and Nova Scotia. Adams came armed with decrees of British Governors and other documents which he argued showed that Maine extended all the way to the St. John's River. Strachey, equally armed, argued that the proper boundary of Maine was at the Penobscot River. In the end, the commissioners agreed that the boundary would run along the St. Croix River from the ocean to its source, and then north from this source. Unfortunately, it later emerged that there were two rivers which could claim to be the St. Croix.[51]

The British argued that "honest debts must be honestly paid in honest money." Adams persuaded his colleagues that it was only fair to repay British merchants who had sold goods to the Americans prior to the war, and to compensate British citizens whose lands in America had been seized. Adams argued that such a provision would "silence the clamors of the British creditors against the peace, and prevent them from making common cause with the refugees." Jay was assigned the difficult task of drafting the provision, which had to compensate British citizens but deny anything to American Loyalists. Jay's draft committed Congress to recommend to the states that they "correct, if necessary" their laws "respecting the confiscation of lands in America belonging to real British subjects." Loyalists, for Jay at least, were not "real British subjects." Jay's draft also provided that British creditors should "meet with no lawful impediment to recovering the full value or sterling amount of such bona fide debts as were contracted before 1775."[52]

Perhaps the most emotional issue was the question of the Loyalists. The British argued that it was only fair for the Americans to compensate those who had been forced to flee to Britain, either with land in the West or with a share of the funds raised through western land sales. The Americans refused to consider land grants. Franklin reported that the British wanted to "bring their boundary down to the Ohio, and to settle their Loyalists in the Illinois country." But the Americans would not have "such neighbors." The

Americans also argued that, if the Loyalists were entitled to compensation, the Americans were equally entitled to compensation for the losses inflicted by the British troops. Strachey reported, with dismay, that the Americans would compensate the Loyalists if "Great Britain would compensate for all the towns, houses, barns etc. destroyed during the war!" The only concession the Americans would make was a six-month period for the Loyalists to leave the United States, and a recommendation to the states to grant "such amnesty and clemency to the said refugees as their respective circumstances and the dictates of justice and humanity may render just and reasonable." [53]

The fisheries were debated at length. As redrafted by Adams, the article provided that both Americans and Britons would have the right to fish off Newfoundland, in the St. Lawrence Gulf, and "all other places, where the inhabitants of both countries used, at any time heretofore, to fish." Both sides would also have the right to dry their fish on the shores of Nova Scotia; Franklin argued that the Americans would only use this right from time to time, "to prevent the fish spoiling before they went home." The Americans yielded on the question of drying fish on Newfoundland itself, and Strachey and Oswald were content with the compromise. [54]

The British suggested, and the Americans agreed, that the discussion of trading relations be postponed until the negotiation of a separate commercial treaty. The British explained that they could not sign anything like the free trade proposal, earlier agreed between Jay and Oswald, without new legislation, and Parliament would be in recess for several more weeks. Two important vestiges of the proposal remained, however: Jay's preamble, with its reference to reciprocity; and the right of the British to navigate and trade along the Mississippi River. [55]

As the discussions progressed, Jay corrected and extended his earlier draft treaty. On November 4, he worked with Adams and Oswald until eleven in the night, drafting and redrafting various provisions. By the end of this long day, the second draft treaty was complete, and Strachey left for England on the next afternoon with a copy in hand. Over the next few days, Jay reviewed the British copy against the American copy, noticed a few minor differences, and raised these with Oswald. Oswald was somewhat surprised; he "did not expect to find Mr. Jay so uncommonly stiff and particular about these matters."

Oswald now advised Strachey that, if possible, "there should not be the least alteration, not a single word, different from the drafts."[56]

The middle two weeks of November were a quiet period, while Oswald waited for official reaction to Jay's second draft. Jay and Adams had some further discussions about their fears of France and Spain. "Our allies don't play fair," Jay told Adams. "They were endeavoring to deprive us of the fishery, the western lands, and the navigation of the Mississippi. They would even bargain with England to deprive us of them." Jay devoted much of this time to a letter to Livingston, nearly ten thousand words long, describing the negotiations day by day, and emphasizing the improper interference of France. Jay stressed that he did not intend to "deviate in the least from our treaty with France." But "if we lean on her love of liberty, her affection for America, or her disinterested magnanimity, we shall lean on a broken reed, that will sooner or later pierce our hands."[57]

While waiting for word from London, Oswald tried, without success, to persuade the Americans to reconsider the Loyalists. Jay responded that "America would carry on the war with England for fifty years rather than subscribe to such evidence of their own iniquity as by making a provision for such cut-throats." Even if the commissioners agreed to compensate the Loyalists, Congress would reject it. "Some of their states," Jay said, "would not in point of conscience think themselves justified in pardoning and providing for those who had burned their towns, and murdered their women and children, and so a treaty signed here would be of no service."[58] Oswald, who feared that the two sides would dig into their positions on this point, suggested that Jay should "go over privately to London" and discuss the issue with Shelburne himself. Jay declined, both because he wanted to avoid "jealousies" among the American commissioners, and because he knew the French would object strongly to any such mission. He discussed the issue with Vaughan, however, who decided to go to England again, giving as the excuse "the critical state of his family, his wife being probably abed."[59]

The negotiations resumed in late November. Once again, Franklin, Adams, Jay, Oswald and Strachey gathered at Oswald's room, surrounded by books and maps. Strachey opened the session with a brief speech. The senior members of the British government, he reported, were "unanimous in their desire of concluding the peace." But they were equally "unanimous" that the Americans were "unreasonable in refusing a general amnesty and restoration of property to the refugees." This was the "grand point upon which a final settlement depends." The other key points were the fisheries, where the British feared future quarrels, and the boundaries, where the British still hoped that the Americans would "admit of the extension of Nova Scotia to the Penobscot."[60]

Strachey also explained that Jay's second draft was "somewhat deficient in point of form and precision." The British had therefore "drawn out the articles as they wish them to stand, and in form similar to all other treaties," and Oswald now passed the British draft across the table. Although Strachey had just requested that Nova Scotia extend to the Penobscot River, the Americans noted that the draft itself referred to the St. Croix River, a gain of many thousands of acres. The fisheries article gave Americans "the liberty" to take fish off Newfoundland and in the St. Lawrence, and to dry fish on certain islands, but prohibited them fishing closer than three leagues from British shores. With respect to the Loyalists, the British now suggested that each side return to the other "all estates, rights and properties in America which have been confiscated during the war" and provide a "full and entire amnesty" for all "acts and offenses" committed during the war. Jay's draft had provided that the British troops would leave America "forthwith"; the British now suggested that their departure be somewhat slower, "with all convenient speed."[61]

Adams immediately launched into the question of fish. He argued that it was impractical for the British fishing vessels to get to Newfoundland in March or April, so there was no reason for the British to deny the Americans this part of the fishing season. Any geographic limits would also, in his view, be unworkable. "How could we restrain our fishermen, the boldest men alive, from fishing in prohibited places?"[62] Towards the end of the day, Jay posed two critical questions to the British. First, he wanted to know whether Oswald "now had power to conclude and sign" the preliminary articles. "Absolutely," Strachey responded. Second, Jay asked "if the propositions now delivered to us were their ultimatum." Strachey did not want to answer this, "but at last said no." The Americans agreed, among themselves, that these were good signs: the British were ready to sign, and ready to negotiate further on the disputed issues.[63]

On the next morning, Adams and Franklin joined Jay at his hotel for breakfast. Franklin read Adams and Jay a letter he had drafted to Oswald on the
question of the Loyalists. Franklin explained again that, if the British insisted
on compensation for the Loyalists, the Americans would insist on compensation for the damage done by the British troops. Congress was in the process of
gathering up evidence on this issue, Franklin reported, and it would "form a
record that must render the British name odious in America to the latest generations." The record would include the destruction of many towns, as well as
miles of "well settled country laid waste, every house and barn burnt, and
many hundreds of farmers, with their wives and children, butchered and
scalped." Franklin urged again that the British "drop all mention of the
Refugees," so that the commissioners could "write to America and stop the
inquiry." [64]

Jay and Adams immediately recognized Franklin's letter as a minor master-
piece, and they urged him to read it to the British later that day. Much of the
day was taken by "endless discussions" about the Tories, in which Jay and
Adams supported Franklin's arguments. There was almost an equally endless
discussion of the fisheries, in which Adams debated with a new member of the
British team, Alleyne Fitzherbert. Although Fitzherbert was only thirty-three,
Adams found him "pretty discreet and judicious." His main mission in Paris
was to negotiate with France and Spain, but he was also charged with watching
over the American negotiation as it approached its conclusion. [65]

The next two days were spent in similar discussions and negotiations,
"endeavoring to come together concerning the fisheries and the Tories."
Although the Americans continued to argue against any compensation for the
Loyalists, they also drafted a clause in which Congress would "earnestly
recommend" to the states that they "provide for restitution of all estates, rights
and properties" both of "real British subjects," and of Americans who had been
under British control during the war but "not borne arms against the United
States." The Americans were encouraged in their approach to this issue by
Vaughan, just returned from London, who reported that the British ministry
did not really expect to recover an immense sum for the Loyalists, but was keen
to preserve its "honor and reputation" by securing something in the treaty for
the Loyalists. [66]

Henry Laurens, the fourth of the five American commissioners, after spending the summer and fall in the south of France, finally arrived in Paris in late November. Jay had quarreled with Laurens while they both served in the Continental Congress, but Laurens was now a broken man, both by his long imprisonment in the Tower of London and by the news of the death of his son John in a recent skirmish with the British. Jay and the other Americans briefed Laurens on the state of the negotiation so that he could join them at the table for the final days.[67]

Although most of the discussion during these days revolved around fish and Tories, there was *some* discussion of other provisions, and there were some interesting changes, probably drafted by Jay. The British draft provided that "British creditors" would meet "no lawful impediment to the recovery of the full value" of debts contracted by Americans "before the year 1775." The Americans insisted that the provision be made bilateral, so that creditors on either side could make use of it, and agreed to remove the time limit, so that it applied to all debts contracted prior to the treaty. The British draft provided a "full and entire amnesty of all acts and offenses which have been, or may be supposed to have been committed on either side, by reason of the war." The Americans apparently feared that this would call into question court judgments rendered before the treaty, and limited the provision so that it only applied to pending or future cases. In general, however, there were few changes from the British third draft, which itself followed on many issues Jay's second draft.[68]

On the day after Laurens arrived, the four Americans and three Britons spent the entire day in negotiations at Jay's rooms at the Hôtel d'Orléans. Adams presented a new draft of the fisheries article, which was debated at length and amended several times. At one point, the British suggested that they should agree on all the other articles, and leave the question of the fishery to the definitive peace treaty. Adams said he "never could put my hand to any articles, without satisfaction about the fishery." Jay agreed, saying that such an agreement "could not be a peace, it would only be an insidious truce." At another point, the British said they did not believe their instructions allowed them to sign the draft as it stood. Adams replied calmly that the Americans could wait while the British sent another courier to London for instructions. Fitzherbert revealed, perhaps injudiciously, that the British team was keen to finish the treaty before Parliament gathered in a few days. Franklin, turning the sword in the wound, said that if a courier went to London, he should take along something about "the sufferers in America," at which he pulled out of his pocket a "claim" for compensation for the destruction in Boston, Philadelphia and elsewhere. The other Americans, including Jay, all added details about destruction with which they were familiar. "After hearing all this," the British team "retired for some time" to confer among themselves. When they returned, Fitzherbert reported that they had decided to accept the American's final draft clauses on the fisheries and the Tories. They all sat down again, "read over the whole treaty and corrected it," and agreed to meet the next day at Oswald's quarters to sign the preliminary articles.[69]

On the next morning, the last day of November, the Americans met at Jay's quarters to read over the fair copies of the preliminary articles which the secretaries had prepared overnight. They noticed a few minor errors, such as the omission of the time limit within which British civilians had to leave the United States. Laurens raised one important new issue; he wanted the treaty to include a "stipulation that the British troops should carry off no Negroes or other American property." Jay would, within a few years, denounce this provision as immoral, at least as it applied to slaves who fled from American masters in response to British promises of freedom. But now, perhaps in an effort to secure southern support for the treaty, Jay and the other two Americans agreed to the suggestion of Laurens. The four Americans walked down the street, the Rue des Petits Augustins, to the Grand Hôtel Muscovite, where they met with the British negotiators. The British agreed to the American changes, including the slave provision, and the preliminaries were "signed, sealed and delivered."[70]

Later in the day everyone went out to Passy to dine with Franklin. One of the Frenchmen present commented on the "growing greatness of America" and predicted that the "thirteen United States would form the greatest empire in the world." Caleb Whitefoord, secretary to the British team, agreed and noted that "they will *all* speak English, every one of them." Whitefoord captured in a phrase Jay's view, that the linguistic and other ties between America and Britain would prove more important over time than the wartime alliance with France. That night, writing in his diary, Adams noted that he had not recorded all the arguments over the past few weeks of his colleagues, who were "very attentive" and "very able." This was "especially" true of Jay "to whom the French, if they knew as much of his negotiations as they do of mine, would very justly give the title with which they have inconsiderately decorated me, that of *le Washington* of the negotiation, a very flattering compliment indeed, to which I have not a right, but sincerely think it belongs to Mr. Jay." [71]

Most Americans, when they learned about the preliminary peace terms between Britain and the United States, were more than satisfied. William Livingston wrote to Jay that the "treaty is universally applauded, and the American commissioners who were concerned in making it have rendered themselves very popular by it." Alexander Hamilton wrote Jay that "the peace, which exceeds in the goodness of its terms the expectations of the most sanguine, does the highest honor to those who made it." In New England, according to Hamilton, there was "talk of making you an annual fish-offering, as an acknowledgment of your exertion for the participation of the fisheries." Thomas Jefferson thanked Jay "for the good work you have completed for us," and congratulated him for "having borne so distinguished a part in the earliest and the latest transactions of this revolution." The terms, Jefferson added, "are indeed great." [72]

Many historians have agreed that the preliminary peace terms were very favorable to the United States. One concluded that the "greatest victory in the annals of American diplomacy was won at the outset by Franklin, Jay and Adams." But others have criticized Jay's work during this period. Several have suggested that he erred by insisting on some form of prior British recognition of American independence. Jay's stubborn demands on this issue delayed the negotiations by about two months, during which Britain's position strengthened, as a result of its victory at Gibraltar, and its sense of the division between France and the United States. It is hard to explain why Jay refused to deal with Oswald, simply because his commission did not refer in proper terms to the United States, after dealing for many months with Floridablanca, who of course did not admit that there *was* any such nation as the United States. It is also hard to explain what Jay thought America would gain by delay. On balance, although one can admire Jay's patriotism in wanting to see early recognition of America's status, one has to question his judgment in insisting that this be dealt with as a precondition.[73]

The most serious question is how much Jay's delay cost the Americans in the treaty terms. Some have suggested that the Americans might have been able to obtain, if they insisted, all of Canada, but most historians now believe that the British were not at all likely to have yielded this much. Others have suggested, more plausibly, that the Americans might have been able to obtain southern Ontario. But the final boundary, the "line of the lakes," apparently devised by Jay, gave the United States a more northerly northern border, and when extended to the Pacific this was ultimately far more important than southern Ontario. The delay may have cost the Americans something in terms of the wording of various provisions, but probably nothing substantial in terms of territory.[74]

Other scholars have criticized Jay's proposal regarding West Florida, arguing that he was wrong to favor an enemy (Britain) over an indirect ally (Spain), and wrong to place a strong power (Britain) on the southern border rather than a weak one (Spain). Here, however, there is far more to be said in Jay's defense. We know today that Spain had provided America secret assistance, but Jay did not know much about that in 1782: he only knew how he had been refused any aid in Madrid. There was every reason for Jay to believe that the British, with whom America had long and deep ties, would prove better neighbors in Florida than the Spanish, with whom America had often been at war. A joint effort to oust the Spanish from Florida would have perhaps led to better relations between America and Britain on other fronts. And the proposal secured the enthusiastic support of Oswald for many of the other terms in Jay's first draft treaty; if this had been enough to secure London's support, the treaty could have been concluded on very favorable terms indeed.[75]

Finally, historians have questioned and criticized Jay for sending an Englishman, Vaughan, as his representative to England. But Jay did not "send" Vaughan to England; he merely urged Vaughan to consider how important it was for his friend and mentor Shelburne to understand the American position. Some have suggested that Jay proposed, through Vaughan, a separate peace with Britain. This is unfair to Jay, who at all times was clear that the Americans would honor their commitment to France, and only sign a final peace treaty at the same time that France signed its final peace treaty with Britain.[76]

Whatever tactical errors Jay made during the Paris peace negotiations should not obscure his great achievements. He secured the trust and admiration of the British negotiators, making them in many cases effective internal advocates for the American position. He bridged the differences between Franklin and Adams, enabling the three Americans to function as an effective team. He prepared the first and second drafts of the treaty, and many of the revisions thereafter, without the benefit of a file of precedents from which to work. Jay and his colleagues secured for the future United States an immense territory, whose boundaries formed the basis of the present outline of the United States. Above all, although there would be one more unfortunate war, Jay helped lay the "permanent foundation" he envisaged for "peace and friendship" between Britain and America. That relationship would prove more important than all the details of the Paris treaty.

CHAPTER 8

American in Paris

As HE SIGNED the preliminary peace terms in November 1782, John Jay believed that much work remained for him in Paris. The first step was to explain and defend the peace terms to the Congress back in Philadelphia. Since the preliminary American terms could not take effect until France and Britain reached their own agreement, and since France would not like some of the American terms, a second task was to defend the American terms against any attempted French revisions. Third, the preliminary terms would have to be turned into a definitive peace treaty between Britain and the United States, a task he expected would involve some further negotiation. And, to cement their peaceful relations, Britain and the United States needed to reach some understanding on trade relations.

Although he worked on all these issues in the eighteen months between November 1782 and his departure from Paris in May 1784, Jay had far more free time than he expected. John and Sarah thus had some time to enjoy life in Paris: to dine with American and French friends, to attend the theater, to explore the shops. John also took two trips during these months, a brief one to Normandy and a far longer one to London and southern England.

For many weeks before the signature of the preliminaries, the American commissioners avoided French questions about their negotiations. The Americans knew, however, that once they actually *signed* with the British, they would not be able to keep the terms from the French. Jay and Adams left to Franklin the delicate task of informing the French Foreign Minister, Vergennes. Vergennes predictably complained that the "abrupt signing of the articles" by the Americans "had little in it which could be agreeable to the King." When he learned that the Americans intended to send the articles to Congress, Vergennes protested that they were promising peace to America "without even informing yourself of the state of our negotiation." Was this, Vergennes asked rhetorically, consistent with the duties of the American commissioners towards the French King? Franklin replied that the first duty of the Americans was to their Congress, which deserved "as early an account as possible of our proceedings." Nothing in the preliminaries was inconsistent with America's obligations to France, although perhaps the commissioners had been impolite in failing to consult more often with the French.[1]

Franklin left to Jay and Adams the equally delicate task of explaining the preliminary terms to Congress. Because the French Minister in Philadelphia had substantial sway over many members of Congress, there would probably be protests in Congress about the failure to consult with France. Also, many members of Congress would likely resent the articles dealing with the debts and the Tories, not appreciating that these concessions were necessary to secure other provisions. Adams apparently drafted most of the joint letter, but Jay handled the critical paragraph regarding France. Jay explained that since the three American commissioners "had good reason to believe that the articles respecting the boundaries, the refugees and the fisheries did not correspond with the policies of this [the French] court, we did not communicate the preliminaries to the Minister until after they were signed." Jay and his colleagues hoped that Congress would "excuse our having so far deviated from the spirit of our instructions." Although this public letter was brief, Jay's private letters had already provided Foreign Secretary Livingston with many of the reasons why he distrusted France at this point.[2]

Jay disliked the French government, but he liked many individual Frenchmen, notably the Marquis de Lafayette. Lafayette and his wife were among the first to welcome the Jays to Paris when they arrived, and the two couples saw one another often thereafter. In late 1782, Lafayette left for Spain, intending to join a force gathering there to attack the British West Indies. When this plan did not work out, he decided to go to Madrid to seek a loan for the United States. Jay wrote to discourage this idea, saying that he would rather borrow elsewhere than "submit to pick up any crumbs" from Spain. By the time he received this letter, however, Lafayette was already in Madrid, where he met with both the King (who had "odd notions" about America) and Floridablanca (who tried to "delay our affairs"). Lafayette was able, during his brief stay, to persuade the Spanish government to receive Carmichael in his official capacity, as chargé d'affaires for the United States, a small step forward in Spanish relations.[3]

Jay feared at this time that he would have to return to Spain himself for further negotiations. Sarah, who far preferred Paris to Madrid, and who was expecting another child, was even more concerned about this possibility. Their young American friend Ridley wrote that "Mr. and Mrs. Jay and the little Spaniard [Maria] are bravely. Whether the next is to be a Spaniard, French or English will depend upon Master Congress." In about June of 1783, however, having heard nothing from Congress about Spain, Jay decided that he would return home in the spring of 1784, and wrote to friends in Congress to ensure that he would not be asked to stay on in Europe.[4]

For many months, Jay had complained to friends and family about his health. He was "neither very well nor very sick" and was "never free from a pain in my breast." In January 1783, he decided to leave Paris for a few weeks with Ridley. For some reason, rather than heading south for the pleasant weather of Provence, the two men headed north for Normandy. Given the season, it is not surprising that they found "rain," "still rain," and then "heavy rain." In Le Havre, they tried to "walk out to see the port, but the weather [was] so bad [they] could not stay."[5] Although the two men knew, when they left Paris, that Britain, France and Spain were negotiating peace terms, they had no sense that agreement was imminent. From Rouen, John reported to Sarah that the "town is daily amused with contradictory reports regarding peace." Two days later, however, news arrived from Paris that the three powers had agreed on preliminary peace terms and would sign them that day. Sarah was overjoyed: she "longed to embrace" her absent spouse both as "as a deliverer of our country" and "as an affectionate and tender husband." She did not have to wait long; finding neither decent weather nor good health, John returned to Paris in late January.[6]

In February 1783, after the other preliminaries were signed, the American commissioners started to consider how to turn their preliminary terms with

Britain into a final treaty. The three commissioners had various ideas about articles which should be added to the definitive articles. Franklin continued to press what the British viewed as his "unfair and unreasonable demand of a compensation from Great Britain for damages sustained by America." Adams and Jay suggested that there should be an article about prisoners, similar to that in the preliminary terms between France and Britain, and an article about the islands in the Bay of Fundy. Adams also wanted to see Britain cede Bermuda to the United States, and suggested that "no forts shall be built or garrisons maintained upon any of the frontiers of America."[7]

The most pressing questions, however, related to trade. In 1782, when the British negotiators deferred discussion of Jay's free trade proposal, there really was not much trade, because of the ongoing war. Now, in early 1783, there were "several Virginia ships loaded with tobacco just arrived in Europe, and others expected hourly," and their captains needed to know whether they could land in Britain. Jay and his colleagues asked their British counterpart for an urgent answer on "whether American vessels, loaded with the produce of that country, will be permitted from this time to enter the ports of England." Ideally, Jay wanted not only the right for American ships to carry American produce to Britain, but also the right to carry the goods of other countries to Britain, and the right to trade with the British West Indies. As he put it in a draft letter at this time, the Americans would agree that "British merchants shall enjoy in America and her ports and waters, the same immunities and privileges" as Americans, "provided that a similar indulgence be allowed to those of our country, in common with British merchants in general." Jay knew this might be more than Britain would concede, but he was prepared to consider alternatives, as long as they ensured reciprocity.[8]

Before there could be any serious discussion of these issues in Paris, however, there was a political upheaval in London. Prime Minister Shelburne was censured by the House of Commons for giving away too much to the Americans in the preliminary peace articles. A few days later he resigned. Jay and his colleagues heard this news with some concern. Franklin reported to Livingston that the "English court is in confusion by another change of ministry, Lord Shelburne and his friends having resigned." Franklin hoped that the new ministry, not yet formed, would not be adverse to America, "but we shall see!" At the end of March, when there was still no new ministry, Jay asked his British friend Vaughan "whence came the idea that the moment a Minister loses a question in Parliament he must be displaced?" Jay was distressed that Parliament did not seem to recognize the advantages that would flow from "the mutual navigation of American waters."[9]

In early April, Jay and his colleagues learned that there was a new ministry in Great Britain, with two former adversaries Lord North and Charles James Fox serving together as Secretaries of State. The Americans also learned that they would have to deal with a new representative in Paris, David Hartley, a Member of Parliament known to favor America. As Franklin reported to Livingston, "Mr. Hartley is an old friend of mine, and a strong lover of peace, so that I hope we shall not have much difficult discussion with him." The Americans also heard reports, however, that Britain and France had agreed that there would be some kind of peace congress including Russia and Austria. If the purpose of this was merely to allow Russian and Austrian representatives to witness the signatures, Jay could not see the point. "Is it probable that a Congress should be called for that poor, simple purpose?" And the Americans equally could not see any role for mediators in their discussions with Britain. "There is nothing in difference between us and Great Britain, which we cannot adjust ourselves, without any mediation."[10]

David Hartley finally arrived in Paris in late April and started meetings with Jay, Adams, Franklin and Laurens. Hartley was about fifty years old, a prosperous Scottish merchant, somewhat stout, with small spectacles on a broad face. He started with the suggestion that trade be resumed on the pre-war terms, allowing American ships to carry American goods to Britain, but denying them the right to bring foreign goods to Great Britain or to carry goods between Britain and the British West Indies. One of the Americans, probably Jay, drafted a far broader proposal, which would have opened all of America's "rivers, harbors, lakes, ports and places" to British ships, and in return opened all British ports, both domestic and overseas, to American ships, excepting only ports reserved for the chartered trading companies. Hartley endorsed Jay's reciprocity proposal and relayed it to London before the end of April.[11]

Two weeks later, Hartley informed the Americans that, although it could not accept their reciprocity proposal, the British government was taking steps to open up the American trade. A new order in council would allow American ships to bring "un-manufactured" American products into British ports and would allow the export of goods from Britain to America, subject to the standard "drawbacks, exemptions and bounties." The Americans were pleased by the trade order, since it would at least allow America to sell and ship agricultural products to Britain.[12] A few days later, Hartley presented a memorandum to the American commissioners, suggesting that they agree on temporary trade terms that would allow American ships to bring any American goods to Britain and the British West Indies on pre-war terms. The Americans, sensing that Hartley was not supported at home, declined to offer any immediate reaction and asked Hartley to seek further instructions. The Americans also urged that American ships should have the right to carry goods between Britain and the British West Indies, a critical leg of the pre-war triangular trade.[13]

Jay and his colleagues were prepared to consider a temporary agreement along the lines suggested by Hartley, and Jay started to draft a few provisions that might be included in such a treaty. One of them would have prohibited British ships from bringing to the United States "slaves from any part of the world, it being the intention of the said states entirely to prohibit the importation thereof." Jay's assertion about American intentions was only partly correct. A number of states had prohibited the import of slaves, including Virginia in 1778 and Maryland in 1783, but South Carolina and Georgia still allowed slave ships, and about eight thousand slaves were imported through Charleston alone between 1783 and 1787. Indeed, the import of slaves into the United States did not end until 1808, more than twenty years after Jay's draft prohibition.[14]

As Jay and his colleagues talked with Hartley in June 1783, news arrived of a second British order in council that allowed the import into Britain of several American articles usually considered "manufactures," and also allowed the import into Britain of American tobacco, subject to the pre-war duty. News also arrived in Paris at about this time that American ships were docking in London; perhaps British ships were similarly docking in America; and since trade was under way, the pressure for compromise was reduced. As Henry Laurens reported to his colleagues from London, to which he had returned, the word "reciprocity" had in recent weeks "undergone a certain degree of refinement," and the British now intended to define the term as "possession of advantages on one side and restrictions on the other." Adams wrote home to Livingston that he saw "no prospect of agreeing upon any regulation of commerce here. The present [British] ministry are afraid of every knot of merchants." [15]

In the middle of July 1783, the American commissioners learned of a third order in council. This one allowed certain American goods to be imported into the British West Indies, and allowed rum, molasses and certain other products to be exported from there to the United States. But American ships were not to be allowed to carry *any* of these goods to or from the British West Indies, a more restrictive policy than had applied before the war. Given the importance of this trade, and Hartley's recent assurances that it would to some extent be open, the American commissioners reacted with understandable anger. It was now quite clear to the American commissioners that Britain did not intend to *negotiate* through Hartley regarding the terms of trade; Britain intended to *dictate* the terms of trade through orders. Indeed, Hartley learned of this latest order from the Americans, rather than from his colleagues in the British government. [16]

If Jay and his colleagues wanted to negotiate, rather than merely accept, trade terms, the United States would have to impose some limits on British trade, which could then be "negotiated away." Jay wrote that the British government was "duped, I believe, by an opinion of our not having decision and energy sufficient to regulate our trade so as to retaliate their restrictions." The British wanted "to be the only carriers between their islands and other countries; and though they are apprised of our right to regulate our trade as we please, yet I suspect they flatter themselves that the different states possess too little of a national or continental spirit, ever to agree in any one national system. I think they will find themselves mistaken." Unfortunately, it was Jay who was mistaken; the various states under the Articles of Confederation could not agree on trade restrictions, and thus the Continental Congress had no leverage in trade negotiations. [17]

Since there was little prospect of a trade agreement, Hartley and the American commissioners discussed other questions that might be addressed in the definitive peace agreement. Hartley presented to the Americans six propositions. He wanted to confirm that the "water line of division" between the United States and Canada, the St. Lawrence River and the Great Lakes, would "be enjoyed fully and uninterruptedly by both countries." Hartley also wanted a provision which would have allowed a certain number of British troops to remain at the British forts along the Great Lakes to secure those living nearby "against the invasion or ravages of the neighboring Indian nations." The Americans were prepared to agree to both these propositions, although they wanted the British troops to leave the forts as soon as American troops arrived to protect the "lives, property and peace" of those nearby.[18]

The Americans in turn had propositions for Hartley to consider. They wanted to provide explicitly that all prisoners would be released upon ratification of the final treaty. They wanted Britain to use its "good offices" to protect Americans against the North African pirates. They wanted a provision in which both nations agreed, in case of future war between them, not to engage in any attacks on private commerce or trade. Jay drafted a revised provision regarding debts, granting a three-year moratorium on repayment, and a complete exemption from interest accrued during the war. Indeed, in early August, Jay drafted a complete definitive treaty, incorporating these and other provisions, which Hartley relayed to London for its consideration.[19]

If accepted and agreed, these draft provisions, especially those on the forts and the debts, would have prevented many future difficulties between Britain and America. But the British government, keen to avoid another debate in Parliament on the American peace terms, was unwilling to agree to any variation from the preliminary terms. Edward Bancroft, the spy who somehow served both Britain and America, reported from London that the definitive treaty would probably "be only a transcript of the provisional articles." As predicted, Hartley soon presented to the Americans in Paris a draft treaty which was almost word for word the same as the provisional articles. Franklin informed Vergennes that, much as they might like to improve the terms, the Americans were "inclined to sign this with Mr. Hartley, and so to finish the affair."[20]

They finished the affair in September 1783. Vergennes planned a grand ceremony at Versailles to sign all the treaties at the same time. But Hartley's instructions did not permit him to negotiate or sign at any place other than in

Paris, so it was agreed that Hartley and the Americans would sign their treaty in Paris in the morning, then go to Versailles to witness as the other treaties were signed in the afternoon. Franklin, Adams and Jay arrived at Hartley's hotel at the early hour of eight in the morning. The four men signed and sealed the definitive British-American treaty and exchanged copies. Then they all went out to Versailles, watched as the other treaties were signed, and dined with Vergennes. The final terms were not all the Americans had hoped for, but they were more than enough. As John Jay put it in a letter home a few days later, "we are now thank God in full possession of peace and independence. If we are not a happy people now it will be our own fault." [21]

Throughout the spring and early summer of 1783, the American commissioners in Paris waited with increasing impatience for reaction from Congress to the preliminary peace terms. Franklin complained to Secretary Livingston in the middle of June that "we know nothing of the reception of the preliminaries, or the opinion of Congress respecting them." A few days later, Adams received a letter from Livingston which, almost in passing, reported that Congress had "agreed to ratify the provisional articles as such, and to release their prisoners." Livingston suggested that there were various questions raised by the wording of the preliminary articles, which he would address in another letter. This other letter, however, did not arrive for several weeks, leaving the Americans in "total darkness" concerning the comments of Congress on the preliminaries. [22]

Finally, in early July, the American commissioners received several letters from Livingston. In one of these letters, Livingston commended the commissioners for the terms they obtained, but attacked them for the way in which they had obtained them, particularly their decision to sign without showing the draft terms to France. "The concealment was, in my opinion, absolutely unnecessary." Livingston also condemned the secret article regarding West Florida, which carried "the seeds of enmity to the court of Spain, and shows a marked preference for an open enemy." In a second letter, Livingston summarized the debate in Congress, in which many had argued against ratification of the provisional articles. He also suggested that "it would be extremely desirable if some ambiguities in the provisional articles should be cleared up," such as the question of when the British troops would leave New York. [23]

Adams and Jay met with Franklin at Passy on the day these letters arrived to discuss how to respond. Adams and Jay were outraged; Adams wrote home a few days later that any man who criticized the preliminary terms should be condemned to re-negotiate them for himself. Franklin was, as usual, more cautious and diplomatic. The three men agreed that Jay would prepare the first draft of a joint response. Jay's initial draft listed four key issues, including the western boundary and the fisheries, on which France had questioned or undermined the American position. Jay explained that the British negotiators were keen, in late November 1782, to sign before Parliament met, giving the Americans unusual and temporary leverage. If the American commissioners had communicated the draft terms to Vergennes, "he would have insisted on our postponing the signature of them," which would have allowed the British time to reconsider and re-negotiate.[24]

When Jay circulated this draft letter, Franklin questioned whether it was necessary to defend their negotiation, or to defend it quite so stridently. Franklin noted correctly that "no letter sent to Congress is ever kept secret," and that Livingston's letters to them were not a formal position of Congress, merely "the private opinion of Mr. Livingston." Jay reluctantly agreed and revised the joint letter. The final letter justified the secret article with respect to Florida, noting that it was a "quid pro quo" for the favorable western boundaries, and it was "both necessary and justifiable to keep this article secret." The letter did not expressly address the issue of separate negotiation, but noted that nothing the American commissioners had written "should be construed to impeach the friendship of the King and Nation." Vergennes was "so far our friend, and is disposed so far to do us good offices, as may correspond with, and be dictated by, his system and policy for promoting the power, riches and glory of France." In other words, France was a friend of America only to the extent that America's interests did not conflict with those of France.[25]

Jay, however, could not resist the temptation to let Livingston know what he really thought of France in a separate, personal letter. Jay argued that the purpose of the instruction to consult with France "was the supposed interest of America, and not of France, and we were directed to ask the advice of the French Minister, because it was thought advantageous to our country that we should receive it." Only Congress, therefore, not France, had "a right to complain of our departure from that line of instruction." Although Jay concluded this letter with some friendly personal remarks, it seems likely that he was hurt by the tone of Livingston's letter. Livingston was not merely the Secretary for Foreign Affairs, and thus Jay's superior; he was his boyhood friend and former law partner. It is probably not a coincidence that Jay started, within a few days of receiving Livingston's letters in early July, to write to friends and family in America that he would return to America in a year's time. Jay wrote to Morris that he was not interested in *any* foreign appointment, since "I mean to return in the spring." To his sister-in-law Kitty he wrote that, "if God preserves my life and grants my prayers, we shall see each other next June or July." [26]

Lewis Littlepage, the young Virginian who had caused Jay so much trouble in Spain, arrived in Paris during the summer of 1783. Littlepage had decided that he was the appropriate person to bear the definitive treaty of peace to the United States, and applied to Jay for this honor. Jay replied that this was an issue to be decided by all the American commissioners, and a few weeks later they settled upon John Thaxter, Adams's private secretary. Littlepage was so incensed by this imagined slight that he sent Jay a long, abusive letter in which he challenged him to a duel. As Jay was reading this letter, first Adams and then Littlepage arrived at his room. Adams and Jay berated Littlepage so thoroughly that Littlepage apologized to Jay, asked for and then burned the offending letter, then "gave Mr. Jay his hand and took his leave." [27]

Jay's letters from this period, indeed from his whole four-year stay in Europe, have remarkably little in them about Europe. Instead they are filled with his affection and concern for America. In one letter, Jay wrote that he had "met with neither men nor things on this side of the water which abate my predilection, or if you please my prejudices, in favor of those on the other." His "affections are deeply rooted in America, and are of too long standing to admit of transplantation." He could "never become so far a citizen of the world as to view every part of it with equal regard, and perhaps nature is wiser in tying our hearts to our native soil." In another letter, he voiced the somewhat "singular" view that young Americans should be educated in America. "The fine and some of the useful arts may doubtless be better acquired in Europe than America, and so may the living European languages." But these could also be learned in America, where young men could form friendships with their counterparts from other states, and above all learn "religion, morality, virtue and prudence."[28]

Jay was concerned about reports of quarrels among the American states, and about the possibility that European nations might try to exploit any divisions. To Washington he wrote that "the increasing power of America is a serious object of jealousy to France and Spain as well as Britain. I verily believe they will secretly endeavor to foment divisions among us." To prevent such divisions, Jay urged that the American states should "proceed to settle the boundaries of such of the states as have disputes about them." He was troubled by reports that the American army was being dismantled, and reminded his readers that "to be constantly prepared for war is the only way to have peace."[29] Jay urged his "nationalist" friends to remain part of the Confederation government. He hoped that Washington would continue to lend his "counsels and application" to the tasks at hand. He regretted that Alexander Hamilton had left Congress, for "the character and talents of delegates to Congress become daily more and more important." He urged Robert Morris to continue handling the nation's finances: "your office is neither an easy nor a pleasant one to execute, but it is elevated and important," and Morris should not "gratify" his enemies by resigning.[30]

More generally, Jay urged his fellow Americans to strengthen the national government. To his father-in-law, he expressed the hope that that a "continental, national spirit [would] pervade our country," and argued that "Congress should be enabled, by a grant of necessary powers, to regulate the commerce and general concerns of the confederacy." Jay wrote to Gouverneur Morris in similar terms. "I am perfectly convinced that no time is to be lost in raising and maintaining a national spirit in America. Power to govern the confederacy, as to all general purposes, should be granted and exercised." As early as 1783, Jay was arguing for a stronger national government, arguments which would ultimately lead to the new federal Constitution.[31]

The Jays generally enjoyed life in Paris, far more than they enjoyed Madrid. One major reason was that they had American friends. Adams spent some of his time in the Netherlands, where he continued to work on obtaining loans,

but when he was in Paris he was often with Jay. He wrote home to his wife
Abigail that "Mr. Jay has been my only consolation. In him I have found a
friend to his country, without alloy. I shall never forget him, nor cease to love
him, while I live." Sarah wrote to her sister that:

> Among all the pleasures which Paris affords (and they are not few) none of them
> gratify me like the frequent opportunity of seeing my countrymen. At present you
> would be surprised to see what a circle we form when collected. We have received
> an agreeable addition to our society by the arrival of Mrs. Ridley the day before
> yesterday. Mrs. Price and Mrs. Montgomery have the suite of rooms over my head
> in this same hotel, and Mrs. Izard lives directly opposite and has two daughters that
> are grown up. There are three days in the week that we take tea and play cards at
> each other's houses, besides meeting upon other occasions.

John Thaxter, secretary to John Adams and cousin to Abigail, spent one
evening "quite agreeably" with this group of ladies, and reported that "Mrs.
Jay is very sensible and amiable," and that she and her husband "live perfectly
happily in each other's society, their tempers and dispositions in unison."[32]

Another reason that the Jays enjoyed Paris was that there was much more
to do than in Madrid: shops, theaters, parks. Sarah shopped not only for herself,
but also for her family, sending silks to her sister and melon seeds to her father.
With her hair dressed high, like the French, Sarah resembled Queen Marie
Antoinette, so much so that on one occasion she was mistaken for the Queen
as she entered a theater.[33]

In July 1783, the Jay family moved out to Passy, to a suite of rooms in
Franklin's house there. The air was "remarkably good" and John soon found
that his health better, "though not yet re-established." The Jays celebrated the
Fourth of July with the Franklins (and presumably other Americans) at Passy.
Sarah reported home to her sister that, in spite of the joy of the occasion, she
"found it difficult to suppress the tears that were ready to flow at the memory
of those who, in struggling to procure that happiness for their country which
we were then celebrating, had fallen in the glorious attempt." John spent some
of his time during the course of the summer interviewing Franklin about early
America. Unfortunately, he did not record any of Franklin's everyday quips;
he was perhaps too serious really to appreciate Franklin. Jay also wrote to
Thomson, long-time secretary of the Congress, urging him to "devote one

hour in the four and twenty to giving posterity a true account" of the Revolution. He thought it would be safe to leave the "battles, sieges, retreats, evacuations etc." to future historians, but he feared that the "political story of the Revolution" would be lost if it were not recorded now. The Jays' little daughter Maria toddled around and developed a "singular attachment" to Franklin. In late August, Sarah gave birth to another daughter, a "perfect cherub" whom they named Ann or Nancy.[34]

John was somewhat restless, however, and in October 1783 he left for England to see if the famous waters of Bath would improve his health. He intended to remain in London only about a week, but in the event stayed there more than a month, largely because he found he had so many friends there. On the day after he arrived, for example, he breakfasted with Peter Van Schaack, the friend who had left New York rather than face continued persecution for his "equivocal" views. Van Schaack had written Jay in Paris, asking whether they could renew their friendship. Jay wrote back warmly, explaining that, although they had differed on the vital question of American independence, "yet be assured that John Jay did not cease to be a friend to Peter Van Schaack." Jay looked forward to their meeting, when they would "as in the days of our youth indulge the effusions of friendship, without reserve and without disguise."[35]

One evening in late October, Jay went to the Drury Lane Theater, where "the celebrated Mrs. Siddons displayed her talents in the character of Belvidera, to which she did ample justice." Jay noted for Sarah that the theater was "neat and well-lighted, but not so magnificent as those at Paris." Jay spent another evening with the "Club of Honest Whigs." He reported with evident pleasure that "their first toast was their absent member Dr. Franklin, of whom they spoke with great respect and affection." The weather, in Jay's view, was dismal. In one letter, he noted that the "season advances, and with it the glooms of this climate, which in this month is particularly unpleasant." In another, he observed that the "English call it an uncommonly fine autumn; it would not be commended in America."[36]

Jay was never much of a tourist: after two weeks in London, he wrote his wife that "as yet I have seen so little of London that I can form but a very imperfect judgment of it." But in late October John Adams and his son John

Quincy Adams arrived in London, and these two tireless tourists took Jay along on a number of outings. Adams obtained permission for the three of them to see Buckingham Palace, "even to the Queen's bedchamber, even to her Majesty's German Bible, which attracted my attention as much as anything else." They admired the King's library, with all its books "in perfect order, elegant in their editions, paper [and] binding." Adams also arranged places for himself and Jay in the gallery of the House of Lords, where they watched the formal presentation of the Prince of Wales on his twenty-first birthday. Adams described these events in detail, but Jay, at least in his surviving letters, does not even mention them. He wrote to his wife in November that "nothing has as yet exceeded my expectations, and I shall probably return to America fully persuaded that Europe collectively considered is far less estimable than America." [37]

Jay found time while in London to sit for two great painters: Benjamin West and Gilbert Stuart. West was born in Pennsylvania, but had lived in London for nearly twenty years, and served for many years as "history painter to the King." He was working at this time on a sketch for a grand painting of the peacemakers, both British and American. West painted Jay standing behind his colleagues, papers in his hands, an intent look in his eyes. The painting was never finished, perhaps because the British negotiators, Oswald and Strachey, declined to sit for West. Stuart was considerably younger at this time, just beginning to be known. He now started a portrait, finished many years later by Trumbull, showing Jay at a desk covered with books and papers, pen in hand, but resting not writing. His eyes are a steely blue; his nose is prominent; his complexion fair; his expression serious, even solemn. [38]

There were some Americans in London in 1783, however, whom Jay avoided. One was Silas Deane, with whom Jay had worked closely in the early days of Congress. Jay had ceased to write to him after letters from Deane, urging that Americans abandon the war, appeared in a Loyalist newspaper in New York. Deane attempted to contact Jay in London, but Jay avoided him. After returning to Paris he explained to Deane by letter that, "I love my country and my honor better than my friends, and even my family, and am ready to part with them all whenever it would be improper to retain them. You are either exceedingly injured, or you are no friend to America, and while doubts remain on that point, all connection between us must be suspended." Jay had hoped to meet Deane in London, to hear what Deane had to say to defend himself, but then Jay had heard from several people that Deane "received visits from, and [was] on terms of familiarity with, General [Benedict] Arnold. Every American who gives his hand to that man, in my opinion, pollutes it." [39]

Another American whom Jay avoided in London was his own brother, Sir James Jay. James had sided with the Americans early in the war and served for several years in the revolutionary New York legislature. But then James had grown unhappy with the American cause, attacked various Patriots in newspaper articles, and finally arranged for himself to be captured by the British, so he could live in New York City and London. When John Jay heard that his brother had "made his peace with Britain," he wrote to a friend that he would "endeavor to forget that my father ever had such a son." Although James Jay was in Paris in early 1783, and in London in late 1783, it appears that the two brothers did not meet in either place. To his nephew, John wrote from London that "Sir James I am told is here, but I have not seen him." [40]

In early November, John Jay learned that Abby, a slave who had served his family for many years, had run away from their rented house in Paris. His reaction shows that, however much he disliked slavery in the abstract, he could not understand why one of *his* slaves would run away. He wrote that her departure was "a measure for which I cannot conceive a motive. I had promised to manumit her upon our return to America, provided she behaved properly in the meantime." He presumed that she had been captured by the Parisian police, and hoped that she would be "punished, though not vigorously." [41] Abby was indeed captured and imprisoned. Peter Jay Munro visited her in prison and "offered her permission to return if she would behave well, but she refused to accept it, saying she was very happy where she was for that she had nothing to do." When John Jay heard this, he wrote that he hoped that "sobriety, solitude and want of employment will render her temper more obedient to reason." Unfortunately, Abby became ill in prison. Although Sarah secured her release in early December, and cared for her carefully at home, she died not long after her release. John wrote to Sarah that he "lamented" Abby's death and that it "would have given me great pleasure to have restored her in health to our own country." [42]

During his absence in England, John and Sarah wrote to one another often, two or three times a week. Sarah described the house she had rented for them in Chaillot, "so gay" and "so lively." She reported on the various hot air balloon experiments at this time, asking her husband in jest whether they should not travel to America "next spring in a balloon?" In another letter, she related an incident which showed Franklin, nearing eighty, had not lost his wit or gallantry. "The other evening at Passy he produced several pieces of steel, the one he supposed you [John] at Chaillot, which being placed near another piece which was to represent me [Sarah], it was attracted by that and presently united." Then Franklin moved "John" away from "Sarah," and placed him "nearer another piece, which the Doctor called an English lady," and "behold! the same effect." Everyone laughed heartily, even Sarah, but she noted that they "could not shake my confidence in my beloved friend." John's letters back to Sarah were filled with questions and concerns about her and their children. "A smile from you and the caresses of our little ones are worth more to me than all the pleasures of this town." [43]

One exchange, in particular, shows the relationship of trust and confidence between John and Sarah. In late November, Sarah wrote that "now that we are a little settled I should like to inoculate the children, if you approve of it." Smallpox inoculation at this time was difficult and dangerous; it required a long quarantine and sometimes resulted in death. John wrote back two weeks later that he "entirely approved" of her plan. But Sarah had not waited for word from John. "Upon more mature reflection," she wrote, she had "concluded that [she] already knew [his] sentiments sufficiently to authorize the operation." The children, she reported, had been quite well for several days, but then the baby had gone into convulsions. The servants were "terrified" but Sarah, "recollecting your fortitude on a former distressing occasion," perhaps the death of Susan in Spain, bathed the child in cool water and walked her up and down to soothe her. Both girls were now "quite recovered." [44]

At the end of November 1783, Jay left London for Bath, the most famous and popular resort in England. People came from everywhere to drink and bathe in the mineral waters and to consult with the famous physicians. People also came to Bath for the social life, which included plays, concerts, dances, parties and sometimes fireworks. "Above all there were the other people, their fashionable clothes, their outrageous hats, their curricles, their horses, their conversation, their shopping and their symptoms." Jay started drinking the waters and taking regular walks. A week after his arrival, he wrote to Adams that the waters "have I think done me some, but as yet not much good." His physician, Jay noted, "tells me more time is necessary."[45]

Jay did not, however, want to wait all winter. After two weeks, he left Bath for Bristol. His father Peter had spent time in Bristol as a youth, more than fifty years ago, and had corresponded throughout his life with his cousins there, the Peloquins. The last of these cousins, Marianne Peloquin, had died childless in 1772, and had left substantial sums in her will to Peter Jay and his children. Jay now met with the Peloquin executors, and explained to them that, since his father had recently died, the Jay children were entitled both to the sums promised them directly, as well as shares of the sum promised to Peter Jay. The executors, however, argued that Peter Jay might have died *before* Marianne Peloquin, causing that gift to lapse. They also asked whether there was "any person in England" who could "prove the handwriting" of either the parties or the witnesses on the powers of attorney Jay presented.[46]

Jay wrote to Van Schaack in London, hoping he could provide an affidavit that would satisfy the executors. He himself returned to Bath at Christmas time and reported to his wife that he was "much better." Indeed, Jay was sufficiently recovered that, the "moment [he could] get that Bristol business dispatched," he would "set out for France." Jay returned to Bristol, armed with papers from Van Schaack, but found he could not budge the executors. As he explained to Sarah, "the unaccountable temper of one of the executors would not permit him to think [the papers] sufficient and [the papers] are now gone to London to be inspected by the Attorney General, whose opinion on them we expect in a day or two." Jay also hinted that he feared his brother James had "thrown obstacles in my way." Jay waited with increasing impatience for the promised opinion, and finally left Bristol for London. There he conferred with Van Schaack about how best to satisfy the executors, saw a few friends, and left for France.[47]

The snow was "thick on the ground" when Jay returned to Paris in February 1784, and the weather remained cold for many weeks thereafter. There was not much for Jay to do. Adams was in the Netherlands, where he was seeking a further loan for the United States, and trying to avoid default on a set of bills. Franklin was confined by gout to his home at Passy. Congress had asked the three American commissioners to negotiate new trade treaties with all the "commercial powers" of Europe. The only "power" interested, however, was Prussia, and Adams handled the face-to-face discussions at the Hague, although Jay provided useful comments on the draft treaty from Paris.[48]

Perhaps moved by the recent death of his slave Abby, Jay prepared and signed at this time a "conditional manumission" of his slave Benoit. He started the document with a bold statement: "the children of men are by nature equally free, and cannot without injustice be either reduced to or held in slavery." It was therefore "right" that Benoit should be free after "the value of his services" would "amount to a moderate compensation for the money expended on him." Since in Jay's view Benoit's "faithful services for three years more" would "be sufficient for that purpose," Benoit would be free after that period. Like Jay's attitudes towards slavery, the document is contradictory: it recognized the injustice of slavery in general, but also required Benoit to serve Jay for another three years.[49]

In late March 1784, the formal ratification of the peace treaty by Congress at last arrived in Paris. Franklin and Jay wrote to Hartley in London to ask when and how the British proposed to exchange ratifications. Even though the six-month period for the exchange provided in the treaty had passed, Hartley responded that the British were still "making out" their ratification, and that he would come to Paris in a few weeks for the exchange. Hartley arrived in Paris in late April, and on May 12, 1784, Franklin, Jay and Hartley exchanged the formal ratifications. As Franklin reported to Congress, "the great and hazardous enterprise we have been engaged in is, God be praised, happily completed."[50]

Jay continued to correspond actively with various Americans, both in America and abroad. From London, John Witherspoon, a former colleague in Congress, now President of Princeton College, wrote to Jay, asking whether he would be able to raise funds for the college in France. Jay's response was that "the diffusion of knowledge among a republican people is and ought to be one of the constant and most important" objects of the new American governments so that, in his view, it was improper "to solicit donations for that or any other purpose, from the subjects of any prince or state whatever."[51] From Philadelphia, Jay heard from Gouverneur Morris, who cautioned him not to judge the new America until he saw it with his own eyes. From New York City, Robert Livingston described how the New York legislature had evicted Benjamin Moore, a Loyalist minister, from the pulpit of Trinity Church. From northern New Jersey, his sister-in-law wrote of the progress his son Peter, now eight years old, was making in reading and writing. John wrote back to Peter, saying he was pleased by the reports of his progress, and hoped that God would "bring us all together this summer, and then I will assist you in your studies."[52]

Jay was understandably eager to return home, but he could not leave until he had resolved the accounts from his mission to Spain. He had asked Carmichael in early 1783 to come to Paris to go through the accounts, but Carmichael had declined, saying he believed he should stay in Spain until directed otherwise by Congress. Even after Jay obtained a resolution from Congress, authorizing him to *require* Carmichael to come to Paris, Carmichael lingered in Madrid. When he finally arrived in Paris in March 1784, Carmichael delayed in providing the relevant papers. Jay complained to a friend in Philadelphia that nothing detained him other than the accounts, "and a mortifying detention it is, considering that this best season for being at sea is passing away." After some angry words between Jay and Carmichael, especially over how Carmichael had treated Jay's private property after his departure, the accounts were finally signed and settled in mid-May.[53]

Jay was not sorry to leave Carmichael, but he regretted that he could not see Adams again before leaving for America. Adams wrote from Holland to a mutual friend that Jay "returns to his country like a bee to his hive, with both legs coated with merit and honor." On a fine May morning, the Jays and their two young daughters left Paris by coach. They traveled to Calais and crossed the Channel to Dover, where they lingered a few days, waiting for their ship. Richard Oswald, Benjamin Vaughan and Henry Laurens traveled down by coach from London to see John Jay one last time, and the four men enjoyed sharing tales of the war and their negotiations. On the first of June, the Jays embarked on an American ship, the *Edward*, under the command of Captain

Matthew Coupar. After a seven-week passage, and almost five years away from the United States, they arrived in New York City. A few weeks later, the City of New York presented to Jay and a few others (including General Washington and Governor Clinton) the "freedom of the city in gold boxes." Jay thanked the City in words which capture his joyful return and hopes for America:

> I consider the day on which I again landed on these shores as one of the happiest with which an indulgent Providence has blessed me; and that satisfaction was increased by finding my fellow citizens in the enjoyment of public tranquility and private security, under the auspices of magistrates who had given early proofs of attention to both . . . If our views be national, our union preserved, our faith kept, war however improbable provided for, knowledge diffused, and our federal government rendered efficient, we cannot fail to become a great and happy people. This being a land of light and liberty, I bless God that it is the land of my nativity. Here my forefathers sought and found freedom and toleration. I am bound to it by the strongest ties, and as its happiness has been the first object of my endeavors from early life, so the most fervent wishes for its prosperity shall be among those of my latest hours.

The gold box itself recently changed hands at auction for more than half a million dollars.[54]

CHAPTER 9

Secretary for Foreign Affairs

W HEN HE RETURNED to New York City in July of 1784, John Jay
learned that the Continental Congress had elected him as its second Secretary
for Foreign Affairs. The position had been vacant for many months, ever since
Robert Livingston had resigned in the spring of 1783, and Jay considered for
several months more before he finally accepted. He needed some time to catch
up with family and friends; he also wanted to negotiate with Congress
regarding the terms of his service, and this was not possible until Congress reconvened late in the year. Jay did not want to move his family from town to
town, or be separated from them for long periods, so his first condition for
accepting the position was that Congress settle itself, preferably in New York
City. His second condition was that he should have the right to appoint his own
staff. He knew that Congress would appoint the ambassadors abroad, but he
wanted to be sure that his immediate assistants were answerable to him, not
being appointed by Congress, like his former secretary Carmichael. Jay's third
condition was that all of the foreign correspondence of Congress pass through
his office. Indeed, not long after he took office, he obtained an order from
Congress allowing him to open any letter in any post office that might involve
the "safety or interest of the United States." It is unclear whether he ever used
this extraordinary authority.[1]

When Congress finally gathered in Trenton, New Jersey, in December 1784,
Jay was there as one of New York's delegates. He discussed his concerns and
conditions with the other delegates: there were only about two dozen of them
present. After some further debate on the location question (which prompted
Sarah Jay to comment that "it is fortunate for the reputation of the ladies that

there are none of our sex in Congress"), it was agreed that Congress would meet for the next few years in New York City, while permanent buildings were built somewhere along the Delaware River. Jay's desire to be in New York City, and Congress's desire to have Jay as its Secretary for Foreign Affairs, no doubt influenced this decision. With this issue resolved, and with an assurance that he could choose his own staff and review the correspondence, Jay agreed to serve as Secretary, and took the oath of office before a justice of the New Jersey Supreme Court. He then returned to New York City to arrange quarters there for the Continental Congress.[2]

Jay served as Secretary for Foreign Affairs from December 1784 through March 1790. In some respects, his role was similar to that of today's Secretary of State: to develop American foreign policy, to supervise America's representatives abroad, and to negotiate with foreign representatives. Of the differences from today, perhaps the most important was that, instead of reporting to a single person, the President, Jay reported to a shifting group of about three dozen people, the Continental Congress. Congress often lacked the quorum of members necessary to act on Jay's reports, and even when a quorum was present, the members often had other priorities. Jay frequently apologized to Adams, America's Minister in Britain, and Jefferson, America's representative in France, about the delays caused by Congress. In late 1785, for example, he wrote to Adams that "a considerable time" had passed since there had been sufficient states represented in Congress to do business. During 1786, he complained to Adams that for the past few months Congress had not had a quorum "for more than three or four days" and to Jefferson that an issue was "now as it has long been, under the consideration of Congress."[3]

Reading these letters, one has the sense that Jay was tied down by Congress, unable to take even the simplest step without congressional instructions. A rather different picture emerges from the reports of the French representatives in New York. The French chargé d'affaires Louis Guillaume Otto reported in early 1786 that "Mr. Jay's political importance increases every day. Congress appears to govern itself only by his impulses, and it is as difficult to obtain anything without the concurrence of this Minister as to have a measure that he has proposed rejected." Otto attributed Jay's "superiority" to the "indolence of most of the members of Congress and the ignorance of some others." The result was that "Mr. Jay's prejudices and passions insensibly become those of Congress, and that without being aware of it this assembly is no more than the instrument of its first Minister." Though Otto regretted that Congress had chosen "a man who does not like us," he also conceded that "there are few men in America more able to fill the position that he occupies. The veneration that he has inspired in almost all members of Congress proves more than anything else that ... he is as circumspect in his conduct as he is firm and unshakeable in his political principles." In early 1789, the French Minister Moustier reported in similar terms that Jay was important because of "the difficulty of replacing him, the perception that he is an industrious person (this in spite of the scantiness of his work), the necessity of transmitting communications through him, the ignorance of the majority of members of Congress above all regarding affairs abroad, and lastly, the rotation of the members, who are often very young men or men of very little importance."[4]

Like Jay's own complaints about his impotence, these French complaints about his dominance must be read with some caution. The French representatives in New York had to explain to their masters back in Paris why they had not been able to achieve much with Congress. It was easier for them to tell a story with a well-known villain, the difficult and dominant Jay, than to tell the more complex story of differing French and American interests. But the French were correct in reporting that Congress often, though not always, deferred to Jay's judgment, just as Jay was correct in reporting that it was hard for him to get Congress to focus on foreign affairs.

Relations with Congress were only one of the difficulties facing Jay as Secretary. The United States had essentially no army or navy, and without military power behind them, the arguments of Jay and other American diplomats were often disregarded. Jay also had a very limited staff with which to work: the few clerks who worked with him in two rooms at Fraunces Tavern and a few ministers, appointed by Congress, stationed abroad. He also faced, from the other side of the Atlantic, the same difficulties and delays of communication he had faced while serving in Europe.[5]

In spite of the difficult conditions, Jay handled an immense amount of work as Secretary for Foreign Affairs. During his five years of service, Jay prepared and submitted more than one hundred reports to Congress and sent more than five hundred official letters.[6] Jay handled an incredible variety of issues as Secretary: he negotiated with foreign representatives in the United States; he established a system of consuls in foreign ports; he helped open up American trade with China; he advised Congress on admiralty cases; he drafted for Congress a law on piracy; he corresponded with diplomats abroad, with governors at home, and with ordinary citizens; and he organized the files, knowing that "it is to papers in this office that future historians must recur for accurate accounts of many interesting affairs respecting the late Revolution." Given the rapid turnover in Congress, and in the presidency of the Congress, Jay provided crucial continuity in the central government during the Confederation years.[7]

Britain was at this time both America's main trade partner and the main threat to American security. In defiance of the provision in the Peace Treaty, which required Britain to remove all its troops from the United States with "all convenient speed," Britain retained several key forts within the boundaries of the United States at Detroit, Niagara and elsewhere. The British troops at these western and northern forts had friendly relations with local Indians, so that Americans feared a combined British-Indian assault. For its part, Britain claimed that America was also guilty of violations of the treaty, and especially that various state statutes improperly hindered British creditors.[8]

As he commenced work as Secretary, Jay had access to reasonably current information about these issues. Henry Laurens, recently returned to the United States from Britain, reported that many Britons seemed to seek a second war against America. James Monroe, a young protégé of Jefferson, had just returned from a tour of the Northwest and Canada. Monroe informed Jay and the others in Trenton that "one reason assigned [by British officials] for detaining the western posts from the United States was because Virginia had not repealed her laws that impede the recovery of British debts." So, as early as December 1784, Jay knew that Britain intended to justify its continued occupation of the western forts by pointing to the state laws on the debts.[9]

Congress took no action on these issues until February 1785, when it decided to appoint a minister or ambassador to Britain, and asked Jay to draw up instructions. Jay suggested that the Minister should "insist that the United

States be put, without further delay, into possession of all the posts and territories within their limits." The Minister should also "remonstrate against the infraction of the Treaty of Peace, by the exportation of slaves and other American property" at the end of the war. Jay evaded the question of the debts, suggesting weakly that both British and American merchants would suffer if Americans were "unseasonably and immediately pressed for the payment of debts contracted before the war." A few weeks later, Congress selected John Adams as Minister to Britain and Jay forwarded these instructions.[10]

Even before he left Paris for London, Adams wrote Jay that "the people in America and their legislatures in the several states should prepare the way for their Minister in England to require a faithful execution of treaties, by setting the example of a punctual execution on their part." Jay wrote back that he was "entirely of opinion with you that the people of this country should, by a punctilious observance of the treaty, enable you to insist with more propriety and energy on its being kept with equal good faith by Britain." If this was really Jay's view, it is odd that he did not immediately urge Congress to act. Perhaps he believed that Britain would withdraw from the forts on its own. In September 1785, however, he received "private intelligence" which suggested that the British, far from withdrawing from the forts, were reinforcing them. At almost the same time, he learned that British authorities in Canada were claiming that certain islands off northern Maine were part of Canada, not of the United States. Jay suggested that Massachusetts, of which Maine was at this time a part, should "proceed without *noise* or *delay* to garrison such places in their *actual* possession as may be most exposed." He was "very apprehensive that to permit these disputes to remain unsettled will be to risk mutual acts of violence which may embroil the two nations in a war."[11]

In early 1786, Jay asked Jefferson whether France "consider[ed] herself bound by her guarantee to insist on the surrender of our posts? Will she second our remonstrances to Britain on that head?" Jefferson raised the question, but he did not press for an answer, because he feared a reciprocal question, that is, whether the Americans considered themselves bound by *their* promises regarding the debts and the Loyalists. Jay was increasingly concerned about the failure of the Americans to live up to their side of the treaty. In March 1786, he advised Congress that "policy as well as justice demands that infractions of the Treaty of Peace should not pass unnoticed, especially when the evidence of them exists in the [state laws] which, being matters of record and of public notoriety, must be supposed to come officially to the knowledge of Congress." Britain was perhaps "well content these [state] infractions should remain uncorrected," since they would give Britain a pretext "to detain from us our frontier posts and countries." [12]

At about this same time, Jay received a copy of a "memorial" which Adams had submitted to the British Foreign Minister, in which he noted that the northwest forts, along with "considerable territory around each of them," were still held by British troops. Adams, on behalf of the United States, "required" Britain to withdraw from these posts, and every other place within the United States, "according to the true intention of the treaties." Although he usually agreed with Adams, Jay was troubled by the word "require." As he explained in a report to Congress, if Britain flatly refused to withdraw from the posts, it would "involve the United States either in war or in disgrace," and the United States "are not prepared for the former, and should if possible avoid the latter." Jay suggested that Adams should "immediately" be instructed to "protract his negotiations" and "avoid demanding a categorical answer." After a month of delay, Congress agreed and Jay sent a letter to this effect to Adams. [13]

Only a few days later, Jay received a letter from Adams with the British response to the memorial. It was not, as Jay had feared, a flat refusal to vacate the posts. Rather, the British Foreign Minister complained about American breaches of article four of the treaty, which provided that creditors would meet with "no lawful impediment to the recovery of the full value in sterling money of *bona fide* debts." The Minister opined that it would be "the height of folly" to suppose "one party alone obliged to a strict observance" of the treaty while "the other might be free to deviate from its own engagements." He enclosed a paper which detailed, state by state, the statutes which the British claimed violated the treaty. [14]

One of Jay's initial steps as Foreign Secretary had been to request, from the Governor of each state, a "complete collection" of state statutes. The Governors had ignored this request. In May 1786, he sent the Governors a more pointed request for statutes relating to debts and Loyalists, and began to advise key leaders of his concerns. He wrote to Jefferson that "the affair of our posts is a serious business, and the more so as in my opinion Britain has too much reason on her side. They who ask equity, should do it." Similarly, Jay wrote to Washington that "it is too true that the treaty has been violated" by the American states. "On such occasions I think it better fairly to confess and correct errors, than attempt to deceive ourselves and others by fallacious though plausible palliations and excuses." Though he did not mention the fact to his two friends from Virginia, all three of them were probably aware that Virginia debtors owed more to British creditors than those of any other state, about half of the total sum owed.[15]

In October 1786, Jay presented Congress with his report on these issues, the most immense and the most interesting report of his five-year term. He began by considering whether state legislatures had any authority to interpret a federal treaty. In his view, the "thirteen independent sovereign states" had "by express delegation of power, formed and vested in Congress a perfect though limited sovereignty for the general and national purposes specified in the Confederation." The states could not participate in this sovereignty "except by their delegates," since the Articles of Confederation gave "Congress the sole and exclusive right and power of determining on war and peace and of entering into treaties and alliances." Once Congress ratified a treaty, "it immediately becomes binding on the whole nation, and super-added to the laws of the land, without the intervention, consent or fiat of state legislatures." It was thus "clear that treaties must be implicitly received and observed by every member of the nation." Today, when the Constitution provides that federal treaties are the "supreme law of the land," and override any inconsistent state law, Jay's remarks seem routine. In 1786, however, Jay's remarks were radical, for most people considered the state legislatures as the only bodies authorized to make laws. Jay presaged not only the Supremacy Clause; he suggested here the novel concept that *both* the national and the state governments could be sovereign, in their separate ways.[16]

Jay then reviewed one by one the various state laws which Britain claimed violated article four. In some cases, he concluded that the state law did not impede proper debt collection efforts, and thus was consistent with the treaty. In other cases, such as North Carolina and Georgia, he had not been able to obtain copies of the state law, so he was unable to form a view. But in several cases, including New York, Virginia, and South Carolina, he concluded that the state laws were contrary to article four. He also considered the British charges that several state laws violated article five (committing Congress to recommend leniency towards the Loyalists) and article six (prohibiting any future penalties based on conduct during the war). He found that certain anti-Tory laws of New York violated article six, condemning one such statute as "a direct violation of the Treaty of Peace, as well as of the acknowledged law of nations." [17]

Given that the British still held the forts, Jay had "no doubt" that the British had violated article seven, which required them to withdraw from American territory. This article also provided (in the language added at the last minute by Henry Laurens) that the British should withdraw without "carrying away any Negroes, or other property of the American inhabitants." Here Jay had more difficulty, not because he doubted that the British had carried away slaves, but because he now questioned the morality of this provision. Jay was "aware that he [was] about to say unpopular things, but higher motives than personal considerations press[ed] him to proceed."

> If a war should take place between France and Algiers, and in the course of it France should invite the American slaves there to run away from their masters, and actually receive and protect them in their camp, what would Congress and indeed the world think and say of France, if on making peace with Algiers, she should give up those American slaves to their former Algerine masters? Is there any other difference between the two cases than this, viz., that the American slaves at Algiers are *white* people, whereas the African slaves at New York were *black* people?

In Jay's view, Britain should not have agreed to the provision, for it had "invited, tempted and assisted these slaves to escape from their masters [so that] it would have been cruelly perfidious to have afterwards delivered them up to their former bondage." Yet Britain *had* agreed to the provision, and to refuse to execute it now would be equally improper. Jay saw only one solution: Britain should "do substantial justice to [the] masters by paying them the value of those slaves." [18]

Some Americans argued that the British had violated the treaty first, so the Americans were justified in their later violations. Jay concluded, however, that the American violations preceded the British violations. Under the circumstances, it was "not a matter of surprise to your Secretary that the posts are detained, nor in his opinion would Britain be to blame in continuing to hold them, until America shall cease to impede her enjoying every essential right secured to her, and her people and adherents, by the treaty." [19]

Jay recommended that Congress take four steps. First, Congress should resolve that no state legislature could pass a law interpreting a national treaty, "nor for restraining, limiting, or in any manner impeding, retarding or counteracting the operation and execution of the same." Second, Congress should urge the state legislatures to repeal "forthwith" all laws which were "repugnant to the Treaty of Peace." Third, to avoid questions about differences between state laws, each state should enact precisely the same repealing law, a draft of which he prepared and provided. Fourth, Congress should instruct Adams to admit the American violations of the treaty, inform Britain of the steps Congress was taking to obtain repeal of the state statutes, and negotiate towards a "convention" that would provide for the removal of the British troops and resolution of the other issues. [20]

Jay submitted this report in October 1786, but it languished in Congress for several months. Jay did not wait for Congress, however. He informed Adams that the "result of my enquiries into the conduct of the states relative to the treaty is that there has not been a single day since it took effect on which it has not been violated in America by one or other of the states." Jay also described the report in general terms to John Temple, the British representative in New York. Temple reported home that Jay conceded that many of Britain's claims about American violations of the treaty "were just" and that Britain was thus justified in "holding the western posts until these states should manifest a fair and honorable disposition to fulfill their part of the said treaty." Several historians have criticized Jay for discussing the report with Temple; one has called this an "inexcusable indiscretion." But the British would have learned of the report soon enough, either through sources in Congress or when Congress acted upon the report's recommendations. By making an early confession to the British, Jay was laying groundwork to persuade both the Americans *and* the British to honor the treaty. [21]

In March 1787, Jay reminded Congress of the case of a Loyalist imprisoned in New York City for his conduct during the war. He viewed the New York law in question, "and all prosecutions under it for military damages committed during the late War, [as] violations of the faith of the Treaty of Peace." This report apparently prompted action, for Congress first adopted unanimously the resolutions he had earlier suggested, and then sent a summary of his report to the states, urging each of them to enact the law drafted by Jay. This circular letter was printed in various American newspapers during April 1787. In the context, the actions of Congress were remarkable. Congress was recommending, almost requiring, that the states pass laws which would enable British creditors to recover immense sums from American debtors. Congress was recommending that the states repeal laws against the hated Loyalists. And Congress was adopting and publishing Jay's views that only the national government had the power to make foreign policy and that national treaties and laws prevailed over any inconsistent state laws. A few weeks later, the delegates of the Philadelphia convention, many of whom were Jay's friends and colleagues, would turn these views into key clauses of the Constitution.[22]

By July 1787, Jay could report to Adams "that several of the states have removed all obstacles to the full and fair operation of the treaty" and that there "is great reason to expect that certain others of them will do the like at the ensuing sessions of their legislatures." He forwarded to Adams laws or resolutions from seven states, including New York. Adams, when he received this letter, wrote back that it "came at a very fortunate moment," that there were now laws from enough states "to furnish something solid to say to this court." Adams would argue the issue with the British, "and there is some reason to believe that the British ministry will listen at this time with attention," particularly in light of worrisome rumors of European war.[23]

Before Jay and Adams could pursue these discussions further, however, Congress acceded to the request of Adams that he be allowed to return home. In words drafted by Jay, Congress thanked Adams for "the patriotism, perseverance, integrity, and diligence with which he has ably and faithfully served his country." In his covering letter to Adams, Jay urged him to return home through New York City, so "that I may have the pleasure of taking you by the hand, and personally assuring you of [my] sincere esteem and regard." Jay recommended that Congress appoint another Minister to Britain, since there were still many unresolved issues, "and the management of them requires prudence and temper." Congress, however, was by this time only meeting from time to time; most members and most Americans were focused on whether to approve the new Constitution. So the position remained unfilled for several years, and the issues remained unresolved.[24]

Historians have generally viewed Jay's efforts to secure compliance with the Peace Treaty as well-intentioned but doomed. But perhaps more remarkable than his failure is how much *progress* he made on these issues during his tenure. Jay not only filed his report, detailing the British and American violations of the treaty; he persuaded Congress to accept the report and publicize its key paragraphs. Through Congress, he persuaded several states to enact the necessary laws, and Adams believed these state laws would give him "something solid" with which to negotiate. Perhaps, with a little more time, and a little more military force behind them, Jay and Adams could have solved at least the questions of the forts and the debts in the 1780s, rather than leaving them for Jay to solve in the 1790s.[25]

Many of the issues Jay faced as Secretary related to France. One of the first was an unusual request for extradition. The request arose from a quarrel between the French Consul General in the United States, François Barbé de Marbois, and another Frenchman, Charles Julien Longchamps. After Marbois declined to certify some papers for him, Longchamps attacked Marbois in the street, calling him a "rascal" and striking him with his cane. The Pennsylvania authorities arrested Longchamps, tried and convicted him, and sentenced him to two years in prison. The French authorities, however, were not satisfied with this; they wanted Congress to remove Longchamps from the Pennsylvania jail and return him to France. In February 1785, Jay received a formal request to this effect from Marbois, who said that he relied "entirely on the justice of Congress, and on its respect for the law of nations, violated in a manner which has never had an example."[26]

In his report on this request, Jay started with first principles: "that every friendly foreigner coming to any country on lawful business is entitled to the protection of the laws of that country on the one hand, and owes obedience to them during his residence, on the other." It followed that a foreigner who violated American law was subject to punishment like any other person, and the "state has undoubted right to punish him in the manner and degree prescribed by the laws of the state." When a foreigner was tried, convicted and imprisoned, the state "has a clear right to hold and detain him in prison," and was not bound to release or deliver him "before he shall have satisfied the laws of the land which he has violated." [27]

In Jay's view, therefore, the request of France was premature. Until Longchamps had served his time in the Pennsylvania prison, he could not properly be returned to France. He noted that if France demanded the return of Longchamps thereafter, it would raise difficult questions under "the laws of nations and the federal compact between the states." Indeed, Congress had no authority at this time to arrest a person and extradite him to another country. But he put off these questions for another day. For now, it was sufficient that Congress had to decline the request of France, with "concern and regret," for the members of Congress would always want to show "their respect, their regard, their gratitude, and their attachment" for France. [28]

Somewhat similar issues were raised by the French consular convention, one of Jay's successes as Secretary. While Jay was in France, his colleague Franklin and counterpart Rayneval discussed from time to time a proposed convention regarding consuls. For the French, a "consul" was a full-time foreign service officer, who served as a sort of judge in cases involving French law or French subjects. For the Americans, a "consul" was generally an American merchant who worked part-time gathering information. These very different views of the role of a consul, as well as the press of other work, delayed the discussions for several years. By the time Jay was leaving France, however, Franklin had reached a tentative agreement with Rayneval on the draft convention. Jay was probably aware of this, but he did not know in December 1784 whether Franklin had in fact *signed* the convention. To buy some time to consider the issues, he moved, and Congress resolved, that if Franklin had not yet signed, he should "delay signing it until he shall receive further instructions on the subject from Congress." [29]

Franklin, however, had signed the convention many months before. When a copy finally arrived on Jay's desk in New York, he found problems in almost every provision. Even the title was wrong: it referred to the "thirteen United States of North America" and thus "excludes from it all such other states as might before the ratification of it or in future be created by or become parties to the Confederacy." The convention did not clearly provide that French consuls, before exercising their functions, should first present their credentials to Congress. Earlier in the year, a Swedish consul had presented himself to the Governor of Massachusetts and had then started work in Boston. With this unfortunate precedent in mind, Jay urged that the French convention be clarified on this point.[30]

Jay had three main objections to the convention. First, he was concerned that France would use the convention to discourage emigration to the United States. The convention would authorize French consuls to arrest the captains, crew and passengers arriving on French ships. He predicted that France would use this authority "whenever passengers attempt to come here in a manner and for purposes not consistent with the ordinances against emigration." Second, he was concerned that the convention gave unnecessary immunity to French consuls and their servants. He recognized that, under international law, ambassadors were entitled to immunity, but consuls and their servants were not similarly protected. In his view, the United States should strive to see that "as few persons as possible should live" in the United States "exempt, in any respect, from the jurisdiction of the laws." Third, he was deeply troubled by the provisions granting French consuls certain judicial functions. If a French subject died in the United States, his creditors would "have no other dependence for payment but the integrity of the consul or vice consul who alone can take possession of his goods." French consuls would have the exclusive right to determine whether someone was a French subject, without any right of someone who considered himself American to appeal to American courts. These provisions violated what Jay viewed as a basic principle of any nation's law: "not to permit any civil power to be exercised in it but by the citizens of the country legally and constitutionally authorized thereto."[31]

In July 1785, Jay recommended that Congress reject the convention and instruct Jefferson to re-negotiate with the French. After a year's delay, Congress asked Jay to reconsider and report again. At this point he did not bother to repeat all his general concerns, but stressed the differences between the convention as signed and the draft Congress had approved in 1782. Although this draft was in his view "far from being unexceptionable," he thought that Congress was bound by its prior approval of the draft, and that it should instruct Jefferson to negotiate "a convention conformable to that scheme," with a ten- or twelve-year time limit. Congress finally approved these recommendations in October 1786, enabling Jay to send to Jefferson both of his reports, as well as authority to negotiate along the lines of the 1782 draft.[32]

Jefferson's initial reaction to Jay's letter was a question: shouldn't Congress authorize him to negotiate *without* reference to the 1782 scheme? The instructions essentially required Jefferson to provide the French with a copy of the 1782 scheme, and "the moment it is produced, [the French] will not abate a tittle from it." But the French might have forgotten the 1782 scheme, and be "willing to reconsider the whole subject," in which case "perhaps we may get rid of something more of it." Jay was delighted to receive Jefferson's letter. He recommended, and Congress now agreed, that Jefferson should receive a general commission to negotiate a consular convention, with an instruction that the new convention should define and limit to the extent possible the role of French consuls.[33]

Jefferson received the revised instructions in December 1787 and started serious discussions with Rayneval in early 1788. Perhaps because the French now realized that the United States would soon have a new and more forceful government, Jefferson was able to achieve in his negotiations much of what Jay had suggested. Consuls, vice-consuls and their servants were subjected to United States law, like all other foreign residents of the United States; only the room in which the consul did his official work was given diplomatic protection. The consul's powers to arrest ships and passengers were greatly diminished, although not eliminated. The consul's power to determine nationality was eliminated. The convention was also limited in duration to twelve years. Jefferson signed the convention in November 1788 and returned it to Jay for the consideration of Congress.[34]

Jay received the signed convention in March 1789, and immediately wrote to Jefferson to praise his work, saying it was "greatly and deservedly commended." There was no Congress, however, to whom he could submit the convention. The Continental Congress had not been able to gather a quorum for many months, and the first Congress under the new Constitution had not yet assembled. The Constitution provided that the President could make

1. John Jay, by Rembrandt Peale and Raphaelle Peale. The Peale brothers apparently painted this in about 1795 from a now-lost portrait by their father, Charles Willson Peale.

2. Sarah Livingston Jay. There do not appear to be any surviving contemporary oil portraits of Sarah Jay; we are left with this type of nineteenth-century print.

3. Sarah, William and Sarah Louisa Jay. Sarah with her two youngest children, from a pastel attributed to John Russell.

4. Peter Jay House, Rye, New York. This image of the house where Jay grew up may well show, in the foreground, some of Peter Jay's slaves.

5. King's College, later Columbia College. The grand new building of King's College, which Jay attended from 1760 through 1764.

6. Southeast Prospect of the City of New York. New York as it looked while Jay was a student in King's College and then a law clerk.

7. Tontine Coffee House, Wall Street, New York. New York later in Jay's life, about 1797, when he was Governor of New York.

8. William Livingston, by John Wollaston. Jay's father-in-law, colleague in the Continental Congress, and then Governor of New Jersey.

9. Robert R. Livingston, by John Vanderlyn. Jay's best friend in their youth, close colleague during the Revolution, and then political enemy in the 1790s.

10. John Jay, by Caleb Boyle. This immense portrait, five by eight feet, depicts Jay with
the Paris Peace Treaty under his right hand. It was painted in 1801 and changed hands
many times before reaching its present home at Lafayette College.

11. John Jay, by Gilbert Stuart and John Trumbull. This painting was started by Stuart while Jay was in England in late 1783 and finished some time later by Jay's friend Trumbull.

12. Benjamin Franklin, by Joseph Siffred Duplessis. Franklin as he looked in France in 1782 and 1783, when Jay worked with him most closely.

13. The American peace commissioners, by Benjamin West. West intended to paint a grand portrait of all those involved, both British and American, in the Paris peace negotiations. He only finished this sketch of the Americans: (left to right) Jay, Adams, Franklin, Laurens and secretary William Temple Franklin.

14. Alexander Hamilton, by John Trumbull. Jay helped Hamilton get his start in America, and they remained close friends and colleagues thereafter.

15. The Poughkeepsie convention, by Gerald Foster. Mural painted for the Poughkeepsie post office at the request of President Franklin Roosevelt, whose ancestor was among those depicted. Below, detail, left to right: Alexander Hamilton, Abraham Bancker, John Jay, James Clinton, Isaac Roosevelt and John Hobart.

16. George Washington, by Charles Willson Peale. The friendship formed between Washington and Jay during the Revolution helped ensure Jay's appointment as Chief Justice and then envoy to England.

17. John Adams, by Gilbert Stuart. When Stuart arrived back in the United States, after many years abroad, it was Jay who introduced and recommended him, leading to this and many other familiar portraits.

18. John Jay, by Gilbert Stuart. Sarah Jay, while her husband was absent in England in 1794, chased Stuart to finish work on this portrait; when it was finally done she pronounced it "inimitable."

treaties "with the advice and consent of the Senate," but since this was one of the first treaties presented to the Senate, no one was quite sure of the process. After Washington transmitted the convention, the Senate asked Jay to attend in person, bringing with him "such papers as are requisite." Jay appeared in July 1789 and "made the necessary explanations." It seems that some of the Senators disliked the convention, for they formally asked him whether "the faith of the United States [was] engaged, either by former agreed stipulations, or negotiations entered into by our Minister at the court of Versailles, to ratify, in its present sense or form, the convention." [35]

In his written response, Jay opined that "this convention will prove more inconvenient than beneficial to the United States, yet he thinks that the circumstances under which it was formed render its being ratified by [the United States] indispensable." He reminded the Senate that the "scheme of 1782, however exceptionable, was framed and agreed to by Congress." He also noted that he had assured Jefferson that Congress would ratify "any convention that is not liable to more objections" than the 1784 convention. Since the 1788 convention was better than either the 1782 draft or the 1784 convention, and since the convention had a twelve-year time limit, the United States should ratify it. [36]

Jay's report was hardly unqualified, but it was sufficient to persuade the Senate, for it now "resolved unanimously" to "consent to the said convention and advise the President of the United States to ratify the same." Washington agreed and ratified the convention. Jay's work on this convention has been called "his most important diplomatic service to his country." This is an overstatement; Jay's most important diplomatic work was in 1782 on the Paris Peace Treaty and in 1794 on the Jay Treaty. But the consular convention was a solid success, made possible by the combination of Jay's careful work in New York and Jefferson's skillful argument in Paris. [37]

Accounts of Jay's negotiations with Spain in 1785 and 1786 are often colored by what happened later. Since we know how important the Mississippi River would prove in American history, Jay's proposal that the United States should yield use of the river for even a brief period seems an error. Moreover, because we know how controversial the proposal would prove in the Continental Congress, the proposal seems impolitic, another example of Jay's lack of political finesse. But when we review the story from Jay's perspective, his actions become far more sensible and defensible.[38]

In June of 1785, after a journey of almost a year, Don Diego Maria de Gardoqui, a new representative of Spain, arrived in New York City. Jay knew Gardoqui from his time in Spain, when the two of them had argued about the Mississippi. The situation, however, had changed since 1780. The United States was an independent nation, albeit a weak and fragile one. Moreover, with the end of the war, thousands of Americans were moving west, over the mountains, and settling along rivers that drained into the Mississippi. They found themselves in direct conflict with Spain, which had closed the southern Mississippi to American traffic.

Most Americans, and in particular many Southerners, viewed the movement west with concern, and were thus ambivalent about the Mississippi. Hugh Williamson, a delegate from North Carolina, wrote to Jefferson that there was a "diversity of opinion" about Spain's closure of the Mississippi. Spain "doubtless" intended to injure the United States, but "I think [Spain's actions] will be favorable in their operations. Should the navigation of the Mississippi continue open, vast bodies of people would migrate thither whose mercantile connections could be of no use to the old states." George Washington was almost obsessed with making the Potomac the main avenue between the East and the West, and so he was concerned that an open Mississippi would result in westerners with "no predilection for us" in the East. James Monroe, who had traveled extensively in the West, reported that "a great part of the territory is miserably poor," merely "extensive plains" without "a single bush on them." Monroe asked what would connect the inhabitants of Kentucky with those of Virginia "once the Mississippi shall be open? Removed at a distance from whatever may affect us beyond the water, they will necessarily be but little interested in whatever respects us."[39]

Jay of course could not read the correspondence among the Southern leaders. But he must have heard similar things in conversations in and out of Congress. As he started his negotiations with Gardoqui, in the summer of 1785, he had both these informal comments in mind, as well as his more formal instructions to insist upon the "right of the United States to their territorial bounds, and the free navigation of the Mississippi, from the source to the ocean."[40]

At first, there was disagreement on almost every issue. On the boundaries, Jay relied upon the terms of English land grants, while Gardoqui relied upon Spanish victories against the English during the war. On the question of navigation of the Mississippi, they "disagreed even more strongly." Gardoqui echoed the arguments that some Americans were making, that the United States "would find it necessary to curtail the growth of settlements so distant from its center," and that "exclusion from all navigation [of the Mississippi] was one of the most efficacious means" to this end. According to Gardoqui, Jay "admitted all this in good faith," but argued that no American leader "would dare to agree to the aforementioned exclusion." Gardoqui argued that America needed trade with Spain, which "was a consumer in Europe and America who makes payments in cash." But when Jay sounded him out on the question of trade with Spain's American colonies, Gardoqui "proved to him the impossibility of such a concession." [41]

According to Gardoqui's reports, by February 1786 he and Jay had reached tentative agreement on several issues, but not on the Mississippi or the boundaries. If they could agree on those issues, Spain was prepared to confirm that its ports in Spain and the Canary Islands would remain open to American ships and products, other than tobacco, for a term of thirty years. Spain would also agree to purchase, for hard currency, a substantial quantity of American timber each year. And Spain would agree to "mediate" between the United States and Britain regarding the northwest forts, and "will see that they get justice, by force of arms if otherwise it cannot be promptly secured." [42]

At about this same time, Jay received a letter from a merchant in Pittsburgh, complaining about the seizure of his goods by the Spanish authorities at Natchez. In his report to Congress on this letter, Jay noted that Spain intended "to exclude all nations from the navigation of that part of the Mississippi which runs between [its] territories." The United States would not be able to use the river "unless by *arms* or by *treaty*." In his opinion, the time for arms "is not yet come," since there was still some hope of obtaining the right by negotiation. "However doubtful the success of these negotiations may be," it was "prudent that they should not be precipitated." Time, he believed, was on the side of the Americans. "As the country adjacent to the river becomes filled with people, and the affairs of the Confederacy become regulated and arranged, the attainment of that and every other object will daily and proportionably become more probable and easy." [43]

In late May 1786, Gardoqui wrote a long letter to Jay on the Mississippi question. He reiterated that "the King will not permit any nation to navigate between the two banks belonging to His Majesty." Spain was entitled to both banks of the southern Mississippi by virtue of its military victories during the war and various prior agreements. Spain could and would help the United States with Morocco and Algiers, but without Spain's assistance, American commerce would suffer not only in the Mediterranean, but also in the Atlantic. Spain was an important market for American goods, but unless the Americans agreed to a treaty, the Spanish King might "find it convenient to prohibit" all American imports into Spain. More generally, the Spanish King was "one of the first sovereigns of Europe" and his recognition would "give consistency to the [American] Confederacy." [44]

Although Jay usually submitted letters from foreign representatives to Congress, he did not submit this letter, at least not immediately. Instead, he suggested that Congress "appoint a committee with power to instruct and advise me on every point and subject relative to the proposed treaty with Spain." Congress appointed a committee of three: Rufus King of Massachusetts, Charles Pettit of Pennsylvania and James Monroe of Virginia. Monroe, who had earlier questioned the value of the Mississippi, was now adamant that the United States should not in any way accept its closure. Indeed, Monroe argued to Jefferson that Jay had "managed this negotiation dishonestly." King, in a letter to Elbridge Gerry, was equally certain that, if necessary, the United States should agree that it would not use the Mississippi for a period. King outlined the benefits that the United States could obtain in a treaty with Spain: access to Spanish ports; purchases by the Spanish government of American timber; and perhaps even access to the Philippines. King was "very sensible that the popular opinion throughout the U.S. is in favor of the free navigation of the Mississippi." But since the United States had neither the will nor the means to fight with Spain, would it not make more sense to consent to the proposal, "considering other benefits to be obtained?" [45]

Not surprisingly, this committee was unable to reach a consensus, and in early August 1786, they returned the question to Congress. At the request of

Congress, Jay appeared before the delegates, in secret session, to discuss the negotiations and how Congress should proceed. Jay started with a review of the effects a treaty with Spain might have on America's relations with other powers: the assistance which Spain could provide the United States with Portugal, with the Barbary Powers, with Britain, and even with France. Jay stressed the advantages the United States enjoyed through its trade with Spain; "there is scarce a single production of this country" that could not be "advantageously exchanged in the Spanish European ports for gold and silver." The continuation of this trade "must depend upon a treaty, for Spain like other nations may admit foreigners to trade with her or not." Jay then summarized the commercial terms he had agreed with Gardoqui, concluding that "by them we gain much, and sacrifice or give up nothing." [46]

With respect to the Mississippi, Jay noted that his letters from Spain, written "when our affairs were the least promising," opposed "every idea of our relinquishing the right to navigate" the Mississippi, and that he still held "the same sentiments of that right." There was a distinction, however, between the *right* to navigate the Mississippi and the *use* of that right. Jay urged that the United States should agree, for a period of twenty-five years, to "forbear to use the navigation of that river below their territories." In his view, the "navigation is not at present important, nor will probably become so, in less than twenty-five or thirty years," so that "a forbearance to use it while we do not want it, is no great sacrifice." Spain "now excludes us from that navigation, and with a strong hand holds it against us." Would it not make more sense "for a valuable consideration" to "forbear to use, what we know it is not in our power to use?" If Spain accepted the proposal, it would in his view accept America's ultimate right to use the river, "for they who take a lease admit the right of the lessor." [47]

Jay argued that, given the current weak state of the American economy and confederation, it could not even think about going to war with Spain. "Unblessed with an efficient government, destitute of funds, and without public credit, either at home or abroad," the Americans could not "plunge into an unpopular and dangerous war with very little prospect of terminating it by a peace either advantageous or glorious." He concluded by noting that he did not know whether Congress would agree with his views, but that he would "always remember that I am to be governed by the instructions, and that it is my duty faithfully to execute the orders, of Congress."[48]

This report started an intense, month-long debate in Congress. The northern delegates, led by Rufus King, argued in favor of the proposal, stressing in particular their need for the Spanish market for fish and other products; the southern delegates, led by James Monroe and Charles Pinckney, argued against the proposal, stressing the importance of the West to the union and the Mississippi to the West. Monroe attacked not only the proposed treaty: he attacked Jay personally and viciously. In a letter to Patrick Henry, at the time the Governor of Virginia, Monroe decried "one of the most extraordinary transactions I have ever known, a minister negotiating expressly for the purpose of defeating the object of his instructions, and by a long train of intrigue and management seducing the representatives of the states to concur in it." In a letter to James Madison, serving in the Virginia legislature, Monroe accused Jay of plotting to divide the union. "Jay and the principal advocates" had "gone too far to retreat." They must "either carry the measure or be disgraced," and "sooner than suffer this they will labor to break the union." Monroe suspected that Jay and others were "intriguing with the principal men in these [northern] states to effect that end in the last resort." Jay was certainly *not* in favor of any division of the union. In a letter to Jefferson, still in France, Jay regretted "an idea that may do mischief," the idea that "the interests of the Atlantic and western parts of the United States are distinct, and that the growth of the latter tending to diminish that of the former, the western people have reason to be jealous of the northern."[49]

In late August 1786, Congress finally voted on the issues raised by Jay's report. With Delaware absent, seven northern states outvoted five southern states, and Congress repealed Jay's instructions and gave him new instructions making no mention of the Mississippi. The southern delegates argued that these instructions were invalid, since the prior instructions had been given by nine states. Jay was well aware of these arguments, but also aware that he had to act in some way upon his new instructions. In early October he wrote to Gardoqui to inform him that he now had "more capacity" to "make and receive propositions," and promised they would resume their discussions soon.[50]

Jay soon found that Gardoqui would not accept his proposed wording about "forbearing to use" the Mississippi. Jay tried various alternatives, all designed to "change the dress but retain the spirit and sense," of his proposal, but none of them were acceptable. They finally tentatively agreed on a provision under which, during the limited term of the treaty, the United States and Spain would each have the right to use the Mississippi River "from its source down to the southern boundary of the said states," and the United States would "not navigate or use the said river below, or further down than the said boundary." Jay cautioned Gardoqui that "he must not conclude that what I might think expedient would also be deemed so by Congress."[51]

In April 1787, Jay submitted two reports to Congress, one on his recent discussions with Gardoqui, and one on the recent violence between Americans and Spaniards in the West. In the first report, although he outlined the terms under discussion, he carefully did *not* recommend that Congress approve these terms, but instead asked for further instructions. In his second report, he said he feared "that the period is not distant when the United States must either decide to wage war with Spain, or settle all differences with her by treaty, on the best terms in their power." If Congress wanted a treaty, he advised Congress "either to place some other negotiator in his stead, or to associate one or more persons with him in the business." If Congress wanted to pursue war, he advised that it "prepare without delay." He ended with a caution: "that a treaty disagreeable to one half of the nation had better not be made, for it would be violated; and that a war disliked by the other half would promise but little success, especially under a government so greatly influenced and affected by popular opinion." In essence, he was recommending that Congress do nothing, and that is what it did. Without further instructions from Congress, Jay himself was not willing to act, and discussions gradually tailed off.[52]

Even today, history books echo Monroe on the Gardoqui discussions, and criticize Jay for his willingness to yield the Mississippi River. In fact, however, Jay was acting in part on the comments of Monroe and others, who feared that an open Mississippi would tend to divide East from West. At most, he was willing to yield the use of the river in a limited way for a limited time, in a way which would confirm the ultimate American right to the river, and would achieve other vital goals. When he realized how divisive even this proposal would be, he wisely abandoned it.

Relations with Britain, France and Spain were difficult, but perhaps the *most* difficult issues were raised in this period by the "Barbary Powers" of Algiers, Morocco, Tripoli and Tunis. The Barbary rulers seized ships in the Mediterranean and enslaved their sailors for several reasons: for the value of the cargoes; for the ransom they could extract for slaves; and, above all, for the payments they could obtain for "peace treaties." The rulers justified their actions with references to religion. As the Ambassador of Tripoli explained to Adams and Jefferson, "it was written in their Koran, that all nations who should not have acknowledged their authority were sinners, that it was their right and duty to make war upon them wherever they could be found, and to make slaves of all they could take as prisoners, and that every [Moslem] who should be slain in battle was sure to go to paradise." The Ambassador described, with some pride, how "each sailor [would] take a dagger in each hand and another in his mouth, and leap on board, which so terrified their enemies that very few ever stood against them."[53]

While the colonies were part of the British Empire, they could rely on Britain to provide naval protection in the Mediterranean and to negotiate treaties with the Barbary Powers. As the war ended, and commerce resumed, informed Americans realized that the Barbary Powers would soon pose a problem. Jay and his colleagues in Paris, during the summer of 1783, had tried to secure continued British protection as part of the final Peace Treaty. The Americans had suggested that Britain commit to "employ [its] good offices and interpositions" with the Barbary Powers to guard the United States "against all violence, insult, attacks, or depredations" by them. Since Britain did not accept any of the American suggestions for changes to the preliminary terms, this provision did not become part of the final treaty.[54]

In early 1785, Congress received a letter from a Connecticut merchant who offered to negotiate with the Barbary Powers. In his report, Jay advised that "the commercial interest of the United States requires that treaties of peace and amity should be formed with the piratical states of Barbary." He recognized that "presents to a considerable amount will be necessary to ensure success to negotiations for such treaties," and he suggested that America offer "naval and military stores." In his view, the negotiations should be entrusted to the American commissioners (Adams, Franklin and Jefferson), not to some self-promoting Yankee merchant. He recognized that one difficulty would be that the main European nations would want to see "the Mediterranean trade divided between as few as possible," and thus would not "receive pleasure from seeing the American merchant ships navigating that sea without interruption."[55] Congress accepted these recommendations and granted the commissioners $80,000 for the negotiations. In his instructions, Jay urged the commissioners to use bribes if necessary, even with "men who may have no other recommendation than their influence with their superiors." He also drafted, at this same time, an obsequious letter praising the "noble" Emperor of Morocco for extending his "friendly regards" across "an amazing length of ocean."[56]

After sending these letters in March 1785, Jay did not think much about the Barbary Powers until October, when news arrived in New York from two sources that "the Algerines had declared war against the United States." In reporting this to the Congress, he commented that "this war does not strike me as a great evil." The war "may become a nursery for seamen, and lay the foundation for a respectable navy, [so] it may eventually prove more beneficial than otherwise." He amplified on these comments in a second, longer report. Since "this declaration of war [was] unprovoked, and made solely with design to acquire plunder" it would not "become the United States to answer it by overtures for peace or offers of tribute." To fight against Algiers, he suggested that every large merchant ship headed for the Mediterranean should be "supplied by the United States with military stores, and with money to pay men necessary to man her." Armed merchant ships were an interim measure; the United States needed a navy, and he urged that "five forty-gun ships should forthwith be built and put under the direction of a brave experienced commodore."[57]

Jay assumed, when he wrote this report, that the states would provide the Confederation the funds necessary to construct such a navy. He realized, within the next few months, that the states would not provide such funds, and so he changed his Barbary policy to fit the reality. Although Algiers was at this time holding more than two dozen American sailors as captives, and although he may have personally favored war, he now knew that the United States had no option other than to try to buy peace and ransom its seamen. He therefore advised Congress that it was "very doubtful" that the funds previously allocated for negotiations with the Barbary Powers would be adequate, "especially as the expense of purchasing peace will naturally be enhanced by the number and value of the captives to be liberated." Adams and Jefferson would need "further funds" for their negotiations.[58]

In May 1786, Jay received a series of letters from Adams, reporting on his discussions in London with the Ambassador of Tripoli. Jay must have smiled at parts of these letters. Adams wrote that "it would scarcely be reconcilable to the dignity of Congress to read a detail of the ceremonies which attended" his first meeting with the Ambassador; "it would be more proper to write them to Harlequin for the amusement of the gay at the New York theater." But the Ambassador's demands were serious: he wanted thirty thousand guineas for a peace treaty, plus the customary commissions and presents. And this was merely *one* of the four Barbary Powers; similar sums would probably be necessary for the other three.[59]

In his report to Congress regarding these letters, Jay focused on the financial question. He doubted whether Congress could borrow the necessary funds in Europe. But even if it could, he advised that Congress should not borrow, since a government "should never attempt a loan without having previously formed and arranged adequate funds for its discharge." The "federal government in its present state is rather paternal and persuasive, than coercive and efficient." Instead of borrowing money first, and finding money from the states later, he suggested "that a fair and accurate state of the matter should be transmitted to the states," and that they should be informed that a substantial sum would "be necessary to purchase treaties from the Barbary States." He explained to Jefferson that the "national character" depended upon payment of the nation's debts, "and I for my part think national character of more importance, than even peace with those pirates."[60]

In October 1786, Jay learned of an unexpected American success with one of the Barbary Powers. Thomas Barclay, an American representative working for Adams and Jefferson, had negotiated a favorable treaty with the Emperor of Morocco. When the signed treaty itself finally arrived, it fully confirmed the early reports. Morocco promised not to attack American ships, indeed promised to assist American ships in distress, and to open its ports to American merchant ships on a "most favored nation" basis. Best of all, perhaps, the treaty did not require any "peace payments" from the United States. Jay strongly recommended that Congress approve the treaty, which it did in July 1787.[61]

With the exception of the Morocco treaty, however, there was no progress with the Barbary Powers. In May 1787, Jay received a letter from Adams and Jefferson, reporting that "the article of money is become so scarce and precious" that they would "be obliged to suspend all further proceedings in the Barbary business, even for the redemption of prisoners." At about this same time, he received a proposal from Lafayette that the United States join a "confederacy" of western nations to fight against the Barbary Powers. (Jay was apparently not aware that the proposal originated with Jefferson, who for some reason did not argue for the proposal personally.) In his report on the proposal, Jay reminded Congress of his personal view that "it would always be more for the honor and interest of the United States to prefer war to tribute." He also reminded Congress that it could not raise the funds for a naval war against the Barbary Powers. Indeed, because of the "inefficiency of the national government" the "public revenue" was not even adequate for the "ordinary exigencies of the Union." It was with "great regret therefore that he is obliged to consider the motion in question as rendered unseasonable by the present state of our affairs." American seamen would remain in Algerian prisons for many, many years.[62]

In some respects Jay's years as Secretary for Foreign Affairs were not successful. Only two treaties were negotiated and signed during his tenure: one with Morocco, in which he had little involvement, and one with France, which was a success mainly because it improved upon the prior treaty. At the end of Jay's tenure, the British still maintained their troops and forts on American soil, the French still shunned American goods, the Spanish still blocked the Mississippi River, and the Algerians still held American prisoners. But one cannot evaluate Jay's work as Secretary without looking at the larger context, including the indecisive and often absent Congress, the limits on the ability of Congress to raise funds or enact laws, and above all the lack of American military power. As Jay observed to Adams near the end of the Revolution, "we shall always find well-appointed armies to be our ablest negotiators." Without either an army or a navy, Secretary Jay found it almost impossible to make any progress through negotiation. Indeed, one of his successes as Secretary was that he ensured that various crises did not lead to war, for war would have been disastrous for America at this point. He also succeeded in laying the groundwork for a stronger national government, which would in time allow a stronger foreign policy.[63]

Sarah Livingston Jay, by James Sharpless.
Sarah Livingston Jay was both a woman of fashion (a visitor observed that she dressed somewhat "showily") and an expert on politics (commenting on one endless debate that it was "fortunate for the reputation of the ladies that none of our sex are in Congress").

CHAPTER 10

Home and Society

DURING the first decade of their married life, John and Sarah Jay were often separated by his official duties; even when they were together, they were often in rented rooms or houses. Whatever home they had in New York City in the first few months of their marriage in 1774 was destroyed at some point during the long British occupation. When the British troops and their Loyalist allies finally left the city in November 1783, they left behind wreckage and ruins. Reconstruction had started by the time the Jays arrived in July of 1784, and they soon started their own construction project, their first real home.[1]

Jay hired Joseph Newton, an architect and builder; he ordered timber from his friend Philip Schuyler; and he confirmed with another friend, James Duane, now Mayor of New York, that his proposed plans would not conflict with city rules. The new house, when it was finished, was "a large square three-story house, of hewn stone, as substantially built within as without, durable, spacious, and commodious." The ground floor rooms were large; for example, the dining room was twenty-seven by eighteen feet. A grand staircase led to the upper floors, where there were bedrooms on the second floor and servants' rooms on the third. The rear of the house looked east over a spacious garden, extending almost ninety feet, and at the handsome stable building, which fronted on New Street.[2]

The Jay family, when they moved into this home in 1785, consisted of John and Sarah and their three children: the two little girls born abroad and Peter Augustus, now nine, re-united with his parents now after many years with his Livingston grandparents. Another son, William, was born in New York in the summer of 1789. There were also about half a dozen slaves and hired servants.[3]

John and Sarah Jay were at this time among the wealthiest people in New York City. Their home on Broadway was valued for tax purposes in 1789 at £3,000 and their personal property there at another £800. This was one of the highest valuations in the tax list. In 1790, when New York State raised funds through a loan, Jay subscribed for about $18,000, a substantial sum, but not as much as his friend Nicholas Low, who subscribed for $38,000. In 1785, Jay opened an account at the Bank of New York, founded by his friend Alexander Hamilton and others. Unfortunately, although the bank's surviving records allow one to see money moving into and out of Jay's account, the entries do not state for what purposes he withdrew sums ranging from a few dollars to several thousand dollars at a time. Jay was also a shareholder of the bank, owning about ten shares at a time during the 1790s. He was not an active spec-ulator in shares, like his friend William Duer, but he was also not an opponent of the emerging system of banks and shares, like his friend Thomas Jefferson.[4]

Jay's wealth was in part the result of his salary, several thousand dollars a year at this time. But even more important were the lands in and around New York City that he had inherited from his father or purchased on his own. Alexander Hamilton's son, writing many years later, said that Jay purchased lots in New York City "and as his means enabled him to hold his lots" this "speculation made him rich." Hamilton, by contrast, purchased lands in upstate New York, investments which did not appreciate during his lifetime.[5]

Wherever they stood on the scale of wealth, it is clear that the John and Sarah Jay were near the top of the social scale. Their position was the result of many factors: his prestigious government position, their combined family connections, and their tireless entertainment. Sarah's dinner and supper list suggests that they hosted more than two hundred different people in 1787 and 1788. Political leaders, foreign diplomats, lawyers, merchants, preachers, aris-tocrats, and democrats: they all gathered in the Jays' spacious stone house on lower Broadway.[6]

Often the guests were relatives. One evening in early January 1787, for example, John's relations at the table included his brother Frederick and sister-in-law Margaret, his first cousin James DePeyster (a prominent merchant), his first cousin Mary DePeyster Charlton (her husband John was the family physician), his second cousin Philip Schuyler (the general and politician), and two second cousins, once removed, John and Robert Watts (one a lawyer and the other a merchant). Sarah's relations at the table included her sister Susan Livingston and three of her first cousins: Walter Livingston, Philip Peter Livingston and Eliza Livingston. Some of the guests were connected with both John and Sarah: John Kean was a delegate to the Continental Congress and his young bride was the former Susan Livingston. New York did not have an aristocracy, at least in the European sense, but it did have a web of prominent families, of which the Jays were a key part.[7]

In May of 1788, Abigail Adams Smith, daughter of John and Abigail Adams, dined with the Jays. Mrs. Smith reported to her mother that "Mr. Jay is a most pleasing man, plain in his manners, but kind, affectionate, and attentive; benevolence is engraved in every feature." Mrs. Jay, according to Mrs. Smith, "dresses showily, but is very pleasing on a first acquaintance." As for the food, it "exhibited more of European taste than I expected to find." The other guests included Cyrus Griffin, President of the Continental Congress, and his wife Lady Christiana Griffin; the French minister Éléonore François Élie, Comte de Moustier, and his mistress the Marquise de Bréhan;[8] Louis Guillaume Otto, the French chargé d'affaires; Don Diego Gardoqui, the Spanish chargé d'affaires; Pieter Johan Van Berckel, the Dutch minister, and his daughter Miss Van Berckel; Sir John Temple, the British consul general, and his wife Lady Temple; General John Armstrong, a delegate to Congress from Pennsylvania; Arthur Lee, at this time one of the commissioners of the Treasury; John Watts, a prominent New York lawyer; William Bingham, now a delegate from Pennsylvania; and John Kean, delegate from South Carolina.[9]

In September of 1788, the Jays' guest of honor was Jacques Pierre Brissot de Warville, the famous French traveler. De Warville described Jay as "a republican remarkable for his firmness and his coolness, a writer eminent for his nervous [energetic] style and his close logic." Once again, there were about twenty guests at the dinner table, including at least nine members of Congress: Nathan Dane, Elbridge Gerry, Rufus King, Samuel Otis and Theodore Sedgwick of Massachusetts, Nicholas Gilman and Paine Wingate of New Hampshire, and Jeremiah Wadsworth and Samuel Huntington of Connecticut. The guests on this evening were mainly from New England, but on other occasions the Jays hosted leaders from other states, including James Madison of Virginia, and Charles Pinckney and John Rutledge of South Carolina. On some evenings, according to the list, the guests were only male, which underscores their political, rather than merely social, nature.[10]

When the new federal government was formed in New York in early 1789, George and Martha Washington naturally became the center of New York society. The Jays and Washingtons were frequently in one another's company. One evening in August 1789, for example, the Jays were among those who dined with the President; the company included John and Abigail Adams, George and Cornelia Clinton, and several members of the Congress. After dinner, and after the ladies retired, Jay "tried to make a laugh" with a modestly risqué joke about how the Duchess of Devonshire had left "no stone unturned" in her effort to get votes for Charles James Fox. A few months later, in November 1789, George and Martha Washington invited John and Sarah Jay to join them for an evening at the theater. Knowing that Jay was severe and reserved, and that theaters were often low and rowdy, Washington added that he would understand if the Jays declined because they had "any reluctance to visiting the theater." But the Jays were "honored and obliged by the President's invitation, which they accept[ed] with pleasure."[11]

For the years 1789 and 1790, we have a fascinating window into the Jays' reading habits in records of the New York Society Library. The library had about 250 members at this time, each of whom paid an initial fee of five pounds and annual fee of ten shillings for the right to borrow any of the library's three thousand books. The circulation ledger shows that, over the course of eighteen months, John Jay borrowed sixty-eight volumes, making him one of the most active members of the library.[12]

A few of the books he borrowed were biographies or memoirs, including Plutarch's *Lives*, Sully's *Memoirs* and Campbell's *Lives of the British Admirals*. Two of the books were early accounts of the American Revolution: *An Essay on the Life of the Honorable Major-General Israel Putnam*, by David Humphreys, and *The History of the Revolution of South-Carolina*, by David Ramsay, a member of Congress in the 1780s. Far more frequently, Jay borrowed travel books, including *Tour Through Sicily and Malta* by Patrick Brydone, *Account of the Pelew Islands* by George Keate, *Memoirs of the Turks and Tartars* by Baron de Tott, and *Travels in the Two Sicilies* by Henry Swinburne.[13]

Jay also borrowed at least nine novels: *Tom Jones* by Henry Fielding, *Candide* by Voltaire, *The Adventures of Peregrine Pickle* by Tobias Smollett, *The Fool of Quality* by Henry Brooke, *Adelaide and Theodore* by Madame de Genlis, *The Independent* by Andrew M'Donald, *Chrysal: or The Adventures of a Guinea* by Charles Johnstone, *Arpasia: or The Wanderer*, and *The Fair Syrian* by Robert Bage. Several of these books were somewhat risqué; *Chrysal* recounts how a coin is passed from pocket to pocket, including the pocket of "the most famous courtesan of the age" from which it witnessed "a scene too sensual for a spirit to describe." At the other end of the spectrum were moral works which Sarah probably used in her instruction of the younger children: *Moral Tales* by Jean-François Marmontel and *The Children's Friend* by Arnaud Berquin. She described the latter work to her father as one in which "the excellence of virtue and the depravity of vice is contrasted by examples ... in so natural and easy a manner as cannot but fail to impress the tender and uncorrupted minds of children." [14]

John and to a lesser extent Sarah found time to keep in touch with friends out of town and out of the country. When Benjamin Franklin returned to Philadelphia in the fall of 1785, John wrote a warm letter, saying that he and Sarah hoped that "the same kind Providence which has restored you to your country may long bless you with health and prosperity in it." Franklin returned an equally warm letter, saying that he was "now so well as to think it possible that I may once more have the pleasure of seeing you both, perhaps at New York, with my dear young friend, who I hope may not have quite forgotten me." (Franklin was alluding to Maria Jay, whom he had loved as a toddler in Paris.) Jay was pleased to hear of Franklin's good health, and his contribution to the Philadelphia convention in 1787. "I see your handwriting has undergone no alteration, and some who were with you in the late convention, told me that the steel was not yet worn off, but that you bore as good an edge as ever." When Franklin died in 1790, he left one final mark of his respect for Jay, naming him as one of the four executors of his famous will. [15]

From Albany, Philip Schuyler wrote to urge Jay to run for Governor against George Clinton. "Not only the lowest but the most unworthy characters are countenanced by [Clinton] and through his influence placed in offices of trust." Jay politely declined, saying he could not, "consistent with my ideas of propriety," leave the service of Congress at this time, that people would think he was quitting "for the sake of a little more pay or a prettier livery." Schuyler responded that his friends would know he was only answering "the general voice of that country disgusted and discontented with an administration ... which does right by accident, and wrong by system, which threatens ruin to the reputation of the state, and distress to its citizens." Jay was flattered but firm: he was not yet ready in 1785 to run for Governor, perhaps because he knew he could not yet beat Clinton.[16]

Another of Jay's main correspondents was his father-in-law, Governor William Livingston of New Jersey. Sarah and the children spent much time with her parents in northern New Jersey, and Governor Livingston wrote often to urge his son-in-law to join them. In February of 1785, for example, Livingston suggested he find "a leisure day or two to see three of the finest children in the country, besides making two very old children very happy with your company." In May of 1786, he asked his son-in-law to come and to bring along "some lobsters, and fish of any sort, but if possible, and at any price, a salmon." A few weeks later, in a similar vein, he said he would be glad if, "instead of the pompous train that usually attends the great in Europe, yours were composed, amongst any others you may choose, of a few lobsters and blackfish." Late in 1788, lying in bed with an injured foot, Livingston wrote that a visit from Jay "would prove more medicinal than all the prescriptions of all the sons of Asclepius."[17]

In November of 1785, Lewis Littlepage, the young man whom Jay had sheltered and supported in Spain, and who still owed Jay substantial sums, arrived in New York City. Littlepage was on his way from Virginia to France, where he was to pay the sculptor Houdon on behalf of Virginia for preliminary work on sculptures of Washington, and then to Poland, where Littlepage intended to join the Polish army. Perhaps concerned that Jay would try to collect the long overdue debt, Littlepage wrote a short note to him, saying that "every exertion has been made on my part to acquit myself of my pecuniary obligations towards you," and that "your reimbursement shall not be delayed longer than circumstances render unavoidable." Jay did not respond to this rather empty promise.[18]

A week later, Littlepage wrote to Jay in his official capacity, requesting a "letter of recommendation" from the Congress that he could present in Poland. In support of this request, Littlepage provided letters from Spanish officials commending has service in Spain. Jay referred this rather unusual request to Congress without comment. When asked for his views, he advised that Congress should not get into the business of writing recommendations. "Congress must look with an equal eye on all such of their citizens as may be of equal merit, [so] they should either refuse such favors to all, or grant them to all, who on equal ground may ask for them." But writing such letters for all who asked "would involve the necessity of frequent and irksome investigations of the real and relative merit of the several applicants." [19]

On the same day that Jay submitted this report, Littlepage wrote to him again, withdrawing his request, and asking for the return of his letters, since Congress was about to adjourn, and he was about to depart. Jay wrote back to say that he could not return the letters since they were now in the files of Congress. On this same day, apparently, he filed a private lawsuit against Littlepage for the thousand dollars. As was the custom when a debtor was about to leave town, he had Littlepage arrested, until he could post bail. Littlepage used some of the funds entrusted to him by Virginia to post bail and, since he would need these funds in France, he asked his friend Brockholst Livingston to provide a substitute bail bond. [20]

Littlepage also protested to Jay, saying that "the catastrophe certainly does honor to the plot, and however incomprehensible it may appear to the world, it is to me no more than your complicated character had taught me to expect." When Jay did not respond, Littlepage wrote again. "Before I proceed to the last extremity, that is, an appeal to the public, be pleased to inform me whether you choose to enter into a discussion more consistent with the character of a gentleman." Jay replied calmly that he was "not conscious of having intentionally committed a single act of injustice or dishonor in the course of my life." Threats to publish "operate on my mind like dust on a balance. Execute them; publish when and what you please." He explained that he had sued Littlepage for a simple reason: "to recover money you honestly owe me, and for which I am not to be satisfied with your assurances." [21]

On the next day, Littlepage published a long attack against Jay in the pages of the *New York Daily Advertiser*. He argued that he did not owe anything, since he had been a minor at the time that Jay had made the advances, and since Jay had made the advances at the request and on the account of Littlepage's uncle. Littlepage said that he respected "the servant of Congress" but "as a man, I pity and despise you." Jay perhaps thought that he was "above the opinion of the world, and secure from censure, under the mask of habitual gravity, and austere importance." Littlepage urged him to "reflect once more," for Jay was "by no means arrived at a period of life which inspires veneration." [22]

Jay responded at length in the newspaper of the next day. He said that he had always sought "to merit the esteem and affection of my fellow citizens," so that whenever "the propriety of my conduct may be arraigned before their impartial tribunal, I shall be ready to put myself on my trial." To refute the suggestion that Littlepage had no personal liability for the amounts in question, he quoted several letters in which Littlepage acknowledged his personal debt. To address the suggestion that he had failed to "support" Littlepage, he described at length their relations in Spain. In particular, he quoted Littlepage's letter seeking permission to join the Spanish army, in which he called Carmichael "a powerful and insidious enemy," and Littlepage's letter claiming that Jay had "left" him in Spain "expressly to be a spy" upon Carmichael. Jay hotly denied this "atrocious falsehood," and argued that Littlepage's "double game" between himself and Carmichael was as dark as that of Iago in the play *Othello*. [23]

Littlepage responded in the *Advertiser* a few days later, reporting that, in the spring of 1784, Jay was "more violently than ever prepossessed against Mr. Carmichael" and expressed his views "in the warmest language of resentment and jealousy." Littlepage also opened up for the public the dispute between Jay and Brockholst Livingston, claiming that Jay had boasted to him about the "parting blow" he had dealt Livingston as the latter left Madrid. Jay had decided to show his "want of confidence" in his personal secretary "by not writing in his favor," and by giving official letters to the care of John Laurens rather than that of Brockholst Livingston. A few days after this newspaper salvo, Littlepage boarded his ship and left for France. [24]

Although Jay's fight against Littlepage was not over, these comments started a new fight, between Jay and Livingston. Livingston, now a young lawyer in New York, demanded that Jay deny Littlepage's comments. Jay refused, but published a brief notice in the newspaper stating that "the motives imputed by Mr. Lewis Littlepage to Mr. Jay, for not sending letters from Spain to America by Mr. B. Livingston, are without foundation." His "family connection with Mr. Livingston renders a public explanation indelicate, and consequently improper," but Jay was ready to explain the matter to Livingston "in the presence of a few friends." Livingston reluctantly agreed.[25]

Livingston still owed Jay a substantial sum on the bond which he had posted to secure Littlepage's freedom and, when this sum was not paid, Jay started another lawsuit, this time against Livingston. In his defense, Livingston argued that he had served Jay faithfully as private secretary in Spain. Jay disagreed, in a statement apparently filed in court, saying that Livingston "did not behave properly in that capacity," that Livingston had insulted and libeled Jay even while serving as his private secretary and "enjoying the rights of hospitality in [his] house." He obtained a judgment against Livingston and pressed for payment. Hamilton, who was acting as Jay's lawyer, told Livingston that he believed Jay would accept a note, so Livingston presented Jay with partial payment and a note for the balance. To Livingston's "astonishment the money and the note [were] brought back." Livingston complained bitterly to his parents about the "the indelicacy which [has] been observed in every stage of the suit, of which by the by, Hamilton must be totally acquitted." Livingston's implication, of course, is that Jay could not be "acquitted" for his conduct.[26]

Meanwhile, in January 1786, Jay published a further response to Littlepage, a seventy-page pamphlet containing the whole correspondence between the two men, along with pointed comments from Jay. He sent copies of this pamphlet to many people, including Washington, Adams and Jefferson. When Adams wrote back from London, supporting Jay's version of the interview with Littlepage in Paris, Jay circulated this letter as well to a few friends. He apparently recognized that people would find it puzzling that he had responded in print and at such length to Littlepage. He offered two related explanations. First, he had to defend his honor. "I should have treated this attack with silent contempt, had not false facts been urged, propagated and impressed with industry and art, and which if not exposed and refuted, might have appeared after my death in the memoirs of some of these people." Second, in his view Littlepage had not acted alone, he had been encouraged by others, especially

French officials in New York. "The attack which produced that pamphlet, was not only countenanced but stimulated by some of the subjects of our good allies [the French] here." A foreign minister could not allow a foreign attack to go unanswered.[27]

Jay's friends generally accepted his explanations and indeed praised his conduct. Washington wrote him that "Littlepage seems to have forgot what had been his situation, what was due to you, and indeed what was necessary for his own character." Jefferson wrote that it was "really to be lamented that, after a public servant has passed a life in important and faithful services, after having given the most plenary satisfaction in every station, it should yet be in the power of every individual to disturb his quiet, by arraigning him in a gazette, and by obliging him to act as if he needed a defense." Peter Van Schaack commented that he could not "help telling you how much I am rejoiced to find that perfect consistency of character and propriety of conduct, which have distinguished you through life displayed in every part of this transaction."[28]

Van Schaack was correct that Jay's conduct was consistent with his earlier conduct. As in the case of John Kempe in 1771, or William Carmichael in 1780, Jay showed in late 1785 that he was sensitive to slights and not averse to a fight. But he should have reflected upon his position before writing for the newspapers. In 1771, he was merely a young lawyer; in 1785, he was the Secretary for Foreign Affairs of the United States of America. Perhaps his official position did not prevent him from filing suit against Littlepage to recover the debt. But surely Secretary Jay could have responded to Littlepage's newspaper article without naming Carmichael, who was at this time America's official representative in Spain. And he should have found some way to resolve his dispute with brother-in-law Brockholst Livingston short of public accusations and litigation. A few years later, during the 1792 election, Robert Livingston would accuse Jay of being "cold," almost "freezing." But as the Littlepage episode shows, on occasion Jay could be warm, even heated.[29]

Many of the founders were religious skeptics, especially about organized religion. Franklin believed in God, and believed that he should be worshipped, but rarely attended church, and expressed doubts about the divinity of Jesus. Jefferson praised Jesus as a moral teacher but did not believe in his divinity or indeed perhaps in any divinity. Washington attended church about once a month but would not take communion.[30] Jay, on the other hand, attended church regularly and clearly believed the central tenets of Christianity. When he returned to New York he returned to Trinity Church, the church where he had worshipped as a boy, and where his father and grandfather had worshipped and served. But he could not return to the particular *building* in which they all had worshipped, for it had burned down in 1776, and the congregation did not yet have the funds to rebuild. More generally, the congregation to which Jay returned was troubled, with its nerves still frayed by a battle over whether a Loyalist should be allowed to remain in the pulpit.[31]

In February 1785, Jay was elected one of the two wardens or lay leaders of Trinity. Although he was more often absent than present at the monthly meetings of the vestry,[32] he provided crucial financial support at this time for Trinity. In October 1785, James Duane informed the vestry that they could not pay the lease on the rector's house because of the "deranged state of the finances of the corporation." Duane reported that "the executors of the late Peter Jay," Jay and his brothers, were prepared to lend the church £1200 "at legal interest." The vestry gratefully accepted the loan. Jay also contributed to fund the impressive new church building. The cornerstone, laid in August 1788, bore not only the name of the rector, Samuel Provoost, but also those of "John Jay and James Duane, Church Wardens." In 1790, when new streets were laid out on Trinity land, they were named after Jay, Duane and the other lay leaders of Trinity.[33]

Jay was also involved at this time in the larger battle over the future of the Episcopal Church. In general, those from the middle and southern states favored a "federal" church, governed by American clergy and laymen, while those from New England favored an "ecclesiastical" church, governed by bishops properly consecrated in Britain. There was a real threat of a split in the church along these lines. Interestingly, Jay, who so strongly feared a split of the nation into separate states, was not so concerned about the potential for a split in his church.

In late 1784, the leader of the ecclesiastical faction, Samuel Seabury, was consecrated Bishop of Connecticut by several Scottish bishops. Jay remembered Seabury from the Revolution, when he had appeared before the conspiracies committee at Fish Kill, and he still disliked him. Moreover, he questioned the need for bishops of any sort, writing to Adams that he "did not consider bishops as very important to our salvation." In the fall of 1785, representatives of many states, but not New England, gathered in Philadelphia to discuss a new constitution for the Episcopal Church. Among other things, they drafted a letter to the English bishops, asking them whether they would consecrate American bishops nominated by the American church. Jay sent the letter along to Adams with a cover letter of his own. Early in the new year, Adams met with the Archbishop of Canterbury and reported back through Jay that the meeting had gone well. Sure enough, a cautious but encouraging letter from the English bishops arrived later in the spring. In May and June 1786, Jay attended meetings in New York City, at which the New York church suggested Samuel Provoost for consecration as bishop, named Jay as a delegate to another national church convention in Philadelphia, and directed the delegates not to "consent to any act which may imply the validity of Dr. Seabury's ordination."[34]

When he arrived in Philadelphia that summer, the national convention asked Jay to assist in revising their response to the English bishops. He prepared a draft overnight which was adopted the next day by the convention. The letter stressed that "we have neither departed, nor propose to depart from the doctrines of your church" and that the American Episcopalians were "anxious to complete our Episcopal system, by means of the Church of England." The convention nominated three ministers, including Jay's close friend Provoost, to become bishops. There was no hint, however, at reconciliation with Seabury and the other New England Episcopalians. Jay helped raise the funds for Provoost to travel to England, where he was consecrated by the English bishops in early 1787, then returned for Easter services in New York, and for a grand ceremony at St. Paul's Chapel in June, where he was formally welcomed as the Bishop of New York.[35]

Although he now had a friend serving as bishop, Jay continued to favor a strong role for laymen in the church. In October of 1789, as delegates were meeting at another church convention in Philadelphia, he moved at a vestry meeting that Trinity should oppose any proposal "that shall not give to the laity equal powers with the clergy in the making of all acts, laws, and regulations binding on the church." There was apparently a lively debate on this

Letter from Jay to Adams regarding the appointment of American bishops. A good example of Jay's penmanship and sometimes elaborate prose. "The convention are not inclined to acknowledge or have any thing to do with Mr. Seabury; his own high church principles, and the high church principles of those who have ordained him, do not quadrate either with the political principles of our Episcopalians in general or with those on which our Revolution and Constitution are founded."

motion and the issue was deferred for a week. By the time the vestry reconvened, news had arrived from Philadelphia of the compromises reached
there, which united the two wings of the American church. One of the
vestrymen moved that they should approve the new church constitution and
"any further measures that may have a tendency to cement the union which has
taken place in the [national] church." Jay argued that this motion was not in
order, but he was outvoted, and outvoted again on the motion itself.
Eventually, Jay reconciled himself with the compromises reached at
Philadelphia, which avoided a split within the church.[36]

Americans today tend to remember slavery as a southern institution, and to
forget that there were, in the late eighteenth century, thousands of slaves in the
northern states. At the time of the first federal census in 1790, there were more
than 8,000 slaves in Delaware, more than 11,000 in New Jersey, more than
21,000 in New York, and more than 100,000 in Maryland. Almost *forty percent*
of the white families in and around New York City owned at least one slave,
a higher percentage of ownership than in the "slave states" of Maryland or
South Carolina. New York's slaves were not only household servants: they
toiled in bakeries, breweries, print shops and shipyards, and above all in the
fields. One contemporary observer commented that, "in the vicinity of
New York, every respectable family had slaves, negroes and negresses who did
all the drudgery." Many people noted that it seemed that the Dutch were
particularly likely to own and rely on slaves. One commented that among the
"dull torpid Hollanders" even the poorest families "has one or two negroes or
negresses, slavery being as strictly maintained in the state of New York as in
that of Virginia."[37]

Jay grew up in a household where slaves did all the heavy work, both
outside in the fields and inside in the kitchen. It is not clear when he first
purchased a slave for his own use, but it was not later than December of 1779,
when he bought Benoit in Martinique. And yet at some point not long after this
Jay's views on slavery began to change. In September of 1780, he wrote from
Spain to his friend Egbert Benson in New York that:

> An excellent law might be made out of the Pennsylvania one for the gradual aboli-
> tion of slavery. Till America comes into this measure her prayers to heaven for liberty

will be impious. This is a strong expression but it is just. Were I in your legislature I would prepare a bill for the purpose with great care, and I would never cease moving it till it became a law or I ceased to be a member. I believe God governs this world, and I believe it to be a maxim in His as in our court that those who ask for equity ought to do it.[38]

In 1784, Quakers and others in Pennsylvania formed the "Society for the Abolition of Slavery, the Relief of Free Negroes, and Improving the Condition of the Colored Race." Perhaps inspired by this example, Jay helped to form in early 1785 the New York Manumission Society. Many of the others present at the organizational meetings were his close friends: James Duane, Alexander Hamilton, Robert Livingston and Philip Schuyler. There were others, however, whom he did not know as well, including several Quakers. The society at its initial meetings elected Jay as its first president and adopted a charter encouraging the manumission of slaves and the legal protection of slaves and free blacks.[39]

The Manumission Society almost obtained, within weeks of its formation, legislation in New York along the lines of the Pennsylvania model. The New York Assembly passed a bill providing that all children born to slave women after 1785 would be free from birth. The Assembly added, however, various provisions to limit the rights of free blacks, including one denying blacks the right to vote, and another prohibiting interracial marriages. The Senate then persuaded the Assembly to drop all but the voting rights provision. The Council of Revision, in a message drafted by Robert Livingston, vetoed the whole bill because of this amendment. Disappointed but not surprised, Jay wrote to an antislavery friend in England that it was "very inconsistent as well as unjust and perhaps impious" for men to "pray and fight for their own freedom" and yet to "keep others in slavery." But "the wise and the good never form the majority of any large society, and it seldom happens that their measures are uniformly adopted." All that men could do was "persevere in doing their duty," being "neither elated by success, however great, nor discouraged by disappointments however frequent or mortifying."[40]

Fourteen years would pass before New York, during Jay's tenure as Governor, finally passed legislation, which itself took many more years to implement, to end slavery in the state. In the meantime, the Manumission society had to be satisfied with partial measures, such as a law prohibiting the importation of slaves for sale in New York, and another law making it easier for New Yorkers to manumit their slaves. During 1786, Jay drafted a petition for the society arguing for legislation that would prohibit the export of blacks or slaves from New York. "It is well known," he argued, "that the condition of slaves in this state is far more tolerable and easy than in many other countries." The petition was signed by more than one hundred men, "a veritable who's who of the city's social, political and economic elites." A year later, Jay drafted another petition, this time to urge that the new federal constitution prohibit the import of slaves. Alexander Hamilton, who was in New York during a recess of the Philadelphia constitutional convention, apparently persuaded Jay and the other members of the society that there would be no point in submitting such a petition.[41]

The Manumission Society was active in various other ways: representing blacks who had to prove in court that they were free not slave; corresponding with similar societies in other states; and above all educating free blacks. Within a few years of its formation, the Manumission Society opened a school for free blacks, and over the next few decades this school and others sponsored by the society educated more than two thousand students. Many of the graduates went on to become leaders of the black community and indeed leaders of the abolition movement.[42]

Throughout the 1780s and the 1790s, Jay continued to own slaves: five at the time of the 1790 census and five (a somewhat different group) at the time of the 1800 one. They appear from time to time in his letters: sometimes almost as objects, other times very much as people. In 1791, for example, while Jay was in Rhode Island, accompanied by his slave Peet, the latter wrote a letter to another slave in New York. Jay asked his son Peter Augustus to have the letter sent on by one of his other slaves. If this was not possible, Jay urged his son to deliver the letter himself to the slave's master. "Providence has placed these persons in stations below us. They are servants but they are men; and kindness to inferiors more strongly indicates magnanimity than meanness."[43]

Jay is often termed an "early abolitionist" and sometimes an "ardent abolitionist." But Jay's views were far more moderate than those of later abolitionists, such as William Lloyd Garrison, or even those of radicals of Jay's own day, such as Anthony Benezet, a Quaker who argued that anyone who owned or traded slaves was involved in the sin of their capture and transportation. Jay presumably read and considered these arguments (we know that he knew Benezet), but he not only kept his own slaves, he also argued against immediate emancipation of slaves. The Pennsylvania law which inspired his famous comment about impious prayers was itself gradual; it did not free living slaves, but only promised liberty to those born after its passage, when they reached the age of twenty-eight.[44]

Because Jay and other New York leaders continued to own slaves, and favored only gradual manumission, some recent scholars have derided their efforts in the Manumission Society. One accused them of "receiving most of the benefits of slavery while avoiding the moral opprobrium with which transatlantic opinion was increasingly regarding slaveholders." Others have praised the Manumission Society and its leaders; one has called the society "the most effective single agency of antislavery in the state." In sum, Jay's record on slavery is mixed. He deserves credit for his public antislavery activities, which helped over time to end slavery in New York and other northern states. He also deserves blame for his delay in freeing his own slaves, for forcing them to earn their freedom over many years.[45]

CHAPTER 11

Federalist

A S HE STARTED WORK as Secretary for Foreign Affairs in late 1784, John Jay was hopeful about the future of America. He wrote to Franklin from Trenton that "the present Congress promises well" because there were "many respectable members," among whom "federal ideas seem to prevail greatly." A few weeks later, he wrote to Lafayette in similar terms, noting that "federal ideas begin to thrive in this city." In March 1785, he wrote to Ridley that, "although much remains to be done, yet we are gradually advancing towards system and order." Within a few months, however, Jay began to express concern about the Confederation, and soon his concern turned almost to despair. In late 1785, he wrote to Adams that "the federal government is incompetent to its objects" and that it was "the duty of her leading characters to cooperate in measures for enlarging and invigorating it." In early 1786, he wrote Jefferson that the Confederation "certainly is very imperfect, and I fear it will be difficult to remedy its defects until experience shall render the necessity of doing it more obvious and pressing." [1]

Although Jay often referred to "federal ideas," he was not in favor of a federation of strong states, but rather in favor of a strong national government. In one letter, he wrote that "it is my first wish to see the United States assume and merit the character of one great nation, whose territory is divided into different states merely for more convenient government and the more easy and prompt administration of justice, just as our several states are divided into counties and townships for the like purposes." In another letter, he wrote that he was pleased to see marriages between people from different states, since they would "tend to assimilate the states" and to make "the people of America become one nation in every respect." In yet another letter, he wrote that the new national government should have as much power as possible, with "the states retaining only so much as may be necessary for domestic purposes, and all their principal officers civil and military being commissioned and removable by the national government." These are remarkable statements, for they show that one of the leading Federalists wanted to see the states reduced to mere subsidiaries of the national government. He was thus a "Federalist leader," since that is the term he and his friends appropriated for their cause, and the term by which we know them today, but he was not at all, at least at this period of his life, a "federalist" as that term is used today.[2]

Within the national government, Jay saw a need for a strong executive and a separate judiciary. The "executive" at this time was only the President of the Congress (as powerless as when Jay held that position) and a few other officers such as the Secretary for Foreign Affairs. The only federal "judiciary" was the Congress itself, which wrestled with boundary issues, and a special court Congress had formed to consider appeals from state decisions in prize cases. Jay wrote to Jefferson in 1786 that:

> I have long thought and become daily more convinced that the construction of our federal government is fundamentally wrong. To vest legislative, judicial and executive powers in one and the same body of men, and that too in a body daily changing its members, can never be wise. In my opinion, those three great departments of sovereignty should be forever separated, and so distributed as to serve as checks on each other.

A few months later, Jay put the issue to Washington more simply and elegantly: "Let Congress legislate. Let others execute. Let others judge."[3]

One of Jay's key services to the nationalist cause was in discussing these ideas with the delegates to Congress. Because of the rapid rotation of delegates, more than 120 served in Congress at some point between late 1784 and early 1787. Jay met these men not only to discuss official business, but also over dinner, often at his home. Because the delegates wrote back and visited their own homes, these meetings in New York had effects far beyond its borders, helping strengthen the consensus that a stronger national government was necessary.[4]

Another of Jay's key services was in helping to persuade his friend

Washington to attend the Philadelphia convention. The two men did not write often while Washington was with the army and Jay was abroad, but they wrote often and at length in 1786 and 1787. Jay started the correspondence with a letter in which he expressed his concern about the "errors in our national government," errors which could "blast the fruit we expected from the tree of liberty." He reported that there was some talk about a national convention to revise the Articles of Confederation, although it was not clear whether "the people are yet ripe for such a measure." But if there was a convention, he was "fervent in [his] wishes, that it may comport with the line of life you have marked out for yourself, to favor your country with your counsels on such an important and single occasion." Washington wrote back that there were indeed "errors in our national government which call for correction," that it was "really mortifying" to see the new nation had "fallen so far." But "virtue," Washington lamented, "has in a great degree, taken its departure from our land."[5]

The two men were gentlemen farmers, so they wrote one another not only about politics but also about plants and animals. Jay sent along some rhubarb seed and asked Washington to report "whether it will flourish in your climate." He suggested that "our country would do well to encourage the breeding of mules, but the difficulty of obtaining good male asses, as yet much retards it." Since Washington had "one of the best kind, would it not be useful to put him to some of the best females now in the country, and by that means obtain a tolerable breed?" Washington responded that he had indeed "disseminated the breed of my Spanish Jack to many of the smaller kind of this country." If his friend had a female, "and should think the trouble of sending her here not too great, she shall have free use of the Jack," and he would "have great pleasure in obliging you." In drafting his reply, Jay considered a joke: "As yet we have no four-footed asses in this state, and I sincerely wish we could exchange some of the other sort for them; we might then obtain a much more valuable race of mules." He deleted this passage, however, and simply wrote to Washington about a society in formation "to promote the breeding of good horses and mules."[6]

In the summer of 1786, Jay wrote that "our affairs seem to lead to some crisis, some Revolution, something that I cannot foresee or conjecture. I am uneasy and apprehensive, more so than during the War." He had faith that "we shall again recover," and "become a great and respectable people," because Providence would not have so "miraculously" made the United States independent "for transient or unimportant purposes." He had little faith, however, in Congress. "Representative bodies will ever be faithful copies of their originals, and generally exhibit a checkered assemblage of virtue and vice, of abilities and weakness." Washington wrote back that "I do not conceive we can exist long as a nation, without having lodged somewhere a power which will pervade the whole Union in as energetic a manner, as the authority of the different state governments extends over the states." He, too, was worried that disorder would lead to some form of dictatorship. "What a triumph for the advocates of despotism to find that we are incapable of governing ourselves, and that systems founded on the basis of equal liberty are merely ideal and fallacious!" As for himself, he warned that "having happily assisted in bringing the ship into port and having been fairly discharged, it is not my business to embark again on a sea of troubles."[7]

Jay and Washington wrote these letters *before* they heard the news of the rebellion in rural New England, where many farmers, frustrated by high taxes, unresponsive legislatures and unfair evictions, marched on nearby towns to close down the courthouses. The authorities responded with force and a few of the rioters were shot and killed. Washington was greatly distressed by the rebellion, as was Jay, who feared that "our posterity will read the history of our last four years with much regret." To Jefferson, he wrote that "the government of Massachusetts has behaved with great moderation and condescension towards the insurgents, more so than in my opinion was wise."[8] ✓

In September of 1786, Hamilton, Madison and a few others met in Annapolis, Maryland, to discuss whether the states should have a uniform system of trade rules. Too few states were represented in Annapolis to do any serious work, but the delegates approved a letter drafted by Hamilton calling for a national convention in Philadelphia starting in May 1787. The purposes of this proposed Philadelphia convention would be far broader than those of the Annapolis convention: to consider measures "to render the constitution of the federal government adequate to the exigencies of the union."[9]

Now that a general convention was imminent, Jay wrote Washington with more detailed thoughts on what the new constitution should look like. In his view, it was critical to "divide sovereignty into its proper departments," namely a legislature, an executive and a judiciary. He then turned to the question of the form of these departments. Should the executive be "a King?" This was not an idle question: some people were seriously arguing that the United States needed an executive as strong as the British King. But in Jay's view this should not be tried "while other expedients remain untried." Rather, he suggested "a Governor General limited in his prerogatives and duration." As to Congress, he suggested that it should be "divided into an upper and lower house." The members of the upper house should perhaps be "appointed for life" and the members of the lower house elected "annually." He did not say much about the judiciary, other than to suggest that there be something like the New York Council of Revision, in which "the great judicial officers" along with the "Governor General" should "have a negative" on the acts of the legislature.[10]

In New York at this time, there was a consensus in favor of appointing delegates for the Philadelphia convention, but a struggle over the scope of their authority, their number and their identity. Governor George Clinton and his supporters were skeptical about the need for general constitutional change, and certainly did not want to see the kind of sweeping changes Jay and Hamilton had in mind. Senator Abraham Yates urged that the New York delegates should only have authority to consider proposals "not repugnant to or inconsistent with the constitution of this state." This motion was only narrowly defeated in February 1787. On the question of the identity of the delegates, Judge Robert Yates was a unanimous choice and Alexander Hamilton was a nearly unanimous choice. There was a struggle over the third member of the delegation, and by a close vote John Lansing was selected rather than James Duane. This assured that Hamilton's known nationalist opinions would be kept in check by two men committed to Clinton and to the current system of government. In April, Hamilton urged that New York should send five delegates rather than three, and argued that Jay's "acknowledged abilities, tried integrity and abundant experience" would make him a particularly valuable delegate. Hamilton's bill to expand the delegation, which would likely have resulted in Jay's attendance in Philadelphia, passed the Assembly but was defeated in the Senate. Jay was clearly entitled, by his national prominence and nationalist views, to be a delegate to the Philadelphia convention. But because the New York legislature wanted to send a small and moderate delegation, he was not among the delegates.[11]

Although he was not present in Philadelphia, many of the leading delegates were men with whom Jay had worked closely. George Washington was present in part at his friend's urging and he had in his pocket a copy of his friend's last letter on the constitution. Others at the convention included Benjamin Franklin (Jay's colleague in Paris), William Livingston (his father-in-law), Alexander Hamilton, Gouverneur Morris, Robert Morris and Rufus King (all personal friends and political allies), and Robert Yates (his colleague from New York convention days). Indeed, Jay had at some point worked with almost *every* important delegate to the Constitutional Convention.

At least two provisions of the Constitution were the result of suggestions by Jay. He had argued in his report on the British treaty that national treaties were "part of the law of the land" and thus "binding and obligatory" upon the states. The Continental Congress agreed and its circular letter to the states with this language was published in the newspapers in early May 1787. During that summer the Philadelphia convention (including many members of the Congress) refined and extended the concept. In its final version, the Supremacy Clause provided (and still provides) that the federal Constitution, laws and treaties "shall be the supreme law of the land," anything in state laws "notwith-standing." Jay's report, and the circular letter based on his report, was the most obvious and direct parent of the Supremacy Clause. From his perspective this was perhaps the most important provision in the whole Constitution; it would not only solve the immediate problem of states declining to honor the Peace Treaty, but ensure that national law would always prevail in a conflict with state law.[12]

In July 1787, midway through the convention, Jay sent a letter to Washington, suggesting that there should be "a strong check to the admission of foreigners into the administration of our national government" and a clause providing "that the command in chief of the American army shall not be given to, nor devolved on, any but a natural born citizen." So stated, his suggestion would have prevented Alexander Hamilton, James Wilson, or any of the many other prominent foreign-born Americans from becoming President. The constitutional convention adopted the idea, but modified the wording, to allow those who were citizens at the time of the adoption of the Constitution to serve as President.[13]

While the convention met in Philadelphia during the summer of 1787, Jay was generally in New York City. The convention's proceedings were secret, but it seems likely that he had some sense, from his many friends there, of how the discussions were progressing. In July, he wrote to Adams in London that "the public attention is turned to the convention. Their proceedings are kept secret, and it is uncertain how long they will continue to sit." In early September, he reported to Jefferson in Paris that the convention "will probably rise next week," after which there will likely be "discussion, debate, and perhaps heat." Indeed, the debate had already started, with some critics attacking the constitution even before it was published. In Jay's view, however, there was "a degree of intelligence and information in the mass of our people, which affords much room for hope that by degrees our affairs will assume a more consistent and pleasing aspect."[14]

On September 19, 1787, the Constitution appeared in a Philadelphia newspaper, marking the end of one phase of the process, the closed drafting session in Philadelphia, and the start of another, the nationwide public struggle over whether to accept and ratify the Constitution. This struggle is hard to imagine today, when the Constitution is enshrined in the National Archives Building in Washington, and copied in the constitutions of many other nations, but in 1787 it was far from clear that the states should accept the work of the Philadelphia convention. Many Americans feared that the powerful national government created by the Constitution would infringe upon their liberties. These people, soon known as the "Antifederalists," argued that the Constitution was defective for various reasons: there was no bill of rights to protect individual liberties; the President would be almost as powerful as the British King; the federal judiciary would disregard state practices and traditions.[15]

To take effect, the Constitution had to be ratified by at least nine states. Although any nine states would work in theory, in practice the new union needed the major states, such as Massachusetts, New York, Pennsylvania and

Virginia. To ratify, a state had to hold a special election to select delegates for a state convention, and this convention had to approve the Constitution. Thus, in one sense the task before Jay and the other Federalists consisted of several stages: they had to ensure that the state legislatures organized elections; they had to campaign to see that Federalist delegates were elected; and they had to persuade the delegates to these conventions to vote in favor of the Constitution. In another sense, however, their task was very simple: the Federalists had to persuade the people to support the Constitution.

As he read it for the first time, there were no doubt aspects of the Constitution which disappointed Jay. The Constitution probably did not go as far as he would have liked to take legislative authority from the states and give it to the central government. He was probably disappointed to see the requirement that all treaties made by the President had to be ratified by a two-thirds vote in the Senate. But Jay only hinted at his concerns in private letters; in public he supported the Constitution without reserve. He wrote to Adams that the Constitution is "much better than the one we have, and therefore we shall be gainers by the exchange, especially as there is reason to hope that experience and the good sense of the people will correct what may prove inexpedient in it." He wrote to Jefferson, who had more doubts about the document, that "the majority seem to be in favor of it, but there will probably be a strong opposition in some of the states," particularly New York.[16]

Hamilton and Jay and perhaps Madison discussed how best to respond to this opposition and agreed to work together on a series of essays. Interestingly, both Alexander Hamilton and James Madison attended a dinner at the Jay household on October 22, along with about a dozen other gentlemen, only five days before the first of the *Federalist* essays appeared in a New York newspaper. Hamilton's overture was followed, in rapid succession, by four essays by Jay, then four by Hamilton, then Madison's famous tenth essay, and so on. All of the essays appeared under a common name, Publius, and the identity of the authors was, for at least the first few months, a closely kept secret. At about the time that Madison's first essay appeared, Jay fell ill, and remained so for many weeks. Jay's illness is the explanation usually offered for why he contributed only five essays to the series, the four that appeared in October and

November 1787 and one that appeared in March 1788. But Jay's health is only a partial explanation, because by February he was again able to handle his work as Secretary for Foreign Affairs. It seems more likely that he realized at that time that Hamilton and Madison had the *Federalist* project well in hand, and decided to focus his own efforts on a different kind of essay.[17]

In the first of his *Federalist* essays, Jay stressed the importance of keeping the states and regions together in one union. Like a lawyer writing a brief, he started with a question: "whether it would conduce more to the interest of the people of America that they should, to all general purposes, be one nation, under one federal government, than that they should divide themselves into separate confederacies, and give to the head of each, the same kind of powers which they are advised to place in one national government." As in most briefs, the question was somewhat unfair, since most Antifederalists were not arguing that the United States should split into separate sections. But it was a key argument of Jay and other Federalists that rejection of the Constitution would *inevitably* lead to such a division.[18]

Jay then described and praised the American union in a passage worth quoting at some length:

It has often given me pleasure to observe, that independent America was not composed of detached and distant territories, but that one connected, fertile, wide-spreading country was the portion of our western sons of liberty. Providence has in a particular manner blessed it with a variety of soils and productions, and watered it with innumerable streams, for the delight and accommodation of its inhabitants ... With equal pleasure I have as often taken notice that Providence has been pleased to give this one connected country to one united people, a people descended from the same ancestors, speaking the same language, professing the same religion, attached to the same principles of government, very similar in their manners and customs, and who, by their joint counsels, arms and efforts, fighting side by side throughout a long and bloody war, have nobly established their general liberty and independence. This country and this people seem to have been made for each other, and it appears as if it was the design of Providence that an inheritance so proper and convenient for a band of brethren, united to each other by the strongest ties, should never be split into a number of unsocial, jealous and alien sovereignties.

The passage was not completely accurate as description: Jay knew well that Americans were descended from various ancestors and practiced various religions. But Jay's purpose was not description but *persuasion*: he was using religious and revolutionary images to persuade reluctant voters.[19]

In his next essay, number three, Jay again started with a slanted question: "whether the people are not right in their opinion that a cordial union, under an efficient national government, affords them the best security that can be devised against hostilities from abroad." The most legitimate reasons for war, he noted, were violations of treaties, violations of "the laws of nations," and "direct violence." He saw several reasons why a united America would be better able to avoid violations of treaties or international law. First, a single national government would attract "the best men in the country," since a "more general and extensive reputation" would be necessary to be elected or selected to serve there. Second, a single federal judiciary would resolve questions of international law "in one sense." Third, the national government was less likely than the states to be tempted from the path of "good faith and justice" in honoring its international obligations. Jay alluded here to the treaty with Britain, but did not develop the point at length, perhaps because he knew that many of his readers would find the idea of paying debts to British merchants distasteful.[20]

In the next essay, number four, Jay turned from just wars to unjust wars, for "nations in general will make war whenever they have a prospect of getting anything by it." He noted some of the current issues between the United States and other nations: the dispute with Spain over the Mississippi; the failure of Britain to evacuate the northwest forts; the tension with France over fisheries. Any of these issues might turn into a war, and for that the United States needed "the best possible state of defense," and that "depends on the government, the arms and resources of the country." It was obvious, he argued, that one American government, rather than several, would be able to develop and maintain the strongest armed forces. He asked where Britain would be if instead of having one army it had three: one English, one Scottish and one Welsh. Danger arose not merely from the weakness of separate states, but from the ability of foreign nations to play the states off against one another. Even if the states could cooperate against a foreign enemy, they would face the same questions which had plagued them in the Revolution: questions of command and contribution and coordination.[21]

In essay number five, Jay amplified on the parallel between the British union and the American union. He noted that it was only relatively recently that England, Scotland and Wales had become a united nation; prior to that the three parts of Britain "were almost constantly embroiled in quarrels and wars with one another." If the United States divided into separate states, they would "always be either involved in disputes and war, or live in the constant apprehension of them." The division Jay saw as most likely was between the North and the South. Jay feared that, as separate nations, these two would find more reasons for conflict than cooperation; they would "neither love nor trust one another, but on the contrary would be a prey to discord, jealousy and mutual injuries." These tensions would open the way for alliances between the separate halves of the nation and foreign nations, and then for conquest by a foreign nation. Jay lived long enough to hear the South threaten to secede, and he deplored the possible division of the union as much in 1825 as he did in 1787.[22]

In November, not long after writing these words, Jay suffered an attack of what was first diagnosed as tuberculosis and then as rheumatism. Jay was essentially incapacitated from the middle of November 1787 through the middle of January 1788, when he resumed writing letters, although he still complained that he was weak. In early February, for example, he wrote to Washington that "a constant pain in my left side continues" but that he was "happy that my long and severe illness has left me with nothing more to complain of."[23]

Although Jay was, from the moment he first read it, an advocate of the new Constitution, his support was not widely known in the fall of 1787. Indeed, in late November there was a report in a Philadelphia newspaper that Jay was "now very decidedly against" the Constitution, and called it "as deep and wicked a conspiracy as has been ever invented in the darkest ages against the liberties of a free people." This report was reprinted in at least a dozen other newspapers. John Vaughan, whom Jay had first met in Spain as an applicant for American citizenship, sent him a copy of this article from Philadelphia on the day it first appeared. Jay immediately responded to Vaughan with a brief letter expressing his strong support for the Constitution. After this letter was printed in the Philadelphia papers in early December, and widely reprinted, Jay's views on the Constitution were known.[24]

As 1787 ended and 1788 began, Jay could see both progress and problems for the Constitution. By mid-January, five states had ratified. Bitter debates were still under way, however, in several major states, including Massachusetts, New York, and Virginia. Indeed, in New York it was not at all clear that the legislature, dominated by Governor George Clinton and his supporters, would call an election to select delegates for a convention.

In early February, Jay wrote to Washington that New York had at last agreed to have a convention. "The opponents to the proposed Constitution are nevertheless numerous and indefatigable, but as the balance of abilities and property is against them, it is reasonable to expect that they will lose ground as the people become better informed." Washington replied that the recent ratification by Massachusetts would, he hoped, strengthen the Federalists in New York. For himself, he said, "I have never entertained much doubt of its adoption, though I am incompetent to judge, never having been six miles beyond the limit of my own farms since my return from Philadelphia." Washington was being too modest; he had correspondents in every state and was as well informed as any man on the progress of the Constitution.[25]

Jay's last *Federalist* essay appeared in the newspapers in early March. In this essay, number sixty-four in the series, Jay considered the provision which authorized the President to make treaties, with the advice and consent of the Senate. One of Shakespeare's characters argued that "there is a tide in the affairs of men which, when taken at the flood, leads on to fortune." Jay adopted and expanded upon the metaphor:

> They who have turned their attention to the affairs of men must have perceived that there are tides in them; tides very irregular in their duration, strength, and direction, and seldom found to run twice exactly in the same manner or measure ... The loss of a battle, the death of a prince, the removal of a minister, or other circumstances intervening to change the present posture and aspect of affairs may turn the most favorable tide into a course opposite to our wishes.[26]

Some Antifederalists had argued that treaties, like all other laws, should be made by the legislature, that is by Congress. Jay responded that these critics "seem not to consider that the judgments of our courts, and the commissions constitutionally given by our governor, are as valid and as binding on all persons whom they concern as the laws passed by our legislature." There were thus many varieties of law, not all of them made by the legislature, and it was perfectly proper to assign to the President and Senate responsibility for this type of law. To those who argued that Congress should have the right to repeal a treaty, he responded that a treaty is a bargain between nations, that it would be "impossible to find a nation who would make any bargain with us, which should be binding on them absolutely, but on us only so long and so far as we may think proper to be bound by it." He had made the same point as Secretary for Foreign Affairs and would have occasions to make it again as Chief Justice.[27]

In mid-April, Jay was almost taken out of the constitutional debate by a rock thrown at a riot. For many months, there had been protests in New York City that doctors and medical students were robbing graves to obtain cadavers for dissection. The protests took fire when a boy saw a discarded limb through the window of a hospital. A crowd stormed the hospital, wrecked the dissection room, and captured several medical students. The crowd later released the students to Mayor Duane, who put them in the city jail that night for their own protection. On the next afternoon, however, a far larger crowd gathered around the jail, which they threatened to attack to get at the students. Jay learned of the threat when his friend Matthew Clarkson burst into the Jays' home and shouted for a sword. According to Sarah, her husband "ran up stairs and handing General Clarkson one sword, to my great concern armed himself with another, and went towards the jail." There they found Governor Clinton, General Von Steuben, and a handful of militiamen defending the jail against an angry mob. The defenders were "bombarded with rocks and brickbats," one of which struck Jay on the forehead, and he dropped to the ground. At about this point, the militia opened fire and killed at least three people. The crowd fled. Jay was taken by his friends first to the nearby poorhouse and then to his home. Sarah was appalled to see her husband returning "with two large holes in his forehead" and feared that some permanent damage might have been done. The family doctor dressed the wound and gave him a strong sleeping potion. He was in bed for several days with black and swollen eyes and "vast pain from his neck and shoulders."[28]

While Jay was still recuperating at home, his unsigned *Address to the People of the State of New York* appeared as a pamphlet. The *Address* was a long essay, about as long as all Jay's *Federalist* essays put together. The *Address* did not focus on particular provisions of the Constitution, but rather on the general political situation, in language aimed at the average reader. Jay once again used rhetorical questions to make his points: whether it was likely that a second convention could devise a better Constitution and "what would be our situation if, after rejecting this [Constitution], all our efforts to obtain a better should prove fruitless?" He answered his own questions: the present Constitution was a careful compromise, devised by America's best men, and now approved by several states. A second convention would likely reflect "the same party views, and the same distrusts and jealousies," that raged in the current debate over the Constitution. He closed with another plea for unity:

> Consider then, how weighty and how many considerations advise and persuade the People of America to remain in the safe and easy path of Union; to continue to move and act as they hitherto have done, as a *Band of Brothers*; to have confidence in themselves and in one another; and since all cannot see with the same eyes, at least to give the proposed Constitution a fair trial, and to mend it as time, occasion and experience may dictate.[29]

This *Address* was the single most persuasive paper in the blizzard of paper produced in New York about the Constitution. One contemporary observer wrote that it had a "most astonishing influence in converting Antifederalists, to a knowledge and belief that the new Constitution was their only political salvation." Another wrote that the pamphlet has "operated very forcibly on the minds of the people here." Washington, to whom Jay sent a copy, found that the "good sense, forcible observations, temper and moderation with which it is written cannot fail, I should think, of making a serious impression even upon the Antifederal mind." Several people tried to persuade Jay to acknowledge that he was the author of the pamphlet. Vaughan wrote from Philadelphia that Franklin, who recognized Jay's style, said that he should put his name on it "to give it additional weight at this awful crisis." Jay replied that, in spite of his "habitual respect for the sentiments of Dr. Franklin," he was inclined to let the pamphlet speak for itself.[30]

On the eve of the New York election, in late April, Jay wrote Washington that the Constitution "still continues to cause great party zeal and ferment, and the opposition is yet so formidable that the issue appears problematical."

Jay's name was at the head of the Federalist list of delegates in New York City, and, given the strong Federalist majority there, he was probably in little doubt about his own election. He had no way of knowing, however, how the voting would go outside New York City. A month later, as the results were still being counted, he wrote Washington again. "There is much reason to believe that the majority of the convention of this state will be composed of Antifederal characters; but it is doubtful whether the leaders will be able to govern the party. Many in the opposition are friends to Union and mean well, but their principal leaders are very far from being solicitous about the fate of the Union." He already realized that he would face an Antifederal majority at the convention in Poughkeepsie and that his task would be to pry individual "friends of union" away from their "principal leaders." He noted that the Antifederalist leaders hope to "reject the Constitution with as little debate and as much speed as can be." Conversely, the Federalists would try to prolong the discussion, to await news from other states, hopefully positive news. An "idea has taken air, that the southern part of the state will at all events adhere to the Union and if necessary to that end seek a separation from the northern." This "idea" would become one of the Federalists' key arguments in Poughkeepsie. In short, even before the election results were announced, Jay was developing his strategy for the convention.[31]

When the election results were announced, the Federalists had won overwhelming majorities in New York City. Jay himself received votes from all but about one hundred of the three thousand men who voted in the city. But elsewhere in the state, the Federalists were handily defeated. Of the sixty-five delegates elected for the convention, only nineteen were Federalists, giving the Antis a better than two-to-one voting majority.[32]

On June 14, 1788, accompanied by a cheering crowd and booming cannon, Jay and the other Federalist delegates boarded sloops to go up the Hudson River. Poughkeepsie was at this time only a village, with a population of less than three thousand. Its main qualifications to serve as the seat of this important convention were its location, about halfway between New York City and Albany, and its new courthouse, completed only the year before. The courthouse had a first floor room large enough for the delegates and about two hundred spectators. Most of the Federalist delegates roomed at Hendrickson's Inn; most of the Antifederalists lodged at Poole's Inn.[33]

The Federalist delegates included John Jay, Alexander Hamilton, Robert Livingston (New York's Chancellor), Richard Morris (Chief Justice of the New York State Supreme Court), and James Duane (Mayor of New York City). These delegates were prominent, prosperous men, mainly from New York City and the surrounding southern counties. On the Antifederalist side, there was only one man of similar prestige: George Clinton, the Revolutionary War hero and long-serving Governor. Most of the other Antifederalists were from the rural, northern counties; many of them were state legislators or small-town lawyers.[34]

Jay knew every member of the small Federalist delegation. But he also knew, and this was to prove far more important, many members of the Antifederalist delegation. Jay had worked with George Clinton, his brother James Clinton and their brother-in-law Christopher Tappen during the war on the committee to obstruct the Hudson River. He had worked with Melancton Smith during the war on the conspiracies committee and more recently in the Manumission Society. He had worked closely with Robert Yates in drafting the New York constitution. Many of these men, within the past few years, had been dinner guests at the Jays' home on Broadway in New York City. In short, Jay had good personal relations with the "other side" even before he arrived in Poughkeepsie.[35]

In their first few days of work, the delegates at Poughkeepsie elected Governor Clinton as their president and various other men as officers and adopted a set of rules to govern their deliberations. The substantive discussion started on the third day, with a long speech from Chancellor Robert Livingston, who urged the delegates to consider not their personal parochial interests but the interests of the state and nation as a whole. Livingston moved that the Constitution be reviewed and discussed section by section, and that no votes be taken until the whole Constitution had been reviewed. A newspaper reported that, "after the Chancellor had concluded, Mr. Jay arose, commanding pleasure and satisfaction; and no doubt, he spoke convincingly on the points he raised ... Fancy, passion, in short everything that makes an orator, he is stranger to; and yet none who hear but are pleased with him, and captivated beyond expression." What the Federalists needed at this stage was time: time to learn of the results of the conventions in New Hampshire and Virginia, either of which might provide the crucial ninth vote in favor of ratification, and time to talk with the Antifederalist delegates one by one.[36]

Livingston's motion passed, with the proviso that amendments could be raised and discussed at any time. John wrote home to Sarah that so far the "debates have been temperate and inoffensive to either party. The opposition to the proposed Constitution seems formidable, though more so from numbers than other considerations. What the event will be is uncertain." Hamilton wrote to Madison, at the Virginia convention, that "there is every appearance that a full discussion will take place, which will keep us together at least a fortnight." Jay and his friends now started "singling out the members in opposition (when out of convention) and conversing with them on the subject" of the Constitution. According to one Antifederalist observer, Jay was particularly dangerous: his "manners and mode of address would probably do much mischief, were the members not as firm as they are." Hamilton was not nearly so effective. "You would be surprised," wrote the same observer, "did you not know the man, what an amazing Republican Hamilton wishes to make himself be considered. *But he is known.*"[37]

The convention began to discuss the Constitution clause by clause. There was an extended debate about the proposed ratio of representation in the House of Representatives, with no more than one member for every 30,000 persons. Jay rose near the end of this debate to emphasize the differences between a state legislature, which would consider "innumerable things of small moment," and the national legislature, which would consider national and international issues. Perhaps more important than his arguments was his conciliatory, compromising tone. This was an issue on which "much may be rationally said on both sides" and "gentlemen ought not to be very strenuous on such points." The delegates "did not come here to carry points. If the gentleman will convince me I am wrong, I will submit."[38]

On June 24, news arrived in Poughkeepsie that New Hampshire had ratified the Constitution. New Hampshire was the ninth state to ratify, so this meant that the Constitution would take effect, although perhaps without some states, such as New York and Virginia, which were still holding their conventions, or

Rhode Island, which had not even called a convention. The Federalists in
Poughkeepsie had hoped that the news from New Hampshire would weaken
the Antis, but at least at first it did not seem to have much effect. Governor
Clinton wrote to a friend that the "Antis are firm and I hope and believe will
remain so to the end." On the next day, as the convention continued to discuss
the provisions regarding Congress, Jay defended the provision giving
Congress the power to set the time and manner of federal elections, which he
viewed as essential to "prevent the dissolution of the union" if one or more
states "by design or accident" should fail to choose a senator or representatives.
In his view, once it was part of the union, no state had the right to secede from
it.[39]

Jay wrote to Washington in late June to report that, in his view, all the
speeches in Poughkeepsie were not having much effect: "there is no reason to
think that either party has made much impression on the other." He also
reported on the results of his own quiet conversations with the Antifederalists:

> The greater number are, I believe, averse to a vote of rejection – some would be
> content with recommendatory amendments – others wish for explanatory ones to
> settle constructions which they think doubtful – others would not be satisfied with
> less than absolute and previous amendments; and I am mistaken if there be not a few
> who prefer a separation from the union to any national government whatever ... The
> accession of New Hampshire does good – and that of Virginia would do more.[40]

On the first of July, Jay opposed an amendment to limit the ability of the
national government to impose direct taxes or excises. It was clear, in his view,
"that a government which was to accomplish national purposes should
command the national resources." He rejected the idea that the states should
have any choice in paying national taxes; the "danger" of this approach "had
already been fully illustrated" in the Confederation. He argued again that
Congress would know more than enough about the situation in the various
states to impose fair, national legislation. "For example, what difficulty or
partiality would there be in the operation of a tax of twenty shillings on all
coaches?" Jay also opposed an amendment which would have required that nine
states approve any federal debt, an early predecessor of the balanced budget
amendments which have received attention in recent years. He was concerned
that "factions" might prevent the federal government from obtaining a loan

"when the exigencies of the state required it or when it would be for the public good." Would it make sense, he asked, to allow the western states to prevent the national government from taking out war loans to support a war to defend the Atlantic states? Noting the small number of Senators, he asked whether it was wise to "put it in the power of five men to disarm a continent?" [41]

On the next day, a rider galloped up to the court house, threw his reins to a boy standing at the door, and handed to the doorkeeper the news that Virginia had ratified the Constitution. Governor Clinton was speaking at the time, but there was "such a buzz through the house, that little of his Excellency's speech was heard." The Federalists cheered, and a Federalist crowd held an impromptu parade around the courthouse. As with the news from New Hampshire, the Antifederalists initially pretended that the news from Virginia did not matter. Virginia might have decided to join the new government, but that did not mean that New York had to do so, at least without some prior changes to the Constitution. The Federalists, however, promptly changed their tactics. Instead of debating every point, they let the Antifederalists introduce their amendments without opposition. As one newspaper put it, since the Federalists had found "the powers of eloquence and argument are unavailing," they would now "refrain from any further exertions in defense of the Constitution." [42]

The convention recessed on the Fourth of July so that all the delegates could celebrate the national holiday. John wrote home to Sarah that, although there were two tables, one for Federalists and one for Antifederalists, the "two parties mingled at each table, and the toasts (of which each had copies) were communicated by the sound of the drum and accompanied by the discharge of cannon." The convention finished its line by line review of the Constitution a few days later, and there was a brief lull while the Antifederalists discussed among themselves how best to frame their amendments. Which of the amendments should be conditions and which merely recommendations? Should the conditional amendments be "conditions precedent" – so that New York's ratification would not take effect until the Constitution was amended as provided – or "conditions subsequent" – so that New York's ratification would take effect but New York could withdraw if the amendments were not adopted within a set time? [43]

Jay reported to Washington that Virginia's ratification had "disappointed the expectations of the opposition here, which nevertheless continues pertinacious. The unanimity of the southern district, and their apparent determination to continue under the wings of the union party, operates powerfully on the minds of the opposite party." Jay was no doubt raising this possibility of internal secession with Antifederalist delegates as well as with Washington, hoping that the prospect of losing New York City would lead them to ratify the Constitution. He also noted that the Antifederalist party "begins to divide in their opinions." This was what he had hoped for: that he would be able to pry *some* Antifederalists away from their leaders and thereby secure *some* form of ratification.[44]

John Lansing, on behalf of the Antifederalists, presented their amendments in three groups: conditional, explanatory, and recommendatory. Lansing suggested that an informal committee be formed to review the amendments. Jay was named a member of this committee; Hamilton and Livingston, who apparently had made enemies during the debates, were not. At the committee session, Jay "declared that the word conditional should be erased before there could be any decision on the merits of the amendment." For New York to say that its ratification would only take effect after its "conditional" amendments had been accepted, when ten of the other states had already ratified the Constitution without any such conditions, would amount "to a virtual and total rejection of the Constitution." The Antifederalists insisted upon their conditions, and the committee disbanded without reaching an agreement. Jay reported back to the whole convention that the committee had been unable to reach agreement. He blamed the Antifederalists for "adhering rigidly to the principle of conditional adoption, which was inadmissible and absurd."[45]

On the next day, Jay moved that the Constitution be ratified, and that "such parts of the said Constitution as may be thought doubtful ought to be explained, and that whatever amendment may be deemed useful, or expedient, ought to be recommended." In other words, Jay accepted that the New York convention would recommend amendments to the Constitution, but he rejected the idea of conditional amendments. He spoke "forcibly" in support of his motion and commanded "great attention." The debate on his motion continued for several days, until Hamilton presented to the convention a list of thirteen amendments the Federalists would support as recommendations to the other states. At least one of them, if adopted, would have had an important effect on Jay's future career: it would have precluded a justice of the Supreme Court from taking any other office, such as the diplomatic assignment Jay later accepted. Now, however, Jay supported Hamilton's list, stressing that the Federalists "wish to accommodate."[46]

On the other side, Melancton Smith moved that the Constitution be adopted "on condition that" a second national convention be held to consider certain amendments. Jay opposed Smith's amendment, again arguing that a conditional ratification would mean that New York would not be part of the new nation. He asked the delegates to consider how other states would treat New York if it was not part of the nation; he hinted at the possibility that the state would divide on north-south lines; and he reminded them of the benefits of having the national capital in New York City. Above all, he urged compromise: "The door is open. Let us agree. *We* will have our Constitution and *you* will have your amendments."[47]

The Federalists now moved an adjournment, hoping that the Antifederalists, when they returned home, would find themselves under pressure to join the union. Lansing, for the Antifederalists, claimed that an adjournment would simply start another partisan newspaper war. Jay, for the Federalists, responded that, although an adjournment might "increase heats," it might not; it would all "depend on the temper with which we go home." The debate continued into the next morning, when Hamilton gave a long speech arguing that adjournment to confer with constituents was far preferable to rejection of the Constitution. The motion to adjourn, however, was rejected by a substantial margin.[48]

The debate turned again to the form of ratification. Clinton gave a long speech in favor of the Smith motion, which he said should not be viewed as a rejection of the new Constitution. But now Smith deserted his own amendment, and suggested that New York should ratify without conditions, but "reserving the right to secede from the Union if amendments were not considered within a specified time." Many of the Antifederalists did not like this form of ratification. One wrote that it "appears to me very little short of an absolute adoption." On the next morning, the convention met but almost immediately recessed. The Antifederalists, evidently, could not agree among themselves on how to proceed. Jay was one of the few speakers on that day: he noted that he considered Smith's proposal to be "less evil" than the prior proposals and that he would support "making it the basis to proceed on." That evening, he reported happily to Washington that the Antifederalists "seemed embarrassed – fearful to divide among themselves, yet many of them very averse to the new plan." [49]

On the next day, a Saturday, rather than take up the divisive issue of the form of ratification, the convention turned to the wording of particular amendments. Jay was quite clear that he was prepared to support amendments, as long as they were not conditional, and would not cause more problems than they would solve. For example, he was prepared to support an amendment allowing Quakers to avoid military service, but only if it was drafted so that it would not "comprehend every person who in time of war will declare they are [a] conscientious objector." In the end the convention reworded the provision. The convention sped rapidly through some important issues. It agreed, for example, to a provision barring suits in federal courts against the states, an issue which Jay would consider as Chief Justice, and to a provision that the "powers of Congress [may] not be extended by implication," an issue which would be debated in the government and the courts for many years to come. [50]

The debate on amendments continued day after day in the late July heat. At times it must have seemed to observers as if the Poughkeepsie convention intended to review and revise every aspect of the work of the Philadelphia convention. Smith proposed that the President be elected to a single eight-year term. Jay supported the amendment; Hamilton opposed it; and Jay said he would not press the point. Jay suggested that only natural-born citizens, and only freeholders, should be eligible to serve as President, Vice-President, or as members of Congress, an even more extreme version of the proposal he had sent to Washington a year earlier. The convention adopted a milder version of this proposal. [51]

The convention at last returned to the central issue of the form of ratification. Samuel Jones, an Antifederalist from Long Island, and occasional dinner guest of the Jays, now moved that the convention ratify "in full confidence" that there would be a second convention to consider amendments. Melancton Smith, another of Jay's friends on the Antifederalist side, spoke in support of the motion; he now believed that the best way to amend the Constitution was for New York to join the new government and then work within it for amendments. Governor Clinton said that "whatever his opinion might be" he was there to represent Ulster County and he would vote as he believed the people of that county would vote. Clinton was perhaps hinting to the other Antifederalists that they were free to support the Jones motion, if that is what they believed their constituents would want. The Jones motion passed by a narrow margin, including a few Antifederalists. Some of the Antifederalists had already "voted with their feet," leaving the convention, perhaps to avoid having to record votes in favor of an unpopular constitution. When one of the Antifederalists passed through Albany, on his way home, he was met there by other Antis with "great surprise and mortification." After the vote on the Jones motion, Jay reported happily to Washington that "if nothing new should occur, this state will adopt unconditionally." With customary caution, he added that the Antifederalists "mean to rally their forces and endeavor to regain that ground."[52]

On the morning of July 24, Jay told the delegates and spectators that he hoped the convention could now come to a unanimous agreement, so that the New York delegates could work "hand in hand" towards amendments. John Lansing, one of the ardent Antifederalists, moved a new form of ratification: New York would join the union but reserve its right to secede if there was no second convention to consider certain amendments within a certain period. Jay said that he regretted this proposal, which would divide the delegates again, for it amounted to a rejection of the Constitution. He argued that the Antifederalists should be pleased "because they have carried all the amendments" and the Federalists should be pleased "because we have adopted such measures as will bring us into the union" and both should be pleased because they would secure important amendments.[53]

To reinforce Jay's argument, Hamilton rose and read to the delegates a letter from James Madison, who opined that "a reservation of a right to withdraw, if amendments be not decided on under the form of the Constitution within a certain time, is a conditional ratification, that it does not make New York a

member of the new union." The debate continued all day, and it seemed that
perhaps the "hard" Antifederalists might have enough votes to force through
their "right to secede" proposal. On this critical day Jay spoke at least eight
times. He pleaded with the Antifederalists not to reject the Constitution; he
reminded them of their past work together on the New York state constitution;
he argued that the proposed right to secede made it appear that New York
did not trust the other states to treat its suggested amendments seriously.[54]

That evening, Jay drafted a short letter, to be sent by the New York convention to all the other states, urging them to call another general convention to
consider amendments to the constitution. The next morning, July 25, Jay was
the first delegate to speak. He did not, he said, intend to debate, because
"yesterday gave the fullest assurances that they meant to go hand in hand with
us." He then read out a "draft of a letter intended to be sent to the other states,"
a letter which explained that New York only ratified because it expected and
hoped that a second convention would correct the defects of the Constitution.
Several of the moderate Antifederalists rose to explain why they would vote
against the "right to secede" proposal. Zephaniah Platt explained that the goal
of the proposal was to find a way in which New York could come into the
union yet force a debate on amendments. Since it now appeared that the
proposal would not serve to bring New York into the union, he would have to
vote against it. The convention then voted on the "right to secede" proposal,
rejecting it by a thirty-one to twenty-eight vote, with several moderate
Antifederalists joining all the Federalists, and with at least four Antifederalists
no longer present. After some further discussion of amendments, the convention adopted the "full confidence" language by the same narrow margin. The
convention then appointed Jay, Smith, and Lansing to revise and refine Jay's
draft letter. The convention recessed for the evening, near but not at the end
of its work.[55]

Jay must have worked hard that evening, drafting, discussing drafts, and
redrafting. The surviving draft is in Jay's handwriting, with some editing by
Hamilton and perhaps one other person. Jay managed to sound both Federalist
and Antifederalist themes, so that both sides could hear their voices. The letter
started by stating that several provisions in the new Constitution "appear so
exceptionable to a majority of us, that nothing but the fullest confidence of

obtaining a revision of them by a general convention, and an invincible reluctance to separating from our sister states, could have prevailed upon a sufficient
number to ratify it, without stipulating for previous amendments."
Amendments had been proposed in several of the state conventions, and "we
think it of great importance that effectual measures be immediately taken for
calling a convention, to meet at a period not far remote; for we are convinced
that the apprehensions and discontents, which those articles occasion, cannot
be removed or allayed, unless an act to provide for it be among the first that
shall be passed by the new Congress." In its conclusion, the letter returned
again to the theme of union: "Our attachment to our sister states, and the
confidence we repose in them, cannot be more forcibly demonstrated than by
acceding to a government which many of us think very imperfect." On the next
morning, the letter was unanimously approved by the convention, and the
convention approved a set of amendments to be circulated with the letter to
the other states. The convention then voted, thirty to twenty-seven, to ratify
the Constitution. The convention was over; New York had ratified; the
Federalists had won.[56]

There has been a tendency, over the years, to give Alexander Hamilton the
credit for the Federalist victory in Poughkeepsie. A few days before the final
vote in Poughkeepsie, there was a grand parade in New York City to celebrate
the Constitution, the centerpiece of which was a float of the federal ship
Hamilton pulled by ten horses. In the mural at the Poughkeepsie Post Office, it
is Hamilton who shakes hands with Clinton while Jay and others look on. But
Hamilton himself conceded that his many speeches did not have much effect,
nor was he very effective in lobbying, because he was not particularly trusted.
It was Jay, well-known and well-trusted, who was most effective in the quiet
after-hours lobbying with the Antifederalists. Jay used both threats and promises: the threat that New York City would secede from the state; the promise
that the Federalists would work together with the Antifederalists to secure the
desired amendments to the Constitution. And it was Jay who, at the eleventh
hour, drafted the side letter which sealed the bargain between the two sides.[57]

John Jay returned to New York City, where in early August he received
a warm letter from George Washington. "With peculiar pleasure I now

congratulate you on the success of your labors to obtain an unconditional ratification of the proposed Constitution in the convention of your state." Washington had been very concerned that New York would reject the Constitution and indeed did not "see the means by which it was to be avoided." Thus, "the exertion of those who were able to effect this great work, must have been equally arduous and meritorious." [58]

Jay also probably heard that his colleague on the *Federalist* project, James Madison, thought the circular letter to the states had "a most pestilent tendency." But Madison was not at the Poughkeepsie convention, and he thus did not appreciate that, without the letter, New York would not have ratified the Constitution. Indeed, from the distance of Virginia, Madison probably did not appreciate that failure at Poughkeepsie could well have led to tension or even civil war in New York. Moreover, the letter did not lead, as Madison feared, to a second constitutional convention; there was essentially no desire to continue the exhausting debate once eleven states had ratified. The letter *did* help strengthen support for a Bill of Rights, which is today viewed as one of the key elements of the Constitution. Indeed it was Madison who, in the first federal Congress, put pen to paper, taking the amendments that had been discussed in New York, Virginia and elsewhere, and turning them into the Bill of Rights. [59]

By late September, Jay could report to Washington that "the opponents in this State to the constitution decrease and grow temperate. Many of them seem to look forward to another convention rather as a measure that will justify their opposition than produce all the effects they pretended to expect from it." In other words, the Antifederalists were still talking about a second convention, but more because they wanted to prove that they had not been wasting time in Poughkeepsie, rather than because they insisted on seeing all their amendments considered and adopted. [60]

It was at about this time that Jay and others realized that, although New York's ancient City Hall had sufficed for the Continental Congress, it would not work in its current form as the seat of the new federal government. The city government was willing to yield the building but not, initially at least, to pay for the renovations. Jay and others did not wait: they raised money themselves, "trusting to future legislation for reimbursement," so that construction could start immediately. It was a major construction project: as many as two hundred men worked through the winter, under the direction of Peter Charles L'Enfant, to expand the building, renovate the interior, and give it an elegant new façade. It was also, like many such projects, plagued by lack of funds: on the last day of 1788 Hamilton reported to Richard Varick (recorder of the City) that work was "nearly at a stand for want of funds" and pleaded for another thousand pounds from the City. It was not until early 1789 that the state legislature passed a law "to indemnify John Jay and the other citizens who had given their notes" to fund the construction. And it was not until a few days before Washington's inauguration itself that the "crowning glory," the eagle on the pediment, was installed.[61]

Everyone knew that Washington would be the first President, but it was unclear who would be the first Vice-President. James Madison reported to Thomas Jefferson in October 1788 that the main candidates seemed to be John Hancock and John Adams. "Mr. Jay or General Knox would I believe be preferred to either, but both of them will probably choose to remain where they are," that is, with Jay in charge of foreign affairs and Knox in charge of the army. A few weeks later, Madison sent a similar letter to Washington, saying that Jay and Knox "have been mentioned, but it is supposed that neither of them will exchange their places for an unprofitable dignity." If there was a contest for the position, Jay was not very conscious of it. In December 1788, when Abigail Adams came to New York to see her new grandson, Jay visited as well, praising the baby as "Grandpa over again." In the end, each of the electors gave one of their votes to Washington, so he became President by unanimous consent. Adams received the next highest vote total, thirty-four electoral votes, and thus became Vice-President. Jay received the next highest total, nine votes. He would no doubt have received more votes but for a dispute which prevented New York from selecting the eight electors to which it was entitled. In other words, Jay came second in the race to be the first Vice-President, a measure of the high esteem in which he was held at this time.[62]

As Washington was preparing to leave Mount Vernon for New York, he received a letter from Jay, who was distressed that arrangements had not been made for Washington's "immediate accommodation" in New York. "Permit me therefore to take the liberty of requesting the favor of you to be with me in

C. Currier, "A View of the Federal Hall of the City of New York as it Appeared in the Year 1797." John Jay was among those who provided funds for the conversion of New York's City Hall into the nation's Federal Hall. When Washington was inaugurated there in April 1789, the crowd on the streets below was "so dense that it seemed one might literally walk on the heads of the people."

the mean time; and if Mrs. Washington should accompany you, we should be still more happy." Jay promised that he would treat Washington "exactly in the way which if in your place, I should prefer," that is, "with a plain and friendly hospitality." The city government soon realized its mistake, and found a house for Washington, but it did not bother to find one for Adams, so he stayed for several weeks with the Jays. He wrote to his wife Abigail that "Mr. Jay, with his usual friendship, has insisted on my taking apartments in his noble house."[63]

In late April 1789, Jay was part of the official delegation that went across from New York to New Jersey to welcome George Washington and to escort him across the Hudson River to Manhattan. Washington entered a barge with a bright red canopy, and was rowed across the river by thirteen men in pure white uniforms, surrounded by dozens of other vessels, and serenaded by a chorus and musicians. As he alighted in New York, Governor Clinton and Mayor Duane, along with hundreds of citizens, welcomed him. It was not unlike the arrival of a king. A few days later, on inauguration day itself, the scene was similar. At about nine o'clock, all the church bells rang for half an hour, and the churches filled with people offering prayers for the new nation. Jay then took his place in the formal parade: a troop of men on horseback, followed by representatives of the Senate, followed by Washington himself in an elegant coach, followed by Jay and the other heads of federal departments, and "several gentlemen of distinction." When the procession reached the Federal Hall, at the intersection of Wall Street and Broad Street, Washington, Jay and the others went into the Senate chamber, where they found the members of Congress respectfully waiting. After some hesitation, Vice-President Adams informed Washington that he could proceed to the balcony to take the oath of office whenever he was ready.[64]

Washington went out, was greeted by the crowd, took the oath, and returned inside, where he read out his inaugural address. The words of the address were agreed by all to be eloquent, but the delivery was less than perfect. "This great man was agitated and embarrassed more than ever he was by leveled cannon or pointed musket," wrote one senator. "He trembled, and several times could scarce make out to read, though it must be supposed he had often read it before." When Washington was finished, all those present walked the short distance to St. Paul's Chapel, where there was another church service.

That night, many of the houses were illuminated with images, "the exhibition at the houses of the French and Spanish Ambassadors being of especial elegance." There was a "display of fireworks at the Fort" which "lasted for two hours and included rockets, wheels, tourbillions, fountains, serpents, cascades, and many other pyrotechnic devices." Afterwards, the crowd was so dense that Washington could not use his carriage and he had to return to his house on foot.[65]

It must have been a supremely satisfying day for John Jay. New York had ratified the Constitution; New York City was (for the time being at least) the national capital; and his friend George Washington was the nation's first President. Twenty years later, Adams would write that, in the process of developing and adopting the Constitution, Jay was "of more importance than any of the rest, indeed of almost as much weight as all the rest." This understates the role of a few other Federalist leaders, notably Madison and Hamilton. But Adams was surely correct that Jay deserved substantial credit for the federal Constitution. He helped form the consensus that strong national government was necessary; he provided several key concepts, such as the supremacy of national laws; he wrote powerful essays in support of the new Constitution; and above all, through quiet compromise, he persuaded the Antifederalists at Poughkeepsie to accept and ratify the Constitution.[66]

CHAPTER 12

First Chief Justice

NEW YORK CITY was filled, during the spring and summer of 1789, with schemes and rumors about who would take the senior positions in the new federal government. Some people suggested that John Jay might well become the first Secretary of the Treasury. James Madison wrote to Thomas Jefferson that, although Alexander Hamilton knew more about finance, Jay was "more known by character throughout the United States." But Jay himself discouraged such talk, saying that he had neither the "qualifications" nor the "least wish" to "be employed in affairs of that kind." Many others assumed that he would continue to handle the nation's foreign affairs. But the man best placed to know Jay's views, his house guest John Adams, thought he should become Chief Justice. Adams noted that although he had "long known and esteemed" James Wilson, an open candidate for the position, "if I had a vote I could not promise to give it to him for Chief Justice." Taking into account "services, hazards, abilities, and popularity, all properly weighed, the balance is in favor of Mr. Jay." A month later, the French Minister Moustier reported that it was likely that Thomas Jefferson "would become, upon his return, Minister of Foreign Affairs, if Mr. Jay obtains the post of Chief Justice, as expected." Moustier was pleased at the prospect, since he viewed Jay as difficult.[1]

When he finally had a conversation with President Washington about the issue, in early August, Jay said he would prefer the position of Chief Justice. It was not an obvious choice, since he had not presided over a trial, or indeed practiced as a lawyer, in more than a decade. But it was from Washington's perspective a very useful choice, because it helped him solve two other problems: Hamilton and Jefferson. Hamilton, with his energy, experience, connections and cunning, was the best man to head the Treasury. But the President could not give Hamilton responsibility for financial matters and then give Jay (a close friend of Hamilton) responsibility for foreign affairs. Moreover, if Jay handled foreign affairs, there would be no sensible senior position for Jefferson, who was packing his bags to leave France at this time. Jay had come to know and respect Jefferson through their correspondence, and he may well have urged Washington to make him the first Secretary of State. It is indicative that it was to Madison, Jefferson's closest friend, that Washington wrote immediately after his conversation with Jay. It is also indicative that, as soon as Jefferson landed in Virginia, Jay wrote to urge him to head the new State Department. "The changes in our government will enable you to employ in that department your talents and information in a manner as useful to the public and honorable to yourself as you have done during your legation in France." [2]

Jay was interested in being Chief Justice not only to help Washington solve his personnel problems, but also because he expected the new federal courts to handle important issues, especially international issues. The state courts were still not allowing British creditors to recover from American debtors. Jay feared that, if the United States did not honor this critical provision of the peace treaty, Britain would not honor the provision requiring it to evacuate the forts, and some frontier incident would lead to a war. From his perspective, therefore, the most pressing problem facing the new federal courts was to enforce the British debts, and thus prevent a second war. The federal courts would enforce the federal tax and revenue laws; many Federalists feared that some states might try to "starve" the federal government by ignoring these laws. The federal courts would also handle boundary and other disputes among the states; Jay knew from his experience with Vermont how bitter and violent these could become. Finally, although he knew that American notions of separation of powers would prevent him from being like Britain's Lord Chancellor, a member of the cabinet, Jay probably expected that he would continue to serve as one of Washington's key informal advisers.

There were other men who hoped to become Chief Justice, including James Wilson and Robert Livingston, and some had more obvious qualifications, such as long service as state court judges. Washington was aware of their interest and their qualifications but also of their limitations. Washington was keen to have as Chief Justice not only an eminent lawyer, but a man well known and well respected throughout the nation. Jay was just such a man, "known by character throughout the United States" according to Madison. Washington explained to Jay that "the love which you bear our country, and a desire to promote general happiness, will not suffer you to hesitate a moment to bring into action the talents, knowledge and integrity which are so necessary to be exercised at the head of that department which must be considered as the key-stone of our political fabric." Washington had to wait to formalize the appointment, while Congress finished work on the Judiciary Act, which formed the federal court system. But on the very day that the bill passed, in late September, the President nominated Jay and five other men (from five different states) to the Supreme Court. The Senate confirmed all these appointments in two days, apparently without debate. A few days later, Washington was able, "with singular pleasure," to send Jay his formal commission as Chief Justice.[3]

The Supreme Court met for the first time on February 1, 1790, in the Exchange Building in New York City. The ground floor of this brick building was an open public market, cleared for the day to keep down the noise, and the upper floor a courtroom, "uncommonly crowded" that day with state judges, members of the bar and others. The justices were not sure how they should dress for the occasion. Justice William Cushing arrived in New York with the standard judicial wig, but it caused such a stir in the street that he "return[ed] to his lodgings, sent for a perruke maker, and obtained a more fashionable covering for his head." Chief Justice Jay may have worn the "ample robe of black silk with salmon colored facings." in which he was later painted by Stuart.[4]

Unfortunately, only three justices were present, so there was no quorum, and the first meeting of the court ended after a few minutes. On the next day, another justice arrived and the court started to handle various administrative matters: appointing a clerk, admitting a few lawyers to the Supreme Court bar, and adopting its first rules. There were no cases to consider, however, so at the end of one week the court closed its first session. That evening the grand jury of the district court "gave a very elegant entertainment" for the justices at

Fraunces Tavern. The guests drank thirteen toasts, including toasts to the national judiciary and the Constitution, which they hoped would "prove the solid fabric of liberty, prosperity and glory."[5]

The justices had finished the first session of the Supreme Court, but they were far from finished with their duties that spring. Congress had created in the Judiciary Act a separate federal circuit court for each state. There was no separate staff for these courts; each of them was to be formed by two Supreme Court justices and one local district judge. Since each circuit court had to meet twice a year, at dates and places fixed by Congress, the six justices had to "ride circuit" twice a year. Given the distances, it was not be possible to return home between court sessions, so a justice would leave on a circuit and return several weeks or even months later.

The circuit courts today are an intermediate level in the federal court system; they handle appeals in cases that have already been considered and decided by district courts. In the early days, however, most of the work of the circuit courts was trial work: hearing witnesses, sifting through evidence, and deciding issues for the first time. There were thus at least two aspects of circuit court duty which Jay and the other justices did not like: it involved a great deal of difficult travel; and the legal issues were often fairly minor. Jay approved in principle of the idea of circuit courts, federal courts that were accessible to the scattered population and yet national in their views. But in practice he found the duties of a circuit court justice tiresome.[6]

The Chief Justice of the United States today has many administrative duties. He administers the court itself; he serves as chairman of the Judicial Conference, helping to set national judicial policy; and he is involved in the preparation of the annual budget for the whole federal court system. With the exception of the circuit rotation question, however, Chief Justice Jay did not have to devote much time to administrative questions. The staffing of the federal court system was essentially complete in September 1789, when Washington nominated and the Senate confirmed the first set of justices, district court judges, and federal attorneys. The annual budget in the early years simply provided for payment of their fixed salaries and fees. There were no federal courthouses to maintain; the federal courts met in state or city buildings or (if none were available) in taverns. There does not appear to have been much controversy over the rules of the federal courts; in many cases their "rule" was simply to follow the local state court rules.[7]

Before they set out on their first circuit tours, Jay and the other justices received letters from Washington, noting that they would probably learn things "which it would be useful should be known," and telling them that it would be "agreeable to me to receive such information and remarks" as they cared to send him. Jay also received from John Hancock, Governor of Massachusetts, an invitation to "take up your residence at my house during your tarry in town." He declined Hancock's invitation, and almost all other similar invitations, because he wanted to avoid the appearance that he owed favors to those whose interests, in one way or another, would come before the federal courts.[8]

In April 1790, Chief Justice Jay presided over his first circuit court, in New York City. With him on the bench were Justice William Cushing (whom he would come to know well through circuit travels) and Judge James Duane (whom he had known since their youth as New York lawyers). He opened the session with a lengthy charge to the grand jury. Today a charge to a grand jury is generally a dull recital of the details of the relevant criminal laws. At this time, however, a grand jury charge was a chance for the judge to discuss general political and legal principles. Jay began by noting that the people of the United States had been blessed with "more perfect opportunities of choosing, and more effectual means of establishing their own government, than any other nation has hitherto enjoyed." America was not only independent, and its population "enlightened," but it was large, which meant "that the personal influence of popular individuals can rarely embrace large portions of it." And the present form of government would be improved as "the good sense of the people" would "discover and correct its imperfections."[9]

It was now "very unanimously agreed" that the powers of government "should be divided into three distinct, independent departments, the executive, legislative and judicial," and each should be kept "within its proper limits." It was also agreed that a "judicial control, general and final, was indispensable" but the "manner of establishing it, with powers neither too extensive, nor too limited," raised "questions of no little intricacy." Although "carrying justice as it were to every man's door" was important, "how to do it in an expedient manner was far from being apparent." And it would prove difficult to "provide against discord between national and state jurisdictions, to render them auxiliary, instead of hostile to each other."[10]

Under the Constitution, international treaties formed part of America's domestic law. An international treaty, like "a fair and legal contract between two men," could not be altered or terminated by only one side. "We are now a nation, and it equally becomes us to perform our duties, as to assert our rights." His audience would have understood the implication; the United States could not expect Britain to observe the treaty of peace unless it also observed the treaty, and in particular the debt provisions. As for federal statutes, he stressed that the proper enforcement of the federal revenue statutes was "very essential to the credit, character and prosperity of our country." He was determined that the new government would not face the same difficulties which the Confederation faced in raising revenues; he would show no leniency on those who violated tax or revenue laws.[11]

In closing, he argued that it "cannot be too strongly impressed on the minds of us all, how greatly our individual prosperity depends upon our national prosperity; and how greatly our national prosperity depends on a well organized vigorous government, ruling by wise and equal laws, faithfully executed." Such a government is not "unfriendly to liberty, to that liberty which is really inestimable." Liberty "consists not in a right to every man to do just as he pleases." Rather, it "consists in an equal right to all the citizens to have, enjoy, and to do, in peace, security and without molestation, whatever the equal and constitutional laws of the country admit to be consistent with the public good." It was thus the duty of "all good citizens" to "support the laws and the government which thus protect their rights and liberties." Jay gave this charge at each circuit court session during the spring and then to the newspapers. It is one of his best political papers: looking back at the ratification debate and forward to the early national government.[12]

The first circuit court session in New York was not just ceremonial. The grand jury indicted two men for conspiring to destroy a vessel, make a revolt, and murder their captain. Although Congress had not yet passed a statute making these actions criminal, the lawyers and judges apparently accepted the notion that there was a federal common criminal law, based on the English common law. On the day after the indictment, the case was tried before a jury, the two defendants were found guilty, and each sentenced to an hour in the pillory, thirty-nine lashes, and six months in jail.[13]

A few days later, Jay left New York City on his circuit, and started keeping a diary of his travels. The first entry was simple and typical: "set out on northern circuit; lodged with my brother at Rye; cloudy and chilly." After a few days at Rye and Bedford, Jay headed east, but it "began to rain," forcing him to stop a mile short of Norwalk, at a tavern "which appears clean and the family obliging." On the next day, as he approached New Haven, "a number of gentlemen of that city met and escorted us to town." He opened the circuit court the day after his arrival, reading the same charge to the grand jury, and admitting several "counselors and attorneys." Over the next few days, according to the diary, the court issued rules of practice and decided various motions. These notes are the most "legal" of any in the diary; it appears he was trying to master the local legal practices.[14]

In late April, Jay and Cushing set out from New Haven for Boston. A spring snow storm held them back, so that they did not reach the outskirts of Boston until the first of May. They stayed the night with federal judge John Lowell, and the three men spent the next day together, with "much interesting conversation," which Jay thought "had better not be written." (Although one can understand his concern that the diary would fall into the wrong hands, one wishes that Jay had sometimes been somewhat less discreet.) On May 3, the three judges opened the Massachusetts circuit court, with Jay giving his standard charge to the grand jury. The grand jury, in its formal reply, said that it hoped "the judicial department will ever be filled, as it now is, with gentlemen of the first character for learning integrity and ability."[15]

A few days later, John wrote home to Sarah that, since the work of the court was finished, he would "have an opportunity of seeing whatever is worthy of notice in and about the place, unless the weather, which is now very disagreeable, should continue so." He stayed on in Boston for almost two weeks, met many people, and generally made a good impression. One of them wrote that "he is a plain dressing man and makes but a poor figure, being rather of a small size, remarkably thin," but went on to say that all "this proves the falsity of judging by appearances." Another noted that he so "delighted the people of Massachusetts [that] they regret that Boston was not the place of his nativity." From Boston, he rode north, stopping on his way to visit with John Quincy Adams, the future President, and "a number of gentlemen of the law." In late May, Jay and the New Hampshire district judge held circuit court in Portsmouth, but there was no work to be done, so that, after seeing some of the sights of coastal New Hampshire, Jay turned south for home. It took him a full week to ride back to New York City.[16]

The second session of the Supreme Court was held in New York in August 1790, again at the Exchange. At their session in February, the justices had agreed that Jay and Cushing would handle the eastern circuit, Blair and Wilson the middle circuit, and Iredell and Rutledge the southern circuit. This division made sense; each justice was assigned the circuit which included his home state. But the southern circuit involved longer distances, over more difficult roads, than the other two. Iredell, who had not been present in February, argued in August that the circuits should be rotated among the justices, so that the burden would be shared equally. Jay argued against rotation, saying that having different judges every few months would lead to different decisions on the same issues. Rotating justices would be inclined to defer decisions on difficult issues, which "would be absurd." And perhaps a partial reform, rotation, would prevent Congress from making a more complete reform, eliminating the circuit duties for the justices. Jay prevailed; the justices agreed to ride the same circuits in the fall as in the spring.[17]

Although the justices could not agree on the question of rotation, they did agree that circuit-riding in general was undesirable. Their concerns were not only personal; they believed that it was inappropriate for a judge to decide a case at one level (the circuit court) and then consider it again at the next level (the Supreme Court). In a draft of a joint letter, Jay argued that the arrangement was not merely unseemly, but actually unconstitutional. "We, for our parts, consider the Constitution as plainly opposed to the appointment of the same persons to both offices nor have we any doubts of their legal incompatibility." He circulated this draft letter to the other justices, asking for comments or corrections, but none responded, so the issue rested for the time being.[18]

Jay left New York in late September for Albany, which he reached after a week, and opened circuit court there in early October. Since there were no cases to consider, he "addressed the grand jurors very handsomely for their punctual attendance and discharged them." From Albany, he rode to Hartford, staying at inns of varying quality: "pretty good," "tolerably clean" and in one case simply "*bad*." In Hartford, in late October, Jay, Cushing and the district judge held circuit court for three days. One of the cases they considered was an action by British merchants based on a bill; the drawer and payee of the bill were from Connecticut, but the bill was drawn and dated in New York. The question was which law should apply; Connecticut law provided for interest at twice the rate of New York.[19]

From Hartford, Jay traveled to Boston, staying at one inn he termed "tolerable" and another he termed "dirty." After holding circuit court for three days in early November, he had some time to enjoy the town. He reported to his wife that "the hospitality and sociability of this place are singular." At almost every table, "you find a clergyman," but they were not "a check to the cheerfulness of the company; they partake in and promote it." A letter from Harvard informed him that the University had, at its June commencement, "conferred upon [him] the degree of Doctor of Laws," although the diploma was not yet ready. In a long letter to the President, the Chief Justice argued that the constitutional power to "establish post roads" implied the power "either to repair these roads themselves or compel others to do it." He was not only commenting on the atrocious quality of the roads: he was creating the legal basis for the federal government to become involved (as it would in later years) in building and maintaining national roads.[20]

Jay left Boston in late November for Exeter, New Hampshire, where he held circuit court with Cushing and the district judge for four days. When he returned to Boston, he had a letter from Hamilton, complaining about resolutions in which the Virginia legislature had criticized his financial plan. Such resolutions, Hamilton argued, were "the first symptom of a spirit which must either be killed or it will kill the Constitution." Should not "the collective weight of the different parts of the government be employed in exploding

the principles" of the Virginia resolutions? Jay did not think there was any call
for alarm, and in particular no need to involve the federal judiciary. "Every
indecent interference of state assemblies will diminish their influence. The
national government has only to do what is right and if possible be silent." [21]

He continued south to Rhode Island, which had finally ratified the
Constitution in May, and thus become part of eastern circuit. According to a
local newspaper, Jay's charge to the Rhode Island grand jury was "full of good
sense and learning, though expressed in the most plain and familiar style." The
paper reported that there were a number of cases filed, but "they were either
settled or continued, without a trial on the merits on any of them." This paper
exclaimed that at last "the mild beams of national justice [have] begun to
irradiate this state, and opened a dawn of hope for better times." He did not
reach New York City until the middle of December. [22]

Early in 1791, Jay wrote to his sister-in-law that his position "takes me from
my family half the year, and obliges me to pass too considerable a part of my
time on the road, in lodging houses and inns." The travel burden increased
for him in 1791 because the national capital moved from New York to
Philadelphia, so that he had to travel there twice a year for the Supreme Court
session. At the February session, there were no cases for the court to consider,
but the justices renewed their discussion of rotation. Iredell argued, in a long
letter to his colleagues, in favor of rotation. "I will venture to say that no judge
can conscientiously undertake to ride the Southern Circuit constantly and
perform the other parts of his duty." Jay responded that, although he was open
to a general review of the question of rotation, he could not handle any other
circuit this spring, since he and Cushing had "points of some importance
reserved on which we expect to decide this spring in the eastern circuit."
Perhaps Wilson or Blair might "be differently circumstanced," and indeed Blair
agreed to ride the southern circuit for that spring, allowing Iredell to travel the
middle circuit. Jay and Cushing traveled together back from Philadelphia to
New York, riding more than fifty miles on what was "said to be the coldest day
of the winter by some degrees." [23]

Sarah and Peter, now fifteen years old, accompanied John as he set out from
New York in late April 1791 for the eastern circuit. From New Haven, Sarah

wrote to the younger children (who remained behind with their aunt) that since "the weather was fine, and we were not hurried, we traveled leisurely, and have been very fortunate in putting up at good houses, clean beds and good fare." She described for them how, at one of the inns along the way, there was "a very pretty spring which the landlord has stoned round and put trout in, whom he keeps tame by feeding." A month later, John wrote to his nephew from Boston that Sarah and Peter were "well and pleased with the jaunt," and that they would join him as he continued on to Portsmouth and Newport.[24]

At the Connecticut circuit court, Jay and the other judges considered a case which presented "the great and much litigated question whether obligations in favor of real British subjects or those who had joined the armies of Great Britain during the war, should draw interest during the time the creditors were inaccessible by reason of war." The court ruled that the Connecticut statute, which prohibited British subjects from recovering such interest, was inconsistent with and invalid in light of the Paris Peace Treaty. It is hard to be sure, since there were so few case reports at this time, but this was probably the first time that a federal court used the federal constitution to override a state law. According to the newspaper, the "learned and ingenious arguments from the bench on this question were highly interesting and gave general satisfaction."[25]

In addition to the British debt cases, Jay and his colleagues had other work in Connecticut; "there were about forty actions entered in the docket, of which about twenty were continued, twelve passed into judgment, and the rest were amicably settled." In May, before the circuit court opened in Boston, there was an elaborate procession, including eight constables with staves, two deputy marshals, the marshal, the justices and district judge, and "barristers, counselors, other gentlemen of the bar and citizens, two and two." Jay, in his charge to the Boston grand jury, noted that there were apparently very few breaches of the revenue laws, and "he took that opportunity, to render to the commercial citizens, the tribute due to their patriotism, honor and integrity." He said that counterfeiting of U.S. government securities had "increased throughout the country, in an alarming degree," and urged the jurors to use their "utmost exertions" to check this crime.[26]

The Jays traveled north from Boston to Portsmouth, New Hampshire, where there was a circuit court in late May, and then south to Newport, Rhode

Island. In one of their cases at this session, the court invalidated a state legal tender statute on the basis of the currency provisions of the federal Constitution. A newspaper reported that the "court in the conduct of the business and in their decisions gave great satisfaction. Justice herself seemed to preside on the bench and inspire it." Jay, apparently without Sarah and Peter, then headed north, for the wilds of Vermont. Vermont had recently joined the union as the fourteenth state, and had thus become the sixth state in the eastern circuit. Jay arrived in Bennington on the last day of June and discovered that the district judge had not yet received his commission. The district judge could not act without a commission, and Justice Cushing had stayed behind, ill in Rhode Island, so there was no quorum. Jay, no doubt annoyed, returned to New York City, which he reached after about another week of travel.[27]

In August 1791, the Supreme Court met in Philadelphia and for the first time heard a case. They dismissed it, however, on a procedural point: the papers for the appeal had been issued by the clerk of the circuit court rather than the clerk of the Supreme Court, as required by the rules. The justices discussed the circuit-riding system both among themselves, and with President Washington, who needed their assurance that they would not condemn a new justice, Thomas Johnson, to repeated service on the southern circuit.[28]

At about this same time, Peter Augustus Jay entered Columbia College, the successor to King's College, which John himself had attended many years before. John advised Peter that those "who wish to write well should write often; and that consideration is one of many motives which induce me to request the favor of your correspondence." Two weeks later, he urged his son to "read more in detail the histories of the great men," and in particular Plutarch's brief biography of Cicero, and "tell me in your next letter to what acts of indiscretion his misfortunes are to be ascribed." Peter dutifully read the text and provided a brief essay. John thanked him and urged him to carry on with Plutarch. "Few books (if properly read) afford more useful lessons than the lives of great men; and among biographers Plutarch is certainly entitled to the first place. To enjoy the experience of others without paying the price which it often cost them, is pleasant as well as profitable."[29]

Jay wrote these letters from his fall circuit, which took him to Hartford in late October, to Boston in early November, to Exeter in late November, and to Providence in early December. In short, he was again away from home for about two months in the fall of 1791, bringing justice "to every man's door."[30]

Friends had often tried, without success, to persuade Jay to run for Governor of New York. In early 1792, when they tried again, he agreed, although he added that "it would be improper for me to make any effort to obtain suffrages." On one level, Jay's decision is difficult to understand; he was a committed nationalist, in a prestigious national position, who viewed the state governments with something like scorn. On another level, however, his decision is not hard to fathom. He was tired of riding circuit and tired of waiting for Congress to change the circuit court system. As Governor of New York, he could live and work in one place, New York City, rather than spending months on the road. One of his friends later wrote that Jay "did not consent to the use of his name until on enquiry he was told there was no likelihood of an alteration of the present arrangement of the judiciary."[31]

National and state political parties were just starting to emerge in 1792. The "Federalist" and "Antifederalist" parties more or less dissolved after the debate on the Constitution was over, although these labels were still sometimes used. More often, those who supported George Clinton, who had served as Governor since 1777, simply called themselves the "friends of Clinton" or "Clintonians;" their opponents in this election were the "friends of Jay." The lack of formal political parties did not make the campaign any less intense. Indeed, the election of the Governor in 1792 was one of the bitterest and closest contests in New York history.[32]

Jay's friends attacked Clinton for his opposition to the Constitution, suggesting that people should even now question how strongly he supported the Constitution. They also argued that it was improper for Clinton to serve in "perpetuity in the chief magistracy," that it was time for a change in the Governor's mansion. At a dinner at Jay's home, attended by a "large set," one of his friends gave a toast to "no perpetual dictator," which was "much applauded." The Clintonians responded that Clinton and his running mate were "old, tried and faithful servants of the public." They attacked Jay as "a high aristocratic Federalist, who wishes the annihilation of the state governments, and to absorb them into the federal union." Jay was fortunate that his private letters, in which he had indeed talked about the subordination of the states, were not public at this time.[33]

One of the main issues in the campaign was slavery. One of Jay's supporters wrote him that the Clintonites were claiming "it is your desire to rob every Dutchman of the property he possesses most dear to his heart, his slaves." He responded, in a letter both bold and cautious, that "every man of every color and description has a natural right to freedom, and I shall ever acknowledge myself to be an advocate for the manumission of slaves in such way as may be consistent with the justice due to them, with the justice due to their master, and with the regard due to the actual state of society. These considerations unite in convincing me that the abolition of slavery must be gradual." His supporters emphasized the caution in this statement, and also pointed out that Clinton was "at least as much for manumitting the slaves as his competitor."[34]

The recent land sales were another major issue. During 1791, the state land office, headed by Governor Clinton, had sold more than five million acres for only a million dollars, most of it payable over time. Many of the grants were immense, including one larger than the state of Connecticut. In April 1792, Philip Schuyler attacked the land sales arguing that the "principle of the republic is a principle of equality," a principle which dictated the sale of small lots. Melancton Smith writing as "Lucius," defended the land sales, arguing that they had raised substantial funds for the state and were less dangerous than Hamilton's proposed national bank. Schuyler responded with a more direct attack on Clinton, listing specific friends of the Governor who had received generous grants. In the countryside, the attack was even more vicious. Judge William Cooper of Otsego County alleged that the Governor was "a rogue" who had "robbed the state of more money than the whole continental war cost." He added that, if he heard anyone disagree, "I will take a firebrand and put his barn on fire."[35]

Clinton probably lost votes because of the land issue, but Jay certainly lost votes because of a stock market scandal. In late 1791 and early 1792, it seemed that everyone in New York City, "the merchant, the lawyer, the physician, [and] the mechanic," was buying bank stocks. To some extent this was speculation, but to some extent it was manipulation, and the main manipulator was William Duer, a long-time friend of Jay and Hamilton. In early March, when share prices started to fall, Duer could not pay his bills. Within two weeks, he was in prison for debt, along with Walter Livingston, who had also bet on the bank shares. The losses extended far more broadly, to "shopkeepers, widows, orphans, butchers, cartmen, gardeners, market women and even the noted bawd, Mrs. McCarty." The atmosphere in New York was electric, explosive. "I expect to hear daily," one man wrote in April, "that they have broken open the jail and taken out Duer and Walter Livingston and hanged them." There was no evidence that Jay or Hamilton had any involvement in Duer's share manipulations, but they were tarnished by association.[36]

One of Jay's main adversaries in the 1792 election was his former friend and law partner, Robert Livingston. In late March, writing under a pseudonym, Livingston described and deplored the close relations among Jay, Hamilton (author of the national bank scheme), and Schuyler ("the most active partisan of Mr Jay"). A few days later an article signed "Timothy Tickler" appeared, arguing that Chancellor Livingston was evidently the author of the prior article, that his talents were slight, and that he was a "traitor" to his principles for supporting Clinton. Livingston responded with another long pseudonymous article, addressed to "Timothy Tickler, C– J– of the U– S–," with some interesting elements of truth under the layers of invective. Livingston started by asking where one should look for the friends of Jay. Not among the "companions of your youth," for "these you have sacrificed to a mere jealousy of their superior abilities, to an overweening ambition, which made you dread them as your rivals." (This was somewhat unfair, for with the exception of Livingston, Jay remained friendly with his King's College friends.) Even among his family, Jay had enemies; "your cold heart, graduated like a thermometer, finds the freezing point nearest the bulb." (Livingston was probably alluding here not only to Brockholst Livingston but also to James Jay and perhaps other family members.) As to political friends, "in the southern district, in which you were born and bred, where of course your character is best known, you will have the least support." (Jay would prevail in New York City over Clinton, but not by a great margin.) Jay should have been careful about calling into question Livingston's talents, since he was "in every walk of science and polite literature ... far, very far behind your compeers." (Jay was indeed not a scientist or an expert on "polite literature.") Even in the state constitution, of which he was the main author, Jay could not "lay [his] finger upon the part of it on which you would build your fame." Would he cite the Council of Appointment, "that wretched blot in our constitution," or would he "bring forward your illiberal arguments for narrowing the grounds of religious toleration?" (Neither the Council nor the Catholic clauses were Jay's finest moments.) Finally, Jay's vocabulary suggested that he believed people owed him some personal loyalty, which was perhaps understandable, since "you have lived abroad, you have seen the courts of princes where every object bowed before the crown [and] it was natural that you should first admire, and then sigh for the bubble" of aristocratic status. Jay probably guessed the identity of the author, but he refrained from responding in kind. Instead, he put only a brief notice in the newspaper stating, apparently truthfully, that he was "not the author of any political paper that has been published this year," nor had he reviewed any of them in draft form.[37]

In mid-April, Jay left for his circuit of New England. He stopped first to visit his brother and sister-in-law on the family farm in Rye, New York, where he planted some trees, and wrote to his son Peter about the pleasure he had in walking among the trees which his own father Peter had planted many years ago. "The time will come when you will probably experience similar emotions." He then continued, visiting Connecticut, Massachusetts, New Hampshire, Rhode Island, and Vermont, before returning to New York on the last day of June. He thus learned of the next phase of the election and dispute through letters and newspapers.[38]

Voting occurred over a week in late April. Even once the voting was done, however, there was no official count for several more weeks. In each district, paper ballots were delivered to local inspectors, who in turn were to deliver them to the local sheriffs, who in turn were to deliver them to the office of the Secretary of State in New York City. There they were to remain until the last Tuesday in May, when a committee of twelve canvassers (members of the state legislature) were to open and count them, making the final "judgment and determination" on the validity of ballots and the election result.[39]

By early May, however, there were estimates of the results of the election. Robert Troup, who had been Jay's law clerk many years before, and was now a leader of the Jay campaign, wrote to him that "the whole election appears to be a majority of 250 for you." Two weeks later, Troup reported that the other side's hopes "rest upon setting aside votes for you; their particular object at present is the votes of Otsego County which are pretty unanimous for you." The Clintonians intended to argue, according to Troup, that the votes of Otsego County could not be counted because they had been delivered by a sheriff whose commission had expired, and whose successor had not received his commission due to a delay. Although it was not part of their formal argument, the Clintonians also argued that the votes of Otsego County were tainted by the illicit pressures used there by Judge William Cooper.[40]

The canvassers met in late May and quickly divided along party lines, with seven supporting Clinton and four supporting Jay. In an effort to avoid a party-line vote, they requested the legal opinions of Rufus King and Aaron Burr, leading lawyers and federal Senators. King's opinion was that the Otsego votes should be counted, as should the votes of two other smaller, disputed counties. Burr's opinion was that the Otsego votes should not be counted. On the day these opinions were made public, Sarah summarized the issues for her husband, in a letter which shows her strong political sense. She was "satisfied that the sentiments of the people are with you; whether you are or are not Governor, it appears that you are the choice of the people." On the next day she reported angrily that "the canvassers have taken upon them to give the people a Governor of their election, not the one the people preferred." And on the next day, in some alarm, she wrote that there was "such a ferment in the city that it is difficult to say what will be the consequences."[41]

Jay was in Hartford, Connecticut, when he learned, not from this letter but from a newspaper, of the decision of the canvassers. He wrote to Sarah that he was pleased that the majority of the electors favored him and not surprised "that injustice has taken place." He continued: "A few years more will put us all in the dust; and it will then be of more importance to me to have governed myself than to have governed the state." Others seemed far more concerned about the election dispute. Jefferson wrote to Madison, for example, that it "does not seem possible to defend Clinton as a just or disinterested man if he does not decline the office." A few days later, he wrote to Monroe that because of "the tumultuous proceedings of Mr. Jay's partisans" the state might "be thrown into convulsions." Hamilton had similar concerns; he wrote to Rufus

King that Jay's supporters had to "beware of extremes." There was danger in the talk of "the convention and the bayonet." [42]

Jay himself was largely out of touch in June, but on the last day of the month he reached Lansingburgh, New York, where his supporters urged him to contest the decision of the canvassers. He was noncommittal. "The people of the state know the value of their rights, and there is reason to hope that the efforts of every virtuous citizen to assert and secure them will be no less distinguished by temper and moderation, than by constancy and zeal." As he progressed down the Hudson, he was greeted in every town, and responded in similar tones. When he reached Harlem Heights, he was met by a group "on horseback and in carriages" that "escorted him into town." They were joined by hundreds more on foot, and passed by various signs, such as one which acclaimed him "Governor by the Voice of the People." When he reached his house on Broadway, he "attempted to say something on the occasion expressive of his feelings," but "the loud and repeated plaudits by the people prevented his being heard." [43]

There was, at this time, not only angry rhetoric in New York, but actual political violence. In Kingston, supporters gathered to toast Jay and parade through the streets; Clinton supporters "offered an insult to some of [Jay's] friends by holding a black flag before their faces. It was resented and a general and promiscuous club battle ensued, both severe and bloody." There was a similar fight between the Jay and Clinton factions in Albany, and a quarrel over the election in a New York City tavern led to a duel between two prominent men. [44]

Jay did not want to lead a mob to attempt to overturn the election. Yet he also did not want to do nothing. King reported to Hamilton, on the day of Jay's return to the city, that he had "an idea of a convention for the sole purpose of canvassing the canvassers and their decision." Hamilton (atypically) counseled moderation. "A ferment may be raised which may not be allayed when you wish it." He also doubted the advisability of a convention; it would have "too much the appearance of reversing the sentence of a court with a legislative decree." King replied (no doubt reflecting Jay's views as well as his own) that there was no harm in asking the legislature to call a convention; the majority of the Assembly was Clintonian, so it would *not* call the convention and "the business will there terminate." As predicted, although the legislature investigated and debated the election for many weeks, it took no action.[45]

The election of 1792 is interesting and important for several reasons. It shows that Jay was already tiring of service on the Supreme Court, already thinking about what he would do next in life. It also suggests that he had learned, from his quarrel with Brockholst Livingston, the virtues of silence and restraint, for that is how he now responded to the anonymous article by Robert Livingston. He showed even more restraint, in a more important situation, when he decided against some kind of protest or contest of the election. However questionable and political the decision of the canvassers, state law provided that their decision would be binding, and he realized the utmost importance of respect for election laws.

Jay did not attend the February 1792 session of the Supreme Court in Philadelphia; he stayed in New York to be with his wife, who gave birth at this time to a daughter, Sarah Louisa. But even though he was not present, he continued to debate by post the question of circuit rotation. Iredell wrote that he would not take the southern circuit again, not only because it was unfair to ask him to undertake "so very unequal a proportion of duty," but also because there were cases pending in North Carolina in which he was a party. A few weeks later, Iredell wrote again to say that he had "some hopes that Congress" would amend the law "to express their sense whether there shall or shall not be rotation." Jay responded that "the objections heretofore stated to a rotation strike me as insuperable; and I think the inconveniences urged as reasons for it, are really too great and unreasonable to be continued." Iredell then suggested that the justices strike a deal with Congress: if they did not have to ride circuit, Congress could reduce their salaries by $500 per year. Jay was favorably inclined, but urged that the "sentiments of Congress on this point should be pretty well ascertained before the proposal is made." He was still concerned to avoid the partial reform of rotation; he hoped to force Congress to consider more radical reform, elimination of the justices' circuit court duties.[46]

Instead of reducing the duties of the justices, however, Congress in early 1792 increased them, through the Invalid Pensions Act. This Act required the circuit courts to hear the claims of Revolutionary War veterans residing in their districts, to decide which of them should receive pensions, and to fix the proper amount of each veteran's pension. The circuit courts were directed to transmit their recommendations to the Secretary of War, who would review them against the military records and make a decision, unless there was reason to suspect fraud or error, in which case the Secretary would refer the case to Congress for final decision.[47]

It is unclear whether, when Jay, Cushing and Duane opened circuit court in New York in early April, there was any particular pension application for them to consider. Yet they immediately considered and opined on the new Pension Act. By modern standards, if there was no pensioner before them, Jay and his colleagues should not have discussed or ruled on the validity of the Act. Perhaps they felt that it was important to let the pensioners in New York and New England know that, in spite of the questions about the Act, the judges would consider applications. If so, they chose an odd way to convey this information: they wrote a letter to the President, who in turn transmitted it to Congress, at which point the letter became public.[48]

Jay and his colleagues considered the Pension Act unconstitutional, although they did not use that dramatic term. They noted that Congress could only assign to the federal courts duties which "are properly judicial," and opined that the duties assigned to the circuit courts under the new Act "are not of that description," because their decisions were subject to review by both the executive and legislative branches. The judges would therefore construe the Act as appointing them as "commissioners," and they agreed to serve as such "between the adjournments" of the circuit courts. In other words, by a clever construction, Jay and his colleagues managed both to signal their concern about the constitutionality of the Act and their willingness to process the applications. This opinion may be the first instance of a federal court reviewing a federal statute to determine whether it was consistent with the Constitution. It was also the first instance of what is now an accepted principle, that courts will if possible construe statutes to avoid finding them unconstitutional.[49]

As Jay and Cushing proceeded on their circuit of New England, they took this opinion and approach with them, and used it in each circuit court. In these courts, they had to consider dozens of cases of actual pensioners. For example, in New Haven, Connecticut, the three judges, sitting as commissioners, decided that Yale Todd of New Haven, who was an artillery private, should receive a pension of "two third parts of his former monthly pay and one hundred and fifty dollars for arrears." In Bennington, Vermont, "a great number of applicants for pensions attended, and many received relief, we would hope adequate to their sufferings, if not to their expectations."[50]

While he was in New Haven, Jay heard that Congress would "probably" set up a system of rotation for the circuits. Indeed, Congress two weeks earlier had passed the Judiciary Act of 1792, which provided that the justices should at each session agree on the circuits so that "no judge, unless by his own consent, shall have assigned to him any circuit which he has already attended, until the same has been afterwards attended by every other of the said judges." Iredell had achieved through legislation the system of rotation Jay had refused to create by negotiation. John wrote hopefully to Sarah that "perhaps it may not take place, or be of short duration."[51]

In Rhode Island, Jay and his colleagues decided an important case regarding the British debts. The plaintiff in the case, a British merchant, had sued several Rhode Island defendants on a loan. The defendants argued that they did not have to pay because of a Rhode Island statute which granted them a stay of three years. The circuit court overruled this defense, apparently because it viewed the statute as impairing contracts, and thus invalid under the contract clause of the Constitution. Today we take it for granted that a federal court may review a state statute under the federal Constitution and, if it decides the statute is unconstitutional, rule that it is invalid. But in the eighteenth and early nineteenth centuries many people viewed the states as sovereigns whose actions could not be reviewed by mere federal judges. For at least the second time, Jay and his colleagues on the circuit court had disregarded this view, reviewed a state statute, and overturned it on the basis of the federal Constitution. Perhaps even more remarkable, the justices had done so in an Antifederalist state without generating popular outcry.[52]

After closing the circuit court in Rhode Island, Jay left for Vermont, which he reached after ten days of difficult travel. Although Cushing was not yet present, Jay and the district judge formed a quorum, and they opened the circuit court with the "a degree of dignity becoming the importance of the institution." Jay delivered to the grand jury the charge he had been giving and refining all spring. In it, he stressed the importance of the federal revenue laws, which at that time did not involve "direct taxation, or burdening the land or any of its productions with the least impost or duty." He also gave a passionate attack on perjury, explaining that "controversies of various kinds exist at all times, and in all communities." Courts are necessary to decide controversies, and "their decision must be regulated by evidence, and the greater part of evidence will always consist of the testimony of witnesses; this testimony is given under those solemn obligations which an appeal to the God of truth impose; and if oaths should cease to be held sacred, our dearest and most valuable rights would become insecure."[53]

The August 1792 session of the Supreme Court in Philadelphia was dominated by the pension case of William Hayburn. Hayburn had applied to the Pennsylvania circuit court for a pension; that court had ruled that the Pension Act was invalid and refused to consider, even informally, the petition. Attorney General Randolph argued to the Supreme Court that it should use a writ of mandamus to direct the circuit court to consider and approve Hayburn's petition. Randolph had scarcely started his argument, however, when Jay asked whether he was "officially authorized to move for a mandamus?" Randolph launched into a long and learned argument about the role of the Attorney General, citing American and English precedents, an argument so long that it carried over for several days. It appears that Jay and the other doubting justices were mainly concerned about whether Randolph could appear in the Supreme Court without specific authority from the President. The court divided evenly on this question, with Jay among those who thought the Attorney General needed specific authorization.[54]

Randolph was determined to have the Supreme Court decide the merits of the case, and so he appeared later on the day of this decision in a new capacity, as Hayburn's private lawyer. He argued that the federal courts had the power to "refuse to execute" a non-judicial duty, but that it was inappropriate, in this case, for them to refuse this duty. After "much consultation on the bench," the justices decided to postpone decision of the case until the next term. Randolph, writing to his friend Madison, was rather unkind about Jay. The Chief Justice was "clear in the expression of his ideas," but they "do not abound on legal subjects," and his decisions showed "no method, no legal principle, no system of reasoning." In the event, however, the decision to postpone consideration of Hayburn's case proved correct. It allowed the Supreme Court to avoid an early confrontation with Congress, which acted over the winter to amend the Pension Act, making the district court judges, and any three commissioners each of them appointed, responsible for considering and acting upon pension applications.[55]

The justices, while they were together in Philadelphia, also discussed their circuit-riding duties. The one point on which they could agree was that it would be better if they did not have to ride circuit, and for the first time they sent formal letters on this issue to the President and the Congress. They said that on "extraordinary occasions we shall always be ready as good citizens to make extraordinary exertions," but in this period of peace and prosperity they could not "reconcile [themselves] to the idea of existing in exile from our families." They did not make the constitutional argument that Jay had made in his draft letter two years ago, but they did argue that "appointing the same men finally to correct in one capacity, the errors which they themselves may have committed in another, is a distinction unfriendly to impartial justice." And the justices agreed on a rotation of the circuits, as required by the new statute, assigning Jay to the middle circuit for the fall of 1792.[56]

Jay left New York for New Jersey in September, "with [the] design after dispatching some private business I had there to proceed from thence on my circuit." He was laid low, however, by a severe eye infection, and had to return to New York. He intended, "the moment I regain sufficient health for the purpose," to "proceed on my circuit," but in the event he could not do so. In late October, he received a letter from Cushing, who reported that he had "rubbed along as well as I could without you." Jay responded that he feared he had "no prospect of seasonably regaining sufficient strength to enable me to be with you either in Maryland or Virginia" and signed the letter "your affectionate friend and servant." Through the trials of their circuit-riding together, these two men had become warm friends.[57]

In February of 1793, the Supreme Court heard and decided the most important case of Jay's tenure, *Chisholm v. Georgia*. The facts were simple. A merchant

had sold cloth and clothing to the state of Georgia during the war. Georgia did
not pay, and Chisholm, the executor of the merchant's estate, sued the state in
the federal circuit court. The state's defense was that as a sovereign it could not
be sued without its own consent.[58]

Attorney General Randolph, acting as private attorney for the executor,
relied on both the Constitution (which gave the federal courts jurisdiction over
"controversies between a state and citizens of another state") and the Judiciary
Act (which gave the Supreme Court jurisdiction over all cases "where a state
shall be a party"). He stressed that neither provision distinguished between
states as plaintiffs and states as defendants. He noted that the Constitution
prohibited the states from taking many actions and asked rhetorically whether
the states should "enjoy the high privilege of acting thus eminently wrong,
without control?" When he was done, and no lawyer appeared for Georgia, the
justices "expressed a wish to hear [from] any gentlemen of the bar, who might
be disposed to take up the gauntlet in opposition to the Attorney General."
Apparently none did.[59]

A few years later, under Chief Justices Ellsworth and Marshall, the Supreme
Court developed the practice of issuing one opinion for the court, or at most
two opinions, a majority opinion and a dissenting opinion. This of course
required consultation among the justices after argument and before the issuance
of the opinion, since they had to decide how to decide the case, and then agree
on the wording of the decision. It also added to the moral and intellectual
power of the Supreme Court, emphasizing its unity rather than the differences
among the justices. Under Chief Justice Jay, however, the court followed the
English common law practice, in which each justice would consider and write
up his own opinion, which were read out in order, from junior to most senior
justice. This arguably reflected a failure of imagination on Jay's part, a failure
to consider whether a more collegial system would strengthen the court.
Certainly the practice did not serve the court well in the *Chisholm* case.[60]

Justice Iredell was the first to read out his opinion to the packed courtroom.
In his view, the court had no jurisdiction, because Congress had not intended
to give it more extensive jurisdiction over states than state courts had previously enjoyed, and it was accepted by all that a state could not be sued in state
court without its consent. Three other justices, Blair, Cushing and Wilson,

concluded that Georgia could be sued in federal court. Finally it was the Chief Justice's turn.[61]

Jay started with a lengthy discussion of sovereignty. In his view, at the time of the Revolution, "the sovereignty of their country passed to the people of it." Although "thirteen sovereignties were considered as emerged from the principles of the Revolution ... the people nevertheless continued to consider themselves, from a national point of view, as one people." When it came time to form a constitution, "the people exercised their own rights, and their own proper sovereignty, and conscious of the plenitude of it, they declared with becoming dignity, 'We the people of the United States, do ordain and establish this Constitution.'" In his view, it was important not to be misled by European notions. In America, the people were "sovereigns without subjects," and state governors and other officials were merely "agents of the people." In Europe, in contrast, the law viewed "the prince as sovereign, and the people as his subjects; it regards his person as the object of allegiance." It was thus "easy to perceive that such a sovereign could not be amenable to a court of justice, or subjected to judicial control or restraint."[62]

Jay then considered whether Georgia, as a state, could be sued. He noted that it was accepted that one person could sue many others, indeed sometimes many thousands, as in the case of a lawsuit against a whole city. He asked whether it was right to view the "fifty odd thousand citizens in Delaware being associated under a state government" as being "so superior to the forty odd thousand of Philadelphia, associated under their charter" that "although it may become the latter to meet an individual on an equal footing in a court of justice, yet that such a procedure would not comport with the dignity of the former?"[63]

Turning at last to the words of the Constitution, he quoted the whole of the article describing the jurisdiction of the federal courts. He noted that the wording of the provision regarding suits involving states and citizens did not make any distinction between cases in which the state is a plaintiff and cases in which it is a defendant. "If the Constitution really meant to extend these powers only to cases in which a state might be a plaintiff, to the exclusion of those in which citizens had demands against a state, it is inconceivable that it should have attempted to convey that meaning in words, not only so incompetent, but also repugnant to it."[64]

Jay's opinion was a decent political argument, and it probably reached the right conclusion, but it was not a particularly powerful legal argument. Its main deficiency, from a modern perspective, is that it assumed that, if there was jurisdiction, if the Supreme Court had authority to *hear* a case against a state, there was a cause of action, a right to recover on a private contract with a state. But before the Constitution it was universally agreed that a private party could not recover on a contract with a state. As Hamilton put it in the *Federalist*, "contracts between a nation and individuals are only binding on the conscience of the sovereign, and have no pretensions to a compulsive force." Jay did not discuss the source of the right to sue a state in contract, but it seems he assumed the right was found in a kind of federal common law, that there was now a federal cause of action on contracts made by states, even though there had been none before the Constitution.[65]

Jay's opinion is often called "Federalist" and the hostile reception which greeted it is often called "Republican," but Federalists and Republicans alike disapproved of the Supreme Court's decision. On the day after the decision was announced, Federalist Representative Theodore Sedgwick proposed in the House an amendment which would have barred suits against states in federal courts by any person, whether individual or corporate, domestic or foreign. On the day thereafter, Federalist Senator Caleb Strong offered an amendment which barred suits in federal court by citizens of another state or of a foreign state. In Massachusetts, the Federalist legislature passed a resolution urging Congress to "remove any clause or article of the said Constitution which can be construed to imply or justify a decision that a state is compellable to answer in any suit by an individual or individuals."[66]

In short, the reaction to the *Chisholm* decision was so universal, and so adverse, that it probably did not matter much what Jay and his fellow justices had said in their opinions. Given existing notions of state sovereignty, and given the substantial debts owed by the states, which they had no means to pay, there was probably little chance that the *Chisholm* decision would be allowed to stand. It took less than two years for Congress to pass, and the required number of states to approve, the Eleventh Amendment to reverse *Chisholm* and protect states from diversity suits in federal courts.[67]

Although there were debtors in every state who owed money to British creditors, Virginia debtors owed more than the residents of any other state, almost half the total amount owed. Jay had been an author of the provision, in the Paris Peace Treaty, guaranteeing that creditors on either side would meet with no "lawful impediment" to recovery of *bona fide* pre-war debts. Jay had also attempted, as Secretary for Foreign Affairs, to persuade the states to repeal the various statutes which hindered British creditors. Some states had passed laws as suggested by Jay and the Congress, and in other states the federal courts were now providing reasonable relief to British creditors, but in Virginia neither state nor federal courts would provide redress.[68]

Starting in 1790, British plaintiffs had filed more than one hundred cases in the federal court against Virginia debtors. The defendants, most of them represented by John Marshall, responded with a set of standard defenses. The key defense was a 1777 statute, which provided that a Virginia debtor who had paid the state, in depreciated colonial currency, an amount equal to the amount owed a British creditor would be relieved from the debt. Another key defense, more political than legal, was that the whole treaty was void because it had been violated by the British, especially when they failed to pay for slaves or vacate the northwest forts.

The British debt cases were first argued before the Virginia circuit court in November 1791. No decision was reached because Justice Blair left before the argument finished and the others were unwilling to proceed without him. In the spring of 1792, a circuit court composed of only two judges postponed consideration of the cases, perhaps because they felt such important issues should be considered by a full court. Again in the fall of 1792, when the circuit court consisted of Justice Cushing and District Judge Griffin, the court postponed the cases. Thus by the time Jay became involved in early 1793, the issue had been awaiting decision for almost three years.[69]

Jay left Philadelphia in the middle of May, armed with letters of introduction from the President, who warned him to "expect the weather to grow warm" as he traveled south in late spring. In Baltimore, Jay met up with Iredell, and they traveled south together by coach. Although they had disagreed about circuit rotation, the two men got along well now, and Iredell wrote to his wife that "Mr. Jay grows infinitely upon intimacy." The two men passed through, but

did not remark upon, the impressive but at this time largely empty site which had been set aside to become the nation's federal district.* They arrived in Richmond "perfectly well but extremely fatigued," and a few days later opened the circuit court session. As was his custom, the Chief Justice gave a lengthy charge to the grand jury, and for those listening closely there were strong hints about his views on the British debt cases. "Justice and policy unite in declaring that debts fairly contracted should be honestly paid … The man or nation who eludes the payment of debts, ceases to be worthy of further credit, and generally meets with their deserts in the entire loss of it." [70]

Patrick Henry and John Marshall argued for the Virginia defendants. Henry, famous for his vivid verbal attacks during the war, was now on the downward slope of his life and career. He tried to turn the case into a trial of British conduct during the war. "Our inhabitants were mercilessly and brutally plundered, and our enemies professed to maintain their armies by these means only. Our slaves [were] carried away, our crops burnt, [and] a cruel war carried on against our agriculture." Given this "mode of warfare," Henry argued, "we had a right to consider British debts as subject to confiscation, and seize the property of those who originated that war." He was, in the words of one local listener, "Shakespeare and Garrick combined." Marshall, a younger man, on the verge of national fame, followed with a more standard legal argument. Virginia, he insisted, was a sovereign nation when it enacted the 1777 statute; it had the right under the law of nations to enact such a confiscation statute; and neither the Treaty of Paris nor the Constitution overruled the Virginia statute. "The discussion," according to one observer, "was one of the most brilliant exhibitions ever witnessed at the Bar of Virginia." [71]

In early June, after the arguments were finished, the judges retired to consider their opinions. This case is unique, among those in which Jay participated as a circuit justice, in that we have a lengthy written opinion by him, as well as one by Iredell. The two justices agreed on many points. They quickly

---

* Washington, D.C., as its visitors know, has a street for every letter in the alphabet, except "J." The usual explanation is that L'Enfant, the Frenchman who designed the new capital, wanted to slight the anti-French Jay. This is incorrect. L'Enfant's plan, completed in late 1791, does not identify the streets by letter. Since most people at this time tended to treat the letters "I" and "J" as one for alphabetical purposes, it seems likely that whoever assigned the letters omitted "J" in order to avoid confusion.

dismissed the idea that the Declaration of Independence had terminated the rights of British creditors. They agreed that a Virginia statute of 1782, which arguably barred a claim by any British creditor, was overturned by the federal Constitution, which made federal treaties the supreme law of the United States. They shied away from the suggestion that the court should decide whether the alleged British violations rendered the treaty invalid. In Jay's view, although the courts could decide questions of "necessary validity," such as whether a treaty had expired by its own terms, courts should avoid questions of "voluntary validity," such as whether a treaty has "been so violated as justly to become voidable by the injured nation." This was the first American discussion of the "political question" doctrine: that federal courts should decline to consider issues better resolved through the political process.[72]

They differed, however, on the critical question of the Virginia statute of 1777. Iredell, joined by District Judge Griffin on this point, held that those Virginians who had made payment into the state treasury, even in debased colonial currency, had discharged their debts. The peace treaty, in their view, did not alter the private rights of the Virginia creditors, which they had acquired by the statute, to pay into the state treasury and be discharged. Jay disagreed. He quoted the leading authorities on international law to show that the United States had the right, in making the Peace Treaty, to alter private property and private rights. He also quoted the provision he had helped to negotiate in 1782: "creditors on either side shall meet with no lawful impediments to the recovery of the full value in sterling money of all *bona fide* debts heretofore contracted." He then proceeded to prove that the plaintiff was a creditor, that the statute was a form of "lawful impediment," and that the debt was a *bona fide* debt contracted before the date of the treaty. He concluded with some pointed comments about the unfairness of expecting Britain to allow Americans to recover in British courts while preventing Britons from recovering in American courts.[73]

Jay was no doubt disappointed that he was not able to clear the way completely for the British creditors to obtain justice against their Virginia debtors. But he must have been pleased that he (together with Iredell and Griffin) had removed several of their defenses; after the circuit court decision only those who had paid into the state were protected, and they were only protected to the extent of such payments. And his position was justified in the end, for when the Supreme Court considered the case in 1796, it agreed with him and overruled the last remaining statutory defense.[74]

Like most Americans, Jay welcomed the first news of the French Revolution, although his welcome was cautious. In late 1789, he wrote that the Revolution "promises much, and I sincerely wish it may perform what it promises." In his view, however, the "general expectations of its influence on other kingdoms appear to me to be rather sanguine; there are many nations not yet ripe for liberty, and I fear that even France has some lessons to learn and, perhaps, to pay for on the subject of free government." In early 1790, he wrote to a French friend that the "people of this country ardently wish success to the Revolution in France," but added that France should beware of the "natural propensity in mankind of passing from one extreme too far towards the opposite one."[75]

The French Revolution from its outset involved violence, but it became more violent and dangerous in late 1792 and early 1793. In September 1792, mobs killed more than a thousand people in Paris, mainly priests and other "reactionaries." Among those killed at this time was Jay's friend and counterpart the Comte de Montmorin, with whom he had worked so closely while they were both in Spain. In January 1793, the National Convention tried and executed King Louis XVI, and the next month France declared war against Britain, a war of the revolutionaries against the reactionaries.[76]

When news of the execution of the King and war against Britain reached America, opinion divided sharply. The emerging Republican party continued to support France. One Republican author exulted in the news of the execution, saying that "the patriots of France can no more be called cruel for putting Louis to death than our laws can for hanging the chief of a gang who had robbed a house." The emerging Federalist party, of which Jay and his friends were leaders, was shocked and horrified by events in France. Hamilton wrote that a struggle for liberty was only "respectable and glorious" if conducted "with magnanimity, justice and humanity." But a revolution "sullied by crimes and extravagances," such as the later French Revolution, "loses its respectability." The French Revolution now seemed for Jay to have "more the appearance of a woe than a blessing. It has caused torrents of blood and tears, and been marked in its progress by atrocities very injurious to the cause of liberty and offensive to morality and humanity." [77]

The war between France and Britain, which would continue with only brief interruptions for more than twenty years, posed serious risks for America. Both sides tried to stop the United States from trading with the other, leading to attacks on American merchant ships, which made it quite possible that the United States would be dragged into the war. Moreover, although there was a broad consensus in America that the nation should not enter the war, there was sharp disagreement over what attitude Americans should take towards the belligerents. Republicans felt that it was perfectly proper for Americans to favor France, and along with Jefferson they deplored "the cold caution of their government." Federalists like Jay feared that such a tilted neutrality would quickly lead America into a war against Britain, a war for which America was in no way prepared. [78]

In early April 1793, Jay received two letters from Hamilton. The first requested advice on whether a Minister from revolutionary France should be received. Hamilton noted that the rest of Europe might not recognize the revolutionary regime, but instead recognize Louis XVI's heir, and that the United States would look foolish receiving envoys from both the revolutionaries and the reactionaries. He concluded with a note that shows how much he respected Jay: "I would give a great deal for a personal discussion with you." In the second letter, Hamilton suggested that Washington should issue a "proclamation prohibiting our citizens from taking commissions on either side." He asked Jay, "if you think the measure prudent," to "draft such a thing as you would deem proper." [79]

Jay immediately took up his pen and drafted a proclamation for the review of Hamilton and Washington. His preamble echoed the Declaration of Independence: noting that "every nation has a right to change and modify their constitution and government in such manner as they may think most conducive to their welfare and happiness" and that "a new form of government has taken place and actually exists in France." In the critical paragraph, he suggested that Washington should "most earnestly advise and require the citizens of the United States to be circumspect in their conduct towards all nations and particularly those now at war" and "expressly require the citizens of the United

States [to] abstain from acting hostilely against any of the belligerent powers under commissions from either of them." [80] Jay was in New York at this time, and thus was not involved in the discussions in Philadelphia on the final wording of the neutrality proclamation. But when he read the proclamation in the newspaper in late April 1793, he would have noticed that it was in many respects similar to his draft. Washington declared that Americans were "to observe a conduct friendly and impartial towards the belligerent powers," that they were not to take up arms against either of them, and that "offenders will not be protected, but on the contrary prosecuted and punished." [81]

In early May, on his way from New York to Richmond, Jay passed through the national capital of Philadelphia. His conversations with Hamilton and others focused on the war and the activities of Edmond Genet. Genet had arrived in April in Charleston, South Carolina, as the first envoy of revolutionary France to the United States. He immediately started to use America as a base for the war against Britain: commissioning American vessels as French privateers; recruiting Americans to serve aboard these vessels; and exhorting Americans to join expeditions against Spain in Florida and Louisiana. As Genet made his way north from Charleston to Philadelphia, toasted and feted in every city, Jay was headed south from Philadelphia for Richmond. They apparently crossed paths, but did not meet, in Baltimore in May. Justice Iredell reported from there to his wife that Jay was in town, and Genet was also in town, indeed that Iredell had "waited on the new French Minister here, in company with many other gentlemen." It is easy to understand why Jay would decline the suggestion that he should "wait" upon the upstart French Minister. A little further south, in Fredericksburg, when one of the locals was "full of zeal" in favor of France, Jay's "enmity" towards France reportedly "broke out in a very decided tone." [82]

At the opening of the court in Richmond, Jay gave a long charge to the grand jury, mainly in praise of Washington's neutrality policy. He quoted the entire proclamation, then quoted from a French authority to prove that the proclamation was "consistent with and declaratory of the conduct enjoined by the law of nations." He argued that the United States should not only "withdraw its protection" from those who violated its neutrality; "it ought also to prosecute and punish them." He noted (and he was clearly alluding to Genet) that "the subjects of belligerent powers are bound while in this country to respect the neutrality of it, and are punishable ... for violations of it within the limits and jurisdiction of the United States." In particular (and again the allusion to Genet must have been obvious) the "right of levying soldiers is a sovereign right" and "no foreign power can lawfully exercise it without permission." He also commented on how the war was causing and sharpening domestic political divisions. As America faced the possibility of war, there was no preparation "more important than union and harmony among ourselves." It was imperative that "such an event not find us divided into parties, and particularly into parties in favor of this or that foreign nation." [83]

Jay was in Richmond in late May and June, hearing and deciding the British debt cases, and then in New York City in early July. In the middle of July, he received a formal letter from Secretary of State Jefferson, saying that President Washington "was desirous of asking the advice" of the justices on certain questions about neutrality. Jay left immediately for Philadelphia, where he dined the day of his arrival with Washington. The President was "embarrassed" that the formal questions for the justices were not yet ready, because they were waiting for review by Attorney General Randolph. Jay apparently suggested to Washington that the justices might not be prepared to answer the formal questions, that they would "have to decide whether the business which it is proposed to ask their opinion upon is, in their judgment, of such a nature as that they can comply with it." [84]

A few days letter, Jay and the other justices received another letter from Jefferson, noting that the war had raised various questions "of considerable difficulty" under treaties, the law of nations, and domestic law, and that these questions "are often presented under circumstances which do not give cognizance of them to the tribunals of the country." Jefferson did not attach the precise questions which he proposed to put to the justices, but it seems that the justices knew at least in outline what they were. The first question, for example, was whether the treaties with France gave that nation the right to fit out and commission vessels from American ports. [85]

Two days later Jay responded, on behalf of himself and the other three justices present in Philadelphia. In their view, the preliminary question posed, whether the justices should answer the detailed questions on neutrality law, was itself a question "of much difficulty as well as importance." They were reluctant "to decide it, without the advice and participation of our absent brethren," Cushing and Blair. But if circumstances required an immediate answer, they would "immediately resume consideration of the question, and decide it." Washington responded a few days later that the questions could await the arrival "of your absent brethren." [86]

While this elaborate exchange was going on, Jay was also having informal conversations with his Federalist friends about how best to handle Citizen Genet. The French envoy had been in Philadelphia since mid-May exciting and enjoying a frenzy of pro-French feeling. On the first of June, for example, there was a dinner for two hundred people including Governor Mifflin. On the same day, a series of newspaper articles started, signed "Veritas," criticizing the President's neutrality proclamation for its failure to distinguish between America's friends (France) and its enemies (Britain). Jay and other Federalists worried that Genet and his Republican friends would soon lead America into war against Britain. And indeed, at a Bastille Day banquet, one of the toasts expressed the hope that, "as France acted with respect to America, so may America act with respect to France." [87]

Genet did not confine himself, however, to dinners and toasts. A French warship had captured a British merchant ship, the *Little Sarah*, and brought her into Philadelphia harbor. Genet renamed her the *Petite Démocrate* and started adding to her guns and arms. Both Alexander Dallas, the Pennsylvania Secretary of State, and Thomas Jefferson warned Genet that the *Petite Démocrate* should not put to sea as a privateer, at least not until Washington returned to Philadelphia. With both men, Genet flew into a rage, and threatened that he would appeal over the President's head to the people. His words would not sound particularly threatening today, when interest groups and for that matter foreign governments appeal to the people all the time. At the time, however, when armed mobs were parading through Paris, they had a far more sinister sound. They suggested, particularly to Federalists, that Genet intended to try to organize the "people" to take violent action against the federal government.

Jefferson came away from his interview with the impression that the *Petite Démocrate* would not put to sea until Washington arrived. Genet, however, was never a man to wait, and he moved the *Petite Démocrate* downriver to Chester, from which she could easily reach the open sea. When Washington arrived in Philadelphia a few days later, and learned all this, he was irate. In a letter to Jefferson, he asked whether Genet was free to "set the acts of this government at defiance *with impunity?* And then threaten the Executive with an appeal to the people?" There was a bitter debate in the cabinet, with Hamilton and Knox arguing that Washington should publicly request that France recall Genet, and Jefferson pleading for more time, and in particular for time for the justices to consider the legal aspects of the matter.[88]

Jay may have learned some of this in his initial interview with Washington, and he certainly learned the details in discussions with Hamilton and others over the next few days. He could also see that, however outrageous his conduct, Genet was still praised by many people. The grand Bastille Day banquet, for example, attended by Governor Mifflin and others, occurred a few days after the first of many angry cabinet meetings to debate Genet's fate. In short, the threat of an attempt by Genet to rally the people against their lawful government seemed real to Hamilton, Jay and their friends. Hamilton urged Jay to go public in some way to defuse the threat posed by Genet.[89]

The Supreme Court met on only two days in early August 1793, fleeing Philadelphia because of the early signs of yellow fever. (This proved a particularly violent epidemic; by the time it abated in the late fall, over five thousand people were dead.) The justices found time, however, to inform the President that they would not answer his neutrality questions. The letter, drafted by Jay, noted that: "The lines of separation drawn by the Constitution between the three branches of government – their being in certain respects checks on each other – and our being judges of a court in the last resort – are considerations which afford strong arguments against the propriety of our extrajudicially deciding the questions alluded to." This letter has often been cited for establishing the principle that federal courts will not answer abstract questions, but only decide concrete cases.[90]

By the time that Jay left for New York in early August, the cabinet had decided to request the recall of Genet; the only remaining question was whether it would be a public request, as Hamilton urged, or a private request, as Jefferson insisted, and the President ultimately decided. Genet, apparently unaware of this debate, arrived in New York, where he was again warmly received. The welcoming committee tendered "to you our hearts and through you to your nation, our warm and undisguised affection." They were "ready and willing" to assist Genet, although only if "consistent with our reciprocal welfare and the duty we owe our country."[91]

Jay had acted wisely by declining to answer the legal questions raised by Genet's activities, but now he acted imprudently, attacking Genet in print. In a brief signed letter to the New York papers, Jay and King said that they were asked, on their return from Philadelphia, whether it was true that Genet "had said he would appeal to the people from certain decisions of the President." They affirmed that he had threatened such an appeal. This allegation, since it was signed by two of New York's leading citizens, was not taken lightly. Indeed, many people assumed that Jay and King must have had the President's sanction to attack Genet in this way.[92]

Jay should have known that his letter would not end, but merely start, a debate with the irrepressible Genet. In late August, a long letter from Genet to the President appeared in the papers. He argued that "certain persons" had "descended to personal abuse" in the hope of "withdrawing from me that esteem which the public feel and avow for the representative of the French republic." The same newspapers carried a short letter from Jefferson, reminding Genet that diplomats were not permitted to correspond directly with the President, and stating that the President saw no reason to respond. Genet was not an easily discouraged man, however; he wrote a public letter to Attorney General Randolph, asking him to prosecute Jay and King for libel. "I am satisfied that it is sufficient for me to acquaint you with the scandalous falsity of the charge against me, to induce you to take such steps, at the ensuing federal court, as the honor of your own country, as well as mine, exact upon such an occasion."[93]

Jay and King, for some reason, felt they had to answer this latest attack. They drafted a long statement explaining how they had heard in Philadelphia of Genet's threats to appeal to the people and decided to publish these threats in New York. They noted that Genet had not initially denied that he had made such threats, merely denied that he had made them directly to the President. They sent the statement in draft to Hamilton and Knox, asking them to prepare and add to it a certificate, and then "cause it to be printed without delay in your papers." Hamilton happily complied, and thus a long statement by Jay and King, with a short certificate by Hamilton and Knox, appeared in the newspapers in early December. Unfortunately, none of these four had personally heard Genet make the critical statements; the two people who had were Alexander Dallas and Thomas Jefferson. Jay regretted that "Mr. Jefferson and Governor Mifflin still remain as it were in a background." He suggested to King that "letters, calculated for publication, from Colonel Hamilton and General Knox to Mr. Jefferson and Governor Mifflin, calling on them to admit or deny the facts in question, would have been, and may yet be useful." [94]

In December, Jefferson sent a brief letter to Randolph regarding Genet's request for a prosecution. Jefferson said that the President was alive to the difficulties of the case: on the one hand, Genet, as a foreign Minister was "peculiarly entitled to the protection of the laws"; on the other hand, Jay and King, like all citizens, were entitled "not to be vexed with groundless prosecutions." Randolph decided that no public prosecution was appropriate, but that Genet could file a private libel suit. Jay and King now wrote a third letter, directly to Washington, complaining of the conduct of Jefferson and Randolph, and requesting publication of Jefferson's notes of his interview with Genet, which they believed would support their side of the story. [95]

The President was again outraged, this time at Jay and King, whom he felt were criticizing *him* for referring Ganet's request to the Attorney General. According to a later account by King, the President met with Jay, and "they conversed freely upon the subject, the President justified his own conduct, and expressed the opinion, that nothing incorrect, or unfriendly, had been intended by Jefferson, or Randolph, and complained of the severity of our letter." It was agreed that Jay and King would deliver to the President the draft of their letter, which King did at a subsequent meeting, and the President then put all the papers "into the fire." The President's action ended the episode, but not the historical debate over whether Jay acted properly, as Chief Justice, in printing the two letters against Genet. If there is any defense of Jay's actions, and perhaps there is none, it lies in the frenzy and fear of those days. Many years later, perhaps with some over-statement, Adams wrote to Jefferson that he had not felt the "terrorism excited by Genet in 1793," when "ten thousand people in the streets of Philadelphia, day after day, threatened to drag

Washington out of his house and effect a revolution in the government." Jay apparently acted on the view that unusual measures were called for to deal with unusual dangers.[96]

In its first years, there was not much work for the Supreme Court as such, since it generally handled appeals, and it took time for cases to make their way to the court on appeal. But in the February 1794 session, the Supreme Court had, by the standards of the day, a full calendar: two pension appeals, a British debt case, and an international admiralty case.

The plaintiffs in the British debt case, Samuel Brailsford and two others, claimed that the defendants owed them over £7000 on a bond. Although it now appears that all three plaintiffs were Americans living in Britain, the courts accepted Brailsford's claim that he was British, and treated his two colleagues as citizens of South Carolina. Because Brailsford was a Briton seeking to recover from the citizens of Georgia, the state of Georgia sought to insert itself into the case. The state argued that the debt was owed not to Brailsford but to it, under a 1782 state statute which provided that all debts owed to British subjects were "confiscated to and for the use of the state."[97]

The court, for reasons that are somewhat mysterious, treated this as a case which required it to decide both legal and factual issues, and summoned a jury of twelve to decide these questions. The lawyers for Georgia argued that the state had the right to confiscate the debt owed to the merchants and that it had done so in the 1782 law. The Paris Peace Treaty, according to Georgia, had simply confirmed existing debts, but the debts in question were not existing, at least not to the merchants, at the time of the treaty. The lawyers for the defendants presented a learned argument, filled with comments about the royal right to swans and sturgeon, which must have puzzled the jurors. Their main argument was that the Peace Treaty was "paramount" and effectively repealed the Georgia statute.[98]

After four days of legal argument, the Chief Justice gave a brief charge to the jury. He began by noting that the case had been argued "with great learning, diligence, and ability" and that the jurors had heard it "with particular attention." The jurors were thus "now, if ever you can be, completely possessed of the merits of the cause." If the jurors were puzzled as to why they were being asked to resolve what seemed a host of difficult legal issues, he noted that although juries are usually "the best judges of facts" and courts "the best judges of law," still "both objects are lawfully, within your power of decision."[99]

The jurors retired to consider, then returned to the courtroom with two questions. First, they asked whether the Georgia statute "completely vest[ed] the debts of [the defendants] in the state?" Second, they asked whether the Peace Treaty "revive[d] the right of the defendants to the debt in controversy." Jay responded that he had intended, in his charge, to address these issues, but since the jury "entertained a doubt, the enquiry was perfectly right." On the first question, he said that the court's view was that the Georgia statute did not vest the debt in Georgia. On the second question (which in fairness to the jurors he had only touched on in his charge), he said that "the mere restoration of peace, as well as the very terms of the treaty, revived the right of action to recover the debt." The jurors, "without going again from the bar," then returned a verdict for the defendants.[100]

This was, no doubt, a satisfying resolution from Jay's perspective. The Supreme Court had vindicated the right of a British creditor, regardless of a state statute, to recover a pre-war debt. By referring the legal issues to the jury, the court had avoided a written opinion or set of opinions, which could well have received the same criticism as the *Chisholm* opinions. Conversely, however, by not issuing a written decision, the court had missed an opportunity to address the issues more generally.[101]

The next case on the calendar was *Glass v. Sloop Betsey*, an admiralty case with international implications. The *Betsey* was captured in June 1793 by one of the ships commissioned by Genet, the modestly named *Citizen Genet*. The *Genet* brought the *Betsey* into Baltimore where, probably after discussion with Genet himself, the French Consul declared that the *Betsey* and cargo were British and thus a legitimate prize. Alexander Glass and others sued in the federal district court, claiming that they were the "true owners" of the *Betsey* and the cargo, that the ship was only two miles off of the coast when it was "forcibly seized," that this seizure was contrary to American and international law, and that they were entitled to the ship, the cargo, and damages. Peter Johannene, the captain of the *Genet*, disputed many of these facts, and argued that only the consul or court of the captor nation, France, could legitimately decide the *Betsey's* fate. Both lower courts agreed with the captain's legal argument, which was indeed the accepted view at the time.[102]

In the Supreme Court, the lawyers for the owners argued that once the captain brought the *Betsey* into Baltimore, he submitted himself "to the American jurisdiction." The lawyers for the captain responded that "by the law of nations, the courts of the captor alone can determine the question of prize, or no prize." The mere act of bringing the ship into an American port did not, in their view, confer any jurisdiction to consider whether it was lawful prize on American courts. And if there was any "American jurisdiction," they argued, it was for the "sovereign, not the judicial, power." In reply, the owners argued that the courts were "sovereign, as to determinations upon property, whenever the property is within its reach." The attempt by France to set up consuls in America to decide such admiralty issues "can never be countenanced."[103]

The Supreme Court took the case under consideration for a few days and then issued a brief, forceful order, drafted by Jay. The court was "decidedly of the opinion" that every federal district court "possesses all the powers of a court of admiralty" and that the captain's argument that the case should be dismissed was "altogether insufficient." The district court was therefore directed to decide the case "consistently with the laws of nations and the treaties and laws of the United States." Moreover, "no foreign power can of right institute or erect any court of judicature of any kind within the jurisdiction of the United States," unless expressly authorized to do so by treaty. The jurisdiction of the French Consul, "not being so warranted, is not of right."[104]

Again, the decision must have been satisfying for Jay, for several reasons. First, the *Glass* case showed that he and the other justices had been right, the prior year, when they declined to answer Jefferson's abstract questions about neutrality. Concrete questions would arise, as in the *Glass* case, for the courts to decide as courts. Second, the *Glass* case allowed the court to support the administration's neutrality policy. The administration had, in 1793, ruled that the French consuls must cease, on pain of expulsion, rendering prize decisions in the United States; the Supreme Court now roundly supported this order. Third, the *Glass* case allowed Jay to frustrate, in a judicial rather than a political way, Edmond Genet's attempts to turn the United States into a base for France's war against Britain. It was surely not lost on Jay that Genet had commissioned the French privateer and had probably encouraged the French consul in Baltimore to rule that the ship was lawful prize. Fourth, the *Glass* case allowed the United States to assert that, on this issue at least, it did not intend to follow standard European legal practice. Other nations might cede jurisdiction over prizes to belligerents; the United States would not.

The first of the two pension cases on the calendar involved John Chandler of Connecticut. Justice Iredell and Judge Law, acting as commissioners under the Pension Act, had recommended that Chandler receive a pension. The Secretary of War, however, had not included Chandler's name on the list of pensions relayed to Congress. Chandler's lawyer now asked the Supreme Court for "mandamus," an order directing the Secretary of War to place Chandler on the list. The Supreme Court ruled, without explanation, that "mandamus cannot issue." [105]

On the next day, the justices heard argument in another pension case, the claim of Yale Todd, also of Connecticut. Chief Justice Jay, Justice Cushing and Judge Law, acting as commissioners, had recommended in May of 1792 that Todd receive a pension. Unlike the recommendation with respect to Chandler, the recommendation with respect to Todd was accepted by the Secretary, and Todd received over $170 as pension. Now, however, the United States claimed that he was not entitled to a pension and owed the money back. The issue, according to the agreed statement of facts, was whether the "said judges of said circuit court sitting as commissioners and not as a circuit court had power and authority" to consider and rule on the pension application. In other words, the Attorney General was now arguing that the "commissioner" compromise devised by Jay in the spring of 1792 was invalid: that either the circuit court judges had to act as a circuit court or not at all. The Supreme Court ruled in favor of the United States, again without explanation, so that later scholars have had to debate whether the court had implicitly declared the Pension Act unconstitutional, or instead decided only that the Act did not allow for decisions by "commissioners." [106]

This cryptic one-line order underlines an important question about the February 1794 session of the Supreme Court. The court decided four important cases, two of them with international implications. In the *Chandler* and *Todd* decisions, the justices were in effect reversing course, deciding that they had *not* in fact had any authority to consider the pension applications as commissioners in the spring of 1792. And yet there were no opinions in any of these four cases; the most the court offered was the brief decree in the *Glass* case. Perhaps the issue was time, since some of the justices left soon after the Supreme Court session ended to start their circuit court duties. Perhaps the issue was reluctance, after the storm caused by the *Chisholm* decision, to write and issue further controversial opinions. Perhaps, however, the court's almost total silence at this time reflects a failure by Jay to force himself and his fellow justices to perform a critical task, not only deciding important cases, but explaining their decisions for other courts and for the public.

When scholars rank the justices of the Supreme Court, Jay is generally rated "average" or "good" but only rarely "great." There are several reasons for this. He did not write many opinions, both because the early court did not have many cases on its docket, and because the court often resolved cases without opinions. His one major opinion, in the *Chisholm* case, was soon overturned by constitutional amendment, a rare rebuke for the Supreme Court. Although not often mentioned, his conduct in the Genet episode was not proper. Above all Jay suffers by comparison with his great successor, John Marshall. To the extent one can forget about Marshall and focus on Jay, however, he accomplished much in his four years on the court. In the pension cases, Jay and his colleagues established that federal courts could review the constitutionality of federal statutes. In the British debt cases, he confirmed that federal courts could review the constitutionality of state statutes, and he helped reduce (but not entirely eliminate) British dissatisfaction with the way in which American courts handled debt cases. In his response to Jefferson's request for an advisory opinion, he established that federal courts would not consider abstract issues, but only concrete controversies. In his brief opinion on the French prize case, he gave support to Washington's neutrality policy, which he had helped form in his role as unofficial political adviser. Both in his work in the Supreme Court, and especially in his work as a circuit justice, he helped to make the federal courts a reality, to bring federal justice to "every man's door." [107]

CHAPTER 13

Envoy to England

I N THE SPRING of 1794, many Americans believed that another war with Britain was imminent and inevitable. The war scare started with reports that British warships were seizing American merchant vessels in the West Indies. The British were forcing the ships into British ports, condemning them there on the basis of a previously secret November order against *any* trade with the French West Indies, and leaving the American seamen without means to support themselves or to return home. It seemed to many Americans, as Madison put it in a letter to Jefferson, that Britain "meditates a formal war as soon as she shall have crippled our marine resources." American concerns increased in late March, when the newspapers printed a speech by the British Governor of Canada, in which he predicted to an Indian delegation that within the year Britain and America would be at war. The Governor hoped that the British and their Indian allies would prevail so that they could, after the war, draw a new border between Canada and the United States. Since the British still held forts in upstate New York and the upper Midwest, there could be little doubt that the Governor had in mind a boundary far to the south of the border Jay and his colleagues had obtained in the 1783 Peace Treaty.[1]

Americans of all political persuasions were outraged by these events, but there were differences between Federalist outrage and Republican outrage. Federalists favored stronger defenses but also favored neutrality and peace. Jay, for example, wrote to his friend Rufus King that "the aspect of the times begins to alarm" and that the defenses of New York harbor were "inadequate and improper." Republicans were much harsher in their criticism of the British; one of them wrote that "every day adds new proofs of the ill will and contempt of Great Britain towards us." But even the Republicans were not quite prepared to declare war, and they were frustrated at the way in which the Federalists seemed to have stolen the war issue.[2]

In early April, Jay traveled to Philadelphia to preside over a circuit court session. Once there, he was immediately drawn into the discussions among the nation's leaders about the war crisis. On the day after he arrived, for example, he dined with Washington, and they discussed the latest dispatches from London. According to one of these reports, the British minister William Grenville characterized the closure of the Caribbean as merely a temporary measure, designed to prepare for a British attack on the French islands. Britain reportedly hoped "to maintain the best understanding and harmony with the United States." Washington may have, at this same dinner, asked Jay whether he was willing to go to England as special envoy. Jay did not mention this, however, in a letter the next day to his wife, saying only that "the question of war and peace seems to be as much in suspense here as in New York when I left you."[3]

Even if the President did not discuss a mission to England with Jay, others did. King said that Jay and Hamilton were the two leading candidates for the mission, and that, although Hamilton was more of an expert on commerce, Jay had more "weight of character abroad, as well as at home." Jay modestly "made no reply respecting himself," but "appeared fully to agree with Hamilton's appointment." A few days later, Hamilton wrote Washington a long letter, stressing the dangers of war, urging the President to send an envoy, withdrawing his own name from consideration, and praising Jay. "Mr. Jay is the only man in whose qualifications for success there would be thorough confidence and him whom alone it would be advisable to send. I think the business would have the best chance possible in his hands."[4]

Hamilton's letter apparently persuaded the President, for on the next day Washington requested that Jay come at "as early an hour this morning, as you can make convenient to yourself." At this breakfast meeting, Washington asked Jay to serve as envoy extraordinary to England. Jay asked for at least a day to consider the question. That afternoon, Alexander Hamilton and four Federalist senators descended upon him. According to King's notes, they "press[ed] upon him the necessity which exists that he should not decline the envoyship; that in short he was the only man in whom we could confide, and that we deemed the situation of the country too interesting and critical to permit him to hesitate." Jay, according to King, "did not decline."[5]

That evening, after a long day in the circuit court, John Jay picked up his pen to write to his "dear, dear Sally." There was, John reported, "a serious determination to send me to England, if possible to avert a war. The object is so interesting to our country, and the combination of circumstances such, that I find myself in a dilemma between personal considerations and public ones." From a personal perspective, nothing could be "more distant from [my] every wish." He expected that it would take at least six months, perhaps longer, to travel to London, negotiate with the British, and return to New York. From a public perspective, however, the mission could help prevent "the effusion of blood, and other evils and miseries incident to war." He had not quite made up his mind, but he was inclined to accept, if it would "please God to make me instrumental to the continuance of peace."[6]

Although John did not mention them to Sarah, he probably considered various other aspects of the issue that night. There was, first of all, the constitutional question: could a Supreme Court justice accept a diplomatic assignment? The Constitution prohibited members of Congress from accepting other federal offices; it was silent on whether justices of the Supreme Court might accept other duties; and Jay and others have read this silence as permitting justices to take on various non-judicial assignments.[7]

Assuming that it was *permissible* for him to undertake this assignment, there was a second question, whether it was *proper* for him to do so. Jay later claimed that he knew all along "that no treaty whatever with Great Britain would escape a partial but violent opposition." If he indeed had this view in April 1794, he should have paused before accepting the assignment, and involving the Supreme Court in a controversial political issue. But he probably did not at this stage understand quite how controversial his nomination and the negotiation would become. And he viewed the court's role as supporting and strengthening the national government, so he probably saw this task as consistent with rather than in tension with the role of the court.[8]

There is a third question which Jay perhaps considered on that April evening: how would this assignment, if he accepted it, affect his own political future? There would be another election for New York Governor in the spring of 1795: would he be able to return to New York in time to serve as Governor if elected? Even more important, there would be an election for President in 1796, and the likely successors to Washington were generally thought to be Adams, Jay or Jefferson. Secretary of State Randolph, writing to President Washington, doubted Jay would accept a longer-term assignment in England because he had his "eye immediately on the government of New York and ultimately on the presidency." Adams viewed the appointment in a similar light, writing to his wife that Jay's peace mission, if successful, would "recommend him to the choice of the people for President as soon as a vacancy shall happen." If Jay himself considered these questions, however, he left no record of it.[9]

On the next morning, Jay again met with Washington, and told him that he would accept. Washington immediately asked the Senate to confirm the appointment. The Senate generally deferred to Washington, but in this case there was a vigorous debate. Senator James Monroe declared that Jay was "not a suitable character," that he was biased in favor of Britain and of Spain. (Monroe apparently believed that Britain and Spain had a secret alliance.) Senator John Taylor opposed the appointment "upon the ground of the incompatibility in the office of Chief Justice and Envoy Extraordinary." In Taylor's view, "such an appointment would destroy the independence of the Judiciary by teaching them to look for lucrative employment from and dependent upon the pleasure of the Executive." Senator Aaron Burr agreed: it was "mischievous and impolitic," and "contrary to the spirit of the Constitution," to allow a justice of the Supreme Court to hold any position "emanating" from the executive branch. After two days of debate, however, the Senate confirmed Jay's appointment by a vote of eighteen to eight.[10]

While this debate was under way, Jay was busy with the work of the federal circuit court. He wrote to his wife that the "court has unceasingly engrossed my time" and that "we did not adjourn until nine" in the evening. He was also considering the question of who would join him on the trip. Sarah urged John to take along their son, Peter Augustus, as private secretary: "it would give him infinite pleasure and me great consolation." John was not persuaded: "the expediency of it does not strike me forcibly; what real advantage will it afford him?" Sarah responded somewhat sharply that she could not "perceive your objections to taking with you our son." Peter had just graduated from college, and not yet started his legal studies, so it seemed "a favorable period to indulge under your auspices a laudable curiosity" with respect to foreign lands. Peter Jay Munro, with whom young Peter was supposed to start a legal clerkship, completely agreed. "Nine months or a year under your eye in Europe will prove more essentially beneficial to [Peter] than the same period spent in my office." John yielded and agreed that Peter could come along as private secretary. For his official secretary, Jay settled on John Trumbull, the painter. He did not really need another lawyer, and thought that Trumbull's "acquaintance with the characters and things of London, his particular intimacy with [Benjamin] West, and his connections to other people of note" would be useful.[11]

Two days after his confirmation, Jay had a long meeting with Secretary Hamilton and Senators King, Cabot and Ellsworth. They talked about his mission, what he should seek from the British (compensation for the recent captures and evacuation of the northwest forts), and what he could offer to them (perhaps as much as half a million pounds for the losses incurred by non-payment of the debts). They all agreed that the President did not have to seek the views of the Senate on the proposed instructions, and that it would suffice if the treaty was signed "subject to the approbation of the Senate." This seems obvious today, but at the time it was far from obvious that the President, who could only enter treaties with the "advice and consent" of the Senate, could send off an envoy without discussing his instructions with the Senate.[12]

On the next day, Jay met with Hamilton alone, and worked with him on the notes that Hamilton presented the following day to the President. They argued that Jay's first priority should be to obtain compensation for the "depredations upon our commerce according to a rule to be settled." The "desirable rule" would be one that allowed the British to seize only "articles by general usage deemed contraband" and that even the presence of contraband on an American ship would not "infect other parts of a cargo." Hamilton and Jay recognized, however, that the British might well not agree to such a rule, and that "in the last resort" Jay should agree to the provisions of the January order, since it reverted to principles "long adhered to by Great Britain." Jay's second priority should be to settle the disputes arising out of the peace treaty: to get the British out of the northwest forts; to obtain compensation for the slaves and other property removed by the British army; and to offer some compensation for the delays suffered by British creditors. Third, Jay should try to obtain a commercial treaty with Britain, and in particular to obtain the right to carry goods to and from the British West Indies. Jay's final instructions were along these lines: he was given broad discretion, subject only to the limit that he not "derogate from our treaties and engagements with France." [13]

Jay returned to New York City in late April to organize his affairs and pack his bags. He may have found time for one or two further sittings for Gilbert Stuart, who was working slowly on a portrait of him in his judicial robes. Stuart had arrived in New York about a year before this time, nearly penniless, knowing only one prominent person: John Jay. The Chief Justice had commissioned a portrait, introduced the painter to various friends, and praised him to President Washington. While Jay was away in England, Stuart would travel to the Philadelphia, to start work on the first of his portraits of Washington, the most famous and familiar images of the first President. Stuart would in time paint almost all the great men of Jay's generation, and it was Jay who helped him get his start in this process. [14]

As he was making final preparations to depart, Jay received a letter from Robert Livingston. In their youth, the two men had agreed their friendship would be indissoluble, but in recent years the friendship had weakened and dissolved. There were various reasons: Jay resented Livingston's criticism of his work in France; Livingston resented Jay's selection as Chief Justice; Livingston opposed Jay in the election of 1792; Jay now viewed Livingston as dangerously pro-French. Livingston's tone therefore was as about as cool as it could be, considering the mortal dangers that Jay was about to face on the North Atlantic. "The Chancellor presents his compliments to the Chief Justice of the United States. Though political differences have excited a coolness between them perhaps inconsistent with the liberality of both, the Chancellor is not so unmindful of past friendships as not to be sincere in wishing the Chief Justice a safe passage, a happy return to his friends and a successful issue to his mission." Jay responded with more warmth: "The Chief Justice of the United States presents his compliments to the Chancellor of the State. It is now late of night and want of time imposes brevity. He assures the Chancellor that while he regrets what is, he will always remember with pleasure what has been their relative situation to each other. Time here or hereafter will correct errors. He thanks him for the kind wishes expressed in his note; and without hesitation reciprocates them." This was their last personal correspondence.[15]

John Jay sailed from New York for England on the *Ohio* on May 12, 1794. The newspaper accounts of that day show how divided Americans were about his mission. On the morning of his departure, a Federalist paper announced in large type that Jay would embark for England "at nine o'clock," and that "such citizens as are disposed to attend him to the place of embarkation are requested to assemble at that hour in front of Trinity Church." That evening, another Federalist paper reported that "an immense concourse of respectable citizens," had accompanied John and Peter Jay from their home to the ship. As he ascended to the deck, Jay turned to the crowd and expressed "his sensibility and gratitude for their attentions" and "his determination to do everything in his power to effect the object of his mission and secure the blessings of peace." The crowd responded with three cheers. After the *Ohio* left the dock, the crowd followed it south, and cheered again from the Battery, as cannons fired.[16]

According to a Republican paper, however, only about two hundred people had actually shown up to "attend" Jay; the others were simply onlookers, curious to see the sight of the ship under sail. Republican papers gave more play to two other events of the same day. In Philadelphia, the Democratic Society denounced Jay's appointment as "contrary to the spirit and meaning of the Constitution" and the "most unconstitutional and dangerous measure in the annals of the United States." In New York harbor, a few hours after Jay's departure, the Tammany Society celebrated its anniversary with a "grand civic feast" onboard a French warship. Governor Clinton and Chancellor Livingston were among those present for this "happy intermingling" of French and Americans. Although Jay was not mentioned by name in the newspaper account, there could be little doubt that this group did not favor closer relations between America and Britain. John sent a note to Sarah, urging her to disregard the resolutions and similar comments. "They give me no concern, and I hope they will be equally indifferent to you."[17]

It took more than a day for the *Ohio* to leave New York harbor. Indeed, the

Jays were able to go ashore, probably on Staten Island, where they "bought two additional sheep and a very large quantity of fresh fish, so that we shall be in no danger of starving." Once the ship caught the wind, however, it made rapid and apparently uneventful progress across the Atlantic, reaching Falmouth in Cornwall in early June.[18]

Falmouth was, according to Peter's diary, "an old town and an ugly one." They started for London, but not in great haste, stopping on the first day for a long tour of a tin mine, then spending the night at Truro. On the next day they traveled to Launceston, where they "found the remnants of a very old castle, formerly of great extent, which before the invention of firearms must have been as impregnable as Gibraltar is now." In Exeter they found an interesting combination of old and new: both factories producing "vast quantities" of clothing for export to China and a "very magnificent Gothic" cathedral, marred in Peter's view by the "figures of saints and bishops without number." Bath impressed and interested Peter, who noted that "persons of every rank and description" came there "to drink of the waters or share in the amusements of the place."[19]

The Jays did not linger in Bath, however, setting out early in the morning, covering about eighty miles, and arriving in Windsor by early afternoon. Because the King was at Windsor Castle, the taverns were "so full that we found it impossible to procure lodging," so the two travelers continued to Salt Hill, "where with some difficulty we got beds." They covered the remaining few miles to London early on June 14, reaching London by nine that morning. They intended to stay at the Bath Hotel, where John Adams had stayed when he was in London, but again they found "no room," so they went to the Royal Hotel on Pall Mall. This "extensive establishment for the reception and accommodation of gentlemen and families of distinction," located in the fashionable West End, would be Jay's home for the next several months.[20]

Jay arrived in London at an extraordinary moment in English and European history. Across the Channel, in Paris, the revolutionaries were killing "counter-revolutionaries" at a sickening pace. Men and women were sentenced to death for "spreading false news," for "depraving morals," even for "impairing the purity and energy of the revolutionary government." More than fifteen hundred people were tried and guillotined in Paris in June and July of

1794. The names, filling column after column in the London newspapers, were sometimes not just names for Jay: they were the Parisians among whom he had lived only ten years before. Thousands of others were arrested, or fled to avoid arrest, including one of Jay's closest French friends, the banker Ferdinand Grand.[21]

France was not only at war with itself; it was at war with England and its allies. On June 11, 1794, the *London Times* reported in bold type that Lord Howe had won an "important naval victory," over the French. (In considerably smaller type, this same paper reported the arrival of the Jays at Falmouth.) Over the next few days, the newspapers printed the details of this naval battle, which would become known as the Glorious First of June, but they also had to report the French successes on the ground in Flanders. Indeed, in late June the French army decisively defeated the Austrian and English forces at Fleurus, leaving more than eight thousand dead on the field. Peter Jay reported home to his cousin Peter Munro, with some exaggeration, that "not less than eighty thousand men have perished since the opening of this campaign, and yet it is but opened." [22]

England too was to some extent at war within itself. A few radicals hoped for an English version of the French Revolution; a far larger group favored reform of Parliament, and this group held several mass meetings in the spring of 1794. William Pitt and his government, however, were in no mood to consider compromise. Not long before the Jays arrived, the government arrested and imprisoned a dozen prominent radicals, charging them with treason, and Parliament approved an eight-month suspension of the right to petition for *habeas corpus*. The government, when the Jays arrived in June 1794, was organizing and arming the militia, to defend both against a possible French invasion and a possible domestic rebellion. In hindsight, it seems the government overreacted, but this was less clear at the time.

It was against this dramatic background that Jay began his attempt to resolve the differences between the United States and Britain.[23]

A few days after his arrival in London, Jay met Lord Grenville, the man with whom he was to negotiate over the next few months. William Wyndham Grenville, not yet thirty-five, was the son of George Grenville, whose stamp tax and other policies had started the process of the American Revolution. The younger Grenville had entered Parliament at the age of twenty-two, served in various junior positions in the government of his cousin William Pitt, and had since 1791 been both Foreign Secretary and leader of the House of Lords. Grenville was in effect deputy Prime Minister for his cousin the Prime Minister, and as such was intimately involved in all the domestic and foreign crises of this time.[24]

Jay presumably learned something about Grenville's background and personality from Thomas Pinckney, the resident American Minister in London. Grenville in turn learned something about Jay from Andrew Elliott, who had known Jay as a young lawyer in colonial New York. Elliott advised that Jay had "good sense and much information; has great appearance of coolness; and is a patient hearer with a good memory. He argues closely, but is long-winded and self-opinioned." Elliott believed that Jay could "be attached by good treatment, but will be unforgiving if he thinks himself neglected; he will expect to be looked up to not merely as an American agent, but as *Mr. Jay*, who was in Spain, who has been in high office from the beginning." On balance, Elliott concluded, the Americans "could not have made a better choice, as he certainly has good sense and judgment, both of which must have been mellowed since I saw him. But almost every man has a weak and assailable quarter, and Mr. Jay's weak side is *Mr. Jay*."[25]

Grenville received Jay, his son and his secretary very politely at their first meeting. In the weeks and months that followed, Grenville and other British leaders often invited the Jays to formal dinners and other entertainments. In early July, for example, Jay was presented to the King and the Queen; he described the King as "well prepared for the occasion" and expressing "many general sentiments that were liberal and proper." As Jay noted in a letter to President Washington, "so far as personal attention to the envoy may be regarded as symptoms of good will to his country, my prospect is favorable." He cautioned, however, that such symptoms "are never decisive; they justify expectation, but not reliance." To Hamilton, he reported "appearances continue to be singularly favorable, but appearances merit only a certain degree of circumspect reliance." He did not intend to be swayed by the personal attention paid to him; he intended to focus on the substance of the negotiation.[26]

At one of their first meetings, Jay described for Grenville how British ships had seized and mistreated American ships and sailors. Grenville claimed that "not a single case under the instructions of November had been presented to him." Jay now realized that he should have brought with him more detailed accounts of the captures. He tried to gather information from American merchants in London, and from lawyers representing American merchants in British admiralty appeals; he also wrote home to Secretary of State Randolph requesting more detailed information.[27]

Two weeks later, Jay and Grenville were meeting amidst daily newspaper reports regarding changes in the composition of the government. Grenville assured Jay that "no unnecessary delays should retard" their discussions, although he cautioned that "the new arrangement of the ministry involved the necessity of time for their being all informed and consulted." Jay raised the question of the western frontier, and in particular the "hostile measures" of British General John Graves Simcoe, who had retaken and rebuilt a fort near Detroit. Grenville and Jay "concurred in the opinion that, during the present negotiation and until the conclusion of it all things ought to remain and be preserved *in statu quo*" and that "all hostile measures, if any such should have taken place, shall cease." Grenville drafted a letter to this effect to the British officials in North America; Jay agreed "on the part of the United States" that the ceasefire would be "faithfully observed and fulfilled."[28]

During July, Jay and Grenville continued to discuss the British seizures and the difficulties Americans faced in the British admiralty courts. At the end of the month, Jay presented Grenville a formal letter on these issues. He noted that "a very considerable number of American vessels have been irregularly captured and as improperly condemned by certain of His Majesty's officers and judges." He explained that various factors had prevented Americans from appealing these decisions in British courts, including the distribution of sale proceeds "among a great number of persons." He expressed the hope that "His Majesty's justice and magnanimity" would "cause such compensation to be made to the innocent sufferers as may be consistent with equity." He also protested the "unusual personal severities" imposed upon American captains and seamen, which extended to "the impressments of American citizens to serve on board of armed vessels."[29]

Jay probably showed this letter in draft to Grenville, for on the next day Grenville responded "that it is His Majesty's wish that the most *complete* and *impartial* justice should be done to all the citizens of America" affected by improper seizures. Grenville believed that a "very considerable part of the injuries alleged to have been suffered by the Americans may ... be redressed in the usual course of judicial proceeding." But to the extent that Americans could not "procure such redress, in the ordinary course of law, as the justice of their cases may entitle them to expect, His Majesty will be anxious that justice should, at all events, be done." As to the impressed seamen, Grenville stressed that Britain did not wish to impress Americans, "though such cases may have occasionally arisen from the difficulty of discriminating between British and American seamen." Grenville would, as Jay requested, send instructions to British naval captains to emphasize that they were not to impress Americans.[30]

Jay was eager to move from these "desultory discussions" and to "fix our attention on certain propositions." In early August, therefore, Jay presented to Grenville a rough first draft of the treaty. Jay proposed that arbitration commissions resolve two disputed boundaries, the northeast boundary of Maine and the northwest boundary of what is now Minnesota. The problem in Maine arose from a confusion over which river was meant, in the Paris Peace Treaty, by the "River St. Croix." The Americans argued that the river was the Magaguadavic; the British maintained it was the Schoodiac. The problem with the northwest boundary arose from a similar confusion. The Peace Treaty provided that the line between Canada and the United States would run "due west" from the northwest corner of the Lake of the Woods to the Mississippi. It now appeared that a line due west from the Lake of the Woods would never hit the Mississippi; it would run west through what is now southern Canada until it reached the Pacific Ocean.[31]

Jay proposed that Britain withdraw all its troops from the northwest forts by June 1795, a somewhat ambitious date, given how long it would take to conclude and ratify a treaty, and get word of the treaty to remote settlements. Echoing the recent letters, Jay suggested that Britain should provide "full and complete satisfaction and compensation" for all "vessels and property of American citizens which have been, or during the course of the present war shall be, illegally captured and condemned." In return, he offered that the

United States would provide "full and complete satisfaction and compensation" to British creditors who had been unable to recover lawful debts through American courts. In both cases, he suggested that an arbitration commission be created to hear cases in which plaintiffs claimed they could not obtain justice in the normal course. If Britain and the United States were ever at war, neither should commission privateers against the other (this was the provision Franklin had urged during the Paris Peace negotiations), nor would they sequester debts of their opponent's citizens (this was perhaps to avoid future state statutes against British creditors).[32]

On commercial issues, Jay urged Britain to allow American ships of up to one hundred tons to trade with the British West Indies. This provision was subject to an ill-advised proviso: "that West India productions or manufactures shall not be transported in American vessels, either from His Majesty's said islands, or from the United States, to any part of the world except the United States, reasonable sea stores excepted, and excepting also rum made in the United States from West India molasses." The context suggested that the proviso only applied to goods from the *British* West Indies, but there was no practical way to distinguish goods from the British, French or Dutch West Indies. The practical effect, therefore, was to prohibit all exports from the United States in American ships of "molasses, sugar, coffee, cocoa or cotton." Even if the proviso were somehow applied only to products from or derived from British islands, it probably gave away more than the main provision obtained. This was the "one great lapse" in the final Jay Treaty, and unfortunately it was Jay who suggested it, in this first draft. Jay proposed that not only the British West Indies, but also the British East Indies, indeed "all the other ports and territories of His Majesty," other than those reserved for the chartered trading companies, would be open to American vessels. Likewise, American ports would be open to British vessels. Although this provision was less noticed at the time, it proved extremely important, providing a basis for American trade with British ports in Asia and elsewhere.[33]

Jay hoped to finish the negotiation as soon as possible. In mid-August, he sent a brief letter to Grenville, noting that Congress would meet in early November, and that "the President must be exceedingly anxious to insert in his speech something satisfactory and decisive relative to our negotiations."

Would it not be possible, Jay asked, to reach an agreement on the basis "of the informal notes which I had the honor of enclosing to your Lordship." Grenville responded the next day, regretting that "the multitude and urgency of other business at the present moment" simply made it "impossible to me to give to our negotiation as entire and undivided an attention as I should wish." Indeed, given all the other demands on his time, especially the total war against France, it is remarkable how *much* time and attention Grenville devoted to his discussions with Jay. A recent biography of Grenville notes that he "responded energetically to the challenge" of securing peace "with a country whose disputes with Britain could be traced back to his father's fateful Stamp Tax." This same biography, however, devotes only three pages to the Jay negotiations. A major event in Jay's life was a minor moment in that of Grenville; a major treaty for the young United States was a minor one for Great Britain.[34]

At the end of August, Grenville presented Jay with two detailed draft treaties, one dealing with the military and legal disputes, the other dealing with commercial issues. Regarding the forts, Grenville proposed evacuation by June 1796. Grenville accepted Jay's suggestion that the northeast boundary should be resolved by an arbitration commission. On the northwest boundary, however, Grenville proposed that the treaty itself should draw the line, and he suggested two alternatives, both of which would have moved the boundary south into what is today Minnesota. Grenville's argument was that the Paris Peace Treaty had promised Britain navigation of the Mississippi River: to achieve this the southern boundary of Canada had to reach the Mississippi. Regarding the debts and seizures, Grenville accepted Jay's formula of "full and complete satisfaction," and he provided the details regarding the composition and powers of the proposed arbitration commissions. Grenville also suggested that each nation should prohibit its citizens from taking up arms against the other nation, a provision probably intended to prevent Americans from enlisting in the French armies or navies.[35]

In the draft commercial treaty, Grenville suggested that there should be a "reciprocal and perfect liberty of commerce and navigation" between Britain and the United States, subject only to payment of whatever duties applied to the most favored third nation. With respect to the British West Indies, Grenville proposed that American ships of up to seventy tons should be allowed to trade with the islands, subject to the proviso that American ships could not carry "any West India productions" either "from his Majesty's Islands, or from the United States, to any part of the world except the United States." Grenville's draft was silent on the question of trade with the British East Indies.[36]

Jay responded immediately to the proposed northwest boundary, a provision of some personal interest, since he had drafted it for the Paris Peace Treaty. Jay argued that there was no need to draw a new line in the treaty, since perhaps the line agreed in the prior treaty worked; that is, perhaps it *was* possible to draw a line west from the Lake of the Woods to the upper reaches of the Mississippi. If this was not possible, then the United States and Britain should let "joint commissioners, at joint expense, upon oath, fix a closing line in the manner which they shall judge most consonant with the true intent and meaning of the Treaty of Peace." Jay rejected the suggestion that Britain's right to navigate the Mississippi implied that the southern boundary of Canada should be on the "navigable part" of the river. "A right freely to navigate a bay, a straight, a sound, or a river, is perfect without, and does not necessarily presuppose, the dominion of lands and property adjacent to it." Grenville conceded the point and the final treaty provided for a joint survey, to be followed if necessary by "amicable negotiation" to resolve the issue "according to justice and mutual convenience, and in conformity to the intent of the [Paris] Treaty." Jay deserves great credit for his stubborn refusal to yield what was, at the time, an unknown bit of forest. Although the immediate issue was the ownership of part of what is today Minnesota, the longer term issue was the starting point for the boundary which would some day run all the way from Minnesota to the Pacific Ocean. By insisting on a more northerly boundary, Jay secured for the United States the northern plains, mountains and coast.[37]

Jay also sent Grenville early in September some "notes" questioning or commenting on other parts of Grenville's draft treaty. For example, Jay noted that Grenville used the term "contraband," and suggested that the treaty should define that controversial term. He continued to press for an article prohibiting the impressments of one another's seamen. He did not, however, question the wording of the provision regarding the West Indies, including the critical proviso.[38]

Jay was reminded at this time that not all Americans would approve of the treaty upon which he was working. James Monroe, recently appointed as American Minister to France, arrived in Paris, was greeted with a kiss by the President of the National Convention, and then gave a stirring speech to the Convention on French-American friendship. Monroe presented, and the British newspapers published, a letter from Secretary of State Randolph which also seemed to support France in its war against Britain. Grenville and Jay were both annoyed. Grenville wrote Jay that "it is not consistent with neutrality to make ministerial declarations of favour and preference." Jay responded that, if he had been in Randolph's place, "I should not have written exactly such a letter." Jay complained to both Washington and Randolph. Everyone was free to have "affections or predilections for persons or nations," Jay wrote to Washington, but "as the situation of the United States is neutral, so also should be their language to the belligerent powers." To Randolph, he wrote bluntly that "your letter by Mr. Monroe, and his speech to the Convention, is regarded here as not being consistent with the neutral situation of the United States."[39]

Jay's discussions with Grenville continued throughout September. On the last day of the month, Jay presented to Grenville a detailed revised draft. The draft included many new provisions, some of which survived into the final treaty, others of which were abandoned. Jay suggested that the treaty should start with peace and friendship: "There shall be a firm, inviolable and universal peace and a true and sincere friendship between His Britannic Majesty, his heirs and successors, and the United States of America, and between their respective countries, territories, cities, towns and people." With some minor wording changes, this provision became article 1 of the final treaty. Jay noted that it was "uncertain" whether the Mississippi River reached the line described in the Paris Peace Treaty and included detailed provisions for a joint survey of the river. The principles of Jay's provision were accepted, although the details were omitted. Grenville had omitted, from his draft, any mention of the British East Indies. Jay insisted upon access to these ports, and a provision along the lines drafted by Jay was included in the final treaty. Jay's revision of the West Indies article was, if anything, worse than his original draft. Jay's new draft provided that, while Britain granted the United States access to the British West Indies, the United States would "prohibit the carrying of any sugar, coffee or cotton in American vessels either from His Majesty's islands or from the United States to any part of the world except the United States." Cotton was not a particularly important product of the West Indies, but it was an increasingly important American product, and it is a mystery why Jay agreed that it could not be exported in American ships.[40]

Other provisions of Jay's draft, however, did not survive into the final treaty. Jay suggested that, if there ever was a war between Britain and the United States, neither side should arm or ally with the Indians. Jay suggested that neither Britain nor the United States should keep armed vessels on the Great Lakes; they would "enter into arrangements for diminishing or wholly withdrawing all military forces from the borders." The border between the United States and Canada is today unarmed, but Jay's suggestion was a radical one for the time, and was not accepted. Jay offered a detailed and narrow definition of contraband: he would have excluded timber, planks, sails and "all other things proper either for building or repairing ships"; he would have clarified that "corn, grain and other provisions" could only be contraband "when a well-founded expectation exists of reducing an enemy by want thereof." The final treaty provided that "timber for shipbuilding" and other similar goods would be contraband, "unwrought iron and fir planks only excepted." The final treaty left the question of when food would be contraband to "the law of nations," but accepted Jay's suggestion that there should always be compensation when food was seized as contraband. Jay's draft did not quite state that "free ships make free goods," but it did limit the ability of British warships to stop and search American merchant ships.[41]

A week later, in early October, Grenville sent Jay a brief letter. He had not been able to consider the draft completely, "but on such attention as I have hitherto been able to give to it, I find so much new matter, and so much variation in the form and substance of the articles proposed in the [draft], that I am very apprehensive the discussion of these points will of necessity consume more time than I had flattered myself might have been sufficient to bring our negotiation to a satisfactory issue." Indeed, there were several points in Jay's draft "which must, if insisted upon on your part" create "insurmountable obstacles to the conclusion of the treaty proposed." Grenville was now using Jay's desire to conclude quickly to force him to make concessions.[42] Jay was keen to reach an agreement, but also keen to avoid a bad agreement. In the middle of October, John Quincy Adams, on his way to serve as America's Ambassador in Holland, stopped in London for two weeks. Jay took advantage of his presence, and that of the American Minister Thomas Pinckney, to go through the draft treaty line by line with them. At the end of these sessions, Adams noted in his diary that the draft was "far from being satisfactory to these gentlemen," but "with some alterations," which the British would probably accept, it seemed to all three Americans "preferable to a war." As Adams was getting ready to leave London, he sought both funds and advice from Jay, both of which the latter provided.[43]

Discussions continued until, on November 19, Jay and Grenville signed the formal treaty now known as Jay's Treaty. Most historians have stressed that the final treaty was "fairly close to Grenville's project" of late August. It was; but it also included several provisions from Jay's draft of late September. Jay was convinced that the final treaty, under the circumstances, was the best that the United States could do. "My task is done," he wrote home, and "my opinion of the treaty is apparent from my having signed it." "Further concessions on the part of Great Britain," he wrote in another letter, "cannot be attained." Whether the terms were acceptable would be for "the President, Senate and public" to decide. Although Jay knew that the fate of the treaty was out of his hands, he hoped that there would be peace between Britain and America. He wrote to Grenville that he prayed "the hatchet [should] henceforth be buried for ever, and with it all the animosities which sharpened, and which threatened to redden it."[44]

When Jay served as America's representative in Spain in 1780 and 1781, he was rarely invited to dinners or other social functions. When he served as envoy extraordinary in England in 1794 and 1795, he was invited out almost every day, and he rarely dined alone. Jay himself did not keep a record of all these dinners, but his son Peter did, in a fascinating daily diary.

Not long after the Jays arrived, they dined with Lord Grenville, whose party that evening included Prime Minister William Pitt and Lord Chancellor Loughborough. The next month they dined one day with "Mr. Hoar, a genteel and very rich Quaker at Hampstead," and on another day with the Russian

Ambassador, who entertained them "with great politeness and extraordinary magnificence." Jay spent a day at the home of Sir John Sinclair, head of the British Agricultural Society, inspecting with him various "ingenious" machines. In September, the Jays dined one day with William Wilberforce, the noted anti-slavery activist, and on another day met Jeremy Bentham, the philosopher and reformer. When they dined with Henry Dundas at Wimbledon, the guests included Lord Macartney, "who has lately arrived from China, and who told us many interesting facts relating to that country." The Jays spent a weekend at Grenville's country house in Dropmore, during which Grenville took them by carriage "to see [William] Herschel and his telescopes," and also to Windsor Castle, where they "walked upon the terrace to enjoy the finest prospect I ever beheld." During October, the Jays dined twice with the Lord Chancellor at his home in Hampstead, and Jay joined him in his box for a performance of *Romeo and Juliet*. He also talked with the Lord Chancellor about the possibility of a treaty or convention between the United States and Britain to make it easier to obtain evidence in one nation for use in the courts of the other.[45]

Jay enjoyed meeting and talking with eminent Britons, but he preferred the company of other Americans, especially that of the Church family. The beautiful and lively Angelica Schuyler Church was the daughter of Philip Schuyler, the sister-in-law and warm admirer of Alexander Hamilton, and indeed a distant cousin of Jay himself. Angelica had married a British businessman, John Barker Church, in 1777, and the family had lived in London since 1784. Their home was quite a social center: their guests included artists such as Benjamin West and politicians like William Pitt. Of particular interest to Peter Jay, the family included two sons about his age and a daughter only somewhat younger. The Church family immediately adopted the Jays when they arrived in 1794; indeed Peter noted that they dined with the Churches four times in the first two weeks of their stay. The Jays continued to see them frequently thereafter: one November evening, for example, they "spent the evening with Mrs. Church, it being Miss Church's fifteenth birthday." [46]

The Jays also spent much of their time during the fall and winter with the family of Thomas Pinckney, the American Minister to Britain. Pinckney had studied law in England before the Revolution, fought as an officer in the

American army, and then served South Carolina as its Governor. Not long after the Jays arrived in London, Pinckney's wife died suddenly, leaving Pinckney with four children. As the family emerged from its mourning, however, there were pleasant evenings with the Jays and others. One February night, for example, the children of the Churches and the Pinckneys performed the "tragedy of Douglas" for the assembled adults. On another evening, the Jays dined "together with a great number of Americans at Mr. Pinckney's to celebrate the birthday of the President."[47]

When he was not meeting with Grenville, or dining or visiting with friends, Jay spent much of his time writing letters. In addition to his lengthy official letters to Randolph, he wrote unofficially to Washington and Hamilton to keep them informed of his progress. He fended off repeated requests from Monroe in Paris for a copy of the treaty, since he knew that Monroe intended to share the treaty with the French, and knew that confidentiality could be critical to the treaty's chances of success. In another instance, however, Jay wrote to Monroe to seek help for a young English girl imprisoned in France. "When I consider what my feelings would be, had I a daughter of that age so circumstanced, I find it impossible to resist this application." He wrote home to his nephew to ask him to be sure to take care of an elderly slave Mary. "She has been so good to my father and mother, and to their children, and for so long a course of years been a faithful, ready and affectionate servant, that in my opinion she has laid us all under obligations which her subsequent faults and errors can never cancel."[48]

John wrote to Sarah at least once a week and sometimes more than once a day. One day he wrote her a letter in the morning and then, when he heard of another ship leaving in the afternoon, wrote a few lines just to wish "health and happiness to you and our dear little flock." Sarah wrote back to report on the children, on the family finances, and on the Gilbert Stuart portrait. In early August she lamented:

> Would you believe that Stuart has not yet finished your picture? I call on him often. I have not hesitated telling him that it is in his power to contribute infinitely to my gratification, by indulging me with your portrait; he has at length resumed the pencil, and your nephew has been sitting with your robe for him; it is now nearly done, and is your very self. It is an *inimitable picture*.

Stuart finally delivered the portrait in November. Sarah wrote to John that the painter, at that time, "insisted on my promising it should be destroyed, when he presented me with a better one, which he said he certainly would, if you would be so obliging as to have a mask made for him." She also noted that "in ten days" Stuart would go to Philadelphia "to take a likeness of the President." (In fact he would not go until the spring of 1795.) She hung the portrait in the dining room, "where the little prints used to hang, and you cannot imagine how much I am gratified in having it." [49]

Although John longed to return home, it was already late November when he finished work on the treaty, and he remembered well, from his ill-fated voyage in 1778, how difficult and dangerous it was to cross the Atlantic in winter. He decided against attempting an immediate return. "Not being fit for a winter voyage," he wrote to Hamilton, "I shall stay here till spring. Indeed, I shall want some repairs before I am quite fit for any voyage." The weather in London in late 1794 and early 1795 was bitterly cold. Peter noted one day that the thermometer stood at only eleven; John reported to Sarah that there "has been so much snow and frost that for a fortnight sleighs might have been used." It was not only cold, it was dark. "The clouds of smoke which constantly hover over the city will not permit us to enjoy much sunshine, even when the sky is free from other clouds." In early February, however, there was a thaw, and the Jays were invited by Sir Clement Cottrell to visit his country house in Oxfordshire. While there, Peter and perhaps John joined in a hunt; Peter's horse was an "old fox hunter" which carried him with "ease" over the hedges and ditches. [50]

As spring came, Jay waited for word about the reaction in the United States to the treaty. In early March, he wrote Sarah that "in the course of this month, towards the latter part of it, I expect to receive advices respecting the treaty, together with instructions relative to the conclusion of my business here. My impatience to receive them increases as the time approaches; not a moment shall then be lost in dispatching what may remain to be done." Peter used somewhat more colorful terms: "We begin now to be a little anxious to hear the fate of the treaty, which must by this time have been decided. It has doubtless been productive of much declamation, clamor and abuse. And I presume a certain party in New York with a worthy senator [Aaron Burr] at their head have been the most forward to reprobate and oppose it." [51]

In February 1795, Thomas Pinckney received instructions to go to Madrid, to attempt to open the Mississippi, define the boundaries between the United States and Spain's territories, and open Spain's ports to American trade. Pinckney and Jay had several long discussions about the Spanish issues before they departed in different directions that spring. Pinckney reached Madrid in June 1795 and was able, quite quickly, to negotiate a very favorable treaty with Spain, and in particular to open the Mississippi River to American trade. Jay's Treaty was a major reason for Pinckney's success. Spain knew of the fact of Jay's Treaty, but not its precise terms, and feared that the treaty was or would lead to an alliance between Britain and the United States. So Jay indirectly, through his treaty, helped Pinckney achieve in Spain what he had been unable to achieve himself, either with Floridablanca or with Gardoqui.[52]

In late March, still without news or instructions from the United States, Jay decided to go home. He wrote to Grenville, asking for a date when he might take formal leave of the King and Queen. Grenville said he feared there was no date, prior to Jay's scheduled departure, when he could see their Majesties. The King learned of Jay's imminent departure, however, and expressed the desire to see him, so Jay and Grenville saw the King and Queen at noon on April 10. That afternoon, Jay took his leave of the hotel staff, leaving five pounds for the head waiter and twenty pounds to divide among the others. The Jays then took the stage west for Bristol, where they boarded the ship *Severn*. Their luggage included six trunks, a paper case, a hat box, three sacks, four boxes, a basket and two swords. The next morning the ship made its way down the Bristol Channel and out into the Atlantic.[53]

Six weeks later, on May 28, the *Severn* sailed into New York harbor. A newspaper reported that, as soon as "the people of the city" learned of Jay's arrival, a "vast multitude" assembled at the wharf and "escorted" him to his house, "with frequent cheers and every possible demonstration of joy and respect." At six o'clock that evening, according to another newspaper account, "a joyful peal was rung from the bells of the city, and at seven a federal salute was fired from the Battery, which was returned from the fort on Governors Island." The crowds cheered for at least two reasons. First, the people knew that Jay had signed a peace treaty with Britain, although they did not yet know any of the details. Second, the people knew that Jay was likely to become their new Governor, once the election returns were fully counted.[54]

Not everyone in New York or the nation welcomed Jay and his treaty. Indeed, long before he returned, and long before the terms of the treaty were known, it was under attack. An author calling himself "Franklin," in a series of essays starting in March of 1795, while Jay was still in England, scorned the very *idea* of a treaty with Britain. "There is not a nation upon earth so truly and justly abhorred by the people of the United States as Great Britain; and if their temper and sensibility were consulted, no treaty whatever would have been formed, especially at the expense of the French Republic." A treaty with Britain, "Franklin" warned, was the first step on the road to ruin. "What has accelerated the destruction of all republics? The corruption of principles which has resulted from the introduction of the fashions, the forms and the precedents of monarchical government."[55]

Washington, when he received the treaty in March, decided to keep its terms secret, and to present it in secret to the Senate. Not long after Jay returned to New York, the Senate began debate on the treaty in Philadelphia, behind closed doors. The Republican newspapers now attacked the Senate's secrecy. "How does the secrecy of the Senate in relation to the treaty," one author demanded, "comport with the sovereignty of the people?" The President and the Senate could make treaties, but surely they could not "hatch those things in darkness." Within the Senate, there were about twenty Federalists and ten Republicans, and although the debate was prolonged, it appears that no votes were changed. In late June, by a party-line vote, the treaty was ratified, with the exception of the article about the West Indies, because of the proviso on exports. The *fact* that the Senate had ratified was reported in the newspapers, but the terms of the treaty were still not public. Benjamin Bache, Franklin's grandson and a Republican newspaper editor, complained bitterly that the people would perhaps not learn the treaty's terms until it "becomes the supreme law of the land, and not an hour sooner."[56]

But within a few days, Bache himself obtained a copy of the treaty, apparently from Virginia Senator Stevens Mason, and published the entire text in early July. There was an outcry and an uproar, not limited merely to newspaper articles. For about six weeks, on almost every day of the week, there was a protest against Jay and his treaty in some city or town. In Charleston, South Carolina, the citizens celebrated Bastille Day by dragging the Union Jack through the mud and then burning it in front of the home of the British consul. In New York City, when Alexander Hamilton tried to defend the treaty at a public meeting, he was hit by a stone, and then retreated, saying he could not respond to such arguments. Jefferson, hearing this, wrote to Madison with evident approval that "the Livingstonians appealed to stones and clubs and beat him [Hamilton] and his party off the ground." [57]

The attacks on Jay were often low and sometimes obscene. One newspaper used a parody of the nativity narrative: "The Chief Justice being overshadowed by the prolific spirit of His Gracious Majesty, at the Court of St. James, conceived and wonderful to relate, after about thirteen months laborious pregnancy, was happily, by the aid of senatorial midwifery, delivered of the long-expected ambassadorial, diplomatic, farci-comical savior of fifteen *fallen* states." Several newspapers reprinted a long poem, by an anonymous author, part of which read as follows:

> May it please your highness, I John Jay
> Have traveled all this mighty way,
> To inquire if you, good Lord will please,
> To suffer me while on my knees,
> To show all others I surpass,
> In love, by kissing of your __;
> As by my 'xtraordinary station,
> I represent a certain nation;
> I thence conclude, and so may you,
> They all would wish to kiss it too;
> So please your highness suffer me
> To kiss, I wait on bended knee.

The King refuses Jay this privilege, but suggests that Grenville might be prepared to allow it. Grenville pays Jay for his treachery, and then:

> Jay took the gold, and well content
> With getting all for which he went
> To Philadelphia bent his way;
> Being there arrived, as some folks say,

Straight to the Senate he repairs,
And putting on some pompous airs,
Told of his vast success, then too,
The money from his purse he drew;
At sight of British gold, some few
Indignant viewed, despised it too;
But others following natures bent
To worship it on knees they went,
With lavish hand he shares it out,
To those who kneeling round about,
Would swear to obey King George's call,
And give up country, soul and all.
Now those who know it to a hair,
Say Jay got the biggest share.[58]

Jay reacted to all this (and there was much more of the same) with philosophic calm. He reportedly joked that he could, if he wanted, make his way from one end of the country to the other by the light of burning effigies of himself. After initially agreeing to help Hamilton in writing a series of essays to defend the treaty, Jay thought better of it, and did not write anything public on the treaty. In private letters, he expressed modest confidence in the treaty's ultimate fate. "The treaty is as it is; and the time will certainly come when it will very universally receive exactly that degree of commendation or censure which, to candid and enlightened minds, it shall appear to deserve." There were protests at present, but it "would be as vain to lament that our country is not entirely free from these evils, as it would be to lament that a field produces weeds as well as corn." Indeed, even though he was the target of vicious public attacks, Jay expressed confidence in the American people, saying they had "a greater portion of information and morals than almost any other people," and that "although they may for a time be misled and deceived, yet there is reason to expect that truth and justice cannot be long hid from their eyes."[59]

In the middle of August 1795, after considering the issue for several weeks, Washington finally signed Jay's Treaty. The debate over the treaty now became more moderate, because it was far harder to attack Washington than Jay. Moreover, as the debate shifted from street demonstrations to newspaper essays, Alexander Hamilton and the other Federalists proved more adept than Robert Livingston and the other Republican writers. Finally, as Jay predicted, although perhaps not for the reasons he envisaged, the American people began to realize that rejecting the treaty would be risky. Many people wanted to move west; that would not be possible while the British retained the forts and supported the Indians. Other people, especially in the Atlantic ports, were enjoying an economic boom; that boom would not continue if there was tension or even war with Britain. One Republican lamented that the treaty, "once reprobated by nineteen twentieths of our citizens, is now approved of, or peaceably acquiesced in, by the same proportion of the people." When the issue finally came up for a vote in the House of Representatives, in late April 1796, the House, even though it had a slight majority of Republicans, approved the funds necessary to implement the treaty. The debate over the treaty helped to divide America into two political parties and solidify those parties, but the Republicans could not prevent its ultimate adoption and implementation.[60]

More than two hundred years later, opinions on Jay's Treaty still differ. Some argue that Jay conceded too much and obtained too little. Others argue that Jay obtained the best treaty he could and "that no other American could have got anything nearly as good." Almost all agree that Jay should not have agreed to the prohibition of the export of cotton and other goods; fortunately the Senate deleted this provision and the British agreed to ratify the treaty without it. The key point, lost perhaps in the review of specific provisions, is that Jay preserved peace and postponed war. Without the treaty, the United States might have had to fight Britain in 1794, rather than in 1812, with no navy, with essentially no army, and with its backcountry laced with British forts supported by Indian allies. How such a war would have ended is impossible to say, but in all likelihood it would have been ended badly for the United States, and it is quite possible that Britain would have demanded some American territory at the peace table. Jay was right to fear such a war and to make concessions to avoid it. Jay's Treaty also helped to cement the West to the East, both by securing the evacuation of the British forts, and, through Pinckney's Treaty, by opening the Mississippi. Viewed in this way, his work on the treaty was a clear success, indeed one of his key contributions to early American history.[61]

CHAPTER 14

Governor of New York

JOHN JAY had come within a few disputed votes of being elected Governor of New York in 1792. He was thus the obvious Federalist candidate in the next election, in the spring of 1795. He played no role in the latter campaign: he was in England when it started and at sea as it concluded. But he was not elected over his objection or without his knowledge. He had almost certainly informed his Federalist friends, before leaving for England, that he would serve if elected. In December of 1794, Peter Munro in New York wrote to Peter Jay in England that, "from what I could see and learn in the upper part of the state," it would be "impossible" for the Republicans to prevent Jay's election. In January of 1795, John Sloss Hobart wrote to urge Jay to return soon, since his absence would make it hard to elect him. Indeed, the election may well have been the main reason Jay left England, rather than waiting for further instructions regarding the treaty. When he arrived in New York City in late May, the first results were being printed in the newspapers. The final results showed that Jay had received more than 13,000 votes and his opponent, Robert Yates, fewer than 12,000.[1]

Now that it was upon him, Jay viewed the prospect of becoming Governor of New York with mixed emotions. Although not quite fifty years old, he had been in active public service for more than twenty years, and he was looking forward to retirement. A few days before taking up his new position, Jay wrote to his friend Egbert Benson that "God only knows, whether my removal from the bench to my present station will conduce to my comfort or not. The die is cast, and nothing remains for me to consider but how to fulfill in the best manner the duties incumbent on me, without any regard to personal consequences." Jay wrote at this same time to Washington, resigning his position as Chief Justice, and thanking the President for "the repeated marks of confidence and attention for which I am indebted to you."[2]

The new Governor entered office very quietly. According to a brief newspaper report, on the second of July the Secretary of State "waited upon John Jay at his home in Broadway, and in the presence of several gentlemen, administered to him the oath of office as Governor of this state." In the afternoon, the new Governor "received the congratulations of a number of his fellow citizens." Jay perhaps sensed the onset of the storm over the treaty; indeed on the very day he took the oath, a newspaper in New York City printed a detailed summary of the treaty, and on the Fourth of July many of the speeches were as much anti-treaty as they were pro-America.[3]

New York, as Jay became its Governor in 1795, was growing and changing rapidly. The population of the state almost tripled over twenty years, from 340,000 in the 1790 census to almost 960,000 in the 1810 census. Much of the growth was in the northern and western parts of the state, around the Finger Lakes and on the southern shores of the Great Lakes. Some of the settlers came north from Pennsylvania; some came north along the Hudson River Valley; but most of them came west from New England. As the population of the state shifted to the north and west, the capital shifted too. When Jay became Governor, the capital was in New York City, but in late 1796 the legislature decided to hold its next session in Albany, and in early 1797 it decided to remain there indefinitely. Albany was at this time a town of only about four thousand people, but an increasingly important transportation and commercial center. One observer hoped that the move of the capital to Albany would "preserve the union of the different part of the state some years longer than it might otherwise have continued."[4]

The first phase of the transportation revolution was starting while Jay was New York's Governor. Roads were being built both by the state government and by private toll road companies. The state chartered more than a dozen toll road companies while Jay was Governor, and by 1807 more than nine hundred miles of turnpike were open.[5] Canals were also under construction, on a modest scale. Various friends of Jay, including Philip Schuyler and Elkanah Watson, were the owners of Western Inland Lock Navigation Company, organized in

1792. The company's goal was to create a water route from Albany to Oswego by clearing and dredging existing rivers and building short canals. In 1795, the company was building a one-mile canal at Little Falls, enabling ships to skirt that obstacle in the Mohawk River. Two years later, the company built another short canal, linking the upper Mohawk River with Wood Creek. The company never made much money, but it did make it far cheaper to move goods east and west.[6] Robert Livingston and others were already working on the problem of how to build a practical steamship. In both 1798 and 1799, the state passed laws promising Livingston a monopoly, if he could get a steam boat in service within a certain period. It would take another decade to solve the problem, but the idea was in the air.[7]

The industrial revolution was also getting under way in New York at this time. In 1793, Eli Whitney invented the cotton gin and started an extraordinary boom in cotton production. Much of this cotton made its way from the South to England via New York City; ships then returned to New York with cloth and other goods for distribution throughout the United States. Duncan Phyfe and others improved the process for making furniture, so that they could use dozens of less skilled workers, rather than a few skilled experts, to turn out chairs and sofas by the hundreds. In 1792, the Lorillard brothers built a snuff plant on the banks of the Bronx River; by the time Jay became Governor, it was the largest tobacco mill in the United States.[8]

The role of a state Governor at this time was in some ways like, and in many ways unlike, the role of a state Governor today. The most dramatic difference was in the scale of state government. New York state in 1795 only employed a few hundred people: a sheriff for each county, a few people to run the state prison, and judges and clerks for the courts. The smallest state government today has thousands of employees. At the end of Jay's tenure, when New York had about 600,000 residents, the annual expenditures of the government were about $300,000 per year. The smallest state governments today, those of Vermont and Wyoming, each with about 600,000 residents, spend more than $1.2 billion per year. Even allowing for inflation, it is clear that government today is far more extensive and expensive than in the late eighteenth century.[9]

Like most state Governors today, Jay could suggest ideas for legislation. He could not, however, influence legislation with the threat of a veto, because he had no veto. He was merely one member of the Council of Revision, and even if he and the others on the Council rejected a bill, the legislature could and often did enact it over their objection. Like state Governors today, he had a role in appointments, but his role was more limited, as merely one member of the Council of Appointment. Jay was also far more of a national and international figure than most of today's Governors, and he devoted considerable time to advising federal officials on international issues.

In late July 1795, a doctor visited a ship in the East River to examine several sick seamen. Within a few days, the doctor and the seamen were dead of yellow fever, and within a few weeks the newspapers were reporting several deaths each day. Jay issued a proclamation, closing the port of New York to ships from the West Indies or Mediterranean. In late August, Pennsylvania imposed a quarantine, banning any ships from New York. Although Pennsylvania's action was understandable, Jay asked the medical society and city council to help him argue against the quarantine. The doctors responded with the grim statistics, but they also opined that the disease was "not contagious," and the Mayor even argued that "a much greater degree of health prevails in this city at present than is usual at this season of the year." Jay sent these reports to his counterpart in Pennsylvania, and urged him to revoke the quarantine, but he was probably not surprised when Pennsylvania ignored his request.[10]

Jay used the epidemic as an excuse to decline an invitation to join the French Consul for a "republican entertainment." He wrote that he "would with great pleasure dine with [the French] on that day, but while general anxiety, distress, and alarm pervade his native city, it will not be in his power to command that degree of hilarity, which becomes such convivial scenes." A friend urged the Governor to move himself and his family to the safety of New Jersey. He declined. "Our situation," he wrote, "affords us considerable security against the disorder, and I think it best that my family should remain here, lest their removal should increase the alarm, which is already too great." By the end of the epidemic, more than seven hundred were dead.[11]

In November, after the disease abated in the cooler weather, Jay issued a thanksgiving proclamation. God had shown "singular kindness" to the

C. Currier, Government House, New York City.
The Jay family lived in Government House from 1795 through 1797, the first years of
Jay's service as Governor. When it became clear that the legislature would remain at
Albany, Jay moved his family there as well, to a rented house on State Street.

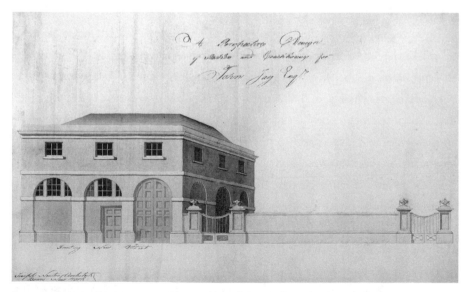

Joseph Newton, Stables and coach house for John Jay, circa 1785.
There does not appear to be any surviving print of the Jay home on Broadway, but this
design for a stables and coach house suggests the magnificence of the main house.

American people: by "protecting our ancestors in their first establishments" and by "leading us, as it were by the hand, through the various dangers and difficulties of the late revolution." The recent plague "reminds us that prosperity and adversity are in His hand." Jay was not sure that he could *require* a day of thanksgiving, but he *recommended* "to the clergy and others my fellow citizens throughout this state, to set apart Thursday the twenty-sixth of November" as a day of prayer and thanksgiving. This was the first November Thanksgiving in New York state.[12]

Governor Jay believed not only in prayer but in action to deal with the disease. He arranged the construction in early 1796 of a "lazaretto" or sick ward on Bedlow's Island, now known as Liberty Island. He urged the legislature to use "every proper measure" not only to prevent the introduction of infectious diseases from abroad but also to "prevent as far as possible their being generated or aggravated by local circumstances or causes." The legislature responded with a law authorizing the suppression of "nuisances." A letter from a doctor during the summer of 1796 provides an example of the kind of "nuisances" that were common: someone had buried two dead horses near the harbor, and the doctor was concerned that the resulting "miasma" would cause disease.[13]

Relatively few people died of yellow fever in New York City in the next two years. In the summer of 1798, however, the disease returned with even more violence than in 1795. Jay was in Albany at this time, but he followed the news of the epidemic closely, and like many others puzzled over its causes. He noted that "intemperance" and "filth" would "doubtless produce diseases as cause and effect." But New York City, he noted, "was never so clean and neat as it has been for this year past, and yet an alarming fever prevails in it." By the time the fever had run its course that year, about two thousand people, out of an urban population of about sixty thousand, were dead. In March 1799, Jay recommended and the state legislature enacted a law to give the city council additional authority to deal with diseases.[14]

Jay was not a doctor, so he could not add much to debates on public health issues. As a lawyer and former judge, however, he could and did improve New York's criminal laws and law enforcement. For several years before he became Governor, there was talk about reform of New York's criminal laws. Death by hanging was the penalty not only for murder but also for burglary, forgery, arson and even malicious mischief. Whipping was another common penalty: a man could get thirty-nine lashes for a simple theft. These punishments were used in part because there was no proper state prison. Reformers argued that the state should make less use of the gallows and more use of prisons, which could punish, deter and perhaps even reform criminals.[15]

The main advocate of reform in New York was Thomas Eddy, a Quaker whom Jay probably knew through common friends. As part of his first message, the Governor asked the legislature to consider whether the "severe penalties prescribed in our laws in particular cases admit of mitigation." He was not opposed to capital punishment in general; indeed he believed it was required by the Bible in cases of murder. But he was opposed to capital punishment for minor crimes. He also argued that proper "establishments for confining, employing and reforming criminals" were now "indispensable." And he noted that, with the increasing size of the state, "the Attorney General cannot possibly manage all the prosecutions (existing at the same time in different counties) which demand his care and attention."[16]

The legislature agreed with this analysis, and passed a law limiting capital punishment to four major crimes: treason, murder, abetting murder and stealing from a church. The legislature also abolished whipping as a punishment. Instead, the new law provided for imprisonment, in serious cases life imprisonment. The legislature also authorized the construction of two new prisons, and appropriated funds to construct one at New York. And, as suggested by Jay, the legislature provided for assistant attorneys to help prosecute criminal cases.[17]

Governor Jay took a personal interest in the construction of this first state prison. He conferred with Caleb Lownes, a leading expert on prisons from Philadelphia, when the latter came to New York. Jay commended the legislature on their choice of the site, four acres in what was then countryside and is today part of Greenwich Village. "Establishments of this kind should have room," he wrote, and it was "an agreeable circumstance that the lot extends to the river." He also urged the legislature, in early 1798, to provide the funds necessary to complete construction, so that the "late benevolent alterations in the criminal law of this state may have a fair and full trial."[18]

The Governor's main role in criminal cases was to consider requests for pardons, and Jay considered these requests carefully, although he seldom granted them. As he explained in one letter, "the power of pardoning is committed by the constitution to the prudence and discretion, and not the wishes or feelings of the governor. If it was confided to the latter, very few convicts would be long imprisoned." In spite of a request from the Governor of Connecticut, Jay declined to pardon a man convicted of forgery. "This is a crime which never has passion, inebriety, or precipitation to plead its excuse; on the contrary, it always indicates some degree, and not infrequently a very high degree, of cool deliberate wickedness." In another case, he refused to pardon a man convicted of a prison escape. The offense involved "disrespect to the laws, opposition and defiance to their authority, and a most unjustifiable combination to break from their control by force of arms, and without regard to the blood and lives of faithful officers and innocent citizens." In yet another case, the "son of a worthy revolutionary officer, who had lost a limb in the public service, had been convicted of forgery and sentenced to imprisonment for life." He resisted the personal plea of the veteran, seconded by "the Governor's most confidential friends," since to pardon the son for the sake of the father "would have been an admission that the children of deserving parents might commit crimes with impunity." [19]

Not long after he became Governor, Jay received a letter from one William Hamilton, believed by some to be the mulatto son of Alexander Hamilton. Hamilton said that, although "my forefathers or ancestors [were] from Africa," he was "a native of New York." He noted that "many of the sons of Africa [were] groaning under oppression," a troubling sight in a state which claimed to be "a land of liberty and equality, a Christian country." He asked what Jay intended to do to end this "scandal." [20]

As the first President of the Manumission Society, Jay had been working for years towards the gradual end of slavery in New York. Governor Jay may well have spoken quietly on this issue to some legislators, but he did not address it in any public way. According to William Jay, his father realized that "in the present state of politics, such a proposition emanating from him would enlist the spirit of party in opposition to a measure, against which the prejudices of a large part of the community were already arrayed." The legislature debated the issue in each of its sessions while Jay was Governor. Finally, in 1799, it passed a law to provide that the slave children born in New York after July Fourth of that year would become free when they reached the ages of twenty-five if they were women or twenty-eight if they were men. The law also prohibited the export of slaves from New York, which was at this time a common form of punishment. According to his son, "no measure of his administration afforded [Jay] such unfeigned pleasure."[21]

Scholars are still debating to what extent Jay deserves credit for this legislation. Some give him substantial credit for developing the moral basis for the legislation. Others argue that there is no contemporary evidence that he did anything to support the legislation by lobbying legislators. But even if he did not personally press for votes, most of those who voted in favor were Federalists, and most of the Federalist legislators revered their Federalist Governor, and knew well his views on slavery. The Republicans, on the other hand, to the extent they considered the views of their Virginian leaders, were not at all inclined to favor the blacks. New York would at some point have passed manumission legislation; but it is not an accident that it passed the law during Jay's tenure as Governor.[22]

Yet John Jay himself continued to own slaves. In 1797, for example, he wrote to his son to lament the death of Mary, "the last of our old family servants." With the exception of some "indiscretions" in her later years, not described in his letters, Mary had served faithfully, which Jay believed proved that "right conduct on the one side, tend[s] to produce it on the other." In 1799, he wrote to his son about the slave Phillis, who was apparently quite difficult. He suggested that they sell Phillis to a new owner "for not more than two years, taking a covenant from the purchaser to manumit her at the expiration of that period." He did not want to free her himself, since then he would be "chargeable with her maintenance."[23]

Jay's letters from this period refer only rarely to African-Americans, but there are frequent references to American Indians. Indeed, an Indian crisis of sorts awaited Jay when he became Governor. After the Revolution, New Yorkers, and especially Jay's second cousin Philip Schuyler, began to purchase vast tracts of lands for tiny sums from the Indians. Schuyler and others then turned around and sold the land to eager settlers, making fortunes in the process. Under a federal law of 1793, however, "no sale of lands made by any Indians, or any nation or tribe of Indians within the United States, shall be valid to any person or to any state ... unless the same shall be made and duly executed at some public treaty held under the authority of the United States." Schuyler did not intend to allow this law to hinder him. In April 1795, he secured from the New York legislature a law authorizing three out of five commissioners, of which he was one, to "make such arrangements with the Oneida, Onondaga, and Cayuga tribes of Indians, respectively, relative to the lands appropriated to their use, as may tend to promote the interests of said Indians." In early June 1795, Schuyler sent a letter to Jay, informing him that he planned to negotiate with the three tribes in the middle of July, and indeed inviting him to join the negotiation if he wished.[24]

When Timothy Pickering, the Secretary of War, learned of the New York law and of Schuyler's plans, he sent letters to both outgoing Governor Clinton and incoming Governor Jay. Pickering cautioned Jay that any contract or treaty which Schuyler entered, without the presence and approval of an authorized federal agent, would be illegal and void. He even provided Jay a copy of an opinion to this effect from the federal Attorney General. Jay, who had for so long advocated the supremacy of national law, should have recognized that the federal law prevailed over inconsistent state law and should have done what he could to halt Schuyler's illegal negotiations. Instead, he responded in mid-July to Pickering with questions about the validity of the federal law and its effect. He also questioned whether, as Governor, he had any authority to interfere, noting that the state constitution charged the legislature with all relations with the Indians.[25]

Jay faced a difficult situation, just a few days into office, caught as he was between state legislators and federal officials. But even if he could not, in practice, stop Schuyler from negotiating, he could have done something, perhaps by a later proclamation, to see that the treaties negotiated in the summer of 1795 did not take effect. Instead, however, he accepted these three treaties as *faits accomplis*. The result was that three Indian tribes were deprived of substantial lands. Of course, even when federal agents were present at state negotiations, they could not prevent the Indians from agreeing to unfair terms. Three more Indian treaties were signed during the course of Jay's tenure as Governor, in each case with a federal agent present, but none of these treaties was notably fair.[26]

Governor Jay's letters suggest that he wanted to see the Indians treated fairly and kindly, that he hoped they would become "civilized," but feared this would take generations. In response to a letter from Joseph Brant, leader of the Mohawks, Jay urged the Mohawks to send "two or three deputies" to New York, and assured them that "nothing on my part shall be wanting to cause what may be right to be done." In his next message to the legislature, Jay expressed the hope that soon "the Indians on our borders, having convincing proof of our justice and moderation, will by good offices and friendly intercourse, be led to rely on our benevolence and protection, and to view our prosperity as connected with their own." In response to a letter from a New England missionary, seeking state aid for mission work among the Oneidas, Jay expressed doubts about such efforts. "Is there not reason to apprehend that, until the savages can be prevailed upon to dwell in fixed habitations, to have separate property, and to depend more on husbandry than the chase for subsistence, little success will attend the best efforts to civilize or christianize them?" He noted that both the state and the Quakers were making efforts, but the "Indian men regard labor as degrading, and fit only for women and slaves. Prejudices associated with a sense of honor are not easily overcome."[27]

During 1777, as they worked on the first state constitution, Jay and the other delegates in Kingston debated different ways to appoint state officials. He devised a compromise, the Council of Appointment, which was still in effect when he become Governor in 1795. As is often the case with compromises, the provision was not precise, perhaps intentionally imprecise. It provided that the Assembly would select one Senator from each of four parts of the state who would, together with the Governor, form a Council of Appointment. The Governor "shall be president, and shall have a casting voice, but no other vote, and, with the advice and consent of the said council, shall appoint" most state officials. Since the "Governor" was the subject of the verb "appoint," some read this sentence to mean that the Governor alone nominated officials, who were appointed if they were approved by a majority of the Council. Others read the sentence to mean that any member of the council could nominate officials, and all of the Council members would vote, with ties resolved by the Governor.[28]

The question was critical because the Council was powerful. The Council appointed almost all central state officials, including the Secretary of State, the Attorney General, the Chancellor and the judges of the Supreme Court. The Council also appointed almost all county officials: the judges, sheriffs and clerks. The chief judge and sheriff of each county were powerful people: "primarily responsible for the regulation of property rights, the preservation of order, and the conduct of elections." The Council also appointed various city officials, including the mayors of New York and Albany. Most of these officials, unless they had specific fixed terms, served at "the pleasure of the Council of Appointment." Thus the Council not only had the power to appoint officials; it had the power to remove them.[29]

Even before Jay became Governor, questions about the Council arose. In January 1794, over the objection of Governor Clinton, the four Federalist senators on the Council nominated and appointed Jay's friend Egbert Benson to the New York Supreme Court. The Council appointed several other Federalists, in some cases removing Republicans to make room, and in other cases creating new positions. Clinton protested "in the most explicit and unreserved manner," arguing that the new approach "renders the constitution unsafe and its administration unstable and whenever parties exist, may tend to deprive men of office because they have too much independence of spirit." Schuyler drafted the Federalist response, arguing that the Council members had as much right as the Governor to nominate officers, and that the Council in removing officers was merely following precedents set by Clinton.[30]

As Governor, Jay of course wanted to read the provision to give the Governor the sole authority to nominate officers, subject only to the consent of the Council. But as a Federalist, Jay could not immediately disagree with the position his friends had taken the prior year. In his first message to the legislature, he noted that the ambiguity of the provision "may give occasion to disagreeable contests and embarrassments." He urged the legislature to adopt a "declaratory act" to resolve the ambiguity and promised to "regard my fellow citizens with an equal eye" and to "cherish and advance merit wherever found." He apparently expected the legislature, dominated by Federalists at this time, to grant their Federalist Governor the exclusive right to nominate. But the legislators (in the words of a contemporary) "had tasted power and were not willing to surrender their assumed prerogatives, not even to a Governor of their own political faith." Perhaps the problem was that the more ardent Federalists feared the Governor was "too high-minded and honorable to use his appointing power to create a powerful political machine." The bill failed and the issue rested for several years.[31]

As promised, Jay generally focused on merit rather than party in considering possible appointments. To be sure, he consulted about appointments with Federalist friends, especially Alexander Hamilton, who was now practicing law in New York City. In one case, Jay asked Hamilton about two candidates for chancery examiner; in another he explained at length why he believed the city did not need another notary. But he also received suggestions from Republicans; in early 1801 Aaron Burr suggested a candidate for Sheriff, saying he hoped Jay would "pardon this intrusion from one old officer in favor of another, his friend and comrade in arms." At one session of the Council, a Senator stressed that a candidate was a zealous Federalist. Jay interrupted: "that, sir, is not the question; is he fit for office?" At another session, a Senator urged Jay to remove from office a Federalist who "had no influence" and replace him with a Republican who would use his "extensive" influence "in behalf of the administration." Jay asked angrily whether the Senator would "advise me to sell a friend, that I may buy an enemy?" Many of his appointments were agreed by all to be excellent. For example, it was Jay who first appointed James Kent, who would go on to become one of New York's most famous judges.[32]

In November 1800, a new legislature convened, and for the first time in many years it had a Republican majority. The Assembly promptly selected four new members for the Council of Appointment, including three Republicans. Their leader was DeWitt Clinton, nephew of former Governor Clinton, and a future Governor in his own right. When the Council met for the first time, in February 1801, Clinton and the other Republicans immediately asserted themselves. Jay nominated first one, then another, and in the end eight different men for one particular office. The Republicans rejected all eight names. Two weeks later, when the Council met again, Jay yielded and nominated a Republican for this office, and he and the Republicans agreed on a few other appointments. But they could not agree upon a Sheriff for Orange County and Jay, in frustration, adjourned the meeting.[33]

Jay then presented his side of the dispute in an address to the Assembly. He explained that it was his "fixed" view that the provision "vested the right of nomination exclusively in the Governor." He cited in support of his view the comments of former Governor Clinton, who had "never yielded or conceded [this right] to the Council." Jay noted that he had raised this issue in his first message to the legislature, that the legislature had not acted at that time, and that now there were "many appointments exceedingly interesting to the public" being delayed because of the controversy. He urged the legislature to resolve the issue by a declaratory law.[34]

As these debates went on in Albany, wild rumors circulated in New York City. Peter Jay heard with some concern that the Assembly had voted to impeach his father. Mayor Richard Varick heard from Brockholst Livingston that a Republican caucus had decided that, "at all events," Varick would be removed from his position as Mayor and replaced by Edward Livingston. Varick added that, "be my fate what it may," he would be "grateful and happy in having merited the confidence and friendship" of the Governor.[35]

When the legislature failed to act, Jay attempted to obtain an advisory opinion from the Chancellor (his old friend and now enemy Livingston) and the judges of the Supreme Court (including his friend Egbert Benson). Jay himself had recently declined to answer Jefferson's neutrality questions, so he was probably not surprised when Livingston, Benson and the other judges declined to answer his appointment questions. Livingston argued that, since the New York constitution did not make the judiciary "an advisory council for the other branches of government, it must have intended that they should lend their support to [the other branches] only in their judiciary capacity." To give advisory opinions at the request of the Governor or the legislature would "by degrees lead [the judges] into political controversies, incompatible with the duties of their offices, and convert them into [shields] to receive the shot, while the leaders of parties fought securely behind their protection." Benson and the other judges explained that they could not see any means "to have the question judicially determined" and they were concerned that a simple advisory opinion would "be without effect." They thus did not view this as a proper case (but would not "pronounce that there cannot be any") for them to advise the Governor. The issue was still unresolved when Jay's second term as Governor ended.[36]

Another provision in the 1777 state constitution made the Governor the "general and commander-in-chief of all the militia, and admiral of the navy, of this state." Under the 1789 federal constitution, the federal government was authorized to form a national army and navy. In the early years of the republic, however, Congress was reluctant to appropriate funds for defense. The result was that, when Jay became Governor in 1795, there was only a limited national army and *no* national navy. The defense of New York thus rested mainly with the state government and upon its Governor.[37]

In January 1796, in his first message to the state legislature, Jay stressed the importance of strong defenses. "It has been often and justly observed that in order to preserve peace, every nation should not only treat others with justice and respect, but also be in constant readiness to resist and repel hostilities." Jay was concerned about the weak state of the defenses of New York harbor, through which "the great mass of our exports and imports pass." Jay was also troubled by the lack of arms and ammunition. Perhaps remembering his effort to secure cannon at the outset of the Revolution, he noted "that the day of alarm and battle was not the best season for seeking and procuring these important stores."[38] He sounded similar themes in his next two messages. "Precarious is the peace and security of that people who are not prepared to defend themselves." New York harbor was vital to the whole state and "its situation cannot yet be deemed secure." Jay called upon the legislature to provide additional funds for arms, ammunition, and the construction of two armories. The legislature was not moved: it voted only $3000 for one armory.[39]

In April 1798, however, New York and the nation were swept by war fever. President Adams had sent three commissioners to Paris to attempt to negotiate peace. Instead of serious negotiations, the commissioners were insulted by demands for bribes from the French negotiators. When the dispatches of the commissioners were sent to Congress, then published in the newspapers, Americans were outraged. As Jay noted in a letter to Pickering, the "demands

354 JOHN JAY

and language of the French government" could not "fail to excite the indignation of honest men in this and every other country." Many Americans favored
an immediate declaration of war. Others feared that French forces, perhaps
from the Caribbean, would soon land in the United States. As one New York
newspaper put it, "the fear of actual invasion is treated by some as a bugbear,
by others as a thing to be expected." Later, Americans would realize that
French invasion was unlikely, but as one expert has put it, "anything and
everything seemed possible in the war crisis of the spring of 1798."[40]

Jay wrote to Ebenezer Stevens, a leader of the defense effort, noting that
$3000 seemed utterly "inadequate" to construct an arsenal. Stevens agreed, and
begged Jay to come from Albany to New York City. "Our citizens I verily
believe are ready to a man, with their lives and fortunes, for their country's
defense, but some one of influence to arouse them, is highly necessary."
Matthew Clarkson, another leader of the defense effort, wrote to urge Jay to
call a special session of the legislature to appropriate more funds for defense.
Jay hesitated for a while, because he recognized that a special summer session
would not be popular, but in the end he called the legislators to meet in early
August.[41]

At about this same time, Congress voted to create a substantial army, and
President Adams asked former President Washington to serve as its leader.
Given Washington's age and health, everyone understood that he would not
command except in an extreme situation, so the question of the second-in-
command was critical. Although Jay generally deferred to Adams as President,
and although he must have known that Adams intensely disliked Hamilton, Jay
was one of the many who urged Adams to appoint Hamilton to this position.
Jay wrote to Pickering that he could not "conceal from you my solicitude that
the late Secretary of the Treasury may be brought forward in a manner corresponding with his talents and services." In the end, Adams was more or less
forced, by Washington and others, to accept Hamilton.[42]

Congress was also, at this same time, considering the proposals that would
become the Alien and Sedition Acts. Although Jay is sometimes said to have
supported these measures, his actual view is difficult to discern. He apparently
only mentioned them once, in a letter to Pickering, in which he said that he had
"for many years" believed that "the right and privilege of being elected or

appointed to, or of holding or executing any office or place of trust or power under the United States, or under any of them, [should] not hereafter be granted to any foreigner." This was simply a restatement of the positions he had urged during the 1787 and 1788 constitutional debates, and considerably less radical than the law adopted by Congress, which allowed the President to deport summarily any alien he deemed dangerous.[43]

When the legislators gathered in Albany in August, Jay described for them the threat, as he saw it, posed by France. "The late very reprehensible and disgusting demands which have been made leave no room for us to believe that peace with the United States is among the objects" of the present French government. The United States, and each state, therefore had to strengthen their defenses. "While security is in question, the expense of providing for it is a secondary consideration." He regretted that the state treasury did not have the necessary funds and squarely argued for tax increases. "Too many of our citizens seem to have inadvertently flattered themselves that, unlike all other people past and present, they were to live exempt from taxes." Defense would be costly, but not as costly as defeat. "The great sovereign of the universe has given us independence, and to that inestimable gift has annexed the duty of defending it." The legislators agreed and voted $150,000 for the Governor to use in fortifying New York harbor, and another $165,000 for the erection of an arsenal and the purchase of weapons. At a time when the annual state budget was generally about $300,000, these were immense sums.[44]

Jay hoped that Hamilton, in addition to his federal duties, would agree to handle the improvement of the defenses around New York City. He raised the subject first with Hamilton's father-in-law, Philip Schuyler, and then with Hamilton himself. Hamilton was not particularly keen on the assignment, but he wrote in September that he would "not decline the trust if you think proper to repose it," since he was "equally disposed to be useful to the public and to second you in the objects of your administration." Having undertaken the assignment, Hamilton threw himself into it with customary energy, although it is doubtful that any forts could have defended New York City if the French navy had arrived and attacked.[45]

By late 1798 and early 1799, most Americans no longer feared a French invasion. Jay continued, however, to view France with suspicion. In a long letter to Adams, he wrote that he believed the French "view of domination comprehends all America, both North and South, and that they wish to place the United States in a situation favorable and auxiliary to those views." Jay urged Adams to remain firm and praised Adams for his work to date. "Your measures have hitherto afforded matter for brilliant pages in our history, and they have inspired a confidence which will greatly facilitate the success of your future ones." [46]

This letter to Adams was only one of many in which Jay advised federal officials on foreign policy. In response to a request from President Washington, in 1795 he had outlined additional provisions that would be desirable in a treaty with Britain, but also noted that "the present moment," in the midst of the anti-treaty protests, seemed "unfavorable" for negotiation. Later that summer, in response to a request from Secretary Pickering, Jay explained at some length his view of the provisions of the treaty regarding compensation for improper seizures. "Perfect justice to all parties is the object" of the provisions in question "and the commissioners are empowered to do it, in terms as explicit and comprehensive as the English language affords." When Washington solicited his views on who should be named to the various arbitration commissions under the treaty, he responded with various names, including that of John Marshall. He corresponded with Rufus King, America's Ambassador in London, and John Trumbull, also in London, serving as one of the treaty commissioners. When the commission regarding the northern boundary solicited his testimony, he declined to go to Boston to testify in person, but provided a detailed written statement. [47]

Jay's six years as Governor were generally pleasant ones for the Jay family. Peter Augustus Jay, after his year abroad with his father, now settled down to read law with his cousin Peter Jay Munro in New York City. Within a few years, Peter Jay passed the bar and joined Peter Munro in private practice. Maria was at a girls' school in Bethlehem, Pennsylvania, while her father was in England, but it appears that she came home about the time her father himself came home. Her sister Ann attended the same school for a short while, but also came home, perhaps because of her weak eyes. Education for girls was becoming far more common in America after the Revolution, and the Jays participated in this trend, but only to the common extent: the Jay girls were not particularly learned. William and Sarah were only six and three when their father returned from England, so they remained at home throughout the next six years.[48]

Home, at least initially, was Government House in New York City. In 1789, when they still had hopes that New York would be the permanent national capital, the city fathers had demolished Fort George, and started construction of a new building to house the federal government. This building, known as Government House, was completed in 1791, not long before the federal government moved to Philadelphia. It was an impressive three-story federal-style building, sitting on the southern tip of Manhattan, with a spectacular view of the harbor. The Jays lived there in 1795 and 1796. Late that year, the state legislature decided that it would hold at least the first session of 1797 in Albany. Not knowing whether the legislature would move again, Jay at first rented only two rooms for himself and left his family in New York. But when the legislature decided later that year to remain in Albany, Jay made Albany his home as well, renting a house at 60 State Street, where he and his family lived for the next four years.[49]

Living in Albany, the Jays naturally met the people of Albany, among them Goldsborough Banyer Jr. Banyer was the son of a prominent colonial official and a colleague of Philip Schuyler in his canal venture; indeed he accompanied Schuyler when he surveyed the wilds of the Mohawk River in the spring of 1792. According to a later account, "young Mr. Banyer's acquaintance with Miss Jay ripened into an attachment, and before the family left Albany, Maria Jay became Maria Banyer."[50]

The one cloud on the wedding day was the poor health of the bride's mother, Sarah Livingston Jay. During the summer of 1800, she spent several weeks at Lebanon Springs, where she enjoyed the baths and the fine air. She was not a total invalid; indeed she wrote to her husband about walking with friends up "one of the highest mountains here," saying it had no effect on her other than a "charming glow" and "quick circulation." But in December 1800, Peter Jay wrote to his father that he was concerned by "the unpleasant intelligence of Mama's illness." A week later, John wrote back that "your mother is nearly as well as she was before her late illness." In April 1801, Peter was again troubled to hear that "Mama continues as when I left her." After leaving

Albany, a few weeks later, John reported that "your mama is not worse but still very feeble." None of these letters explain Sarah's illness.[51]

At about this same time, and perhaps not coincidentally, there was at last a truce between John Jay and his brother-in-law Brockholst Livingston. Livingston apparently made the first move; he wrote to Jay that "considering how nearly we are connected, and that you justly sustain the character of a virtuous and honorable man, I wish for an interview with you, for the purpose of a reconciliation." Livingston traveled to Albany and, upon his return to New York City, called upon Peter Augustus, thus bridging the gap with the younger as well as the older generation.[52]

Like many people, Jay hoped that Washington would serve as President for a third term. He wrote to Washington in April 1796, urging him not to "leave the work unfinished," but rather to "remain with us at least while the storm lasts, and until you can retire like the sun in a calm unclouded evening." Washington responded that he was worn out from "the trouble and perplexities" of his office and from "the weight of years which have passed upon me." He firmly intended to retire to his farm unless there were circumstances, "which I hope and trust will not happen," that would "render a retreat dishonorable."[53]

When Washington asked Hamilton to comment on a draft farewell address, Hamilton, with typical energy, both commented on Washington's draft and prepared his own new draft. Although Hamilton was the principal "speech-writer" for this famous speech, Jay played a supporting role. After Hamilton had prepared his first draft, he and Jay reviewed it together and agreed upon a number of changes, which Jay later characterized as minor. In September, just before providing the address to the printer, Washington sent a copy to Jay for his comments. Jay was troubled by the suggestion that United States should *never* expect favors from other nations; he suggested Washington say simply that such favors could not be counted upon. By the time Washington received this letter, however, it was too late: the address was already in the newspapers.[54]

Washington's farewell address started the final phase of the presidential election campaign of 1796. In New York and a few other places, however, the campaign was effectively over. New York law at this time provided for elections in the spring of a legislature, which would in the fall select the presidential electors. The New York election in the spring of 1796 was to some extent a referendum on Jay's Treaty. Since by this time most New Yorkers approved of the treaty, they voted Federalist. Judge Lowell of Massachusetts congratulated Jay that "your state elections have been closed so favorably to order," that is, with such a substantial Federalist majority. Jay responded in similar key: "It is happy for the United States that so great a part of the people are able to discern their true interests." He added that in his view the United States would be safer "when a greater proportion of our people become well-informed. Schools, colleges and churches are in my opinion absolutely essential to governments like ours."[55]

When the New York legislature assembled in November 1796, Jay noted in his address that this was really America's first presidential election. "Hitherto the embarrassments arising from competitions, and from the influences incident to them, have not been experienced; they have been excluded by the uniform and universal confidence reposed in that illustrious patriot," George Washington. As expected, the New York legislature selected twelve Federalist electors. On his way from Quincy to Philadelphia in December 1796, still not knowing how the overall election would come out, Adams stopped to spend an evening with Jay, a "very happy" evening spent sharing stories of old times and political comments. When all the votes were finally counted in early 1797, John Adams received seventy-one electoral votes and Thomas Jefferson sixty-eight, so that Adams was President and Jefferson Vice-President. The votes of New York had ensured that Jay's friend Adams prevailed over his former friend Jefferson.[56]

No sooner was the presidential election over than New Yorkers began to think about the next election of their Governor. In November 1797, Peter Jay reported to his father that the "democratic agents" had already "begun to electioneer in Westchester." They made some "ingenious accusations" against Jay: "removing the seat of government to Albany," "creating the new office of comptroller," and "abolishing all justice courts in New York." From the tone of this letter, it seems that Jay had already decided that he would run again for Governor in the spring. "Run" is of course too strong a word for Jay's campaign; he gave no speeches and made no tours. The critical moment was probably the publication, in early April 1798, of the American dispatches from

France. Jay's opponent, Robert Livingston, was known to be pro-French, and his chance of election disappeared in the wave of anti-French anger. Jay reported at this time from Albany to Peter Augustus that "nobody here on our side seems to doubt the success of the election, and there prevails a degree of confidence and security, which may expose it to hazard." He claimed that he was "neither sanguine nor anxious." When the votes were counted a few weeks later, Jay had prevailed over Livingston by a substantial margin, more than two thousand votes out of thirty thousand votes cast.[57]

Jay played a quiet but critical role in the presidential election of 1800. As the election year opened, many expected that New England would support John Adams, the Federalist candidate, and the South would support Thomas Jefferson, the Republican candidate. New York was expected to be the pivotal state and New York City to be the pivotal part of the state. Peter Jay reported from New York to his father in Albany that on the day of the election "all business was suspended, even the workmen deserted the houses they were building." In prior elections, candidates had generally remained indoors; in this election, some of them solicited votes in the streets. Brockholst Livingston "made speeches to the mob, though he was himself one of the candidates." When it was all over, and the ballots were counted, it appeared that the Republicans had won a solid majority in the new Assembly, and would thus be able to select Republican electors in the fall. Peter feared this would "ensure" the election of Jefferson; "the prospect is gloomy indeed."[58]

It was at this moment that Hamilton wrote Jay an extraordinary letter, urging him to call the existing state legislature, with a Federalist majority, into session, so that it could pass a law changing the state's system for selecting presidential electors. If there were a new election, in which New Yorkers elected electors by districts, rather than through an "all or none" vote in the legislature, Hamilton was sure that Adams would obtain several New York electors, and probably be re-elected as President. Hamilton conceded that there were "weighty objections to the measure," but argued that "in times like these in which we live, it will not do to be over-scrupulous." He quickly added that he was not suggesting anything "which integrity will forbid." He was merely suggesting that "delicacy and propriety" ought not "to hinder the taking of a *legal* and *constitutional* step, to prevent an *atheist* in religion and a *fanatic* in

politics from getting possession of the helm of state." Philip Schuyler sent Jay
a similar letter, arguing that the proposal was the "only way to save a nation"
from the "disasters" which would occur under Jefferson, "a man pervaded with
mad French philosophy." Schuyler claimed that John Marshall was "one of
those who has recommended the measure." [59]

Jay refused all these requests. He did not explain his reasons, beyond a brief
note on the back of Hamilton's letter, that it was "proposing a measure for
party purposes which I think it would not become me to adopt." Jay rightly
recognized that it was improper to change the rules of an election once the
votes were cast and counted. He also probably disagreed with the standard
Federalist view of Jefferson. Jay knew Jefferson, through their professional and
personal correspondence while Jefferson was in France, and he knew that
Jefferson was not "mad." [60]

Jay played one other minor but interesting role in this presidential campaign.
In August 1800, Hamilton asked him for copies of two letters: the official
instruction to the American peace commissioners to be governed by French
advice, and the unofficial suggestions Hamilton provided him for his British
peace mission. Hamilton said only that he needed these letters "for a public
purpose." Jay rummaged among his papers in Albany and found both letters
for Hamilton. Hamilton used these letters, and much other material, in an
amazing attack on President Adams, published as a pamphlet in late October.
Hamilton's basic argument was that Adams did not "possess the talents adapted
to the administration of government, and that there are great and intrinsic
defects in his character, which unfit him for the office of Chief Magistrate." One
of his points was that Jay and not Adams deserved credit for the Paris Peace
Treaty. Jay, like almost all Federalists, was shocked and dismayed by
Hamilton's attack on the Federalist President. As Jay's former law clerk Robert
Troup noted, "the general impression at Albany among our friends was that
[the letter] would be injurious, and they lamented the publication of it." Adams
did not respond in public to Hamilton, but he did write to Jay that "among the
very few truths in a late pamphlet there is one that I shall ever acknowledge
with pleasure, viz., that the principal merit of the negotiation for peace was Mr.
Jay's." It was a generous word from a true friend. [61]

By this time, late November of 1800, it was still unclear whether Adams would be re-elected, but Jay's own political career seemed to be at an end. For many months, he had not disguised from friends that he hoped to retire after a second term. In May and June of 1799, Troup wrote to King about who would run if, as he expected, Jay declined to run for a third term. In the summer of 1800, newspapers reported that Jay was busily improving his farm in Bedford, and suggested that he intended to retire there soon. A frontier Federalist wrote to him in distress: "Pray sir, should you wish to retire, who is the man fit for so important a station?" In November, a committee of Federalists formally asked Jay to stand again for Governor. Whether he could win was unclear: the Republicans had won the legislative election in early 1800, but Jay was personally popular, and New Yorkers were already politically fickle. But he was not interested in making the attempt. "The period is now nearly arrived at which I have for many years intended to retire from the cares of public life, and for which I have for more than two years been preparing. Not perceiving, after mature consideration, that any duties require me to postpone it, I shall retire accordingly." [62]

By early December, it was clear that Adams would not be re-elected. (If New York had given Adams even a few electoral votes, as it would have under the scheme proposed by Hamilton, Adams would have prevailed.) It seemed likely, however, that there would be a tie in the electoral college between the two Republicans, Jefferson and Aaron Burr. The Constitution provided that, in this case, the election would be decided in the spring by the House of Representatives, voting by states. The Federalists did not control enough state delegations in the House to elect a Federalist President, but they had enough votes to delay the election of either Republican. Some Federalists hoped to negotiate with Burr, so that, in return for Federalist support in the House, Burr would become a quasi-Federalist President. Thomas Jefferson feared that the Federalist Congress would try to "pass a bill giving the government to Jay, appointed Chief Justice, or to Marshall, as Secretary of State." [63]

At this critical juncture, Jay received another extraordinary letter, this time from Adams. The President wrote that he had nominated, and the Senate had confirmed, Jay as the next Chief Justice of the United States. "In the future administration of our country," Adams wrote, "the firmest security we can have against the effects of visionary schemes or fluctuating theories, will be in a solid judiciary; nothing will cheer the hopes of the best men so much as your acceptance of this appointment." The vacancy on the Supreme Court provided Adams with an opportunity "of marking to the public the spot where, in my opinion, the greatest mass of worth remained collected in one individual" and provided Jay with "a great opportunity to render a most signal service to your country." A few days later, Jay received the formal commission, under a cover letter from the Secretary of State John Marshall, who hoped "that you may be prevailed upon to accept it." [64]

Many people expected that he would decline the appointment. According to Robert Troup, "no one believes [Jay] will accept the appointment" because he had already stated "his fixed determination to devote the remainder of his life to retirement." Timothy Pickering commented that it was "impossible that Mr. Jay should consent to take the office of Chief Justice" and that "it is deeply to be regretted that the President will so often *sport* in serious things." Peter Jay wrote to his father that he could "hardly congratulate you on your new appointment; to accept it will be contrary to all your views and wishes, and yet perhaps it may not be pleasant to decline." Peter "supposed," however, that "after so many years of laborious service, you have fully discharged your duty to your country and may justly claim as your right the enjoyment of quiet and repose." [65]

John Jay was in Albany, so that he was not aware of the rumors in Philadelphia or Washington, indeed not aware of the views of his son in New York City. All that he had was the letter from the President, summoning him to duty. He did not like to decline duty, so that, in answering Adams, he did not mention his desire to retire. Instead, he stressed his concern over the circuit court duties imposed upon the justices. When the Judiciary Act was passed, he noted, it was expected that "it would be amended as the public mind became better informed and composed." These expectations "have not been realized," and indeed "the efforts repeatedly made to place the judiciary department on a proper footing have proved fruitless." Given this, he doubted "the propriety or expediency of my returning to the bench under the present system," indeed feared "it would give some countenance to the neglect and indifference with which the opinions and remonstrances of the judges on this important subject have been treated." He added that his health was "clearly and decidedly" too

weak for him to undertake the "fatigues incident to the office." He wrote separately to Marshall, returning the commission and pleading ill health.[66]

It took about a week for Jay's letter to Adams to make its way from Albany
to the new national capital in Washington. When it did, Secretary Marshall
handed the letter to President Adams, who read it through, then turned to
Marshall and asked "who shall I nominate now?" Marshall replied that he really
did not know. "After a moment's hesitation," Marshall later recalled, Adams
said "I believe I must nominate you." Adams did so the next day, and the
Senate confirmed the appointment, after some grumbling that Marshall was not
sufficiently Federalist. Thus it was Jay, by declining this appointment, who
opened the way for Adams to appoint Marshall, America's greatest Chief
Justice.[67]

Many Federalists were, at this time, scheming to use the tie in the electoral
college in their favor. Jay was not among them. On the contrary, he urged
Federalists to abide by the election results. In a letter from Albany to New
York, perhaps intended for publication, he argued that Federalists should give
"full and fair effect to the known sense and intention of a majority of the
people, in every constitutional exercise of their will," and that they should
"support every administration of the government of our country which may
prove to be intelligent and upright, of whatever party the persons composing
it may be." It was a fitting statement of the principles which had guided him
when he refused to contest the outcome of the gubernatorial election of 1792
or to interfere in the presidential election of 1800.[68]

CHAPTER 15

Retirement

Many of Jay's colleagues, during or after the Revolution, had a few years in retirement or semi-retirement. Washington spent the years after the war at Mount Vernon, "under the shadow of my own vine and my own fig tree." Jefferson spent several years building his home and tending his farm at Monticello. But Jay served in various public positions almost without interruption from May of 1774, when he was elected to the first New York revolutionary committee, through June of 1801, when his second term as Governor of New York ended. Many of these years involved difficulty, danger and separation from his family. He was thus more than ready, in the spring of 1801, to retire to his farm. Indeed, six years earlier, he had written to his wife Sarah that "much of our lives is spent. A few years of leisure and tranquility are very desirable. Whether they will fall to our lot, cannot be known ... If they come, let us enjoy them; if not let us be resigned."[1]

He could not retire to the farm where he grew up in Rye, because that farm was now the home of his brother Peter and his sister-in-law Polly. But John owned another farm, at Bedford, New York, about twenty miles northeast of Rye. The land at Bedford had been purchased in about 1700 by his grandfather, Jacobus Van Cortlandt, from the Indian chief Katonah. The land passed to John at the time of the death of his father Peter, but he leased it to tenants, and only visited from time to time. John's plan was to turn the existing modest farmhouse into a substantial three-story home. Sarah's health, however, was too weak at this time to stand the strain of living at a construction site, so the family separated for the summer. John and his daughter Ann, now seventeen, traveled to Bedford in early May; Sarah went to stay with her sister

Catharine at Oak Hill along the Hudson River; Maria remained with her new husband in Albany; and young William also stayed in Albany, to study with a tutor.[2]

Jay, now fifty-five, did not wield a hammer himself, but he spent the summer and fall supervising the work. He wrote to his wife to describe the "noise and hurry of carpenters, masons and laborers in and about the house." Sarah suffered from "restlessness" and "night sweats" at Oak Hill. She was so weak that, for a time, she could not even dress and undress herself. But she could not bear to be so far from her husband. So in July she took a seat on a sloop headed down the Hudson River, then traveled overland to Rye, where she stayed with Peter and Polly, only a short ride from John at Bedford. Sarah was still at Rye in early October, when she wrote to John that "most sincerely do I regret the impediments that have separated us for these five or six months past." By early December, however, she was at Bedford, writing to her daughter Maria that her sister Ann was "at this moment in the garden planting peach stones." Sarah added in a postscript that "my health continues to improve."[3]

The house at Bedford, when it was built, was a three-story farmhouse, substantial and comfortable, but in no way as grand as Jefferson's Monticello or Washington's Mount Vernon. From the large front porch, which the family called the "piazza," they could enjoy a view of the surrounding countryside and the distant mountains. Bedford was remote, a two-day ride from New York City. The newspapers arrived only once a week, giving Jay what he called "a history of the times." Sarah must have missed the company of her friends in New York and Albany, but she wrote in late 1801 that "I can truly say I have never enjoyed so much comfort as I do here."[4]

In February 1802, Jay set out from Bedford for New York City to sit for a portrait requested by the city council. He stopped to visit his brother in Rye, and was delayed there first by a severe snowstorm, and then by a severe cold. Sarah wrote to her husband in early March, describing the effects of the storm at Rye, and closing as she always did, "sincerely and affectionately yours, Sarah Jay." In early May, Sarah wrote to her daughter Maria in Albany, expressing the hope that the latter could spend several weeks with the family in the summer, and adding "with the greatest sincerity" that "my health and appetite increase daily." A few days after this, however, she was "seized with a severe illness" and a few days later she died, at the age of forty-five.[5]

Sarah had lived a remarkable if brief life. An ardent American patriot, perhaps more vocal than her reserved husband, she contributed to the creation of the new nation in many ways: by running the household during her husband's frequent absences on public business; by advising him on personal and political issues; and by gathering at their dinner table the leaders of various parties and states. Above all she is remembered, and rightly so, for her brave decision to accompany her husband on his revolutionary diplomatic mission to Spain and France. America had Founding Mothers as well as Founding Fathers, and Sarah Livingston Jay deserves her place in this pantheon.

John Jay was at his wife's side, "calm and collected," when she died. He then led their children "into an adjoining room, and with a firm voice but glistening eye, read to them the fifteenth chapter of Paul's first letter to the Corinthians, thus leading their thoughts to that day when the lifeless but beloved form they had just left would rise to glory and immortality." He could not and did not write letters for many weeks. In one of the few from that year in which he mentioned Sarah, he said that she endured a "long and painful illness" and then, "when she appeared to be fast recovering," suffered "unexpected death." He was a faithful Christian and his faith supported him at this time, but nothing could fill the void left by Sarah's death. John was ten years older than Sarah, but in some ways he was thirty years older: serious, sober, even severe. Sarah provided the light and the life in their household, and now that light was gone, and John was left to face many years alone.[6]

He was comforted by his five children, of course, but they had lives and difficulties of their own. Peter Augustus, a young lawyer in New York City, fell ill in the fall of 1802, and the family feared the illness was tuberculosis. On the advice of his doctors, Peter spent one winter in southern Europe and the next in Bermuda. He spent much of the next two years with his father and sister at the family farm in Bedford. Peter regained his health, returned to New York City, married a distant cousin and started his own family. By 1810, Peter Augustus Jay was one of the leading lawyers of New York City and a member of various social and political organizations. Peter also served as his father's agent in New York City, much as John had served as agent for his own father Peter, handling all sorts of personal and business tasks for his father in Bedford.[7]

Maria Jay Banyer lived with her family at Albany. The Banyer household included not only her husband but also her elderly father-in-law and her younger sister, Sarah Louisa. In 1804, the Banyers had a son, but the boy soon died. Jay, thinking no doubt of his wife, wrote to Maria that "we have indeed reason to grieve for the comforts we lose by [the boy's] absence, but not that he is where he is. His happiness is now certain, complete, eternal. Happy shall we all be to arrive finally at the same blest abodes; and there to be received by him, and many others of our best and dearest friends and kindred." In 1806, Maria's husband died, and not long thereafter the couple's remaining child, a daughter Sarah, died. Maria remained in Albany, however, until about 1815, caring for her father-in-law and raising her sister.[8]

The one child who remained at home with Jay at Bedford throughout his retirement was his daughter Nancy, nineteen years old the summer her mother died. It seems that, even before her mother's death, Nancy was more concerned about her parents than about finding a husband. She wrote to her mother during the summer of 1800 that "if all were equally blessed with myself in such tender and indulgent parents, they would look for happiness at home, and not seek for it in the world, where they can never find it." Nancy was a religious girl who became a religious woman. In 1812, writing to her brother to console him after the death of a child, she observed that they could "take courage and comfort in knowing that we are in the hands of a merciful God." In 1818, she wrote about her father that "his continued peace of mind and habitual trust in an overruling Providence ... more strongly recommends the blessings of religion, than volumes written in its praise."[9]

William was at home the summer that his mother died, and his father then tried to find a suitable place for him to study near Bedford. When this proved impossible, Jay decided that Yale, which was undergoing an educational and religious revival under Timothy Dwight, was the proper place for him. Jay wrote to Dwight, asking whether he would accept William into his family, both as he prepared for and then attended the college. Dwight responded that his own household was not suitable, because he was away from home so often, but that Henry Davis, one of the senior tutors, had several boys in his house, and

Jay Homestead, Bedford, New York.
(*New York Department of Parks and Recreation*)

would be glad to care for and instruct William. In early 1803, young William set off for New Haven, carrying a letter in which his father asked his new master to emphasize "habits of punctuality and industry." William remained at New Haven, with only intermittent visits to home at Bedford, until his graduation from Yale College in 1808. He then went to Albany, where he worked as a law clerk, but found that his eyes were too weak for all the reading. He returned home to Bedford, and for a while his father fretted that the boy would become a "mere farmer." He need not have worried, however. William married in 1812, founded the American Bible Society in 1816, was named county judge in 1818, and was a leader in local and national affairs for many years thereafter.[10]

The youngest daughter, Sarah or Sally, spent most of her time with her sister Maria in Albany, although she visited her father in Bedford and her friends and relatives in New York from time to time. Her letters to her father were generally filled with news about the weather and friends; she noted in one that the discussion in Albany was often political and "I am no politician." Like many young women, she was torn between her love of social life and her desire to "do my duty and be useful to others." In one letter to her father from New York City, she noted that it was "much more difficult to keep the straight path here than at home" since "the temptations to expense, amusements and vanity are very many and almost irresistible." During another visit to New York City, in early 1818, Sarah fell ill and died. Her brother invited dozens of family and friends to the funeral, but her father did not feel up to coming into town for the event.[11]

In addition to Jay's children, and after 1813 his grandchildren by William, the household at Bedford included slaves and servants. At the time of the 1810 census, the household included one slave and four "other free persons," former slaves now working as servants. As late as 1809, Jay sold Zilphah, a slave whom he found difficult and disobedient. Zilphah's mother begged to have her daughter back with her, and Jay wrote to Peter Augustus that he was willing to "make the experiment" with the daughter for the sake of the mother. When his brother Peter asked whether he should let go one of his servants, Jay observed that "a faulty servant is better than none" and "for my part I do not think that a new set that would suit him could be had." He included his servants

in the evening prayers. One visitor remembered joining "the venerable patriarch and his children, and the household within his gates, uniting in
thanksgiving, confession and prayer. Sir, it was more like Heaven upon earth
than anything I ever witnessed or conceived." [12]

After his retirement, Jay was only rarely involved in state and national politics.
The Federalist party never regained power after its losses in 1801, so there were
few Federalist leaders to seek his advice. Even when Federalists did seek his
advice, he responded sometimes with platitudes, and other times with barbed
words. In April 1807, for example, a New York Federalist wrote to him, probably hoping for some stirring words that could be used in the imminent election
for Governor. The response was a long lament about the "vices and violences
of parties and the corruptions which they generate and cherish." According to
Jay, "*all* parties have their demagogues, and demagogues never were nor will
be patriots." Indeed, in his view the problem was not just a few individuals, but
the whole system. "The rulers in democratic societies are generally men of
more talents than morals. There can be but little connection between cunning
and virtue, and therefore (except now and then in particular instances) our
affairs will commonly be managed by political intrigues." It was a long and
interesting letter, but not at all the kind of thing which one could print in a
Federalist newspaper. [13]

At about this same time, Jay discussed the election with his old friend Egbert
Benson. Benson described the conversation to a Federalist editor, William
Coleman, who reported in his newspaper that Jay "cannot possibly conceive
how any man who calls himself a Federalist can ever give a vote for a candidate set up by the Clinton party." Jay immediately sent a short, sharp letter to
Benson, saying that his view was quite the "reverse of the illiberal one ascribed
to me." Benson responded that he thought they were only talking about this
election, and that people had understood the comment in that way, but that he
would be happy to help get a correction published. Benson must have been
taken aback, after knowing him for forty years, to be rebuked in this way by
his friend. [14]

In June 1812, at the request of President Madison, Congress declared war on
Great Britain. Federalists at the time, and historians more recently, have

viewed the war as unjustified and ill-advised. Jay, who had devoted so much of his life to negotiating and maintaining peace between Britain and America, found this war particularly painful. As he put it in a letter to Peter Van Schaack, the "declaration of war was neither necessary, nor expedient, nor seasonable." He was not one of those such as his friend Gouverneur Morris, who talked about the possibility that New York and New England would secede from the union. "Commotions tending to dissolution of the union, or to civil war, would be serious evils." But he did not speak out, either against the war or against secession. Indeed, he cautioned Van Schaack that he did not want "to be quoted in newspapers, or hand-bills, or public speeches." [15]

The debate over the war was conducted in all these fora as well as in the streets. In Baltimore, Democrats attacked a Federalist editor and his supporters, killing several people, injuring others and destroying many houses. DeWitt Clinton, who had emerged as Madison's main rival in the presidential election, solicited the support of New York's Federalists. In early August 1812, at the very moment of the Baltimore riots, John Jay, Rufus King and other Federalist leaders gathered at the home of Gouverneur Morris, in what is today the Bronx, and Clinton came out to meet with them one evening. Some of the Federalists, especially Morris, emerged from these meetings as enthusiastic Clinton supporters. Jay was more subdued. He wrote to his son Peter that "if we must have either Mr. Madison or Mr. Clinton, I prefer the latter, and for reasons which have less relation to his personal qualifications, than to the existing state of things." Morris tried to persuade Jay to attend a statewide anti-war meeting, but he declined, pleading ill health. [16]

The one exception to Jay's political silence, the one case in which he took a public stance, was in the Missouri controversy. In the fall of 1819, anti-slavery activists started a campaign to prevent the admission of Missouri as a slave state. Their concern was not only to prevent the extension of slavery to another state, but also to preserve the balance of power in the Senate. Elias Boudinot, with whom Jay had served in the Continental Congress, wrote seeking his support for this campaign. He responded with a strong letter. Slavery "ought not to be introduced nor permitted in any of the new states" and "it ought to be gradually diminished and finally abolished in all of them." He refuted the argument, advanced by Madison among others, that Congress could not under the Constitution prohibit slavery in any particular state. He even quoted, in support of his argument, the Declaration of Independence, with its ringing statement that "all men are created equal." [17]

This letter was printed in many newspapers, and it was "read in the North with a feeling akin to veneration." In the South, however, it was read with disgust, and reminded people of his "anti-Southern" attitude in the negotiations with Spain. President James Monroe complained privately that Jay was once again seeking "a monopoly of power in the eastern portion of the union, to be perverted to improper purposes." The Missouri question was resolved in 1820 by compromise, in which Missouri was admitted as a slave state, Maine was admitted as a free state, and slavery was prohibited in the Louisiana Territory or any new states there north of the thirty-sixth parallel. [18]

In early 1818, after a long silence, Jay received a letter from John Adams, who like Jay had been living in retirement since 1801, in his case in Quincy, Massachusetts. Adams was eager for Jay to comment on a paragraph from a recent biography of Patrick Henry. The author asserted that it was Richard Henry Lee who had, in late 1774, prepared for Congress the first draft of the address to the British people, that Congress had received Lee's draft with "silence" and "disappointment," that Congress had asked Livingston and Jay to prepare another draft, and that Congress had adopted this draft "with scarcely an alteration." Jay responded at length. It was he, not Livingston and not Lee, who had prepared the draft of the address to the British people. There was, he insisted, no first draft by Lee, who was busy with "other avocations in and out of Congress." Jay admitted that there were amendments to his draft, but commented that the first Congress was so careful about the "force and latitude of expressions" that it amended every draft. He signed himself "your affectionate friend." [19]

In early 1821, it was his own turn to write to Adams with a similar question. He noted that a Philadelphia publisher claimed he would soon publish the "journals" of Jay and Adams for the Paris peace negotiations. Adams responded that he had not kept a journal during that period, "except the one that was sent to Congress, which General Hamilton made somewhat notorious by the exquisite satire which he, so justly, did it the honor to confer upon it." (Adams was referring to Hamilton's attack upon Adams during the 1800 election, a "satire" he did not find so "exquisite" at the time.) Adams added that Jay need not be worried about publication of his letters, "for your letters will do you honor wherever they go." Jay wrote the publisher, saying that neither he nor Adams kept journals of this period, and asking him to describe these "journals." The publisher said he had two documents, each "very short," captioned the journals of Jay and Adams. Adams was satisfied with this but Jay was still troubled. "It appears to me that the journals which he calls ours, cannot be exact copies of our official letters to the Secretary for Foreign Affairs, for he mentions these journals as being 'very short indeed,' whereas our letters were very far from being short." He believed that the "journals" were probably just "extracts" or "abridgments" of their letters and he was concerned about "how judiciously such extracts have been selected and combined, or how correctly such abridgments have been made." He wrote again to the publisher, asking him to provide copies of the purported "journals." The publisher declined, apparently concerned about revealing his source.[20]

In the course of this second correspondence, there were some interesting asides between Jay and Adams. Adams commented that the "beauty and firmness" of Jay's handwriting was "equal to the best of your former days." Adams wished he could "give you a specimen of mine as beautifully written, but a pen will not obey the command of my paralytic nerves." Adams also reported that he had just, for the first time, read Jay's "elegant and masterly" address to the Kingston grand jury in 1777. The address "revived a thousand painful, and as many pleasant, recollections. The snare is broken, and we have escaped, but heaven alone knows how." Jay commended Adams on the work of the recent constitutional convention in Massachusetts and lamented that, in New York, "certain of our demagogues seem to regard checks and balances as inconvenient obstacles." Adams hoped Jay would be able to attend the imminent New York constitutional convention: "it will want some such heart of oak pillar." Jay responded that, although he would like to play his part, his health would not allow him to go to the convention in Albany. The last letter in this series was a note from Jay to Adams, covering a copy of the official record of this convention. But it was Adams who had the last word, at the Fourth of July celebration in Quincy in 1823, when he rose to offer a toast to "the excellent President, Governor, Ambassador and Chief Justice, John Jay, whose name by accident was not subscribed to the Declaration of Independence, as it ought to have been, for he was one of its ablest and faithfulest supporters." According to the newspaper report, this toast was greeted not with the customary American roar, but rather with near-silence, as each person present offered a prayer that "the two illustrious sages might pass the remainder of their days in tranquility and ease, and finally be landed on the blissful shores of a happy eternity." [21]

Jay's most regular correspondent, aside from family members, was Richard Peters. Jay knew Peters from the Revolution; he was the clerk of the Board of War while Jay was the President of the Congress. Peters was now the federal district judge in Philadelphia, and the head of the local agricultural society, and the two often wrote one another on agricultural issues. In one letter, for example, Jay reported to Peters that some of his neighbors were using crushed sea shells as a fertilizer. Peters described his Tunisian sheep, and Jay responded that he would "like to have some of them, if they would remain quietly in fields fenced only by stone walls. My farm was from its first settlement occupied by tenants; they have left no trees fit for rails, nor can I obtain a supply in the neighborhood." A few months later, Peters sent Jay two of the sheep, male and female. Jay feared the sheep might suffer from the local dogs, "who occasionally do much mischief. I wish they were well taxed, for the number of them is too great." A few years later, Jay had to report not only the death of the sheep, but also the death of "a favorite mare, which I had rode for twenty-three years with great satisfaction." The mare was the third in succession which Jay had owned and ridden; the grandmother "was given to me by my father in 1765." [22]

Jay and Peters corresponded about current affairs, both American and international. In 1809 Jay described Europe, then torn by war, as "a tempestuous and raging ocean; and who can tell what governments afloat upon it will escape destruction or disaster?" America too, would "experience deep distress, but I do not believe you or I will live to see it." There were too many people, in his view, who "love pure democracy too dearly; they seem not to consider that *pure* democracy, like *pure* rum, easily produces intoxication, and with it a thousand mad pranks and fooleries." For him, the wars in Europe and the problems in America were linked. "There came forth with the French Revolution a spirit of delusion which, like an influenza, passed over and infected all Europe. Even our distant country has not entirely escaped ... Delusions have their errands, and are sent for some purpose different from that of promoting unanimity and peace." [23]

Jay and Peters also wrote one another about historical issues and characters, especially Washington. In 1811, Peters asked Jay to comment on reports that Hamilton had written Washington's Farewell Address. He responded with a long letter, one of the longest he wrote during his retirement. He stressed Washington's virtue and intelligence, which allowed him to "lead and govern an army, hastily collected from various parts," to "meet and manage all those perplexing embarrassments" of the war, including "the frequent destitution and constant uncertainty of essential supplies." He described how "at a subsequent and alarming period, [when] the nation found that their affairs had gone into confusion," the people "instituted under his auspices a more efficient government, and unanimously committed the administration of it to him." He noted that Washington, at all stages of his life, wrote well, and knew how to solicit advice to improve his writing. [24]

After this long preamble, he finally came to the point: what role did Hamilton play in drafting Washington's Address? Jay was initially inclined to avoid the question, but "on more mature reflection" he had decided that Washington, if he were still alive, would want Jay to commit to paper now what he knew, for the sake of history. So he described how, a short time before the Address appeared in 1796, he had met with Hamilton to review the draft. "We proceeded deliberately to discuss and consider it, paragraph by paragraph, until the whole met with our mutual approbation." In 1826, when the Pennsylvania Historical Society asked Jay similar questions, he referred them to this letter, but asked that if it were published, it be published in full, not in mere extracts. [25]

Peters was not the only friend with whom Jay discussed history. His friend Jedidiah Morse, the Boston minister and author, was considering writing a history of the United States. Jay encouraged him, noting that a "proper history" would "develop the great plan of Providence, for causing this extensive part of our world to be discovered, and these 'uttermost parts of the earth' to be gradually filled with civilized and Christian people and nations." A few years later, when Morse still had not done much on the project, Jay noted that "time will not wait, but will proceed in the usual way to impair memory, to diminish and obscure evidence, to introduce doubt, and enable error to impose upon credulity." In person, Jay's views on American history could be less complimentary. According to family tradition, one day after dinner at Bedford, Gouverneur Morris turned to Governor Jay and called the members of the Continental Congress "a set of damned scoundrels." To which Jay heartily agreed.[26]

As Jay grew older, requests for historical information came more often from the younger generation, those whose fathers had fought in the Revolution. James Fenimore Cooper, the son of Judge William Cooper, spoke with Jay about Revolutionary spies. Jay's stories provided Cooper with the basis for *The Spy*, a novel which proved "instantaneously and phenomenally popular," and provided the model for many future accounts of the Revolution.[27] George Alexander Otis, son of a Massachusetts revolutionary, sought comments on his translation of Botta's *History of the War of Independence*. Jay responded with a long letter, mainly refuting the suggestion that Americans aimed, from the outset, for independence. "During the course of my life and until after the second petition of Congress in 1775, I never did hear any American of any class, or of any description, express a wish for the independence of the colonies." In his view, "our country was prompted and impelled to independence by necessity and not by choice."[28] Richard Henry Lee, grandson of the Revolutionary of the same name, asked about the authorship of various documents during the Continental Congress. Jay again responded at some length, with both quotations from the Journals of Congress and his own recollections about who penned which documents. He added that "the memoirs you are preparing would derive advantage from deliberation and frequent revision." A few weeks later, Charles DeWitt wrote to seek memories of his grandfather. Jay wrote back to describe how, when he was in desperate need of a horse in Kingston, to ride to northern New Jersey to check on his wife and her family, the elder DeWitt "immediately supplied me with a good one that was working in his plough," for which he was still grateful. When James Morris requested material for a biography of his late father, Jay urged him to proceed carefully. "Biographical narratives require time for the collection, selection and arrangement of the materials; and it is more important that they should be interesting and accurate, than that they should be quickly compiled and speedily published." [29]

Jay was well-off, but not wealthy, in his retirement. He had earned solid salaries in his various public positions: $4000 per year as Secretary for Foreign Affairs, as Chief Justice, and as Governor of New York. American custom, however, did not allow him to hold multiple offices, and it does not appear that he used his public positions to find lucrative private investment opportunities. During his retirement, he lived mainly off the income from his land, especially in New York City, where he owned several substantial plots. He was not so wealthy that he did not have to worry about money. In 1819, for example, he wrote to his son Peter noting that they would have to raise a "large sum" to pay the tax assessments on their land in New York City, and asking for his son's views on whether they should "sell lots, sell stocks, or borrow." A year later, he wrote to Peter again, noting that the recent assessments, and the debts he had incurred to pay them, "have so reduced my income, that if the assessments should demand large additional sums, I shall be constrained to make very inconvenient retrenchments." At his death, he left a substantial estate to his children, but nothing like the fortune of £250,000 that his contemporary Lord Ellenborough, Chief Justice of England, left upon his death. [30]

Jay devoted much of his time to religion and to religious causes. When he arrived in Bedford, there was a small Episcopal congregation, but no Episcopal church building and no regular minister. For a few years, he attended services at the Presbyterian church, but he provided financial support to the Episcopal congregation, which enabled them to build the church building which still stands as St Matthew's in Bedford. He declined a position on the vestry, but attended the church regularly and supported it financially. According to parish tradition Jay sometimes brought along to church his dog, Bob. Jay also devoted much of his time to reading the Bible, too much time in the view of some of his friends. Adams, in a letter to Jefferson, said he would not want to see his son "retire like a Jay to study prophecies to the end of his life." [31]

Even in church matters, Jay sometimes showed his sharp side. In 1804, he heard that Trinity Church was interested in acquiring some of his land in New York City for a new church. Trinity probably hoped that he would donate the land, or at least some of it, for this purpose, but he was not prepared to be quite so generous. He responded that he was willing to sell two lots to Trinity Church, at fair market value, and would donate the third, if Trinity would pay the Bedford church an imputed "rent" on this third lot. After considering the question, the Trinity vestry rejected this proposal. Jay resented the tone of the vestry's resolution, which seemed to him to suggest that he was merely out for "a good opportunity for disposing of his lots to advantage." [32]

A similar case involved the Methodist priest at Bedford, Reverend Nathan Felch. After he had served the Episcopal congregation for several months, Jay and others recommended that Felch be ordained as an Episcopalian. Shortly thereafter, however, Jay heard that Felch would sometimes "tell tales" about his horse or his farm. He joined the vestry for several meetings, at which they apparently took testimony for and against Felch, and he drafted for the vestry resolutions stressing that "a minister should deserve and sustain a reputation of constantly adhering to the truth." But the vestry decided that Felch should still be ordained. Jay disagreed, and wrote to Bishop Moore in New York to explain why. Felch remained at Bedford for three more years, then departed when the vestry refused to increase his salary. Jay wrote his son that there was "no reason to regret" the departure. [33]

Jay often received letters with religious questions as well as political and historical ones. He was asked, for example, whether he agreed that all wars were forbidden by the Bible. He disagreed. "Praise is due to those who endeavor to turn public opinion against unjust wars, but zeal against any and every war, without exception, does not appear to me to be a 'zeal according to knowledge.'" He was asked whether he agreed that the death penalty was inconsistent with the commandment against taking life. He disagreed. "As to murderers, I think it not only lawful for government, but that it is the duty of government, to put them to death." [34]

As he became more religious, Jay became less tolerant of popular pastimes. Before his retirement, he enjoyed the theater, finding time for performances in Paris, in New York, in Philadelphia, and in London. In March of 1795, for example, he and Peter had gone twice to the Drury Lane Theater in London to see Mrs. Siddons, once playing Isabella in *Measure for Measure* and once playing Portia in *The Merchant of Venice*. In early 1813, however, Jay wrote to his daughter Maria that "you know my opinion of theaters. From me they neither have received nor will receive encouragement." [35]

Jay's "causes" in his retirement were generally moral and religious: societies for founding missions or suppressing vice. It appears that his involvement in these organizations was generally limited to lending his prestigious name and reviewing draft petitions. In the case of the American Bible Society, however, his role was much more substantial. In the early part of the nineteenth century, new printing technologies made it possible to print thousands of Bibles at modest cost. There were far more Bible readers than ever before, because the population, the literacy rate and religious enthusiasm were all increasing. William Jay was one of those, from various denominations, who helped form the American Bible Society in 1816, with the stated goal of printing and distributing Bibles "without note or comment." Although his father did not attend the initial meeting of the society, he was so keen about its work that he made an exception to his normal practice, and agreed to serve as a vice-president. In late 1821, when the society's President died, the managers of the society asked Jay to become the next President. He was initially reluctant, because he would not be able to attend the meetings of the society, but the leaders persuaded him that even as an absentee he could provide valuable service. [36]

His main duty was to prepare an address, really a short sermon, each year for the spring meeting. He praised, in several of these messages, the new missionary efforts in Asia and Africa. "We now see Christians, in different countries, and of different denominations, spontaneously and cordially engaged in conveying the scriptures, and the knowledge of salvation, to the heathen inhabitants of distant regions." He encouraged Christians to recognize "that persons of great worth and piety are [often] attached to sects different from their own." Above all, Jay talked about the Bible and its distribution. The Bible, for him, was the record of the experience of God's chosen people, the Jews, as well as of "every material event and occurrence respecting our Redeemer, together with the Gospel he proclaimed." If one viewed "the Bible in this light, it appears that an extensive and increasing distribution of it has a direct tendency to facilitate the progress of the Gospel throughout the world. That it will proceed, and in due time be accomplished, there can be no doubt; let us therefore continue to promote it with unabated zeal." [37]

From time to time a visitor would arrive to vary the routine. In the summer of 1826, two gentlemen arrived and found the Governor "on his piazza in a large arm chair." He invited them "into his sitting parlor," where they were joined by his two daughters (Maria Banyer and Nancy Jay) and his daughter-in-law (Augusta McVickar Jay). Although he was "thin and infirm," he had "his memory hearing and understanding," and indeed spoke at length about what he viewed as the errors of the recent New York constitutional convention. After a mid-afternoon dinner, when the Governor took up his pipe, the ladies "kindly pressed us to smoke, saying they were used to the flavor." The visitors "bid adieu to this great and good man and his excellent family" at around four in the afternoon.[38]

Although he had activities, interests and visitors, Jay was, in comparison with some of his contemporaries, very *retired* in Bedford. Thomas Jefferson, during his retirement, advised Presidents, founded the University of Virginia, and hosted the steady stream of visitors who showed up at Monticello. In one year, by his own count, he received more than a thousand letters. John Adams defended his reputation in newspaper articles, attended celebrations and events in Boston, and kept up with many correspondents, including Jefferson.[39] Jay had fewer visitors, fewer letters and fewer projects. He amused himself by "little improvements, occasional visits, the history which my recollections furnish, and frequent conversations with the 'mighty dead'" in his library. In 1816, he noted that he had not been to New York City during the past eight years. A few years later, he wrote that "my health has been declining for twelve years past; my excursions from home have long been limited to short distances; such are my maladies that they often confine me to my house, and at times to my chamber." Even his correspondence was limited; he apparently received and wrote only a few dozen letters a year during his retirement.[40]

Jay's isolation in Bedford was to some extent caused by his severity, even in dealing with family and friends. In 1803, for example, he chided his nephew Munro for his handling of a minor business question. Munro wrote back that his letter had "given him much pain" and attempted to justify himself. Jay said that his "meaning was not to accuse but to correct, as he would any of his own children." Munro, who was of course not one of Jay's children, nor a child at all, had to come out to Bedford to "come to a better understanding." In 1806, Sarah

Louisa questioned her sister's conduct in a letter. Jay chastised her: "there is a wide difference between confiding sentiments to me, and confiding sentiments to a letter to me. Letters not infrequently miscarry, and are sometimes read by those for whose inspection they were not intended. Prudence is one of the cardinal virtues, and well deserves our constant attention." In 1813, Gouverneur Morris wrote to ask whether Jay would serve as godfather for his infant son. The godfather might not live to see the child become a man, but "should you be mingled with the dust, he shall learn, from the history of your life, that man must be truly pious to be truly great." In spite of the generous compliment, Jay declined. Since he did not expect to live long, "it appears to me advisable that some proper person not so circumstanced should be selected." [41]

In 1826, every city and town planned a grand celebration of the fiftieth Fourth of July. New York City invited its most famous native son to attend its celebration. Jay declined, but added his "earnest hope that the peace, happiness, and prosperity enjoyed by our beloved country, may induce those who direct her national affairs to recommend a general and public return of praise and thanksgiving to Him from whose goodness these blessings descend." On the same occasion, Jefferson wrote that he hoped America's independence would be "the signal of arousing men to burst the chains under which monkish ignorance and superstition had persuaded them to bind themselves, and to assume the blessings and security of self-government." Jay saw the Revolution as mainly American history, not world history, and saw it as God's particular gift to America. Jefferson looked forward to world revolution, against not only kings but also against religious superstition. [42]

Even in the early years of his retirement, when he was in his late fifties and early sixties, Jay complained in his letters of ill health. In early 1807, for example, he told Peter Van Schaack that "for some weeks during the winter I was much indisposed." In 1809, he told Jedidiah Morse that he had "become sick last autumn, and have not had a well day since. Although better, I am still feeble; and can neither bear much exercise, nor much employment of any kind." In early 1810, he wrote to Judge Peters that "since the middle of November I have been confined to the house." But Jay cannot have been entirely an invalid, for his son William later wrote that he generally "rose with or before the sun at all seasons, and when the weather permitted, was frequently on horseback before breakfast."[43]

In later years, as his health declined and his friends died off, Jay became more appreciative of his own health and life. He wrote to his son Peter that weakness was "common to old age, and mine though unpleasant is not very troublesome; to wear away, at my time of life, by a gentle decay, has more of favor than affliction in it." A few years later, he wrote to his friend Lindley Murray, whom he had known since they were clerks more than fifty years earlier, that the "term of my lease has expired, and I am holding over. How long I shall be permitted to do so, depends on Him, without whose will not a sparrow falls to the ground."[44]

In 1825, he suffered a slight stroke, and William reported to Peter that their father's "articulation was perfect, but he found it difficult to express himself, from a forgetfulness of the words he wished to use. He frequently called things by the wrong names, was conscious of his mistake, but unable to correct it." He apparently soon recovered his speech, however, for there is no further mention of this in the family letters. In 1827, he injured his hand while taking a piece of firewood off the stack for his fire. He thought nothing of it at first, but within a few days "the hand was dreadfully swelled, of a dark purple color, and extremely painful." His children feared that he would die, but he himself did not seem fearful, merely serious. The doctors treated him with "wine, porter, and quinine, and have ordered that his feet and legs be rubbed with brandy." Whether because of or in spite of these treatments, he recovered.[45]

In the spring of 1829, as his health failed further, Jay prepared his last will and testament. He thanked God for blessing him "with excellent parents, with a virtuous wife and with worthy children." "His protection has accompanied me through many eventful years, faithfully employed in the service of my country, and His providence has not only conducted me to this tranquil situation, but also given me abundant reason to be thankful." He asked that, instead of the customary funeral scarves and rings, his family should give two hundred dollars "to any one poor deserving widow or orphan of this town, whom my children shall select." There was a long provision regarding his papers and manuscripts, some of which he hoped would be destroyed immediately, and others preserved by his sons.[46]

In the last few days, he could scarcely speak. At one point, he managed to say to Maria "the Lord is good" and at another point "the Lord is better than we deserve." Mainly, however, he lay silent in his bed, attended by his daughters, wearing an expression Maria described as "like a saint ripened for glory." On May 17, 1829, he died peacefully, aged eighty-three. His son Peter, writing to Cooper, reported that "my good old father has paid the debt of nature." His death "was attended by every circumstance which can lighten affliction for such a loss" and yet it was a loss, especially for the family.[47]

As he requested, Jay was buried quietly in the family cemetery at Rye. (He had established this cemetery by a deed in 1815, a few yards from the house where he had grown up as a boy, to provide for the descendants and spouses of descendants of his father and mother.) There were a few obituaries after his death, but nothing like the number that had marked the deaths three years earlier of Adams and Jefferson. One newspaper reported of Jay that "few of the great men of this country have enjoyed a higher or more deserved reputation." Another commented that his "fine talents, displayed in every department of government, as a legislator, a jurist, and a diplomatist, were unaccompanied by that sordid ambition which too frequently degrades the greatest genius." The New York Supreme Court observed that "few men in any country, and perhaps scarce one in this, have filled a larger space, and few ever passed through life with such perfect purity, integrity and honor."[48]

CHAPTER 16

Conclusions

ALTHOUGH he was not a historian, John Jay was conscious of history, both the example of the past and the judgment of the future. In 1774, he reminded his British readers of how their "great and glorious ancestors" had through many years and wars "maintained their independence, and transmitted the rights of men and the blessings of liberty to you, their posterity." Arguing in 1776 about why the Americans would prevail, he cited the examples of the Netherlands and Switzerland, small nations which had secured and preserved liberty. Freedom was a gift from God, for which Americans were responsible and answerable. "If the means of our defense are in our power and we do not make use of them, what excuse shall we make to our children and our Creator?" He often linked religion and history in this way, viewing them as related forms of final judgment. The task of historians was to discern and describe the truth, but truth and error would, he feared, "imperceptibly become and remain mixed and blended until they shall be separated forever by that great and last refining fire." [1]

While doubtful about the possibility of writing "true history," Jay believed that history was an important endeavor. He urged Charles Thomson, secretary of the Continental Congress, to spend an hour a day on an account of the "rise, conduct, and conclusion of the American Revolution," especially on the "political story of the Revolution." He carefully recorded some of the stories Benjamin Franklin told about various figures he had known in his youth, an early example of oral history. While he was Secretary for Foreign Affairs, he gathered and organized the papers of the office, commenting to Adams that "it is common, you know, in the course of time for loose and detached papers to be lost, or mislaid, or misplaced." Regrettably, he did not take steps to ensure that his own papers would be preserved for history, and many of them were destroyed or lost over the years.[2]

Some of his contemporaries attempted to identify their key contributions to American history. Late in life, Adams wrote to a friend that, without his efforts:

> this country would never have been independent; Washington would not have been commander of the American army; three hundred millions of acres of land which she now possesses would have been cut off from her limits; the cod and whale fisheries ... would have been ravished from her; the Massachusetts constitution, the New York constitution ... the Constitution of the United States would never have been made.

Jefferson directed that his tombstone state that "here is buried Thomas Jefferson, author of the Declaration of Independence, of the Statute of Virginia for Religious Freedom, and Father of the University of Virginia." Jay apparently never attempted a similar list, but it is not hard to construct one for him. He was the principal author of the first constitution of New York state, the most balanced of the early state constitutions. He drafted and negotiated the extensive American boundaries secured by the Paris Peace Treaty. He played a critical role in forming the federal Constitution and securing its ratification. He negotiated the treaty which bears his name, Jay's Treaty, which avoided a disastrous war with Britain.[3]

He made several contributions which are more elusive but also important. He was not as gifted an author as Thomas Jefferson or Thomas Paine, but his political papers, starting with his address to the British people and running through his grand jury charges, helped define and inspire the nation. His year as President of the Continental Congress was not a good year for the Congress, but perhaps his tact prevented even more damage. During his five years as Secretary for Foreign Affairs, he provided crucial continuity and solidity to the confederation government. His prominent anti-slavery stance helped not only to end slavery in New York but also to establish the moral foundation for its end throughout America. He did not make the Supreme Court the power it would become under John Marshall, but he helped define what federal courts could do, such as review statutes for constitutionality, and what they could not do, such as decide abstract questions.

Jay was part of a great generation, and one way to approach his place in history is to compare his contributions with those of some of his contemporaries. He was not as important as Franklin, rightly called the "First American," or Washington, the "Father of His Country." He also ranks behind Adams, Hamilton, Jefferson and Madison. After these six men, however, no other American of the revolutionary generation contributed more than Jay. Samuel Adams and Patrick Henry helped start the Revolution, but once it was underway they played limited roles, and almost no role in the early republic. Robert Morris provided crucial financial management during the early 1780s, but then devoted most of his efforts to his private affairs, and indeed spent several of his last years in debtors' prison. Aaron Burr played a minor military role in the Revolution, then served as a Senator and Vice-President. But for his famous duel with Hamilton, he would be as forgotten today as any other nineteenth century Vice-President.[4]

Jay rose to prominence, and then remained in senior positions, because of certain talents and qualities. His legal training and experience gave him a facility for words; he could write quickly and precisely and persuasively; he could grasp and resolve complex issues. Once he was in public life, his contemporaries recognized not only these skills, but other qualities. He worked hard, not only day by day but year after year. Few men would have had the patience to spend two years seeking Spanish aid or five years handling the chaotic foreign affairs of the young nation. He was a serious and sober man, but he had many friends, including friends with whom he sometimes disagreed on political issues. He had a gift for developing compromises, for finding the way out of an apparently impossible conflict. He ensured that the process was fair, whether in interrogating suspected spies or in negotiating a draft treaty. He used his religious faith to rally other Americans and to sustain himself in difficult hours. From a very early stage, he recognized that America could and would be a great nation, and others recognized him as a man who would help lead them to that future.

Perhaps the best brief summary of Jay's life and temper was by his son, Peter Augustus, who placed these words on his father's tombstone:

> In memory of John Jay, eminent among those who asserted the liberty and established the independence of his country, which he long served in the most important

offices, legislative, executive, judicial and diplomatic, and distinguished in them all by his ability, firmness, patriotism, and integrity. He was in his life and death an example of the virtues, the faith and the hopes of a Christian.[5]

Notes

Letters cited without identification are at Columbia University, either in manuscript in the Rare Book and Manuscript Room, or in facsimile, on the new Jay Papers website.

The following abbreviations are used for frequently cited works:

ASPFR	*American State Papers: Foreign Relations.*
DHFFC	Linda De Pauw et al., eds., *The Documentary History of the First Federal Congress.*
DHSC	Maeva Marcus, ed., *The Documentary History of the Supreme Court of the United States, 1789–1800.*
EN	Mary A. Giunta et al., eds., *The Emerging Nation: A Documentary History of the Foreign Relations of the United States under the Articles of Confederation, 1780–1789.*
JCC	Worthington C. Ford, ed., *Journals of the Continental Congress, 1774–1789.*
JPC	*Journals of the Provincial Congress, Provincial Convention, Committee of Safety and Council of Safety of the State of New York.*
JPJ	Henry P. Johnston, ed., *The Correspondence and Public Papers of John Jay.*
1 JPM	Richard B. Morris, ed., *John Jay: The Making of a Revolutionary. Unpublished Papers, 1745–1780.*
2 JPM	Richard B. Morris, ed., *John Jay: The Winning of the Peace. Unpublished Papers, 1780–1784.*
LDC	Paul H. Smith, ed., *Letters of Delegates to Congress, 1774–1789.*
PAH	Harold C. Syrett, ed., *The Papers of Alexander Hamilton.*
PBF	Leonard W. Labaree et al., eds., *The Papers of Benjamin Franklin.*
PGW	W. W. Abbot et al., eds., *The Papers of George Washington* (separate series identifiable by date).

PTJ   Julian P. Boyd et al., eds., *The Papers of Thomas Jefferson.*

RDC   Francis Wharton, ed., *The Revolutionary Diplomatic Correspondence of
               the United States.*

Notes to Introduction

1. Thomas E. V. Smith, *The City of New York in the Year of Washington's Inauguration,
   1789* (Riverside, Conn.: Chatham Press, 1973), 231–33; William A. Duer, Description
   of the Inauguration, 15 DHFFC 395–96; Comte de Moustier, Description of the
   Inauguration, ibid. 403. Although there does not appear to be a contemporary account
   which places Jay on the balcony, it seems likely that he was there based on his prominent place in the procession to Federal Hall and the presence of his counterpart,
   Henry Knox, among those on the balcony. See Order for Inauguration, March 1789,
   8 DHFFC 772–73; Gazette of the United States, 29 April – 2 May 1789, 15 DHFFC
   410–11; North Callahan, *Henry Knox, General Washington's General* (New York:
   Rinehart, 1958), 274–75.

2. Cokie Roberts, *Founding Mothers* (New York: William Morrow, 2004).

3. George Washington to John Jay, 5 October 1789, 4 PGW 137; Charles
   F. Adams, ed., *The Works of John Adams, Second President of the United States,* 10
   vols. (Boston: 1856), 10:115; John Marshall, *The Life of George Washington,* 5 vols.
   (London: 1807), 5:183; Louis Guillaume Otto to Vergennes, 10 January 1786, 3 EN
   64–65.

4. Joseph J. Ellis, *Founding Brothers: The Revolutionary Generation* (New York: Alfred
   A. Knopf, 2000), 17, 109; A. J. Langguth, *Patriots: The Men Who Started the American
   Revolution* (New York: Simon and Schuster, 1988); David McCullough, *John Adams*
   (New York: Simon and Schuster, 2001), 231; Richard B. Morris, *The Peacemakers:
   The Great Powers in Search of American Independence* (New York: Harper and Row,
   1965), 1–26; Gordon S. Wood, *The Creation of the American Republic, 1776–1787*
   (New York: W. W. Norton, 1969).

Notes to Chapter 1: New York

1. Carl Bridenbaugh, *Cities in Revolt: Urban Life in America, 1743–1776* (New York:
   Alfred A. Knopf, 1955); Edwin G. Burrows and Mike Wallace, *Gotham: A History of
   New York City to 1898* (New York: Oxford University Press, 1999); D. W. Meinig,
   The Shaping of America, Atlantic America, 1492–1800 (New Haven: Yale University
   Press, 1986); Alan Taylor, *American Colonies: The Settling of North America* (New
   York: Penguin, 2002).

2. Burrows and Wallace, *Gotham,* 167–70; Fred Anderson, *Crucible of War: The Seven
   Years' War and the Fate of Empire in British America, 1754–1766* (New York: Alfred
   A. Knopf, 2000); James G. Lydon, *Pirates, Privateers, and Profits* (Upper Saddle
   River, New Jersey: Gregg Press, 1970).

3. William Jay, *The Life of John Jay*, 2 vols. (New York: 1833), 1:2–10; John Jay to Gouverneur Morris, 29 April 1778, 1 JPM 476; Laura Jay Wells, *The Jay Family of La Rochelle and New York* (New York: Order of the Colonial Lords of Manors in America, 1938); Jon Butler, *The Huguenots in America: A Refugee People in New World Society* (Cambridge: Harvard University Press, 1983), 13–49; Joyce D. Goodfriend, *Before the Melting Pot: Society and Culture in Colonial New York City, 1664–1730* (Princeton: Princeton University Press, 1992), 46–51.

4. Jacob Judd, "Frederick Philipse and the Madagascar Slave Trade," *New-York Historical Society Quarterly* 55 (1971): 354–74; John A. Garraty and Mark C. Carnes, eds., *American National Biography*, 24 vols. (New York: Oxford University Press, 1999), 17:439–40.

5. Jay, *Life of John Jay*, 1:7–8; Goodfriend, *Before the Melting Pot*, 22–23; Wells, *Jay Family*, 9.

6. Augustus Jay listed only four children in his family Bible: Judith, born in 1698, Marie, born in 1700, John Jay's father Pierre or Peter, born in 1704, and Anne or Anna, born in 1706. Edward F. DeLancey, "Original Family Records, Jay," *New York Genealogical and Biographical Record* 7 (1876): 112. The records of the French Church show a fifth child, Françoise, born and baptized in 1701. Alfred V. Wittmeyer, ed., *Registers of the Births, Marriages, and Deaths of the Eglise Françoise à la Nouvelle York* (Baltimore: Genealogical Publishing Co., 1968), 74–75, 87. For Augustus Jay's service to Trinity Church, see William Berrian, *An Historical Sketch of Trinity Church, New York* (New York: 1847), 356.

7. L. Effingham de Forest, *The Van Cortlandt Family* (New York: Historical Publication Society, 1930); Goodfriend, *Before the Melting Pot*, 62, 106.

8. Peter Jay to David and John Peloquin, 8 January 1724; David Peloquin to Peter Jay, 19 September 1724; David Peloquin to Peter Jay, 19 July 1725; Berrian, *Historical Sketch*, 357.

9. Samuel Johnson to Peter Jay, 27 July and 29 December 1739, in Frank Monaghan, "Dr. Samuel Johnson's Letters to Peter Jay," *Columbia University Quarterly* 25 (1933): 88, 91.

10. Jay, *Life of John Jay*, 1:111; Susan Mary Alsop, *Yankees at the Court: The First Americans in Paris* (Garden City, New York: Doubleday and Company, 1982), 194; Peter Jay to James Jay, 3 July 1752, 1 JPM 34–35.

11. Peter Jay to David and John Peloquin, 9 November 1745; Peter Jay to James Jay, 1 November 1748; Frank Monaghan, *John Jay: Defender of Liberty* (New York: Bobbs-Merrill Co., 1935), 22; City of New York, "Fraunces Tavern Historic District Designation Report," 1978.

12. Alsop, *Yankees*, 194; Charles W. Baird, *Chronicle of a Border Town: A History of Rye, Westchester County, New York, 1660–1870* (New York: 1871).

13. Peter Jay to John Jay, 26 March 1765.

14. Peter Jay to Chafin Grove, 5 May 1747; Peter Jay to David and John Peloquin, 20 July 1747 and 20 April 1748; Peter Jay to John Adlam, 26 June 1749.

15. Peter Jay to James Jay, 13 May 1749, 12 July 1749 and 17 November 1754.

16. Peter Jay to James Jay, 13 March 1751, 7 June 1751 and 4 May 1752; Jay, *Life of John*

Jay, 1:1–9; Wells, *Jay Family*, 9 n. 8; Patricia U. Bonomi, "John Jay, Religion, and the State," *New York History* 51 (2000): 9–18.

17. Peter Jay to David and John Peloquin, 17 June 1746, 1 November 1748, 23 September 1754, 24 November 1756, 10 October 1760, 12 December 1761 and 1 December 1762; Anderson, *Crucible of War*.

18. Peter Jay to James Jay, 3 July 1752, 1 JPM 34–35; Peter Jay to David and John Peloquin, 24 October 1753, 1 JPM 36–37.

19. Butler, *Huguenots*, 137, 170–72, 186–92; Bonomi, "John Jay, Religion, and the State."

20. Jay, *Life of John Jay*, 1:12.

21. Robert Bolton, *The History of the Several Towns, Manors and Patents of the County of Westchester*, 2 vols. (New York: 1881), 1:645–46.

22. Monaghan, *John Jay*, 24.

23. David C. Humphrey, *From King's College to Columbia, 1746–1800* (New York: Columbia University Press, 1976).

24. Joseph J. Ellis, *The New England Mind in Transition: Samuel Johnson of Connecticut, 1696–1772* (New Haven: Yale University Press, 1973); Humphrey, *King's College*, 19–28, 163–64.

25. Humphrey, *King's College*, 166–68; Jay, *Life of John Jay*, 1:13.

26. Humphrey, *King's College*, 168–78.

27. Ibid. 122–25.

28. Ibid. 126–30, 177–80.

29. Michael Kammen, *Colonial New York: A History* (Milwood, New York: KTO Press, 1975), 279–92; Carl Bridenbaugh, *Cities in Revolt: Urban Life in America, 1743–1766* (New York: Alfred A. Knopf, 1955), 156–61, 314–18.

30. Peter Jay to David Peloquin, 14 April 1763, 1 JPM 46–47; Peter Jay to Nicholas Stuyvesant, 21 September 1763; Walter DuBois Jr. to Robert R. Livingston, 7 September 1763, Livingston Papers, New-York Historical Society.

31. George Dangerfield, *Chancellor Robert R. Livingston of New York, 1746–1813* (New York: Harcourt, Brace, 1960), 25–45; Cynthia Kierner, *Traders and Gentlefolk: The Livingstons of New York, 1675–1790* (Ithaca: Cornell University Press, 1992), 4–5.

32. Walter DuBois Jr., to Robert R. Livingston, 6 January 1764, Livingston Papers, New-York Historical Society; John Jay to Robert R. Livingston, 1 January 1775, 1 JPM 138–39.

33. Leonhard F. Fuld, *Kings College Alumni* (New York: 1913), 24–36; Milton H. Thomas, *Columbia University Officers and Alumni, 1754–1857* (New York: Columbia University Press, 1936), 99; Humphrey, *King's College*, 208–24.

34. Jay, *Life of John Jay*, 1:14–15; John Jay, Note, 1 JPM 55.

35. Humphrey, *King's College*, 186.

36. Peter Jay to John Jay, January 1763, 1 JPM 41–42; Peter Jay to John Jay, 16 January and 22 May 1764, 1 JPM 51–52, 64; *New York Mercury*, 30 January 1764, 1 JPM 52.

37. Peter Jay to David Peloquin, 16 May 1762, 1 JPM 38–39; Peter Jay to John Jay, 23 August 1763, 1 JPM 48–49; William H. Adams, *Gouverneur Morris: An Independent Life* (New Haven: Yale University Press, 2003), 21–22.

38. Peter Jay to James Jay, 15 February 1763 and 14 April 1763, 1 JPM 44–45; Peter Jay to David Peloquin, 14 April 1763, 1 JPM 46–47; David Peloquin to Peter Jay, 26 July 1763, 1 JPM 47–48; Peter Jay to James Jay, 12 November 1763 (typescript); Peter Jay to David Peloquin, 15 November 1763, 1 JPM 50–51.

39. Peter Jay to John Jay, 16 January 1764, 1 JPM 51–52.

40. *New York Mercury*, 28 May 1764, 1 JPM 62–63; Herbert A. Johnson, *John Jay: Colonial Lawyer* (New York: Garland Publishing, 1989), 1–9; Burrows and Wallace, *Gotham*, 177.

41. *New York Mercury*, 28 May 1764, 1 JPM 62–63; Johnson, *Colonial Lawyer*, 10–11.

Notes to Chapter 2: The Law

1. Paul Hamlin, *Legal Education in Colonial New York* (New York: New York University Press, 1939), 43; Johnson, *Colonial Lawyer*, 15–17; Lindley Murray, *Memoirs of the Life and Writings of Lindley Murray* (New York: 1827), 33–34.

2. Peter Jay to David Peloquin, 9 October 1764; Murray, *Memoirs*, 34; Johnson, *Colonial Lawyer*, 111–14; E. B. O'Callaghan, "John Chambers," *New York Genealogical and Biographical Record* 3 (1888): 57–62.

3. John Jay to Robert R. Livingston, 2 April 1765, 1 JPM 71–72; John Jay to Robert R. Livingston, 19 April 1765, 1 JPM 74–76; John Jay to Robert R. Livingston, 31 October 1765, 1 JPM 77–79; see Kenneth R. Bowling, *Peter Charles L'Enfant: Vision, Honor and Male Friendship in the Early American Republic* (Washington, D.C.: George Washington University Libraries, 2002); Clare A. Lyons, "Mapping an Atlantic Sexual Culture: Homoeroticism in Eighteenth Century Philadelphia," *William and Mary Quarterly* 60 (2003): 119–54.

4. John Jay to Benjamin Kissam, 12 August 1766, 1 JPJ 4; Benjamin Kissam to John Jay, 25 August 1766, 1 JPM 82–84.

5. Rules of King's College, March 1763, 1 JPM 60; *New York Mercury*, 1 June 1767, 1 JPM 85–86.

6. Minutes of the Debating Society, 1768, 1 JPM 87–95.

7. License to Practice Law, 26 October 1768, 1 JPM 95; Johnson, *Colonial Lawyer*, 58–59, 62–63.

8. Petition to the House of Commons, 18 October 1764, in Edmund S. Morgan, ed., *Prologue to Revolution: Sources and Documents on the Stamp Act Crisis, 1764–1766* (Chapel Hill: University of North Carolina Press, 1959), 8–14; Anderson, *Crucible of War*, 572–79, 608–09 (errs in arguing that *Forsey* trial preceded assembly petition); John W. Tyler, *Smugglers and Patriots: Boston Merchants and the Advent of the American Revolution* (Boston: Northeastern University Press, 1986), 65–83.

9. Herbert A. Johnson, "George Harison's Protest: New Light on *Forsey v. Cunningham*," *New York History* 50 (1969): 50–82; Milton M. Klein, "Prelude to Revolution in New York: Jury Trials and Judicial Tenure," *William and Mary Quarterly* 17 (1960): 453–54; Joseph H. Smith, *Appeals to the Privy Council from the American Plantations* (New York: Columbia University Press, 1950), 390–412.

10. Kammen, *Colonial New York*, 345–46; Johnson, "Harison's Protest"; Klein, "Prelude to Revolution"; Smith, *Appeals*, 394–99.

11. John Watts to Robert Monckton, 10 November 1764, Aspinwall Papers, *Massachusetts Historical Society Collections*, 4th series (Boston: 1871), 10:542–43; *New York Gazette*, 14 March 1765 and 18 July 1765, quoted in Klein, "Prelude to Revolution," 458–59; Dorothy R. Dillon, *The New York Triumvirate: A Study of the Legal and Political Careers of William Livingston, John Morin Scott and William Smith, Jr.* (New York: Columbia University Press, 1949), 68–81.

12. Peter Jay to David Peloquin, 7 May 1765; Peter Jay to David Peloquin, 19 September 1765; Edmund S. and Helen M. Morgan, *The Stamp Act Crisis: Prologue to Revolution* (New York: Collier Books, 1962), 96–98.

13. Anderson, *Crucible of War*, 679–85; Morgans, *Stamp Act*, 139–44; F. L. Engelman, "Cadwallader Colden and the New York Stamp Act Riots," *William and Mary Quarterly* 10 (1953): 560–78.

14. Peter Jay to David Peloquin, 25 November 1765.

15. *New York Mercury*, 23 December 1765, and *New York Journal*, 19 April 1770, quoted in Carl L. Becker, *The History of Political Parties in the Province of New York, 1760–1776* (Madison: University of Wisconsin Press, 1960), 40; Morgans, *Stamp Act*, 223–25; Johnson, *Colonial Lawyer*, 27–28; John Jay to Robert R. Livingston, 31 October 1765, 1 JPM 79–80.

16. John Jay to Robert R. Livingston, 31 October 1765 and 4 March 1766, 1 JPM 79–81; Benjamin Kissam to John Jay, 25 April 1766, 1 JPM 82.

17. Benjamin Kissam to John Jay, 25 August 1766, 1 JPM 82–84; de Forest, *Van Cortlandt Family*; Johnson, *Colonial Lawyer*, 40–44; Sung Bok Kim, *Landlord and Tenant in Colonial New York: Manorial Society, 1664–1775* (Chapel Hill: University of North Carolina Press, 1978); Irving Mark and Oscar Handling, "Land Cases in Colonial New York, 1765–1767: The King v. William Prendergast," *New York University Law Quarterly* 19 (1942): 164–94.

18. Anderson, *Crucible of War*, 691–708; Morgans, *Stamp Act*, 327–52; Smith, *Appeals*, 408–09; Joseph A. Ernst, "The Currency Act Repeal Movement: A Study of Imperial Politics and Revolutionary Crisis, 1764–1767," *William and Mary Quarterly* 25 (1968): 177–211.

19. Gordon S. Wood, *The Radicalism of the American Revolution* (New York: Alfred A. Knopf, 1991).

20. Johnson, *Colonial Lawyer*, 62–65.

21. Boundary Commission files, Columbia; Philip J. Schwarz, *The Jarring Interests: New York's Boundary Makers, 1664–1776* (Albany: State University of New York Press, 1979), 179–90; Smith, *Appeals*, 453–63; Johnson, *Colonial Lawyer*, 65–75.

22. Anderson, *Crucible of War*, 529–34, 719–24; David G. Hendrickson, *Peace Pact: The Lost World of the American Founding* (Lawrence: University Press of Kansas, 2003); Johnson, *Colonial Lawyer*, 75–76; Monaghan, *John Jay*, 42; Smith, *Appeals*, 417–63.

23. Benjamin Kissam to John Jay, 6 November 1769, 1 JPJ 9–10.

24. Moot Minutes, Columbia; Hamlin, *Legal Education*, 96–97, 201–03; Johnson, *Colonial Lawyer*, 116–24.

25. John Jay to Peter Yates, 23 March 1772, 1 JPM 110—11; James D. Sumner, Jr., "The Full-Faith-and-Credit Clause: Its History and Purpose," *Oregon Law Review* 34 (1955): 224—49.

26. John Jay to Samuel Kissam, 27 August 1771, in Frank Monaghan, "Samuel Kissam and John Jay," *Columbia University Quarterly* 25 (1933): 131.

27. John Jay to John Tabor Kempe, 27 December 1771, John Tabor Kempe to John Jay, 27 December 1771, John Jay to John Tabor Kempe, 2 January 1772, 1 JPM 106—09; Catherine Crary, "The American Dream: John Tabor Kempe's Rise from Poverty to Riches," *William and Mary Quarterly* 14 (1957): 176—95; Dillon, *Triumvirate*, 49—52; Johnson, *Colonial Lawyer*, 126—30.

28. Johnson, *Colonial Lawyer*, 98—101.

29. Johnson, *Colonial Lawyer*, preface, tables.

30. John Jay to John Vardill, 23 May 1774, 1 JPM 130—31; William H. Sabine, ed., *Historical Memoirs of William Smith*, 2 vols. (New York: New York Times, 1956), 1:129—32.

31. Hamlin, *Legal Education*, 94; Milton M. Klein, "The Rise of the New York Bar: The Legal Career of William Livingston," *William and Mary Quarterly* 15 (1958): 354.

32. John Jay to Robert Randall, 2 February 1773, 1 JPM 116—18; Note, 1 JPM 112—13.

33. Patricia U. Bonomi, *A Factious People: Politics and Society in Colonial New York* (New York: Columbia University Press, 1971); Humphrey, *King's College*, 99; Klein, "Rise of the New York Bar,"; Carl E. Prince, ed., *The Papers of William Livingston*, 5 vols. (Trenton: New Jersey Historical Commission, 1979—88), 1:xxvi, 1—7.

34. Gouverneur Morris to Catharine Livingston, 11 January 1773, Ryder Papers, Massachusetts Historical Society; Henry Livingston Jr. to Catharine Livingston, 12 March 1773; Max M. Mintz, *Gouverneur Morris and the American Revolution* (Norman: University of Oklahoma Press, 1970), 40—41.

35. Thomas Jones, *History of New York during the Revolutionary War*, 2 vols. (New York: 1879) (ed. Edward DeLancey), 2:223, 474; see Peter Jay to William Livingston, 31 January 1774, 1 JPM 124.

36. Sarah Jay to Susannah Livingston, 6 May 1774, 1 JPM 124—25.

37. *New-York Gazette and Weekly Mercury*, 9 May 1774.

Notes to Chapter 3: Resistance Leader

1. *New-York Gazette and Weekly Mercury*, 25 April 1774; Becker, *History*, 95—111; Bernard Mason, *The Road to Independence: The Revolutionary Movement in New York, 1773—1777* (Lexington: University of Kentucky Press, 1966), 3—22; Robert Middlekauff, *The Glorious Cause: The American Revolution, 1763—1789* (New York: Oxford University Press, 1982), 221—24; Thomas J. Wertenbaker, *Father Knickerbocker Rebels: New York City during the American Revolution* (New York: Charles Scribner's Sons, 1948), 31—33.

2. Sarah Jay to Susannah Livingston, 6 May 1774, 1 JPM 124; John Jay to John Vardill, 23 May 1774, 1 JPM 130; Becker, *History*, 112—17.

3. New York Committee to Boston Committee, 23 May 1774, 1 JPJ 13–15; Note, 1 JPM 132.

4. John Jay to Sarah Jay, 29 June 1774, quoted in Monaghan, *John Jay*, 55 (not in Columbia index); John Jay to John Morin Scott, 20 July 1774, 1 JPM 135; Peter Force, ed., *American Archives*, 9 vols, 4ᵗʰ Series, 1:298–24 (Washington: Government Printing Office, 1837–53); Becker, *History*, 120–41.

5. Edward P. Alexander, *A Revolutionary Conservative: James Duane of New York* (New York: Columbia University Press, 1938); United States Congress, *Biographical Directory of the American Congress, 1774–1971* (Washington: Government Printing Office, 1971).

6. David Ammerman, *In the Common Cause: American Response to the Coercive Acts of 1774* (Charlottesville: University Press of Virginia, 1974), 53–55; Jerrilyn Greene Marston, *King and Congress: The Transfer of Political Legitimacy, 1774–1776* (Princeton: Princeton University Press, 1987), 67–77; Jack N. Rakove, *The Beginnings of National Politics: An Interpretive History of the Continental Congress* (New York: Alfred A. Knopf, 1979), 21–41.

7. Samuel Ward Diary, 1 September 1774, 1 LDC 14; John Adams Diary, 1 September 1774, 1 LDC 6; Silas Deane to Elizabeth Deane, 4 September 1774, 1 LDC 18; *New-York Gazette*, 5 September 1774; Bridenbaugh, *Cities in Revolt*; Carole Shammas, "The Space Problem in Early American Cities," *William and Mary Quarterly* 57 (2000): 505–42.

8. John Adams Diary, 30 August 1774, 1 LDC 5; Silas Deane to Elizabeth Deane, 31 August 1774, 1 LDC 15; Rakove, *Beginnings*, 42–44.

9. Robert Treat Paine Diary, 5 September 1774, 1 LDC 13; John Adams Diary, 5 September 1774, 1 LDC 9–10; James Duane Notes, 5 September 1774, 1 LDC 25–26; Joseph Galloway to William Franklin, 5 September 1774, 1 LDC 27; Silas Deane to Elizabeth Deane, 5 September 1774, 1 LDC 23.

10. John Adams Notes, 6 September 1774, 1 LDC 27–29; James Duane Notes, 6 September 1774, 1 LDC 30–32; Marston, *King and Congress*, 76–77.

11. Ammerman, *In the Common Cause*, 89–101; Rakove, *Beginnings*, 42–45, 61–62; Monaghan, *John Jay*, 58.

12. John Adams to Abigail Adams, 16 September 1774, 1 LDC 74; John Adams Diary, 7 September 1774, 1 LDC 33; Silas Deane to Elizabeth Deane, 7 September 1774, 1 LDC 34.

13. John Adams Diary, 6 September 1774, 1 LDC 27; Silas Deane to Elizabeth Deane, 6 September 1774, 1 LDC 29–30; James Duane Notes, 6 September 1774, 1 LDC 32; Robert Treat Paine Diary, 6 September 1774, 1 LDC 32; John Adams to Abigail Adams, 8 September 1774, 1 LDC 49; Silas Deane to Elizabeth Deane, 8 September 1774, 1 LDC 50–51; Marston, *King and Congress*, 82–83.

14. John Adams Notes, 8 September 1774, 1 LDC 46–48, 60; John Adams Diary, 8–10 September 1774, 1 LDC 45, 60; Samuel Ward Diary, 14 and 16 September 1774, 1 LDC 72, 75.

15. Suffolk Resolves, 6 September 1774, 1 JCC 32–38; Robert Treat Paine Diary, 16 September 1774, 1 LDC 75.

16. 1 JCC 39–40.

17. Rakove, *Beginnings*, 46–48; Marston, *King and Congress*, 84–86.

18. John Adams Diary, 14 September 1774, 1 LDC 69; Robert Treat Paine Diary, 16 September 1774, 1 LDC 75; Thomas Cushing to Deborah Cushing, 4 October 1774, 1 LDC 142.

19. John Jay to John Vardill, 24 September 1774, 1 JPM 137–38.

20. Becker, *History*, 164 ("Jay, Duane and Low [signed] the Association which they had opposed during the proceedings of Congress"); Monaghan, *John Jay*, 63 ("Why did Jay, essentially conservative, sign the Association, a radical measure of revolutionary consequence?").

21. John Adams Notes, 26 September 1774, 1 LDC 105.

22. John Adams Notes, 26–27 September 1774, 1 LDC 103–04; Ammerman, *In the Common Cause*, 79–81; Marston, *King and Congress*, 113–16.

23. Ammerman, *In the Common Cause*, 103–24; Marston, *King and Congress*, 100–30.

24. Richard Henry Lee, Proposed Resolution, 3 October 1774, 1 LDC 140; Silas Deane Diary, 3 October 1774, 1 LDC 138–39; Robert Treat Paine Diary, 6 October 1774, 1 LDC 154; Samuel Adams Draft Letter, 7–8 October 1774, 1 LDC 158–60; 1 JCC 60–61; Ammerman, *In the Common Cause*, 74–75.

25. Thomas Jefferson to William Wirt, 4 August 1805, in Edmund C. Burnett, ed., *Letters of Members of the Continental Congress* (Washington: Carnegie Institution of Washington, 1921), 1:57; Notes, 1 LDC 179, 220.

26. Address to the People of Great Britain, 1 JCC 84–85. Although the printed journal refers to the Stamp Act, the law described is clearly the Revenue Act.

27. Ibid. 86–88.

28. Ibid. 90.

29. John Adams Diary, 26 October 1774, 1 LDC 246; Robert Treat Paine Diary, 26 October 1774, 1 LDC 248; John Dickinson to Arthur Lee, 27 October 1774, 1 LDC 250; Ammerman, *In the Common Cause*, 89.

30. Alexander Hamilton to Catharine Livingston, 11 April 1777, 1 PAH 225–27; Ron Chernow, *Alexander Hamilton* (New York: Penguin Press, 2004), 41–61; James T. Flexner, *The Young Hamilton: A Biography* (Boston: Little Brown, 1978); Becker, *History*, 158–61; Philip Ranlet, *The New York Loyalists* (Knoxville: University of Tennessee Press, 1986), 52–53.

31. John Jay to Robert R. Livingston, 1 January 1775, 1 JPM 139; Force, *American Archives*, 4th Series, 1:987; New York Delegates to the Mechanics Committee, 18 November 1774, 1 JPJ 31–32; John Jay Draft, New York Committee to New Haven Committee, 17 April 1775, 1 JPM 143–44.

32. William Laight to John Vardill, 27 March 1775.

33. Benjamin Franklin to Joseph Galloway, 25 February 1775, 21 PBF 508.

34. Force, *American Archives*, 4th Series, 2:351–58.

35. Ibid. 400, 427, 446–49; Burrows and Wallace, *Gotham*, 223–24; Wertenbaker, *Knickerbocker Rebels*, 53–55.

36. Force, *American Archives*, 4th Series, 2:427–28, 471; Becker, *History*, 196–97.

37. Force, *American Archives*, 4th Series, 2:468, 470, 479, 481, 509, 510, 529, 530, 531 and 532.

38. John Adams to Abigail Adams, 23 July 1775, 1 LDC 648–49; Carl Van Doren, *Benjamin Franklin* (New York: Viking Press, 1938), 527–39; Dumas Malone, *Jefferson: The Virginian* (Boston: Little Brown, 1948), 201–03; Gordon S. Wood, *The Americanization of Benjamin Franklin* (New York: Penguin Press, 2004).

39. John E. Ferling, *John Adams: A Life* (Knoxville: University of Tennessee Press, 1992), 120–28; Marston, *King and Congress*, 145–48; Middlekauff, *Glorious Cause*, 276–81; Rakove, *Beginnings*, 69–74.

40. Silas Deane Diary, 16, 23 and 24 May 1775, 1 LDC 351–52, 371, 401; John Dickinson Notes, 23–25 May 1775, 1 LDC 371–86.

41. 2 JCC 49–52, 68–70, 74, 80; New York Delegates to New York Provincial Congress, 16 May 1775, 1 LDC 353; Connecticut Delegates to William Williams, 31 May 1775, 1 LDC 423–24; Marston, *King and Congress*, 146–47; Rakove, *Beginnings*, 71–76.

42. Frederick Jay to John Jay, 11 May 1775, 1 JPM 144–45; John Jay to Sarah Jay, 16 May 1775; John Jay to Sarah Jay, 23 May 1775, 1 JPM 145–46; John Jay to Sarah Jay, 30 May 1775; Peter Jay to John Jay, 30 May 1775, 1 JPM 146–47; John Jay to Sarah Jay, 22 June 1775, 1 JPM 154; John Jay to Sarah Jay, 10 July 1775.

43. Draft Petition to the King, June 1775, 1 LDC 440–42; Middlekauff, *Glorious Cause*, 260–61.

44. Compare Jay Draft, 1 LDC 440–41, with Final Petition, 2 JCC 158–61.

45. Rakove, *Beginnings*, 76–77; 2 JCC 76–79, 83–84.

46. 2 JCC 97–99, 105–06, 111–23; Silas Deane Diary, 22 June 1775, 1 LDC 532; Middlekauff, *Glorious Cause*, 280–81; Ferling, *Adams*, 123–30.

47. Thomas Jefferson to William Wirt, 4 August 1805, in Burnett, *Letters*, 1:158.

48. Plan of Accommodation, 27 June 1775, Force, *American Archives*, 4th Series, 2:1326–29; Gouverneur Morris to John Jay, 30 June 1775, 1 JPM 156–57; New York Delegates to New York Provincial Convention, 6 July 1775, 1 LDC 596–97; Rakove, *Beginnings*, 77.

49. John Adams Notes, 12 and 13 October 1775, 2 LDC 167, 174; John Jay to Alexander McDougall, 17 October 1775, 2 LDC 197–98.

50. John Adams Notes, 20 October 1775, 2 LDC 212.

51. Provincial Congress to New York Delegates, 1 September 1775, 1 JPM 165; New York Delegates to New York Committee of Safety, 20 September 1775, 2 LDC 38.

52. John Jay to Alexander McDougall, 4 December 1775, 2 LDC 436–37; 3 JCC 308, 314; Force, *American Archives*, 4th Series, 3:1309, 1315.

53. William Laight to John Jay, 3 October 1775, 1 JPM 168–71; Eliga H. Gould, *The Persistence of Empire: British Political Culture in the Age of the American Revolution* (Chapel Hill: University of North Carolina Press, 2000).

54. John Jay to Alexander McDougall, 4 December 1775, 1 JPM 193–94; John Jay, Proofs, December 1775 or January 1776, 1 JPM 198–201; Milton M. Klein, "Failure of a Mission: The Drummond Peace Proposal of 1775," *Huntington Library Quarterly* 35 (1972): 343.

55. Klein, "Failure," 347–57; Note, 3 LDC 24–25. The full text of Drummond's plan is at Klein, "Failure," 377–80.

56. Lord Drummond Notes, January 1776, 3 LDC 23–24.

57. Lord Drummond Notes, 5–6 January 1776, 3 LDC 32–40.

58. 3 JCC 392; Benjamin Franklin et al. to Charles William Frederic Dumas, 9 December 1775, 2 LDC 465–69; Benjamin Franklin et al. to Arthur Lee, 12 December 1775, 2 LDC 474–76; Benjamin Franklin to Don Gabriel of Bourbon, 12 December 1775, 2 LDC 478.

59. Henri Doniol, *Histoire de la Participation de la France à l'Etablissement des Etats-Unis d'Amérique* (Paris: 1887), 1:267–68, 287–91 (author's translation); Alsop, *Yankees at the Court*, 26–32.

60. John Jay to Sir James Jay, 4 January 1776, 3 LDC 29.

61. John Jay to Sarah Jay, 18 and 29 September 1775, 26 October 1775, 4 and 23 December 1775, 1 JPM 166–68, 172–73, 187, 212–13.

62. Peter Jay to John Jay, 18 December 1775, 1 JPM 205; Robert R. Livingston to John Jay, 29 December 1775, 1 JPM 218–19; John Jay to Robert R. Livingston, 6 January 1776, 1 JPM 222–23.

63. Robert Troup to John Jay, 30 October 1775, 1 JPM 177–78; New York Delegates to Provincial Convention, 3 November 1775, 2 LDC 294–95; John Jay to Sarah Jay, 23 December 1775, 1 JPM 212; John Jay, Receipt, 12 June 1776.

64. New York Delegates to Provincial Convention, 5 January 1776, 3 LDC 37; John Jay to James Duane, 6 January 1776, 3 LDC 46; John Jay to Robert R. Livingston, 6 January 1776, 3 LDC 47; John Jay to Robert R. Livingston, 26 January and 25 February 1776, 1 JPM 223, 230; Frederick Jay to John Jay, 6 March 1776, 1 JPM 233; Peter Jay to John Jay, 12 March 1776.

65. Alexander Hamilton to John Jay, 31 December 1775, 1 PAH 178–79; Edward Nicholl to John Jay, February 1776; John Jay to Alexander McDougall, 17 February 1776; John Jay to Robert R. Livingston, 25 February 1776, 1 JPM 229–31; Becker, *History*, 241–43; Bruce Bliven, Jr., *Under the Guns: New York, 1775–1776* (New York: Harper and Row, 1972), 96–98.

66. Force, *American Archives*, 4th Series, 4:1153–54; Bliven, *Under the Guns*, 91–94, 98–101, 120–22; Middlekauff, *Glorious Cause*, 307–08, 315–16.

67. Committee of Secret Correspondence, 2 March 1776, 3 LDC 320–23; John Jay to Robert R. Livingston, 4 March 1776, 3 LDC 327; Richard Smith Diary, 5 March 1776, 3 LDC 335; John Jay to Robert Morris, 15 September 1776, 1 JPM 315–16; Klein, "Failure," 368–69.

68. Richard Smith Notes, March 1776, 3 LDC 375, 387, 411; Resolution on Privateers, 23 March 1776, 3 LDC 430; John Jay to Alexander McDougall, 27 March 1776, 3 LDC 452–53.

69. John Jay to Alexander McDougall, 13 March 1776, 3 LDC 373–74; 4 JCC 195; Michael Kammen, "The American Revolution as a *Crise de Conscience*: The Case of New York," in Richard M. Jellison, ed., *Society, Freedom, and Conscience: The American Revolution in Virginia, Massachusetts, and New York* (New York: W. W. Norton and Co., 1976), 177–78.

70. John Jay to Alexander McDougall, 21 March 1776, 3 LDC 424–25; John Jay to Alexander McDougall, 11 April 1776, 3 LDC 505–06; Chernow, *Hamilton*, 72.

71. Alexander McDougall to John Jay, 20 March 1776, 1 JPM 238; John Jay to Alexander McDougall, 23 March 1776, 1 JPM 243; Marinus Willett to John Jay, before 27 April 1776, 1 JPM 260–61; John Jay to Marinus Willett, 27 April 1776, 1 JPJ 56.

72. Congress to George Washington, 2 April 1776, 1 JPM 247 (Jay draft).

73. John Jay to Alexander McDougall, 21 March 1776, 1 JPM 241; John Jay to Alexander McDougall, 11 April 1776, 1 JPM 253–54.

74. John Jay to Philip Schuyler, 5 May 1776, 3 LDC 624; James Duane to John Jay, 11 May 1776, 1 JPM 264–65.

75. Burrows and Wallace, *Gotham*, 229; Judith Van Buskirk, *Generous Enemies: Patriots and Loyalists in Revolutionary New York* (Philadelphia: University of Pennsylvania Press, 2002), 13–16; Wertenbacker, *Knickerbocker Rebels*, 76–81.

76. Becker, *History*, 257–61.

77. Force, *American Archives*, 4th Series, 6:1364–70; Bliven, *Under the Guns*, 271–72, 279–83; Ranlet, *New York Loyalists*, 153–54; Wertenbaker, *Knickerbocker Rebels*, 80–81.

78. Force, *American Archives*, 4th Series, 6:1154–58; Bliven, *Under the Guns*, 302–05.

79. Force, *American Archives*, 4th Series, 6:1163–66; Bliven, *Under the Guns*, 309–10; Douglas Southall Freeman, *George Washington*, 7 vols. (New York: Charles Scribner's Sons, 1948–57), 4:115–20.

80. Force, *American Archives*, 4th Series, 6: 1410; 1 JPC 590; Bliven, *Under the Guns*, 311–12; Van Buskirk, *Generous Enemies*, 16–17; Wertenbaker, *Knickerbocker Rebels*, 81–82.

81. Resolve on New Governments, 15 May 1776, 3 LDC 677; John Adams to James Warren, 15 May 1776, 3 LDC 676; James Duane to John Jay, 18 May 1776, 1 JPM 266–67.

82. Becker, *History*, 268.

83. Ibid. 270–72; Force, *American Archives*, 4th Series, 6:1362–63, 1396.

84. Robert R. Livingston to John Jay, 4 June 1776, 1 JPM 272–74; Edward Rutledge to John Jay, 8 June 1776, 1 JPM 275–76; Edward Rutledge to John Jay, 29 June 1776, 1 JPM 280–81; Pauline Maier, *American Scripture: Making the Declaration of Independence* (New York: Alfred A. Knopf, 1997), 41–46.

85. John Jay to Edward Rutledge, 6 July 1776, 1 JPJ 68; Barnet Schecter, *The Battle for New York: The City at the Heart of the American Revolution* (New York: Walker and Co., 2002), 97–101; Freeman, *Washington*, 4:127.

86. John Jay to Robert R. Livingston, 1 July 1776, 1 JPM 281–82.

87. Resolutions, 9 July 1776, 1 JPC 518.

88. Gordon S. Wood, *The American Revolution* (New York: Modern Library, 2002), 76–79.

Notes to Chapter 4: Revolutionary Leader

1. 1 JPC 522–28; George Washington to John Hancock, 12 July 1776, 5 PGW 283–84; Nathaniel Woodhull to George Washington, 13 July 1776, 5 PGW 300–01; George

Washington to New York Convention, 14 July 1776, 5 PGW 312–13; Schecter, *Battle for New York*, 104–06.

2. Minutes of the Secret Committee, 19–20 July 1776, 1 JPM 296–97; Secret Committee to George Washington, 20 July 1776, 1 JPM 298–99; John P. Kaminski, *George Clinton: Yeoman Politician of the New Republic* (Madison: Madison House Publishers, 1993), 19–21.

3. Minutes of the Secret Committee, 22 July 1776, 1 JPM 296–300; Notes on Mission to Connecticut, July 1776, 1 JPM 300; Report to the Secret Committee, 7 August 1776, 1 JPM 301–03; Robert R. Livingston to John Jay, 12 August 1776, 1 JPM 303–04; E. M. Ruttenber, *Obstructions to the Navigation of Hudson's River* (Albany: 1860), 75–77; Secret Committee to George Washington, 13 August 1776, 6 PGW 7–9.

4. John Jay to Sarah Jay, 21 and 29 July 1776, 1 JPM 305–07; John Jay to Sarah Jay, 28 July 1776 (quoted in Monaghan, *John Jay*, 88–89, but not in Columbia index).

5. John Morin Scott to New York Convention, 6 September 1776, 1 JPM 310–14; Middlekauff, *Glorious Cause*, 339–48; Schecter, *Battle for New York*, 140–67.

6. 1 JPC 599.

7. 1 JPC 600–12; H. L. Barnum, *The Spy Unmasked: or The Memoirs of Enoch Crosby* (reprint, Harrison, New York: Harbor Hills Books, 1975), 81–82.

8. 1 JPC 612–33.

9. Peter Jay to John Jay, 22 September 1776; John Jay to Susannah Livingston, 29 September 1776; Frederick Jay to John Jay, 1 October 1776, 1 JPM 318–19; Frederick Jay to John Jay, 19 October 1776, 1 JPJ 89–90; John Jay to Sarah Jay, 19 October 1776; John Jay to Catharine Livingston, 8 November 1776, 1 JPM 320–21.

10. Enoch Crosby Pension Application, 15 October 1832, 1 JPM 338–40.

11. Ibid. 342–44.

12. Barnum, *The Spy Unmasked* (introduction); James Fenimore Cooper, *The Spy: A Tale of the Neutral Ground* (New York: Penguin Books, 1997) (introduction); Michael Kammen, *A Season of Youth: The American Revolution and the Historical Imagination* (New York: Alfred A. Knopf, 1978), 24, 153–55; Alan Taylor, *William Cooper's Town: Power and Persuasion on the Frontier of the Early American Republic* (New York: Random House, 1995), 408–12; Van Buskirk, *Generous Enemies*, 73–105; Note, 1 JPM 333–37.

13. William A. Benton, "Peter Van Schaack, The Conscience of a Loyalist," in Robert A. East and Jacob Judd, eds., *The Loyalist Americans: A Focus on Greater New York* (Tarrytown, New York: Sleepy Hollow Restorations, 1975).

14. Benton, "Van Schaack," 48–49; Kammen, *"Crise de Conscience,"* 167.

15. Sarah Jay to Susannah Livingston, 6 May 1774, 1 JPM 125; Minutes of the Committee for Detecting Conspiracies, 1 JPM 346–48.

16. Beverly Robinson to John Jay, 4 March 1777, 1 JPM 349–50; John Jay to Susanna Philipse Robinson, 21 March 1777, 1 JPM 352–54.

17. John Jay to Edward Rutledge, 11 October 1776, 1 JPJ 92–93; Middlekauff, *Glorious Cause*, 349–56; P. K. Rose, "The Founding Fathers of American Intelligence," *The Intelligencer: Journal of U.S. Intelligence Studies* 11 (2000): 9–15; Schecter, *Battle for New York*, 243–66.

18. Address of the Convention of the Representatives of the State of New York to Their Constituents, December 1776 (Evans 14,921).

19. Ibid.

20. Thomas Jefferson to Thomas Nelson, 16 May 1776, 1 PTJ 292; John Jay to Edward Rutledge, 6 July 1776, 1 JPJ 68; John Jay Charge to the Grand Jury of Ulster County, July 1777, 1 JPJ 161; Willi Paul Adams, *The First State Constitutions: Republican Ideology and the Making of the State Constitutions in the Revolutionary Era* (Lanham, Maryland: Rowman and Littlefield, 2001) 1–24; Wood, *American Revolution*, 65–70.

21. Charles Z. Lincoln, *The Constitutional History of New York*, 5 vols. (Rochester: Lawyers Cooperative Publishing Co., 1906), 1:490–91; Stefan Bielinski, *Abraham Yates, Jr., and the New Political Order in Revolutionary New York* (Albany: New York State American Revolution Bicentennial Commission, 1975), 27–29; United States Congress, *Biographical Directory*.

22. Edward Rutledge to John Jay, 24 November 1776, 1 JPM 322–23; Robert Morris to John Jay, 12 January 1777, 1 JPM 363–64; John Jay to Gouverneur Morris, 17 March 1778, 1 JPM 468. See also Mason, *Road*, 213–49; Allan Nevins, *The American States During and After the Revolution, 1775–1789* (reprint, New York: Augustus M. Kelley, 1969), 149–56; Alfred H. Young, *The Democratic Republicans of New York: The Origins, 1763–1797* (Chapel Hill: University of North Carolina Press, 1967), 17–22.

23. Abraham Yates, quoted in Mason, *Road*, 230 n. 57; Robert R. Livingston to William Duer, 12 June 1777, Livingston Papers, New-York Historical Society; Lincoln, *Constitutional History*, 1:490–95; Peter J. Galie, *Ordered Liberty: A Constitutional History of New York* (New York: Fordham University Press, 1996), 37–38.

24. Ray B. Smith, ed., *History of the State of New York: Political and Governmental*, 10 vols. (Syracuse: Syracuse Press, 1922), 1:44; Galie, *Ordered Liberty*, 38–40; Mason, *Road*, 228; Monaghan, *John Jay*, 94–98.

25. 1 JPC 838, 850; Sarah Jay to John Jay, 23–24 March 1777, 1 JPM 380–81; John Jay to Sarah Jay, 25 March 1777, 1 JPM 381–82; Robert Troup to John Jay, 29 March 1777, 1 JPM 382–84.

26. The states with mere "Presidents" at this time were Delaware, New Hampshire, Pennsylvania and South Carolina. See Adams, *First American Constitutions*, 264–66, 320–21.

27. 1 JPC 873–75; Lincoln, *Constitutional History*, 1:531–35; John Jay to Gouverneur Morris and Robert R. Livingston, 29 April 1777, 1 JPM 397–98; Galie, *Ordered Liberty*, 44–48.

28. 1 JPC 843, 860; Lincoln, *Constitutional History*, 1:504–05, 554–56; Galie, *Ordered Liberty*, 46–48, 59–61.

29. 1 JPC 866–69; Lincoln, *Constitutional History*, 1:501–24; Galie, *Ordered Liberty*, 40–41.

30. Lincoln, *Constitutional History*, 1:535.

31. Ibid. 554; John Jay to Gouverneur Morris and Robert R. Livingston, 29 April 1777, 1 JPM 397–98; 1 JPC 873–75.

32. 1 JPC 844–46; Lincoln, *Constitutional History*, 1:541–45; Patricia U. Bonomi, "John

Jay, Religion, and the State," *New York History* 51 (2000): 9–18; New York Constitution, Article 1, Sec. 3.

33. 1 JPC 846; Lincoln, *Constitutional History*, 1:547–52.

34. 1 JPC 898; John Sloss Hobart to the New York Convention, 24 April 1777, 1 JPM 393–94.

35. Robert R. Livingston and Gouverneur Morris to John Jay, 26 April 1777, 1 JPM 395–96.

36. John Jay to Robert R. Livingston and Gouverneur Morris, 29 April 1777, 1 JPM 397–402.

37. John Jay to Abraham Yates Jr., 16 May 1777, 1 JPJ 136–37; John Jay to Leonard Gansevoort, 5 June 1777, 1 JPJ 140–41; Committee of Safety to County Committees, 2 June 1777, in Hugh Hastings, ed., *Public Papers of George Clinton, First Governor of New York, 1777–1795, 1801–1804*, 10 vols. (Albany: State of New York, 1899–1914), 1:855–56.

38. John Jay to Philip Schuyler, 20 June 1776, 1 JPJ 142–43; Philip Schuyler to John Jay, 30 June 1776, 1 JPJ 144; Philip Schuyler to John Jay, 14 July 1776, 1 JPJ 147; Don R. Gerlach, *Proud Patriot: Philip Schuyler and the War of Independence, 1775–1783* (Syracuse: Syracuse University Press, 1987), 230–33; Kaminski, *Clinton*, 23–25; Young, *Democratic Republicans*, 22–25, 33–39.

39. John R. Alden, *A History of the American Revolution*, 309–16 (New York: Alfred A. Knopf, 1969); Richard M. Ketchum, *Saratoga: Turning Point of America's Revolutionary War* (New York: Henry Holt and Co., 1997); Middlekauff, *Glorious Cause*, 370–77.

40. New York Committee of Safety to George Washington, 27 July 1777, 1 JPC 1019; Mintz, *Gouverneur Morris*, 82–83.

41. John Jay to Philip Schuyler, 26–28 July 1777, 1 JPM 429–31; John McKesson to George Clinton, 29 July 1777, Hastings, ed., *Clinton Papers*, 2:144–16; James Duane to John Jay, 3 August 1777, 7 LDC 409; George Washington to New York Committee of Safety, 4 August 1777, John C. Fitzpatrick, ed., *The Writings of Washington from the Original Manuscript Sources*, 39 vols. (Washington: Government Printing Office, 1931–44), 9:12–15; Report of John Jay and Gouverneur Morris, August 1777, Hastings, ed., *Clinton Papers*, 2:233–36; 1 JPC 1046; 8 JCC 649; George Washington to Daniel Morgan, 16 August 1777, Fitzpatrick, ed., *Writings of Washington*, 9:71; Sarah Jay to Brockholst Livingston, 18 August 1777, 1 JPM 438; Gouverneur Morris to Philip Schuyler, 27 August 1777, in Jared Sparks, *The Life of Gouverneur Morris*, 1:141–42 (Boston: 1832); Mintz, *Gouverneur Morris*, 83–84.

42. The Charge of Chief Justice Jay to the Grand Inquest of the County of Ulster, 9 September 1777 (Evans 15,376).

43. Ibid.

44. *Votes and Proceedings of the Senate of the State of New York* (Fish Kill, New York: 1777), 5–6; Kaminski, *Clinton*, 27; Minutes of the Supreme Court of Judicature, September 1777, New York County Clerk's Office, Division of Old Records.

45. Robert Troup to John Jay, 14 September 1777; John Jay to Charles DeWitt,

8 October 1777; Mary Isabella Forsyth, "The Burning of Kingston," *Journal of American History* 7 (1913): 1137–48; Freeman, *Washington*, 4:470–500; Kaminski, *Clinton*, 30–35; Ketchum, *Saratoga*, 350–72, 390–404; Middlekauff, *Glorious Cause*, 378–96; George W. Pratt, *An Account of the British Expedition above the Highlands of the Hudson River* (Albany: 1861), 33.

46. Susan Livingston to Sarah Jay, 1 November 1777, 1 JPM 446; James Duane to John Jay, 2 December 1777, 1 JPM 451–52; Alden, *Revolutionary War*, 326–27; Samuel Bemis, *The Diplomacy of the American Revolution* (Bloomington: Indiana University Press, rev. ed. 1957), 58–69; Brands, *First American*, 539–44; Middlekauff, *Glorious Cause*, 396–404.

47. Susan Livingston to Sarah Jay, 1 November 1777, 1 JPM 447; James Duane to John Jay, 23 December 1777, 1 JPM 458–59; John Jay to Robert Morris, 26 December 1777, 1 JPM 460; Van Buskirk, *Generous Enemies*, 55–57.

48. John Jay to Gouverneur Morris, 29 April 1778, 1 JPM 475; Report of the Judges, April 1778, Hastings, ed., *Clinton Papers*, 3:180–83; Report of the Judges, 19 May 1778, 1 JPM 480–81. Jay was named to several other courts, but it is unclear whether he attended. See *Minutes of the Committee and of the First Commission for Detecting and Defeating Conspiracies* ... (New York: New-York Historical Society, 1924), 2:20–21, 46–47, 50–51.

49. Report of the Judges, 19 May 1778, 1 JPM 480–81; George Clinton to Gouverneur Morris, May 1778, Hastings, ed., *Clinton Papers*, 3:309.

50. Alfred B. Street, *The Council of Revision of the State of New York: Its History ... and its Vetoes* (Albany: 1859), 203–08; John Jay to Gouverneur Morris, 3 June 1778, 1 JPM 483; John Jay to Gouverneur Morris, 21 October 1778, 1 JPM 500.

51. Street, *Council of Revision*, 208–13. Street attributes the first message to Jay, but the original minutes state that it was drafted by Yates and presented by Jay.

52. Minutes, Council of Revision, 22 June 1778, New York State Library; John Jay to Gouverneur Morris, 21 October 1778, 1 JPM 500.

53. Street, *Council of Revision*, 214–19; *Mistretta v. United States*, 488 U.S. 361, 371–72 (1989).

54. Hint to the Legislature, January 1778, 1 JPM 461–63; Laws of the State of New York, 1st Sess., ch. xxix.

55. John Jay to James DeLancey, 2 January 1778, 1 JPJ 171–72; John Jay to Peter Van Schaack, 18 April 1778, 1 JPM 470; John Jay to Peter Van Schaack, 26 June 1778, 1 JPJ 181–82; Peter Van Schaack to John Jay, August 1778, in Kammen, *"Crise de Conscience,"* 167–70; Benton, "Van Schaack," 44–55.

56. Gouverneur Morris to John Jay, 1 February 1778, 1 JPJ 173–75; John Jay to Gouverneur Morris, 17 March 1778, 1 JPM 468; John Jay to Gouverneur Morris, 14 April 1778, 1 JPM 468–69; Gouverneur Morris to John Jay, 28 April 1778, 1 JPM 471; Gouverneur Morris to John Jay, 29 April 1778, 1 JPM 471–73; John Jay to Gouverneur Morris, 29 April 1778, 1 JPM 475–77; Gouverneur Morris to John Jay, 3 May 1778, 1 JPM 477–78; John Jay to Gouverneur Morris, 7 May 1778, 1 JPM 482; Gouverneur Morris to John Jay, 23 July 1778, 1 JPM 486–87.

57. Gouverneur Morris to John Jay, 16 August 1778, 1 JPM 487; James Duane to John

Jay, 22 August 1778, 1 JPM 494; John Jay and Sarah Jay to Susannah Livingston, 16 March 1778, 1 JPM 466–67.

58. Matt B. Jones, *Vermont in the Making, 1750–1777* (Cambridge: Harvard University Press, 1939); Michael A. Bellisiles, *Revolutionary Outlaws: Ethan Allen and the Struggle for Independence on the Early American Frontier* (Charlottesville: University Press of Virginia, 1993); Note, 1 JPM 102–04.

59. George Clinton to Henry Laurens, 7 April 1778, Hastings, ed., *Clinton Papers*, 3:144–46; James Duane to John Jay, 22 August 1778, 1 JPM 493; George Clinton to Henry Laurens, 8 July 1778, Hastings, ed., *Clinton Papers*, 3:533–35; 12 JCC 1196–97; Bellisiles, *Ethan Allen*, 156–58.

60. John Jay to Gouverneur Morris, 14 April 1778, 1 JPM 469; John Jay to Gouverneur Morris, 29 April 1778, 1 JPM 476; John Jay to Gouverneur Morris, 3 June 1778, 1 JPM 484; John Jay to Gouverneur Morris, 13 September 1778, 1 JPM 498.

61. John Jay to Gouverneur Morris, 3 June 1778, 1 JPM 483; John Jay to George Clinton, 19 February 1779, 1 JPM 561; George Pellew, *John Jay* (Boston, Houghton Mifflin, 1890), 76 (citing William Jay).

Notes to Chapter 5: President of the Continental Congress

1. John Jay to Philip Schuyler, 8 December 1778, 11 LDC 302; John Jay to Rawlins Lowndes, 18 December 1778, 11 LDC 354; Thomas M. Doerflinger, *A Vigorous Spirit of Enterprise: Merchants and Economic Development in Revolutionary Philadelphia* (Chapel Hill: University of North Carolina Press, 1986), 204–05, 226–28; John W. Jackson, *With the British Army in Philadelphia, 1777–1778* (San Rafael, California: Presidio Press, 1979), 265–73; Leonard Lundin, *Cockpit of the Revolution: The War for Independence in New Jersey* (Princeton: Princeton University Press, 1940), 409–12; Middlekauff, *Glorious Cause*, 541–45.

2. *Pennsylvania Packet*, 5 December 1778; Robert Middlekauff, *Benjamin Franklin and his Enemies* (Berkeley: University of California Press, 1996), 148–67; Louis W. Potts, *Arthur Lee: A Virtuous Revolutionary* (Baton Rouge: Louisiana State University Press, 1981), 160–92; Rakove, *Beginnings*, 249–53.

3. Henry Laurens Speech, 9 December 1778, 11 LDC 312–17; see Charles Thomson Notes, 31 October 1778, 11 LDC 153.

4. 12 JCC 1202; Nathaniel Scudder to R. H. Lee, 9 December 1778, 11 LDC 321; John Fell Diary, 10 December 1778, 11 LDC 324; James Duane to George Clinton, 10 December 1778, 11 LDC 322–24; Gouverneur Morris to George Clinton, 10 December 1778, 11 LDC 328; Samuel Adams to Elizabeth Adams, 13 December 1778, 11 LDC 334.

5. Articles of Confederation, Sec. 2; Rakove, *Beginnings*, 164–76; Wood, *American Revolution*, 70–74.

6. Compare 3 LDC (table of delegates) with 11 LDC (table of delegates).

7. Rakove, *Beginnings*, 216–39; Calvin Jillson and Rick K. Wilson, *Congressional*

Dynamics: Structure, Coordination and Choice in the First American Congress, 1774−1789 (Stanford: Stanford University Press, 1994), 155−63.

8. Henry Laurens to Rawlins Lowndes, 17 May 1778, 9 LDC 702; William Carmichael to Charles Carroll, 16 January 1779, 11 LDC 471; Henry Laurens Notes, 10−11 June 1779, 13 LDC 44−45; Jillson and Wilson, *Congressional Dynamics*, 71−86; Herbert E. Klingelhofer, "The Presidents of the United States in Congress Assembled," *Manuscripts* 28 (1976); Jennings B. Sanders, *The Presidency of the Continental Congress, 1774−1789* (Chicago: University of Chicago Press, 1930), 33−34.

9. Estimate of 500 based on John Butler, ed., *Index to the Papers of the Continental Congress, 1774−1789*, 5 vols. (Washington: Government Printing Office, 1978), 2:2592−607. On Brockholst, see John Jay to William Livingston, 18 December 1778, 11 LDC 354.

10. See John Jay to Philip Schuyler, 8 December 1778, 1 JPM 503; John Jay to Lafayette, 3 January 1779, 11 LDC 408−09; John Jay to Philip Schuyler, 15 January 1779, 1 JPM 532−33; Anthony Benezet to John Jay, 2 February 1779, 1 JPM 544−45; John Jay to Robert R. Livingston, 16 February 1779, 1 JPM 556−58; Robert R. Livingston to John Jay, 4 March 1779, 1 JPM 570−71; Alexander Hamilton to John Jay, 14 March 1779, 2 PAH 17−19; John Jay to Robert R. Livingston, 14 March 1779, 1 JPM 575; John Jay to Philip Schuyler, 21 March 1779, 1 JPM 579−80; 13 JCC 386 (part of resolution in John Jay's hand); Gregory D. Massey, *John Laurens and the American Revolution* (Columbia: University of South Carolina Press, 2000), 140.

11. Henry Laurens to John Gervais, 15 July 1778, 10 LDC 282; 12 JCC 1213, 1220; John Jay to Sarah Jay, 21 March 1779, 1 JPM 578; Edmund C. Burnett, "Perquisites of the President of the Continental Congress," *American Historical Review* 35 (1935): 69−76.

12. Professors Jillson and Wilson have proved that there were no consistent parties through their detailed study of voting. See Jillson and Wilson, *Congressional Dynamics*. Professor Rakove came to a similar conclusion. Rakove, *Beginnings*. For the "party" argument, see H. James Hendersen, *Party Politics in the Continental Congress* (New York: McGraw-Hill, 1974); Monaghan, *John Jay*, 107−14. For an example of the delegates' views, see Gouverneur Morris Speech, 7 January 1779, 11 LDC 426.

13. Rakove, *Beginnings*, 243−74; William C. Stinchcombe, *The American Revolution and the French Alliance* (Syracuse: Syracuse University Press, 1969), 32−47, 62−76.

14. John Jay to Conrad Gérard, 11 December 1778, 11 LDC 329; James Lovell to Horatio Gates, 1 March 1779, 12 LDC 128−29. For other examples of Jay's tone, see John Jay to Conrad Gérard, 10 January 1779, 25 April 1779 and 4 May 1779, 11 LDC 445, 12 LDC 381 and 426. For a brief biography, see John J. Meng, ed., *Despatches and Instructions of Conrad Alexandre Gérard* (Baltimore: Johns Hopkins Press, 1939), 35−42, 78−90.

15. Juan de Miralles Reports, Aileen Moore Topping Papers, Library of Congress; Light T. Cummins, *Spanish Observers and the American Revolution, 1775−1783* (Baton Rouge: Louisiana State University Press, 1991); Helen Matzke McCadden, "Juan de Miralles and the American Revolution," *The Americas* 29 (January 1973): 359−75.

16. Don Juan de Miralles to José de Galvez, 28 December 1778, 11 LDC 381−83.

17. *Pennsylvania Packet*, 3 and 5 January 1779; Conrad Gérard to John Jay, 5 January 1779, 3 RDC 11–12; Note, 11 LDC 445–46; John Keane, *Tom Paine: A Political Life* (Boston: Little, Brown, 1995), 175–78.

18. Samuel Holten Diary, 5 January 1779, 11 LDC 417; 13 JCC 30–31; Gouverneur Morris Speech, 7 January 1779, 11 LDC 425–30.

19. 13 JCC 36–38.

20. Conrad Gérard to John Jay, 10 January 1779, 11 LDC 445–46; John Jay to Conrad Gérard, 13 January 1779, 11 LDC 459–60; 13 JCC 54–55; Keane, *Paine*, 178–80.

21. On Paine, Morris, Laurens and Penn, see Robert Morris to the Public, 7 January 1779, 11 LDC 430–35; Henry Laurens Notes, 9 January 1779, 11 LDC 439–41.

22. Conrad Gérard to Vergennes, 15 and 17 February 1778, Meng, ed., *Gérard Despatches*, 521–32; William Henry Drayton Notes, 15 February 1779, 12 LDC 71–73.

23. Bemis, *Diplomacy*, 81–102; Stinchcombe, *American Revolution*, 62–76.

24. 12 JCC 241–43; Rakove, *Beginnings*, 255–57.

25. James Lovell to John Adams, 27 September 1779, 13 LDC 565; Rakove, *Beginnings*, 255–70; Jillson and Wilson, *Congressional Dynamics*, 223–30.

26. *Pennsylvania Gazette*, 2 and 23 June 1779 ("Americanus"); ibid. 30 June 1779 and 14 and 21 July 1779 ("Common Sense"); see Stinchcombe, *American Revolution*, 66–71.

27. Meng, ed., *Gérard Despatches*, 777–83; Rakove, *Beginnings*, 268–69.

28. 14 JCC 896–97, 909–10; Jillson and Wilson, *Congressional Dynamics*, 228–30.

29. 13 JCC 363–68 (committee report); Gérard to Vergennes, 12–14 December 1778, in Meng, ed., *Gérard Despatches*, 422; Thomas Burke Statement, 16 April 1779, 12 LDC 336–39; Henry Laurens Notes, 21 April 1779, 12 LDC 364–67; William Paca and William Henry Drayton to Congress, 30 April 1779, 12 LDC 410–11; Rakove, *Beginnings*, 256–65.

30. John Fell Diary, 6 April 1779, 12 LDC 301–02; Richard Henry Lee to William Shippen, Jr., 18 April 1779, 12 LDC 350–51 (criticizing Gérard and Jay); Henry Laurens Notes, 26 April 1779, 12 LDC 387–88; Henry Laurens Notes, 30 April 1779, 12 LDC 408–09; 14 JCC 542–43; Rakove, *Beginnings*, 256–57.

31. 14 JCC 542–43; *Pennsylvania Packet*, 6 and 8 May 1779; Rakove, *Beginnings*, 263–67.

32. Henry Laurens Notes, 10–11 June 1779, 13 LDC 44–45; William Whipple to R. H. Lee, 23 August 1779, 13 LDC 403–04; *Pennsylvania Packet*, 14 September 1779 ("Common Sense").

33. Morris, *Peacemakers*, 10–13; Rakove, *Beginnings*, 258–59.

34. Henry Laurens Notes, 25–27 September 1779, 13 LDC 556–57; John Fell Diary, 26 and 27 September 1779, 13 LDC 558, 562; Henry Laurens to John Laurens, 27 September 1779, 13 LDC 563–65; James Lovell to John Adams, 27 September 1779, 13 LDC 565–567; Juan de Miralles to José de Galvez, 26–27 September 1778, 13 LDC 567–68; James Lovell to Richard Henry Lee, 27 September 1778, 13 LDC 568–69; Elbridge Gerry to John Adams, 29 September 1779, 13 LDC 588–89. There is some disagreement among the sources: Laurens states that the first ballot was five to four to three; Fell that it was five to four to one for Lee.

35. James Lovell to John Adams, 27 September 1779, 13 LDC 566; Conrad Gérard to Vergennes, 25–27 September 1779, Meng, ed., *Gérard Despatches*, 897; Juan de

Miralles to José de Galvez, 26 September 1779, 13 LDC 568; Jay, *Life of John Jay*, 1: 95–99.

36. E. James Ferguson, *The Power of the Purse: A History of American Public Finance, 1776–1790* (Chapel Hill: University of North Carolina Press, 1961), 32.

37. Edmund C. Burnett, *The Continental Congress: A Definitive History of the Continental Congress from its Inception in 1774 to March, 1789* (New York: Macmillan Co., 1941), 379–85, 405–09; Ferguson, *Power of the Purse*, 25; Rakove, *Beginnings*, 207–09.

38. John Jay to the States, 10 January 1779, 11 LDC 446. See John Fell Diary, 16 December 1778, 11 LDC 349; Francis Lewis to George Clinton, 31 December 1778, 11 LDC 391–92; 13 JCC 20–23, 28–29.

39. George Washington to John Jay, 23 April 1779, Fitzpatrick, ed., *Writings of Washington*, 14:435–37; John Jay to George Washington, 26 April 1779, 1 JPM 588; John Fell Diary, 13 May 1779, 12 LDC 468; John Jay to the States, 22 May 1779, 12 LDC 510; John K. Alexander, "The Fort Wilson Incident of 1779: A Case Study of the Revolutionary Crowd," *William and Mary Quarterly* 31 (1974): 593–97.

40. John Jay to George Clinton, 2 September 1779, 13 LDC 446–47; 15 JCC 1013–14, 1019, 1036, 1051, 1062.

41. 15 JCC 1052–53; Rakove, *Beginnings*, 210–11.

42. 15 JCC 1054.

43. 15 JCC 1054–55.

44. 15 JCC 1056.

45. 15 JCC 1058–59.

46. 15 JCC 1061–62; see *Compania de Tabacos v. Collector*, 275 U.S. 87, 100 (1904).

47. Burnett, *Continental Congress*, 413; Ferguson, *Power of the Purse*, 32.

48. Silas Deane to Elizabeth Deane, 10 September 1774, 1 LDC 61–62; George Washington Address, 16 June 1775, 1 PGW 1–3; Eliphalet Dyer to Joseph Trumbull, 17 June 1775, 1 LDC 499–500; Lyman H. Butterfield, ed., *Diary of John Adams*, 4 vols. (Cambridge: Harvard University Press, 1961): 3:322–23; Richard Brookhiser, *Founding Father: Rediscovering George Washington* (New York: Free Press, 1996), 20–23; John E. Ferling, *The First of Men: A Life of George Washington* (Knoxville: University of Tennessee Press, 1988), 103–04, 113–14.

49. Congress to George Washington, 2 April 1776, 1 JPM 247 (Jay draft); Robert Troup to John Jay, 23 November 1778, 1 JPM 502–03; Robert Troup to John Jay, 21 January 1779, 1 JPM 536–37; Robert Troup to John Jay, 7 February 1779, 1 JPM 551–52; Ferling, *First of Men*, 260–66.

50. John Jay to George Washington, 12 and 18 December 1778, 11 LDC 331, 355; Freeman, *Washington*, 5:90–91.

51. Samuel Holton Diary, 25 and 30 December 1778, 11 LDC 381 and 387; Nathaniel Greene to Alexander McDougall, 11 February 1779, in Freeman, *Washington*, 5:91 n. 35; George Washington to Benjamin Harrison, December 1778, Fitzpatrick, ed., *Writings of Washington*, 13:462–68.

52. George Washington to the Committee of Conference, 8 January 1779, Fitzpatrick, ed., *Writings of Washington*, 13:487; John Jay to Lafayette, 3 January 1779, 11 LDC 409.

53. John Jay to George Washington, various dates, February, 1779, 12 LDC 75, 105, 107, 111.
54. John Jay to George Washington, 6 April 1779, 12 LDC 287; George Washington to John Jay, 14 April 1779, Fitzpatrick, ed., *Writings of Washington*, 14:378–88.
55. John Jay to George Washington, 21 April 1779, 12 LDC 363–64.
56. George Washington to John Jay, 23 April 1779, Fitzpatrick, ed., *Writings of Washington*, 14:435–37.
57. John Jay to George Washington, 26 April 1779, 12 LDC 386–87.
58. George Washington to John Jay, 7 October 1779, 1 JPM 656–57; George Washington to Sarah Jay, 7 October 1779, 1 JPM 656.
59. John Jay to George Clinton, 10 December 1778, 11 LDC 324–25; John Jay to George Clinton, 25 September 1779, 13 LDC 547–48; Michael A. Bellisles, *Revolutionary Outlaws: Ethan Allen and the Struggle for Independence on the Early American Frontier* (Charlottesville: University Press of Virginia, 1993), 192–93.
60. John Jay to George Clinton, 22 May 1779, 12 LDC 509–10; John Jay to George Clinton, 25 September 1779, 13 LDC 548; 14 JCC 631–33.
61. John Jay Notes of Debates, 29 May 1779, 12 LDC 552–53; 14 JCC 667–68; Kaminski, *Clinton*, 66–67.
62. Gouverneur Morris to George Clinton, 30 May 1779, 12 LDC 555–56; John Jay Notes, 29 May 1779, 12 LDC 552–53; 14 JCC 667–68.
63. John Jay to George Clinton, 1 June 1779, 13 LDC 3; New York Delegates to George Clinton, 1 June 1779, 13 LDC 7–8; John Jay to Committee, 2 June 1779, 13 LDC 13; 14 JCC 673–76; Bellisles, *Revolutionary Outlaws*, 181–85.
64. Committee of Congress to John Jay, 4 July 1779, 13 LDC 143–44; Committee of Congress Report on Vermont, 13 July 1779, 13 LDC 201–03; George Clinton to John Jay, 23 June 1779, Hastings, ed., *Clinton Papers*, 5:93–95.
65. John Jay to George Clinton, 27 August 1779, 13 LDC 419; John Jay to George Clinton, 2 September 1779, 13 LDC 446.
66. Resolutions, 24 September 1779, 13 LDC 551–54.
67. John Jay to George Clinton, 24 September 1779, 13 LDC 547–51.
68. John Jay to Egbert Benson, 26 August 1782, 2 JPM 326; Kaminski, *Clinton*, 70–77.
69. Sarah Jay to John Jay, 28–30 December 1778, 1 JPM 516–18.
70. Sarah Jay to John Jay, 3 January 1779, 1 JPM 520–21; John Jay to Sarah Jay, 18 January 1779, 1 JPM 534; Sarah Jay to John Jay, 12 February 1779, 1 JPM 554 55.
71. Catharine Livingston to John Jay, 20 February 1779, 1 JPM 563–64; John Jay to Catharine Livingston, 27–28 February 1779, 1 JPM 567–69; Sarah Jay to John Jay, 5 March 1779, 1 JPM 572–73; John Jay to Sarah Jay, 21 March 1779, 1 JPM 578.
72. On Francis Gurney, see *Poulson's American Daily Advertiser*, 8 September 1815; *Pennsylvania Magazine of History and Biography* 47 (1923): 175–76. Gurney acquired a lot with thirty-four feet of Front Street footage, and eighty-two feet of Union Street footage, in 1771 from one John McPherson. See Philadelphia Deed Book I–10, 67 (Pennsylvania Historical Society). Gurney was living at "1 Union Street" in 1785, when the first city directory was compiled. *McPherson's Directory* (Philadelphia: 1785). This section of Union Street later became DeLancey Street.

73. See John Fell Diary, 17 April 1779, 12 LDC 343; Samuel Holten Diary, 5 May 1779, 12 LDC 433; John Fell Diary, 16 July 1779, 13 LDC 231. For Jay's "allowance," see 13 JCC 38 ($8000), 13 JCC 286 ($5000), 13 JCC 487 ($5000), 14 JCC 629 ($5000), 14 JCC 847 ($1000) and 14 JCC 919–20 ($5000).

74. Don Juan de Miralles to José de Galvez, 5 July 1779, Aileen Moore Topping Papers, Library of Congress; Samuel Holten's Diary, 4–5 July 1779, 13 LDC 145; *Pennsylvania Packet*, 8 July 1779, 13 LDC 144–45.

75. McCadden, "Juan de Miralles," 362; William Livingston to Sarah Jay, 12 July 1779, Prince, *Livingston Papers*, 3:151–52; William Livingston to Catharine Livingston, 9 August 1779, ibid. 159–60.

76. Alice DeLancey Izard was with her husband Ralph Izard in Paris when the latter received, in October 1777, a commission as America's Minister to Tuscany. Izard, however, was advised that he would not be well received in Florence, and remained in Paris, where he had no official role. When Izard finally returned to the United States in the spring of 1780, his wife and daughters remained in Paris. Abigail Adams did finally travel to Europe to join her husband, but only after the War was over; she left Massachusetts in June of 1784. Ralph Izard to Committee of Foreign Affairs, 6 October 1777 and 18 December 1777, 2 RDC 403–04, 455–56; Robert Middlekauff, *Benjamin Franklin and His Enemies* (Berkeley: University of California Press, 1996), 161–65; Ferling, *John Adams*, 263–64.

77. William Livingston to Sarah Jay, 21 August 1781, 2 JPM 199–200; Note 2 JPM 252–54.

78. William Livingston to Sarah Jay, 7 October 1779, 1 JPM 675; Susannah Livingston to Sarah Jay, 9 October 1779, 1 JPM 676; William Livingston Jr. to Sarah Jay, 16 October 1779, 1 JPM 677.

79. Rakove, *Beginnings*, 255–65.

Notes to Chapter 6: Minister to Spain

1. William Livingston Jr. to Sarah Jay, 16 October 1779, 1 JPM 677; Pere Gifra-Adroher, *Between History and Romance: Travel Writing on Spain in the Early Nineteenth-Century United States* (Madison: Fairleigh Dickinson University Press, 2000); Herbert S. Klein, *The American Finances of the Spanish Empire: Royal Income and Expenditures in Colonial Mexico, Peru, and Bolivia, 1680–1809* (Albuquerque: University of New Mexico Press, 1998); Henry Swinburne, *Travels Through Spain* (London: 1779).

2. Anderson, *Crucible of War*, 487–90, 497–505, 515–17; Morris, *Peacemakers*, 16–17.

3. Samuel F. Bemis, ed., *The American Secretaries of State and their Diplomacy*, 10 vols. (New York: Alfred A. Knopf, 1928), 1:294–99 (translation of convention); Jonathan R. Dull, *The French Navy and American Independence* (Princeton: Princeton University Press, 1975), 126–43; Jonathan R. Dull, *A Diplomatic History of the American Revolution* (New Haven: Yale University Press, 1985), 107–13; W. N. Hargreaves-Mawdsley, *Eighteenth Century Spain, 1700–1788: A Political,*

Diplomatic and Institutional History (London: Macmillan, 1979); Stanley J. Stein & Barbara H. Stein, *Apogee of Empire: Spain and New Spain in the Age of Charles III* (Baltimore: Johns Hopkins University Press, 2003), 175.

4. *Pennsylvania Gazette*, 25 August 1779, 1 September 1779 and 27 October 1779; Dull, *French Navy*, 143–58; Piers Mackesy, *The War for America, 1775–1783* (Cambridge: Harvard Univesity Press, 1965), 279–97, 322; Morris, *Peacemakers*, 27–42.

5. 15 JCC 1118–20 (instructions); Arthur Lee to Committee of Secret Correspondence, 18 March 1777, 2 RDC 292; Benjamin Franklin to Committee for Foreign Affairs, 26 May 1779, 29 PBF 554; John Jay to George Washington, 14 October 1779, 1 JPJ 248; John Jay to Samuel Huntington, 9 June 1780, 3 RDC 117; Potts, *Arthur Lee*, 169–72; Morris, *Peacemakers*, 13–21.

6. Marine Committee to Seth Harding, 17 September 1779, 13 LDC 510–11; Marine Committee to Seth Harding, 17 October 1779, 14 LDC 88–89; James L. Howard, *Seth Harding, Mariner* (New Haven: Yale University Press, 1930), 105–16; Morris, *Peacemakers*, 1–7; Monaghan, *John Jay*, 125–29.

7. Passengers: John Jay to Samuel Huntington, 24 December 1779, 3 RDC 437. Brockholst Livingston: William Livingston to Brockholst Livingston, 4 January 1778, Prince, ed., *Livingston Papers*, 2:158–59; William Livingston to John Jay, 22 December 1778, ibid. 518; Garraty and Carnes, eds., *American National Biography*, 13:764–66. Peter Jay Munro: James Grant Wilson and John Fiske, eds., *Appleton's Cyclopedia of American Biography* (New York: 1888), 4:461. William Carmichael: Samuel G. Coe, *The Mission of William Carmichael to Spain* (Baltimore: Johns Hopkins University, 1928); Jonathan R. Dull, *Franklin the Diplomat: The French Mission* (Philadelphia: American Philosophical Society, 1982), 37–40; Garraty and Carnes, eds., *American National Biography*, 4:406–07.

8. Brockholst Livingston to Susannah Livingston, 25 October 1779, 1 JPM 678–79; John Jay to Robert R. Livingston, 25 October 1779, 1 JPM 665–66; Sarah Jay to Susannah Livingston, December 1779, 1 JPM 680.

9. Sarah Jay to Susannah Livingston, December 1779, 1 JPM 680–81; John Jay to Samuel Huntington, 24 December 1779, 3 RDC 436–38; Howard, *Harding*, 105–09; Morris, *Peacemakers*, 3–4.

10. Sarah Jay to Susannah Livingston, December 1779, 1 JPM 681.

11. John Jay to Samuel Huntington, 24 December 1779, 3 RDC 436–45; Council of Commissioned Officers of the Confederacy, 23 November 1779, 1 JPM 666–68; Morris, *Peacemakers*, 4–5.

12. John Jay to Samuel Huntington, 24 December 1779, 3 RDC 443; Sarah Jay to Susannah Livingston, December 1779, 1 JPM 682–83; Sarah Jay to William Livingston, 24 June 1781, 2 JPM 192; Monaghan, *John Jay*, 127.

13. Sarah Jay to Susannah Livingston, December 1779, 1 JPM 685–86; Sarah Jay to Peter Jay, 9 January 1780, 1 JPM 687–89; John Jay to Robert R. Livingston, 19 February 1780, 1 JPM 735–36; John Jay to Peter Jay, 23 May 1780, 1 JPM 702; Robert C. Alberts, *The Golden Voyage: The Life and Times of William Bingham, 1752–1804* (Boston: Houghton Mifflin, 1969), 37–38, 75–76; Monaghan, *John Jay*, 130; Morris, *Peacemakers*, 5–6.

14. William Bingham to Benjamin Franklin, 3 March 1779, 29 PBF 29–31; Benjamin Franklin to the Committee for Foreign Affairs, 26 May 1779, 29 PBF 547–61; Benjamin Franklin to William Bingham, 4 October 1779, 30 PBF 463; John Jay to Samuel Huntington, 25 December 1779 and 26 December 1779, 3 RDC 446–49; William Bingham to Benjamin Franklin, 28 February 1780, 31 PBF 557–58; John Jay to Samuel Huntington, 3 March 1780, 3 RDC 530; Alberts, *Bingham*, 77–79.

15. Sarah Jay to Peter Jay, 9 January 1780, 1 JPM 687–89; Sarah Jay to Catharine and Susan Livingston, 4 March 1780, 1 JPM 692–93; Sarah Jay to Susan Livingston, 28 August 1780, 1 JPM 705.

16. John Jay to Benjamin Franklin, 26 January 1780, 31 PBF 409; John Jay to George Clinton, 1 February 1780, 1 JPM 723; John Jay to Robert R. Livingston, 19 February 1780, 1 JPM 736; Dull, *French Navy*, 178–79; Mackesy, *War for America*, 322–23; Donald MacIntyre, *Admiral Rodney* (New York: W. W. Norton, 1962), 98–106.

17. John Jay to Don José de Galvez, 27 January 1780, 1 EN 14–16; John Jay to William Carmichael, 27 January 1780, 1 JPM 720–22.

18. John Jay to George Clinton, 1 February 1780, 1 JPM 723; Brockholst Livingston to Susannah Livingston, 20 February 1780, 1 JPM 693; Sarah Jay to Catharine and Susan Livingston, 4 March 1780, 1 JPM 692–93; John Jay to Margaret Meredith, 12 May 1780, 1 JPM 753–54; Sarah Jay to Susan Livingston, 28 August 1780, 1 JPM 705; Linda K. Kerber, *Women of the Republic: Intellect and Ideology in Revolutionary America* (Chapel Hill: University of North Carolina Press, 1980), 73–113

19. William Carmichael to John Jay, 15 February 1780, 1 JPM 729–31; William Carmichael to John Jay, 18 February 1780, 1 JPM 732–33.

20. Floridablanca to John Jay, 24 February 1780, 1 JPM 737–38; John Jay to Samuel Huntington, 3 March 1780, 1 EN 39–40.

21. John Jay to Peter Jay, 23 May 1780, 1 JPM 699; Brockholst Livingston to Susannah Livingston, 30 April 1780, Massachusetts Historical Society; Sarah Jay to Susannah Livingston, 28 August 1780, 1 JPM 705–06.

22. John Jay to Peter Jay, 23 May 1780, 1 JPM 699–702; Sarah Jay to Susannah Livingston, 28 August 1780, 1 JPM 706.

23. Sarah Jay to Catharine and Susan Livingston, 4 March 1780, 1 JPM 692–93; John Jay to Samuel Huntington, 26 May 1780, 3 RDC 710; Sarah Jay to Susannah Livingston, 28 August 1780, 1 JPM 706–07.

24. Sarah Jay to Susannah Livingston, 13 May 1780, 1 JPM 694; Sarah Jay to Catharine Livingston, 1 December 1780; Sarah Jay to William Livingston, 14 March 1781, 2 JPM 178; Richard Herr, *The Eighteenth-Century Revolution in Spain* (Princeton: Princeton University Press, 1958), 87; Charles E. Kany, *Life and Manners in Madrid, 1750–1800* (Berkeley, University of California Press, 1932); Robert W. Kern, *Historical Dictionary of Modern Spain, 1700–1988* (New York: Greenwood Press, 1980), 316–17; Alsop, *Yankees*, 207.

25. Floridablanca to John Jay, 9 March 1780, 1 EN 41–42; John Jay to Floridablanca, 25 April 1780, 1 JPJ 280–303. Although Morris states that Jay met with Floridablanca "the very next morning after his arrival at Madrid," Morris, *Peacemakers*, 49–50, Jay's letters from this period indicate that they had not met. John Jay to John

Adams, 26 April 1780, 1 JPJ 304–06; John Jay to Benjamin Franklin, 27 April 1780, 32 PBF 316.

26. Benjamin Franklin to John Jay, 22 February 1780, 31 PBF 513; Benjamin Franklin to John Jay, 7 April 1780, 32 PBF 222–25; John Jay to Benjamin Franklin, 14 April 1780, 32 PBF 252–54; John Jay to Benjamin Franklin, 27 April 1780, 32 PBF 315–17.

27. Committee of Foreign Affairs to John Jay, 11 December 1779, 1 JPM 668–69; Gouverneur Morris to John Jay, 3 January 1780, 1 JPM 712–13; John Jay to Samuel Huntington, 26 May 1780, 3 RDC 721.

28. John Jay to Floridablanca, 29 April 1780, 3 RDC 721–22.

29. John Jay to Margaret Cadwalader Meredith, 12 May 1780, 1 JPM 753–54; John Jay to Robert Morris, 25 April 1782, 2 JPM 155–57.

30. John Jay to Samuel Huntington, 26 May 1780, 3 RDC 722; Joseph Townsend, *A Journey Through Spain in the Years 1786 and 1787*, 2 vols. (London: 1791), 1:292; Morris, *Peacemakers*, 48–49; Kern, *Historical Dictionary*, 213–14; Herr, *Eighteenth-Century*, 22–23; Rebecca Gruver, "The Diplomacy of John Jay" (Ph.D. diss., University of California at Berkeley, 1964), 76–77.

31. John Jay to Samuel Huntington, 26 May 1780, 3 RDC 722–25; John Jay to Samuel Huntington, 6 November 1780, 4 RDC 112.

32. John Jay to Robert R. Livingston, 23 May 1780, 1 JPM 757; John Jay to Samuel Huntington, 6 November 1780, 4 RDC 112–15; Morris, *Peacemakers*, 51–66.

33. John Jay to Samuel Huntington, 6 November 1780, 4 RDC 115–19.

34. Ibid. 123–25.

35. John Jay to William Livingston, 14 July 1780, 1 JPM 703; John Jay to Benjamin Franklin, 17 July 1780, 33 PBF 84; John Jay to Benjamin Franklin, 16 August 1780, 33 PBF 200; Sarah Jay to Susannah Livingston, 28 August 1780, 1 JPM 709–11.

36. John Jay to Samuel Huntington, 6 November 1780, 4 RDC 125–31.

37. Ibid. 131–32.

38. Ibid. 133–39.

39. John Jay to Vergennes, 22 September 1780, 1 JPJ 409–15; John Jay to Benjamin Franklin, 22 September 1780, 33 PBF 317–18.

40. John Jay to Samuel Huntington, 6 November 1780, 1 JPM 825–32.

41. Ibid. 833–34.

42. John Jay to Robert R. Livingston, 23 May 1780, 1 JPM 758–59; John Jay to Samuel Huntington, 26 May 1780, 1 EN 69–70; John Jay to Benjamin Franklin, 25 October 1780, 33 PBF 462; John Jay to Benjamin Franklin, 21 February 1781, 34 PBF 386; John Jay to Benjamin Franklin, 1 April 1781, 34 PBF 511.

43. John Jay to William Carmichael, 27 June 1780, 1 JPM 777–79; William Carmichael to John Jay, 28 June 1780, 1 JPM 780–82; John Jay to William Carmichael, 29 June 1780, 1 JPM 782–83; John Jay to Silas Deane, 16 June 1781, 2 JPM 84; John Jay to Gouverneur Morris, 28 September 1781, 2 JPM 108–09; Alsop, *Yankees*, 98–99; Monaghan, *John Jay*, 157–59; Gruver, "Diplomacy of John Jay," 87–93.

44. Sarah Jay to William Livingston, 24 June 1781, 2 JPM 188–89.

45. Ibid. 189–91.

46. Lewis Littlepage to John Jay, 15 July 1780, 2 JPM 220–21; John Jay to Benjamin

Lewis, 21 November 1780, in John Jay, *Letters: Being the Whole of the Correspondence ... Lewis Littlepage* (New York: 1786); John Jay to Lewis Littlepage, 26 October 1781, 2 JPM 223–33; Curtis C. Davis, *The King's Chevalier: A Biography of Lewis Littlepage* (New York: Bobbs-Merrill, 1961), 30–38.

47. Lewis Littlepage to John Jay, 3 July 1781; Lewis Littlepage to John Jay, 8 October 1781; John Jay to Lewis Littlepage, 26 October 1781; John Jay to Lewis Littlepage, 29 December 1781; Lewis Littlepage to John Jay, 20 January 1782; John Jay to Lewis Littlepage, 6 March 1782; Lewis Littlepage to John Jay, 17 March 1782, all in Jay, *Littlepage Letters*.

48. Sarah Jay to Catharine Livingston, 14 May 1780, 1 JPM 696–98; John Jay to Silas Deane, 26 October 1780, 2 JPM 57; John Jay to Gouverneur Morris, 5 November 1780, 2 JPM 35–36; Sarah Jay to Susannah Livingston, 28 August 1780, 1 JPM 704–09; Sarah Jay to John Jay, 22 September 1780; John Jay to Samuel Huntington, 21 April 1781, 2 JPM 67.

49. John Jay to Benjamin Franklin, 21 February 1781, 34 PBF 386; John Jay to Floridablanca, 15 March 1781, 2 JPJ 25; John Jay to Benjamin Franklin, 28 March 1781, 34 PBF 492–94; John Jay to Benjamin Franklin, 1 April 1781, 34 PBF 509–11; John Jay to Samuel Huntington, 25 April 1781, 2 JPJ 25.

50. Benjamin Franklin to John Jay, 12 April 1781, 34 PBF 532–35; John Jay to Samuel Huntington, 21 April 1781, 2 JMP 64–70; Samuel Huntington to John Jay, 5 July 1781, 2 JPM 90.

51. Samuel Huntington to John Jay, 15 February 1781, 2 JPM 62–63; James Lovell to John Jay, 20 February 1781, 4 RDC 261; Gouverneur Morris to John Jay, 7 May 1781, 2 JPM 76; Samuel Huntington to John Jay, 28 May 1781, 2 JPJ 32–35; John Jay to Floridablanca, 2 July 1781, 2 JPJ 93–94; John Jay to President of Congress, 3 October 1781, 2 JPJ 77–97.

52. John Jay to Floridablanca, 3 September 1781, 2 JPM 98–99; John Jay to Montmorin, 16 September 1781, 2 JPM 99–100; John Jay to Floridablanca, September 1781, 2 JPM 100–04 (draft); John Jay to President of Congress, 3 October 1781, 2 JPJ 101–28.

53. John Jay to President of Congress, 3 October 1781, 2 JPJ 121–28.

54. John Jay to Gouverneur Morris, 28 September 1781, 2 JPM 109–10.

55. Elbridge Gerry to John Jay, 20 September–9 October 1781, 2 JPM 106–08; John Jay to President of Congress, 3 October 1781, 2 JPJ 130; George Washington to John Jay, 22 October 1781, 2 JPJ 137–38; John Jay to Henry Knox, 10 December 1781, 2 JPJ 159–60; John Jay to George Clinton, 11 December 1781, 2 JPM 115–16; John Jay to Matthew Ridley, 8 January 1782, 2 JPM 122; John Jay to Elbridge Gerry, 9 January 1782, 2 JPM 123; John Jay to Robert R. Livingston, 28 April 1782, 2 JPJ 216, 237–40; Middlekauff, *Glorious Cause*, 559–70.

56. John Jay to Benjamin Franklin, 11 January 1782, 36 PBF 424–25; John Jay to Robert R. Livingston, 28 April 1782, 2 JPJ 243–45.

57. John Jay to Robert R. Livingston, 28 April 1782, 2 JPJ 253–61.

58. John Jay to Floridablanca, 2 March 1782, 2 JPM 142–43; John Jay to Robert R. Livingston, 28 April 1782, 2 JPJ 265–74.

59. John Jay to Benjamin Franklin, 18 March 1782, 2 JPM 143-44; John Jay to Robert R. Livingston, 28 April 1782, 2 JPJ 275-78.

60. Benjamin Franklin to John Jay, 16 March 1782, 37 PBF 5-6; John Jay to Robert R. Livingston, 28 April 1782, 2 JPJ 281-84.

61. Benjamin Franklin to John Jay, 19 January 1782, 2 JPM 138; John Jay to Benjamin Franklin, 11 February 1782, 2 JPM 141; John Jay to Robert R. Livingston, 28 April 1782, 2 JPJ 281.

62. Benjamin Franklin to John Jay, 22 April 1782, 37 PBF 198; Benjamin Franklin to John Jay, 23 April 1782, 37 PBF 201-02; John Jay to Robert R. Livingston, 28 April 1782, 2 JPJ 294; John Jay to Benjamin Franklin, 8 May 1782, 37 PBF 288.

63. Bemis, *Diplomacy*, 104; John Walton Caughey, *Bernardo de Galvez in Louisiana, 1775-1783* (Berkeley: University of California Press, 1934); Dull, *Diplomatic History*, 110-11; Mackesy, *War for America*, 322-23, 436-38, 482-84.

Notes to Chapter 7: Peace Commissioner

1. John Jay to Robert Livingston, 14 June 1782, 2 JPM 242; John Jay to Montmorin, 26 June 1782, 2 JPM 244-45; Sarah Jay to Susannah Livingston, 28 August 1782, 2 JPM 464-65; Christopher Hibbert, *The Days of the French Revolution* (New York: Morrow Quill Paperbacks, 1981), 29-31.

2. David Garrioch, *The Making of Revolutionary Paris* (Berkeley: University of California Press, 2002).

3. John Jay Diary, 23 June 1782, 2 JPM 446; John Jay to Robert R. Livingston, 25 June 1782, 1 EN 437-38; H. W. Brands, *The First American: The Life and Times of Benjamin Franklin* (New York: Doubleday, 2000), 545-70; Walter Isaacson, *Benjamin Franklin: An American Life* (New York: Simon and Schuster, 2003), 325-81; Claude-Anne Lopez, *Mon Cher Papa: Franklin and the Ladies of Paris* (New Haven: Yale University Press, 1965), 1-28; Edmund S. Morgan, *Benjamin Franklin* (New Haven: Yale University Press, 2002), 243-51.

4. Benjamin Franklin, *The Morals of Chess*, before June 1779, 29 PBF 750-59; Brands, *First American*, 606-07; Isaacson, *Franklin*, 372-73.

5. Benjamin Franklin to John Adams, 2 June 1782, 1 EN 417; Mackesy, *War for America*, 436-38, 479-80; Middlekauff, *Glorious Cause*, 571.

6. Richard Oswald to Lord Shelburne, 9 and 12 June 1782, 1 EN 427-30; Thomas Grenville to Charles James Fox, 21 June 1782, 1 EN 434-35; John Jay to Robert R. Livingston, 28 June 1782, 1 EN 442; Morris, *Peacemakers*, 248-81.

7. Thomas Jefferson to Thomas McKean, 4 August 1781, 6 PTJ 113; John Adams to Benjamin Franklin, 2 May 1782, 1 EN 371; Henry Laurens to Benjamin Franklin, 17 May 1782, 1 EN 393; John Jay to Robert R. Livingston, 25 June 1782, 1 EN 438; Benjamin Franklin to Thomas Jefferson, 15 July 1782, 6 PTJ 194; John Jay to John Adams, 2 August 1782, 1 EN 489-90; Alleyne Fitzherbert to Lord Grantham, 17 August 1782, 1 EN 533; Dull, *Diplomatic History*, 58.

8. Instructions to the Peace Commissioners, 15 June 1781, 1 EN 199; John Jay to

President of Congress, 20 September 1781, 1 EN 235; John Jay to Benjamin Franklin, 29 March 1782, 1 EN 323.

9. Richard Oswald Journal, 18 April 1782, 1 EN 345-48; Benjamin Franklin Diary, 28 May 1782, 37 PBF 316.

10. John Jay to Robert R. Livingston, 25 June 1782, 1 EN 437; John Jay to Lafayette, 25 June 1782, 2 JPM 244; John Jay Diary, June 1782, 2 JPM 446-47.

11. John Jay to John Adams, 2 August 1782, 1 EN 489; John Jay to Robert R. Livingston, 13 August 1782, 2 JPM 317-18; Sarah Jay to Catharine Livingston, 14 August 1782, 2 JPM 461; John Jay to Egbert Benson, 26 August 1782, 2 JPM 326; John Jay to William Livingston, 13 October 1782, 2 JPM 472-73.

12. Richard Oswald to Lord Shelburne, 10 July 1782, 1 EN 462-64; Benjamin Franklin to Richard Oswald, 12 July 1782, 1 EN 469-71; Frank W. Brecher, *Securing American Independence: John Jay and the French Alliance* (Westport, Connecticut: Praeger, 2003), 178-79.

13. John Jay to Benjamin Franklin, 31 May 1781, 2 JPM 80-81; Benjamin Franklin to Benjamin Vaughan, 11 July 1782, 1 EN 464-65; John Jay Diary, 25 July 1782, 2 JPM 447; Benjamin Vaughan to Lord Shelburne, 31 July 1782, 1 EN 484-85; Benjamin Vaughan to Lord Shelburne, 3 October 1782, *Massachusetts Historical Society Proceedings*, 2nd Series, 17 (1903): 410; Mary Vaughan Marvin, *Benjamin Vaughan, 1751-1835* (Hallowell, Maine: 1979); Morris, *Peacemakers*, 291-93.

14. John Jay to Montmorin, June 1782, 2 JPM 246; Aranda Notes, 3 August 1782, 2 JPM 270-72; John Jay to Robert R. Livingston, 17 November 1782, 6 RDC 22-23; Note 2 JPM 382-84; Jay, *Life of John Jay*, 1:140-41; Robert W. Kern, *Historical Dictionary*, 35-37.

15. David Hancock, *Citizens of the World: London Merchants and the Integration of the British Atlantic Community, 1735-1785* (Cambridge: Harvard University Press, 1995), 59-69, 153-70; Charles R. Ritcheson, "Britain's Peacemakers, 1782-1783: 'To an Astonishing Degree Unfit for the Task?,'" in Ronald Hoffman and Peter J. Albert, eds., *Peace and the Peacemakers: The Treaty of 1783* (Charlottesville: University Press of Virginia, 1986).

16. Draft Commission, 3 August 1782, 2 JPM 286 note; Richard Oswald Notes, 7 August 1782, 2 JPM 287.

17. Richard Oswald Notes, 7 August 1782, 2 JPM 289-91.

18. Ibid. 292.

19. John Jay to Robert R. Livingston, 17 November 1782, 6 RDC 14-15.

20. John Jay to Robert R. Livingston, 18 September 1782, 1 EN 581; John Jay to Gouverneur Morris, 13 October 1782, 1 EN 613; John Jay to Robert R.Livingston, 17 November 1782, 6 RDC 15; Morris, *Peacemakers*, 309-10; Monaghan, *John Jay*, 195-97.

21. Richard Oswald Notes, 11 August 1782, 2 JPM 301; John Adams to John Jay, 13 August 1782, 1 EN 527-28.

22. Richard Oswald Notes, August 1782, 2 JPM 303-08; John Jay to Robert R. Livingston, 17 November 1782, 6 RDC 16-17.

23. Benjamin Vaughan to Lord Shelburne, 24 August 1782; 1 EN 542-43; Morris, *Peacemakers*, 291-92, 313-15; Ritcheson, "Britain's Peacemakers," 72-77.

24. Aranda Notes, 26 August 1782, 2 JPM 278–81; John Jay to Robert R. Livingston, 17 November 1782, 6 RDC 23–24.

25. John Jay to Robert R. Livingston, 17 November 1782, 6 RDC 24–28.

26. Thomas Townshend to Richard Oswald, 1 September 1782, 1 EN 545; Benjamin Franklin to John Jay, 4 September 1782, 1 EN 551–52; John Jay to Richard Oswald, 10 September 1782, 1 EN 561–62 (draft); Richard Oswald to Thomas Townshend, 10 September 1782, 1 EN 563–68; John Jay to Robert R. Livingston, 17 November 1782, 6 RDC 18–21.

27. Herbert E. Klingelhofer, "Matthew Ridley's Diary during the Peace Negotiations of 1782," *William and Mary Quarterly* 20 (1963): 104–06; John Jay to Robert R. Livingston, 17 November 1782, 6 RDC 28–29.

28. François Barbé de Marbois to Vergennes, 13 March 1782, 1 EN 313–16; John Jay to Robert R. Livingston, 17 November 1782, 6 RDC 29.

29. Benjamin Vaughan to Lord Shelburne, 9 September 1782, 2 JPM 338; John Jay to Robert R. Livingston, 17 November 1782, 6 RDC 29–31; Klingelhofer, "Ridley Diary," 104–05.

30. John Jay to Vergennes, September 1782, draft, 6 RDC 32–44.

31. John Jay to Robert R. Livingston, 17 November 1782, 6 RDC 45; Klingelhofer, "Ridley Diary," 114–15.

32. Commission of Richard Oswald, 21 September 1782, 2 JPM 360–62; John Jay to Robert R. Livingston, 28 September 1782, 1 EN 590–91; John Jay to John Adams, 28 September 1782, 2 JPM 367; John Jay to Robert R. Livingston, 17 November 1782, 6 RDC 47; Klingelhofer, "Ridley Diary," 113–15; Marvin, *Benjamin Vaughan*, 18–19; Morris, *Peacemakers*, 339–40.

33. Richard Oswald to Thomas Townshend, 7 October 1782, 1 EN 603–05.

34. Richard Oswald to Thomas Townshend, 2 October 1782, 1 EN 593–95; Richard Oswald to Thomas Townshend, 7 October 1782, 1 EN 605–06; Charles Ritcheson, "Britain's Peacemakers," 93–95.

35. Klingelhofer, "Ridley Diary," 116–17.

36. First Draft Articles, 5 October 1782, 2 JPM 389–90.

37. Ibid. 390–91.

38. Ibid. 391–92.

39. Richard Oswald to Thomas Townshend, 7 October 1782, 1 EN 603–05; Richard Oswald to Thomas Townshend, 8 October 1782, 1 EN 606–08; Richard Oswald to Thomas Townshend, 11 October 1782, 1 EN 610–12; Benjamin Vaughan to Lord Shelburne, 11 October 1782, *Massachusetts Historical Society Proceedings*, 2nd Series 17 (1903): 414–18.

40. John Jay to Gouverneur Morris, 13 October 1782, 2 JPM 393; John Jay to Robert R. Livingston, 13 October 1782, 1 EN 612; John Jay Diary, 24 October 1782, 2 JPM 449.

41. John Jay Diary, 24 October 1782, 2 JPM 449–50.

42. Ferling, *John Adams*, 203; James H. Hutson, *John Adams and the Diplomacy of the American Revolution* (Lexington: University Press of Kentucky, 1980), 118; Klingelhofer, "Ridley Diary," 122–23.

43. John Adams to John Jay, 28 February 1782, 2 JPM 128–29; John Adams to Abigail Adams, 17 August 1782, Butterfield, ed., *Adams Family Correspondence*, 4:365–66; John Adams Diary, 26–27 October 1782, Butterfield, ed., *Diary*, 3:37–38, 82; Klingelhofer, "Ridley Diary," 121–22; Hutson, *Adams Diplomacy*, 118–19.

44. John Adams Diary, 26–29 October and 30 November 1782, Butterfield, ed., *Diary*, 3:37–38, 82; Klingelhofer, "Ridley Diary," 121–22.

45. John Jay Diary, 29 October 1782, 2 JPM 450–51; Morris, *Peacemakers*, 351–57; Ritcheson, "Britain's Peacemakers," 72–77.

46. John Jay Diary, 29 October 1782, 2 JPM 450–51; Richard Oswald to Lord Shelburne, 29 October 1782, 1 EN 629; Henry Strachey to Thomas Townshend, 29 October 1782, 1 EN 629; John Adams Diary, 3 November 1782, Butterfield, ed., *Diary*, 3:43–44.

47. John Adams Diary, 30 November 1782, Butterfield, ed., *Diary*, 3:82.

48. John Jay Diary, 29 October 1782, 2 JPM 450–51; John Adams to Robert R. Livingston, 31 October 1782, 1 EN 631; John Adams Diary, 4 November 1782, Butterfield, ed., *Diary*, 3:46; Henry Strachey to Thomas Townshend, 8 November 1782, 2 JPM 412; *Boston Patriot*, 31 July 1811; Klingelhofer, "Ridley Diary," 123.

49. Second Draft Articles, 4 November 1782, 2 JPM 401–02 (forty-five degrees); Alternative Boundary, 7 November 1782, 2 JPM 415–16 (line of lakes); John Adams to Robert R. Livingston, 6 November 1782, 1 EN 640; Morris, *Peacemakers*, 362–63.

50. Second Draft Articles, 4 November 1782, 2 JPM 404.

51. John Adams Diary, 2 November 1782, Butterfield, ed., *Diary*, 3: 46; John Adams to Robert R. Livingston, 6 November 1782, 1 EN 641; Morris, *Peacemakers*, 363–64.

52. Lord Shelburne to Richard Oswald, 21 October 1782, 1 EN 621; John Adams Diary, 3–4 November 1782, Butterfield, ed., *Diary*, 3:44–46; Second Draft Articles, 4 November 1782, 2 JPM 402–03.

53. Lord Shelburne to Richard Oswald, 21 October 1782, 1 EN 621; Richard Oswald to the American Commissioners, 4 November 1782, 1 EN 633–34; Second Draft Articles, 4 November 1782, 2 JPM 404; American Commissioners to Richard Oswald, 7 November 1782, 1 EN 645–46; Henry Strachey to Thomas Townshend, 8 November 1782, 2 JPM 414; Benjamin Franklin to Robert R. Livingston, 5 December 1782, 1 EN 709; James H. Hutson, *John Adams and the Diplomacy* (Lexington: University Press of Kentucky, 1980), 127–28.

54. John Adams Diary, 4 November 1782, Butterfield, ed., *Diary*, 3:45–46; Richard Oswald Note, 7 November 1782, 1 EN 653; Henry Strachey to Thomas Townshend, 8 November 1782, 1 EN 650.

55. Lord Shelburne Notes, 20 October 1782, 1 EN 619; Second Draft Articles, 4 November 1782, 2 JPM 401–03.

56. John Adams Diary, 4 November 1782, Butterfield, ed., *Diary*, 3:45–46; Henry Strachey to American Commissioners, 5 November 1782, 1 EN 638; Richard Oswald to Thomas Townshend, 6 November 1782, 1 EN 642; Richard Oswald to Henry Strachey, 8 November 1782, 2 JPM 417–19.

57. John Adams Diary, 5 November 1782, Butterfield, ed., *Diary* 3:47; John Jay to Robert R. Livingston, 17 November 1782, 6 RDC 11–49.

58. Richard Oswald to Lord Shelburne, 15 November 1782, 1 EN 657–60; Richard Oswald to Lord Shelburne, 16 November 1782, 1 EN 660–61.

59. Richard Oswald to Lord Shelburne, 16 November 1782, 1 EN 661; John Adams Diary, 17 November 1782, Butterfield, ed., *Diary* 3:57–58; Benjamin Vaughan to John Jay, 18 November 1782, 2 JPM 423–24.

60. John Adams Diary, 25 November 1782, Butterfield, ed., *Diary* 3:72; Henry Strachey Remarks, 25 November 1782, 1 EN 686–87.

61. Third Draft Articles, 25 November 1782, 6 RDC 74–77.

62. John Adams Diary, November 1782, Butterfield, ed., *Diary* 3:72–74.

63. Ibid. 75.

64. Ibid. 75; Benjamin Franklin to Richard Oswald, 26 November 1782, 6 RDC 77–80.

65. Thomas Townshend to Richard Oswald, 19 November 1782, 1 EN 678–79; John Adams Diary, 26 November 1782, Butterfield, ed., *Diary*, 3:75–77; Ritcheson, "Britain's Peacemakers," 73–75.

66. John Adams Diary, November 1782, Butterfield, ed., *Diary*, 3:77–81; Klingelhofer, "Ridley Diary," 131–32; Preliminary Articles, 30 November 1782, 1 EN 699; Morris, *Peacemakers*, 375–76.

67. Henry Laurens to John Adams, 27 August 1782, in David R. Chesnutt and C. James Taylor, eds., *The Papers of Henry Laurens*, 16 vols. (Columbia: University of South Carolina Press, 1976–2003), 15:592–96; Henry Laurens to President of Congress, 5 September 1782, ibid. 16:7–9; John Adams to Henry Laurens, 6 November 1782, ibid. 16:52–53; Henry Laurens to John Adams, 12 November 1782, ibid. 16:55; Daniel J. McDonough, *Christopher Gadsden and Henry Laurens: The Parallel Lives of Two American Patriots* (Cranbury, New Jersey: Associated University Presses, 2000), 260–63.

68. Compare Third Draft Articles, 25 November 1782, 6 RDC 74–77, with Preliminary Articles, 30 November 1782, 6 RDC 96–99.

69. John Adams Diary, 29 November 1782, Butterfield, ed., *Diary*, 3:79–81.

70. Ibid. 3:82–84; Report re: State Laws, 13 October 1786, 3 EN 343–45; Morris, *Peacemakers*, 381–82.

71. John Adams Diary, 30 November 1782, Butterfield, ed., *Diary*, 3:85; W. A. S. Hewins, ed., *The Whitefoord Papers ... from 1739 to 1810* (Oxford: 1898), 187.

72. Thomas Jefferson to John Jay, 11 April 1783, 6 PTJ 260–61; William Livingston to John Jay, 21 May 1782, 2 JPM 533; Alexander Hamilton to John Jay, 25 July 1783, 3 PAH 416.

73. Bemis, *Diplomacy*, 212–13, 256; Brecher, *Securing*, 236; Dull, *Diplomatic History*, 148–49; Morris, *Peacemakers*, 301–02; Perkins, "Peace of Paris," 200–05; Andrew Stockley, *Britain and France at the Birth of America: The European Powers and the Peace Negotiations of 1782–1783* (Exeter: University of Exeter Press, 2002), 62–63.

74. Richard B. Morris, "The Durable Significance of the Treaty of 1783," in Hoffman and Albert, *Peace and the Peacemakers*, 249 n. 38; Perkins, "Peace of Paris," 208; Stockley, *Britain and France*, 64.

75. Dull, *Diplomatic History*, 149; Ritcheson, "Britain's Peacemakers," 94; Stockley, *Britain and France*, 69.
76. Brecher, *Securing*, 193–98; Dull, *Franklin the Diplomat*, 58.

Notes to Chapter 8: American in Paris

1. Benjamin Franklin to Vergennes, 29 November 1782, 1 EN 688; Vergennes to Benjamin Franklin, 15 December 1782, 1 EN 720; Benjamin Franklin to Vergennes, 17 December 1782, 1 EN 721–22; Morris, *Peacemakers*, 382–85.
2. John Jay to Robert R. Livingston, 17 November 1782, 6 RDC 11–49; John Jay to Robert R. Livingston, 12 December 1782, 6 RDC 130; American Commissioners to Robert R. Livingston, 13 December 1782, 2 JPM 440–43; John Jay to Robert R. Livingston, 14 December 1782, 2 JPM 443–44; Robert R. Livingston to American Commissioners, 31 May 1783, 1 EN 859.
3. Lafayette to John Jay, 25 June 1782, 2 JPM 243–44; Madame de Lafayette to Sarah Jay, 29 June 1782, 2 JPM 248; Lafayette to the American Commissioners, 21 November 1782, 2 JPM 508–09; American Commissioners to Lafayette, 27 November 1782, 2 JPM 511; Lafayette to John Jay, 26 December 1783, 2 JPM 512–13; John Jay to Lafayette, 19 January 1783, 2 JPM 513–14; Lafayette to John Jay, 15 February 1783, 2 JPM 517–18; Lafayette to Robert R. Livingston, 2 March 1783, 6 RDC 268–70; John Jay to Lafayette, 5 March 1783, 2 JPM 518–19; John Jay to Robert R. Livingston, 22 April 1783, 1 EN 831–32; Louis Gottschalk, *Lafayette and the Close of the American Revolution* (Chicago: University of Chicago Press, 1942), 394–413.
4. Sarah Jay to Catharine Livingston, 16 March 1783; Matthew Ridley to Catharine Livingston, 26 March 1783, Massachusetts Historical Society; Sarah Jay to Susan Livingston, 16 April 1783; John Jay to Egbert Benson, 10 July 1783, 3 JPJ 51–52; John Jay to Gouverneur Morris, 17 July 1783, 3 JPJ 53–54; John Jay to Robert R. Livingston, 19 July 1783, 2 JPM 561–63;
5. John Jay to William Livingston, 13 October 1782, 2 JPM 472; Sarah Jay to Catharine Livingston, 16 November 1782; John Jay to Robert R. Livingston, 12 December 1782, 6 RDC 130; Matthew Ridley Diary, January 1783, 2 JPM 487–88; John Jay to Sarah Jay, 9 January 1783, 3 JPJ 20.
6. John Jay to Sarah Jay, 18 January 1783, 3 JPJ 23; John Jay to Lafayette, 19 January 1783, 2 JPM 514; Matthew Ridley Diary, January 1783, 2 JPM 487–88; Sarah Jay to John Jay, 21 January 1783, 3 JPJ 26; Morris, *Peacemakers*, 408–10.
7. John Adams Diary, 10 December 1782, Butterfield, ed., *Diary*, 3:95; Alleyne Fitzherbert to Lord Grantham, 9 February 1783, 1 EN 765–66; Morris, *Peacemakers*, 416–17.
8. American Commissioners to Alleyne Fitzherbert, 20 February 1783, 2 JPM 494 (draft); Alleyne Fitzherbert to Lord Grantham, 22 February 1783, 2 EN 70.
9. Benjamin Franklin to Robert R. Livingston, 7 March 1783, 1 EN 779; John Jay to Benjamin Vaughan, 28 March 1783, 1 EN 812–13; John Jay to Robert R. Livingston, 7 April 1783, 3 JPJ 38; Morris, *Peacemakers*, 418–22.

10. John Jay to Benjamin Vaughan, 28 March 1783, 1 EN 814; John Jay to Robert R. Livingston, 11 and 14 April 1783, 1 EN 818, 822–23; Benjamin Franklin to Robert R. Livingston, 15 April 1783, 1 EN 825.

11. David Hartley to Charles James Fox, 27 and 29 April and 20 May 1783, 2 EN 93–94, 99–101, 121–24; see George H. Guttridge, *David Hartley, M. P.: An Advocate of Conciliation* (Berkeley: University of California Press, 1926); Vincent F. Harlow, *The Founding of the Second British Empire* (London: Longmans, Green, 1952), 466–88.

12. Order in Council, 14 May 1783, 2 EN 117–18; Charles James Fox to David Hartley, 15 May 1783, 2 EN 118–21; David Hartley to Charles James Fox, 20 May 1783, 2 EN 121–24.

13. David Hartley to Charles James Fox, 22 and 23 May 1783, 2 EN 124–32; John Adams to Robert R. Livingston, 24 May 1783, 2 EN 132–33.

14. John Jay to Robert R. Livingston, 1 June 1783, 6 RDC 464–65; Draft Treaty, June 1783, 2 JPM 540–41; David B. Davis, *The Problem of Slavery in the Age of Revolution, 1770–1823* (New York: Oxford University Press, 1999), 119–23; James A. Rawley, *The Transatlantic Slave Trade: A History* (New York: W. W. Norton and Co., 1981), 400–18; Hugh Thomas, *The Slave Trade: The Story of the Atlantic Slave Trade, 1440–1870* (New York: Simon and Schuster, 1997), 499–503.

15. Charles James Fox to David Hartley, 10 June 1783, 2 EN 146–49; Henry Laurens to the American Commissioners, 17 June 1783, 6 RDC 493; John Adams to Robert R. Livingston, 23 June 1783, 6 RDC 501.

16. John Adams to Robert R. Livingston, 14 July 1783, 2 EN 188–90; John Adams to Robert R. Livingston, 16 July 1783, 2 EN 192–94; John Adams to Robert R. Livingston, 17 July 1783, 2 EN 194–96; David Hartley to Charles James Fox, 17 July 1783, 2 EN 196–97.

17. John Adams to Robert R. Livingston, 16 July 1783, 2 EN 193; John Jay to Gouverneur Morris, 17 July 1783, 3 JPJ 54; John Jay to Robert Morris, 20 July 1783, 3 JPJ 66; John Jay to William Bingham, 29 July 1783, 2 JPM 571.

18. David Hartley Propositions, 19 June 1783, 1 EN 864; American Commissioner Comments, July 1783, 1 EN 870.

19. American Propositions, July 1783, 1 EN 871–73; John Jay Draft Provision, 17 July 1783, 2 JPM 547–48; David Hartley to Charles James Fox, 6 August 1783, 1 EN 905–06; Draft Definitive Treaty, August 1783, 1 EN 906–13.

20. John Adams to Robert R. Livingston, 27 June 1783, 6 RDC 504–05; Edward Bancroft to John Jay, August 1783, 2 JPM 575–77; John Adams to Robert R. Livingston, 13 August 1783, 1 EN 917–18; Benjamin Franklin to Vergennes, 16 August 1783, 1 EN 921–22.

21. Vergennes to John Jay, 28 August 1783, 2 JPM 581; Rayneval to Benjamin Franklin, 30 August 1783, 6 RDC 662; David Hartley to the American Commissioners, 30 August 1783, 6 RDC 662; American Commissioners to David Hartley, 30 August 1783, 6 RDC 662–63 (fixing time as eight o'clock); David Hartley to Charles James Fox, 1 September 1783, 1 EN 930–31; John Adams to Elias Boudinot, 5 September 1783, 1 EN 932; John Jay to Robert Morris, 12 September 1783, 1 EN 940–41; Morris, *Peacemakers*, 435–37.

22. John Jay to Montmorin, 3 April 1783, 2 JPM 524; John Adams to Robert R. Livingston, 14 April 1783, 6 RDC 373; Robert R. Livingston to John Adams, 14 April 1783, 6 RDC 375; Benjamin Franklin to Robert R. Livingston, 12 June 1783, 6 RDC 480; John Adams to Robert R. Livingston, 16 June 1783, 6 RDC 488–90; John Adams to Robert R. Livingston, 23 June 1783, 6 RDC 501–02.

23. Robert R. Livingston to American Commissioners, 25 March 1783, 6 RDC 338–40; Robert R. Livingston to Benjamin Franklin, 26 March 1783, 6 RDC 343–44; Robert R. Livingston to American Commissioners, 21 April 1783, 6 RDC 386–87; John Adams to Robert R. Livingston, 3 July 1783, 6 RDC 510–13.

24. John Adams to Robert R. Livingston, 3 July 1783, 6 RDC 510–13; John Adams to Robert Morris, 5 July 1783, 6 RDC 515; John Jay Draft Response, July 1783, 2 JPM 550–53.

25. Franklin's Observations on Jay's Draft, July 1783, 2 JPM 553–54; American Commissioners to Robert R. Livingston, 18 July 1783, 2 JPM 554–58.

26. John Jay to Robert R. Livingston, 30 May 1783, 3 JPJ 48; John Jay to Egbert Benson, 10 July 1783, 3 JPJ 51–52; John Jay to Gouverneur Morris, 17 July 1783, 3 JPJ 53–54; John Jay to Robert R. Livingston, 19 July 1783, 2 JPM 558–63; John Jay to Catharine Livingston, 20 July 1783, 3 JPJ 67.

27. Jay, *Littlepage Letters*, 40–41; John Adams to John Jay, 14 February 1786, William A. Weaver, ed., 7 vols., *Diplomatic Correspondence of the United States* (Washington: 1833–34), 5:485; Monaghan, *John Jay*, 223–24.

28. John Jay to Robert Morris, 13 October 1782, 2 JPM 473–74; Sarah Jay to Mary Morris, 14 November 1782, 2 JPM 475–76; John Jay to Catharine Livingston, 1 July 1783, 2 JPM 608; John Jay to Gouverneur Morris, 24 September 1783, 3 JPJ 82–84.

29. John Jay to George Washington, 6 April 1783, 2 JPM 525; John Jay to William Livingston, 19 July 1783, 2 JPM 564–65; John Jay to Gouverneur Morris, 24 - September 1783, 3 JPJ 82–85.

30. John Jay to George Washington, 13 June 1783, 3 JPJ 50; John Jay to Robert Morris, 20 July 1783, 2 JPM 566; John Jay to Alexander Hamilton, 28 September 1783, 3 PAH 459–60.

31. John Jay to William Livingston, 19 July 1783, 2 JPM 564–65; John Jay to Gouverneur Morris, 24 September 1783, 3 JPJ 82–85.

32. John Thaxter to Abigail Adams, 19–20 November 1782, Butterfield, ed., *Adams Family Correspondence*, 5:43; John Adams to Abigail Adams, 16 April 1783, ibid. 124; Sarah Jay to Catharine Livingston, 14 August 1782, 2 JPM 460; Sarah Jay to Catharine Livingston, 14 December 1782, 2 JPM 590–91.

33. Sarah Jay to Susannah Livingston, 28 August 1782, 2 JPM 464–66; Sarah Jay to William Livingston, 18 July 1783, 2 JPM 610–12; Monaghan, *John Jay*, 227.

34. John Jay to William Livingston, 21 May 1783, 2 JPM 606; John Jay to Catharine Livingston, 1 July 1783, 2 JPM 607; Sarah Jay to Catharine Livingston, 16 July 1783 (encloses toast erroneously identified as September 1783 at 2 JPM 581); John Jay to Frederick Jay, 18 July 1783, 2 JPM 609–10; John Jay to Robert R. Livingston, 19 July 1783, 2 JPM 563; John Jay to Charles Thomson, 19 July 1783, Thomson Papers, Library of Congress; John Jay Notes, July 1783, 2 JPM 713–14; John Jay to Frederick

Jay, 26 August 1783, 2 JPM 614; Sarah Jay to John Jay, 12 November 1783, 2 JPM 640; Benjamin Franklin to John Jay, 10 May 1785, Bigelow, ed., *Works of Franklin*, 9:325.

35. John Jay to Peter Van Schaack, 17 September 1782, 2 JPM 466–68; John Jay to Peter Van Schaack, 16 June 1783, 2 JPM 542–43; John Jay to Sarah Jay, 15 October 1783; John Jay to Sarah Jay, 28 October 1783, 2 JPM 628; John Jay to Sarah Jay, 14 November 1783, 2 JPM 642.

36. John Jay to Sarah Jay, 28 October 1793, 2 JPM 628; John Jay to Sarah Jay, 14 November 1783, 2 JPM 642; John Jay to Sarah Jay, 18 November 1783, 2 JPM 645.

37. John Adams Diary, 26–27 October 1783, Butterfield, ed., *Diary*, 3:148–49; John Adams to *Boston Patriot*, 17 February 1812, ibid. 3:150; John Jay to Sarah Jay, 28 October 1783, 2 JPM 627; John Jay to Sarah Jay, 14 November 1783, 2 JPM 643.

38. John Jay Ide, *The Portraits of John Jay* (New York: New-York Historical Society, 1938), 12–13, 18–19, 52; Dorinda Evans, *The Genius of Gilbert Stuart* (Princeton: Princeton University Press, 1999), 53–60.

39. John Jay to Silas Deane, 23 February 1784, 2 JPM 620; Note, 2 JPM 49–50.

40. John Jay to Peter Van Schaack, 17 September 1782, 2 JPM 468; John Jay to Peter Jay Munro, 26 October 1783, 2 JPM 626; Morris, *Peacemakers*, 298–99.

41. Sarah Jay to John Jay, 6 November 1783, 2 JPM 635–36; John Jay to William Temple Franklin, 11 November 1783, 2 JPM 639.

42. Sarah Jay to John Jay, 18 November 1783, 2 JPM 643; John Jay to Sarah Jay, 23 November 1783, 2 JPM 647; Peter Jay Munro to John Jay, 7 December 1783, 2 JPM 658–59; John Jay to Sarah Jay, 26 December 1783, 2 JPM 669–70.

43. Sarah Jay to John Jay, 6 November 1783, 2 JPM 634–36; Sarah Jay to John Jay, 18 November 1783, 2 JPM 644; John Jay to Sarah Jay, 23 November 1783, 2 JPM 647; Sarah Jay to John Jay, 27 November 1783, 2 JPM 649; John Jay to Sarah Jay, 29 November 1783, 2 JPM 651–52.

44. Sarah Jay to John Jay, 27 November 1783, 2 JPM 649; John Jay to Sarah Jay, 8 December 1783, 2 JPM 660; Sarah Jay to John Jay, 11 December 1783, 2 JPM 683.

45. John Jay to Sarah Jay, 23 November 1783, 2 JPM 647; John Jay to John Adams, 9 December 1783, 2 JPM 662; Claire Tomalin, *Jane Austen: A Life* (New York: Alfred A. Knopf, 1997), 146–47.

46. John Jay to Egbert Benson, 15–18 December 1783, 2 JPM 665–67; Note, 2 JPM 620–21.

47. John Jay to Sarah Jay, 20 December 1783, 2 JPM 667–68; John Jay to Sarah Jay, 5 January 1784; John Jay to Peter Van Schaack, 8 January 1784; John Jay to Frederick Jay, 22 January 1784; John Jay to John Adams, 6 February 1784, 2 JPM 690; John Jay to Frederick Jay, 6 February 1784.

48. Benjamin Franklin to Henry Laurens, 12 February 1784, 6 RDC 766; John Adams to John Jay, 13 February 1784, 2 JPM 693; John Adams to John Jay and Benjamin Franklin, 20 February 1784; Benjamin Franklin to Charles Thomson, 9 March 1784, 6 RDC 785; John Adams to John Jay and Benjamin Franklin, 10 April 1784, 2 EN 331; John Jay and Benjamin Franklin to John Adams, 29 April 1784, 2 EN 352.

49. Conditional Manumission of Benoit, 21 March 1784, 2 JPM 705–06.

50. Benjamin Franklin to John Jay, 30 March 1784, 2 JPM 706; American Commissioners to David Hartley, 31 March 1784, 2 JPM 707; David Hartley to Benjamin Franklin and John Jay, 9 April 1784, 1 EN 971; Benjamin Franklin to Thomas Mifflin, 12 May 1784, 1 EN 971–72; Benjamin Franklin to Charles Thomson, 13 May 1774, 6 RDC 806.

51. John Witherspoon to John Jay, 27 March 1784, 3 JPJ 118–19; John Jay to John Witherspoon, 6 April 1784, 3 JPJ 120–22.

52. Catharine Livingston to John Jay, 30 December 1784, 2 JPM 670–72; Gouverneur Morris to John Jay, 10 January 1784, 2 JPM 674–75; Charles Thomson to John Jay, 15 January 1784, 2 JPM 677–78; Robert R. Livingston to John Jay, 25 January 1784, 2 JPM 678–81; John Jay to Peter A. Jay, 8 April 1784, 2 JPM 709–10.

53. John Jay to William Carmichael, 14 August 1783, 2 JPM 688; John Jay to William Carmichael, 28 January 1784, 2 JPM 688–89; John Jay Notes, March-April 1784, 2 JPM 690; John Jay to Charles Thomson, 7 April 1784, Thomson Papers, Library of Congress.

54. John Jay to John Adams, 27 April 1784, 2 JPM 720–21; John Adams to John Jay, 11 May 1784, 2 JPM 724; Richard Oswald to Caleb Whitefoord, May 1784, Hewins, ed., *Whitefoord Papers*, 192; John Adams to Thomas Barclay, 24 May 1784, 2 JPM 16; John Jay to William Vaughan, 25 May 1784; John Jay to Matthew Ridley, 26 May 1784; John Jay to President of Congress, 25 July 1784, 3 JPJ 128; John Jay to Matthew Ridley, 3 September 1784; John Jay to New York Council, 4 October 1784; Laura Verlaque, "The John Jay Freedom Box," *Christie's Magazine*, January–February 2001; *Wall Street Journal*, March 16, 2001.

Notes to Chapter 9: Secretary for Foreign Affairs

1. Charles Thomson to John Jay, 18 June 1784, 3 JPJ 126; John Jay to Charles Thomson, 12 August 1784; John Jay to Charles Thomson, 20 October 1784, Papers of the Continental Congress; James Monroe to James Madison, 6 December 1784 and 1 February 1785, 22 LDC 52, 157; Joseph L. Davis, *Sectionalism in American Politics, 1774–1787* (Madison: University of Wisconsin Press, 1977), 59–75; John P. Kaminski, "Honor and Interest: John Jay's Diplomacy during the Confederation," *New York History* 83 (2002): 293.

2. John Jay to Benjamin Vaughan, 30 November 1784, 3 JPJ 134–35; James Monroe to James Madison, 6 December 1784, 22 LDC 52; Sarah Jay to John Jay, 10 December 1784; John Jay, Oath of Office, 21 December 1784; Elbridge Gerry to James Warren, 23 December 1784, 22 LDC 82–83; Kenneth R. Bowling, *The Creation of Washington D.C.* (Fairfax: George Mason University Press, 1991), 62–67; Sidney I. Pomerantz, *New York as an American City, 1783–1803* (New York: Columbia University Press, 1938), 94–95.

3. John Jay to John Adams, 26 November 1785, Weaver, ed., *Diplomatic Correspondence*, 4:357; John Jay to John Adams, 4 May 1786, ibid. 4: 483; John Jay to John Adams, 21 February 1787, 3 EN 430–31; John Jay to Thomas Jefferson, 19 August 1786, 3 EN

267; Richard B. Morris, *The Forging of the Union, 1781–1789* (New York: Harper and Row, 1987), 194–219; Jennings B. Sanders, *Evolution of the Executive Departments of the Continental Congress* (Chapel Hill: University of North Carolina Press, 1935), 119–27.

4. Louis Guillame Otto to Vergennes, 10 January 1786, 3 EN 64–66; Comte de Moustier to Montmorin, 19 January 1789, 3 EN 915–16.

5. Staff List, 16 February 1786, Papers of the Continental Congress; Michael McShane Burns, "John Jay as Secretary for Foreign Affairs, 1784–1789" (Ph.D. diss., University of North Carolina, Chapel Hill, 1974), 42–53; Morris, *Forging*, 194–95.

6. Estimates based on Butler, ed., *Index to the Papers of the Continental Congress*, 2:2616–49.

7. Report re: Ordinance on Piracy, 29 September 1785, 2 EN 833–35; Congress to Samuel Shaw, 27 January 1786, 3 EN 76–77; Samuel Shaw to John Jay, 31 December 1786, 3 EN 376–86; John Jay to John Adams, 25 July 1787, 3 EN 560.

8. Samuel F. Bemis, *Jay's Treaty: A Study in Commerce and Diplomacy* (New Haven: Yale University Press, rev. ed. 1962); Kaminski, "Honor and Interest"; Morris, *Forging*, 196–206; Charles R. Ritcheson, *Aftermath of Revolution: British Policy towards the United States, 1783–1795* (New York: W. W. Norton, 1971).

9. Henry Laurens to Thomas Mifflin, 24 April 1784, 2 EN 348–49; James Monroe to Thomas Jefferson, 1 November 1784, 22 LDC 3–5; John Francis Mercer to James Madison, 12 November 1784, 22 LDC 15–17; James Monroe to James Madison, 15 November 1784, 22 LDC 18–21; Richard Henry Lee to James Madison, 20 November 1784, 22 LDC 24–25.

10. Report re: Instructions for Minister to Britain, 5 February 1785, 2 EN 541; John Jay to John Adams, 15 March 1785, Weaver, ed., *Diplomatic Correspondence*, 4: 164; John Jay to John Adams, 18 March 1785, ibid. 165.

11. John Adams to John Jay, 24 April 1785, 2 EN 609–10; John Jay to John Adams, 3 August 1785, 2 EN 719–21; John Jay to Richard Henry Lee, 2 September 1785, 2 EN 793–94; Report re: Eastern Boundary, 21 April 1785, 2 EN 887–89; James Avery to James Bowdoin, 23 August 1785, 2 EN 903–04; Report re: Eastern Boundary, 22 September 1785, 2 EN 902–03; John Jay to John Adams, 1 November 1785, 2 EN 886; John Jay to Thomas Jefferson, 2 November 1785, 9 PTJ 8–9; Morris, *Forging*, 204–05.

12. John Jay to Thomas Jefferson, 19 January 1786, 3 EN 69–70; Report re: British Consuls, 8 March 1786, 3 EN 121; Thomas Jefferson to John Jay, 12 March 1786, 3 EN 126–27.

13. John Adams Memorial, 30 November 1785, 2 EN 930; Report re: British Posts, 30 March 1786, 3 EN 137–38; John Jay to John Adams, 1 May 1786, 3 EN 161.

14. Lord Carmarthen to John Adams, 28 February 1786, 3 EN 110–11; John Adams to John Jay, 4 March 1786, Weaver, ed., *Diplomatic Correspondence* 5:7; David Ramsay to John Adams, 14 May 1786, 23 LDC 287–88.

15. John Jay to the Governors, 29 January 1785, Papers of the Continental Congress; John Jay to the Governors, 16 May 1786, ibid.; John Jay to Thomas Jefferson, 16 June 1786, 3 EN 200–01; John Jay to George Washington, 27 June 1786, 4 PGW 130–32;

Charles F. Hobson, "The Recovery of British Debts in the Federal Circuit Court of Virginia," *Virginia Magazine of History and Biography* 94 (1984): 176–79.

16. Report re: State Laws, 13 October 1786, 31 JCC 797–874 or 3 EN 333–49; see Cathy D. Matson and Peter S. Onuf, *A Union of Interests: Political and Economic Thought in Revolutionary America* (Lawrence: University Press of Kansas, 1990).

17. 31 JCC 806–62; 3 EN 334.

18. 31 JCC 863–66; 3 EN 344–45.

19. 31 JCC 867–69.

20. 31 JCC 869–74.

21. John Jay to John Adams, 1 November 1786, 3 EN 362–63; John Temple to Lord Carmarthen, 7 December 1786, 3 EN 371–72; Bailey, *Diplomatic History*, 58; Bemis, *Jay's Treaty*, 284–85; Burns, "Jay as Secretary," 148–51.

22. Report re: Richard Lawrence, 14 March 1787, 3 EN 451–52; Resolutions re: State Observance of the Treaty of Peace, 21 March 1787, 3 EN 454–55; Arthur St. Clair to the State Governors, 13 April 1787, 3 EN 472–77; *Pennsylvania Gazette*, 2 May 1787.

23. John Jay to Thomas Jefferson, 24 April 1787, 11 PTJ 312; John Jay to John Adams, 31 July 1787, Weaver, ed., *Diplomatic Correspondence*, 5:258–61; John Adams to John Jay, 22 September 1787, ibid. 327.

24. Resolutions re: Adams Recall, 5 October 1787, 3 EN 613–14; John Jay to John Adams, 16 October 1787, 3 EN 631–32; John Adams to John Jay, 21 February 1788, Weaver, ed., *Diplomatic Correspondence*, 5:366.

25. John Temple to Lord Carmarthen, 3 May 1787, 3 EN 492–93; Peter Allaire to George Young, 4 June 1787, 3 EN 520–22; Monaghan, *John Jay*, 249–54; Morris, *Forging*, 197–98.

26. Chevalier de la Luzerne to John Dickinson, 19 May 1784, 2 EN 374; Chevalier de la Luzerne to Vergennes, 19 June 1784, 2 EN 393; François Barbé de Marbois to John Jay, 10 February 1785, 2 EN 549–50.

27. Report re: Longchamps, 16 February 1785, 2 EN 554–56.

28. Ibid.; Thomas Jefferson to John Jay, 14 August 1785, 2 EN 742; John Jay to Thomas Jefferson, 14 September 1785, 2 EN 815.

29. Proposed Consular Convention, 24 July 1781, 3 EN 8–15; Benjamin Franklin to Vergennes, 31 May 1784, 3 EN 27; Resolution re: Consular Convention, 14 December 1784, 3 EN 36.

30. Report re: Richard Soderstrom, 2 March 1785, 2 EN 565–66; John Jay to Richard Henry Lee, 23 June 1785, 3 EN 38; Report re: Consular Convention, 4 July 1785, 3 EN 38–51.

31. Report re: Consular Convention, 4 July 1785, 3 EN 38–51.

32. Report re: Consular Convention, 18 August 1786, 3 EN 264–66; John Jay to Thomas Jefferson, 18 August 1786, 3 EN 266–67; John Jay to Thomas Jefferson, 3 October 1786, 3 EN 323–24.

33. Thomas Jefferson to John Jay, 9 January 1787, 3 EN 388–89; Report re: Consular Convention, 10 May 1787, 3 EN 495–97; John Jay to Thomas Jefferson, 27 July 1787, 11 PTJ 627–29.

34. Thomas Jefferson to Montmorin, 20 June 1788, 3 EN 795–99; Thomas Jefferson to John Jay, 14 November 1788, 3 EN 858–62; Consular Convention, 14 November 1788, 3 EN 862–68.

35. John Jay to Thomas Jefferson, 9 March 1789, 14 PTJ 689; Senate Executive Journal, June-July 1789, 2 DHFFC 7–10; Stanley Elkins and Eric McKitrick, *The Age of Federalism: The Early American Republic, 1788-1800* (New York: Oxford University Press, 1993), 55–58; Burns, "Jay as Secretary," 109–10.

36. Report re: Consular Convention, 22 July 1789, 2 DHFFC 10–12.

37. Senate Executive Journal, 29 July 1789, ibid. 12; Samuel F. Bemis, "John Jay," in Bemis, ed., *American Secretaries of State*, 1:259; Burns, "Jay as Secretary," 109–10.

38. Samuel F. Bemis, *Pinckney's Treaty: America's Advantage from Europe's Distress* (New Haven: Yale University Press, 1960), 60–79; Davis, *Sectionalism*, 109–26; John Ferling, *A Leap in the Dark: The Struggle to Create the American Republic* (New York: Oxford, 2003), 264–66; Middlekauf, *Glorious Cause*, 586–88; Morris, *Forging*, 232–44; Phelan Powell, *John Jay: First Chief Justice of the Supreme Court* (Philadelphia: Chelsea House, 2001), 49–50.

39. Richard Henry Lee to James Madison, 20 November 1784, 22 LDC 24–26; Hugh Williamson to Thomas Jefferson, 11 December 1784, 22 LDC 62–65; George Washington to Richard Henry Lee, 22 August 1785, 3 PGW 195–97; James Monroe to Thomas Jefferson, 25 August 1785, 22 LDC 599–601; James Monroe to Thomas Jefferson, 19 January 1786, 23 LDC 92–95; Joel Achenbach, *The Grand Idea: George Washington's Potomac and the Race to the West* (New York: Simon & Schuster, 2004).

40. 29 JCC 658.

41. Gardoqui to Floridablanca, 23 August 1785, 2 EN 764–66.

42. Bemis, *Pinckney's Treaty*, 77–79.

43. Alexander Fowler to John Jay, 1 October 1785, 2 EN 835–36; Report re: the Mississippi, 25 February 1786, 3 EN 106.

44. Gardoqui to John Jay, 25 May 1785, 3 EN 181–83.

45. John Jay to Congress, 29 May 1786, 3 EN 190; James Monroe to James Madison, 31 May 1786, 23 LDC 323–25; Rufus King to Elbridge Gerry, 4 June 1786, 23 LDC 331–34; James Monroe to Thomas Jefferson, 16 June 1786, 23 LDC 359–60; James Monroe to Thomas Jefferson, 16 July 1786, 23 LDC 404–05.

46. Rufus King to James Monroe, 30 July 1786, 23 LDC 423; John Jay to Congress, 3 August 1786, 3 EN 247–55; James Monroe to Patrick Henry, 12 August 1786, 23 LDC 462–66.

47. John Jay to Congress, 3 August 1786, 3 EN 247–55.

48. Ibid.

49. James Monroe to Patrick Henry, 12 August 1786, 23 LDC 462–66; Charles Thomson Notes, 18 August 1786, 23 LDC 494; James Monroe to James Madison, 3 September 1786, 23 LDC 544–46; John Jay to Thomas Jefferson, 14 December 1786, 3 EN 373–74.

50. 31 JCC 574–613; James Monroe to James Madison, 29 September 1786, 23 LDC 575–76; John Jay to Gardoqui, 6 October 1786, 3 EN 328; James Monroe to James Madison, 7 October 1786, 23 LDC 583–84.

428 NOTES TO PAGES 217-222

51. Gardoqui to Floridablanca, 28 October 1786, quoted in Bemis, *Pinckney's Treaty*, 105–06; John Jay to Congress, 11 April 1787, 3 EN 466–68.

52. John Jay to Congress, 11 April 1787, 3 EN 466–68; Report re: George Rogers Clark, 12 April 1787, 3 EN 469–72; Bemis, *Pinckney's Treaty*, 91–107.

53. John Adams and Thomas Jefferson to John Jay, 28 March 1786, 3 EN 135–36; H. G. Barnby, *The Prisoners of Algiers: An Account of the Forgotten American–Algerian War* (London: Oxford University Press, 1966); Ray Irwin, *The Diplomatic Relations of the United States with the Barbary Powers, 1776–1816* (Chapel Hill: University of North Carolina Press, 1931).

54. American Commissioners' Propositions, 1 July 1783, 1 EN 872.

55. John Lamb's Memorial to Congress, February 1785, 2 EN 546–47; Report re: John Lamb, 10 February 1785, 2 EN 548–49.

56. Giacomo Crocco to Congress, 16 November 1784, Papers of the Continental Congress; John Jay to the American Commissioners, 11 March 1785, 2 EN 574–76; Congress to Emperor of Morocco, 11 March 1785, 2 EN 578–80; John Jay to Giacomo Crocco, 11 March 1785, 2 EN 580–81.

57. John Paul Jones to John Jay, 6 August 1785, Papers of the Continental Congress; John Jay to Congress, 13 October 1785, 2 EN 862; Pierse Long to John Langdon, 14 October 1785, 22 LDC 686–87; Report re: Algerine Declaration of War, 20 October 1785, 2 EN 868–70.

58. Richard O'Bryen to Thomas Jefferson, 24 August 1785, 2 EN 767–68; Report re: American Prisoners in Algiers, 2 January 1786, 3 EN 58–59; John Jay to Thomas Jefferson, 19 January 1786, 3 EN 69–70; Report re: Anglo-American Relations, 31 January 1786, 3 EN 83.

59. John Adams to John Jay, 17 February 1786, 3 EN 96–97; John Adams to John Jay, 20 February 1786, 3 EN 99–101; John Adams to John Jay, 22 February 1786, 3 EN 104–06; John Adams and Thomas Jefferson to John Jay, 28 March 1786, 3 EN 135–36.

60. Report re: Relations with Barbary States, 29 May 1786, 3 EN 188–89; John Jay to Thomas Jefferson, 16 June 1786, 3 EN 200–01.

61. Treaty of Peace Between Morocco and the United States, 15 July 1786, 3 EN 227–33; John Jay to Thomas Jefferson, 27 October 1786, 10 PTJ 488; John Henry to William Smallwood, 5 November 1786, 22 LDC 635–36; John Jay to Thomas Jefferson, 9 February 1787, 3 EN 418; Report re: Morocco Treaty, 5 May 1787, Papers of the Continental Congress; Ratification of Morocco Treaty, 18 July 1787, 3 EN 551–52.

62. John Adams and Thomas Jefferson to John Jay, 27 January 1787, 3 EN 404; Thomas Jefferson to John Jay, 1 February 1787, 3 EN 410; Report re: American Captives, 1 May 1787, 3 EN 487; Report re: Confederacy Against Algiers, 2 August 1787, 3 EN 563–64; Note, 10 PTJ 563–65; Barnby, *Prisoners of Algiers*, 264–301.

63. John Jay to John Adams, 2 August 1782, 2 JPM 267–68.

Notes to Chapter 10: Home and Society

1. Edward P. Alexander, *A Revolutionary Conservative: James Duane of New York* (New York: Columbia University Press, 1938), 156–57; Burrows and Wallace, Gotham, 265–66.

2. Philip Schuyler to John Jay, 22 January and 21 February 1785; John Jay to Philip Schuyler, 17 March 1785; John Jay to James Duane, 30 September 1785; *The Talisman* 3 (1830): 343; Monaghan, *John Jay*, 232–33.

3. Shane White, *Somewhat More Independent: The End of Slavery in New York City, 1770–1810* (Athens: University of Georgia Press, 1991), 4–5, 82–83; Jan Horton, "Listening for Clarinda" (Bedford: John Jay Homestead, 2000) (typescript).

4. New York City Tax List 1789 (microfilm at Library of Congress); Account and Stock Ledgers, Bank of New York, New York; Chernow, *Hamilton*, 199–202; Forrest McDonald, *We The People: The Economic Origins of the Constitution* (Chicago: University of Chicago Press, 1958), 302–03 (loan amounts).

5. Peter Jay Will, 28 January 1778; Chernow, *Hamilton*, 186.

6. The original of Mrs. Jay's list is at the John Jay Homestead. For partial printed versions, see Elizabeth Fries Ellett, *The Queens of American Society* (New York: 1867), 71–77 (chapter by John Jay II); Rufus W. Griswold, *The Republican Court: or American Society in the Days of Washington* (New York: 1856), 98–99.

7. Sarah Jay Dinner List, 8 January 1787, John Jay Homestead; John Kean to John Jay, 23 LDC 164; Humphrey, *King's College*, 196–97; Kierner, *Traders and Gentlefolk*, 255–61; de Forest, *Van Cortlandt Family*.

8. See John Jay to Thomas Jefferson, 25 November 1788, 3 EN 881; James Madison to Thomas Jefferson, 8 December 1788, 3 EN 896–97.

9. Ellett, *Queens of American Society*, 75–76.

10. Ibid.; J. P. Brissot de Warville, *New Travels in the United States of America* (London: 1792), 139; Dixon Wecter, *The Saga of American Society* (New York: Charles Scribner, 1970), 199–204.

11. William Maclay's Journal, 27 August 1789, 9 DHFFC 136–37; George Washington to John Jay, 30 November 1789, 4 PGW 340–41; John Jay to George Washington, 30 November 1789, ibid.; Joseph J. Ellis, *After the Revolution: Profiles of Early American Culture* (New York: W. W. Norton and Co., 1979) 128–34.

12. Frank Monaghan and Marvin Lowenthal, *This Was New York: The Nation's Capital in 1789* (Garden City: Doubleday, Doran, 1943), 148–53.

13. Ibid. 297–98 (citations expanded).

14. Ibid. 297–98 (citations expanded); Sarah Jay to William Livingston, 18 July 1783, 2 JPM 611–12; Charles Johnstone, *Chrysal: or The Adventures of a Guinea* (London: 1785), 132.

15. John Jay to Benjamin Franklin, 16 September 1785; Benjamin Franklin to John Jay, 21 September 1785; John Jay to Benjamin Franklin, 28 March 1788.

16. Philip Schuyler to John Jay, 22 January 1785; Philip Schuyler to John Jay, 21 February 1785; John Jay to Philip Schuyler, 17 March 1785; Philip Schuyler to John Jay, 30 May 1785, 3 JPJ 151–52; John Jay to Philip Schuyler, 10 June 1785, 3

JPJ 154–56; Philip Schuyler to John Jay, 10 September 1785; Monaghan, *John Jay*, 234–35.

17. William Livingston to John Jay, 13 February and 1 May 1786; William Livingston to John Jay, 28 August 1786, 3 JPJ 211–12; William Livingston to John Jay, 24 December 1788. Asclepius was the Greek god of medicine.

18. Lewis Littlepage to John Jay, 17 November 1785; Lewis Littlepage to John Jay, 25 November 1785, in Nell H. Boand, *Lewis Littlepage* (Richmond: Whittet and Shepperson, 1970), 78–79.

19. Lewis Littlepage to John Jay, 30 November 1785, Papers of the Continental Congress; Report re: Lewis Littlepage, 2 December 1785, ibid.

20. Lewis Littlepage to John Jay, 2 December 1785, Papers of the Continental Congress; John Jay to Lewis Littlepage, 3 December 1785, ibid.; Boand, *Littlepage*, 79–80.

21. Lewis Littlepage to John Jay, 3 December 1785; John Jay to Lewis Littlepage, 5 December 1785, in *New York Daily Advertiser*, 6 December 1785.

22. *New York Daily Advertiser*, 6 December 1785.

23. Ibid. 7 December 1785. Monaghan asserts, without support, that Littlepage on this day challenged Jay to a duel. Monaghan, *John Jay*, 237–38.

24. *New York Daily Advertiser*, 10 December 1785.

25. *New York Daily Advertiser*, 16 December 1785; John Vaughan to Brockholst Livingston, 3 January 1786; Brockholst Livingston to John Jay, 13 January 1786; Gerald T. Dunne, "Brockholst Livingston," in Leon Friedman and Fred L. Israel, eds., *The Justices of the United States Supreme Court, 1789–1969*, 4 vols. (New York: Chelsea House Publishers, 1969).

26. Draft Declaration, January 1786 (typescript in Jay papers project file at Columbia); Robert Morris to John Jay, 16 January 1786; Alexander Hamilton to John Jay, 3 May 1787, 4 PAH 155–57; Brockholst Livingston to Susannah Livingston, 27 June 1787; Brockholst Livingston to Lewis Littlepage, 30 November 1801, in Boand, *Littlepage*, 285.

27. John Jay to Thomas Jefferson, 9 December 1785, 9 PTJ 86–87; John Jay to Catharine Livingston, 28 December 1785; John Jay to John Adams, 2 February 1786, in Jay, *Life of John Jay*, 1:225–26; John Adams to John Jay, 14 February 1786, ibid. 227–28; John Jay to George Washington, 2 March 1786, 3 PGW 577–78; John Jay to Jacob Read, 16 March 1786; John Jay to Peter Yates, 1 March 1787; John Jay to George Mason Jr., 9 August 1787.

28. Thomas Jefferson to John Jay, 25 January 1786, 9 PTJ 215; Peter Van Schaack to John Jay, 21 February 1786; George Washington to John Jay, 18 May 1786, 4 PGW 55–56; George Mason Jr. to John Jay, 23 July 1787, Jay, *Life of John Jay*, 1:229.

29. *New York Journal*, 4 April 1792 (Robert R. Livingston writing as "Aristedes").

30. Brands, *First American*, 677–78, 706–07; Joseph J. Ellis, *American Sphinx: The Character of Thomas Jefferson* (New York: Alfred A. Knopf, 1997), 215–16, 259; Ferling, *First of Men*, 75–76; James Hutson, "James Madison and the Social Utility of Religion: Risks vs. Rewards" (on Library of Congress website); Wood, *American Revolution*, 129–30.

31. Morgan Dix, *A History of the Parish of Trinity Church in New York City*, 6 vols. (New York: 1898), 2:1–25, 77–82, 133–39.

32. Jay was elected warden in February 1785, and apparently served until early 1791. The vestry met about once a month at this time, but Jay attended only ten meetings during this period. Minutes of the Vestry, Trinity Church Archives, New York City, February 1785 through April 1791.

33. Minutes of the Vestry, 7 October 1785, 14 February 1791 (requesting punctual payment of interest); Alexander, *Revolutionary Conservative*, 178–79; Dix, *History of Trinity*, 2:133–39.

34. John Jay to John Adams, 1 November 1785; John Adams to John Jay, 4 January 1786; English Bishops to American Convention, 24 February 1786, in Protestant Episcopal Church, *Journals of the General Conventions of the Protestant Episcopal Church in America* (Philadelphia: 1814), 19–20; John Jay to John Adams, 4 May 1786; Episcopal Church of New York, *Proceedings of the Convention of the Protestant Episcopal Church, in the State of New-York* (New York: 1787); Clara O. Loveland, *The Critical Years: The Reconstitution of the Anglican Church in the United States of America, 1780–1789* (Greenwich: Seabury Press, 1956).

35. Protestant Episcopal Church, *Journals of the General Conventions*, 26–28; Loveland, *Critical Years*, 192–94.

36. Episcopal Church of New York, *Proceedings of the Convention*; Dix, *History of Trinity*, 2:110–14, 128–29; Loveland, *Critical Years*, 236–72; Minutes of the Vestry, Trinity Church Archives, October 1789.

37. Federal Census 1790; White, *Somewhat More Independent* (quotes on pp. 16, 19).

38. John Jay to Peter Jay, 23 May 1780, 1 JPM 702; John Jay to Egbert Benson, 18 September 1780, 1 JPM 822–23.

39. Minutes of the New York Manumission Society, February 1785; Edgar J. McManus, *A History of Negro Slavery in New York* (Syracuse: Syracuse University Press, 1966), 162–69; Richard S. Newman, *The Transformation of American Abolitionism: Fighting Slavery in the Early Republic* (Chapel Hill: University of North Carolina Press, 2002); Arthur Zilversmit, *The First Emancipation: The Abolition of Slavery in the North* (Chicago: University of Chicago Press), 147–48, 162–63.

40. John Jay to Richard Price, 27 September 1785, 3 JPJ 169; Street, *Council of Revision*, 258; McManus, *Negro Slavery*, 162–69; Zilversmit, *First Emancipation*, 146–50.

41. Petition to the New York Legislature, in Frank Monaghan, "Anti-Slavery Papers of John Jay," *Journal of Negro History* 17 (1932): 489–90; *New York Daily Advertiser*, 14 March 1786 (petition); Minutes of the New York Manumission Society, August 1787; Morris, *Forging*, 183; White, *Somewhat More Independent*, 79–93; Zilversmit, *First Emancipation*, 165–67.

42. Charles C. Andrews, *History of the New-York African Free-Schools* (New York: 1830); Newman, *Transformation*, 18–19; White, *Somewhat More Independent*, 81–88.

43. John Jay to Peter Augustus Jay, 17 June 1791.

44. John Jay to Anthony Benezet, 5 March 1779, 1 JPM 572; John Jay to Benjamin Rush, 24 March 1785, 3 JPJ 139–40; *Columbia Spectator*, May 3, 2004 ("ardent abolitionist"); Henry Mayer, *All on Fire: William Lloyd Garrison and the Abolition of Slavery* (New

York: St. Martin's Press, 1998); George S. Brookes, *Friend Anthony Benezet* (Philadelphia: University of Pennsylvania Press, 1937); Zilversmit, *First Emancipation*, 124–32.

45. McManus, *History of Negro Slavery*, 168–72; White, *Somewhat More Independent*, 80–87; Zilversmit, *First Emancipation*, 147, 150–51, 160.

Notes to Chapter 11: Federalist

1. John Jay to Benjamin Franklin, 13 December 1784, 22 LDC 69; John Jay to Lafayette, 19 January 1785, 3 JPJ 138; John Jay to Matthew Ridley, 31 March 1785; John Jay to John Adams, 14 October 1785, 3 JPJ 172; John Jay to Thomas Jefferson, 19 January 1786, 9 PTJ 185–86.

2. John Jay to James Lovell, 10 May 1785, 3 JPJ 142; John Jay to John Adams, 4 May 1786, 3 JPJ 194–95; John Jay to George Washington, 7 January 1787, 4 PGW 503.

3. John Jay to Thomas Jefferson, 18 August 1786, 3 EN 267; John Jay to George Washington, 7 January 1787, 4 PGW 503; John Jay to John Adams, 21 February 1787, 3 JPJ 233–35.

4. See Jillson and Wilson, *Congressional Dynamics*, 330–42; Wecter, *Saga of American Society*, 199–204.

5. John Jay to George Washington, 16 March 1786, 3 PGW 601–02; George Washington to John Jay, 18 May 1786, 4 PGW 55–56; Rakove, *Beginnings*, 369–75.

6. John Jay to George Washington, 3 February 1788, 6 PGW 80; George Washington to John Jay, 3 March 1788, 6 PGW 138; John Jay to George Washington, 20 April 1788, 6 PGW 217.

7. John Jay to George Washington, 27 June 1786, 4 PGW 130–32; George Washington to John Jay, 15 August 1786, ibid. 212–13.

8. John Jay to John Adams, 1 November 1786, 3 EN 362–63; John Jay to John Adams, 21 February 1787, 3 EN 430–31; John Jay to Thomas Jefferson, 14 December 1786, 10 PTJ 597; Richard B. Bernstein, *Are We To Be a Nation? The Making of the Constitution* (Cambridge: Harvard University Press, 1987), 92–97; Morris, *Forging*, 260–65.

9. Bernstein, *Are We To Be?*, 100–05; Richard B. Morris, *Witnesses at the Creation: Hamilton, Madison, Jay and the Constitution* (New York: Henry Holt and Co., 1985), 165–69.

10. John Jay to George Washington, 7 January 1787, 4 PGW 502–04. On the question of a King, see Matson and Onuf, *Union of Interests*, 86–89.

11. Motion and Remarks, 16 April 1787, 4 PAH 147–48; John P. Kaminski, "New York: The Reluctant Pillar," in Stephen L. Schecter, ed., *The Reluctant Pillar: New York and the Adoption of the Federal Constitution* (Albany: New York State Commission on the Bicentennial of the United States Constitution, 1985), 59–60.

12. Report on State Laws, 13 October 1786, 3 EN 334–35; Resolutions re: State Laws, 21 March 1787, 3 EN 454–55; Arthur St. Clair to the State Governors, 13 April 1787, 3 EN 472–77; *Pennsylvania Gazette*, 2 May 1787; U.S. Constitution, art. VI.

13. John Jay to George Washington, 25 July 1787, 5 PGW 271–72; U.S. Constitution, art. II, sec. 1, cl. 4.

14. John Jay to John Adams, 4 July 1787, 3 JPJ 248; John Jay to Thomas Jefferson, 8 September 1787, 12 PTJ 105–06; Kaminski, "Reluctant Pillar," 66–68.

15. Bernstein, *Are We To Be?*, 199–242; Robert A. Rutland, *The Ordeal of the Constitution: The Antifederalists and the Ratification Struggle of 1787–1788* (Norman: University of Oklahoma Press, 1963).

16. John Jay to John Adams, 16 October 1787, 3 JPJ 258; John Jay to Thomas Jefferson, 24 October 1787, 12 PTJ 265–66.

17. Sarah Jay Dinner List, 22 October 1787, Jay Homestead; Douglas Adair, "The Authorship of the Disputed Federalist Papers," in *Fame and the Founding Fathers: Essays by Douglas Adair*, ed. Trevor Colbourn (Indianapolis: Liberty Fund, 1998); Lance Banning, *The Sacred Fire of Liberty: James Madison and the Founding of the American Republic* (Ithaca: Cornell University Press, 1995); Richard Brookhiser, *Alexander Hamilton: American* (New York: Free Press, 1999), 68–70; Jensen et al., eds., *The Documentary History of the Ratification of the Constitution*, 17 vols. to date (Madison: State Historical Society of Wisconsin, 1973–), 13:486–90.

18. John Jay, *Federalist* 2, Jacob E. Cooke, ed., *The Federalist* (Middletown: Wesleyan University Press, 1961), 8–9; Robert A. Ferguson, "The Forgotten Publius: John Jay and the Aesthetics of Ratification," *Early American Literature* 34 (1999): 223–40.

19. John Jay, *Federalist* 2, Cooke, ed., *Federalist*.

20. John Jay, *Federalist* 3, ibid. 15–17.

21. John Jay, *Federalist* 4, ibid. 20–23.

22. John Jay, *Federalist* 5, ibid. 24–27.

23. John Jay to George Washington, 3 February 1788, 6 PGW 81.

24. Philadelphia *Independent Gazetteer*, 24 November 1787; John Jay to John Vaughan, 1 December 1787, Jensen et al., eds., *Documentary History of Ratification*, 14:208–09.

25. John Jay to George Washington, 3 February 1788, 6 PGW 79–80; George Washington to John Jay, 3 March 1788, ibid. 139–40.

26. John Jay, *Federalist* 64, Cooke, ed., *Federalist*, 434–35.

27. Ibid. 435–37; Shakespeare, *Julius Ceasar*, act IV.

28. Sarah Jay to Susannah Livingston, 17 April 1788; Burrows and Wallace, *Gotham*, 386–87; Paul A. Gilje, *The Road to Mobocracy: Popular Disorder in New York City, 1763–1834* (Chapel Hill: University of North Carolina Press, 1987), 78–81; Kaminski, *Clinton*, 109–11; Monaghan, *John Jay*, 290–91; Pomerantz, *New York*, 401–02.

29. An Address to the People of the State of New York, 15 April 1788, Jensen et al., eds., *Documentary History of Ratification*, 17:106–20.

30. Samuel B. Webb to Joseph Barrell, 27 April 1788, ibid. 103; William Bingham to Tench Coxe, 30 May 1788, ibid. 103; John Vaughan to John Jay, June 1788, ibid. 102; John Jay to John Vaughan, 27 June 1788, ibid. 102; George Washington to John Jay, 15 May 1788, 6 PGW 275–76; Bernstein, *Are We To Be?*, 221; Linda G. DePauw, *The Eleventh Pillar: New York State and the Federal Constitution* (Ithaca: Cornell University Press, 1966), 114–17; Ferguson, "Forgotten Publius"; Kaminski, "Reluctant Pillar," 72.

31. John Jay to George Washington, 20 April 1788 and 29 May 1788, 6 PGW 217, 303–04; Kaminski, "Reluctant Pillar," 77–80.

32. Kaminski, "Reluctant Pillar," 79–80.

33. Burrows and Wallace, *Gotham*, 291; DePauw, *Eleventh Pillar*, 187–88; Edmund Platt, *The Eagle's History of Poughkeepsie* (Poughkeepsie: Platt and Platt, 1905), 56–57.

34. DePauw, *Eleventh Pillar*, 187–88; Burrows and Wallace, *Gotham*, 291.

35. Kaminski, "Reluctant Pillar," 100.

36. *New York Daily Advertiser*, 28 June 1788; Richard B. Morris, "John Jay and the Adoption of the Federal Constitution in New York: A New Reading of Persons and Events," *New York History* 63 (1982): 151.

37. Alexander Hamilton to James Madison, 19 June 1788, 5 PAH 10; John Jay to Sarah Jay, 21 June 1788; Charles Tillinghast to James Lamb, 21 June 1788, Documentary History of Ratification Files; DePauw, *Eleventh Pillar*, 190.

38. Jonathan Elliot, ed., *The Debates in the Several States on the Adoption of the Federal Constitution*, 2 vols. (Philadelphia, 1876), 2:282–86.

39. Kaminski, "Reluctant Pillar," 105; Elliot, *Debates*, 2:325–27.

40. John Jay to George Washington, June 1788, 6 PGW 367–68.

41. Elliot, *Debates*, 2:380–81; Morris, "Adoption," 154.

42. *New York Daily Advertiser*, 7 July 1788; DePauw, *Eleventh Pillar*, 214–16; Kaminski, "Reluctant Pillar," 107.

43. John Jay to Sarah Jay, 5 July 1788, 3 JPJ 347–48; DePauw, *Eleventh Pillar*, 219; Kaminski, "Reluctant Pillar," 107.

44. John Jay to George Washington, 4–8 July 1788, 6 PGW 371–72.

45. *New York Daily Advertiser*, 15 July 1988; Morris, "Adoption," 156; Kaminski, "Reluctant Pillar," 108; DePauw, *Eleventh Pillar*, 219–20.

46. Proposed Amendments, 15 July 1788, 5 PAH 167–70; Notes of Gilbert Livingston, 15 July 1788, New York Public Library; Elliot, *Debates*, 2:410–11; Morris, "Adoption," 157; Kaminski, "Reluctant Pillar," 108.

47. Morris, "Adoption," 158–59; DePauw, *Eleventh Pillar*, 222–23.

48. Gilbert Livingston Notes, 16–17 July 1788.

49. Gilbert Livingston Notes, 18 July 1788; John Jay to George Washington, 17–18 July 1788, 6 PGW 383–84; DePauw, *Eleventh Pillar*, 224–27; Kaminski, "Reluctant Pillar," 108–09, 159.

50. Gilbert Livingston Notes, 19 July 1788.

51. Gilbert Livingston Notes, 19–23 July 1788; Morris, "Adoption," 160–61.

52. DePauw, *Eleventh Pillar*, 247; Kaminski, "Reluctant Pillar," 111; Kaminski, *Clinton*, 163–64; Abraham Lansing to Abraham Yates, 20 July 1788, Documentary History of Ratification Files; John Jay to George Washington, 23 July 1788, 6 PGW 394.

53. Morris, "Adoption," 161; Kaminski, "Reluctant Pillar," 112–13; DePauw, *Eleventh Pillar*, 243–45.

54. Gilbert Livingston Notes, 24 July 1788; Alexander Hamilton, Speech, 24 July 1788, 5 PAH 193–94; James Madison to Alexander Hamilton, 20 July 1788, 5 PAH 185.

55. Gilbert Livingston Notes, 25 July 1788; DePauw, *Eleventh Pillar*, 245; Kaminski, "Reluctant Pillar," 112–13.

56. Letter to the States, 26 July 1788, Elliot, *Debates*, 2:413–14; Kaminski, "Reluctant Pillar," 114.

57. Charles Tillinghast to James Lamb, 21 June 1788, Documentary History of Ratification Files; Alexander Hamilton to James Madison, 2 July 1788, 5 PAH 140; Kaminski, "Reluctant Pillar," 112–15; William Rhoads, "The President and the Sesquicentennial of the Constitution: Franklin Roosevelt's Monument in Poughkeepsie," *New York History* 90 (1990): 318–19.

58. George Washington to John Jay, 3 August 1788, 6 PGW 419–20.

59. James Madison to George Washington, 11 August 1788, ibid. 437–38; Bernstein, *Are We To Be?*, 261–72.

60. John Jay to George Washington, 21 September 1788, 6 PGW 527–28.

61. Alexander Hamilton to Richard Varick, 31 December 1788, 5 PAH 240; Note, 15 DHFFC 26–31; Kenneth R. Bowling, *Peter Charles L'Enfant: Vision, Honor and Male Friendship in the Early American Republic* (Washington: Friends of the George Washington Libraries, 2002), 14–20; Smith, *City of New York*, 40–44.

62. James Madison to Thomas Jefferson, 8 October 1788, William T. Hutchinson et al., eds., *Papers of James Madison*, 30 vols. to date (Chicago: University of Chicago Press, 1962–), 11:276–77; James Madison to George Washington, 5 November 1788, ibid. 334–35; Tench Coxe to James Madison, 27 January 1789, ibid. 431–33; Abigail Adams to John Adams, 15 December 1788, quoted in Page Smith, *John Adams*, 2 vols. (Garden City: Doubleday, 1962), 2:742; Senate Journal, 6 April 1789, 1 DHFFC 1–9; Young, *Democratic Republicans*, 124–28.

63. John Jay to George Washington, 14 and 17 April 1789, 2 PGW 53–54, 66; Comte de Moustier Diary, 20 April 1789, 15 DHFFC 302; John Adams to Abigail Adams, 22 April 1789, ibid. 322.

64. Richard B. Bernstein, "The Inauguration of George Washington," in Stephen L. Schecter and Richard B. Bernstein, eds., *Well Begun: Chronicles of the Early National Period* (Albany: New York State Commission on the Bicentennial of the United States Constitution, 1989), 45–51; Burrows and Wallace, *Gotham*, 296–98; James T. Flexner, *George Washington and the New Nation* (Boston: Little Brown and Co., 1970), 185–91; Monaghan and Lowenthal, *This Was New York*, 263–81.

65. William Maclay Journal, April 30, 1789, 9 DHFFC 13; Smith, *City of New York*, 234–35; Monaghan and Lowenthal, *This Was New York*, 263–81.

66. Adams, *Works of John Adams*, 10:115.

Notes to Chapter 12: First Chief Justice

1. John Adams to Benjamin Rush, 17 May 1789, 15 DHFFC 574; James Madison to Thomas Jefferson, 27 May 1789, 15 PTJ 153; Comte de Moustier to Comte de Montmorin, 29 June 1789, 16 DHFFC 882; John Jay to Charles Pettit, 15 July 1789; Francis Dana to John Adams, 31 July 1789, 16 DHFFC 1182; Comte de Moustier to Comte de Montmorin, 9 September 1789, 17 DHFFC 1493.

2. George Washington to James Madison, 9 August 1789, 3 PGW 405; John Jay to

Thomas Jefferson, 12 December 1789, 16 PTJ 20; Elkins and McKitrick, *Age of Federalism*, 50–55; Ferling, *First of Men*, 378–81; Miller, *Federalist Era*, 30–34.

3. James Madison to Thomas Jefferson, 27 May 1789, 15 PTJ 153; George Washington to Edmund Randolph, 28 September 1789, 4 PGW 95; George Washington to John Jay, 5 October 1789, 4 PGW 137; Casto, *Supreme Court*, 54–70; Charles Warren, *The Supreme Court in United States History*, 2 vols. (Boston: Little, Brown, 1926), 1:33–36; James R. Perry, "Supreme Court Appointments, 1789–1801: Criteria, Presidential Style, and the Press of Events," *Journal of the Early Republic* 6 (Winter 1986), 371–410.

4. Warren, *Supreme Court*, 1:46–47. Warren states that these robes reflect an honorary degree from Dublin; others that they reflect his honorary degree from Harvard. Carrie Barratt and Ellen Miles, *Gilbert Stuart* (New York: Metroplitan Museum, 2004).

5. Warren, *Supreme Court*, 1:50–51.

6. Dwight F. Henderson, *Courts for a New Nation* (Washington: Public Affairs Press, 1971), 88; Note, 2 DHSC 2–3.

7. Henderson, *Courts*, 27–34, 51–54; Julius D. Goebel, *History of the Supreme Court: Volume 1, Antecedents and Beginnings to 1801* (New York: Macmillan Co., 1971), 569–89. On halls and taverns, see 2 DHSC 102–03, 136, 154.

8. John Jay to Edward Rutledge, 16 November 1789, 2 DHSC 10; George Washington to the Justices, 3 April 1790, 2 DHSC 21; John Hancock to John Jay, 31 March 1790, 2 DHSC 19; John Jay to John Hancock, 20 April 1790, 2 DHSC 48.

9. John Jay, Charge to the Grand Jury, 12 April 1790, 2 DHSC 25–26; William R. Casto, *The Supreme Court in the Early Republic: The Chief Justiceships of John Jay and Oliver Ellsworth* (Columbia: University of South Carolina Press, 1995), 126–29; Ralph Lerner, "The Supreme Court as Republican Schoolmaster," *Supreme Court Review* (1967) 127.

10. 2 DHSC 26–28.

11. Ibid. 27–30.

12. Ibid. 31.

13. Note, 2 DHSC 8; Casto, *Supreme Court*, 129–30.

14. Jay Diary, April 1790, 2 DHSC 47–51.

15. Jay Diary, April-May 1790, 2 DHSC 54–55; Reply of the Grand Jury, 4 May 1790, 2 DHSC 61.

16. Jay Diary, May 1790; John Jay to Sarah Jay, 6 May 1790, 2 DHSC 61–62; Joshua Loring to Jonathan Palfrey, 13 May 1790, 2 DHSC 67; Christopher Gore to Rufus King, 15 May 1790, 2 DHSC 67–68.

17. John Blair to John Jay, 5 August 1790, 2 DHSC 84; Sarah Jay to Catharine Ridley, 8 August 1790, 2 DHSC 86; Wythe Holt, "'The Federal Courts Have Enemies in All Who Fear Their Influence on State Objects': The Failure to Abolish Supreme Court Circuit-Riding in the Judiciary Acts of 1792 and 1793," *Buffalo Law Review* 36 (1987): 312–14.

18. John Jay Draft Letter, 13 September 1790, 2 DHSC 89–91; John Jay to William Cushing, 13 September 1790, 2 DHSC 88; John Jay to George Washington, 13 November 1790, 2 DHSC 108.

19. Jay Diary, September-October 1790; *Pennsylvania Packet*, 19 October 1790, 2 DHSC 99; *Connecticut Courant* (Hartford), 25 October 1790, 2 DHSC 102.

20. Jay Diary, 27 October and 1 November 1790, 2 DHSC 105; *Independent Chronicle* (Boston), 4 November 1790, 2 DHSC 105; John Jay to George Washington, 13 November 1790, 2 DHSC 107–10; Joseph Willard to John Jay, 3 November 1790; Henry Jackson to Henry Knox, 7 November 1790, 2 DHSC 106; John Jay to Sarah Jay, 10 November 1790.

21. Alexander Hamilton to John Jay, 13 November 1790, 7 PAH 149–50; John Jay to Alexander Hamilton, 28 November 1790, 7 PAH 166–67; Elkins and McKitrick, *Age of Federalism*, 133–61.

22. *Providence Gazette*, 11 December 1790, 2 DHSC 115–16.

23. John Jay to Catharine Ridley, 1 February 1791, 2 DHSC 126; James Iredell to John Jay et al., 11 February 1791, 2 DHSC 131–35; John Jay to James Iredell, 12 February 1791, 2 DHSC 135–36; William Cushing to Theodore Sedgwick, 21 February 1791, 2 DHSC 139–40; John Jay to Iredell, 16 March 1791, 2 DHSC 154; Holt, "Federal Courts," 317–18.

24. Sarah Jay to Maria Jay, 23 April 1791; John Jay to Peter Jay Munro, 19 May 1791; John Jay to Peter Jay Munro, 20 June 1791.

25. *Connecticut Courant*, 9 May 1791, quoted in Warren, *Supreme Court*, 65–66; Scott D. Gerber, "Deconstructing William Cushing," in Scott D. Gerber, ed., *Seriatim: The Supreme Court before John Marshall* (New York: NYU Press, 1998).

26. *General Advertiser* (New Haven), 4 May 1791, 2 DHSC 160–61; *Columbian Centinel* (Boston), 14 May 1791, 2 DHSC 164–65.

27. *Newport Mercury*, 25 June 1791, 2 DHSC 195; Notes, 2 DHSC 192–94; John Jay Diary, June–July 1792.

28. Warren, *Supreme Court*, 56; Holt, "Federal Courts," 318–19.

29. John Jay to Peter A. Jay, 29 October and 12 November 1791; Peter A. Jay to John Jay, 23 November 1791; John Jay to Peter A. Jay, 29 November 1791.

30. *Dunlap's American Daily Advertiser*, 14 November 1791, 2 DHSC 226; *Columbian Centinel*, 16 November 1791, 2 DHSC 231–32; Notes, 2 DHSC 213, 229, 232 and 234.

31. James Duane to Walter Livingston, 8 January 1792 (misdated 1791 in Columbia index); John Jay to J. C. Dongan, 27 February 1792, 3 JPJ 413–14; William Loughton Smith to Edward Rutledge, February 1792, 1 DHSC 732; Benjamin Bourne to William Channing, 21 February 1793, 1 DHSC 733; Egbert Benson to Rufus King, 18 December 1793, in C. R. King, ed., *The Life and Correspondence of Rufus King*, 6 vols. (New York: 1894), 1:506–07.

32. Alan L. Blau, "New York City and the French Revolution, 1789–1797: A Study of French Revolutionary Influence" (Ph.D. diss., City University of New York, 1973), 54–55, 66–70, 88–91, 281–82; Elkins and McKitrick, *Age of Federalism*, 257–302; Young, *Democratic Republicans*, 227–80.

33. Blau, "French Revolution," 67–70; Kaminski, *Clinton*, 208–11; Young, *Democratic Republicans*, 287–88.

34. J. C. Dongan to John Jay, February 1792, 3 JPJ 413; John Jay to J. C. Dongan, 27 February 1792, 3 JPJ 414; Kaminski, *Clinton*, 204–06.

35. Kaminski, *Clinton*, 195–97; Taylor, *Cooper's Town*, 170–73; Young, *Democratic Republicans*, 293–98.

36. Blau, "French Revolution," 64–68; Burrows and Wallace, *Gotham*, 307–10; Young, *Democratic Republicans*, 298–99; Robert F. Jones, *"The King of the Alley:" William Duer, Politician, Entrepreneur and Speculator, 1768–1799* (Philadelphia: American Philosophical Society, 1992), 170–84, 200–01.

37. *New-York Journal*, 31 March 1792; *New-York Journal*, 4 April 1792; John Jay to the Public, April 1792, 3 JPJ 415–16; Dangerfield, *Livingston*, 256–61; Young, *Democratic Republicans*, 291–93.

38. John Jay Diary, April 1792; John Jay to Peter A. Jay, 25 April 1792, 3 JPJ 421.

39. N.Y.Laws, 10th Sess., Chap. 15; Mary-Jo Kline, ed., *Political Correspondence and Public Papers of Aaron Burr*, 2 vols. (Princeton: Princeton University Press, 1983), 1:106.

40. Robert Troup to John Jay, 6 and 20 May 1792, 3 JPJ 423–24; Kline, *Burr Papers*, 1:106–08; Young, *Democratic Republicans*, 305–10; Taylor, *Cooper's Town*, 171–76.

41. Robert Troup to John Jay, 10 June 1792, 3 JPJ 426–30; Sarah Jay to John Jay, 10–12 June 1792, 3 JPJ 431–33; Young, *Democratic Republicans*, 307–09.

42. John Jay to Sarah Jay, 18 June 1792, 3 JPJ 434–35; Thomas Jefferson to James Madison, 21 June 1792, 23 PTJ 105; Thomas Jefferson to James Monroe, 23 June 1792, 23 PTJ 114; Alexander Hamilton to Rufus King, 28 June 1792, 11 PAH 588–89; Elkins and McKitrick, *Age of Federalism*, 288–89.

43. John Jay to the People of Lansingburgh, 3 JPJ 437; *New-York Journal*, 7 July 1792; Rufus King to Alexander Hamilton, 10 July 1792, 12 PAH 20–21; *Daily Advertiser*, 11 July 1792, 3 JPJ 441.

44. Taylor, *Cooper's Town*, 181.

45. Rufus King to Alexander Hamilton, 10 July 1792, 12 PAH 20–21; Alexander Hamilton to Rufus King, 25 July 1792, 12 PAH 99–100; Rufus King to Alexander Hamilton, 29 July 1792, 12 PAH 125–26; Young, *Democratic Republicans*, 313–23; Taylor, *Cooper's Town*, 180–98.

46. James Iredell to John Jay, 17 January 1792, 2 DHSC 238–39; John Jay to George Washington, 27 January 1792; Catharine Ridley to John Jay, 7 February 1792; James Iredell to John Jay, 16 February 1792, 2 DHSC 239; John Jay to James Iredell, 3 March 1792, 2 DHSC 243; John Jay to James Iredell, 19 March 1792, 2 DHSC 249; Holt, "Federal Courts," 328–30.

47. 1 Stat. 243; Note, 2 DHSC 235.

48. Notes, 6 DHSC 33–34, 372.

49. Minutes of the Circuit Court, 5 April 1792, 6 DHSC 370–71; Casto, *Supreme Court*, 176; Maeva Marcus and Robert Teir, "Hayburn's Case: A Misinterpretation of Precedent," *Wisconsin Law Review* (1988): 527–46; Scott, "Deconstructing William Cushing." 114.

50. Proceedings of the Commissioners, 3 May 1792, 6 DHSC 373–74.

51. Judiciary Act of 1792, 1 Stat. 252–53; Holt, "Federal Courts," 330; John Jay to Sarah Jay, 24–25 April 1792, 2 DHSC 261.

52. Goebel, *Supreme Court*, 589; *Crosby v. National Foreign Trade Council*, 530 U.S. 363 (2000); *Cohens v. Virginia*, 19 U.S. 264 (1821).

53. John Jay to Sarah Jay, 18 June 1792, 3 JPJ 434–35; John Jay, Charge to the Grand Jury, 25 June 1792, 2 DHSC 282–86; *Herald of Vermont*, 2 July 1792, 2 DHSC 286.

54. Note, 6 DHSC 35–38; Edmund Randolph to James Madison, 12 August 1792, 6 DHSC 67–68; David P. Currie, "The Constitution in the Supreme Court, 1789–1801," *University of Chicago Law Review* 48 (1981): 823.

55. Edmund Randolph to James Madison, 12 August 1792, 6 DHSC 67–68.

56. Justices of the Supreme Court to George Washington, 9 August 1792, 2 DHSC 288–89; Justices of the Supreme Court to Congress, 9 August 1792, 2 DHSC 289–90; Note, 2 DHSC 292.

57. John Jay to Alexander Hamilton, 28 September 1792, 2 DHSC 301; William Cushing to John Jay, 23 October 1792, 2 DHSC 319–20; John Jay to William Cushing, 27 October 1792, 2 DHSC 325.

58. Richard B. Morris, *John Jay, the Nation, and the Court* (Boston: Boston University Press, 1967), 49–50.

59. *Chisholm v. Georgia*, 2 U.S. 419, 421–27 (1793); Goebel, *Supreme Court*, 728.

60. See Casto, *Supreme Court*, 110–12; Goebel, *Supreme Court*, 728; 777–78; Smith, *Marshall*, 293, 448.

61. *Chisholm v. Georgia*, 2 U.S. 419 (1793).

62. Ibid. 471–72.

63. Ibid. 470–73.

64. Ibid. 476.

65. Alexander Hamilton, *Federalist* 81; Akhil Reed Amar, "Of Sovereignty and Freedom," *Yale Law Journal* 96 (June 1987): 1425.

66. 5 DHSC 444–45, 607–08; William A. Fletcher, "A Historical Interpretation of the Eleventh Amendment: A Narrow Construction of an Affirmative Grant of Jurisdiction Rather than a Prohibition Against Jurisdiction," *Stanford Law Review* 35 (July 1983): 1058; Monaghan, *John Jay*, 308–09; Richard Norton Smith, *Patriarch: George Washington and the New American State* (Boston: Houghton Mifflin, 1993), 205.

67. Fletcher, "Historical Interpretation," 1058–63.

68. Charles F. Hobson, "The Recovery of British Debts in the Federal Circuit Court of Virginia, 1790 to 1797," *Virginia Magazine of History and Biography* 92 (1984):176–79; Smith, *Marshall*, 575 n. 47.

69. Hobson, "Recovery," 185–88.

70. George Washington to John Jay, 12 May 1793, 2 DHSC 376; James Iredell to Hannah Iredell, 16 May and 20 May 1793, 2 DHSC 378–80; John Jay Charge to the Grand Jury, 22 May 1793, 2 DHSC 380–90; Kenneth R. Bowling, *The Creation of Washington, D.C.* (Fairfax: George Mason University Press, 1991), 228–29.

71. Henry Mayer, *A Son of Thunder: Patrick Henry and the American Republic* (New York: Franklin Watts, 1986), 464–65; William Wirt, *The Life of Patrick Henry* (New York: 1846), 341–43; Charles F. Hobson, ed., *The Papers of John Marshall* (Chapel Hill: University of North Carolina Press, 1974), 5:300–07; Smith, *Marshall*, 157.

72. *Jones v. Walker*, 13 Fed. Cas. 1060, 1062 (1793); see *Baker v. Carr*, 369 U.S. 186 (1962) (political question doctrine).

73. *Ware v. Hylton*, 3 U.S. 256, 262–80 (1796) (circuit court opinion of Iredell); *Jones v. Walker*, 13 Fed. Cas. 1067–69 (circuit court opinion of Jay).

74. *Ware v. Hylton*, 3 U.S. 199 (1796).

75. John Jay to David Hartley, 14 December 1789, 3 JPJ 382–83; John Jay to Ferdinand Grand, 1 March 1790, 3 JPJ 386–87.

76. See Simon Schama, *Citizens: A Chronicle of the French Revolution* (New York: Alfred A. Knopf, 1989), 441–47, 619–75; Christopher Hibbert, *The Days of the French Revolution* (New York: Morrow Quill, 1980), 165–89; Samuel F. Scott and Barry Rothaus, eds., *Dictionary of the French Revolution* (Westport: Greenwood Press, 1985), 679–81.

77. *National Gazette*, 20 April 1793; Alexander Hamilton to George Washington, 2 May 1793, 14 PAH 386; John Jay to Robert G. Harper, 19 January 1796, 4 JPJ 201.

78. Elkins and McKitrick, *Age of Federalism*, 335–55; Smith, *Patriarch*, 154–77.

79. Alexander Hamilton to John Jay, 9 April 1793, 14 PAH 299–300.

80. John Jay to Alexander Hamilton, 11 April 1793, 14 PAH 307–10.

81. 1 ASPFR 140; Charles M. Thomas, *American Neutrality in 1793: A Study in Cabinet Government* (New York: Columbia University Press, 1931), 42–45.

82. George Washington to John Jay, 12 May 1793, 2 DHSC 376; James Iredell to Hannah Iredell, 16 May 1793, 2 DHSC 378; James Madison to Thomas Jefferson, 17 June 1793, Hutchinson et al., eds., *Papers of James Madison*, 15:31–32; Harry Ammon, *The Genet Mission* (New York: W. W. Norton, 1973), 4–5, 44–46, 52–53.

83. John Jay Charge to the Grand Jury, 22 May 1793, 2 DHSC 380–91.

84. Thomas Jefferson to John Jay, 12 July 1793, 2 DHSC 744; George Washington to Thomas Jefferson, 18 July 1793, 2 DHSC 745.

85. Thomas Jefferson to the Supreme Court Justices, 18 July 1793, 2 DHSC 747; Draft Questions, 18 July 1793, 2 DHSC 747–51.

86. Supreme Court Justices to George Washington, 20 July 1793, 2 DHSC 752–53; George Washington to the Supreme Court Justices, 23 July 1793, 2 DHSC 753.

87. *National Gazette*, 17 July 1793; Elkins and McKitrick, *Age of Federalism*, 343–50; Ammon, *Genet Mission*, 54–58.

88. Elkins and McKitrick, *Age of Federalism*, 350; Ammon, *Genet Mission*, 90–93.

89. Ammon, *Genet Mission*, 97.

90. Justices of the Supreme Court to George Washington, 8 August 1793, 6 DHSC 755; J. H. Powell, *Bring Out Your Dead: The Great Plague of Yellow Fever in Philadelphia in 1793* (Philadelphia: University of Pennsylvania Press, 1993 reprint).

91. Young, *Democratic Republicans*, 356–57.

92. *New York Journal*, 12 August 1793; Ammon, *Genet Mission*, p. 135.

93. Edmond Genet to George Washington, 13 August 1793, 15 PAH 234; Thomas Jefferson to Edmond Genet, 16 August 1793, 26 PTJ 684; Edmond Genet to Edmund Randolph, 14 November 1793, 15 PAH 235; Young, *Democratic Republicans*, 357–58.

94. John Jay and Rufus King, Statement, 26 November 1793, 15 PAH 236; John Jay and Rufus King to Alexander Hamilton and Henry Knox, 26 November 1793, 15 PAH 411–14; *Dunlap's American Daily Advertiser*, 9 December 1793, quoted in 15 PAH 237–28; John Jay to Rufus King, 19 December 1793, 15 PAH 238.

95. Thomas Jefferson to Edmund Randolph, 18 December 1793, 15 PAH 238; Rufus King, Statement, February 1794, 15 PAH 238.

96. Rufus King, Statement, February 1794, 15 PAH 238–39; John Adams to Thomas Jefferson, 30 June 1813, in Lester J. Cappon, ed., *The Adams-Jefferson Letters: The Complete Correspondence between Thomas Jefferson and Abigail and John Adams*, 2 vols. (Chapel Hill: University of North Carolina Press, 1959), 2:346–47.

97. Note, 6 DHSC 73–78.

98. William Bradford's Notes, 4 February 1794, 6 DHSC 158–70; Note, 6 DHSC 84–85.

99. John Jay's Charge to the Jury, 7 February 1794, 6 DHSC 86, 173.

100. *Dunlap's American Daily Advertiser*, 17 February 1794, 6 DHSC 174.

101. Note, 6 DHSC 87–88.

102. Note, 6 DHSC 301–03; Libel, 16 July 1793, 6 DHSC 314–16; Plea to Jurisdiction, 6 August 1793, 6 DHSC 320–22; District Court Opinion, 15 August 1793, 6 DHSC 324–32; *Maryland Journal*, 12 November 1793, 6 DHSC 341.

103. Notes, 6 DHSC 309, 343.

104. Decree of the Supreme Court, 18 February 1794, 6 DHSC 347–49.

105. 6 DHSC 292–95.

106. Proceedings of the Supreme Court, 15 February 1794, 6 DHSC 377–80.

107. Robert C. Bradley, "Who Are the Great Justices and What Criteria Did They Meet?," in William D. Pederson and Norman W. Provizer, eds., *Great Justices of the U.S. Supreme Court* (New York: Peter Lang, 1992), 19–31; Casto, *Supreme Court*, 247–53; Scott D. Gerber, "The Supreme Court before John Marshall," in Gerber, ed., *Seriatim*; Robert G. McCloskey, *The American Supreme Court* (Chicago: University of Chicago Press, 1960), 30.

Notes to Chapter 13: Envoy to England

1. James Madison to Thomas Jefferson, 12 March 1794, Hutchinson et al., eds., *Papers of James Madison*, 15:278; *Gazette of the United States*, 26 March 1794; Elkins and McKitrick, *Age of Federalism*, 388–95; Bemis, *Jay's Treaty*, 239–40, 266–67.

2. Alexander Hamilton to George Washington, 8 March 1794, 16 PAH 134–36; James Madison to Thomas Jefferson, 12 March 1794, Hutchinson et al., eds., *Papers of James Madison*, 15:278–79; James Madison to Horatio Gates, 24 March 1794, ibid. 287; John Jay to Rufus King, 22 March 1794, in King, ed., *Rufus King*, 1:555–56.

3. Thomas Pinckney to Edmund Randolph, 9 January 1794, 1 ASPFR 430–31; John Jay to Sarah Jay, 9 April 1794, 4 JPJ 2–3; Elkins and McKitrick, *Age of Federalism*, 392–94.

4. King, ed., *Rufus King*, 1:519; Alexander Hamilton to George Washington, 14 April 1794, 16 PAH 266–79.

5. George Washington to John Jay, 15 April 1794, Fitzpatrick, ed., *Writings of Washington* 33:329; King, ed., *Rufus King*, 1:520.

6. John Jay to Sarah Jay, 15 April 1794, 4 JPJ 3–5.

7. U.S. Constitution, Article I, section VI, clause 2.

8. John Jay to Sarah Jay, 15 April 1794, 4 JPJ 5; James Madison to Thomas Jefferson, 28 April 1794, Hutchison et al., eds., *Madison Papers*, 15:315–16; John Jay to George Washington, 30 April 1794, 4 JPJ 9–10; John Jay to Richard Henry Lee, 11 July 1795, 4 JPJ 178–79; John Jay to Edmund Randolph, 20 August 1795, 4 JPJ 186.

9. James Madison, Notes, 5 May 1792, Hutchison et al., eds., *Madison Papers*, 14:302–03; John Adams to Abigail Adams, 19 April 1794, quoted in Smith, *Adams*, 2:859; Edmund Randolph to George Washington, 28 April 1794, Washington Papers, Library of Congress; George Washington to John Jay, 29 April 1794, Fitzpatrick, ed., *Writings of Washington*, 33:345–46; John Jay to George Washington, 30 April 1794, 4 JPJ 9–10; Alexander Hamilton, *The Defense* No. 1, 22 July 1795, 16 PAH 482.

10. George Washington to the Senate, 16 April 1794, Fitzpatrick, ed., *Writings of Washington*, 33:32–33; King, ed., *Rufus King*, 1:521–22; Kline, ed., *Burr Papers*, 1:177–78; Senate Executive Journal, 19 April 1794; Harry Ammon, *James Monroe: The Quest for National Identity* (New York: McGraw Hill, 1971), 110–13.

11. Sarah Jay to John Jay, 18 April 1794; John Jay to Sarah Jay, 20 April 1794; John Trumbull to John Jay, 21 April 1794; Sarah Jay to John Jay, 22 April 1794; Peter Jay Munro to John Jay, 22 April 1794; Samuel Bayard to Alexander Hamilton, 23 April 1794, 16 PAH 314.

12. King, ed., *Rufus King*, 1:523; Elkins and McKitrick, *Age of Federalism*, 55–58, 396–97.

13. Alexander Hamilton to George Washington, 23 April 1794, 16 PAH 319–23; Alexander Hamilton to John Jay, 6 May 1794, 16 PAH 381; Edmund Randolph to John Jay, 6 May 1794, 4 JPJ 9–21.

14. There is no surviving letter from Jay to Washington about Stuart, but the painter's daughter stated that it was Jay who made the introduction, and historians have accepted this. Evans, *Genius of Gilbert Stuart*, 53–60; Charles M. Mount, *Gilbert Stuart: A Biography* (New York: W. W. Norton, 1964), 167–73.

15. Robert R. Livingston to John Jay, 11 May 1794; John Jay to Robert R. Livingston, 11 May 1794; Dangerfield, *Chancellor Livingston*, 237–45, 264–68; Monaghan, *John Jay*, 304–05; Young, *Democratic Republicans*, 385–86, 571.

16. *New-York Daily Gazette*, 12 May 1794; *American Minerva*, 12 May 1794; *New-York Daily Gazette*, 13 May 1794; *Gazette of the United States*, 14 May 1794.

17. *General Advertiser* (Philadelphia), 10 May 1794; John Jay to Sarah Jay, 12 May 1794, 4 JPJ 21–22; *New York Journal*, 14 May 1794, *Columbian Gazetteer*, 15 May 1794, quoted in Blau, "French Revolution," 346–48; Young, *Democratic Republicans*, 386.

18. Peter A. Jay to Sarah Jay, 13 May 1794 (two letters); Peter A. Jay Diary, 8 June 1794.

19. Peter A. Jay Diary, June 1794.

20. Peter A. Jay Diary, June 1794; F. H. W. Sheppard, ed., *Survey of London: Parish of St. James Westminster, Part One, South of Piccadilly* (London: Athlone Press, 1960), 352.

21. John Jay to Sarah Jay, 16 August 1794; Hibbert, *Days of the French Revolution*, 244–48; R. R. Palmer, *Twelve Who Ruled: The Year of the Terror in the French Revolution* (Princeton: Princeton University Press, 1970), 364–70; Schama, *Citizens*, 830–39.

22. *Times* (London), June 1794; Peter A. Jay to Peter Munro, 22 June 1794; Schama, *Citizens*, 839; Scott and Rothaus, eds., *Dictionary of the French Revolution*, 75–76.

23. John Ehrman, *The Younger Pitt: The Reluctant Transition* (Stanford: Stanford University Press, 1983), 387–402; Frank O'Gorman, "Pitt and the Tory Reaction to the French Revolution, 1789–1815," in H. T. Dickinson, ed., *Britain and the French Revolution, 1789–1815* (New York: St. Martin's Press, 1985).

24. Peter Jupp, *Lord Grenville, 1759–1834* (Oxford: Oxford University Press, 1985).

25. Lord Auckland to Lord Grenville, 22 June 1794, in Historical Records Commission, *The Manuscripts of J. B. Fortescue, Esq., Preserved at Dropmore*, 3 vols. (London: 1892–99), 2:578.

26. John Jay to Edmund Randolph, 23 June and 6 July 1794, 1 ASPFR 476–77; John Jay to Alexander Hamilton, 11 July 1794, 4 JPJ 29–30; John Jay to George Washington, 21 July 1794, 4 JPJ 33–34; Peter A. Jay Diary, June-September 1794.

27. John Jay to Edmund Randolph, 6 July 1794, 1 ASPFR 476–78.

28. *Times* (London), 8 and 11 July 1794; John Jay to Edmund Randolph, 12 and 16 July 1794, 1 ASPFR 479–80.

29. John Jay to Lord Grenville, 30 July 1794, 1 ASPFR 481.

30. Lord Grenville to John Jay, 31 July 1794, ibid. 481–82.

31. John Jay Draft Treaty, 6 August 1794, ibid. 486.

32. Ibid. 486–87.

33. Ibid.; Elkins and McKitrick, *Age of Federalism*, 412–13.

34. John Jay to Lord Grenville, 16 August 1794; Lord Grenville to John Jay, 17 August 1794; Jupp, *Grenville*, 161–63; Elkins and McKitrick, *Age of Federalism*, 401–03.

35. Lord Grenville Draft Treaty, 30 August 1794, 1 ASPFR 487–89.

36. Lord Grenville Draft Commercial Treaty, 30 August 1794, 1 ASPFR 489–90.

37. John Jay to Lord Grenville, 1 and 4 September 1794, 1 ASPFR 490–91; Lord Grenville to John Jay, 5 September 1794, 1 ASPFR 492; Bemis, *Jay's Treaty*, 330–31; Jerald A. Combs, *The Jay Treaty: Political Battleground of the Founding Fathers* (Berkeley: University of California Press, 1970), 156.

38. John Jay Notes, 6 September 1794, 1 ASPFR 492.

39. Lord Grenville to John Jay, 7 September 1794; John Jay to Lord Grenville, 7 September 1794; John Jay to George Washington, 13 September 1794, 4 JPJ 38–39; John Jay to Edmund Randolph, 13 September 1794; Elkins and McKitrick, *Age of Federalism*, 409–10, 499.

40. See Bemis, *Jay's Treaty*, 392–93, 395–400, 417, 454, 458–59, 469–71 (compares draft with final); Elkins and McKitrick, *Age of Federalism*, 412–14.

41. Bemis, *Jay's Treaty*, 394–95, 418–30, 474–78; Elkins and McKitrick, *Age of Federalism*, 410.

42. Lord Grenville to John Jay, 7 October 1794, in Historical Manuscript Commission, *Fortescue Manuscripts*, 3:516.

43. Allan Nevins, ed., *The Diary of John Quincy Adams, 1794–1845* (New York: Longmans, Green, 1928), 5–7.

44. John Jay to Oliver Ellsworth, 19 November 1794, 4 JPJ 133; John Jay to Alexander Hamilton, 19 November 1794, 4 JPJ 135; John Jay to Edmund Randolph, 19

November 1794, 4 JPJ 138; John Jay to Lord Grenville, 22 November 1794, 4 JPJ 147; Bemis, *Jay's Treaty*, 344–45; Elkins and McKitrick, *Age of Federalism*, 410; Monaghan, *John Jay*, 378–81.

45. Peter A. Jay Diary, June-September 1794; John Jay to Judge Hobart, 12 August 1794, 4 JPJ 46–49; Monaghan, *John Jay*, 385.

46. Brookhiser, *Hamilton*, 45–49; University of Virginia Library, *Muse and Confidante: Angelica Schuyler Church* (online exhibit); Helene C. Phelan, *The Man Who Owned the Pistols: John Barker Church and his Family* (Almond, New York: 1981); Peter A. Jay Diary, 29 June 1794 and 7 February 1795. Jay's great-grandfather, Oloff Stevense Van Cortlandt, was also the great-great-grandfather of Angelica Schuyler Church. De Forest, *The Van Cortlandt Family*.

47. John Jay to Thomas Pinckney, 31 August 1794; Peter A. Jay Diary, 25 August 1794 and 7 and 23 February 1795; John Jay to Yranda, 7 April 1795; Bemis, *Pinckney's Treaty*, 245–50; Garraty and Carnes, eds., *American National Biography* 17:539–40.

48. John Jay to George Washington, 11 August 1794; John Jay to James Monroe, 28 August 1794, 4 JPJ 53–54; John Jay to Peter Jay Munro, 14 September 1794; John Jay to Alexander Hamilton, 17 September 1794, 17 PAH 240; John Jay to John Langdon, 17 September 1794; Ammon, *Monroe*, 142–44.

49. John Jay to Sarah Jay, 21 June, 2, 6, 17 and 18 July, 13 and 16 August 1794; Sarah Jay to John Jay, 2 August 1794, 15 November 1794 and 5 December 1794; Mount, *Gilbert Stuart*, 178–85.

50. John Jay to Alexander Hamilton, 19 November 1794, 4 JPJ 135; John Jay to Sarah Jay, 3 February 1795; Peter A. Jay Diary, January-February 1795.

51. John Jay to Sarah Jay, 6 March 1795; Peter A. Jay to Sarah Jay, 7 March 1795.

52. Bemis, *Pinckney's Treaty*, 227–29, 284–93; Elkins and McKitrick, *Age of Federalism*, 439–40.

53. John Jay to Lord Grenville, 15 March 1795, in Historical Records Commission, *Fortescue Manuscripts*, 3:34; King George III to Lord Grenville, 8 April 1795, ibid. 49; John Jay to Lord Grenville, 31 March 1795; John Jay to Edmund Randolph, 28 May 1795, 1 ASPFR 519; Monaghan, *John Jay*, 386–87.

54. *American Minerva*, 28 and 29 May 1795; Blau, "French Revolution," 449–54; Young, *Democratic Republicans*, 440–42.

55. Elkins and McKitrick, *Age of Federalism*, 416–18; Donald H. Stewart, *The Opposition Press of the Federalist Period* (Albany: State University of New York Press), 190–94.

56. Elkins and McKitrick, *Age of Federalism*, 418–20; Stewart, *Opposition Press*, 198.

57. Chernow, *Hamilton*, 486–90; Elkins and McKitrick, *Age of Federalism*, 420–21; Monaghan, *John Jay*, 388–404; Stewart, *Opposition Press*, 200–21.

58. Stewart, *Opposition Press*, 214–19.

59. John Jay to Henry Lee, 11 July 1795, 4 JPJ 178–79; John Jay to Edmund Randolph, 20 August 1795, 4 JPJ 186–87; John Jay to James Duane, 16 September 1795, 4 JPJ 191–94; John Jay to Robert Harper, 4 JPJ 198–203; Chernow, *Hamilton*, 487–93; Todd Estes, "John Jay, the Concept of Deference, and the Transformation of Early American Political Culture," *The Historian: A Journal of History* 65 (2003) 293–317; Smith, *Adams*, 2:873.

60. Benjamin Rush to Samuel Bayard, 1 March 1796, in Lyman H. Butterfield, ed., *Letters of Benjamin Rush*, 2 vols. (Princeton: Princeton University Press, 1951), 2:768–69 n. 2; Elkins and McKitrick, *Age of Federalism*, 431–49; Monaghan, *John Jay*, 403; Note, 18 PAH 475–49 (on the Camillus essays).

61. Bemis, *Jay's Treaty*, 346–73 (quote on page 372); Burrows and Wallace, *Gotham*, 321; Elkins and McKitrick, *Age of Federalism*, 410–14; Monaghan, *John Jay*, 381–82; Ritcheson, *Aftermath of Revolution*, 352–59.

Notes to Chapter 14: Governor of New York

1. Peter Jay Munro to Peter A. Jay, 28 December 1794; John Hobart to John Jay, 7 January 1795; Young, *Democratic Republicans*, 429–42.

2. John Jay to Sarah Jay, 12 March 1795; John Jay to Egbert Benson, 27 June 1795; John Jay to George Washington, 29 June 1795, 4 JPJ 177.

3. *American Minerva*, 2 and 3 July 1795; Blau, "French Revolution," 470–76.

4. Stefan Bielinski, "Episodes in the Coming of Age of an Early American Community: Albany, New York, 1780–1793," in Stephen L. Schecter and Wendell Tripp, eds., *World of the Founders: New York Communities in the Federal Period* (Albany: New York State Commission on the Bicentennial, 1990); Burrows and Wallace, *Gotham*, 333–52; James F. Cronin, *The Diary of Elihu Hubbard Smith* (Philadelphia: American Philosophical Society, 1973), 292; Codman Hislop, *Albany: Dutch, English, and American* (Albany: Argus Press, 1936), 228–30; Milton M. Klein, ed., *The Empire State: A History of New York* (Ithaca: Cornell University Press, 2001), 257–68; Monaghan, *John Jay*, 412–15.

5. Joseph Durrenberger, *Turnpikes: A Study of the Toll Road Movement in the Middle Atlantic States and Maryland* (Valdosta, Georgia: 1931), 41–43, 58–61; Laurence M. Hauptman, *Conspiracy of Interests: Iroquois Dispossession and the Rise of New York State* (Syracuse: Syracuse University Press, 1999), 6–7, 95–97; Mary-Jo Kline, "The 'New' New York: An Expanding State in a New Nation," in Manfred Jonas and Robert V. Wells, eds., *New Opportunities in a New Nation: The Development of New York after the Revolution* (Schenectady: Union College Press, 1982).

6. Hauptman, *Conspiracy*, 15–16, 82–87; Klein, ed., *Empire State*, 270–71; Ronald E. Shaw, *Erie Water West: A History of the Erie Canal, 1792–1854* (Lexington: University of Kentucky Press, 1966), 3 21.

7. Burrows and Wallace, *Gotham*, 341–43; Dangerfield, *Livingston*, 276, 287–89, 403–22.

8. Burrows and Wallace, *Gotham*, 340–46; Paul A. Gilje and Howard B. Rock, eds., *Keepers of the Revolution: New Yorkers at Work in the Early Republic* (Ithaca: Cornell University Press, 1992), 1–23.

9. Population figures from the U.S. Census Department web site; current budget figures from state web sites; historical budgets from Don C. Sowers, *The Financial History of New York State from 1789 to 1912* (New York: AMS Press, 1969), 302–05; appointees from Franklin B. Hough, *The New York Civil List* (Albany: 1855).

10. *American Minerva*, 14 August 1795; John Jay to John Charlton, 4 September 1795;

John Charlton to John Jay, 5 September 1795; John Jay to John Broome, 6 September 1795; John Jay to Richard Varick, 6 September 1795; John Broome to John Jay, 8 September 1795; Richard Varick to John Jay, 8 September 1795; John Jay to Thomas Mifflin, 9 September 1795; John Duffy, "An Account of the Epidemic Fevers that Prevailed in the City of New York From 1791 to 1822," *New York Historical Society Quarterly* 50 (1966): 333–64; Pomerantz, *New York*, 338–43.

11. John Jay to French Consul, 19 September 1795; John Jay to John Blanchard, 3 October 1795.

12. *American Minerva*, 12 November 1795.

13. John Jay to John Charlton, 22 April 1796; John Jay to Richard Varick, 7 June 1796, 4 JPJ 217; Richard Bayley to John Jay, 1 July 1796, quoted in Duffy, "An Account," 342; Charles Z. Lincoln, ed., *Messages From the [New York] Governors*, 11 vols. (Albany: J. B. Lyon, 1909), 2:364, 371–72, 382; Pomerantz, *New York*, 345–49.

14. John Jay to Peter A. Jay, 4 September 1798; John Jay to Jedidiah Morse, 4 September 1798; Burrows and Wallace, *Gotham*, 357–58; Duffy, "An Account," 342–49; Lincoln, ed., *Messages*, 2:433.

15. Burrows and Wallace, *Gotham*, 365–66; Young, *Democratic Republicans*, 526–28.

16. Lincoln, ed., *Messages*, 2:363–64; John Jay to John Murray Jr., 15 April 1818, 4 JPJ 406; Arthur A. Ekirch, Jr., "Thomas Eddy and the Beginnings of Prison Reform in New York," *New York History* 24 (July 1943): 376–91; W. David Lewis, "Newgate of New-York: A Case History of Early American Prison Reform," *New-York Historical Society Quarterly* 47 (1963): 137–48.

17. Ekirch, "Thomas Eddy," 379–81; Lincoln, ed., *Messages*, 2:363–64; Pomerantz, *New York*, 318–20; Young, *Democratic Republicans*, 528–29.

18. Benjamin Rush to John Jay, 9 July and 2 August 1796; John Jay to the Assembly, 1 August 1796; John Jay to Peter Jay Munro, 21 January 1797; Lincoln, ed., *Messages*, 2:405, 426–27; Burrows and Wallace, *Gotham*, 366–67.

19. John Jay to Oliver Wolcott, 20 October 1797; John Jay to the Justices of Norfolk, 2 July 1798, 4 JPJ 245–48; Alexander Hamilton to John Jay, 17 August 1798, 22 PAH 163–64; John Jay to Alexander Hamilton, 30 August 1798, 22 PAH 169–70; Jay, *Life of John Jay*, 1:396–400.

20. William Hamilton to John Jay, 8 March 1796, in Frank Monaghan, "Anti-Slavery Papers of John Jay," *Journal of Negro History* 17 (1932) 491–93; Daniel C. Littlefield, "John Jay, the Revolutionary Generation, and Slavery," *New York History* 81 (2000): 91–96; Chernow, *Hamilton*, 735.

21. N.Y. Session Laws, 22nd Sess., ch. 62 (29 March 1799); Burrows and Wallace, *Gotham*, 348–49; Jay, *Life of John Jay*, 1:390–91, 407–08; White, *Somewhat More Independent*, 24–31, 145–50; Young, *Democratic Republicans*, 529–32; Zilversmit, *First Emancipation*, 176–84.

22. Graham R. Hodges, *Root and Branch: African Americans in New York and East Jersey, 1613–1863* (Chapel Hill: University of North Carolina Press, 1999), 162–86; Paul Finkelman, "The Problem of Slavery in the Age of Federalism," in Doron Ben-Atar and Barbara B. Oberg, eds., *Federalists Reconsidered* (Charlottesville: University Press

of Virginia, 1998); White, *Somewhat More Independent*, 83–84, 234–35; Young, *Democratic Republicans*, 529–32.

23. John Jay to Peter A. Jay, 2 November 1797; John Jay to Peter A. Jay, 26 January 1799.

24. Philip Schuyler to John Jay, 9 June 1795; Barbara Graymont, "New York State Indian Policy after the Revolution," *New York History* 57 (1976): 438–74; Hauptman, *Conspiracy*, 58–81.

25. William Bradford to Timothy Pickering, 16 June 1795, quoted in Graymont, "Indian Policy," 466; John Jay to Timothy Pickering, 13 July 1795 (answers missing letter from Pickering); Graymont, "Indian Policy," 465–72; Hauptman, *Conspiracy*, 76–81.

26. Graymont, "Indian Policy," 470–71; Hauptman, *Conspiracy*, 76–81.

27. John Jay to Joseph Brant, 1 August 1796; John Jay to Legislature, 1 November 1796, Lincoln, ed., *Messages*, 2:381; Peter Thacher to John Jay, 19 April 1797; John Jay to Peter Thacher, 25 April 1797.

28. John Jay to Robert R. Livingston and Gouverneur Morris, 29 April 1777, 1 JPM 397–402; New York Constitution of 1777, Section 23; Hugo M. Flick, "The Council of Appointment in New York State," *New York History* 15 (1934): 253–65.

29. New York Constitution of 1777, Section 28; Flick, "Council of Appointment," 256–60; Hough, *New York Civil List*; Taylor, *Cooper's Town*, 163.

30. Flick, "Council of Appointment," 263–64; Kaminski, *Clinton*, 244–46; Young, *Democratic Republicans*, 536–37.

31. Lincoln, ed., *Messages*, 2:360–61; Flick, "Council of Appointment," 265; Jabez D. Hammond, *The History of Political Parties in the State of New York* (Syracuse: 1852), 1:97–98.

32. John Jay to Alexander Hamilton, 5 December 1797, 21 PAH 321–22; Aaron Burr to John Jay, 23 February 1801; Jay, *Life of John Jay*, 1:392.

33. Flick, "Council of Appointment," 266–67; Lincoln, ed., *Messages*, 2:472–76, 491–94.

34. Lincoln, ed., *Messages*, 2:472–76.

35. Peter A. Jay to John Jay, 21 February 1801; Richard Varick to John Jay, 2 March 1801.

36. Lincoln, ed., *Messages*, 2:479–90.

37. New York Constitution of 1777, Section 18; Elkins and McKitrick, *Age of Federalism*, 593–95, 643–47; Richard W. Kohn, *Eagle and Sword: The Beginnings of the Military Establishment in America* (New York: Free Press, 1975), 174–89.

38. Lincoln, ed., *Messages*, 2:359–60.

39. Ibid. 382–83, 398–401.

40. John Jay to Timothy Pickering, 19 April 1798; Frederick C. Leiner, *Millions for Defense: The Subscription Warships of 1798* (Annapolis: Naval Institute Press, 2000), 15–19; Elkins and McKitrick, *Age of Federalism*, 581–618.

41. John Jay to Ebenezer Stevens, 26 May 1798; Ebenezer Stevens to John Jay, 30 May 1798; Matthew Clarkson to John Jay, 10 June 1798; John Jay to Matthew Clarkson, 14 June 1798; Lincoln, ed., *Messages*, 2:420.

42. John Jay to Timothy Pickering, 18 and 26 July 1798; Timothy Pickering to John Jay, 20 July 1798; Elkins and McKitrick, *Age of Federalism*, 593–606.

43. John Jay to Timothy Pickering, 13 May 1798, 4 JPJ 241; James M. Smith, *Freedom's Fetters: The Alien and Sedition Laws and American Civil Liberties* (Ithaca: Cornell University Press, 1956), 55 n. 14.

44. Lincoln, ed., *Messages*, 2:420–24; New York Laws, 22nd Sess., ch. 5 (27 August 1798); Dominick de Lorenzo, "The New York Federalists: Forces of Order" (Ph.D. diss., Columbia University, 1979), 305–09.

45. Philip Schuyler to Alexander Hamilton, 17 August 1798, 22 PAH 79–81; John Jay to Alexander Hamilton, 30 August 1798, 22 PAH 169–70; John Jay to Alexander Hamilton, 26 September 1798, 22 PAH 190–91; John Jay to John Adams, 26 September 1798, 4 JPJ 250–51.

46. John Jay to John Adams, 2 January 1799.

47. George Washington to John Jay, 31 August 1795, 4 JPJ 187; John Jay to George Washington, 3 September 1795, 4 JPJ 190; John Jay to George Washington, 4 September 1795; Timothy Pickering to John Jay, 10 October 1795; John Jay to Timothy Pickering, 14 October 1795; George Washington to John Jay, 21 December 1795; John Jay to George Washington, 26 January 1796; Rufus King to John Jay, 10 January and 6 February 1797; John Trumbull to John Jay, 7 September and 16 December 1796; John Jay to John Trumbull, 27 October 1797, 4 JPJ 232; John Trumbull to John Jay, 6 March 1798, 4 JPJ 236; John Trumbull to John Jay, 20 September 1798, 25 March and 3 June 1799; John Jay to James Sullivan, 28 July 1797, 4 JPJ 228–29; John Jay Statement, 21 May 1798.

48. John Jay to Sarah Jay, 6 March 1795; John Jay to Anne Jay, 8 June and 3 August 1796; Peter A. Jay to John Jay, 24 October 1797 and 22 February 1800; Jay, *Memorials of Peter A. Jay*, 34–35, 44–48: Kerber, *Women of the Republic*, 185–232.

49. Dirck ten Broeck to John Jay, 14 December 1796; John Jay to Peter Jay Munro, 21 January 1797; John Jay to Peter A. Jay, 2 November 1797; Burrows and Wallace, *Gotham*, 299–300, 368–69; Monaghan, *John Jay*, 412.

50. Jay, *Memorials*, 47; Klein, ed., *Empire State*, 270.

51. John Jay to Sarah Jay, 6 June 1800; Sarah Jay to John Jay, 28 July 1800; Peter A. Jay to John Jay, 11 December 1800; John Jay to Peter A. Jay, 18 December 1800; Peter A. Jay to John Jay, 5 April 1801; John Jay to Peter A. Jay, 17 May 1801.

52. Brockholst Livingston to John Jay, 10 March 1801; Peter A. Jay to John Jay, 5 April 1801.

53. John Jay to George Washington, 18 April 1796, 4 JPJ 207–08; George Washington to John Jay, 8 May 1796, 4 JPJ 211–12.

54. Alexander Hamilton to George Washington, 10 May 1796, 20 PAH 169–74; John Jay to George Washington, 19 September 1796; John Jay to Richard Peters, 29 March 1811.

55. John Lowell to John Jay, 1 August 1796; John Jay to John Lowell, 24 August 1796; Elkins and McKitrick, *Age of Federalism*, 513–28; Young, *Democratic Republicans*, 465–67.

56. Lincoln, ed., *Messages*, 2:379–80; Elkins and McKitrick, *Age of Federalism*, 519; Smith, *Adams*, 2:903–04.

57. Peter A. Jay to John Jay, 26 November 1797; John Jay to Peter A. Jay, 18 April 1798; Dangerfield, *Chancellor Livingston*, 274–76; Monaghan, *John Jay*, 415–16.

58. Peter A. Jay to John Jay, 3 May 1800; Elkins and McKitrick, *Age of Federalism*, 732–34; Joanne B. Freeman, *Affairs of Honor: National Politics in the New Republic* (New Haven: Yale University Press, 2001), 230–33; John Ferling, *Adams v. Jefferson: The Tumultuous Election of 1800* (New York: Oxford University Press, 2004) 127–31.

59. Alexander Hamilton to John Jay, 7 May 1800, 24 PAH 464–67; Philip Schuyler to John Jay, 7 May 1800, 4 JPJ 273; *Albany Register*, 25 May 1800, quoted in De Lorenzo, "New York Federalists," 337; Chernow, *Hamilton*, 609–10.

60. John Jay Note, May 1800, 24 PAH 467 n. 4.

61. Alexander Hamilton to John Jay, 19 August 1800, 24 PAH 72–73; John Jay to Alexander Hamilton, August 1800, 24 PAH 82–83, 91–92, 96; Alexander Hamilton, Statement re: John Adams, 24 PAH 169–234; John Adams to John Jay, 24 November 1800; Chernow, *Hamilton*, 619–29; Elkins and McKitrick, *Age of Federalism*, 737–40; Ferling, *Adams*, 397–99.

62. Robert Troup to Rufus King, 6 May and 5 June 1799, De Lorenzo, "New York Federalists," 312–13; Joshua Mercereau to John Jay, 15 July 1800; John Jay to Joshua Mersereau, 6 August 1800; John Jay to Richard Hatfield, 8 November 1800, 4 JPJ 278–79.

63. Elkins and McKitrick, *Age of Federalism*, 746–50; Ferling, *Adams*, 403–05; Miller, *Federalist Era*, 266–76.

64. John Adams to John Jay, 19 December 1800, 1 DHSC 145–46; William Cooper to John Jay, 29 December 1800, 1 DHSC 902–03; Henry Glen to John Jay, 19 December 1800, 1 DHSC 905; John Marshall to John Jay, 22 December 1800.

65. Abigail Adams to Thomas Adams, 25 December 1800, 1 DHSC 907; Thomas Jefferson to James Madison, 26 December 1800, 1 DHSC 908–09; Thomas Jefferson to Tench Coxe, 31 December 1800, 1 DHSC 908; Robert Troup to Rufus King, 31 December 1800, 1 DHSC 912; Peter A. Jay to John Jay, 2 January 1801; Timothy Pickering to Oliver Wolcott, 3 January 1801, 1 DHSC 912.

66. John Jay to John Adams, 2 January 1801, 1 DHSC 146–47; John Jay to John Marshall, 2 January 1801.

67. Smith, *Marshall*, 14–16.

68. John Jay to Committee of Federal Freeholders, 27 January 1801, 4 JPJ 288–89.

Notes to Chapter 15: Retirement

1. John Jay to Sarah Jay, 13 March 1795; Ferling, *First of Men*, 323–54; Dumas Malone, *Jefferson the Virginian* (Boston: Little, Brown, 1948), 371–423; Dumas Malone, *Jefferson and the Ordeal of Liberty* (Boston: Little, Brown, 1962), 167–244.

2. John Jay to Peter A. Jay, 17 May 1801; John Jay to Sarah Jay, 17 May 1801; Sarah Jay to John Jay, 27 and 31 May 1801; Wells, *Jay Family*; Note, 1 JPM 211–12.

3. John Jay to Sarah Jay, June 1801; Sarah Jay to John Jay, 13 July 1801; Sarah Jay to

Maria Jay, 14 July 1801; Sarah Jay to John Jay, 6 October 1801; Sarah Jay to Maria Jay, 2 December 1801.

4. Sarah Jay to ?, November 1801, quoted in Ellett, *Queens*, 84 (not in Columbia index); John Jay to Rufus King, 20 January 1803.

5. Sarah Jay to John Jay, 2 March 1802; John Jay to Robert Lenox, 3 April 1802, 4 JPJ 295–96; Sarah Jay to Maria Jay, 5 May 1802; Goldsborough Banyer Jr. to John Jay, 4 June 1802; Jay, *Life of John Jay*, 1:430.

6. John Jay to Rufus King, 30 January 1803; Jay, *Life of John Jay*, 1:431.

7. Peter A. Jay to John Jay, 26 November 1802, 28 December 1802, 14 May 1803, 30 June 1803, 2 December 1803, 10 February 1804; Jay, *Memorials of Peter A. Jay*, 54–57, 82–88.

8. John Jay to Maria Jay Banyer, 25 July 1803 and 2 November 1804, 4 JPJ 299–300; John Jay to Sarah Louisa Jay, 28 January 1806; John Jay to Maria Jay Banyer, 1 August 1806; Maria Jay Banyer to John Jay, 14 November 1809; John Jay to Maria Jay Banyer, 3 January 1812; Maria Jay Banyer to John Jay, 16 September 1812; Maria Jay Banyer to John Jay, 8 May 1815.

9. Anne Jay to Sarah Jay, 27 July 1800; Anne Jay to Peter A. Jay, 9 April 1812; Anne Jay to Margaret Maclay, 12 March 1818.

10. John Jay to Timothy Dwight, December 1802 and 10 February 1803; John Jay to Henry Davis, 10 February 1803; Henry Davis to John Jay, 25 May 1803; John Jay to Maria Jay Banyer, 23 April 1810; Bayard Tuckerman, *William Jay and the Constitutional Movement for Abolition* (New York: 1893).

11. Sarah Louisa Jay to John Jay, 24 April 1809 and 7 March 1816; Peter A. Jay to John Jay, 22 April 1818; Peter A. Jay, List of Persons Invited to Sarah Jay's Funeral, 24 April 1818, John Jay Homestead; John Jay to Peter A. Jay, 20 May 1818.

12. John Jay to Peter A. Jay, 16 April and 24 October 1811; Federal Census, Bedford, New York, 1810; Horton, *Listening for Clarinda*; Monaghan, *John Jay*, 430–31.

13. William P. Beers to John Jay, 2 April 1807; John Jay to William P. Beers, 18 April 1807.

14. John Jay to Egbert Benson, 12 May 1807; Egbert Benson to John Jay, 19 May 1807; John Jay to Egbert Benson, 2 June 1807; William Coleman to John Jay, 6 June 1807; John Jay to William Coleman, 18 June 1807.

15. John Jay to Peter Van Schaack, 28 July 1812, 4 JPJ 360–61; Donald R. Hickey, *The War of 1812: A Forgotten Conflict* (Urbana: University of Illinois Press, 1989).

16. Gouverneur Morris Diary, August-September 1812, Morris Papers, Library of Congress; Peter A. Jay to John Jay, 11 September 1812; Gouverneur Morris to John Jay, 11 September 1812; Maria Jay Banyer to John Jay, 16 September 1812; John Jay to Gouverneur Morris, 21 September 1812, 4 JPJ 362–64; John Jay to Peter A. Jay, 23 September 1812; Dixon Ryan Fox, *The Decline of the Aristocracy in New York Politics, 1801–1840* (rev. ed. New York: Harper and Row, 1965), 168–72; Hickey, *War of 1812*, 52–71, 100–05; Jay, *Life of John Jay*, 1:443–48; Mintz, *Gouverneur Morris*, 237–38; Norman K. Risjord, "Election of 1812," in Arthur M. Schlesinger Jr., ed., *History of American Presidential Elections, 1789–1968* (New York: Chelsea House, 1985), 1:249–54.

17. John Jay to Elias Boudinot, 17 November 1819, 4 JPJ 430–31; Glover Moore, *The Missouri Controversy, 1819–1821* (Lexington: University of Kentucky Press, 1953), 67–72.

18. Moore, *Missouri Controversy*, 5–6, 72–80.

19. John Adams to John Jay, 8 January 1818, 4 JPJ 395–97; John Jay to John Adams, 31 January 1818, 4 JPJ 397–402.

20. John Jay to John Adams, 27 February 1821; John Adams to John Jay, 5 March 1821; John Jay to William Duane, 13 March 1821; John Jay to John Adams, 20 March 1821; John Jay to John Adams, 27 March 1821; John Adams to John Jay, 31 March 1821; John Adams to John Jay, 30 April 1821; John Jay to John Adams, 7 May 1821; John Adams to John Jay, 13 May 1821; John Jay to William Duane, 22 May 1821; William Duane to John Jay, 30 May 1821.

21. John Adams to John Jay, 5 March 1821, 31 March 1821, 30 April 1821, 13 May 1821 and 19 June 1821; John Jay to John Adams, 7 May 1821, 11 June 1821 and 11 March 1822; *Niles' Weekly Register* (Baltimore), July 26, 1823.

22. John Jay to Richard Peters, 24 July 1809, 26 February 1810, 21 November 1810 and 25 January 1819, 4 JPJ 315–19, 327–29, 338–41, 425–28; Richard Peters to John Jay, 5 September 1810 and 16 October 1811; Dumas Malone, ed., *Dictionary of American Biography* (New York: 1934), 8:509–10.

23. John Jay to Richard Peters, 25 July 1809, 26 February 1810, 9 January 1811 and 14 March 1815, 4 JPJ 315–19, 327–29, 380–81, 386–88.

24. Richard Peters to John Jay, 14 February 1811, 4 JPJ 344–46; John Jay to Richard Peters, 29 March 1811, 4 JPJ 346–58.

25. John Jay to Richard Peters, 29 March 1811, 4 JPJ 356–58; Pennsylvania Historical Society to John Jay, 10 February 1826; Richard Peters to John Jay, 21 February 1826; John Jay to Pennsylvania Historical Society, 21 February 1826; John Jay to Richard Peters, 3 March 1826.

26. John Jay to Jedidiah Morse, 16 August 1809 and 1 January 1813, 4 JPJ 322–23, 365–67; Note by William Jay, 1867, John Jay Homestead.

27. Kammen, *Season of Youth*, 40–50; Taylor, *Cooper's Town*, 406–09; James D. Wallace, *Early Cooper and his Audience* (New York: Columbia University Press, 1986), 100–14.

28. John Jay to George Alexander Otis, 13 January 1821; Carlo Botta, *History of the War of Independence of the United States of America*, 3 vols. (trans. by George Alexander Otis) (Philadelphia: 1820–21).

29. Richard Henry Lee to John Jay, 30 January 1823, 4 JPJ 465–67; John Jay to Richard Henry Lee, 12 February 1823, 4 JPJ 468–72; Charles DeWitt to John Jay, 4 August 1823; John Jay to Charles DeWitt, 18 August 1823; John Jay to James Morris, 1 November 1823.

30. John Jay to Peter A. Jay, 12 October 1819 and 30 October 1820; Compensation Act of 1789, 4 DHSC 19–21; Sowers, *Financial History*, 185; Lord John Campbell, *The Lives of the Chief Justices of England*, 6 vols. (New York: J. Cockcroft and Co., 1873–76), 4:254.

31. John Jay to Peter Jay Munro, 4 April 1803; John Adams to Thomas Jefferson, 16 July 1813, in Lester J. Cappon, ed., *The Adams-Jefferson Letters: The Complete*

Correspondence between Thomas Jefferson and Abigail and John Adams (Chapel Hill: University of North Carolina Press, 1959), 359–60; Robert Bolton, *The History of the Several Towns, Manors and Patents of the County of Westchester*, 2 vols. (New York: 1881), 1:66–67; Jay, *Life of John Jay*, 1:434–35.

32. John Jay to Benjamin Moore, 9 March 1804; Benjamin Moore to John Jay, 7 April 1804; John Jay to Benjamin Moore, 22 April 1804.

33. Vestry Resolution, St. Matthew's Church, Bedford, New York, January 1810; John Jay to Benjamin Moore, 8 February 1810; John Jay to Peter A. Jay, 22 March 1813; John Jay to Maria Jay Banyer, 30 March 1813; John Jay to William Miller, 30 March 1813.

34. John Jay to John Murray, 12 October 1816, 4 JPJ 391–93; John Jay to Eleazor Lord, 7 February 1817; John Jay to John Murray, 15 April 1818, 4 JPJ 403–19.

35. Peter Jay Diary, 7 and 10 March 1795; John Jay to Maria Jay Banyer, 2 February 1813.

36. John Jay to Samuel Bayard, 15 February 1816; John Jay to Rev. Romeyn, 12 June 1816, 4 JPJ 389; John Jay to S. S. Woodhull, 7 December 1821, 4 JPJ 459–61; Jay, *Life of John Jay*, 1:450–55; Jon Butler, *Awash in a Sea of Faith: Christianizing the American People* (Cambridge: Harvard University Press, 1990), 277–78; Nathan O. Hatch, *The Democratization of American Christianity* (New Haven: Yale University Press, 1989); Peter J. Wosh, *Spreading the Word: The Bible Business in Nineteenth-Century America* (Ithaca: Cornell University Press, 1994).

37. John Jay, Addresses to the American Bible Society, 9 May 1822, 8 May 1823, 13 May 1824 and 12 May 1825, 4 JPJ 478–504.

38. Henry Van Der Lyn to Gerardus Van Der Lyn, 22 July 1826, in Van Der Lyn Diary, vol. 1, p. 91, New-York Historical Society.

39. Thomas Jefferson to John Adams, 27 June 1822, in Cappon, ed., *Adams–Jefferson Letters*, 580–81; Joseph J. Ellis, *Passionate Sage: The Character and Legacy of John Adams* (New York: W. W. Norton, 1993); Joseph Ellis, *American Sphinx: The Character of Thomas Jefferson* (New York: Alfred A. Knopf, 1997), 228–35; Dumas Malone, *Jefferson: The Sage of Monticello* (Boston: Little, Brown, 1977); David McCullough, *John Adams* (New York: Simon and Schuster, 2001), 568–651.

40. John Jay to Richard Peters, 30 August 1808, 4 JPJ 311–13; John Jay to Samuel Bayard, 5 February 1816; John Jay to S. S. Woodhull, 7 December 1821, 4 JPJ 459–61; Columbia index.

41. John Jay to Peter Jay Munro, 31 March 1803; Peter Jay Munro to John Jay, 30 April 1803; John Jay to Peter Jay Munro, 6 May 1803; Peter Jay Munro to John Jay, 20 May 1803; John Jay to Sarah Louisa Jay, 28 November 1806; Gouverneur Morris to John Jay, 15 February 1813, 4 JPJ 369; John Jay to Gouverneur Morris, 22 February 1813, 4 JPJ 370–71.

42. John Jay to the New York Committee, 29 June 1826, 4 JPJ 476–77; Thomas Jefferson to Roger G. Weightman, 24 June 1826, in Ford, ed., *Writings of Jefferson*, 10:390–92.

43. John Jay to Peter Van Schaack, 4 May 1807, 4 JPJ 309–10; John Jay to Jedidiah Morse, 16 August 1809, 4 JPJ 322–23; John Jay to Richard Peters, 26 February 1810, 4 JPJ 327–29; Jay, *Life of John Jay*, 1:443.

44. John Jay to Peter A. Jay, 11 July 1820; John Jay to Lindley Murray, 24 April 1821, 4 JPJ 446–47; John Jay to Edward Livingston, 26 February 1823.

45. William Jay to Peter A. Jay, 31 May 1825; William Jay to Peter A. Jay, 28 March 1827; William Jay to Richard Peters, 28 June 1828; Anne Jay to Peter A. Jay, 1829.

46. John Jay Will, 18 April 1829, Jay, *Life of John Jay*, 1:519–20.

47. Peter A. Jay to James Fenimore Cooper, 29 May 1829; Anne Jay to Peter A. Jay, 1829.

48. *New York Mirror: A Weekly Gazette*, 22 November 1828 and 30 May 1829; *Casket* (Philadelphia), August 1829; *The Jay Family Cemetery at Rye, New York* (New Haven: Yale University Press, 1947).

Notes to Chapter 16: Conclusions

1. Address to the People of Great Britain, 5 September 1774, 1 JPJ 18; Address of the New York Convention to Their Constituents, December 1776, 1 JPJ 102–20; John Jay to Jedidiah Morse, 28 February 1797, 4 JPJ 225.

2. John Jay to Charles Thomson, 19 July 1783, Thomson Papers, Library of Congress; John Jay Notes, July 1783-March 1784, 2 JPM 712–19; John Jay to John Adams, 25 July 1787, 3 EN 559–60; Note, 1 JPM 1–10.

3. John Adams to William Sumner, 29 March 1809, quoted in John Ferling, *Setting the World Ablaze: Washington, Adams, Jefferson, and the American Revolution* (New York: Oxford University Press, 2000), 302; Thomas Jefferson, Epitaph, quoted ibid.

4. Brands, *The First American*; Ellis, *Founding Brothers*; Ferling, *Setting the World Ablaze*; Richard B. Morris, *Seven Who Shaped Our Destiny: The Founding Fathers as Revolutionaries* (New York: Harper Row, 1973).

5. Epitaph quoted in Bolton, *History of Westchester*, 2:204.

Bibliography

There are three sets of published Jay papers, each useful in its way. John Jay's son William published *The Life of John Jay: With Selections from his Correspondence and Miscellaneous Papers* (1833). William omitted almost all family letters and edited other letters mercilessly. The volumes are still useful, however, for documents which have since been lost, and for the stories Jay told to his family. At the end of the nineteenth century, Henry Johnston published four volumes of the *Correspondence and Public Papers of John Jay* (1893). Johnston's volumes cover Jay's entire life, in chronological order, in reasonable detail. Again, however, the letters are edited, sometimes without indication. In the late twentieth century, Richard Morris of Columbia University published two volumes of Jay papers. These volumes are superb, but they only cover the period up to 1784, and even for the years they cover they omit much material. For the year in which Jay was President of the Congress, for example, Morris omitted almost all the official letters.

Although many of Jay's papers have been published, many remain unpublished. By far the largest and most useful collection is at Columbia, which has many originals, and copies of most other letters to and from Jay. Richard Morris and his students prepared abstract cards of all this material, and Jean Ashton and her colleagues have recently made some of it available on the Columbia Library internet website. Morris also prepared, but never published, volumes three and four of his intended four-volume set of Jay papers; the typescript is at Columbia.

Various other printed primary sources provide the "official" framework of Jay's life. For the years 1774 through 1776, the key sources are Peter Force's *American Archives*, the *Journal of the Continental Congress*, and the impressive *Letters of Delegates to Congress*. For 1776 through 1778, when Jay was in New York, the key sources are the various official journals; the records of the New York Supreme Court are almost non-existent. For 1779, when Jay was President of the Congress, the *Journal of the Continental Congress* and *Letters of Delegates* are critical, as is John Meng's edition of the dispatches of Conrad Gérard. Morris provides quite full coverage of Jay's years in Spain and France. Useful for this period, and vital for Jay's years as Secretary for Foreign Affairs, is *Emerging Nation: A Documentary History of the Foreign Relations of the United States under the Articles of the Confederation*. The ratification process is receiving careful and thorough treatment in *The Documentary History of the Ratification of the Constitution*, but only two of the volumes on

New York are available. The early Supreme Court is the subject of the six superb volumes to date of *The Documentary History of the Supreme Court of the United States, 1789–1800*. The key documents relating to the negotiation of Jay's Treaty are printed in *American State Papers: Foreign Relations*. Jay's addresses to the New York legislature are in *Messages of the Governors*. Most of Jay's papers as Governor were lost, unfortunately, in a fire in Albany in the early twentieth century.

The best biography to date is Frank Monaghan, *John Jay: Defender of Liberty Against Kings and Peoples* (1935). Although there are some errors, and citations are often missing, there is also much useful material, including quotes from some letters which are apparently no longer available. An earlier, shorter biography is Frank Pellew, *John Jay* (1890). Richard Morris never wrote a biography of Jay, but he touched on Jay in many books, essays and articles, all of which are illuminating. Other useful essays include the chapter on Jay in Joseph Dorfman and Rex Tugwell's book on Columbia, Herbert Johnson's *John Jay* (1970), and Sandra Van Burkleo's chapter in Scott Gerber's book on the Supreme Court.

The following bibliography is partial; other sources are cited in the notes and many others were consulted.

Manuscript Sources

Bank of New York, New York
   Archives

Columbia University, New York, New York
   John Jay Papers
   John Jay Papers Project

George Washington University, Washington, D.C.
   First Federal Congress Project Files

Library of Congress, Washington, D.C.
   Papers of the Continental Congress (microfilm)
   Aileen Topping Moore Papers
   Gouverneur Morris Papers
   Charles Thomson Papers
   George Washington Papers (internet)

New-York Historical Society, New York
   John Jay Papers
   Rufus King Papers

Robert Livingston Papers

New York Public Library, New York
  Gilbert Livingston Papers

Pennsylvania Historical Society, Philadelphia
  Land Records

Trinity Church, New York, New York
  Vestry Minutes

University of Wisconsin, Madison, Wisconsin
  Documentary History of the Ratification of the Constitution Files

Printed Primary Sources

American State Papers: Foreign Relations. 6 vols. Washington: 1832–59.

Abbot, W. W., et al., eds. *The Papers of George Washington*. 52 vols. to date. Charlottesville: University Press of Virginia, 1983—.

Adams, Charles F., ed. *The Works of John Adams, Second President of the United States*. 10 vols. Boston: 1856.

Boyd, Julian P., et al., eds. *The Papers of Thomas Jefferson*. 29 vols. to date. Princeton: Princeton University Press, 1950—.

Burnett, Edmund C., ed. *Letters of Members of the Continental Congress*. 8 vols. Washington: Carnegie Institution of Washington, 1921–36.

Butterfield, Lyman H., ed. *The Adams Papers: Diaries and Autobiography of John Adams*. 4 vols. Cambridge: Harvard University Press, 1961.

——, ed. *Adams Family Correspondence*. 6 vols. Cambridge: Harvard University Press, 1963–93.

Chesnutt, David R., and C. James Taylor, eds. *The Papers of Henry Laurens*. 16 vols. Columbia: University of South Carolina Press, 1976–2003.

De Pauw, Linda, et al., eds. T*he Documentary History of the First Federal Congress*. 17 vols. to date. Baltimore: Johns Hopkins University Press, 1972—.

Elliot, Jonathan, ed. *The Debates in the Several State Conventions on the Adoption of the Federal Constitution*. 2 vols. Philadelphia: 1876.

Ferguson, James, et al., eds. *The Papers of Robert Morris, 1781–1784*. 9 vols. Pittsburgh: University of Pittsburgh Press, 1973–1999.

Fitzpatrick, John C., ed. *The Writings of George Washington*. 39 vols. Washington: Government Printing Office, 1931–44.

Force, Peter, ed. *American Archives: Consisting of a Collection of Authentick Records, State*

Papers, Debates, and Letters and Other Notices of Publick Affairs. 9 vols. Washington: Government Printing Office, 1837–53.

Ford, Worthington C., et al., eds. *Journals of the Continental Congress, 1774–1789.* 35 vols. Washington: Government Printing Office, 1904–76.

Freeman, Landa M., et al., eds. *Selected Letters of John Jay and Sarah Livingston Jay: Correspondence by or to the First Chief Justice of the United States and his Wife.* Jefferson, North Carolina: McFarland & Co., 2004.

Giunta, Mary A., et al., eds. *The Emerging Nation: A Documentary History of the Foreign Relations of the United States under the Articles of Confederation, 1780–1789.* 3 vols. Washington: Government Printing Office, 1996.

Hastings, Hugh, ed. *Public Papers of George Clinton, First Governor of New York, 1777–1795, 1801–1804.* 10 vols. Albany: State of New York, 1899–1914.

Hobson, Charles F., ed. *The Papers of John Marshall.* 11 vols. to date. Chapel Hill: University of North Carolina Press, 1974—.

Hutchinson, William T., et al., eds. *The Papers of James Madison.* 30 vols. to date. Chicago: University of Chicago Press, and Charlottesville, University of Virginia Press, 1962–.

Jay, John. *Letters: Being the Whole of the Correspondence between the Hon. John Jay, Esquire, and Mr. Lewis Littlepage.* New York: 1786.

Jay, William. *The Life of John Jay: With Selections from his Correspondence and Miscellaneous Papers.* 2 vols. New York: 1833.

Jensen, Merrill, et al., eds. *The Documentary History of the Ratification of the Constitution.* 17 vols. to date. Madison: State Historical Society of Wisconsin, 1976—.

Johnston, Henry P., ed. *The Correspondence and Public Papers of John Jay.* 4 vols. New York: 1890–93.

King, Charles R., ed. *The Life and Correspondence of Rufus King.* 6 vols. New York: 1894.

Labaree, Leonard W., et al., eds. *The Papers of Benjamin Franklin.* 37 vols. to date. New Haven: Yale University Press, 1959—.

Lincoln, Charles Z., ed. *Messages from the Governors ... to and Including the Year 1906.* 11 vols. Albany: J. B. Lyon, 1909.

Marcus, Maeva, ed. *The Documentary History of the Supreme Court of the United States, 1789–1800.* 6 vols. to date. New York: Columbia University Press, 1985—.

Meng, John J., ed. *Despatches and Instructions of Conrad Alexandre Gérard.* Baltimore: Johns Hopkins Press, 1939.

Morris, Richard B., ed. *John Jay: The Making of a Revolutionary. Unpublished Papers, 1745–1780.* New York: Harper and Row, 1975.

Morris, Richard B., ed. *John Jay: The Winning of the Peace. Unpublished Papers, 1780–1784.* New York: Harper and Row, 1980.

New-York Historical Society. *Minutes of the Committee and of the First Commission for Detecting and Defeating Conspiracies in the State of New York.* 2 vols. New York: New-York Historical Society, 1924.

New York State. *Journals of the Provincial Congress ... of the State of New York*. 2 vols. Albany: 1842.

——, *The Votes and Proceedings of the Assembly of the State of New-York, at Their First Session ... 1777*. Kingston, New York: 1777.

——, *The Votes and Proceedings of the Assembly of the State of New-York, at Their Second Session ... 1778*. Poughkeepsie, New York: 1779.

——, *The Votes and Proceedings of the Senate of the State of New-York, at Their First Session ... 1777*. Kingston, New York: 1777.

Prince, Carl E., ed. *The Papers of William Livingston*. 5 vols. Trenton: New Jersey Historical Commission, 1979–88.

Smith, Paul H., et al. eds. *Letters of Delegates to Congress, 1774–1789*. 27 vols. Washington: Government Printing Office, 1976–99.

Syrett, Harold C., ed. *The Papers of Alexander Hamilton*. 27 vols. New York: Columbia University Press, 1961–1987.

Weaver, William A., ed. *Diplomatic Correspondence of the United States of America From the Signing of the Definitive Treaty of Peace, September 10, 1783, to the Adoption of the Constitution, March 4, 1789*. 7 vols. Washington: 1833–34.

Wharton, Francis, ed. *The Revolutionary Diplomatic Correspondence of the United States*. 6 vols. Washington: 1889.

Books

Alsop, Susan Mary. *Yankees at the Court: The First Americans in Paris*. Garden City, New York: Doubleday and Company, 1982.

Ammerman, David. *In the Common Cause: American Response to the Coercive Acts of 1774*. Charlottesville: University Press of Virginia, 1974.

Ammon, Harry. *The Genet Mission*. New York: W. W. Norton, 1973.

Anderson, Fred. *Crucible of War: The Seven Years' War and the Fate of Empire in British America, 1754–1766*. New York: Alfred A. Knopf, 2000.

Becker, Carl L. *The History of Political Parties in the Province of New York, 1760–1776*. Madison: University of Wisconsin Press, 1960.

Bemis, Samuel. *The Diplomacy of the American Revolution*. Bloomington: Indiana University Press, rev. ed. 1957.

——, ed. *The American Secretaries of State and Their Diplomacy*. New York: Pageant Book Co., 1958.

——, *Pinckney's Treaty: America's Advantage from Europe's Distress*. New Haven: Yale University Press, rev. ed. 1960.

——, *Jay's Treaty: A Study in Commerce and Diplomacy*. New Haven: Yale University Press, rev. ed. 1962.

Ben-Atar, Doron, and Barbara B. Oberg, eds. *Federalists Reconsidered*. Charlottesville: University Press of Virginia, 1998.

Bernstein, Richard B. *Are We To Be a Nation? The Making of the Constitution*. Cambridge: Harvard University Press, 1987.

Berrian, William. *An Historical Sketch of Trinity Church, New York*. New York: 1847.

Blau, Alan L. "New York City and the French Revolution, 1789–1797: A Study of French Revolutionary Influence." Ph.D. diss., City University of New York, 1973.

Bliven, Bruce. *Under the Guns: New York, 1775–1776*. New York: Harper and Row, 1972.

Bolton, Robert. *The History of the Several Towns, Manors and Patents of the County of Westchester*. 2 vols. New York: 1881.

Brands, H. W. *The First American: The Life and Times of Benjamin Franklin*. New York: Doubleday, 2000.

Brecher, Frank W. *Securing American Independence: John Jay and the French Alliance*. Westport, Conn.: Praeger, 2003.

Brookhiser, Richard. *Alexander Hamilton: American*. New York: Free Press, 1999.

———, *Gentleman Revolutionary: Gouverneur Morris – The Rake Who Wrote the Constitution*. New York: Free Press, 2003.

Burns, Michael McShane. "John Jay as Secretary for Foreign Affairs, 1784–1789." Ph.D. diss., University of North Carolina, Chapel Hill, 1974.

Burrows, Edwin G., and Mike Wallace. *Gotham: A History of New York City to 1898*. New York: Oxford, 1999.

Casto, William R. *The Supreme Court in the Early Republic: The Chief Justiceships of John Jay and Oliver Ellsworth*. Columbia: University of South Carolina Press, 1995.

Chernow, Ron. *Alexander Hamilton*. New York: Penguin Press, 2004.

Combs, Jerald A. *The Jay Treaty: Political Battleground of the Founding Fathers*. Berkeley: University of California Press, 1970.

Countryman, Edward. *A People in Revolution: The American Revolution and Political Society in New York, 1760–1790*. Baltimore: Johns Hopkins University Press, 1981.

Dangerfield, George. *Chancellor Robert R. Livingston of New York, 1746–1813*. New York: Harcourt, Brace and Co., 1960.

De Lorenzo, Dominick. "The New York Federalists: Forces of Order." Ph.D. diss., Columbia University, 1979.

De Pauw, Linda Grant. *The Eleventh Pillar: New York State and the Federal Constitution*. Ithaca: Cornell University Press, 1966.

Dull, Jonathan R. *A Diplomatic History of the American Revolution*. New Haven: Yale University Press, 1985.

Dorfman, Joseph, and R. G. Tugwell. *Early American Policy: Six Columbia Contributors*. New York: Columbia University Press, 1960.

Elkins, Stanley, and Eric McKitrick. *The Age of Federalism: The Early American Republic, 1788–1800*. New York: Oxford University Press, 1993.

Ellis, Joseph J. *American Sphinx: The Character of Thomas Jefferson*. New York: Alfred A. Knopf, 1997.

———, *Founding Brothers: The Revolutionary Generation*. New York: Alfred A. Knopf, 2000.

Ferling, John E. *The First of Men: A Life of George Washington*. Knoxville: University of Tennessee Press, 1988.

———, *John Adams: A Life*. Knoxville: University of Tennessee Press, 1992.

———, *Setting the World Ablaze: Washington, Adams, Jefferson and the American Revolution*. New York: Oxford University Press, 2000.

———, *A Leap in the Dark: The Struggle to Create the American Republic*. New York: Oxford University Press, 2003.

———, *Adams vs. Jefferson: The Tumultuous Election of 1800*. New York: Oxford University Press, 2004.

Freeman, Douglas Southall. *George Washington*. 7 vols. New York: Charles Scribner's Sons, 1948–57.

Gerber, Scott D., ed. *Seriatim: The Supreme Court before John Marshall*. New York: New York University Press, 1998.

Goebel, Julius D. *History of the Supreme Court of the United States*: Volume I, *Antecedents and Beginnings to 1801*. New York: Macmillan Co., 1971.

Gruver, Rebecca. "The Diplomacy of John Jay." Ph.D. diss., University of California at Berkeley, 1964.

Hamlin, Paul M. *Legal Education in Colonial New York*. New York: New York University Press, 1939.

Henderson, Dwight F. *Courts for a New Nation*. Washington: Public Affairs Press, 1971.

Hobart, Lois. *Patriot's Lady: The Life of Sarah Livingston Jay*. New York: Funk and Wagnalls Co., 1960.

Hoffman, Ronald, and Peter J. Albert, eds. *Peace and the Peacemakers: The Treaty of 1783*. Charlottesville: University of Virginia Press, 1986.

Humphrey, David C. *From King's College to Columbia, 1746–1800*. New York: Columbia University Press, 1976.

Ide, John Jay. *The Portraits of John Jay (1745–1829)*. New York: New-York Historical Society, 1938.

Isaacson, Walter. *Benjamin Franklin: An American Life*. New York: Simon and Schuster, 2003.

Jay, John. *Memorials of Peter A. Jay Compiled for his Descendants*. N.p.; 1905.

Jensen, Merrill. *The New Nation: A History of the United States during the Confederation, 1781–1789*. New York: Alfred A. Knopf, 1950.

Jillson, Calvin, and Rick K. Wilson. *Congressional Dynamics: Structure, Coordination, and Choice in the First American Congress, 1774–1789.* Stanford: Stanford University Press, 1994.

Johnson, Herbert A. *John Jay, 1745–1829.* Albany: University of the State of New York, 1970.

———, *John Jay: Colonial Lawyer.* New York: Garland Publishing, 1989.

Jupp, Peter. *Lord Grenville: 1759–1834.* Oxford: Clarendon Press, 1985.

Kaminski, John P. "New York: The Reluctant Pillar," in Schecter, Stephen L., ed., *The Reluctant Pillar.*

———, *George Clinton: Yeoman Politician of the New Republic.* Madison: Madison House Publishers, 1993.

Kammen, Michael. *Colonial New York: A History.* New York: Oxford University Press, 1986.

Ketchum, Richard M. *Divided Loyalties: How the American Revolution Came to New York.* New York: Henry Holt, 2002.

Lincoln, Charles Z. *The Constitutional History of the State of New York.* 5 vols. Rochester: Lawyers Co-operative Publishing Co., 1906.

Loveland, Clara O. *The Critical Years: The Reconstitution of the Anglican Church in the United States of America, 1780–1789.* Greenwich: Seabury Press, 1956.

Mackesy, Piers. *The War for America, 1775–1783.* Lincoln: University of Nebraska Press, 1993.

McCullough, David. *John Adams.* New York: Simon and Schuster, 2001.

Middlekauff, Robert. *The Glorious Cause: The American Revolution, 1763–1789.* New York: Oxford University Press, 1982.

Mintz, Max M. *Gouverneur Morris and the American Revolution.* Norman: University of Oklahoma Press, 1970.

Monaghan, Frank. *John Jay: Defender of Liberty Against Kings and Peoples, Author of the Constitution and Governor of New York, President of the Continental Congress, Co-Author of the Federalist, Negotiator of the Peace of 1783 and the Jay Treaty of 1794, First Chief Justice of the United States.* New York: Bobbs-Merrill Co., 1935.

Monaghan, Frank, and Marvin Lowenthal. *This Was New York: The Nation's Capital in 1789.* Garden City, New York: Doubleday, Doran and Co., 1943.

Morgan, Edmund S., and Helen M. Morgan. *The Stamp Act Crisis: Prologue to Revolution.* New York: Collier Books, 1963.

Morris, Richard B. *The Peacemakers: The Great Powers in Search of American Independence.* New York: Harper and Row, 1965.

———, *John Jay, the Nation, and the Court.* Boston: Boston University Press, 1967.

———, *Seven Who Shaped Our Destiny: The Founding Fathers as Revolutionaries.* New York: Harper and Row, 1973.

————, *The Forging of the Union, 1781–1789*. New York: Harper and Row, 1987.

Pellew, Frank. *John Jay*. Boston: Houghton Mifflin and Co., 1890.

Pomerantz, Sidney I. *New York as an American City, 1783–1803*. New York: Columbia University Press, 1938.

Rakove, Jack N. *The Beginnings of National Politics: An Interpretive History of the Continental Congress*. New York: Alfred A. Knopf, 1979.

Ruttenber, E. M. *Obstructions to the Navigation of Hudson's River*. Albany: 1859 (includes committee minutes).

Schecter, Barnet. *The Battle for New York: The City at the Heart of the American Revolution*. New York: Walker & Co., 2002.

Schecter, Stephen L., ed. *The Reluctant Pillar: New York and the Adoption of the Federal Constitution*. Albany: New York State Commission on the Bicentennial of the United States Constitution, 1987.

Schecter, Stephen L., and Richard B. Bernstein, eds. *Well Begun: Chronicles of the Early National Period*. Albany: New York State Commission on the Bicentennial of the United States Constitution, 1989.

Smith, Thomas E. V. *The City of New York in the Year of Washington's Inauguration, 1789*. reprint, Riverside, Conn.: Chatham Press, 1973.

Street, Alfred B. *The Council of Revision of the State of New York: Its History … and its Vetoes*. Albany: 1859 (includes text of veto messages).

Taylor, Alan. *William Cooper's Town: Power and Persuasion on the Frontier of the Early American Republic*. New York: Alfred A. Knopf, 1995.

Wells, Laura Jay. *The Jay Family of La Rochelle and New York*. New York: Order of the Colonial Lords of Manors in America, 1938.

Wertenbaker, Thomas J. *Father Knickerbocker Rebels: New York City during the American Revolution*. New York: Charles Scribner's Sons, 1948.

White, Shane. *Somewhat More Independent: The End of Slavery in New York City, 1770–1810*. Athens: University of Georgia Press, 1991.

Wood, Gordon S. *The Creation of the American Republic, 1776–1787*. New York: W. W. Norton, 1969.

Young, Alfred H. *The Democratic Republicans of New York: The Origins, 1763–1797*. Chapel Hill: University of North Carolina Press, 1967.

Zilversmit, Arthur. *The First Emancipation: The Abolition of Slavery in the North*. Chicago: University of Chicago Press, 1967.

Articles

Blackmun, Harry A. "John Jay and the Federalist Papers." *Pace Law Review* 8 (1988): 237–48.

Bonomi, Patricia U. "John Jay, Religion, and the State." *New York History* 81 (2000): 9–18.

Currie, David P. "The Constitution in the Supreme Court, 1789–1801." *University of Chicago Law Review* 48 (1981): 819–85.

Estes, Todd. "John Jay, the Concept of Deference, and the Transformation of Early American Political Culture." *The Historian: A Journal of History* 65 (2003): 293–317.

Ferguson, Robert A. "The Forgotten Publius: John Jay and the Aesthetics of Ratification." *Early American Literature* 34 (1999): 223–39.

Graymont, Barbara. "New York State Indian Policy after the Revolution." *New York History* 57 (1976): 438–74.

Hobson, Charles F. "The Recovery of British Debts in the Federal Circuit Court of Virginia, 1790 to 1797." *Virginia Magazine of History and Biography* 92 (1984): 176–201.

Holt, Wythe. "'The Federal Courts Have Enemies in All Who Fear Their Influence on State Objects': The Failure to Abolish Supreme Court Circuit-Riding in the Judiciary Acts of 1792 and 1793." *Buffalo Law Review* 36 (1987): 301–40.

Johnson, Herbert A. "George Harrison's Protest: New Light on *Forsey v. Cunningham*." *New York History* 50 (1969): 61–82.

——, "John Jay: Lawyer in a Time of Transition, 1764–1775." *University of Pennsylvania Law Review* 124 (1970): 1260–92.

——, "John Jay and the Supreme Court." *New York History* 81 (2000): 59–90.

Kaminski, John P. "Shall We Have a King? John Jay and the Politics of Union." *New York History* 81 (2000): 31–58.

——, "Honor and Interest: John Jay's Diplomacy during the Confederation." *New York History* 83 (2002): 293–321.

——, and C. Jennifer Lawton. "The Grand Jury Charges of Chief Justice John Jay, 1790–1794." Forthcoming.

Klein, Milton M. "The Rise of the New York Bar: The Legal Career of William Livingston." *William and Mary Quarterly* 15 (1958): 334–58.

——, "Failure of a Mission: The Drummond Peace Proposal of 1775." *Huntington Library Quarterly* 35 (1972): 343–80 (includes Drummond's plan).

——, "John Jay and the Revolution." *New York History* 81 (2000): 19–30.

Klingelhofer, Herbert E. "Matthew Ridley's Diary during the Peace Negotiations of 1782." *William and Mary Quarterly* 20 (1963): 95–133.

Littlefield, Daniel C. "John Jay, the Revolutionary Generation, and Slavery." *New York History* 91 (2000): 91–132.

Monaghan, Frank. "Anti-Slavery Papers of John Jay." *Journal of Negro History* 17 (1932): 481–96.

——, "Dr. Samuel Johnson's Letters to Peter Jay." *Columbia University Quarterly* 25 (1933): 88.

——, "Samuel Kissam and John Jay." *Columbia University Quarterly* 25 (1933): 131.

Morris, Richard B. "The John Jay Court: An Intimate Profile." *Journal of Contemporary Law* 5 (1979): 163–79.

——, "John Jay and the Adoption of the Federal Constitution in New York: A New Reading of Persons and Events." *New York History* 63 (1982): 151–64.

Index

References in italics are to tables, maps or prints